ACCLAIM FOR Randall Rothenberg's

WHERE THE SUCKERS MOON

"*Where the Suckers Moon* is ... entertaining and instructive ... a revealing job of reporting."
—*The New York Times*

"The great strength of *Where the Suckers Moon* is that it provides an authentically messy internal sense of how advertising is conducted."
—*Boston Globe*

"In his engaging deconstruction of the advertising business ... Rothenberg discovered the essence of Madison Avenue."
—*New York Observer*

"An interesting and ... illuminating narrative ... reveals the tense, funny and fun business of being creative, sometimes with more honesty than meets the eye."
—*The Nation*

"If the advertising executives who people this book could manufacture a campaign for it, they would trumpet: *Riveting story! Vivid characters! Reads like a novel!* But, unlike many of their ads, this one would be anchored in truth."
—Ken Auletta, author of *Three Blind Mice*

BOOKS BY Randall Rothenberg

The Neoliberals:
Creating the New American Politics

Where the Suckers Moon:
The Life and Death of an Advertising Campaign

Randall Rothenberg

WHERE THE SUCKERS MOON

Randall Rothenberg is the author of *The Neoliberals: Creating the New American Politics*. At *The New York Times*, Rothenberg was the science, politics, and food editor of the Sunday magazine until he left in 1991. Previously, he was a contributing editor at *Esquire* and wrote extensively for other national magazines. During the writing of this book, he served as a residential Fellow at the Freedom Forum Media Studies Center at Columbia University. He lives with his wife in New York City.

WHERE
THE SUCKERS
MOON

The Life and Death
of an Advertising Campaign

Randall Rothenberg

VINTAGE BOOKS

A Division of Random House, Inc.

New York

FIRST VINTAGE BOOKS EDITION, NOVEMBER 1995

The Library of Congress has cataloged the Knopf edition
as follows:
Rothenberg, Randall.
Where the suckers moon: an advertising story / by Randall
Rothenberg.—1st ed.
p. cm.
Includes bibliographical references and index.
ISBN 0-679-41227-1
1. Advertising—United States. 2. Advertising campaigns—United
States. 3. Advertising agencies—United States. 4. Wieden &
Kennedy—Case studies. 5. Advertising—Automobiles—United
States—Case studies. 6. Subaru automobile—Case studies.
I. Title.
HF5813.U6R57 1994
659.1'96292222—dc20
94-496
CIP
Vintage ISBN: 0-679-74042-2

Manufactured in the United States of America
10 9 8 7 6 5 4 3 2 1

For Susan Roy

... Fortune swims, not with the main stream of letters,
but in the shallows, where the suckers moon.

—A. J. Liebling,
The Honest Rainmaker

CONTENTS

CONTENTS

PART I

THE MISSION

Ford. Worth more when you buy it. Worth more when you sell it . . . When better automobiles are built, *Buick* will build them . . . Take the key and see. You'll find none so new as *Nash Airflyte* . . . Dollar for dollar you can't beat a *Pontiac* . . . Small spaces seem bigger, long drives seem shorter with *De Soto* full power steering . . . The action car for active Americans. Dependable *Dodge* . . . *Mercedes-Benz*. Engineered like no other car in the world . . . The new *Packard*. America's new choice in fine cars . . . The *Cadillac* car is a vacation in itself . . . *Oldsmobile*. Where the action is! . . . See the U.S.A. in your *Chevrolet* . . . *BMW*. The Ultimate Driving Machine . . . Look what they've gone and done to the new *Renault*. It's shiftless . . . *MG*. The sports car America loved first . . . Wouldn't you really rather have a *Buick?* . . . *Pontiac*. The wide-track people have a way with cars . . . *Nash Airflyte*. Great cars since 1902 . . . *Austin Marina*. The tough economy car from British Leyland . . . The heartbeat of America, today's *Chevrolet* . . . *Chrysler*. Better engineered. Better made! . . . The new *Honda Civic*. It will get you where you're going . . . We don't make compromises. We make *Saabs* . . . *Pierce-Arrow*. America's finest motor car for America's finest families . . . *Ford* has a better idea . . . *Volvo*. Fat cars die young . . . Baseball, hot dogs, apple pie and *Chevrolet* . . . You'll step into a New Automotive Age when you drive your *Tucker '48* . . . *Datsun* saves and sets you free . . . The *Dodge* Rebellion wants you! . . . *Toronado*. The all-car car for the all-man man . . . There's a *Ford* in your future . . . I love what you do for me, *Toyota* . . . *Nissan*. Built for the human race . . . The Motoramic *Chevrolet*. Stealing the thunder from the High-Priced Cars . . . Have you driven a *Ford* lately? . . . *Subaru* . . .
Subaru?

Chapter 1

Where's the Beef?

AT 7:30 A.M., Christopher Wackman was a lonely presence on Madison Avenue. Farther north and later in the day, fondling the ties at a Brooks Brothers counter or admiring Paul Stuart's wingtips, he would have melted into a crowd of other tall and troubled executives. Here, in a cramped coffee shop on the edge of the bluff that carries Madison south from midtown, he seemed a very solitary figure.

But on this street, of course, a marketing man is never really alone.

Chris Wackman, vice president for marketing at Subaru of America, an automobile company, like thousands of troubled vice presidents for marketing at hundreds of companies before him, had come to Madison Avenue to find an advertising agency.

"We've got a problem," he said, rehearsing a guilty plea he had voiced before and would soon repeat. His two companions hurried through their breakfasts. "We screwed up," Chris continued. "Now we're trying—some would say a little later than we should have—to correct things."

Chris's journey to Madison Avenue had begun two and a half hours earlier, when he left his rustic home in Tabernacle, on the border of New Jersey's Pine Barrens, drove past his company's headquarters in Cherry Hill, crossed the Delaware River into Philadelphia, parked and lowered himself into a seat on Amtrak's Metroliner. A short walk northeast from Penn Station led the forty-seven-year-old executive to America's legendary highway of hype. There he and his advertising manager, a buoyant fellow named Mark Dunn, joined their advertising search consultant, Gene Van Praag, for some java and some jive.

"To tell you the truth, we don't know *what* we're looking for," Chris said.

Mark agreed. "Our minds are open."

"Advertising agencies," said Gene, "can do *anything*."

For others, perhaps. But no longer for themselves. There had been a period, decades before, when "men said that they are in the advertising business with just as much pride as the man who says, 'I am a professor at Yale' or 'I am President of the United States.' " Now, as Subaru came calling, that self-esteem had virtually vanished. "Fear and loathing," moaned one agency chief executive, "is the tenor of the times."

To the casual visitor, the transformation was invisible. Madison Avenue looked as it had for so many years, an imperious blend of looming office towers, grand hotels and smart shops, larded with vest-pocket stationery stores and busy hasheries. This setting had its origins nearly a century earlier, when small advertising agencies—eager to flee the constraining environment of Park Row, where the city's newspaper publishers battled—migrated north. A few agencies alighted on Madison Square, in the East 20s. Gradually, with commissions from national magazines, then radio, later television making them wealthy, the agencies sought plusher quarters farther uptown, settling along a one-mile stretch of Madison in the 40s, 50s and 60s, like fat crows on a concrete high wire.

By 1923, "Madison Avenue" was already a synonym for the advertising industry—although advertising people, then as now, preferred the term "agency business"—and by the 1950s, some three-quarters of the advertising spending in the United States was controlled by agencies with headquarters or branch offices in the immediate vicinity of "Ulcer Gulch." So entwined were the industry and its location that when Erwin, Wasey & Company (the agency that renamed the malady tinea pedis "athlete's foot") moved from Madison Avenue to a new building on Third Avenue, the defection was considered a watershed in advertising history.

But if the Madison Avenue called on by Chris Wackman remained, in fable, the wellspring of high ambition and low art, of fast deals and boozy lunches, of national neuroses and corporate cynicism, the agencies that had furnished that reputation were now mostly absent. A decade of agency mergers (and the cost-trimming that followed) plus a slowdown in advertising spending by American marketers had prodded agencies to seek relief from the avenue's high rents. Batten, Barton, Durstine & Osborn ("Better things for better living . . . through chemistry") joined a conglomerate called Omnicom and moved to Seventh Avenue. Saatchi & Saatchi, a British-owned advertising giant, acquired both the Dancer-Fitzgerald-Sample ("Where's the beef?") and the Compton ("Ninety-nine and forty-four one-hundredths percent pure") agencies and moved its American headquarters from Madison near 62nd Street to a postmodern cakebox in an old warehouse district in downtown Manhattan. From their windows, copywriters and account executives could look west to the Hudson River and see a barge moored there by the city's Department of Corrections to shelter prisoners awaiting trial. The symbolism did not escape notice.

Two big agencies remained on Madison's curbs, but they served only to reinforce the mood of bitter nostalgia. There was DDB Needham— once known as Doyle Dane Bernbach. It was started by an Irishman and two Jews. They made funny ads ("You don't have to be Jewish to love Levy's" rye bread) and grew rich. Then they merged with a big midwestern agency, fired people and started making boring ads. And there was Young & Rubicam. It, too, once did great advertising ("Eastern Airlines—The Wings of Man") and good works ("Give jobs, give money, give a damn" for the New York Urban Coalition). It reaped profits. It bought other agencies. It hit the skids. It pleaded guilty to conspiring to bribe foreign officials to secure a tourism account.

Madison Avenue had become a kind of Delaware Canal of capitalism: a once-essential commercial conduit now little more than a quaint memory. "Today, Madison Avenue is more a symbol than a stronghold," noted a French tourist guidebook.

Dreams die hard. There remained on the street a small agency determined to rekindle the avenue's glory. Its name hung limply on a flag draped from an upper window of a building across from the coffee shop. The agency was called TBWA. It was twenty-one years old, but remained a cipher in the business. The agency's executives intended to transform their reputation by persuading, begging or forcing Subaru of America to let TBWA pitch the car company's account.

Chris Wackman and his two colleagues crossed the avenue and rode up the elevator to an alternative future.

The nature of an advertising agency can be ascertained by the look of its conference room or, if it has one, its executive dining room. For it is in these chambers, where current and potential clients are entertained, that an agency communicates its contrived verities. TBWA's conference room was comfortable yet not intimate. Recessed lighting, set above walls the texture of burlap, bathed the space in a warm, muted glow, but the wide table assured that people remained distant from one another. The cantilevered chairs and the 330-milliliter bottles of Evian water (an agency client) placed discreetly with the monogrammed pads and pens at each seat gave the setting an air of Continental propriety—a sign of the agency's roots. For at a time when "global marketing" was quite the boardroom buzzword, TBWA proudly trumpeted the fact that its four acronymic founders were a Frenchman, Claude Bonnange; a German, Uli Wiesendanger; an Italian, Paolo Ajroldi; and a Greek-American from St. Louis, William Tragos, the agency's chairman.

In its cool comfort, the space could not have been more different from one of the ad industry's more famous chambers, the J. Walter Thompson agency's New England Room. That compartment had been taken apart and removed, board by board, from an eighteenth-century farmhouse in Ipswich, Massachusetts, and meticulously reassembled and appointed with period furnishings each time the agency moved its New York headquarters—a total of four times since the 1920s. The New England Room was the manifestation of J. Walter Thompson's Yale roots, a silent signal to clients that they and the agency were of the same seed. After its shrinking profit margins made Thompson the victim of the ad industry's first hostile takeover in 1987, one of the first acts by its new chairman, Burt Manning, a driven Jew off the streets of Chicago, was the dismantling of the New England Room—an act one former Thompson executive called "an attack on the culture," which, indeed, it was.

Seven TBWA executives filed into their Eurostyle conference room and established themselves in a tight row, Tragos in the center, across the table from the Subaru representatives. When Chris and his partners doffed their suit jackets and wrapped them around the backs of their chairs, three admen immediately did the same. Richard Costello, TBWA's president, lowered the lights and, standing next to a sparkling white screen in the front of the room, narrated a slide presentation of the agency's history and growth.

His patter rapid and salesmanlike, Costello told of TBWA's work for the Anheuser-Busch brewery. (The agency had found a new name— Eagle Snacks—for the client's potato-chip-and-pretzel division and, to flog the "new" products, hired television's Odd Couple, Jack Klugman and Tony Randall.) He spoke of other clients: Beiersdorf, for which TBWA did sleekly sensuous ads for Nivea skin cream; Dannon, the yogurt maker; Air France.

Costello flashed the complete client list on the screen. "I think," he said, his round face beaming, "there's an opening in the 'S' category."

He went on to describe TBWA's expansion. The agency's billings—the amount its clients spent to put ads on the air, the page, billboards and elsewhere, and the standard measure of an agency's prowess—had grown some 36 percent in 1990, to $214 million in the United States alone. Within the past four months, TBWA had lured the New York

Mets and Carvel ice cream onto its client roll. A month before the Subaru meeting, TBWA had been named Agency of the Year for the Eastern United States by the trade magazine *Adweek*.

Tragos interrupted his president's monologue. "Agency of the East is okay," he said slowly, a bit sternly. "But we want 'of the world,' 'of America.'"

Chris Wackman pulled a black folder from a maroon briefcase with his initials monogrammed on its fabric cover and, his half-lens reading glasses pushed far down his nose, jotted down the figures.

TBWA followed with its trump card: a detailed case study of its work for Absolut vodka, the most memorable and most honored print advertising campaign of the past decade.

The agency had had the good fortune to pick up the account shortly before the 1980 Moscow Olympics, when anti-Soviet sentiments in the United States were beginning to crest and Americans who fancied imported vodka were starting to look beyond Stolichnaya. Later, with public opinion inflamed by Ronald Reagan's "evil empire" rhetoric and the Soviet downing of a Korean passenger jet, the Swedish vodka in the odd, stubby bottle was perfectly positioned to replace the Russian brand in American cocktails.

The agency's contribution to the liquor cabinet was its repudiation of verbal tag lines in favor of using the bottle's distinctive squat shape as a kind of visual slogan, underscored by a two-word pun on the product's name. A graffiti-art rendering of the bottle was titled "Absolut Haring," after Keith Haring, the noted street artist whom the agency had paid to sketch the bottle. "Absolut New York" was done as a map of Manhattan, the green expanse of Central Park forming the outline of the bottle.

Arnie Arlow, a copywriter and TBWA's co-creative director, presented the Absolut story. A big man with a barrel chest accentuated by a buttoned, double-breasted suit jacket and white pocket square, he pointed to the agency's awards for their work. There was the $100,000 Kelly Award for the best magazine ad campaign in the country, then the Grand Effie from the American Marketing Association's New York chapter for the industry's most effective ad campaign.

"The results are incredible," Arlow said. "We're now approaching three million bottles—"

"Cases!" Tragos interrupted harshly.

Peter Lubalin, Arlow's art director partner and the agency's other co–creative director, silently attached the ads to the fabric walls. (Lubalin had invented Renault's image as "Le Car," Dick Costello told the Subaru executives.)

Taken together, the Absolut ads that lined one wall of TBWA's conference room formed a map of fresh, witty advertising creativity. One ad in particular caught Mark Dunn's eye, a three-page, glossy foldout titled "Absolut Centerfold."

"You did that ad specifically for *Playboy* magazine?" Mark asked.

"We often do ads for specific magazines," Arlow replied, putting enough punch in "often" to indicate that he knew he'd scored a point. Mark raised his eyebrows and nodded.

Tragos let the quiet humor of the Absolut ads sink in. Turning serious, he took a barely hidden swipe at the advertising Subaru had been receiving for the past sixteen years from its current ad agency, which he named only by implication. "There's a New York school of advertising that always has to be funny, always has to be smartass." TBWA's different offices, by contrast, had mastered a variety of styles. "Our Italian agency does wonderful emotional work. St. Louis is very homey. The German agency bonks you over the head. You don't always have to be funny."

"New York agencies," Tragos added with contempt, "have a problem with that."

TBWA had everything going for it. Absolut Vodka's importer had increased its ad spending twentyfold in a decade, to $25 million a year. The agency was making its way into pitches for airline accounts, camera accounts, cigarette accounts. It had awards, prestige, profits. It lacked only one thing.

Fame. The fame a car account could bestow.

Dick Costello, the session's narrator, turned from the screen to face Chris, Mark and Gene. He vowed to take a six-month leave of absence from his administrative responsibilities as president of TBWA to devote himself fully to Subaru. His face red with passion and the veins in his bald head popping, Costello concluded his presentation by thumping his fist on the table.

"It drives me absolutely *nuts* that an agency of our quality does not have a car!" he thundered. "It is a personal crusade."

Later, squeezed into the backseat of a taxi carrying him to another meeting downtown, Chris Wackman recalled that final thump as the moment TBWA lost its chance for the Subaru account.

"When Costello said, 'I won't rest until I get a car account!' " Chris said, halting slightly between words, "I don't know *what* that does for *me*."

Chris Wackman had few predispositions about what, or whom, he was looking for. He had been shown advertising that was "creative"—the term ad people use for work that kisses the irrational, emotional cheek of the human brain instead of appealing to its just-give-me-the-facts-

and-the-price-over-and-over-if-you-must side. Chris liked creative advertising, but he was willing to consider hard sell. He had seen passion at TBWA, and God knows he wanted passion for his company and his account. But the executives there had missed the point. Their presentation was about their agency. It should have been about Subaru. For, as Chris had told them inside the muted conference room, "We feel we have an opportunity to launch our company off, perhaps in a totally new direction."

His goals were modest, if vague. "There isn't anybody who would stand up right now and say we want to have the same volumes Toyota and Honda have"—some 650,000 cars sold each, annually, in the United States in the late 1980s, about six times Subaru's sales. "But we definitely believe, no question about it, that we can improve our lot in the world."

Mark Dunn—an ebullient man nine years younger than Chris who had never been hardened, as Chris had, by years in Detroit—was more optimistic.

"There's no reason we couldn't be at 300,000, 400,000 sales like the Toyota Camry," he said, referring to Toyota's compact car, a particular nemesis of Subaru's, which had actually sold 284,595 units in 1990.

"What's the difference?" Mark asked. "Image."

IMAGES ARE THE WAY we define ourselves and our world. Whether in tandem with words or absent their influence, images provide us the reference points of our history, our emotions, our memories.

For so many of us, the very idea of childhood is embodied in a black mouse with a big white snout and large round ears. The Jazz Age of the 1920s is evoked by the trim lines and unadorned curves of a typeface called FuturaBold. The power of American multinationalism courses through Paul Rand's logo for International Business Machines Corp., the initials' slab serifs creating a solid, modern foundation for growth, wealth and greatness.

But what *is* image? Most certainly, an image encompasses the physical appearance of an object—its shape, contours, color, interior and exterior attributes as grasped by our senses. But when an object becomes a subject, tangibility grows hazy; drawing a detergent box is easy, but try to scratch a picture of cleanliness on an Etch-A-Sketch and disputes are bound to follow. Moreover, as long ago as Heracleitus, we learned that sight, smell, touch and hearing were poor measures of knowledge and being.

George Lois, an art director whose startling designs (like Andy

Warhol drowning in a can of Campbell soup) graced dozens of *Esquire* covers in the 1960s, says an image is a one-shot representation of a thing's essence. "Imagery is the conversion of an idea into a theatrical cameo, an indelible symbol, a scene that becomes popular folklore, an iconographic image," he has written. True, but also incomplete. Lois finds an image only in its translation, and it was Plato who informed us that the reification of an idea is not the idea itself.

The classic how-to texts of advertising devote nary a word to the meaning of images, preferring to dwell either on their component parts or their impact. You can read Claude C. Hopkins (from whom we learned that Quaker Oats Puffed Rice was "shot from guns") and discover that "the right name is an advertisement in itself." David Ogilvy, the creator of the eyepatched "Man in the Hathaway Shirt," told his industry that "photographs sell more than drawings." And while he was a spirited proponent of the use of "brand image" in advertising, he got bogged down in the minutiae: An image is a "complex symbol" and "a long-term investment in the total personality" of a brand; images should be "consistent," of "one style in the face of all the pressures to come up with something new"; brand image "is the result of many different factors—advertising, pricing, the name of the product, its packaging, the kind of television shows it has sponsored, the length of time it has been on the market. . . ."

But the parts are not the whole, as the historian Daniel Boorstin pointed out in *The Image*. "An image . . . is not simply a trademark, a design, a slogan or an easily remembered picture," Boorstin wrote. "It is a studiously crafted personality profile of an individual, institution, corporation, product or service." Yet even Boorstin's definition is lacking, for it relies on the intentions of the image's makers.

Missing from these efforts at definition are two elements. The first is the human mind, which, in Milton's words, "is its own place, and in itself / Can make a Heav'n of Hell, a Hell of Heav'n"—especially when influenced by the interpretations and misinterpretations, mass delusions and news reports, smudged ink and flawed videotape, heavy accents and bad lighting and press conferences and spin doctors and the myriad other things that can inadvertently affect the way images are perceived.

And then there is the image itself. Endowed not only with form and color, representative characteristics and iconographic meaning, but with abilities and quirks vested in it by its perceivers, the image can take upon itself roles its presumably omnipotent creators never intended. Far from being an inanimate, unchanging manifestation of a writer's or artist's or strategist's or ideologue's desires, the image can become a willful being, capable of mischief beyond the ken of its inventors.

That's what happened to Subaru of America. Its image—the vast array of notions and perceptions and commercials and stories and looks and hues and shapes that, taken together, *were* the company—had risen up and bitten the corporation, its Creator, in the ass.

It had occurred virtually overnight. Nine years before, when Chris Wackman had joined Subaru, the company's stability and spirit could not have been more refreshing. There was no pretense to the cars Subaru imported. Manufactured by Fuji Heavy Industries, the Japanese company that had built the airplane engines used in Japan's World War II Zeroes, they were rugged little sedans and wagons that could go on forever and, if equipped with the four-wheel-drive transmissions that Fuji had perfected, on any terrain. Nor were there any airs about Subaru's chief executive and co-founder, Harvey Lamm, a street-smart *hondler* from Philadelphia who imbued his company with an entrepreneurial vitality so unlike the M.B.A. culture that had stymied Wackman's ascent at Ford Motor Company, where the marketing executive had spent the earlier part of his automotive career.

Subaru of America manufactured nothing; it merely imported Fuji's cars and wholesaled them to a dealer network it had assembled. But the niche market it had found proved fabulously remunerative. With the rest of the automobile industry staggering under the burden of the Carter-era energy crisis, Subaru's durable and efficient cars made it the most profitable company in American industry, earning an unheard-of 72 percent return on equity.

Subaru's stock, which traded over-the-counter at about $55 a share when Wackman joined the company in 1982, surged, month by month, almost day by day. By the mid-1980s, employees in the company's New Jersey headquarters stopped greeting each other with "hello" but with knowing nods and citations of the day's opening share price, which reached a high of $273 before an eight-for-one split in May 1986.

Then, within a year, Subaru went from darling to dog in the eyes of Wall Street. Even as financial prosperity danced across much of the American map, Subaru's sales fell, from a high of 183,242 cars in 1986 to 177,000 in 1987; its $94 million profit became a $30 million loss; the stock price plunged to one-sixth its peak.

As sales plummeted, Subaru's once-ample cash reserves dwindled. The company and Fuji Heavy Industries (which owned 49.6 percent of its importer's shares) tried frantically to lower costs and attract consumers.

In 1989, having concluded that their decline was due to the lack of a compact car that could compete with the popular, midpriced vehicles offered by Toyota, Honda and other rivals, Subaru of America and Fuji Heavy Industries unveiled the Legacy, as mainstream as their earlier cars had been quirky. "This is a bet-your-company car," one securities analyst said at the time. "If the Legacy fails, no more Subaru."

The cars did not sell. Sales tumbled to 108,547 vehicles in 1990. Many culprits were identified: the Japanese yen, inelegant styling, misdirected investment, poor product planning, the ads. The cognoscenti, however, knew differently. "The real problem that Subaru has," a prescient automobile industry analyst named Christopher Cedergren said in 1988, "is one of image."

So in January 1990, Fuji Heavy Industries made a public offer to acquire the 50.4 percent of Subaru of America it did not own. The offering price was $6 a share, or a total of $147 million—a fraction of the stock's peak value during its halcyon days. The offer, subsequently raised to $8 a share, was duly approved.

Left in his job was Thomas R. Gibson, Subaru's president and chief operating officer, an even-tempered, silver-haired man who had been Chris Wackman's idol at DePauw University (where Gibson had been a Big Man on Campus and upperclass fraternity brother when Wackman was a wide-eyed freshman) and later at the Lincoln-Mercury division of the Ford Motor Company. It was Gibson who had brought Chris over to Subaru, and who had overseen Chris's rise up the ranks to marketing director. And it was Gibson who was protecting Chris, not to mention himself, in the chaotic midst of falling sales, a failing domestic economy and the skepticism of the new Japanese owners.

The price for that protection, both men understood, was a new image for their company and its cars. Aside from the occasional minor imperfections that plague even the Hondas of the world, they believed, to the core of their souls, that their products, their cars, were unassailable. The company even had a mantra that calmed whatever doubts its executives or dealers or salesmen may have had about their vehicles. The cars were "bulletproof." Only the image had holes.

Whether the new image required a new advertising agency was an open question. Few large companies in the United States handle their own advertising. Some, to be sure, purchase their own broadcast time and print space. But with the exception of a handful of significant clothing and cosmetics companies like Calvin Klein and Revlon (which, after all, are selling pure images, just barely tethered to physical products), most corporations believe they lack the expertise to communicate their virtues to consumers. They retain ad agencies for the task.

"We're really car people before we're advertising people," Chris explained. "I grew up in the car business, on the sales and promotional side, and I feel comfortable with that. What I don't feel comfortable with is that I know all the nuances of the creative side and the media side. I know what I like, but to be honest, I haven't bought a car in ten, twelve years"—his cars came free, from the company—"so what I like may not be relevant."

Subaru of America had been served faithfully and well since 1975 by a smallish New York agency named Levine, Huntley, Schmidt & Beaver. Although little known by name to the general public, Levine, Huntley had for years been a shining star in the exclusive galaxy of New York agencies that were deemed by their peers to be "creative," not least because of its funny, cinematic work for Subaru. Much of Levine, Huntley's advertising emphasized Subaru's expertise at producing economical, utilitarian cars whose four-wheel-drive transmissions made them especially good at traversing ruts, ascending mountains and overcoming snow and rain. The slogan, in place for years, identified Subarus as "inexpensive, and built to stay that way."

Despite the quality of the agency's ads, once Fuji disclosed its plans to acquire Subaru of America, the ad industry took it as a given that Levine, Huntley's days were numbered. Subaru's new Japanese owners were sure to force the company to find a new agency. New management always compelled changes in advertising strategy, if for no other reason than to show who was boss.

Chris bridled at the suggestion that Fuji had compelled the search. The decision to investigate other agencies, he said, was made even before the final merger papers were signed (albeit after the deal was announced). "Fact is, we hadn't gone anyplace but down for four years." The marketing plans—*his* marketing plans—and Levine, Huntley's advertising had lost credibility among Subaru's dealers and among Subaru of America's regional representatives, the executives responsible for wholesaling cars to those dealers.

Levine, Huntley pleaded for one more chance, and was allowed to mount a solo presentation in early April, based on a detailed assignment that had been drawn up by Gene Van Praag. The agency came back with mountains of research, a new analysis of current Subaru drivers and potential new ones, and two full campaigns based on a single, fresh strategy. One labeled the Subaru "the uncommon car for the commonsense driver." Or, if the corporation preferred, it could tout itself with "We make cars that make better drivers."

Subaru of America's ten-person advertising search committee, mostly

Americans with a few Japanese sprinkled in, was unimpressed. The headlines in the print ads were not simple enough and the copy was too long. The new image Levine, Huntley had crafted was not different enough to lift Subaru out of the cellar.

So sixteen months after the Japanese declared their intention to take control of Subaru's purse strings, the quest for that new! improved! so easy to love! image began with Wackman's journey to Madison Avenue.

The voyage he, his colleagues and some tenscore advertising workers, marketing consultants, public relations executives and others were to make in their search for Subaru's new image was, in no small way, central to America's understanding of itself as the twentieth century dragged to a close. For everywhere—in economics, in government, in public and private life—image seemed to have taken precedence.

In leadership, image had superseded substance. One hundred and thirty years after Henry Clay earned the sobriquet "The Great Compromiser" for his effort to stave off the Civil War, Ronald Reagan gained the White House and *his* nickname, "The Great Communicator," for his ability to make Americans feel good.

In business, image had replaced machinery and organization. Six decades after Alfred P. Sloan, Jr., had fashioned a new system of production and management that had built General Motors into the world's largest corporate enterprise, the investment firm of Kohlberg Kravis Roberts paid more than $20 billion, the most ever tendered for a company, for RJR Nabisco. The extravagance of the sum hinged on the value inherent in brand names like Oreo cookies and Camel cigarettes.

In politics, image had replaced action. Forty years after Harry Truman won election by calling a recalcitrant Republican Congress back into session to review his proposals, George Bush bested Michael Dukakis for the presidency by skillfully deploying a handful of television commercials. His image-makers' spots, pundits maintained, had transformed the vice president from "wimp" to gallant, and demonized the Massachusetts governor by linking him to the photograph of a menacing rapist-murderer.

The best minds of a generation were stirred to fabricate illusions. As the century drew to its close, young men and women were increasingly using their creative powers not to convey high truths or poetry but to dream up five-word slogans. After all, the economists were saying, products and services were now so much alike, in category after category, that the only element which could distinguish one company's wares from another's was image. Image, they said, could add actual value to a firm's yield. Why else would someone charge with Visa over MasterCard, lather with Ivory instead of Dial, drive an Accord rather than a Camry, or vote for Clinton, not Bush?

This paradox was perfectly embodied in one of the more celebrated advertising campaigns of the 1980s, a trade promotion for *Rolling Stone* that extolled its virtues to the young men and women who put together media plans—suggested rosters of magazines and television programs in which ads should appear—for advertising agencies. *Rolling Stone* was the bible of rock and roll and 1960s-style countercultural mores. By the eighties, though, its values seemed terribly out of step with the dominant acquisitive culture—the very culture from which emerged the young agency media planners, who were increasingly loath to recommend to their clients a publication they deemed a relic of the low-rent decades.

The print campaign to correct their misconception was devised by a Minneapolis agency, then called Fallon McElligott Rice. Against a white background on the left page of a double-page spread, the agency placed an icon of the 1960s—a Volkswagen bus inscribed with peace signs, for example, or a bearded and beaded hippie. On the right were their latter-day equivalents—a snazzy BMW, or a short-haired yuppie in a slick sports jacket. Whatever the illustrations, the headline always consisted of the same two words, which were meant to distinguish *Rolling Stone*'s lingering past from its allegedly vibrant present. Over the left-side illustration was "perception"; over the right, "reality."

The campaign's brilliance lay in its alchemical power. Nothing about *Rolling Stone* had changed. Its audience, the commodity the magazine was selling to advertisers, was exactly the same before the Minneapolis agency's ads ran as after. The only thing that changed was media planners' opinions about that audience. Fallon McElligott knew the ad industry's greatest secret: In the modern world, perception *is* reality.

Or is it? Subaru of America at the moment of its reinvention provided an opportunity to ponder whether the pixel is indeed more important than the product. The company certainly thought so. In its distress, its executives continually insisted that they needed to find what one advertising agency in its account review called the "soul" of the company and its products. The word was apt. Three thousand years before, in a wooded glade somewhere beyond the Athenian Acropolis, Socrates had told his disciple Phaedrus of the intimate connection between images and souls. "The dialectician," the philosopher said, "selects a soul of the right type, and in it plants and sows his words founded on knowledge, words which can defend both themselves and him who planted them, words which instead of remaining barren contain a seed whence new words grow up in new characters. . . ."

Survival was the predominant concern of Subaru's executives as they began their pursuit of a new image. They had come through a long, debilitating period of upheaval and emerged bruised. Finding the soul of Subaru, they believed, would heal their wounds.

Chapter 2

I'm Not a Doctor,
but I Play One on TV

EVERYBODY LIKED CHRIS WACKMAN. His ad agency called him a gentleman. He was a true Christian, they said—for once setting aside the cynicism so rampant in the ad game. He was self-effacing to a fault. He still sang baritone in his church choir, in a voice only slightly rougher than the tenor that had once moved Ethel Merman, his prep-school roommate's mother, to tears. He had the look of power: the sharp nose, perfectly chiseled looks, clear blue eyes and smoothly swept-back hair of a matinee idol.

Yet his manner was one of accommodation. When he spoke, he would begin slowly, pausing frequently between words, and as often as not, he finished his sentences with a verbal uptick that made affirmations sound like questions. He looked like Cary Grant but seemed like Ronald Reagan—the sidekick, the guy who never got the girl, the knowledge-able and pleasant manager who could never force himself to be tough enough. That was the price of his decency.

So was his schedule, which was so tight as to be almost unworkable. Normally, a company and its advertising agency would spend months carefully plotting every stage in a campaign intended to relaunch a cor-poration's image. Because Chris and his colleagues, out of kindness, had given Levine, Huntley an unfettered, albeit ultimately futile, chance to retain the account, they were allowing themselves only four months be-tween the start of their agency search and the introduction of the new campaign. Having only begun to examine the names of advertising agencies in mid-April, Subaru was determined to select five to compete with Levine, Huntley by May 10. On June 10, after a week of final pre-sentations by the agencies, it would pick the victor. On August 6, Subaru of America would unveil its new campaign by presenting two television commercials at its annual dealers meeting in Denver. The spots were to go on the air around Labor Day, complemented by print advertisements in the October issues of several national magazines, which had advertising deadlines in late July or early August and would hit newsstands in mid-September.

"We have set out for ourselves, created for ourselves," Chris said dryly, "a scintillating challenge for the summer."

This process of finding a new image through the reinvigoration of an existing ad agency or the hiring of a new one is called an "advertising account review." The phrase is a prettified disguise for reality. A marketer no more reviews its advertising agency than the *New York Times*'s theater critic reviews a Broadway play. However dispassionate and analytical the examination might seem, both the critic and the show's producer know that single review will sustain or crush the production.

So it is in advertising. For companies—"clients," in the quaintly self-centered world of the agency business—account reviews are meant to add life to a lackluster brand and to the workforce that attends to it. For ad agencies, account reviews are a continual struggle for nourishment or survival.

The words agencies use to describe the process seem culled from anthropology texts: Accounts are "pursued," like animals in the hunt; the executives charged with finding accounts through the interpretation of street gossip are "rain makers"; "headhunters" are retained to locate marketing or creative experts who can be dragged in, at a price, to help the pursuit.

Yet for all this tribal lingo, the procedure itself more often than not is associated with sports. Once an ad agency makes it through the initial screenings and onto the short list of finalists for an account, the only thing separating it from triumph or loss is the final presentation: the "pitch." And pitching an account can be as arduous and as exhilarating as a baseball team's season-long trek to the World Series, and sometimes as lonely and cold as a figure skater's preparation for the Winter Olympics.

"Aside from the agony and the risk involved, the review is probably the most fun there is in the business," said Jack Taylor, the vice chairman of an agency that was eager for the Subaru account. "After you get the account," he sighed, "there's baggage and politics."

Despite the longevity of a few client-agency relationships, which rival the strongest of marriages between the healthiest of people—Chevrolet, for example, has stuck with Lintas Campbell-Ewald since 1914—there was, as Subaru began its review, a broad perception inside the agency business that account-switching had become pandemic. According to a once-a-decade survey, in 1985, by the American Association of Advertising Agencies, the industry's main trade association, an account stayed at an agency for 7.2 years on average, with the largest agencies maintaining their client relationships for 14 years. Yet after 1985, anecdotally at least, a panic seemed to begin. Large and prestigious accounts transferred repeatedly from agency to agency. When Burger King took its $200 million account from J. Walter Thompson to N. W. Ayer in 1987, in what was then said to be the largest account transfer in history, the new agency celebrated its gain with champagne and Whoppers. The empty Styrofoam cases were still tumbling across landfills when, less than two years later, the fast-food company pulled its business from Ayer and divided it between D'Arcy Masius Benton & Bowles and Saatchi & Saatchi. In 1989, DMB&B won the Maxwell House coffee account from Ogilvy & Mather, only to lose the $80 million account back to Ogilvy in 1990.

It wasn't merely the appearance of rampant account switching and client disloyalty that contributed to the terror. There was the very real fact of plummeting advertising expenditures. From 1976 to 1988, ad spending in the United States advanced much more rapidly than the total domestic economy, consistently tallying double-digit growth even as the economy stagnated. Indeed, in 1981 and 1982, in the depths of America's worst post–World War II recession, with unemployment reaching 9 percent and then 10 percent of the workforce, advertising spending was barely touched, growing 12.8 percent and 10.2 percent, respectively. No wonder that, when the nation emerged from the recession in the mid-1980s, it was admen, culled from the industry's largest and most creative agencies, who crafted the "it's-morning-again-in-America" pitches on behalf of Ronald Reagan. They had been spared the worst of it, and could muster patriotic enthusiasm with little strain.

The descent from those heights was dizzyingly rapid. In 1989, ad spending, only 5 percent greater than a year before, barely kept pace with inflation; in 1990, it did not even reach that threshold. Nineteen-ninety-one was darker yet. Local and network television revenues declined 7 percent in the first three months of the year. During the same period, profits at several of the nation's most stable media companies, those whose incomes derive largely from advertising, plunged: by 28 percent at Dow Jones & Company, 42 percent at the Washington Post Company, and a staggering 87 percent at The New York Times Company. Magazines—the glamour medium of the 1980s, what with the renaissance at *Esquire* and the revival of *Vanity Fair*—shuttered their offices for lack of ad support, no matter whether their franchises were regional (*New England Monthly*), physical (*Health*), spiritual (*Psychology Today*), or psychosexual (*Smart for Men*). Ad spending would finish the year down 1.5 percent, to $126.7 billion—the first time in thirty years that expenditures for radio commercials, billboards, TV spots, newspaper promos and magazine spreads declined.

Anguished agency executives, marketing experts and finger-wagging academics debated the reasons for advertising's decay. The agencies, recalling the not-too-distant days when novel products and services like personal computers and deregulated airlines fueled ad spending, attributed their debilitated state to the lack of such novelties. They also blamed the Persian Gulf War, which dried up spending like the sun on a puddle.

Others said the responsibility for their impairment lay with the agencies themselves. Over the years, in pursuit of high profits, they had cut back, gradually but perceptibly, on their services, most notably research. Advertising agencies used to serve as their clients' eyes and ears in the marketplace. Was there a need for a new product? Was a service now more popular in the suburbs than the cities? Were more men using a household cleanser than women? The ad agency's research department was usually the first, and often the only, source for such information.

Figures gathered by the American Association of Advertising Agencies showed that research-department salaries, which had accounted for 3.16 percent of agency payroll costs in 1968, constituted less than 1 percent of payroll twenty years later. Ad agencies ceded this ground, diminishing their own importance.

Further, agencies had organized their businesses so tightly around revenues from network television advertising that they had nowhere to turn when the networks' share of the viewing audience shrank from more than 90 percent in 1979 to barely more than 60 percent as the 1990s bloomed. Clients eager to stake out positions closer to their consumers were abjuring their agencies and turning to specialists in junk mail or couponing. One study, a survey of three hundred marketing executives by Myers Marketing and Research, found that mainstream advertising, which in 1976 accounted for more than three-fifths of corporate marketing expenditures, now comprised only 31 percent of the executives' budgets. The rest was devoted to the publicizing of discounts and other sales promotions.

Advertising agencies have few of the cushions other businesses maintain to protect them from economic blows; there are no machines to idle and no inventory to unload for a quick revenue boost. There are only people: people who write or draw, people who schmooze or calculate, people who process or produce. People—the largest proportion of them middle-aged men in the account services area, who had spent twenty or thirty years bargaining with clients, negotiating with copywriters, agreeing with their superiors—found themselves thrust from a business that no longer had room for them.

At first the layoffs seemed too large and too fast to be assimilated by a shell-shocked industry. Bozell fired 35 people at the end of 1990; so did Young & Rubicam, on its way to eliminating 223 positions between the end of that year and late 1991. Then the unemployed crowds grew larger: N. W. Ayer dismissed 60 people in mid-1991, then DDB Needham let go 59. Ogilvy & Mather fired 51 people, 7.3 percent of its New York office, when it lost the $60 million American Express Green Card ("Don't leave home without it") account.

Needless to say, advertising agencies craved Subaru of America's account. Car advertising is an ad agency's best advertisement for itself. "For the agency long-term, it can mean a lot more visibility—the opportunity for advertising to be much more visible," said Wilder Baker, one of the dozens of advertising executives pursuing Subaru's account. "Because you bring out new models, cars allow you to refresh a campaign on an ongoing basis."

The history of American advertising brims with agencies whose reputations were anchored to automobile accounts. For Doyle Dane Bernbach, it was Volkswagen ("Lemon"). For McCaffrey & McCall, Mercedes-Benz ("Engineered like no other car in the world"). Volvo launched the Carl Ally agency ("Fat cars die young"). But, more than the chance for recognition, more than the possibility of profit in straitened times, a car account has greater meaning still in the advertising world: It represents power.

"The reason you want something like this," said Jim Dale, president of the Baltimore agency W. B. Doner, "is you see an opportunity to change the destiny of a product on a grand scale."

WINNOWING A MANAGEABLE LIST of suitors from the myriad of auto-less bachelors was the Subaru review's first task. The job seemed daunting. The term "advertising agency" can cover an array of businesses; it can be applied with equal legitimacy to the world's largest marketing-communications conglomerates (like the WPP Group P.L.C., whose subsidiaries include the J. Walter Thompson and Ogilvy & Mather empires and dozens of smaller specialty units), and to tiny printing shops whose sole proprietors occasionally write headlines for the posters they reproduce.

Altogether, the Department of Commerce estimates that there are some twenty thousand companies in the United States that deserve to be called advertising agencies. The Standard Directory of Advertising

Agencies, a thick guide known in the industry as "The Red Book," listed 5,150 advertising agencies in its February–May 1991 edition. William M. Weilbacher, a marketing consultant, recommends in his authoritative handbook, *Choosing and Working with Your Advertising Agency*, that marketers looking for an agency limit themselves to the narrower list of "*bona fide* advertising agencies" published annually in *Advertising Age* magazine. But even this more selective catalogue numbers 533 companies.

Yet the assignment for Subaru was easier than it looked. The truth is, there aren't that many ad shops in the United States that the industry itself deems capable of creating a new image for a car company, even by the relatively broad standards Subaru and its consultant used to narrow their search. "We didn't want to be the only account at the shop, but we didn't want to be lost, either," said Gene Van Praag, whom Subaru had hired to guide it through this portion of the review. He decided to limit the search to agencies with at least $50 million in billings. That decreased the choice to some 130 agencies. When others, including several agencies that Gene had worked with and respected, were thrown in, Subaru's "scan list" included about 150 ad agencies.

Three dozen or more had to be eliminated because they already had car accounts, or were part of agency networks that had them. Numerous others were local or regional shops that had never handled anything larger than a small retail chain, or knew nothing about how to buy network television time. "It wasn't too tough to figure out the top thirty-six to forty prospects," Mark Dunn said. Immediately after Levine, Huntley's solo pitch, Van Praag sent twenty-eight of them a questionnaire. The thirty-six questions on it were designed to assess the agencies' specific abilities and their interest in Subaru's business. Van Praag gave the agencies three days to reply.

On Friday, April 19, twenty-four responses flooded into the offices of Ernst-Van Praag. Despite the time pressures, several of the agencies had clearly spent late evenings on the job. The weightiest response came from Earle Palmer Brown in Bethesda, Maryland, which sent two large loose-leaf binders filled with data. The most creative came from the Weightman Group, a Philadelphia ad agency known best, if at all, for its advertisements for ALPO pet foods. Weightman cut a model car out of Styrofoam, carved a hole in it and stuck its questionnaire answers inside.

Gene and four of his employees came in on Saturday and reviewed the questionnaires. By Federal Express, he sent the surveys, his analyses and copies of the various agencies' television commercials and print ads to Chris Wackman, who met on Monday with Mark Dunn and

Karen Allen, Subaru's television-commercial production manager. The car company and its consultant then agreed that ten of the agencies—exclusive of Levine, Huntley, which they already knew well and were including in the review automatically—were worthy of personal visits. These trips are known in the agency business as "credentials visits," for they allow ad agencies an opportunity to establish their capabilities, introduce their executives and expound on their philosophies.

The ten agencies ran a geographical and creative gamut of midsized shops. Earle Palmer Brown, of the compulsively long reply, made it; so did the Weightman Group, the locals with the creative flair. From Baltimore, the W. B. Doner agency was slated for a visit, as was a Chicago shop, Eisaman, Johns & Laws, which, like Doner, knew the car business through its work for several automobile dealer associations and a tire company. Wieden & Kennedy, an agency from Mark Dunn's hometown of Portland, Oregon, was also scheduled for a call, even though its experience was limited largely to work for Nike, the shoe manufacturer.

Five New York agencies, each representing a different gestalt, made the semifinals. Warwick, Baker & Fiore specialized in advertising packaged goods, as household commodity products, distinguishable mostly by their packaging, are called. Jordan, McGrath, Case & Taylor also did packaged goods—it was part of the distinguished roster of Procter & Gamble agencies—but was also known as one of the largest remaining independent agencies with offices only in New York. Altschiller Reitzfeld / Tracy-Locke was part of the ad industry's creative elite, but the industry's slow growth had forced it to sell out to the Omnicom Group, America's second-largest advertising conglomerate. DCA Advertising was also conglomerate-owned; its parent was Dentsu, the world's largest single advertising agency and (not incidentally) Subaru's agency in Japan, where Dentsu was headquartered. And there was TBWA, a strong favorite as the visits began but whose credentials were found lacking.

Subaru asked each agency to present two case studies: a history of one new-product introduction the agency had managed, and the story of one brand repositioning. Every other detail of the three hours the agency would have with the visiting Subaru representatives was left to the agency itself.

Chris, Mark and Gene, of course, had other things they wanted to see. For Gene, the crucial element was evidence of rationality, of what he called "left-brain thinking."

"A right-brain solution is an art director who wakes up at three a.m., writes down his dream and goes out and shoots it for a million dollars," he explained. "People come up with ideas and make statements. A lot of times they're based on feelings. Some feelings are legitimate. Some are not." He mentioned a production technique, borrowed from rock-music videos, in which frames of film are removed from a sequence, giving the piece a kind of stop-action effect. "Skip-framing is a big trend right now. A client has to ask, Why? What is it about this that makes it work? If you can't answer that, you can't respond when problems arise. The emphasis on the rational is really a communications link. To make sure assertions are proven. To make sure the risk is minimized."

Chris, on the other hand, wanted relevance. At no point had he or his colleagues asked any of the ten agencies to relate their case studies to Subaru's problems. But that was what he wanted to see and hear. To make it into the finals for Subaru's account, an agency had to "close the sale," and make its expertise germane to Subaru. "I want some closure," Wackman said.

TBWA had failed to provide closure. Subaru's advertising budget, a probable $70 million in 1992, was less than half that of competitors like Nissan and Toyota. Its money would have to be stretched, through creative media planning and tough negotiations with networks, stations and magazines. Yet very little of TBWA's talk addressed "media"—marketing shorthand for the venues in which advertising is placed. Moreover, while the agency's advertising for Absolut vodka was undeniably impressive, the Subaru people were hard-pressed to figure out how alcohol could clean their wounds.

Before the credentials visits, Mark, who was as concerned with rationality as Gene, had developed a computer spreadsheet program to help him cull from the long list of agencies the few worthy of visits. Of the thirty-six questions on that survey, seventeen were graded on a 1 to 5 scale (5 being the highest) and four were crucial: What was the agency's perception of Subaru? Of the Subaru customer? What was the agency's philosophy in developing a campaign? And (considering how distant the Subaru executives sometimes felt from Levine, Huntley) how often would the agency review its situation with the client? On his office computer, Dunn not only calculated the scores of each agency on each question, but weighted the responses according to their importance, aggregated them and determined each agency's deviation from the mean response in each category.

For the credentials visits, Dunn had created yet another scoring sheet, grading each agency (again on a 1 to 5 scale) on eight factors in its live presentation. This "Credential Meeting Scoresheet" was designed to facilitate an analysis of the case studies the agencies were presenting. How difficult was the challenge facing the agency? Was the product at an extreme price disadvantage against the competition? How finely and economically did the agency reach the product's target audiences? At the top of this form was a diagram that looked like a child's pinwheel, with letters representing the questions inside each blade of the fan. In the hub was the letter that stood for the crucial issue at this stage of the search: Did the agency relate the case study to Subaru?

For all the science, though, the Subaru representatives understood that their questionnaires, scorecards and spreadsheets lacked one thing. "It doesn't give a way to grade gut feelings," Chris acknowledged.

TBWA had received the highest score on the initial, thirty-six-question questionnaire. But it had failed the gut test. There was no empathy. The agency's performance had been completely self-absorbed. Lack of humility was okay; that was an occupational hazard of the business. Self-absorption, though, was another matter. Subaru, like any marketer in trouble, wanted to be embraced. It wanted its troubles addressed; it wanted the reassurances that all could be and would be right with the world. That was not TBWA's style. The agency had gone on a blind date and talked only about itself.

"It is just not like a regular vendor relationship," Mark Dunn said of the agency-client union. "It is almost a marriage. And you've got to like these people as individuals."

Chapter 3

The Closer He Gets,
the Better You Look

THERE WAS EMPATHY to spare at Altschiller Reitzfeld/Tracy-Locke. It oozed from the curls that bounced from the shoulders of David Altschiller, a shaggy, bearded, passionate man. It flowed from the soft, soothing voice of Robert Reitzfeld, a pale fellow with white hair whose pallor was balanced by a trim black suit and a black shirt buttoned up to the neck. From every pore of the agency's presentation—from the carefully calligraphed name tags at each seat of the conference table to the opening request by the agency that each of the Subaru representatives "tell us something about yourself," from the disclosure that Reitzfeld had flown back from a Caribbean vacation for the meeting to the presence of two female agency executives at the performance (TBWA's had been stag)—came the message, *We are caring people and we care about you.*

They studded their presentation with code phrases signifying their accommodating natures. When they introduced James Hutchinson, the agency's fresh-faced, toothy general manager, they pointedly told the Subaru representatives that Hutchinson had "worked on the P&G account at Benton & Bowles." Superficially, this was meant to convey that Hutchinson understood marketing strategy inside out: P&G—Procter & Gamble—has long been America's first- or second-largest advertiser, with an expertise at moving undifferentiated commodity products unmatched by any other marketer; D'Arcy Masius Benton & Bowles was one of its oldest agencies, handling Crest toothpaste among many other brands.

Hutchinson's introduction also had a deeper meaning. Procter & Gamble, America's oldest soap company, the corporation that pioneered the selling of mass products to mass audiences through mass media, was notorious for compelling its agencies to leap through more hoops than a circus lion. Every element of an agency's creative plans had to be quantified, the most ephemeral of qualitative decisions had to be justified. For a self-styled creative advertising shop—and Altschiller Reitzfeld prided itself on the wit of its words and the beauty of its layouts—telling a potential client that one of its account men had been on P&G at B&B was shorthand for saying the executive had, uncomplainingly, put up with copious amounts of torment.

Immediately after his introduction, Hutchinson punched a few buttons on a console in front of him and displayed a slide that read, "Good News For Subaru."

"Here's where I'm going to stick my neck out a little bit," he said. "But we think the market may be moving in your direction." The agency's observations were "part intuitive, part Yankelovich, part Faith Popcorn, part the reading we digest all the time," he added, lumping together a distinguished public opinion researcher (Yankelovich) and a self-made trend analyst (Popcorn). (Advertising agencies willingly appropriate insights from any source.)

Hutchinson flashed a series of slides and ran through a handful of the most-repeated marketing clichés of the young decade.

He said: "People are returning to traditional values, but updated. Not Ozzie and Harriet, but not the Me Decade of the 1980s." This meant that people who, during the Reagan Boom, could afford live-in housekeepers, now, in the Bush Bust, had to take care of their kids themselves.

He said: "People expect, recognize and demand quality." This meant that consumers were no longer willing to pay $28 for a broiled chicken just because it was served in a fancy French restaurant, as they had a few years earlier.

He continued: "There is a new price/value consciousness." This meant that people wanted to pay less for everything than they had in the eighties.

He added: "Time is the luxury, not possessions." This meant that people were working longer hours just to make ends meet.

He concluded: "There is less luxury badging." "Badging," a very popular marketing term in 1991, signified conspicuous consumption with a purpose; it was shorthand for keeping up with the Joneses. To say there was less badging meant that fewer driveways boasted Mercedes Benzes.

All of that, Hutchinson said, worked to Subaru's advantage, for the company, he believed, offered good cars at a fair price. Nonetheless, the little import company had severe problems. "The consumer is bombarded with more than 350 car choices. Your cars are viewed as practical, reliable, inexpensive and, I have to say, dowdy. It's a word you read in the buff books. Your dealers are agitated because they haven't been selling cars."

"We haven't been the shining light of success with our ideas so far," Chris Wackman acknowledged. "So far, you have taken our understanding and spit it back to us. You've done your homework. But how to do this? That's why we're on the road."

The question played to the agency's strength. Unlike TBWA, Altschiller Reitzfeld understood that a credentials presentation was a place for an ad agency to position itself, like a product, against the confusing array of seemingly similar products on the market.

"We believe the key to selling product is emotional—understanding the needs of the prospect in relation to what the product can offer," David Altschiller said. "So we would work very hard to find what Subaru is all about, what makes it relevant. Essentially, we find that if we can make that link, we'll make a sale. We can find you a different place to live."

He turned to Richard Newman, a young vice president at the agency, who wore a tie embroidered with tiny pastel snails. Newman told the Subaru men how Altschiller Reitzfeld had taken a toilet tissue named Coronet, renamed it Angel Soft, and through television commercials featuring the soothing voice of Sterling Holloway and fat babies with softly flapping wings, transformed the lackluster brand into one of the giants of the toilet tissue business.

"For the premium bath roll user, there is only one issue: softness, softness, softness," Newman said. "We realized through our research that we could create a new product attribute around the concept of softness, and also give the brand a personality that was happy, positive, whimsical and loving." It was the most successful new bath tissue launch in twenty years, Newman concluded.

As the Subaru men departed, walking beneath the exposed girders and through the massive metal doors of the high-tech-style office, Mark and Gene felt warmth and excitement from the agency's presentation, sentiments they shared with Wackman as they stood in a clutch in the lobby of the building.

Chris thought differently. "No closure yet," he sighed, shaking his head.

"The problem in dealing with an agency that has not had a car account is the products they deal with are very disposable," he explained in the taxi en route to the next credentials presentation. "You can buy a year's worth of Liz Claiborne fragrances, it doesn't work, you throw it away. People spend $15,000 on a Subaru, they don't like it, they're angry at you, they can't throw it away, and they tell everybody they know.

I'm not sure how to translate case studies about bath tissue into selling a car."

By the time they reached the Moondance Diner and had given their orders to a waitress with purple highlights in her hair and a stud in her nose, Mark Dunn's ardor for Altschiller Reitzfeld had also cooled. Indeed, to Mark, the agency's failure to link its case studies to Subaru's problems, as well as TBWA's complete ignorance of those problems, constituted two counts of a broader indictment of the culture of New York advertising.

Subaru's dealers, whose approval of the company's agency choice was crucial, already believed that no adman or adwoman who took a subway or taxi to work could comprehend their business; Chris had warned Altschiller Reitzfeld that "car dealers don't believe that anyone coming from New York understands how to sell cars, especially on the West Coast." He and Mark, their familiarity with the agency business more intimate than that of the dealers, knew that New York agencies had resources that small, out-of-town shops often could not match, chief among them easy access to a large pool of creative talent. But they were souring on what they interpreted as the intellectual laziness of the city's advertising community.

"The out-of–New York agencies felt they had to drive home their agency point. New York agencies seem to think they're *New York*—they don't have to do that," Mark told his colleagues over sandwiches. "The ones outside New York really try to do something memorable, so you'll remember them. New York doesn't do that. Maybe because they do so many new-business presentations."

The men were still reeling from a credentials presentation that had been made to them by W. B. Doner, the Baltimore agency. Doner had prepared it with all the precision of a military mission and all the ostentation of a Broadway musical. Immediately upon receiving the invitation to participate, the agency had assigned a score of people to work on the presentation, either full- or part-time. Some of them made calls to twenty-one Subaru dealers around the U.S. and taped their conversations about the company and its cars, customers and advertising. Others questioned consumers, in person or by phone, a total of four hundred interviews. Still others prepared a "ride-and-drive," an event in which potential auto buyers are somehow induced to come to a dealership to test-drive a car.

When Chris, Mark and Gene arrived at the small building—about five blocks from the Johns Hopkins Medical School campus—that housed Doner, they knew immediately that something was up. In the first-floor reception area, Doner had added a plate to the bottom of the wall that listed the cities in which it operated. Beneath "Baltimore," "Detroit," "Cleveland," "St. Petersburg, Fla.," "Boston," "Toronto," "Montreal" and "London" (where the agency maintained a tiny office to service the British Petroleum account) they had hung another sign, brazenly inscribed "Cherry Hill."

The attention to detail continued in the presentation. Doner took advantage of the lack of specificity in Gene's letter to present not two but six case studies outlining product introductions or repositionings on which the agency had worked. The products in question, to be sure, were not cars: Doner told how it had transformed the Klondike ice-cream bar from a kids' snack to an adult treat, for example, and how it broadened the appeal of the Arby's fast-food restaurant chain. When each of the case histories was concluded, each one timed to run exactly three minutes and each accompanied by print ads and statistical references posted on a wall, there appeared over the illustrations a cardboard sign that read "Subaru similarities." The agency then proceeded to relate what it had done for the other client to what it could do for Subaru. As a topper, the agency then brought into the room the marketing director of Arby's and the chief executives of Klondike and the Jos. A. Bank retail clothing chain, another client, to vouch for Doner's prowess—a touch that reminded Gene of the scene in the movie *Annie Hall* where Woody Allen supports his side of a debate on media theory by dragging Marshall McLuhan in from off-screen.

Finally, Doner switched on the large television set in its conference room. The picture focused on an auto dealership. More than two dozen people were milling around a Subaru Legacy, inspecting and talking about the car. After the Subaru reps had puzzled over the scene for a moment, the Doner executives explained that immediately after they had learned they were going to be visited, they called R. L. Polk, a market-research company specializing in automotive research, and bought from it a list of eight thousand people who lived in the Detroit suburbs. Within three days, the agency had prepared and mailed to these prospective customers an invitation to a dealership to test-drive a Subaru Legacy. As a lure, Doner told the potential buyers that a drawing would be held at the dealership, the winner to receive a television set. The event was set to coincide with the visit to Doner of the Subaru team. What the car company executives were watching, they were told, was a television broadcast from the Detroit-area dealership, live via satellite.

Wackman and his colleagues were still absorbing the spectacle when they left the conference room. They were led down the elevator and

out of the building, not through the front door but through the employees' entrance in Doner's basement garage. There, in every stall,
were Subaru Legacies, spanking-new (albeit, unknown to the Subaru
execs, rented), the license plates reading "WBD 1" to "WBD 36," in
succession.

"Doner," said Gene, breaking a stunned silence. "A killer agency."

"It blew us away," Chris Wackman said as he finished his sandwich at
the Moondance Diner. "Even if it was glitz, it was meaningful glitz.
And," he added, reemphasizing a point of consternation, "nobody in
New York did it."

Doner was a shoo-in for the finals of the Subaru pitch. By Mark
Dunn's mathematical calculations, it scored 128.75 points, the top
among the credentials presenters and nearly 50 points more than the
arguably more famous New York agency, TBWA. Not that Subaru abjured New York agencies entirely; Jordan, McGrath, Case & Taylor provided the Subaru executives with a reasoned analysis of how a car,
Chris's apprehensions to the contrary, could be sold like one of the
soaps made by the agency's client, Procter & Gamble. That merited 108
points and an invitation to the finals of the Subaru pitch.

Both Doner and Jordan, McGrath had exhibited "retail strength,"
Mark said, by showing exactly how they could increase sales, car by car,
through various methods and through close contact with car dealers.
"We looked at our current experience and asked what we were missing. From Levine, it was the retail experience."

At the opposite extreme, Mark Dunn prevailed on his colleagues to
invite Wieden & Kennedy into the finals as a creative wild card. Wieden
& Kennedy's ads for Nike athletic shoes had garnered just about every
major advertising award during the previous three years. Although
Subaru's dealers were skeptical of the whimsy that was the agency's
strong suit, Mark persuaded Chris that the creative impulse needed
representation in the review. Chris, in turn, successfully argued the case
to Tom Gibson.

Levine, Huntley received its promised last shot at the account. And
to mollify Subaru's new owners, tiny DCA was invited in. Its credentials
presentation had been less than impressive. The case histories it chose
to present were all for parity products, goods (like Canon camcorders)
that had no real differences from others in their categories. Chris, Mark
and Gene were unable to see how the agency would create advertising
to exploit real technological differences in a product. Moreover, DCA
had barely attempted to draw from its work inferences about what it
might be able to do for Subaru. By Mark's ranking, DCA scored only a

66.5. But that was enough for Subaru's Japanese overlords—with implications that were not unrecognized on Madison Avenue. When Gene made his courtesy calls to the also-rans, TBWA's Dick Costello exploded when he heard mention of the Japanese agency. *Is this a setup?* he asked.

"The final-analysis truth is that it is a fair situation," Chris Wackman replied. "Every agency has an equal chance to earn this business based on merit."

In reality, though, he was worried.

THEY PAID THE LUNCH BILL and walked quickly up the Avenue of the Americas, past young men in square-shouldered suits and black T-shirts, past sleekly dressed young women carrying leather artists' portfolios, to the renovated industrial building that housed the last agency Subaru was scheduled to visit, Warwick, Baker & Fiore.

NoHo, SoHo, TriBeCa, Chelsea, lower Park Avenue—these were New York's trendiest neighborhoods. Years ago, the cheap rents had attracted the artists, who were followed by the galleries, which, in time-honored fashion, were followed by bistros, fashion marts, luxury co-operative apartments, Korean groceries and, late in the line, advertising agencies. Most of the agencies that had made the move to these areas were newer, populated by young, iconoclastic writers and graphic artists, and associated with clothing designers, alcoholic-beverage companies and those clients who were, traditionally, more willing than others to experiment with unconventional advertising.

Warwick, Baker & Fiore was not that type of agency. This was immediately apparent upon entering the large, high-ceilinged echo chamber that served as its conference room. On a back wall that cantilevered out at a thirty-degree angle from the rest of the space like the top of a child's jack-in-the-box were several rows of white-on-black cards naming, with slogans, the agency's clients. "*Parade*: 61,000,000 readers in 48 hours," read one. "BVD: You're better off with them on," read another. "Midol: Helps it all go away," said a third. Clearly, this was an agency that specialized in old-fashioned, unapologetic sloganeering.

The room's large size and the constant hum of the ventilation system contributed to a deadened feeling as the meeting started. The impression was augmented by the presence of only four executives from the agency and by the eerie blue glow of two enormous television screens, capitalism's sentinels, which dominated the wall at right angles from the agency people and across from the three Subaru reps. There were perfunctory introductions, with the Warwick execs, as their advertising competitors had before them, bandying their previous agency affiliations the way old grads wear their prep school pedigrees; chief creative officer Bob Fiore had been at Kenyon & Eckhardt, "where he did the initial advertising for Dodge Colt," research director Susan Small-Weil was "formerly of McCann" and media director Mike Haggerty "worked on Procter & Gamble at Benton & Bowles" (there's one in every crowd). But it was the chief executive, Wilder Baker (who graduated from Andover and Yale a few years after President Bush), who led the presentation. And his first words broke through the room's torpor.

"We've chosen case histories that we think may be relevant to you," he said. "This agency is very, very experienced in turning brands around in difficult environments."

With buttressing commentary by Fiore, a gnomish, bearded man with an ardent manner, and by Small-Weil, a petite, efficient woman, Wilder, employing advanced advertising jargon, ran through Subaru's marketing problems, all of them identified using videotaped interviews with consumers or salesmen inside dealerships.

The first problem was "becoming part of a considered set"—getting on the short list of cars people think about when they're in the market for a new one. A button was pressed, and the words "CrossLand Savings" appeared on the television screens. Chris looked at Mark and gave a barely perceptible smile. The loop was about to be closed.

"Banks," said Fiore, before explaining how the agency had helped give this one a new name, "are not like cars, but in the broadest sense, there is a considered set." With these few words, he answered the objection Wackman had had to so many other presentations: What did they have to do with *his* business?

The second problem Subaru faced, according to Warwick, was "making the brand for me," a shorthand way of saying that the car company's identification with a handful of niche markets was so tight that the general audience of import buyers ignored it. Up on the TV screens appeared spots for Coty's Stetson cologne, depicting (to the country-rock melody "Easy for You") cowboy-boot-wearing, jeep-driving men splashing smell on their faces. Most men, the agency explained, did not think cologne was "for them." These spots, it claimed, enabled men to think of a fragrance as an appropriate product.

Then there was the issue of "addressing the trend surfers"—younger people, influential among their peers, who darted from novelty to novelty. Here, Warwick's evidence was not detailed market research but a six-four, 245-pound agency art director who owned a Subaru, was (according to Small-Weil) "the ultimate trend surfer—he has a house in Vermont" and was thinking of giving his wife the Subaru and trading up to another car. The agency followed with its campaign for Heineken beer, a brew whose image had grown stodgy amidst the onslaught of Mexican *cervezas*, "party animals" and the Swedish Bikini Team. War-wick's ads ridiculed the trend-seeking bar-hoppers, using the slogan, "When you're done kidding around. Heineken." The result was the reversal of a five-year sales decline.

Finally, Subaru faced a lack of dealer support. In a taped interview played for the executives, one car buyer recalled that a Subaru salesman told him Subaru was the car for him if he liked to take ski vacations in Vermont. In another interview, a saleswoman recounted how she could "tell a Subaru buyer when they walk in the door."

"What we found," said Small-Weil, "is that dealers look for the Subaru type. If you're not the type, they won't push you."

Wackman shook his head in discomfort and spat one word: "Whew!"

That was Wilder Baker's cue. On the television screens appeared the words, "Crafted With Pride in the U.S.A. Council"—a coalition of garment manufacturers and unions that had banded together to combat sales of cheaper imported clothing. "This may raise some sensitivities, because you're a Japanese company," Baker warned.

Chris brushed away his concern. "It doesn't bother us," he said.

"I just wanted to put it out there," responded Baker. "For if it were ever to become an issue, you could come to us. But a lot of this advertising is—" He punched his open hand, while looking Chris directly in the eye.

The problem and the strategy were simple. Unlike cars, American clothes were better than foreign clothes, consumers believed. But retailers, for whom the profit margins were the same regardless of the product's origin, would not help consumers distinguish foreign from American clothes. So Warwick developed for the council a campaign that featured celebrities like Bob Hope pointing to "Made in the U.S.A." labels on their garments and declaring, "It matters to me." War-wick's goal was to scare retailers into stocking the goods—a strategy reinforced by the agency's recommendation (followed by the council) that it sign on as a sponsor of the Miss America Pageant and retain the reigning Miss America as a spokeswoman for the campaign. Warwick ran a tape of the beauty queen plugging domestically manufactured clothing in an appearance on the ABC television program "Good Morning, America." Chris Wackman's response was again limited to one word: "Wow!"

The three Subaru representatives were downright cheerful as they shook hands with the four Warwick executives in the lobby of the agency's office. The elevator doors opened, and the car men got in. As soon as the doors closed, Chris looked up, shook his head slightly and said one word, prayerfully: "Closure."

PART II

THE COMPANY

Chapter 4

Cheap and Ugly

IT WAS AN EXPORT-IMPORT SCHEME, plain and simple. Didn't need to know exchange rates, currency fluctuations, port duties—

No. Harvey Lamm wanted nothing to do with it.

To Mal, it was a perfect plan. *A game.* But Harvey, this dutiful son of North Philly, was comfortable, y'know? Lamm's Furniture, his dad's store, was doing well—desk and swivel chair supplier to half of Center City's finest offices. It was 1967. He was thirty-one, a newlywed, the store was *forallintensivepurposes* his. *Whaddoo I wan' with some import deal?*

Mal had an answer. Mal had an answer for everything. *You were meant for more than conference tables, Harv,* he told his new friend not long after he moved back from Florida to Merion. *It's easy. Bring the stuff in, wholesale it at a profit and move on. You're not challenging your brain. Economy's booming. Wall Street à go-go. Whatever we're sellin', they're buyin'.*

Well . . . maybe. Malcolm Bricklin, he was something, after all. Tall, distinguished-looking, a great dresser—wide ties, wide lapels, wide flares. He was a furrier's son who had made a million in the hardware business, so he said, although why he moved to the fourth floor of an apartment building and not a Main Line mansion, he didn't say.

They golfed. *Started with a drive-in hardware store in Orlando,* Malcolm told Harvey, *and before I sold it, had 147 stores in the chain.* Some said it was more like sixteen, and hadn't been sold but went belly up. *But who's askin'?* He was so cultured, Mal was. Harvey had never got over his lack of education; Mal had never looked back after dropping out of the University of Florida.

Lookin' for a partner, Harv. Got this Italian company buildin' a juke-box plays music and movies at the same time.

No. Harvey wasn't interested in jukeboxes. Still, he was intrigued. Sure, Malcolm was flighty, Harvey conceded to his friends. But he was a brilliant idea man. *He's got the right addeetood. I could see starting a business with him.*

Got this Italian scooter deal, Harv. Lambretta. Givin' me $5,000 a week and a chauffeured Rolls-Royce to sell 'em in.

No. Harvey didn't care about scooters. Yet Mal was a doer, Harvey could see that. Did the Lambretta deal himself. (Unloaded the scooters on the New York Police Department, so he said.) Then Lambretta pulled out of the market. Malcolm found a substitute.

Got this Japanese scooter deal, Harv. Fuji Heavy Industries. Calls 'em the Rabbit. They got automatic transmission. We'll wholesale 'em to gas stations, tell 'em—ever been to Bermuda?—the scooter rental business is gonna explode. Sell 'em signs, service—

Well . . . maybe. It was after dinner, late 1967. Harvey was browsing through a brochure Malcolm had received from Fuji Heavy Industries. *Yo, Mal. They don't just make scooters. They make buses. They make jet fighters. They make this car.*

Whaddabout the car, Harv?

Harvey thought about it. *I'll tell you what,* he said, mostly to get Malcolm to change the subject. *You get 'em to give ya the car, we can talkaboudit.*

Are you serious? Malcolm quickly replied.

Harvey stopped and thought a long bit. Whatever he said next could cost him money.

Yeah, I'm serious, he said at last. *I think it'd be fun.*

They looked together at the photograph of the automobile in the brochure. The car was called the Subaru 360. . . .

ADVERTISING, IN THE MINDS OF ITS PRACTITIONERS, is a con-trolling science. *Perception is reality,* the admen and -women confi-dently declare; there is no truth outside consumers' beliefs, the convictions that advertising's technicians are trained to create. From Bishop George Berkeley, who 250 years ago held that nothing could ex-ist independent of human cognition, it was just a short step to Arthur Miller's hapless salesman, Willy Loman, who cried when his most ex-pensive appliance died, "I told you we should've bought a well-advertised machine! Charley bought a General Electric and it's twenty years old and it's still good. . . ."

In their view that advertising transforms reality, those in the business adhere to a theory that media scholars term the "transmission view of communication": the belief that interactions among people exist foremost for the purpose of change and control. But some sages hew to an alternative model, which James W. Carey calls the "ritual view of communication." We engage in social intercourse, Carey says, not to control but to commune with each other, to share information and beliefs for the purpose of maintaining a society over time.

Companies, as all who work for them know, are nothing if not little societies, each with its own rich creation mythology, rites, demons and gods. Advertising, the process by which a company communicates not only to its customers but to itself as well, is in the "ritual view" less a scientifically devised effort at control than an evolving collection of allegory and fable, created by one independent society, the agency, for another, the client. Advertising is not a science but a study in anthropology. Its basis is not perception as reality; it is image as history, and culture as destiny.

As the six finalists for Subaru of America's advertising account commenced their battle for the auto company's business in May 1991, they thumbed through reams of market data, buried themselves in tearsheets and videotapes of automobile advertising, tore through the archives of *Motor Trend* magazine and *Automotive News*, even inspected under the hoods of Subaru cars. What they *should* have done in addition was pay heed to what Subaru *was*. "A good and successful discourse," Socrates said in Plato's *Phaedrus*, "presupposes a knowledge in the mind of the speaker of the truth about his subject."

For the truth was, Subaru was a game. . . .

THE OBJECT OF HARVEY'S ARDOR was an automobile whose name neither he nor Malcolm Bricklin could pronounce. It was the Subaru (enunciated, they would soon learn, with the accent on the second syllable, as Soo-BAH-roo) 360. It was, simply put, wretched. Its headlights sat recessed inside cylinders that looked like late-model stovepipes, on two sides of a distended hood that resembled an anteater's snout. The rolling pitch of the front fenders, which continued across the sides of the stubby car all the way to its attenuated rear, made the sedan look as if it had the mumps.

It was among the world's tiniest autos. At 71 inches from the center of its front wheels to the center of the rear wheels, and 118 inches overall, the car "occupied one-third the road space of a Cadillac Eldorado," as *Road & Track* magazine derisively pointed out. The "360" indicated the vehicle's engine displacement—the volume of the space, in cubic centimeters, inside the car's two cylinders through which the engine's pistons moved during a single stroke. By contrast, the Volkswagen Beetle's engine displacement was 1,500 cubic centimeters. The Beetle, despite its plodding, Mr. Magoo–like appearance, was also quite a bit more powerful than the 360, its engine boasting more than twice the little Subaru's 25 horsepower.

But the Subaru 360 was small where it counted, too. Harvey and Malcolm quickly calculated that they could earn $660 per vehicle by selling it, at retail, for $1,297, a price about $500 below the Beetle's. They never thought about going retail, though. Much better to remain a distributor—wholesaling the cars, taking the profits, leaving the aftermarket headaches to the dealers.

The VW Beetle could still be a selling point for them. Despite the 360's deficiencies, it could be compared favorably to America's most popular car. The 360 had a rear-mounted engine, just like the Volkswagen, that was air-cooled, and thus not susceptible to overheating or freezing, just like the Volkswagen. It could seat four people, just like the Volkswagen; achieve, according to Fuji, a top speed of 63 miles per hour (not much less than the Volkswagen); and get 66 miles per gallon of fuel in its 4.7-gallon gas tank, which was *better* than the Volkswagen.

Best of all, after a little bit of research, Harvey and Malcolm discovered that the Subaru 360 was not a car.

Federal motor vehicle safety standards applied only to vehicles weighing 1,000 pounds or more. Despite its quartet of wheels and hydraulic brakes, its rack-and-pinion steering and four-wheel independent suspension, the Subaru 360 weighed only 965 pounds. It was, in the eyes of the U.S. government, a covered motorcycle. Malcolm and Harvey could import it with virtual impunity.

They hatched a deceptively simple scheme. As Mal had done with his scooters, the idea was to avoid the consumer marketplace altogether. *Why mess with warranties? Why screw around with repairs? Become an importer-distributor instead!* They proposed to obtain exclusive agreements from foreign manufacturers who didn't know any better and wholesale their vehicles to dealers. Then bolt.

Fuji was the perfect place for Malcolm and Harvey to start. Germans, Swedes, French—everybody knew those countries' cars. Volkswagen was already selling half-a-million cars stateside. The Japanese . . . no one knew they existed. They had been exporting their cars to the States for ten years, but their tin-box junkers were so mechanically unsound that outside of California, where people were culturally more willing to experiment, they never caught on. The time had come, the two Philadelphians believed, to bring Japanese cars back to the East Coast. The market, they thought, was good for maybe 25,000 cars a year within five years.

The one obstacle was that Fuji Heavy Industries was not interested in exporting its cars to the United States. Indeed, it was planning to stop production and export of the Rabbit motor scooter whose import contract Mal had acquired—a fact that Malcolm was able to use to wedge open Fuji's door. He went to Tokyo to confront his wouldn't-be partners.

You owe me one! he charged. Technically, this was not true. Malcolm had started a company, American Rent-A-Scooter, in hopes of wholesaling Fuji's Rabbits to gas station owners. But his deal wasn't with Fuji; he had picked up the scooter-import contract from a fellow in Boston, who had neglected to tell Malcolm when he sold him the deal that Fuji was stopping production of the Rabbit. Still, Malcolm figured it was worth a shot.

Least you could do, leavin' me inna lurch like that, is gimme the car to sell.

He was persuasive—especially when he reminded the Japanese that, as their new scooter importer, he also controlled the parts and servicing of their existing stateside Rabbits, and that they had a legal obligation to make sure their scooters continued to work. *Shame if owners couldn't get repairs. . . .* He could also pontificate like a statesman. Later, his colleagues would joke that Malcolm could hand you a bucket and make you think it was filled with jewels when it was really a bucket full of holes and whatever was in it was leaking. Fuji agreed to sell him the cars. Malcolm wanted more. He always wanted more. He demanded an exclusive contract, and got it.

On February 15, 1968, Malcolm and Harvey incorporated themselves as Subaru of America. Harvey put up $25,000, and Malcolm $50,000. Eight days later, they signed their hastily negotiated contract with Fuji Heavy Industries. The manufacturer appointed the two-man firm its sole distributor for the Subaru 360 in the United States, charged with wholesaling the car (through, the Philadelphians explained, a series of regional distributors wholly or partly owned by the new company) to independent auto dealers around the country. The contract would run for one year, but could be automatically renewed each year for four years.

Fuji protected itself from its new market and its new partners by requiring Subaru of America (or S.O.A.) to purchase at least two thousand vehicles in 1968—less than half the number Volkswagen sold *each month*. The number was to increase by a thousand units in each of the contract's subsequent years. The agreement allowed Fuji to cancel the contract at any time if the U.S. or Japanese governments altered their import or export regulations, if "circumstances" made performance by either party "physically or financially infeasible or extremely difficult" or if Fuji simply decided to stop making the Subaru 360.

The piece of paper was only the first part of Malcolm and Harvey's scheme. The second part was even *bigger*. With nothing but their Fuji contract, the two men took their company public.

Even during Wall Street's go-go years, it was unlikely that a company whose only asset was an unfulfilled contract would have been able to obtain a listing on one of the major stock exchanges. But S.O.A. found another route. The rules of the Philadelphia Stock Exchange, one of several local exchanges around the country, allowed companies to sell shares to residents of the Commonwealth of Pennsylvania if they restricted their trading in the shares to fellow residents. Pennsylvania regulators were not as stringent as the governors of the major national exchanges. The risk was on the underwriter, if one could be found, and the buyers. At least one investment banking firm approached by Harvey and Malcolm wouldn't touch the issue, but in less than a month, in exchange for ordinary fees and commissions and fifteen thousand shares of stock, the pair located a Philadelphia investment banker who agreed to underwrite the offering. Eventually, through peculiarities in securities regulation, the Philadelphia listing allowed Subaru of America shares to be sold over-the-counter on the NASDAQ exchange in New York.

Banks were willing to lend Mal and Harvey only $100,000. The two men conceded that they had no idea whether the additional money they were trying to raise was adequate to open their business. They had already agreed with nine dealers to provide them with "prompt and competent service" and "service facilities and trained mechanics," but admitted that they had "not yet created the training courses" for the dealers and mechanics "nor acquired the personnel" to conduct the courses, nor even rented the warehouse space to store the spare parts they didn't have the money to train the nonexistent mechanics to install. Yet with a contract arbitrarily valued at $12,000, no land, no factory, no equipment and no product, the Philadelphians were able to raise nearly $1 million by selling 300,000 shares of stock to trusting Pennsylvanians. *See Harv, I told you it was easy.*

Naturally, they rewarded themselves. Malcolm took an annual salary of $30,000 and 882,000 shares to serve as Subaru of America's president. Harvey got 258,000 shares, plus $25,000 per annum to be secretary-treasurer. Two of Harvey's associates, both manufacturer's reps in the furniture business (one a governor of the Eastern States National

Wholesale Furniture Association, the other a past president of the Philadelphia Furniture Club), together got 60,000 shares.

They were on their way. Harvey and Malcolm set up a new corporate headquarters in Bala Cynwyd, a Philadelphia suburb, installed Bricklin's mother, Gertrude, as bookkeeper and got Harvey's dad, Ed, to help with the ordering. (He bought a bunch of adding machines at liquidation, but soon found they were dysfunctional; they moved the decimal point one space too far to the left. When S.O.A.'s auditor complained about the expenditure, Ed whined. *Is it really important?* he asked. *I got a deal.*) They also bought automobiles. The first shipment of Subaru 360s from Fuji, three cars that barely came up to Harvey Lamm's chest, arrived at the port of Philadelphia even before the papers were signed. Others, hundreds of others, soon followed.

Some of the cars were easy to sell. Malcolm plied his old haunts—repair shops, gas stations, bicycle stores, used car dealers—and offered them the deal of the decade. A thousand dollars down for a franchise, signs, tools, brochures and trade advertising. ("Cheap and ugly does it," read the headline Malcolm wrote, under the photo of the 360.) Nine hundred dollars and change for the car. Sell the 360 at suggested retail price of $1,297, and that meant an unheard-of profit of more than $300 a vehicle. Twenty dealers on the East Coast and another sixty in California took the bait.

"I remember putting thirteen or fourteen little Subarus in the showroom, putting them in like wheelbarrows," recalled Marty Pizza, an Orangeburg, New York, auto repairman who could not resist the come-on. "You'd back them all up, then lift up the front bumper, and push them in."

With the 360s beginning to sell, S.O.A. needed more money to make the purchases from Fuji. Mal found a New York investment firm willing to underwrite a private placement, but not if S.O.A.'s contract with Fuji could lapse after only five years. What kind of security was there in that?

They had a point. Malcolm went back to Japan. *We need an agreement in perpetuity.* Fuji was reluctant. He pushed. *Whaddya gonna do? You can't take 'em back. They got the steering wheel on the left. You people like 'em on the right.* Later, Fuji executives would grumble that they had been tricked. Neither Malcolm nor Harvey cared. They had their eternal contract. Now they could *really* hustle dealers.

Fuji was able to extract several concessions in return for the new arrangement. All payment, the manufacturer told Subaru of America, must now be up front. If the Americans could not get the cash from their dealers, then they would have to get the money from banks.

S.O.A., the new contract read, could "order vehicles or equipment only upon the presentation to Fuji of an irrevocable letter of credit to cover the invoice price and in some cases freight for all items ordered." The letters of credit would be opened the moment Fuji placed vehicles on the boats in Yokohama, and would be payable no later than 180 days from the shipment date.

The Japanese also demanded that S.O.A. purchase a minimum of ten thousand vehicles during the first year of the new contract, and at least three thousand additional vehicles each year for the next thirteen years. From 1984 on, Subaru of America would be required to buy from Fuji at least fifty thousand cars annually.

Harvey and Malcolm were undaunted by the new numbers. Whether it was the rising price of the VW Beetle, Americans' growing familiarity with Japanese cars, or the confidence dealers felt in the renegotiated contract, S.O.A. was having no trouble moving the metal. During the first few months of 1969, dealers were selling about a thousand of the 360 minicars each month—bringing revenues of a few hundred thousand dollars every new moon into Bala Cynwyd.

The future looked bright and the next step was clear: *Build a headquarters! Show the world we've arrived!* Mal hired his brother-in-law to supervise construction of a new headquarters across the Delaware River in Pennsauken, New Jersey. On the lawn, space was set aside for a helicopter pad.

Malcolm's office was a push-button-remote-control-automatic-all-in-one-007-fantasy chamber. Its imposing, ten-foot-tall oak doors swung open without visible human intervention when Mal pressed a button on the underside of his palette-shaped, Formica-topped desk. Other buttons caused half a dozen miniature television sets to rise from beneath the desk, and still other buttons allowed Mal to view activities, courtesy of hidden cameras, in every part of his Jersey empire. In front of the magic desk was a recessed conversation area. In it, eggshell-shaped chairs surrounded the sitter with stereophonic music, again controlled by a Bricklin button. Harvey's office was nearby. He covered his desk—the whole thing, the top as well as all four sides—in animal fur.

The partners began dressing the roles their offices dictated, sporting Nehru jackets, orange bodysuits and heavy gold chains that reached to their exposed navels. They made sure their Asian suppliers were thematically represented, too. Between Malcolm's office and the service department was an atrium filled by an elaborate Japanese garden, replete with bonsai trees, water pools and bulging goldfish. A visitor to the headquarters not long after it opened was struck less by Malcolm's toys than by the garden. "The plants there were absolutely dead," she recalled.

Details, it seemed, were not the men's strong suit. In April 1969, just four months after S.O.A. signed the renegotiated contract with Fuji, *Consumer Reports*, the publication of Consumers Union, issued its "Annual Auto Issue." Young drivers looking for an inexpensive first car or families seeking a cheap second car had to look no further than the magazine's table of contents for the verdict on the Fuji-S.O.A. minicar: "The Subaru 360: Not Acceptable."

Consumer Reports was not opposed to minicars per se. Urban traffic, limited parking and poor public transportation cried out for an American equivalent of Europe's Isetta, Messerschmidt and Goggomobile. The 360, however, was not that car: "The Subaru is, in *CU*'s judgment, unacceptably hazardous."

The vehicle's fundamental problem was speed: It had none. From a standing start, it took the 360 "an agonizing" 37.5 seconds to reach 50 miles per hour. The 1968 Beetle, by contrast, took only 14.5 seconds. "Vehicles moving substantially slower than the surrounding traffic are an even more frequent cause of road accidents" than speeders, the magazine warned. "They frustrate drivers behind them into rash passing maneuvers."

Consumer Reports found fault with the automobile's emergency handling. A sudden turn at 55 miles per hour caused the outside rear wheel to tuck under as the back end of the car pitched up, causing sudden, violent oversteering. Straight roads were little better. "Crosswinds caused the car to swerve alarmingly." The brakes locked on slippery surfaces, controlled short stops were hard to manage, and the windshield defroster melted a hole barely larger than a Boy Scout's merit badge. When a controlled, 30-mile-per-hour head-on collision was arranged between the 360 and an American car, the domestic suffered only minor damage. But "the Subaru was collapsed back to its window line," the magazine reported, "and the U.S. car's bumper ended up in the Subaru's passenger department."

"It was a pleasure," *Consumer Reports* concluded, "to squirm out of the Subaru, slam the door and walk away."

At the time the magazine hit the stands, there were some six thousand Subaru 360s in the United States—about two thousand at S.O.A. or its ports of entry, the rest in dealers' lots or owners' garages. Wild spending on the Pennsauken headquarters and overambitious ordering had given the company a negative cash flow of $750,000 and pushed several previously accommodating banks into rejecting requests for letters of credit. No problem, thought Mal, Harvey and their investors. As long as sales continued, the debt would take care of itself. Consumers Union put a halt to that.

Less than a year after they had opened, the pyramid was collapsing around Malcolm and Harvey. S.O.A.'s dealers and its distribution partners were terrified. They froze their orders. Its wholesale payments gone, Subaru couldn't pay cash to Fuji. So the manufacturer collected on the letters of credit. Since S.O.A. had no money, it could not reimburse the banks, and defaulted on the credit agreements. That blocked further borrowing from its current banks and from every other financial institution within sight of a credit report. Since it couldn't obtain letters of credit or other forms of financing, S.O.A. could not obtain additional cars to sell, which was the only way the company saw to extricate itself from its predicament.

Sales slowed to a trickle. The two-door sedans did not move at all. Some dealers were able to unload a few vans and tiny pickup trucks by selling them to large manufacturing companies for use as in-plant transportation. But even these vehicles soon lost their marketability. Toward the end, when S.O.A. was trying to dump them, dealers were able to buy rusting 360s, right off the docks, for $500 apiece. One enterprising entrepreneur in Long Island City, New York, bought several, cut them apart with a welding torch and turned them into motorized hot-dog wagons.

At the end of February 1970, Subaru sales ground to a virtual halt. S.O.A. had lost $3.9 million. By the end of the year, the company had 2,800 minicars in inventory. On paper, the vehicles were worth about $1.06 million net; in reality, they were worth nothing.

For Malcolm, this was all part of the game. He had been through difficult times with other entrepreneurial ventures before. For Harvey, though, this situation was a touch more desperate. He had tied up his family's money, his friends' money. On his own, Harvey decided not to fight the bad publicity, but to work with it. He called on the automotive trade press, consumer publications and Philadelphia-area newspapers. He cited Japanese statistics that, he said, proved the minicar actually had a better history of safety than other cars. *We're not saying that this car is as safe as a big car. What we're really selling is something one step above a motorcycle, something that could be used as a commuter car, an around-town kind of car.*

Malcolm took measures more immediately aimed at seeing the company through what he insisted on calling its "liquidity problem." The company's advertising agency, a tiny local shop, owed $57,000 to printers and publications for work and space they had given for Subaru ads;

customarily, the vendors and the media front an agency their services and space and receive their money immediately after the agency collects from its client. When Len Epstein, the agency owner, called on Bricklin for his fees, Malcolm took his hand. *Len,* he said, *in one month you'll have all your money.* "The way he put it," Epstein said a few years later, "I felt there was no way I wasn't going to get my money. That was the last I ever saw or heard of him." The overdue bills eventually forced Epstein to close his agency.

You could only stall so much, of course. Subaru had to let independent auditors review its books; its lenders required it, and so did securities regulators. This presented a problem. If the banks ever found out how badly Subaru was doing, they would never lend it any more money or back its credit letters. And if Fuji found out, it could cancel S.O.A.'s import agreement.

For a time, Subaru was saved from having to face its financial backers through the sheer mismanagement of its records. Legend had it that Malcolm's mother—the company bookkeeper, "Ma Bricklin," as the staff called her—would throw away invoices and receipts with which she found fault. Inventory control—accounting for the number and location of the vehicles S.O.A. bought from Fuji—was nonexistent. (Years later, long after the company had grown respectable, a Subaru executive received a call from a woman in Oklahoma. *When are you fellas gonna come for them cars?* she wanted to know. An S.O.A. representative traveled west to find thirty minicars, tire-deep in mud, on her farm. Subaru—most likely to hide them from the banks so it could continue to borrow money, ostensibly to buy new cars but probably to pay old bills—had parked them there and forgotten about them.) Simply reconstructing the financial and inventory records so they could be audited took months and months. The Subaru account's senior auditor at Arthur Andersen & Co., a man with nervous bowels, took to spending one to two hours on the toilet every morning before he started in on the company's books. Altogether, the problems helped delay S.O.A.'s 1970 annual meeting for nearly a year.

Even after the auditors reassembled the books, S.O.A. managed to delay a final accounting. Malcolm and Harvey devised a game to rid themselves of unwanted visitors. Confronted by a disagreeable guest, Mal would excuse himself, pick up his phone and call Harvey. They'd start arguing. At a prearranged signal, Harvey would slam down the phone, rush in and continue the argument in person. Malcolm would then pull a gun from his drawer and shoot his partner. The guest—auditor, supplier, whoever—would flee, never to learn that the pistol was filled with blanks.

The bottom line, though, was that only Fuji could bail them out. Harvey and Malcolm flew back and forth to Japan. They had set their sights on the next car up in Fuji's model line, the FF1. It, they believed, could save them.

The discussions began cordially. *We can't stay in business if we don't have the bigger car, and if we don't stay in business, you won't have an export market in the United States,* they told the Japanese. Fuji was unyielding. Malcolm and Harvey turned up the heat. *There's no saving the 360. If we don't get the larger car, we're dead.* Nothing. So at dinner one night, at a restaurant atop a Tokyo office building, Malcolm loosed a tirade on two senior Fuji executives. *If you think Hiroshima was bad, wait until you see what happens to Subaru inna United States!* Finally, Fuji agreed to sell S.O.A. the FF1.

Harvey took charge of the effort to line up new dealers and distributors. He concentrated his efforts in the southern, midwestern and mountain states—less trendy areas of the country where, he assumed, *Consumer Reports* had less influence than in the sophisticated East, where small-time dealers with dreams of millions were less prone to panic.

Malcolm, meanwhile, went out and found a new source of financing, a Binghamton, New York, family by the name of Koffman, whose business was lending, often in huge amounts, usually for short periods of time, occasionally for controlling interests in companies that, sometimes, they would run, sometimes pull apart and sell. Mal's connection to the Koffmans was a friend named Weiss who lived in the same Merion apartment complex in which he and Harvey resided.

The Koffmans soon found themselves owning, in payment for defaulted loans they had made and letters of credit they had backed, more than 36 percent of Subaru's shares. It didn't take them long to determine that their investment was sour. They wanted out, but figured there was no way they could dump their shares unless they could also distance themselves from Subaru's highly visible, highly voluble and highly troublesome president. Malcolm, though, wasn't budging. They offered him a $120,000, three-year consulting contract and relief from his last, $40,000 personal debt to the company. But Malcolm wanted one more thing: FasTrack.

FasTrack was a wholly owned subsidiary of Subaru. It was a typical Malcolm scheme. If the Subaru 360 was unsafe for the open road, he reasoned, then sell it as a racing car—and franchise the racing courses to go along with it.

Next to S.O.A.'s Pennsauken headquarters, Malcolm constructed a prototype track. He took a handful of 360s, removed the windshields and windows, and surrounded the vehicles with thick bumpers. He painted racing stripes and numbers on them, then invited potential franchisees to come take a look.

"Once behind the wheel, you rev up the throaty engine while waving a salute to the crowd in the grandstands," read the prospectus Malcolm gave them. "And then it's all up to you. . . . It's just you and that stripped-down racer against the clock." All it would cost, he told them, was $25,000. *You get 10 refurbished minicars, a sign, a racing clock, helmets, uniforms and an annual profit we project at more than $135,000.*

Malcolm had developed FasTrack as a way of dumping S.O.A.'s financially draining inventory of 360 minicars. But now, as he prepared his exit from the company, he envisioned it as a grand venture, one that could easily eclipse his previous undertakings. FasTrack would become the center of a string of theme parks strewn across America, combinations of Disneyland and the Indianapolis Speedway that would appeal to kids and adults alike. He had already talked the owner of a resort hotel in Pennsylvania's Pocono Mountains into financing his first "FasTrack Leisure Land." *I'll leave,* Malcolm told his board of directors, *but give me FasTrack.* The Koffmans acceded. They gave Malcolm all "assets and equipment" the FasTrack division owned—$978,000 worth of matériel, by Subaru's calculation.

In this way, in June 1971, Subaru of America got rid of the last vestiges of its flirtation with the disastrous and dangerous Subaru 360: 454 rusting sedans, 391 miniature trucks and vans, 55 other vehicles . . . and Malcolm Bricklin.

CULTURE IS DESTINY. The life span of the Subaru 360 in the United States was less than three years. Yet the measures taken to stave off the bankruptcy and dissolution threatened by the little car affected Subaru of America for the next two decades, influencing the way the company conducted its business and, more important, the way consumers perceived it well into its 1991 search for a new image.

Because of the 360's mechanical deficiencies and, later, *Consumer Reports'* criticism of those flaws, Subaru of America began assembling, then catering to, a network of dealers removed from the nation's great cities and their suburbs. "In the earlier years, with the 360 and the FF1, they took anybody as a dealer. I mean, they didn't even know where the dealers were," said Marvin S. Riesenbach, who became the company's comptroller in the early 1970s.

Harvey Lamm, at twenty years' remove, recalled that the need for a "rural strategy," as he termed it, became apparent almost as soon as he and Bricklin took possession of their first 360s. "We had our own experience seeing what the driving condition of the car was, what it was like to get on the Philadelphia Expressway," he said. "The car wasn't best suited to most metro areas, because most metro areas had high-speed highways that you almost *had* to go on in normal daily transportation. It wasn't that we didn't think we could sell them [in urban areas]. We didn't think that's where we could build a real future."

The problems were compounded by the notoriety. "The metro markets suffered very, very early on from the bad publicity," Harvey said. The attention hurt most in the nation's largest single market for imported automobiles—California. Harvey had spent much of his time there, even living in an ocean-view apartment in Newport Beach, courting dealers and distributors. But California was an early incubator of the consumers movement. The assault on the Subaru 360 drove a sharp, heavy wedge between the car's importer and the "motorist's paradise."

The back roads, where consumer publications barely circulated, provided an escape. "What we found was that the dealers in the rural markets, were able to do a better job selling the product because it was an unknown car and they traded on their reputation," Harvey recalled. "Local dealers in metro markets . . . they don't have that kind of market relationship. They're not members of the Kiwanis Club or the church. They're just not as involved in the same way in the community."

Built by necessity, this complex of showrooms and salesmen off the beaten track proved beneficial to Subaru when Fuji began exporting to America its unusual front-wheel-drive car and, a bit later, its unique four-wheel-drive vehicles, automobiles peculiarly suited to the rigors of unpaved roads, steep hills and snowy climes. Moreover, dealers in these markets, unencumbered by high real-estate or advertising costs, could make do with less, especially in the mid- and late-1970s, when energy crises made consumers wary of new automobiles.

So Subaru of America began to exploit the market into which it had, unceremoniously, been thrust. If, in the future, its vehicles would no longer be "cheap and ugly," they would still be cheap—and utilitarian.

The liabilities of that message, and the tactics that led to and later supported it, would not become apparent for a long, long time. Rural dealers were also, often, weak dealers, "weaker than other Japanese manufacturers' dealers and the domestics' dealers," according to Ronald Glantz, an automobile industry analyst, because they "were not located as well, and their facilities were not as nice." As early as 1974, Subaru owners were complaining en masse about poor service and neglect by their dealers. In one survey, a third of Subaru drivers rated dealer service as "poor." But because these dealers were able to sell the automobiles Subaru of America was importing, the company had little incentive to improve its sales network. Nor did it feel great pressure to tinker, or ask Fuji to tinker, with its product line.

None of this would have mattered, of course, if Subaru of America had chosen the sensible route and gone out of business; if the shareholders had written off their losses and bailed out; if Harvey Lamm had tucked his tail between his legs and returned to the furniture business. But Harvey had a different vision. He'd tasted failure, but he'd also supped, however briefly, on success. He could run this company.

It took him some time, but eventually he persuaded Fuji, the once-reluctant exporter, to buy out the Koffmans, take just shy of 50 percent of S.O.A. and assure itself a market in the United States. Then Harvey convinced his new "partner" to name him president, then chief executive officer, and finally chairman. Then he got Fuji to leave him alone to run the company as he saw fit.

Or so he thought. If Subaru's rural strategy was the defining element of its marketing effort for years to come, its relationship with Fuji Heavy Industries would similarly mark the company's structure and strategy. On the surface, the two companies were independent of each other, an unacknowledged symbiosis that defied managerial and financial logic. Years later, Takeshi Higurashi, Fuji's liaison to S.O.A. in its earliest years and later its chairman, was asked why Fuji had allowed its American importer to remain so distant. "Oriental mysticism," he replied, with only partial irony.

The mutual independence was illusory, of course. Every move either company made was severely circumscribed by the other company's decisions. Subaru's ability to communicate a consistent image to the American public was continually confounded by Fuji's reticence in sharing product-planning intelligence, technical details or pricing information until it was too late to incorporate the data into advertising and promotional campaigns. Fuji claimed it had no choice but to withhold the information, lest it give S.O.A. an unfair advantage when the two companies negotiated product prices.

But Harvey was willing to overlook these obstacles as he worked toward his greater goal—success. He grew to understand that Subaru was, first and foremost, a niche marketer, blessed with an ardent, if inexperienced, dealer base in relatively uncluttered markets. It also had a product whose front-wheel drive and, later, four-wheel-drive transmissions made it, for a time, unique.

How Harvey characterized S.O.A.'s niche was, however, conditioned as much by his background and the tumult of the company's origins as by the products it received over the years from Japan. Instead of identifying Subaru by its engineering technology or its regional biases, the former Philadelphia furniture salesman—who, having stared failure in the face without blinking, believed he could sell anything to anyone—came to identify Subaru's niche by his own character: feisty, street-smart, tough and quirky.

We want to be the people who go out at night and go to where nobody else isn't! he bellowed, Goldwynesquely, to his troops. *We want to go into jungles, into woods—all the places they are not. Their weakest places is where we want to be successful.*

He had to communicate that message, of course. So Harvey went out and hired an advertising agency.

Chapter 5

Inexpensive, and
Built to Stay That Way

HISTORIANS TRACE THE JEWISH AFFINITY for salesmanship to the Middle Ages, when European Jews were prevented from
joining the crafts guilds and were forced to find sustenance in trade and
finance, endeavors from which Christians, for religious and cultural reasons, were largely barred. To wind their way around the anti-Semitic
proscriptions, Jews learned the art of innovation—the creation of new
financial instruments, the location of new market opportunities. To lure
customers who would otherwise spurn their entreaties, Jews traded low
prices and low margins for high volume, and therefore traveled far to
develop the widest markets possible for their goods and services. They
thus developed expertise in understanding and exploiting consumption
trends. Finally, where tradition and law (like a 1761 Parisian regulation
which forbade traders to issue leaflets about their goods) hindered Gen-
tile self-promotion, Jews, writes the historian Paul Johnson, having little
social standing, "were among the leaders in display, advertising and
promotion."

Harold Levine was a product of this history, although he was quite
unaware of it. An impressionable youth of fifteen in the summer of
1936, Harold was attracted to advertising for a more immediate reason:
Uncle Charlie's Cord.

The Cord was the long, smooth glamour car of its day. When
Levine, a Manhattan kid vacationing away from the city's heat in Long
Branch, New Jersey, saw his next-door neighbor's Uncle Charlie pull up
in one, he was mesmerized. What, he stammered, did Uncle Charlie
do?

Uncle Charlie did the "I-was-a-98-pound-weakling" advertising for
the Charles Atlas Company. Harold had found his future.

After high school and the Army, he went to a family friend, who gave him a list of Jewish advertising agencies—the only ones, he told Harold, that would hire him. At one, then another, the young man learned the art of advertising. He wrote five "goodwill" letters a week, thanking every vendor, every salesman, every printer who came by for a visit: You never knew who might lead to a prospective client. He learned to generate "ideas"—promotional or marketing schemes that could be explained in less than a paragraph and sold to prospects as original bursts of inspiration made *especially* for them.

In 1952, Harold met Mervin Levine (no relation), who, with his brother Jesse, ran an agency called Fashion Advertising. It was a typical Jewish agency. Mervin and Jesse had started it as a printing shop, doing brochures and handbills for the dressmakers surrounding their office at 34th Street and Eighth Avenue. Mervin told Harold that he wanted his agency to grow beyond the garment trade. The prospect appealed to Harold. He joined the shop as a $9,000-a-year account executive, recommended a name change from Fashion Advertising to Mervin & Jesse Levine (the better to suggest its broadening purview) and advertised it in the *New York Times*'s financial pages as a provider of "advertising from the businessman's viewpoint."

By the early 1960s, Harold was the agency's president, with a small ownership position in the firm. But he was restless. Mervin & Jesse Levine had not managed to break away from the dry-goods advertising to which the Jewish agencies had been consigned. Ship 'n' Shore clothing was still his major client. Enormous national accounts still went to the white-shoe agencies. But, looking around, Harold saw a way out—a path to riches, perhaps even fame.

"I wasn't a member of The Club," he said of the large agencies. "But I could become a member of the Other Club."

The Club—that was Madison Avenue. Ivy League educations, homes in Greenwich, woods and irons, alcoholic lunches. The Club's members—McCann-Erickson, J. Walter Thompson, Young & Rubicam, names that reeked of Presbyterianism and privilege—said they were in the business of advertising. The reality was, they were in manufacturing. They made relationships—relationships between themselves and their clients.

Madison Avenue was as much a product of the Industrial Revolution as Ford cars. Before the 1840s, when production was largely based on craftsmanship or imperfect commodity manufacture, demand for most goods exceeded supply. Since almost all communication was local (it wasn't until May 1, 1844, that the telegraph was used to transmit a news message—that the Whigs had chosen Henry Clay as their presidential nominee), most selling involved a personal conversation between merchant and buyer.

The Industrial Revolution made possible the manufacture of vast quantities of identical goods, more than could be sold through the inefficient process of local-store distribution. The new manufacturing processes also enabled a variety of companies to create similar goods, more than the small local store could carry. Furthermore, to staff the new factories, Americans left the countryside and began concentrating in cities. For all these reasons, department stores, retail emporia furnished with a wide array of goods, capable of serving a large and diverse clientele, where the owner was not a neighbor but a distant figure, began to open.

Manufacturers found that to sell the products their factories were disgorging, they now had to do more than depend on a store owner to announce he had them. The manufacturer had to distinguish his goods, give them brand names and make those names stand for something. He needed to bypass the retailer and make customers request his goods, so the grocer and the department-store magnate alike felt compelled to carry them. That meant using the newspapers to communicate not just a product's existence (a responsibility that had always been undertaken by the merchants anyway), but its virtues. Since the merchant and the manufacturer were obviously too busy to become specialists in newspapers (and because the number of newspapers in America, under pressure from the new communications needs, was soaring, from 75 to 1,400 in the half-century after 1790), there existed a yawning gap into which an enterprising middleman could step, someone who could find where newspapers were operating, how widely they circulated and what they charged for advertising.

The advertising agent was a product of these times. The first agent of any repute, Volney B. Palmer, who started in the trade selling ad space for his father, a newspaper publisher in Mount Holly, New Jersey, represented numerous publications and offered his services as a convenience to them and them alone. He forwarded their circulation data and other information to potential advertisers, brought the ads back to them and deducted a commission from the advertiser's fee to the paper in return for his effort. Soon, agents like Palmer became brokers, buying space from newspapers and reselling it at a markup to advertisers. To publishers and advertisers alike, that markup was still termed a "commission" for services rendered. Before too long, Francis Wayland Ayer, an enterprising schoolteacher's son from Philadelphia, realized he could land more business placing ads if he stopped acting as a space broker and started representing clients exclusively. The commission was kept, but it was standardized; after Ayer, newspapers, magazines and, later, radio and television stations and networks kicked back up to 15 percent of their charges to the ad agencies that brought them their clients' advertising.

The fixed commission virtually guaranteed excess profits to advertising agencies. It took the same four people to construct an advertisement—a writer, a layout man, a space-sales representative and an account handler—regardless of whether the ad ran ten times or ten thousand times. The earnings from additional client spending would always outpace the need for more staff to attend to the client. As James Rorty, a former copywriter and early critic of the agency business, wrote in 1934: "The commission method of compensation . . . is a factor in the endless chain of selling that links the whole advertising business." The most important link in that chain, the sine qua non of the entire industry—the copywriter James Webb Young identified it as the true "art of the advertising business"—was selling the agency to its clients.

Once the 15 percent commission was established, advertising agents could no longer vie for companies' placement business by undercutting their rivals' commissions. They were forced to compete by other means, the most effective of which was to offer clients more services for their money. Wayland Ayer began the trend in 1875 by opening a printing department that manufactured his clients' advertisements. By 1900, N. W. Ayer & Son (although Nathan Ayer never worked at the agency, his son, in an early example of the industry's willful duplicity, named it for him to give it maturity and credibility) was providing its clients rudimentary market research in the form of geographical information on consumption trends, most of it culled from U.S. Census Bureau data.

The creative side of the agency business developed in much the same way. At Ayer, for example, copywriting began as an adjunct to the "Business-Getting Department." But it was a rival, Albert D. Lasker, the spiritual founder of the Lord & Thomas (later Foote, Cone & Belding) agency, who turned the task into a standardized function. In 1898, Lasker persuaded the Wilson Ear Drum Company of Louisville, Kentucky, to pay his agency a 15 percent commission, instead of the 5 percent it was then paying, in return for having a copywriter at Lord & Thomas compose the ads the agency was already placing for the company. At the time, Wilson Ear Drums was spending $10,000 a year on advertising. The client so liked the agency's line—"You Hear! When you use *Wilson's* Common Sense *Ear Drums*"—that "within four months they were spending $15,000 *a month*, a thing unheard of in our house, and were paying us 15 percent," Lasker recalled in 1925.

The lesson he learned was quite clear. "My idea of this business," Lasker said, "was to render service and make money."

Over the years, agencies continued to increase the services they provided to clients in return for their commissions. These came to include the development and production of broadcast programming, psychological research, new product design, sales promotion, public relations and a thousand other supplementary tasks. The historian Roland Marchand has labeled these activities "benign deceptions," for they masked the agencies' real intent—maintaining the excess profits the 15 percent commission provided—and covered the agents' cynical disbelief in the efficacy of those services.

Advertising's leaders continually sought new theoretical rationales to encourage greater client spending. "The time has come when advertising in some hands has reached the status of a science," wrote Claude C. Hopkins, the president of Lasker's Lord & Thomas agency, in 1923. "We know what is most effective, and we act on basic laws."

Hopkins's "scientific advertising" was based on his analysis of mail-order ads. He created test advertisements, placing ads that were substantially the same save for a variation in, say, the headline, in different issues of the same newspaper or magazine. The ad that drew the greatest number of paid responses was the superior ad among those being tested, and its single distinction was deemed the key to its pulling power. Through successive tests of such variants, it was possible to create the perfect advertisement.

In the 1940s and '50s, Ted Bates Worldwide promoted one of the industry's most enduring theories, the Unique Selling Proposition. According to the U.S.P. approach, one factor alone determined the success of an ad campaign: the memorability of a single message. "The consumer tends to remember just one thing from an advertisement—one strong claim, or one strong concept," Rosser Reeves, the Bates agency's chairman and creative overseer, maintained.

In practice, Reeves's principle meant the endless repetition of a single product attribute—the perpetual drone of the same slogans, the continual assault of the same images, year after year. A child's clenched fist opened and—behold!—there were no smudge marks around the morsels in her palm. "M&M's—melts in your mouth, not in your hands!" proclaimed Bates's ads. A little boy expanded into a big boy against the Mom-carved notches near the kitchen door. "Wonder Bread helps build strong bodies 12 ways!" thundered Bates.

Reeves boldly asserted the immortality of superior advertising. "Unless a product becomes outmoded, a great campaign will not wear itself out," he claimed. Even consumer boredom was no obstacle to the power of the U.S.P. "I never tried to make *interesting* advertising," the burly Virginian once said. To clients who wanted to change long-running campaigns to circumvent the risk of public disenchantment, Reeves counseled, "If 90 percent do not remember it, the story is certainly not worn out."

Reeves was being disingenuous. Even in the 1950s, when the Bates agency was growing at a furious pace, there was ample evidence showing that much of a brand's sales came from existing heavy users, not from incremental sales to consumers who had not previously heard the manufacturer's message. Heavy users, of course, could be reinforced in their patterns by hearing the same message over and over; they might also be the customers most offended by the continual repetition of a message they already knew.

Confronted by such problems in logic, other advertising executives strove to develop theories that were less subject to testing or syllogism. Their debates took on the rancor of sectarian disputes. David Ogilvy, a onetime disciple (and brother-in-law) of Rosser Reeves, eventually stopped talking to him over their professional disagreements. Ogilvy promoted the theory of brand personality, arguing that the association of a company or product with consistent and appealing images, "rather than any *trivial product difference*," could thread it into the woof of the consumer's psyche.

The specific content of these theories was less important than the mere fact that they *were* theories—promoted in speeches, published in books, asserted to clients, claimed to prospects and proved, over and over again, in case studies that just happened to cite the agency's *other* clients. Apostasy being harder to explain than a temporary shift in the business cycle, once a client company bought into an agency's theory, its executives would be hard-pressed to justify at some future date why they might want to switch to another ad agency. A theory of advertising became one of the surest ways for an agency not only to win but to keep clients. A theory was a relationship builder.

Away from industry meetings, off the written page, safely buried in the bar cars and the bitterness of their sullied dreams, the advertising men knew their theories were Copernican claptrap. Everything they did was to maintain the relationship. No lie, no subterfuge, no humiliation was too low to strike or too base to endure, so long as the client remained content. Always, they were surrounded by The Fear. The Fear of saying the wrong thing. The Fear of not doing what the client wanted. The Fear of violating some unspoken rule. "Fear is as much a part of the air as the pollution along Madison Avenue," said Patricia Tierney, a copywriter who toiled at several white-shoe agencies in the postwar period. Lee Bristol, a founder of the Bristol-Meyers consumer-products company, once said he could describe an adman in five words: "Yes, sir! No, sir! Ulcer!"

Impediments to relationship-building were banished from the main-stream agencies. Jews (and, needless to say, other ethnic minorities and women) were exiled from Madison Avenue; one review of the five thou-sand men listed in the 1931 edition of *Who's Who in Advertising* found only ninety-two with identifiably Jewish names. This discrimination lasted well into the 1950s, long after Jews had begun to break the barrier in other industries. Some clients—Four Roses whiskey was one—expressly banned Jews from their accounts.

The Jews accepted and worked within their advertising ghetto, form-ing agencies to pull threads of profit from the garment manufacturers and retailers who wouldn't discriminate against their own. Some, like the Biow Agency and Mervin & Jesse Levine, proudly trumpeted their ethnic origins; others, like Grey Advertising (which was founded by two men named Fatt and Valenstein) hid them. The arrangement held fast until the end of World War II, when several factors—the G.I. Bill, suburbanization, the return of consumer production, television— enabled advertising's Jews to form the Other Club. The delicious irony was that a Nazi car was their membership ticket.

As copy chief at Grey Advertising, Bill Bernbach had chafed under the pseudo-scientific duplicities of his profession. "Advertising is funda-mentally persuasion and persuasion happens to be not a science, but an art," Bernbach said. David Ogilvy, his elegant, British-born contempo-rary, declaimed that in advertising, content superseded form: "*What* you say in advertising is more important than *how* you say it." To which Bernbach responded: "Execution can *become* content. It can be just as important as what you say."

In 1949, Bernbach fled Grey, and with an Irish account man named Ned Doyle and a Jew with a good financial *kop* named Mac Dane, he formed Doyle Dane Bernbach to test his own theory: that in advertis-ing, the only thing that mattered was creativity. "Properly practiced, creativity *must* result in greater sales more economically achieved," Bernbach told members of the American Association of Advertising Agencies at their 1961 annual meeting. "Properly practiced, creativity can make one ad do the work of ten." Artful writing and graceful design could "lift your claims from the swamp of sameness and make them ac-cepted, believed, persuasive, urgent. Is creativity some obscure, esoteric art form? Not on your life. It's the most practical thing a businessman can employ."

Volkswagen, the "people's car" that had been the inspiration of Adolf

Hitler himself, was to be the proof of Bernbach's theory. The company had been exporting to the United States for about nine years before it initiated the search that led it to Doyle Dane. At the time, American automobile advertising was under the thrall of a faux Jungian discipline called motivational research. Its message was less "you-are-what-you-drive" than "you-are-what-you-fantasize." In the prosperous 1950s, with the empty hopes of the war years replaced by a consumerist cornucopia, the automobile had come to symbolize the new America's fantasies. Astride constricted cities with belching buses were now verdant suburbs with homes, garages, driveways! Instead of rationed gasoline, there was mobility. The look of Detroit's cars became longer, lower, leaner; the cars reflected "an almost limitless sense of possibility." As the 1950s sped on, automobiles became manifestations of the nation's restless yearning for more. They grew gaudier, decked with enough chrome (forty-four pounds, Detroit's peak, on the 1958 Buick) to outshine the sun.

Advertising agencies encouraged Detroit in its pursuit of the subliminal, and did their best to make it liminal. One typical 1956 Dodge ad posed an exotic and demure woman next to a car that was shot at ground level from the rear right side; its tail fin was hoisted high in a classic tart's come-on, an automotive cheesecake shot that was a favorite of the time. The copy made little show at hiding what the scene was about: Its headline talked of a "magic touch," and the first sentence of the body text boasted of "The *look* of success! The *feel* of success! The *power* of success!"

Doyle Dane proposed that Volkswagen depart from such convention by marketing itself honestly, and by using self-deprecation to impart that message. Bernbach, his art director Helmut Krone and the copywriter Julian Koenig broke every sacrosanct rule of automotive promotion. At that time, virtually all automobile print advertisements (most of Volkswagen's advertising would be print) used illustrations, not photographs. Advertising people believed that the fantasies they inflated in automobile ads were pricked and burst by the intrusion of metallic reality. "When you take a photograph, you do something to an automobile which makes it look different from the way it looks when you look at it," Fairfax Cone of Foote, Cone & Belding, the Edsel agency, said at the time. To Krone, a photograph of the Beetle would stand in dramatic contrast to these hyperreal paintings, the more so because the little spheroid car would be shot against a stark white background.

Koenig's copy was laid out to buttress the empty look of the photograph. It was set in a narrow Gothic typeface, without serif flourishes. Paragraphs ended with half-lines, to avoid the ponderous, overblown look of solid text-blocks. The writer filled his text with negatives and half-sentences. He presented the corporation as a first-person plural, not the Orwellian monolith proffered by Ford or G.M. Koenig took cherished American icons and inverted them: He dared to intrude the unpleasant realities of automotive ownership, things like insurance, breakdowns and used cars, into the fantasyland of automotive advertising. He defiantly challenged Detroit's and Madison Avenue's psychosexual allusions to size.

"Think small," read the headline of Koenig's most famous ad. With the little Beetle taking up a small fraction of the upper-left corner of the white page, stationary and forlorn, the copy continued:

> Our little car isn't so much of a novelty
> any more.
> A couple of dozen college kids don't
> try to squeeze inside it.
> The guy at the gas station doesn't ask
> where the gas goes.
> Nobody even stares at our shape.
> In fact, some people who drive our little
> flivver don't even think 32 miles to the gal-
> lon is going any great guns.
> Or using five pints of oil instead of five
> quarts.
> Or never needing antifreeze.
> Or racking up 40,000 miles on a set of
> tires.
> That's because once you get used to
> some of our economies, you don't even
> think about them anymore.
> Except when you squeeze into a small
> parking spot. Or renew your small insur-
> ance. Or pay a small repair bill.
> Or trade in your old VW for a new one.
> Think it over.

The selling proposition, the strategic foundation on which all these ads were constructed, was truthfulness. Volkswagen was going to be known as "the honest car."

The campaign, like any advertising campaign, wasn't particularly honest, of course. The ads never mentioned the Beetle's awful safety record. As an advertising proposition, "honesty" was, its proponents understood, merely a relative term. "We didn't tell lies," Bob Levenson, a copywriter who followed Julian Koenig onto the account and thereafter became its creative director, said in 1992. "Our mission was to sell merchandise, not to reveal big truths."

Nor was Bernbach's theory of creativity any more empirically sound than Claude Hopkins's "scientific advertising" or Rosser Reeves's "Unique Selling Proposition." True, Doyle Dane was credited with Volkswagen's success—"once the campaign was launched, sales never looked back," a trade magazine editor wrote in 1984. But the fact was that between 1953 and 1959, the year Doyle Dane initiated its legendary campaign, Volkswagen on its own managed to build sales from 2,000 to 150,000 vehicles a year, "without advertising, without big deals, without fat trade-in allowances and with only 400 dealers," *Popular Mechanics* magazine noted at the time. Surveying Volkswagen's spectacular sales growth prior to its association with Doyle Dane Bernbach and its slower (but still striking) growth after the agency and the automaker joined, the sociologist Michael Schudson concluded, "The campaign caught the crest of a sales wave."

The Volkswagen advertising campaign's true importance lay less in what it did for Volkswagen than in what it did for the agency business. It changed the rules. Agencies were now no longer punished but *rewarded* for arguing with clients, for breaking the guidelines of art direction, for clowning around in the copy, for using ethnic locutions and academic references and a myriad of other once-forbidden formulae. Seemingly overnight, a great wave of originality engulfed the advertising profession, transforming agencies and agency-client relationships and, in turn, the impressions made on millions of Americans.

The Volkswagen campaign, in short, changed the culture of advertising. Agencies, particularly the Jewish agencies that had been relegated to selling Seventh Avenue's *shmattes*, no longer saw themselves in Madison Avenue's business of manufacturing relationships. With the Creative Revolution (as Bernbach's rebellion was called) they were in a new business. These agencies manufactured entertainment. Writers who once chose agency work because they could not support a family on a newspaper reporter's salary now leapt at advertising. They considered it an opportunity to make millions laugh. Art directors who sullenly contemplated Kandinsky on weekends in their garages could now experiment with form and function at the office. And clients who believed they had no choice but to torture their customers with televised banalities had something else to live for.

"In the beginning, there was Volkswagen," Jerry Della Femina, a copywriter-turned-agency-head, wrote. "That's the first campaign where everyone can trace back and say, 'This is where the changeover began.' That was the day when the new advertising agency was really born."

THAT WAS THE OTHER CLUB Harold Levine wanted to join. All around him, small agencies were popping up—more than a hundred in the peak revolutionary year of 1969 alone, many led by Jewish copywriters and Italian art directors who thought of themselves as the next Bernbach. Harold wanted to be among them.

Before he could effect the transition, he needed a crackerjack salesman, one who could locate clients willing to gamble that the old Levine Bros. shop was on a creative par with those run by these new Bernbachs. Through a fellow Long Island Railroad commuter who ran an investment firm, Harold met Bob Schmidt.

Schmidt was just a kid, not yet thirty, who, with his unruly black hair, buck teeth and constant motility, seemed barely removed from the blacktop basketball courts of Queens. His voice was raspy from too much talking. He had a feral look: Except for those moments when he displayed the salesman's gaze of sincerity, his small eyes were always darting up, down and sideways, scanning for prey. If he lacked the signs of breeding that, in the Madison Avenue agencies, made for an agreeable account executive, he nonetheless had an obvious hunger . . . and three accounts that would follow him anywhere: John's Bargain Stores, Irvington Place Dresses, and Investor's Planning, a mutual-fund sales firm. Harold Levine hired him to be hustler-in-residence.

Schmidt lived with the telephone in his ear; no pretense was too vague for a sales call. Rejections rolled off him like marbles on tilted mirrors; he would call again in a week, and again, in person, in a month, and again, with a merchandising plan, the next month.

Schmidt also possessed a hunger for recognition that suited Harold's needs and the changes taking place in the industry. He was enamored by Harold's promise of creative prestige. *I want to do great work*, was Schmidt's goal. *I want to do something people will react to.*

Unlike most account executives, who saw creatives as necessary aggravations, Schmidt lived vicariously through his copywriters and art directors. When his ad agency moved from the West Side to East 53rd Street, then to Park Avenue and finally to Park Avenue South, Schmidt placed his own office not among the account people but with the creative department. His agency's philosophy was a call-to-arms borrowed from the creative revolutionaries who had readied the industry for him: *It's not a great campaign unless it makes the blood drain from the client's face.*

To prove their mettle to the business world, however, Harold and Schmidt needed a television account. TV advertising cost more to produce and place than print, so under the commission system television was more remunerative. And it attracted the most energetic creative people, who did the fanciest work. But TV ads required clients with fat wallets.

Through a mutual friend, Harold met Chet Huntley, the retired co-anchor of NBC's evening news broadcast, who needed guidance in marketing his Montana property, the Big Sky Ranch. "I saw in Chet Huntley the answer to all our problems," Harold recalled. "One, instant fame. Two, a television identification for an agency that was doing no television. And three, an entrée to new business. How could I miss?" Huntley also enabled Harold and Schmidt to get the bank loan they needed to buy the agency from Mervin and Jesse. Harold offered Huntley 10 percent of the agency in return only for his presence in New York a few days a month and on other occasions, for account pitches, as might be necessary.

Huntley also attracted the attention of one of the ad industry's hottest young creative teams, Allan Beaver and Larry Plapler. They had gained their reputation working on the fabulous Talon Zippers campaign at Delehanty, Kurnit & Geller, a series whose most famous ad featured an executive crouched in embarrassment, covering his crotch on the steps of the New York Stock Exchange. "A prominent New York stockbroker just went public," read the headline. Beaver, a sad-eyed, quiet, thirty-four-year-old art director with a refined typographic sense, had gone through the Cartoonists and Illustrators School (later renamed the School of Visual Arts), several small agencies and the fabled design department of CBS before landing at Delehanty. Plapler was a wiry, argumentative/Manhattanite six years Beaver's senior who had started in advertising as a print broker, then made stops at Benton & Bowles, McCann-Erickson and Doyle Dane before alighting at Delehanty. The partners' work had won a spate of awards and, at their next agency, the princely salary of $60,000 each, when Harold and Schmidt called on them. The offer was paltry—$30,000 each, and the promise of partnership shares two years down the road if the association proved satisfactory. But Chet Huntley's presence cinched the deal. "It got us out of the small-agency syndrome and gave us, at least, 'here is a small agency with a well-known name on it,'" Allan Beaver said. "We thought that gave us a little bit of an edge, at least in p.r."

In 1972, the sale of the agency finally consummated, Mervin & Jesse Levine was renamed, cumbrously, Levine, Huntley, Schmidt, Plapler & Beaver. Harold took 60 percent, Schmidt 20 percent, Plapler and Beaver (after Huntley died in 1974 and his shares were divided) 10 percent each.

Theirs was an unhappy family virtually from the start. The partnership was artificial, built on a shrewd construct but not on real affinities. Plapler and Schmidt, both of them fiery and opinionated, took a rapid dislike to each other; Plapler, with Beaver in tow, even approached Harold at one point to seek to force Schmidt out of the agency. Schmidt privately called Harold a "bigoted Socialist" because Harold, so involved in philanthropic causes, evinced disdain for so many with whom he worked. Harold, for his part, disliked Schmidt for the very reasons he'd hired him: He was a hustler, a Sammy Glick, a money-obsessed salesman with no concern for anything but profits.

Professionally, though, the partnership worked exceedingly well. Levine, Huntley landed Jockey underwear, which led to Timme fake furs, which led to Matchbox toy cars, all of them ready and able to do the television advertising the agency craved! New York Yankees great Yogi Berra did a Levine, Huntley spot; so did the milquetoastish actor Wally Cox. But still Bob Schmidt was dissatisfied. He was on television, but he was not yet Bernbach. He didn't have the recognition of his peers. For that, he needed his own Volkswagen.

BOB SCHMIDT had been hustling Subaru of America for months—to an ambivalent reception. Harvey Lamm and his executives knew they needed advertising, because their dealers and distributors expected it. They had also been put off by the overpromising, overselling and outright charlatanism which advertising agencies were prone to employ.

Subaru's first national advertising agency (aside from the Philly shops it had stiffed) gave the company its name. Green Dolmatch had been formed by Paula Green, who hoped to capitalize on the fame that had accrued to her when, as a Doyle Dane Bernbach copywriter, she'd penned the line "We're only No. 2, so we try harder" for Avis rental cars. S.O.A. gave her the account to avert the dealer rebellion that was mounting in the wake of the 360 fiasco. Among the first things she decided was that the name "Subaru," with the accent on the second syllable, sounded too foreign. Unilaterally, she shifted the accent to the third syllable, as in "kangaroo." At the dealers' meeting at which she introduced her campaign, she got an auditorium full of rambunctious auto salesmen to shout in unison, "One, two—Soo-ba-ROO."

Green also provided one other lasting component of Subaru's image: its positioning against Volkswagen. After the failure of the 360, S.O.A. had managed to persuade Fuji to provide it with the car one step up its model line, the FF1, whose most significant feature was its front-wheel-drive transmission, an attribute then meaningless to most Americans but one which would rapidly become familiar and important. Where virtually all the cars available at the time were pushed by their rear wheels, the Subaru FF1 was pulled by its front wheels. That benefited drivers in three ways: It gave them more space by eliminating the drive shaft which, in most cars, ran from the engine in front to the rear wheels and took up precious interior room; it saved gasoline, because without the drive shaft, the frame and the engine could be lighter; and it rendered the vehicle more responsive, especially around turns and in tight squeezes. Its maneuverability made the FF1 safer than other cars in emergency situations, an advantage Subaru greatly needed after the attacks on the 360. Other automakers had worked with front-wheel drive in the past, but most had abandoned it. By 1971, Subaru was the only company importing front-wheel-drive cars to the United States.

. Yet Green Dolmatch chose not to spotlight the FF1's engineering in its advertising. In the contorted way marketers occasionally think, they believed that by identifying "The Subaru" (as the agency named it) as *not Volkswagen*, they would attract Volkswagen's customers. "The Subaru is not a Japanese Beetle," read the agency's most memorable ad. It did little for the company, and Paula Green was fired. Nevertheless, for years afterward, S.O.A. and its dealers would try to sell their cars as less expensive versions of Volkswagen, and later of other imports.

S.O.A.'s next ad agency, Spiro & Associates of Philadelphia, contributed the theme of durability to Subaru's image. A Spiro testimonial advertisement featured a photograph of a sweatered Massachusetts salesman leaning on a cream-colored Subaru parked outside his comfortable country house, grinning in total satisfaction. "John Kelley put 91,000 miles on his Subaru," the headline read. "And spent less than $20 on repairs." For a time, those ads—or something—appeared to work. In the 1972 calendar year, Subaru dealers sold 24,056 cars at retail, about 10,000 more than the previous year. In 1973, they sold 37,793 vehicles, far exceeding the overly optimistic five-year projection of 25,000 cars that Harvey and Malcolm had put forward when they first sought financing. But then the first Arab oil embargo turned the economy and the automotive industry upside down. Americans stopped buying cars, and S.O.A. sacrificed Spiro to its angry minions.

Desperate, Subaru next turned to the Marat of the Creative Revolution, George Lois. The son of a Greek florist from the Bronx, Lois had been the first and most notorious Doyle Dane Bernbach expatriate, having left the Mother Agency in 1960 to start one of several renegade creative shops, which became known as much for their antics as their ads. He once pummeled a copywriter who was quitting his agency, prompting the scribe to sue the shop for "creating an atmosphere of physical violence" that impeded his creative abilities. Lois's belligerence extended to clients. He once climbed out on the third-story ledge of a matzo-maker's office and threatened to jump if the client didn't accept a poster he'd designed. A big, powerfully built art director, Lois was an alchemist determined to lixiviate a purified, combustible version of Bill Bernbach's advertising-is-entertainment philosophy. "Advertising is poison gas," Lois believed. "It should bring tears to your eyes. It should unhinge your nervous system. It should knock you out!"

To Subaru, he was blunt. *Your problem,* the car company's latest savior told its top brass, *is nobody knows who the fuck you are. Your awareness is shit. I've got a campaign that'll take you from no awareness to total awareness in just a few months.* His plan was to sign up Sadaharu Oh, the most famous baseball player in Japan, as Subaru's American spokesman. *The whole idea is to say, "We're a Japanese car," and that this car is the culmination of Eastern technology. "You taught us baseball; we're teaching you how to make cars."* Lois concluded with his summary claim that the campaign would do what advertising is supposed to accomplish. *It'll make you famous!* he boomed.

Subaru liked the idea, not least because a campaign extolling the Japanese might flatter Fuji into easing its payment policies and the prices S.O.A. paid for its supply. The importer gave Lois the go-ahead. After he got to Japan, however, he found that Sadaharu Oh would not even meet with him. So he went and found a substitute.

Subaru of America introduced its third advertising campaign in five years at a press conference in January 1975. The first television spot in the campaign opened on still photographs of Cy Young and Walter Johnson, which appeared sequentially on the screen. "Everybody knows the three winningest pitchers of all time," said the announcer, in a voiceover. "Cy Young . . . Walter Johnson . . . And of course—"

The scene shifted to a thoroughly unfamiliar Asian face, leaning in from the left, squinting and smiling under a baseball cap.

The voiceover continued: "—Masaichi Kaneda, the winningest pitcher alive."

"Who, me?" Kaneda asked, in heavily accented English.

Kaneda, according to the publicity release Lois wrote for Subaru, had won more games—four hundred—than any player in the history of Japanese baseball. A southpaw, he was, to the adman, the perfect pinch hitter for Sadaharu Oh. In the commercial, he spoke in Japanese for several seconds, his facial gestures a portrait of sumo-like exaggeration. Soon, an English translation filtered in over the foreign tongue. "In Japan, we have adopted both of America's national pastimes: baseball and—"

Kaneda's face dissolved into the front passenger side of a car. The word "Subaru" was visible. The narrative continued. "—Cars. We have learned about your baseball, and you have learned about Japan's economical Toyota and Datsun. But the best is still to come. The culmination of Japanese technology—Subaru!"

The camera pulled back, revealing the entire car in an appealing profile. "The car that proves that Eastern economy and Western luxury can meet," the narration concluded. "Subaru! The star of Japanese cars!" The image faded as unmistakably Japanese music swelled.

Dealers were given a brochure showing "the winningest pitcher alive, Masaichi Kaneda—now pitching for Subaru!" They were provided showroom material with Kaneda, in uniform, his arms outstretched in a victory pose, sitting atop a coupe. "The incredible front-wheel-drive Subaru! The Star of Japanese cars!" the brochure read, putting a salesworthy word to the company's stellar nameplate and to its entire, meager model line. The two-door coupe would be called the Shooting Star. The two-door hardtop was now the Evening Star. The four-door sedan would take the name Star Cruiser. All-Star became the name of the standby, front-wheel-drive station wagon. And the new four-wheel-drive wagon came in as the Superstar. "If you want Eastern economy with Western luxury," the sales brochure concluded, "reach for the Subaru Stars!"

Lois left the most appropriate name out of his constellation: Falling Star. Subaru's dealers and distributors, when they saw the ads, were outraged. A conservative lot, some of them World War II veterans from rural areas, they wanted to know, *How is a Jap going to bring people into MY showroom!* The final straw came from Tokyo. Fuji was disturbed. Masaichi Kaneda, the spokesman the Americans were using, was not Japanese. He was Korean.

Within weeks of the fanfare-filled introduction, S.O.A. pulled its new campaign from the air and fired George Lois.

With hustle and intuition, Bob Schmidt had put himself in the proper place to accept the Bernbachian mantle that Subaru was about to bestow. Schmidt had first called on S.O.A.'s advertising director, Alan Ross, when Spiro & Associates had the car company's account. He refused to take the auto executive's initial disinterest at face value. Ross was a man who liked to express his passions—he was once chosen "bachelor of the month" by *Cosmopolitan*, and allowed the women's magazine to publish his interest in girls who were "not zaftig, but not skinny, either"—and Schmidt saw he could bide his time by playing willing receptacle to Ross's vituperations. First, he called every few weeks. Then, he finagled an invitation to Pennsauken to show Levine,

Huntley's reel of Jockey and Matchbox commercials. Then he managed to get a lunch with Ross every two weeks or so. When Ross dumped Lois, Schmidt was the only person he thought of calling.

Schmidt's creative team devised a slogan and a concept—the two were indistinguishable—during a session of "garbageball" in the office of Allan Beaver, the quiet art director. Beaver and Larry Plapler stood at one corner of the room, taking turns tossing a rubber ball into a trash can at the opposite corner—five shots each time, loser pays a buck. Plapler was babbling disconnectedly about what seemed to be the only strategy Subaru could use: Its cars were cheaper than everyone else's. Beaver, as usual, grunted. When Plapler, on his eighteenth or twentieth try, described Subaru as "the economy car for today's economy," Beaver did not grunt. He said, "That's it."

The idea was a new articulation of Subaru's on-again, off-again position against Volkswagen. When S.O.A. had tried it in 1971, there was no evidence that Americans wanted or needed a better Beetle. But Volkswagen had continued to raise the price of its cars, despite the mid-'70s recession, making the company an inviting target. Levine, Huntley was betting the time was ripe to sell not a better Beetle but a markedly cheaper Beetle.

The campaign was tart and pointed. The agency's initial print advertisements displayed a VW with a price tag hanging from it, an explicit reminder that the car was no longer the bargain it once had been. The copy was smart and sassy. "On a Subaru, the only thing affected by inflation is the tires," read one headline. An early television commercial used the screen as a glass wall between the viewer and the announcer, who with a Magic Marker created a graph to illustrate Subaru's new tack. "When the economy goes this way," he said, drawing a line that plunged south, "Subaru"—he reversed directions—"goes this way."

A year later, with America pulling out of the recession, Levine, Huntley replaced the "economy car" campaign with one that did not refer directly to the nation's economic travails. The new campaign maintained the implicit positioning against Volkswagen, but added to it the durability theme that had been broached, then dropped, two agencies earlier. The new image was captured by another slogan that came to Larry Plapler during a garbageball game. Henceforth, Subaru's cars would be known as "Inexpensive, and built to stay that way."

In the beginning, television stations and national magazines would only accept advertising on the agency's account, not on S.O.A.'s questionable credit. Moreover, Subaru's advertising and promotion spending in 1975, $3.1 million, was actually a half-million dollars below the 1974 level.

Even with the lower spending, though, Subaru unloaded 41,587 cars at retail in 1975, a striking increase over the 23,000 sold the year before. Rebates the company was giving consumers were probably the reason, but S.O.A., relieved, granted Levine, Huntley and its "economy car" campaign the credit. The client-agency relationship, which was supposed to last only for six months before Subaru placed the account into review, was extended indefinitely.

Over the long haul, this campaign, whose life followed Subaru's steep trajectory up the western side of a bell curve, hurt the car company, although no one could have predicted it when the slogan was introduced. Inasmuch as image had anything to do with Subaru's rise and fall, it was the "inexpensive, and built to stay that way" slogan—or, more exactly, this slogan's *interpretation*—that led to both.

For six years, Subaru's dealers had been battered by frequent shifts in sales and strategy. When they finally achieved a measure of success and stability, it was with a campaign whose meaning seemed unambiguous: Subarus were cheaper than the competition's products. Because most of S.O.A.'s by now seven-hundred-plus dealers sold two lines of cars, they took the advertising strategy as dispensation to make Subaru their budget line. Whatever Subaru of America may have intended to convey with its brand advertising over the years, its dealers were reinforcing one message: Buy a Subaru because it's cheap.

Selling bargains is a time-honored strategy at retail. But S.O.A., at least implicitly, encouraged it at the national brand level by resting its identification on words that could easily be translated into "buy us for what we cost," not "buy us for what we are." Harvey Lamm's training in the retail furniture business had led him to this strategy; he was a salesman, not a marketer. When he engineered Subaru's turnaround in 1975, it was through pricing and deals; the cars themselves, their technology, their attributes, were, beyond a benchmark standard of functionality and reliability, not relevant. The lesson was not lost on Harvey. "Product was never the issue," Marvin Riesenbach said. "His view is we always sold product that wasn't competitive."

That was, in retrospect, a shame. For in 1976 and 1977, at exactly the time Subaru encased in amber its image for inexpensiveness, the company introduced a technology that, if used properly, might later have pulled it from the rut in the bargain basement of the automotive industry. That mechanism was four-wheel drive.

World War II veterans knew it from their Jeeps, which had to travel through deep mud and over studded terrain. Long-haulers knew it because it was the only way to grind heavy rigs up steep grades. But, like front-wheel-drive transmissions before the Arab oil embargo, four-wheel drive was, to the average consumer in the mid-1970s, a little-known curiosity. Unlike rear-wheel drive or front-wheel drive, four-wheel drive distributes power to all wheels simultaneously, giving the vehicle stability and (because its traction is evenly apportioned) a firm grip on slippery surfaces. But because most four-wheel-drive vehicles were big and bulky, the technology remained mostly within the domain of truckers and sportsmen.

Fuji had developed a different kind of four-wheel drive after a utility company in northern Japan approached the company and asked for help in obtaining a vehicle that would allow its personnel to perform routine maintenance tasks in the country's mountainous and snowy northern region. Because the men would be spending a great deal of time in the vehicles, the electric company wanted a car more comfortable than the typical off-road trucks then in existence. Fuji used its basic, front-wheel-drive station wagon (called the Leone in Japan) as the framework, and simply split the driveline, delivering equal amounts of power from the engine to all four, independently suspended wheels. Unlike other four-wheel-drive vehicles, this new wagon was also suitable for routine driving. Under normal conditions, the car would operate as a front-wheel-drive vehicle; pulling a lever when in motion would engage the four-wheel drive. The finished prototype, which took a year of research and development and was introduced in late October 1971 at the Tokyo Motor Show, weighed only thirty-seven pounds more than the front-wheel-drive Leone wagon. Volume production began in 1972, with Fuji selling about a hundred of the "little bastards," as the Japanese head of its engineering team proudly called it, per month.

Harvey Lamm wanted the car as soon as he saw it. His preponderantly rural dealers, especially those in New England, could use it. The question was: How to market it? There was, after all, nothing else like this in the United States. Early cracks at the puzzle—including one Levine, Huntley commercial which depicted a photographer chasing a mountain goat across a rock-strewn, hilly desert—did not adequately distinguish Subaru's odd wagon from Jeep or other, similar, existing off-road vehicles. The company wanted something that visually set its unusual vehicle apart from the rugged competition.

The solution came from a Los Angeles public relations executive who was working with Subaru at the time. Watching a ski competition on television one Sunday night, he had an inspiration and called Alan Ross at home. *Maybe,* he said, *Subaru could sponsor the U.S. Ski Team?*

The idea was brilliant. Subaru's strength was in New England and the Pacific Northwest—snow country. Skiing was growing in popularity, and it carried a cachet that could help an unfamiliar little foreign car. Best of all, the p.r. man discovered that the ski team's current automotive sponsor was pulling out. A foreign auto manufacturer supporting an American athletic team? As long as the company could come up with some vehicles to help the team haul its members and equipment, the skiers didn't care.

Levine, Huntley, Schmidt, Plapler & Beaver made the most of the ski team sponsorship, creating a spot which, with updates and variations, ran for years and became known in the ad industry as a classic of the "demo," or product demonstration, genre.

The thirty-second commercial opened on a beautiful but forbidding landscape: a mountain trail so snowed under that even the trees on its border listed under the weight. A piano struck deliberate diminished-chord arpeggios, lending the sun-dappled setting an otherworldly cast. Suddenly, the music changed; a guitar and a bass guitar started pounding out a steady rock beat. It sounded like a chase scene from a James Bond movie. Sure enough, a quartet of debonair skiers, clad in blue, caps and sunglasses obscuring their faces, paralleled in from the upper right. Just as suddenly, another scene interrupted: a red Subaru wagon, a ski rack on its roof, a white racing stripe on its side, gripped its way, slowly but confidently, along and up this seemingly impassable trail. The scenes shifted back and forth: closeups of the speeding skiers, in slow motion, shot from the front; closeups of the car, its six-star Subaru logo barely visible as it passed; closeups of the skiers, their legs swerving left, then right; closeups of the wheels, buried in snow, but climbing; closeups of the skiers; closeups of the car's comfortable interior. In the background, the swooshing of the skis and the grating of the car supplanted each other, back and forth. Finally, a male voice:

"Did you ever wonder how the U.S. Ski Team gets up those snowy mountains?"

The camera focused on the smiling skiers as they emerged from the car and slammed its doors, then pulled back to reveal the vehicle poised on top of the isolated peak. The voiceover concluded: "The remarkably inexpensive, practical family car. The Subaru four-wheel-drive wagon. Official car of the U.S. Ski Team."

The ski team affiliation and the advertising promoting it was a textbook case study of how a niche marketer could exploit a geographical peculiarity with an unusual technology. But as good as it was, the campaign had a kink built into its spine. Subaru marketed *nationally*; Harvey and Malcolm had pieced together a pyramid of dealers around the country to save S.O.A. from bankruptcy years before. Without the budget to sell different cars in different parts of the United States, or to create discrete regional campaigns to market a single car differently in disparate areas, Subaru had to make one effort mean all things to all consumers and all dealers. This, of course, was impossible.

The distributors and dealers in the southern tier of the United States looked on the ski team sponsorship as proof that S.O.A. favored the northern states. One Texas distributor got up at the meeting where Alan Ross first described the promotion and complained, "Now you've convinced us that you *really* have no interest in the South at all." Try as S.O.A. did in ensuing years to mollify southern dealers, the money and advertising time spent on the ski team sponsorship made them feel, forever, like unwanted stepchildren. In the long run, the ski team promotion helped diminish the vigor with which southern and even midwestern dealers retailed Subarus. In later years, when Subaru's sales were soaring, many southern dealers, instead of capitalizing on the brand's rising popularity by augmenting their sales efforts, simply sold their allotments, at cost plus built-in profit, to northern dealers who were hungry for any Subarus they could get their hands on.

That, however, was years in the future. At the time, to Harvey, Subaru's destiny had never looked more luminous. Was it the new slogan? The ski team sponsorship? Confident dealers, national pride and economic stabilization in a Bicentennial year? Or his own genius? No matter. Subaru sold nearly 49,000 vehicles in 1976 and moved up from the twelfth largest automobile importer to number six. The company registered $166.3 million in sales of cars and parts, a 98 percent increase over 1975. Its net income of $3.8 million was triple that of the year before. As S.O.A. trumpeted to its recently restive shareholders in its annual report, "1976 was the year in which Subaru came of age."

Levine, Huntley, Schmidt & Beaver (Larry Plapler eventually left with the People Express airline account and his name was struck from the door) was growing along with its car client. Harvey Lamm allowed his advertising agency control over Subaru's image because in Bob Schmidt he had hitched up with a man who was capable of gaining for him the recognition of a world beyond the Philadelphia furniture marts. Harvey had finally found his Bernbach.

Schmidt played the role to the hilt. He had found his Volkswagen, and there was no way he was going to lose it and let himself slip back into the ignominy of fashion advertising. He devoted himself soul and substance to the Subaru account and to Harvey.

During Levine, Huntley's first five years on the account, Schmidt learned, by sight and by first name, each of Subaru's seven-hundred-plus dealers. Even in good times, their complaints were many. Schmidt was a superb listener. As much as he coddled his creatives, he became S.O.A.'s eye on its customer base, the dealers. He was Lamm's amanuensis. Schmidt was able to balance these delicate tasks because he and Harvey were, in management and personal style, twins—coarse, proudly of the streets, instinctive, inspirational men who motivated their employees with infectious excitement, not oppressive fear. They plotted marketing strategy in home-to-home telephone calls that lasted from 9 p.m. to 1 a.m., three nights a week. Subaru's advertising account became a Lamm-Schmidt relationship—no others need apply.

More than once, S.O.A. marketing executives discovered that a Levine, Huntley storyboard they thought they had killed was in production. "Some behind-the-scenes decisions were made just strictly between Bob and Harvey," Chris Wackman recalled.

The Harvey-and-Bob alliance left Levine, Huntley's creatives blissfully free to create. The Subaru account's creative directors, Lee Garfinkel and Tony DeGregorio—the former a Jewish copywriter, the latter an Italian art director, in the time-honored tradition—made the most of their privilege. Lee, a short, quiet man, had joined Levine, Huntley a year after graduating from Queens College. He had tried standup comedy, then discovered that copywriting was a more remunerative avenue for his humor. Gags infused his work. Lee's idea of a good ad was one which delivered empathy by way of a laugh. When Subaru marketing executives demanded more metal and engineering talk in their spots, Lee argued, *Couch it in the story of a boy who wants to drive to his girlfriend's house so he can get laid, something that everyone can relate to, and the only way he's going to get laid is if he's got a Subaru four-wheel drive.* Tony, nine years Lee's senior, came to the agency with wide professional experience, having already passed through BBDO, McCann-Erickson and Scali, McCabe, Sloves. He was Lee's opposite. Where Lee was mild-mannered bordering on cuddly, Tony was prickly, with a bruising aggressiveness that made him enemies both at his agency and at Subaru. Lee was a slob; Tony was fastidious: When they worked over lunch in the art director's office, Tony would cover his desk with paper lest Lee drop a sliver of moo shu pork on it. For all their differences, the two men, indeed, virtually every creative at Levine, Huntley, agreed on one thing: "If it wasn't funny, we wouldn't do it," Tony said later.

Funny was a legacy of the Creative Revolution. The recession of the mid-1970s, the economic downturn that had nearly shut Subaru down, ended much of the ad industry's love affair with uninhibited creativity. "Hard times demand hard selling," Mary Wells, one of the insurrection's leaders, announced, declaring an end to the revolt. Yet funny remained. Young creatives, the spiritual descendants of Wells and Bill Bernbach, justified it through marketing logic. Punch lines were memorable. With products and services increasingly indistinguishable, maybe the only way to sell something was with a laugh.

The real reason funny prevailed, though, was cultural. "The main outlet for a sense of pride and accomplishment," wrote Roland Marchand in his study of the ad industry between the World Wars, "lies in in-group displays of virtuosity."

If the Harvey-Schmidt relationship bred resentment inside S.O.A., if the "funny" advertising occasionally rubbed minor Subaru executives and dealers the wrong way, that was of small concern, for however flawed the advertising may have been, it seemed, to all outward appearances, to be working. S.O.A.'s sales and profits continued climbing. In 1977, 80,826 Subarus were sold at retail, up from 49,000 the year before. Profits rose to $4.3 million on sales of $236.7 million. Subaru moved up to fifth best-selling import, behind only Toyota, Datsun, Volkswagen and Honda. In 1978, S.O.A. retailed more than 100,000 vehicles for the first time, more than half of them in its core, rural markets. Sales rose 86 percent, to $440 million.

With its American sales climbing, Fuji made some minor adjustments in the design of the Leone, redoing the front grille and ornament, repositioning the lights and lowering the hood to make its mainstream auto line look sleeker and less clumsy. It called its regular Leones the "DL" series, and introduced the "GL" series, which was actually nothing but a more luxurious and expensive version of the Leone, with AM/FM radios and electric clocks as standard equipment. Unit sales rose to 127,871 in 1979, to 142,968 in 1980 and to 152,062 in 1981. Profits climbed concomitantly, to $10.4 million, $17.7 million and $26.3 million. With this remarkable period of growth came, finally, recognition. *Road & Track* reported: "Subaru rates as one of the most trouble-free cars we've surveyed." *Car & Driver* said: "A month with a Subaru DL wagon was an eye-opener."

To Subaru of America, there was little mystery behind this outstanding record: The company had finally built itself an image. It was a somewhat hip, occasionally insouciant but more often folksy car company, in a New-Yorkers-traveling-to-their-country-home-with-a-wood-stove-in-Vermont kind of way. The cars were inexpensive, durable, friendly little autos, especially where the weather and the terrain could ruin a beckoning weekend. In 1980, 40 percent of Subaru's sales were four-wheel-drive vehicles, and 60 percent of those were retailed in small towns and rural backwaters. More than one-fourth of all its four-wheel drives were sold in Colorado, Maine and New Hampshire, which together accounted for but 2 percent of the country's population. Subarus were nothing less than the perfect car for the back-to-the-country, less-is-more, cardigan-wearing Carter era. It was an image that advertising had certainly helped to create, as evidenced by the $21.8 million S.O.A. spent on promoting itself in 1980—almost seven times the budget when Levine, Huntley had won the account five years before.

Levine, Huntley could not prove that its advertising had anything to do with Subaru's remarkable renaissance. Like all entertainment agencies, it did little research, either to assess campaigns or to develop them. The creatives preferred inspiration to hard data. "How did we find research?" Tony DeGregorio asked years later. "Looked for letters, consumer letters to Subaru that people wrote in. 'Here's how I use my Subaru. It's very reliable. I'm a veterinarian in Wisconsin and I deliver cows.' And so we did a nice commercial on that." Lee Garfinkel, his co-creative director, said the research underlying the work "was coming from our gut and how we felt about the car, really. That was it."

There were other factors beyond image contributing to Subaru's dizzying spiral of growth. The energy crisis precipitated by the first Arab oil embargo never really dissipated, despite an initial postembargo return to large, American cars. With the rise of Islamic fundamentalism and the Iranian revolution, Americans realized they would never again have secure access to Middle East oil. Between 1978 and 1981, gasoline prices at the pump increased 109 percent. Operating a car became half again as expensive—from 4.11 cents per mile in 1978 to 6.74 cents a mile in 1982. Small cars were consumers' permanent response to the economic changes. The small-car share of the American market, 27 percent in 1978, surged to 61.5 percent by 1981. The gains accrued mostly to foreign manufacturers, especially the Japanese; import penetration of the U.S. market increased from 17.7 percent the year Jimmy Carter was elected to nearly 28 percent the year after he left office.

As much as Subaru's executives believed it was image selling their cars, many dealers knew the truth. "I'd drive around, people would say, 'How do you like that car? What is it? How do you like it?' " recalled Marty Pizza, the Rockland County, New York, dealer. "People were looking for small cars. Subarus hit the market at the right time."

That Subaru's image was barely relevant to the average American automobile buyer became clear after S.O.A. commissioned its first "Advertising and Image Evaluation Study" in late 1980. The study, conducted by Burke Marketing Research, a Cincinnati, Ohio, company, purported to measure the impact and effectiveness of S.O.A.'s advertising by testing consumers' recall of various elements in the Subaru ads.

Of a theoretically representative sample (drawn from 17,435 randomly dialed telephone numbers) of 301 licensed drivers between the ages of twenty and fifty-four, who lived in households where at least one member had a college degree, and who were considering buying a small car within two years, "Subaru rates low in unaided awareness of import and small cars," the survey concluded. Without prompting, only 7 percent of the respondents named Subaru among the list of small cars they could think of on the market at that time. Toyota was named by 62 percent, Datsun by 55 percent and Volkswagen by 35 percent.

Among its chief competitors, Subaru's advertising awareness was the lowest. Fifty-nine percent told the interviewers they had seen it—nothing more, just that they had seen it. More than 80 percent said they had seen the ads for Toyotas, Datsuns and VWs.

Whether Subaru's self-proclaimed ad watchers got anything from the ads was questionable. Only 8.5 percent said they knew Subaru had a four-wheel-drive station wagon. Forty-four percent said, yes, they remembered specific sales messages in the company's ads, but few could say what those messages were, and only 10 percent remembered that the company produced four-wheel-drive cars.

Asked to rate specific attributes of competitive makes on a scale of 1 to 10, Subaru fared worse than any of its competitors. All of the import brands, except Subaru, stood out for something. Even Mazda, then as unfamiliar to the broad public as Subaru was, managed to shine when consumers were asked about the small cars' exterior design. But nothing shined on Subaru. "The Subaru image is not superior to the competition" in any way, Burke reported.

Subaru's advertising even failed to communicate the attribute specified in the first word of the company's slogan, inexpensiveness. When asked to guess the manufacturer's suggested retail prices of two Subaru models, nearly 65 percent of those surveyed thought the $3,999 hatchback was at least $5,999, and more than half figured the $5,149 station wagon cost more than $7,000. Consumers were substantially more accurate in judging the costs of Subaru's competitors. "An artificially high price preconception about Subaru may keep potential customers from the showroom," the study warned. "This lack of correct pricing information could easily become a serious liability."

But, then, Subaru's slogan was not very well known. Thirty-one percent of those surveyed knew that Volkswagen's tag line was "Volkswagen does it again." Thirty percent remembered Datsun's "We are driven." Asked if they knew Subaru's slogan, a mere 1.7 percent repeated, "Inexpensive, and built to stay that way"; more—2.3 percent—confidently recited, "Whoop-de-doo for my Subaru."

It was the closing line to a commercial for a chain of muffler-repair shops.

Chapter 6

We Built Our Reputation
by Building Better Cars

BAD LUCK HAD BLINDSIDED Chris Wackman often. And good
luck, mixed with not a little hard work and common decency, had managed to raise him from the depths each time. Chris needed his luck to
turn, for times were pretty dismal in early 1982, what with 20 percent
consumer-lending rates and a virtual halt in auto sales, just when he
needed a job again. *Did I make a mistake leaving Ford?* he wondered,
as he made his way East to visit his old mentor, Tom Gibson.

Life wasn't supposed to twist this much. It was supposed to be
steadier. That's what he had been brought up in Scarsdale to believe. A
boy who worked hard was supposed to achieve what he wanted. And
what Chris had wanted more than anything else in life was to fly.

He started at age fifteen and his talent showed early. On his sixteenth
birthday, after only four hours in the air, he soloed. One year later to
the day, he received his pilot's license. All through DePauw University,
he dreamed of becoming a jet fighter pilot. God and chromosomes even
conspired to ease him on his way—he was a fairy-tale portrait of the flyboy, a strapping six-footer with daring, nonchalance and love of country.
In 1967, immediately after his graduation, despite the raging Vietnam
War, ignoring his pacifist brother's imprecations, Chris joined the U.S.
Navy to realize his fantasy.

Whereupon a doctor told him that he was missing a vertebra in his
back. Although otherwise in fine health, Chris would not fly in this
man's navy. It was the worst thing that had ever happened to him.

He became an analyst in Naval Intelligence, charting the movement
of Soviet submarines, and eventually rose to the rank of lieutenant. He
moved with his wife, Nancy (the college sweetheart whom he'd married
ten days before starting his hitch), to San Francisco. But his life's plans
again started unraveling. With the Vietnam War ending, the pace of ad-

vancement in the military slowed. Chris began looking into civilian careers, only to discover that in the real world his military-intelligence training qualified him for very little. Finally, a civilian friend, a zone manager at Lincoln-Mercury, recommended Chris to the car company. *We prefer M.B.A.s*, he was told, but Ford wanted to do its bit for the boys in uniform, especially one who claimed a potentially transferable talent for analysis.

Lincoln-Mercury was still the Ford Motor Company's little gem in those days. The Continental Mark IV was retailing for $7,100, and selling well. The division was immensely profitable. Then the Arab oil embargo hit and Easy Street became Skid Row. Chris's job—selling cars to dealers and showing dealers how to sell gas guzzlers to consumers—became a challenge. Chris found a small dealer in Watsonville, California, who took a liking to him and let the earnest young man come in and look at his books, to learn about the car business from the dealers' viewpoint. Chris studied. He wholesaled cars and, especially when American consumers started buying big cars again in the immediate-post-embargo euphoria, he prospered. When he was called to the "Vatican"—Ford Motor Company headquarters in Detroit—four years later, Chris didn't hesitate.

The move was exhilarating. Chris and Nancy traded their one-story, two-bedroom Bay Area residence for a large, two-bath center-hall colonial on eight-tenths of an acre; their sons, Peter and David, not only had a yard now but their own bedrooms. The domestic manufacturers in those days were subject to two-year cycles of prosperity and depression, and the Wackmans arrived in Detroit during an up cycle, which made the transition headier. There was money to spend developing sales promotions for the cars; budgets were so large that Chris, like his colleagues, starting talking nonchalantly of "tenths"—"five-tenths" being a half-million-dollar promotional campaign.

By 1980, he had bumped into the top of Ford's hierarchy. Without an M.B.A., he was stymied. Chris left Lincoln-Mercury and joined a sales incentive company as an account executive, hawking Owens Corning Fiberglass and Gulf & Western Manufacturing and even General Motors on programs designed to assist them in selling their products to the trade. These giant corporations needed the help. The American economy was sinking into its deepest recession since the end of World War II. Detroit, especially, was in the pits. Which meant, of course, that no one was buying anything—not even sales-incentive programs. Having bounced, with hope each time, from flyboy to navy careerist to Ford sales exec to incentive salesman, Chris, after two years, was fired.

Desperate, he returned to the automobile business, but in a far less lofty position. The car companies had to keep their factories running, because idle capacity was more expensive to maintain than excess inventory. But those cars kept piling up. Chrysler, which was in the worst shape of all, had fields and fields where thousands of cars sat, fender to fender, with no dealers willing to take them and few drivers willing to buy them. Out of this miasma of industrial despair grew a new specialty: tent sales. A few hardy entrepreneurs offered to take hundreds of cars at a time from the factories' back lots, put them under canvas and fill the airwaves and newspapers with ads for giant sales extravaganzas. They sold the cars for a little over the wholesale cost, taking their profits on the volume. Tent sales became a thriving business.

This huckster's underground welcomed Chris Wackman. He found a company with a new product called "Sale in a Box," a kit which provided local dealers everything they needed to set up their own tent sales, including templates for the ads and direct-mail lists of potential car buyers in their areas. Unfortunately, Chris's new employer hadn't paid payroll taxes for some time, a problem that led the Internal Revenue Service temporarily to padlock the business. Chris began beating the bushes for employment. Tom Gibson, his old boss from Lincoln-Mercury in the Bay Area, dangled an offer. *Come to Subaru*, said Gibson, whom Harvey Lamm had hired to bring smooth experience to his ragged-edged company. *Leave the domestics. We're selling 'em as fast as we can import 'em.*

Chris was Gibson's third hire from Ford Motor Company. The old guard at S.O.A. began to lump the newcomers together, derisively, calling them "the Fords." The Fords were resented because they hadn't been through the desperate days at Subaru. But they prevailed. The stalwarts soon left or were fired, and the Fords brought in more of their own. Gibson eventually promoted Chris to the position of marketing director.

His influence, however, was tightly circumscribed. Harvey Lamm had acquired a gorgeous boat, on which he was spending more and more time; there were trips to the Bahamas with his family, long weekends in Cape Cod with friends. As time passed, only one, adjunct member of the Old Guard continued to have Harvey's ear: Bob Schmidt. The Schmidt-Harvey alliance remained as strong as ever, perhaps stronger, despite the presence of the Fords. The new S.O.A. executives were a little too smooth, a little too bureaucratic, for a Philly boy to feel comfortable with. Schmidt was a more *haimisher* confidant—a role that gave the agency executive and his staff more influence than ever over Subaru's image, more than Chris Wackman, more than Tom Gibson.

"I included Tom in everything I did, but he wasn't always with me when I had my discussions with Bob," Harvey said of his successor and his adman. "But what I was telling Bob I had already told Tom. If I hadn't, when I came back from talking to Bob, I would tell Tom. And I'd make sure he was understanding everything I was saying to Bob."

The festering morale troubles failed to tamp Subaru's fortunes. Quite the contrary, the arrival of the Fords heralded a new period of prosperity for S.O.A. The company sold 150,300 cars in 1982, 156,800 in 1983, 157,400 in 1984 and 178,175 in 1985. Profits kept pace with the tally. In 1982, *Forbes* magazine ranked Subaru's five-year return on capital second, and its market-value appreciation third, among all the publicly held companies it investigated.

The company's investors prospered, and Subaru's shares became traders' favorites. From a low of about 50 cents a share during the company's period of near-insolvency in 1975, the price hit $3 a share in 1977. It zoomed to $9.875 in 1978. Two years later, it reached as high as $15.625. In 1981, share-price growth was breathtaking, the stock climbing from $21.625 in the first quarter to $39.25 in the final quarter. Many investors grew wealthy; Harvey Lamm, for one, risked the disapprobation of Wall Street by unloading 72,000 of his own shares over a one-year period ending February 1982. The stock still rose: $56.75 in 1982, $87 in 1983, reaching, in 1984, a high of $110 per share. That year, Harvey's holdings were worth $8.4 million.

Wall Street's rosy assessment of Subaru's prospects was not hard to understand. Despite protectionist pressures, the Japanese were on their way to taking over the American automobile market. Subaru had a unique niche with its four-wheel-drive station wagon that fairly well guaranteed it substantial margins. Automotive industry financial analysts expected Subaru's earnings to continue to grow at a 12–15 percent annual rate. On the strength of such projections, institutional investors snapped up the shares—at one point, institutions owned some 60 percent of the company's publicly traded shares—driving the price even higher, to a top of $171.50 in 1985 and, finally, to a peak of $273 per share before an eight-for-one split in May 1986. Inside Subaru of America, the atmosphere was understandably heady. As the company grew in personnel, people gauged their colleagues' length of service by asking what the share price was when they joined.

Out in the regions, dealers were taking every car they could get their hands on and conniving to obtain more. Dealer profits were even higher than in earlier years, because so many of the cars were presold before they arrived. Customers simply came in and picked up their already ordered cars the day they came in; local advertising was unnecessary. And there was no need for dealers to take out short-term loans to purchase the cars from the manufacturer, a process known in the auto-motive business as "floor planning."

In Orangeburg, New York, Marty Pizza was closing his showroom at 6 p.m. "We had no cars to show, I had no brochures to give away," he said. "So all you did if you sat there at night was antagonize people, you know?"

S.O.A. continued to believe that its popularity was a function of the right products, with the right image, at the right prices. The company failed to consider a fourth component: Thanks to the American political system, it was also the right time.

Despite years of warning, by the late 1970s Detroit still had not man-aged to invent a decent, inexpensive, fuel-efficient car. Frightened by the 1979–80 oil shock, Americans turned to Japanese cars in greater numbers than ever before. The domestic manufacturers and their un-ions panicked, and, with the American economy tumbling into reces-sion, their calls for protection against imports began to receive a more favorable hearing in Washington.

Aware of the growing antagonism, the Japanese government agreed "voluntarily" to limit exports of automobiles to the United States, a sug-gestion that had first been advanced under the Carter administration but which only reached fruition during the first months of the militantly free-trade Reagan administration. Tokyo agreed to restrict for two years the number of cars exported to the U.S. to 1.685 million units annually, 7.7 percent fewer cars than the 1.82 million vehicles Japanese compa-nies sold in America in 1980. In return, the Japanese insisted that the number be fixed for two years, and that, within the set limit, they not be restricted in the sizes or prices of the vehicles. The agreement be-tween the two governments was announced on May 1, 1981. Later, this voluntary restraint agreement—the quotas took its initials, and were called "V.R.A.s" in the auto business—was extended to a third, then a fourth year.

Fuji Heavy Industries was a party to the agreement, to the annoyance of Subaru of America. S.O.A. felt that, as a small, American-founded, American-owned importing company, it should not be made to suffer for the piggishness of far-larger competitors like Toyota and Nissan and their wholly-owned subsidiaries in the United States. S.O.A. knew from the start that the V.R.A.s could depress sales. But the company reas-sured shareholders that it would maintain strong operating margins by importing more high-priced models from Japan, and by emphasizing "a higher volume of factory-installed accessories."

The tactic worked better than the company had imagined. The V.R.A.s made Japanese cars scarce at the very time the U.S. began pulling out of the recession and Americans were once more entering the market for new cars. With demand exceeding supply, dealers raised prices on imported cars. Several Japanese manufacturers used these windfall profits to develop larger, more expensive and more profitable luxury models. Meanwhile, the American manufacturers, whose sales also blossomed with the economic upswing, rejected the opportunity to entice Americans back to American cars by keeping their prices low. Instead, they raised prices to match the Japanese. Then, rather than taking their own profits and using them to build more efficient factories or more competitive cars, the Detroit manufacturers gave the money to shareholders in the form of dividends. The V.R.A.s helped assure Japanese dominance of the American automobile market for the rest of the decade.

Subaru was among the beneficiaries. In 1983, for the first time, its sales exceeded $1 billion. S.O.A. considered this a favorable judgment on the company's acumen and its image.

Its research told a partly different story. On a per-car basis, Subaru's advertising spending was the highest in the auto industry. Its 1984 ad budget of $34 million worked out to $250 for every car sold, far outstripping the $137 General Motors spent to advertise each of its vehicles. Yet the image study released toward the end of that year showed that Subaru's image had improved hardly at all since the 1981 report. When consumers were asked, "If you were to buy a new car today, which one make do you think you'd consider looking at first? What other makes would you consider looking at?," only 5 percent of the respondents mentioned Subaru—putting it in twelfth place, behind all the other Japanese imports save lowly Mitsubishi. Hardly anyone knew anything about Subaru. Only 3 percent of those surveyed mentioned Subaru when they thought of trouble-free cars, the same percentage that considered it the best value for the money; a mere 2 percent considered it among the most durable makes. Yet these were the very qualities the company's slogan was trying to sell. Its most familiar attribute was, again, four-wheel drive—7 percent of those surveyed said Subaru was the one that popped to mind when they thought of it. Unfortunately, four-wheel drive was last on a list of fourteen attributes that consumers considered when hunting for a car. Only 3 percent of all the people knew without prompting that Subaru's slogan was "Inexpensive, and built to stay that way." While that was more than the ratio who knew the slogan in the 1981 image survey, it had cost S.O.A. nearly $100 million in advertising and promotions to get a bump of 1.3 percentage points in unaided recall.

"Most domestic and imported competitors currently outstrip Subaru by comfortable margins on these scores," reported Factline Inc., the New York company that conducted the survey. "Results of this benchmark study show that Subaru has a long way to go in (a) building awareness and predisposition to consider Subaru and (b) establishing a clear image of the characteristics of its cars in the minds of U.S. motorists." It wasn't image that was selling Subarus.

The company overlooked a more likely explanation: With the V.R.A.s limiting the availability of Japanese cars, people were buying Subarus because they couldn't get Toyotas and Nissans.

SUBARU'S PROSPERITY WAS DUE, of course, to more than a mere accident of timing. Harvey Lamm was essential to it. Harvey had not simply traded in the shaggy hair and gold chains of 1970 for the sartorial conservatism of the 1980s; he had also learned the automotive business, from the showroom floor up, and he applied his knowledge with a craftiness that rendered him a formidable negotiator and a charisma that made him a beloved boss. His haggling with Fuji kept prices low, ensuring a continuing market for Subaru's cars. His firmness with the distributors—his willingness to challenge their duplicities and to force them to honor agreements with dealers and their customers—kept Subaru a respected name among automotive marketers. The president of S.O.A.'s independent New York–area distributorship, Tom O'Hare, who tangled with him dozens of times, called Harvey "in terms of street smarts, probably the smartest man I've ever met."

Yet even smart people have blind spots. Harvey's was his unwillingness to distinguish what Subaru *was* from what he wanted Subaru *to be*. He embodied his error in a decision he made during S.O.A.'s period of expansion in the early 1980s. He decided to ask Fuji to build a car that the Japanese called the Alcyone and the Americans dubbed the XT.

The XT was the ultimate symbol of Subaru's niche, as Harvey interpreted it. Subaru was the Vietcong of automotive marketers, *the people who go out at night and go where nobody else isn't,* as he put it. His vision for the company, now that it had succeeded in selling no-frills "econoboxes" and chug-along four-wheel-drive station wagons, was a sports car. But not just any sports car. Harvey wanted a vehicle with all the sharp edges and high-tech dash gadgetry of a sporty auto, but without all the frightening, useless power. The XT, as one of his marketing executives, David Wager, later described it, was designed to be "a sports car for people who don't like sports cars."

Building it, though, meant abandoning the pursuit of other niches; Fuji was a small manufacturer with limited resources. Harvey decided not to battle the Japanese manufacturer to build either a minivan or a four-wheel-drive sport-utility vehicle, two conveyances many in his inner circle were begging him to obtain. Both vehicles would become the auto industry's best-selling new products in the late eighties, in large part because of their appeal to young families, an important Subaru constituency. To serve consumers who might want to trade up to an antispeed sporty car, Harvey turned his back on the people who had been buying S.O.A.'s four-wheel-drive autos.

The neglected opportunities had a measurable effect on Subaru of America. With other companies now carving reputations for four-wheel-drive engineering by building minivans or "4x4" sport-utility vehicles, Subaru's primacy began to slip. By late 1985, S.O.A. still accounted for half the 101,542 four-wheel-drive passenger cars retailed in the United States—"a formidable market share," cautioned the *New York Times*, "but of a market it once owned."

The XT was meant to take up the slack, to open new and more profitable consumer markets and lessen S.O.A.'s dependence on four-wheel drive. Unfortunately, though, the XT was an exercise in ambivalence.

Everything about the car reeked of speed, from its flying-wedge shape to its exterior colors, including bright red and sky blue, which were, to car buffs, sports-car hues. Yet the XT's engine, in the initial model, was the old Subaru four-cylinder job, a steady, stable piece of equipment that made the vehicle perform less like a Corvette than a Corolla. Among the equipment in its digital interior was a warning buzzer that sounded when the car exceeded a preset speed—hardly the accoutrement for a sports-car fanatic's dash. "An uninspired effort in wild clothes," declared *Car & Driver*.

Fuji developed the XT with little input from or understanding of the American market. "There was no U.S. arm in terms of styling, research on future trends in styling," said Kei Ono, a young Japanese product planner at S.O.A. Predictably, this deficiency manifested itself as soon as the car arrived in America and S.O.A.'s executives saw that it had a checkerboard interior, a weird remnant of the muscle cars of the 1960s. With something approaching horror, Ron Will, a product development executive at S.O.A., tracked down the Japanese designer responsible for the tic, and found that the fellow had based his design on an understanding of America gleaned from fifteen-year-old movies. *This,* the designer told Will, in proud, halting English, *is for the American dude.*

Levine, Huntley amplified the XT's dissonant character with a launch advertisement that focused almost entirely on speed. The spot, a typically witty Lee Garfinkel–Tony DeGregorio narrative, opened on a grizzled farmer walking from a hay-strewn barn with his twenty-something son as a lazy harmonica filled the background. "Remember when you were my age, Dad?" the kid asked. "Come on, Dad, you understand what I mean. It's my first car." "It's your money, son," replied the father, walking up to his old-faithful station wagon. "But if you want my advice, buy a Subaru. It's been good to us." The boy assented.

In a split second, the music shifted to a throbbing rock beat, a wailing guitar and an unseen singer shouting, "Take me to the limit, take me where it's hot." From below the screen, a gleaming silver sports car moved into view, the farmer's lad, in aviator sunglasses and bouncing to the beat, behind the wheel. His new car had everything—speed, a sun-roof, a turbo-charged engine, speed, astronautical digital displays, four-wheel drive, speed. As the kid barreled back onto the farm, his father looked on in consternation. "I thought we agreed you'd buy a Subaru," the farmer said.

"But, Dad," replied the son, smiling ingenuously, "I did."

The spot, titled "Farmboy," built on Subaru's central value of durability and added some new elements, notably styling. Set on a farm, it called, perhaps unintentionally, to S.O.A.'s core rural market. Tom Gibson, S.O.A.'s president, called it his favorite automobile ad of all time. "It was the transition from 'cheap and ugly' to upscale." The dealers loved it; more than a few wrote "But Dad, I did," in soap, on the wind-shields of XTs on their lots. The ad garnered a Clio Award as the best automobile commercial of the year, one of three in a row Levine, Huntley and Subaru won.

But the commercial lacked a certain rigor. It identified the XT's audience as young, first-time car buyers who lived in the country—hardly the type to appreciate the XT's relatively high cost. So, too, the XT was not, as the closing slogan claimed, "Inexpensive, and built to stay that way." At retail prices of up to $14,000, the car cost almost twice as much as the average Subaru. The spot was also constructed on the assumption that consumers knew enough about frumpy old Subaru to understand why this radical new Subaru was a departure. But as the company's image studies had shown, Subaru was little known to the car-buying public.

There is an adage in the agency business that nothing will kill a bad product faster than good advertising. S.O.A. sold 27,000 XTs during the introductory year, after which the car gradually dropped from sight. "It wasn't this and it wasn't that, so to speak," one dealer complained. "It wasn't a sports car and it wasn't a sedan, a coupe, or a two-door sedan. It was something in-between."

The XT's schizophrenic design was only partly Harvey's fault. The

aloof relationship between S.O.A. and Fuji was ripening into an antagonism that hindered the companies' ability to make and market autos.
In public, Harvey praised Fuji (*They would do anything for us, and we
would do anything for them*) and affirmed the two companies' mutual
respect (*It's an unbelievable relationship and an exciting one*). Privately,
he and his fellow Americans cursed Fuji's engineers who, the Americans
complained, designed engines and transmissions to meet their own ego-
istic desires and then reluctantly built bodies—often ugly, sometimes
ghastly—around them. Fuji, in turn, thought of its American marketing
arm as an operation staffed with dishonest philistines who understood
little of an automobile's native beauty.

The hostility worsened after June 1985, when Toshihiro Tajima, a
sixty-six-year-old banker, became Fuji's president. Until Tajima's ascendancy, the path between Subaru and Fuji had been kept smooth by
Shoji Kikuchi, the Japanese company's longtime head of export operations and a gentle, reflective man who became something of an uncle
to Harvey and secretly advised him on how to negotiate with his own
Japanese superiors.

Once Tajima became president, though, Kikuchi's mediation ceased.
On their first visit to Tokyo after Tajima's ascension, Harvey and Tom
Gibson took lunch with the executive. Fuji's silver-haired, handsome
president looked at them sternly and said: *From now on, I am in
charge. You will not talk to Kikuchi. You will report to me.* Tajima had
his own visions of glory for Subaru. "We want," Tajima told an interviewer, "to be more like Audi and BMW."

LEVINE, HUNTLEY was of only limited use in helping S.O.A. bridge
the gaps in its marketing program. Not only did the agency have its own
agenda, but it, too, like its largest client, was torn by internal strife that
hindered concerted efforts on Subaru's behalf.

Outwardly, the agency reminded Madison Avenue of the antic atmosphere of Doyle Dane Bernbach and Papert, Koenig, Lois during the
halcyon days of the Creative Revolution, what with the spontaneous
water-gun fights, romantic couplings and desecration of the agency
bosses' hallway photographs. Landing a job at Levine, Huntley was like
arriving in Camelot. Michael Moore, the research director, called the
agency "Camp Levine."

Yet new arrivals rapidly became aware of the seething rivalries. The
rest of the agency despised the Subaru group, which it believed received benefits (like private Christmas parties and salary increases) denied others. Even within the Subaru group, there was tension. Terry

Bonaccolta, the punctilious account director, was angered by Lee Garfinkel's slovenly dress. Lee chafed at Bonaccolta's creative demands (shoot the cars at a three-quarter front angle; no profile shots; do not cock the wheels when a car pulls to a curb) which Lee complained "weren't conceptual, or really smart," just "by-the-book." Harold Levine didn't like Bob Schmidt, and, ever since Larry Plapler's departure, Schmidt hadn't trusted Allan Beaver. The four highest-ranking account executives fought constant battles over turf, making and breaking alliances among the creatives and media staff and warring for control of the new-business and research departments.

Bob Schmidt was fully aware of the chaos and unhappiness. *What the fuck is wrong with these people?* he'd complain to confidants as tensions grew. But he refused to end the fighting. He figured that more growth would quell the hostilities and bring back the loving family that Schmidt, in his personal mythology, believed the agency had once been. So he threw himself into the pursuit of new business, using the profits thrown off by the growing Subaru account to fuel the quest. New accounts arrived, but they were always also-rans in coveted categories—the Whataburger fast-food chain instead of McDonald's—and they always departed quickly. The agency remained unbalanced, with Subaru accounting for more than half its income through the decade. Schmidt tried to mollify his contentious underlings, telling each, out of earshot of the others, *You're the best. Those others stink.* To pacify them, he gave them elevated titles and higher salaries. "He became the sugar daddy, and when things went wrong, everybody would run to Daddy," Michael Moore said. Even after the agency sold out in 1985 to Grey Advertising—the dull, plodding $1.7 billion giant that Bill Bernbach had fled thirty-six years earlier—to finance Harold Levine's retirement, the battling continued, for Schmidt, stepping into Harold's chairmanship, kept dangling the firm's presidency in front of different senior executives. He wanted to placate his fractious minions. Instead, he only made them more rancorous. "The agency was like a series of fiefdoms," said Philippe Krakowsky, its communications director.

Preoccupied by their own bitter contests, Schmidt and his staff were unable to provide S.O.A. with the marketing counsel the car company required. Neither Levine, Huntley nor Subaru thought to change S.O.A.'s decade-old slogan, which was becoming manifestly inaccurate. Between 1981 and 1985, the average price of a Subaru rose from $6,025 to $8,000—not that the vehicles were really worth the extra cash. Following the strategy it disclosed to shareholders in 1981, S.O.A., with Fuji's acquiescence, refrained from asking for fundamental styling or engineering changes in its model line. Instead, the two companies kept profits high by plastering the otherwise unchanged Leones with more and more factory-installed accessories (called "trim" in the trade). In 1983, Subaru offered the GL-10, which was nothing more than the old GL hardtop with power steering, power brakes and a sunroof. (The "10" had no real meaning; Harvey named the car for the Bo Derek movie *10*.) For the 1985 model year, Subaru upped the ante even more, offering its old sedan in a "turbo-traction model," with aluminum-alloy wheels and a "sport-suspension system." More than merely maintaining the level of profit, the scheme nearly tripled Subaru's per-car profits. S.O.A.'s customers—the distributors and dealers—greedily competed for their own pieces of the expanding pie. Distributors overcharged dealers for the most desirable cars. Dealers took advantage of the limited availability of Japanese cars under the V.R.A.s by charging consumers more than the manufacturer's suggested retail price for Subarus; some even had the audacity to add a line on the window sticker that read "additional profit." In 1986, close to one-third of the cars S.O.A. imported into the U.S. were its most expensive, top-of-the-line models.

Yet the price hikes still did not dampen sales. Subaru sold 183,242 cars at retail in '86, more than ever before, and earned $94 million on $1.9 billion of sales, a 29 percent increase over the previous year.

But while sales and profits were climbing, a time bomb was ticking. It had been set in the fall of 1985, when U.S. Secretary of the Treasury James A. Baker III persuaded finance ministers and central bankers from West Germany, Britain, France and Japan to agree to a program to drive down the value of the American dollar. The United States deemed the dollar's strength in foreign currency markets responsible for the nation's mushrooming trade deficit, because the strong dollar made American goods more expensive than comparable foreign goods both in the U.S. and in other countries. Within a year, the American dollar, the value of which stood at 242 Japanese yen on the day before the agreement, plunged to 150 yen.

Most of Japan's automakers kept their export prices low in the United States, instead of raising them to account for the weakened dollar. These exporters were determined to maintain their market-share gains from the first half of the decade. They used their tremendous profits from those years to subsidize continued low prices. In the first year after the currency accord, Japanese export prices rose just 61 percent of the yen's appreciation. Even though the dollar continued to slide in value, these large Japanese companies managed to stem much of the impact.

Fuji Heavy Industries was not a large company. It had no choice (so it said) but to raise the prices it charged Subaru of America for its automobiles. Subaru, in turn, had to raise the prices it charged distributors. Distributors then increased prices to dealers, who, naturally, stuck consumers with the bill. Within an eighteen-month period, loyal Subaru owners who had paid $8,000 for a loaded four-wheel-drive wagon confronted an unfamiliar monstrosity: a $17,000 Subaru.

Built to stay that way? Maybe. Inexpensive? No.

THE "SITUATION," as he called it, ran over Chris Milhous like a speeding truck. An unflappable young man who only a few years before, just out of college, had had a tough time finding a dealer who would finance a car for him without his father's signature, Milhous now wholesaled cars in the South for the nation's most profitable automobile company—nice title (district manager), easy job (ravenous dealers), neat surroundings (suburban Atlanta). When he prepared to place the first calls to his dealers to take their orders for the '87 models, he steeled himself for the most difficult part of the task: fending off those who wanted more cars. But Subaru's "turn-and-earn" system was strict; vehicles were allocated based on each dealer's sales from the previous year. Milhous readied his lecture and called his top dealer, who had earned more than fifty cars.

The dealer didn't want a single vehicle.

Puzzled, Milhous called his number-two dealer, who was good for just under fifty cars. *Not one, Chris.*

The rejections were troubling, but what really shocked Milhous was the discovery that the two dealers, venomous rivals, had broken bread together to hash over their mutual unhappiness with Subaru. They were disgusted by the rising prices, fed up with the lack of sales incentives, sickened by the company's inadequacies. They wanted to teach S.O.A. a lesson.

As 1987 dawned, Subaru confronted a haunting specter from its distant past: automobiles that would not sell.

S.O.A. looked to the domestic manufacturers for inspiration. In late August 1986, General Motors had offered 2.9 percent annual financing on three-year loans for its new cars, four percentage points lower than the rates then in effect and the lowest financing terms ever offered in the auto industry. The next day, Ford followed suit. Chrysler went both one better, extending 2.4 percent financing on twenty-four-month loans. A few days later, American Motors sweetened the pot, extending free financing to buyers of its 1986 models.

The Japanese manufacturers, whose vehicles were still highly coveted by American buyers, did not have to fight the rebate wars as strenuously as Detroit. All, that is, except Subaru. After a decade of denials, it now confronted the fact that its customers bought its cars not because of high image but because of low prices. Subaru's consumers were concentrated in poorer areas, in "C" and "D" counties—A.C. Nielsen designations for consolidated statistical areas with populations of 150,000 or below. They were "salt-of-the-earth types, not country club," Chris Wackman said. They weren't urban lawyers or Silicon Valley techies. They read the labels and bought generic brands. "When the dollar and yen flipped, so did they." To maintain Subaru's popularity among these wallet-watchers, S.O.A., virtually alone among the Japanese import companies, was forced to offer them incentives and rebates.

Subaru started advertising rebates in February 1987, when twelve thousand 1986 models were still left on dealer lots. Through the year, the company spent $106 million on dealer and consumer incentives. The strategy was of limited effectiveness because, as the yen rose in value, Subaru's competitors—Honda, Toyota, Nissan—stripped the frills from their compact cars to keep prices low. Eventually, these barebones compacts were selling for prices barely above those for subcompacts—Subaru's subcompacts.

By the end of 1987, S.O.A. managed to retail 177,000 cars, only a slight fall from the year before. But its wholesales to dealers dropped 8 percent from 1986. The company lost $30 million—its first loss since the days of Masaichi Kaneda and the "Who, me?" campaign. Worse, Subaru was left with inventories worth $133 million.

Yet Fuji, with the fervor of an addict in a pharmacy, was unable to stop making cars. Subaru pleaded with its manufacturer to curtail production, or to let S.O.A. out of its previous commitments to purchase specific—and high—numbers of cars. At the very least, S.O.A. begged, Fuji should hold on to some of the cars in Japan. The Japanese refused to listen. *They're like a salt machine by the ocean,* Marv Riesenbach, the chief financial officer, thought, relentlessly churning out more and more product, piling it in stacks, then going back to make more.

Fuji argued that if it closed the plants, then when the market turned around, it would have difficulty hiring new staff, Japan facing chronic shortages of workers. Fuji also said that if S.O.A. didn't buy cars, the manufacturer would have no capital to invest in developing new products, leading to eventual failure anyway. Indeed, Fuji was so desperate to keep its factories running that it even released Subaru from the two-decades-old requirement that the Americans back their purchases with bank letters of credit. Fuji, breaking another tradition, also proffered S.O.A. money to help with the rebates, giving $12 million in 1987. The

Japanese tendered another $20 million in 1988, a year when S.O.A. rebated $112 million to dealers and consumers.

The scheme had little effect. Subaru lost $57.8 million. Retail sales plummeted 12 percent, to 155,956, and wholesale trade dropped 13 percent. Inventories totaled thousands of cars, worth a staggering $210 million. Subaru's shareholders proved as fickle as its customers. From a high of $39 after the May 1986 stock split, the share price collapsed. At the end of 1988, shares bottomed out at $4.625 each.

As the debacle was taking shape, Fuji Heavy Industries forged ahead with a plan that was mind-numbing in its costs and implications. The manufacturer decided to build a plant in the United States.

Fuji was the last of the Japanese import manufacturers to conclude it needed a stateside factory. Honda had begun producing Accords in Marysville, Ohio, in 1982. Nissan came next with a plant in Smyrna, Tennessee. Mazda, and then Toyota, followed. They all feared the growth of protectionism in the United States, especially domestic-content legislation that might require a percentage of their cars' parts to be American-made. The continued strength of the yen also was making it cheaper to manufacture in the U.S. than in Japan. If the competition could do it, why not Fuji?

Answers flooded back, from S.O.A., consultants and analysts. Fuji's sales were but a fraction of its competitors'. Fuji was small enough to withstand protectionism's impact. Fuji's success had always depended on an undersupply of cars, enhancing their value in the limited geographic market Subaru had carved for itself in the U.S. The half-billion-dollar factory would double, at the least, the supply of Subarus in the United States. Investing in the plant would mean a delay of several years in developing a new subcompact to replace Subaru's boxy Leone.

Harvey pleaded with Tajima. *You need to build a factory in the United States like I need a fourth arm!* he shouted. *It's ridiculous! 'Cause all you're doing is violating one of the rules you never do—you never move into an oversupply situation when you're a niche marketer. You always have to be short of supply.*

Tajima thought differently. The factory—and the new compact car it was to produce—would push his company from the fringes of the niche market directly into the mainstream of the automotive world. At last, he could sit proudly as a brother among the Hondas and Toyodas and the other gray-suited titans of the Japanese auto industry.

Tajima had another project, also formulated from observations of his competitors, of which the Americans were only slightly aware. Just as Toyota and Nissan were developing luxury models, Fuji, too, wanted to enhance its appeal to more affluent consumers. The company was developing a replacement for the XT, the meteoric sporty car that flamed and fizzled because its wedge-shaped styling and snazzy interior raised expectations of performance which the vehicle never met. S.O.A. had agreed to a plan to build a new XT, because it believed that a car with superior performance, a rounder, more subtle styling and a retail price around $18,000 would fill in a gap in its model line and provide worthy competition to the Honda Prelude and the Toyota Celica.

Fuji's engineers, however, had a different idea. They wanted to build a car which would showcase their superiority, but which would end, once and for all, the auto critics' continual carping about the poor quality of Fuji's styling. They turned the project over to an Italian designer whose specialty was Ferraris. His composition was almost impossibly modern—a sleek, forward thrust; a high-bustle rear; a wide, low, road-hugging chassis; and, most noticeably, windows-within-windows that made the vehicle's upper body look like a glassed-in jet cockpit. Fuji's engineers, emboldened by President Tajima, decided to bring the vehicle to life. They widened the car from a planned 67 inches to 70 inches and increased the length. Now heavier, the vehicle needed a more powerful engine, which increased the production cost, of course. The new vehicle would not cost $18,000, as proposed; it would retail for $25,000 to $30,000. Named SVX, for Specialty Experimental Vehicle, the car was the ultimate expression of Fuji's (and S.O.A.'s) create-a-niche philosophy. Unfortunately, it conflicted with the new corporate strategy of going mainstream.

"It was engineers' ego," lamented Kei Ono, the young Japanese product planner. "Definitely engineers' ego. Nothing more than that." Subaru of America found out about the car only a few months before the new Subaru-Isuzu joint-venture factory began spitting out a new compact car, the Legacy, a $13,000-to-$17,000 rival to two of America's best-selling cars, the Toyota Camry and the Honda Accord.

From the start, analysts were leery of the Legacy. "Trying to take on Camry, Accord and 626 [Mazda's compact] looks like swimming in shark-infested waters to me," said Charles Brady, an automotive-industry analyst with Oppenheimer & Company. Subaru, however, gamely made the best of it. Fuji had provided the car with antilock brakes and smooth, low styling more than reminiscent of the much more expensive Acura Legend. J. Paul Bubernak, S.O.A.'s group vice president for parts and service, was so excited when he inspected the Legacy that he termed the compact car "bulletproof." The tag stuck, becoming an expression of S.O.A.'s faith in the car that was supposed to save it.

Harvey knew to whom he wanted to advertise the car—men and

women, twenty-five to forty-nine, with household incomes above $40,000, a level 33 percent higher than that of buyers of the Leone (which was renamed the Loyale in America). Harvey also knew *how* he wanted to advertise the car. Inexpensive and durable? *That's dead. We'll market the Legacy as the most powerful Subaru ever!*

Highlighting the Legacy's power, like many of Subaru's earlier marketing decisions, was an idea that came from Harvey's gut. "You sometimes got to do a lot of market research when you're trying to dot *i*'s or cross *t*'s. That's not Subaru," Harvey would explain years later. "Because the expense of dotting those *i*'s and crossing those *t*'s, as it relates to what comes back to you, is not the business." Most market research was "a total waste. It didn't get anything accomplished. I happen to feel I am perceptive about general markets. Most entrepreneurs and most people who are more subjective think that they can do good evaluations of people, good evaluations of markets. You don't need research to do those kinds of things."

Levine, Huntley's introductory Legacy commercial, the "launch spot" in ad-speak, was a direct homage to the earlier "Farmboy" launch ad for the XT that S.O.A. so loved. It, too, opened with a leisurely harmonica, purring "The Old Gray Mare." The camera zoomed in, in increasing speed, over an expansive green field, across a stream, over a broken fence and down a dirt road. The music, in counterpoint, slowed and the harmonica was replaced by a cello, which rendered the folk tune in an ominous adagio. The camera zipped past a haystack and right up to the closed door of a dilapidated barn. The music ceased. The doors flashed open, and over stacked bales of hay burst forth . . . a silver Subaru Legacy, its headlights shining despite the daylight. With only the sound of wind behind it, the car, in slow motion, sailed along, its wheels two feet from the ground. It landed, and rode off. "The old gray Subaru," the announcer intoned, as the words "Subaru Legacy" appeared on screen, "ain't what she used to be."

The launch was a failure. Legacy sales were slow from the start. Subaru blamed the continuing rebate ads for the Loyale, which were also running. They diminished the impact of the new car's introduction and, said Mary Treisbach, the company's onetime advertising manager, "cheapened the image at the time we needed to move up." Compounding the confusion was S.O.A.'s belated introduction of a new Levine, Huntley slogan, "We built our reputation by building better cars." But the Legacy launch faltered on its own terms, too. Harvey's desired image of power had nothing to do with the real reasons—economy, functionality, safety and social acceptance—millions of Americans were flocking to imported compact cars.

Subaru's misfortunes were a boon to Levine, Huntley, though. All the advertising—the rebate ads, the Legacy launch, the Leone-Loyale renaming, the promos for a new minicar called the Justy, the revised slogan—were like powdered manure sprinkled liberally on the agency's commissions. The agency renovated and moved into a stylish new headquarters on Park Avenue South, in the heart of a trendy neighborhood just beginning to fill with publishing companies, p.r. firms, ad agencies and chic bistros to feed them. Before long, senior executives on the Subaru account were crowing that S.O.A.'s ad spending had exceeded $100 million a year—the first Levine, Huntley client to pierce this proud barrier.

Bob Schmidt, however, knew the Subaru work was inadequate. He could hear the desperation in Harvey's voice and he saw the seething hostility toward the company and his agency whenever he made his customary stops at dealerships. He begged his Subaru creative directors for another blockbuster commercial to relaunch the Legacy and retake the hearts of Subaru's dealers. Lee and Tony complied, with a spot that took off from a favorite Garfinkel theme, coitus interruptus. In the commercial, a couple drove hard down a smooth road, the man shifting, shifting, shifting, at higher and higher speeds, as his woman friend *ooh*ed and *aah*ed at higher pitch and growing intensity. As she was about to climax, they reached the end of the pavement. He looked at her. She looked at him. He smiled and said, "It's a four-wheel drive." They took off into the dirt, and to orgasmic satisfaction.

The spot was never produced. S.O.A. was adamant about not promoting four-wheel drive, a quirky technology, on this, its new, mainstream luxury car. That was the end for Lee. He had already received an offer from BBDO to become a senior creative executive on the Pepsi-Cola campaign.

In charge on his own, Tony fired several creatives who he felt were loyal to his predecessors. Allan Beaver, tired of all the infighting, decided to retire. But Tony alone was no more successful in positioning the new Subaru than he and Lee together had been. He presented one ad that had the Legacy swerving in and out among wrecking balls in the desert. That spot had already been approved for production when an astute S.O.A. executive intervened, calling attention to the fact that it showcased the Legacy's handling—an attribute they were not supposed to be spotlighting. Another Tony commercial depicted a couple driving their Legacy from Houston to New Orleans and then, having enjoyed the ride so much, driving immediately back again. That one was actually produced, at a cost of several hundred thousand dollars. It was broadcast only a few times.

In 1989, despite continued incentive spending of $76 million, S.O.A. sold only 136,112 cars, a drop of more than 12 percent from 1988. Of those, a mere 35,000 were Legacies. For the third year in a row, the company lost money—$42.7 million. In 1990, Subaru of America sold just 108,542 cars.

If the advertising was not wholly to blame, it certainly had not helped S.O.A. The hundreds of millions of dollars of rebate ads, the shifting slogans and the wandering positions had taken their toll. Subaru's image, indistinct to begin with, had, according to its last image survey for the year, virtually disappeared.

Subaru was last on the list of makes the company's target consumers said they would consider when shopping for a new car, behind Toyota, Ford, Honda, Chevrolet, Nissan, Buick, Chrysler, Mazda, Pontiac, Dodge, Oldsmobile, GMC and Mitsubishi. More people than ever before were rejecting Subaru out of hand, including once-loyal present and former Subaru owners, a fifth of whom now said they would not buy another. Ad recall had plummeted. Less than 3 percent of the target consumers could call up any visuals, slogans or messages associated with the Legacy.

To Factline Inc., the company that had conducted these surveys for Subaru for years, the conclusion was depressingly clear. "The new advertising strategy," it reported, "was not capable of generating any incremental Subaru purchase consideration—or building any favorable attitudes toward—the Subaru product line."

"The energy, the positive energy that existed toward the Legacy didn't exist anymore," said Tom O'Hare, the independent distributor. "Now, all of a sudden, we had dealers looking on the car not as the savior, but as shit."

IN JANUARY 1990, Fuji Heavy Industries bid $6 a share, or a total of $147 million, for the 50.4 percent of Subaru of America it did not own. Tetsuo Miyaji, a Fuji executive vice president, explained to Harvey Lamm that the Japanese company wanted to strengthen its market position in the U.S. "We will be able freely to integrate the manufacturing and distribution process in the same way as our Japanese competitors," Miyaji said.

Fuji eventually sweetened the offer by another $60 million, but only to smooth the road to an inevitable conclusion. There would not be—could not be—any other contenders for S.O.A. "What would another bidder end up with?" asked Wendy Beale Needham, an analyst with Smith Barney, Harris Upham & Co. She answered her own question:

"The exclusive right to sell a product in North America that's losing its appeal and is supplied by the rival bidder."

Perception, as they say, is reality.

Nine months later, Harvey resigned from Subaru, the company that had nearly bankrupted him several times during two decades of plotting, before it had made him rich. In turning over the reins to Masahiru Masumitsu and Takeshi Higurashi, two Fuji lifers, Harvey spoke graciously of wishing to "provide a clear path" for the unification of importer and exporter. He did not reveal that Fuji wanted him out, to resurrect a product and a market that *it* had invented and *it* knew best how to revive.

Culture, after all, is history.

Bob Schmidt hung around for a little more than a year after the departure of his friend and client Harvey Lamm, but the agency business had lost its tug. The young creatives he had protected and nurtured were deserting him. He no longer ran the agency with his name on the door; Grey Advertising did. So one day in January 1991, without warning his staff, his corporate overseer or the new management at Subaru, he left to take a job with a client. Grey soon found another senior advertising figure, Edward H. Vick, a man with both packaged-goods and automotive-advertising experience, to take over the shop. Schmidt's name was stripped from the agency. When Subaru put its advertising account into review that April, it was to be a life-or-death matter for Levine, Huntley, Vick & Beaver. Ed Vick and executives at five other agencies willingly, if nervously, accepted the assignment with which they'd been charged: to find a way to transform the reputation of Subaru's cars from inexpensive and reliable to luxurious and, most of all, mainstream.

For image, of course, is destiny.

PART III

THE PITCH

Chapter 7

When You're Having
More Than One

WILDER BAKER was not on top of the world, but he looked it. Through the eight large windows on the north side of his office, he could peer uptown, toward the giant agencies and their gray-flanneled denizens, whom he had forsaken for downtown's calmer confines. To the west, more windows overlooked the majestic flows of the Hudson River and the cheerful halo of the setting sun, whose rays bounced off the collection of ceramic owls that festooned his office. The Metropolitan Life blimp floated lazily by, its intrusive slogan—"Get Met"—a reminder of the pervasiveness of Wilder's chosen profession. And Wilder, who was dressed in the khaki slacks, blue pinpoint oxford-cloth button-down shirt and red tie that constitute the uniform of Ivy Leaguers at rest, had just been invited to pitch what could be the most significant account of his career.

But Wilder was anything but happy. "This came," he said, as he stood at the 111-year-old chrome-and-maple artist's easel that was his desk, "at the worst time for us."

For Warwick, Baker & Fiore, the news that it had been tapped for the finals of Subaru of America's advertising account was unexpected. "We never had a car account, and no car experience to speak of," Wilder conceded. "I didn't have anybody in account management to speak of with car experience. I've never had any car experience. I'm a packaged-goods guy, basically." To compound his unease, the month leading up to the final pitch for the Subaru account just happened to be Warwick's busiest of the year. The agency was putting together a new campaign for Heineken and Amstel beer, a new campaign for Shady Brook Farms, a new campaign for Knorr soups, "brand visions" for Midol analgesics and the Sterling Drug retail chain, and a pitch for the Steak & Ale/Bennigan's restaurant account. With all that work, Wilder could have—a management consultant might have argued *should* have—turned down Subaru's surprising invitation.

But Wilder Baker rose to the challenge. Because, like every other advertising person at each of the agencies summoned by Subaru, Wilder had something to prove, to the advertising world and to himself.

In 1991, America's five hundred largest advertising agencies, a group that included all but the tiniest and most obscure, took in $7.7 billion in revenues, from clients who spent $56.2 billion on advertising. More than seventy thousand men and women toiled at these agencies, writing copy, laying out pictures, schmoozing with clients, *hondling* with space sales reps and fathoming the intricacies of consumer culture. Despite its impressive size, though, the agency business is more like a small town where the residents know one another, if not personally then certainly by standing; where they meet in the pages of *Advertising Age*; where they compete in the sporting events called account reviews. And, as in small towns, where reputation paves the road that branches off to triumph or to ruin, no better forum exists to support or repair or resurrect a reputation than one big pitch.

Warwick, which stood at the fifty-ninth position on the list of largest American agencies, with 160 employees and $160 million in billings, wanted more than anything else to *have* a reputation. In that tiny burg girded by Madison Avenue, the agency was a cipher, the nondescript fellow who paid for his paper every morning but left the drugstore without a word. "Part of that is we're involved with the management of our clients. We haven't done much on the outside," explained Wilder. "We're not known for cutting-edge creative. But our clients aren't, either." Wilder had tried to infuse some particular vigor into the shop; six years before, he took the staff on a retreat and developed a "mission statement" for the agency: "Committed to creating a superb creative product." That sense of purpose had helped pull Warwick through its most dire period, the loss of its flagship client, Seagram's liquors. But making a reputation, even more than remaking one, is a slow process. A car account would be an amphetamine injection. "It can mean a lot more visibility," Wilder said.

W. B. Doner, on the contrary, was renowned in the agency business, although its fame, paradoxically, caused it discomfort. Doner was known as a "great retail agency," the title sticking to it like a military commission. Retail agencies are said to know the little tricks that can boost a product's sales in an eyewink. This legerdemain is deemed by advertising people to be distinct from image building, the power of which is felt only at a remove. Doner, whose main offices, in Baltimore and Detroit, set it physically apart from the haunts of New York's awards-show judges, was desperate to prove that it could craft a glorious image campaign for a national auto company *and* sell cars at the same time. "Image and sales go hand in hand," said Jim Dale, Doner's president. The goal was as much personal as professional; Dale, a well-tailored, introspective man, who peppered his conversation with alternately haughty and jealous references to "New York agencies," wanted his shop's creative prowess recognized and revered by the creative Mafia up north.

Jordan, McGrath, Case & Taylor was also known for moving products off store shelves. But Jordan, McGrath could not have been less interested in image—not if image meant pretty pictures and fancy production and music-video editing. To this agency, and especially to James J. Jordan, Jr., its bombastic chairman, advertising was about words. "Words," Jordan said, "are still the primary means of communication and will be for the foreseeable future. Words give you a medium, if you will, and make your message part of the human thought process. Words are as portable as the human being who hears them."

Jordan considered himself the bulwark against the onslaught of the image, the Ahab of language set to slay the phosphorescent leviathan of MTV. In his Park Avenue office (a chamber washed in crimson, his favorite color) he surrounded himself with his words. On one shelf was a framed newspaper cartoon whose caption identified U.S. Supreme Court Justice Anthony M. Kennedy as "Zest-fully clean"—a Jim Jordan soap slogan. In a hallway outside his office was a black Yamaha piano, on which he could plunk "Schaefer is the one beer to have when you're having more than one"—another Jordan slogan. During a twenty-five-year career at BBDO, his enviable oeuvre also grew to include "How do you handle a hungry man?" for Campbell's Manhandlers soups, "Delta is ready when you are" for the airline, "Ring around the collar" for Wisk detergent, "Us Tareyton smokers would rather fight than switch" for the cigarette brand and, for the breakfast cereal, "Quaker Oats. It's the right thing to do." When he lost out in a leadership struggle in 1978, at the dawning of the age of video trickery, he started his own agency to combat the ascendancy of the image.

Jordan and his colleagues had even trademarked a name for their advertising methodology. They called it "nameonics." And if some of nameonics's more recent tests (e.g., "Renuzit Doozit!" for the household cleanser) were less memorable than Jim Jordan's earlier work, the agency nonetheless stood as proof that the principle had legs. Jordan, McGrath, Case & Taylor had grown from nothing to $350 million in billings—the thirty-second largest agency in the nation—by 1991.

All it needed was a car account. For, as Jack Taylor, the account-handling partner, put it, "In this business, you tend to mirror your own successes. We're primarily a packaged-goods agency. That doesn't define the limit of our ability; it defines our client list. Our vision is to grow as big as our energy and talent can take us."

Geographically, Wieden & Kennedy was clear across the country from Jordan, McGrath—in Portland, Oregon. Spiritually and professionally, the nine-year-old agency was on the other side of the universe. Unlike the other agencies in the Subaru pitch, which concealed their ambitions under a cloak of client-centered concern, Wieden & Kennedy did little to hide its selfish interest in the Subaru account. At one point, Dan Wieden, the agency's copywriting co-founder, even told the Subaru executives that for him, their account meant an opportunity "to stretch our wings creatively."

Although only the seventy-second-largest agency in America, Wieden & Kennedy was, arguably, the nation's hottest shop at the moment the Subaru review was moving to its conclusion. It had taken a multitalented athlete, Bo Jackson, and rendered his prowess in football and baseball in a two-word phrase, "Bo knows . . . ," that had become a schoolyard anthem. It had retained the black film director Spike Lee, long before he moved from cult figure to celebrity, and asked him to direct and star in several spots, which were aimed not at an African-American audience (the reason most black entertainment professionals are hired in advertising) but at a multiracial consumer population. The agency had a knack for identifying the tiniest carbon dioxide bubbles on the bottom of the bottle of popular culture, and riding them as they rose, expanded and burst on the surface of public consciousness. In the advertising world, where attention to detail is keen, Wieden & Kennedy was known for employing the hippest young designers, using Hollywood's most daring imagists and scoring with the newest music. To the consternation of New York agencies, the Portland shop was not only confident in its solipsism, but wildly profitable, too.

Wieden & Kennedy's problem was that virtually all its successes had derived from one client, Nike Inc., the shoe company—a tenuous link, at best, to financial (if not psychic) reward. Wieden & Kennedy possessed a barely hidden passion for something—almost anything of prominence, really—that could reduce its reliance on its single, massive client. "Subaru," Wieden admitted without self-consciousness, "is an incredibly important piece of business for this agency. It brings us outside of Nike."

DCA, the small New York outpost of Tokyo's mammoth Dentsu agency, was motivated neither by ideological enthusiasm nor by creative ardor. Being Japanese, DCA was worried about honor.

For at least a year, DCA's most senior executives, lifers who had joined Dentsu in Tokyo immediately after college, and for whom the foray in New York was another ticket punch on the way home and up to the top, had been in conversation with Subaru's new Japanese leaders. They had shuttled from DCA's office on West 42nd Street, across from the New York Public Library, to Dentsu's headquarters in the Ginza, to Fuji Heavy Industry's offices in Shinjuku, to S.O.A.'s domain in Cherry Hill. No one revealed what exact requests were conveyed, what specific promises were made. But when DCA ended up in the finals for Subaru's account, the gossipy citizens of Madison Avenue assumed what was indeed the truth: Pressure had successfully been brought to bear on the car company by its Japanese chiefs to include the agency, the United States' 125th-largest shop, in the review. The industry chatter proved a burden to DCA, especially to the Americans who had been hired to run the shop and direct the Subaru pitch. They knew that Subaru's American executives resented the agency's presence in the review. And they understood that Fuji, which had extended itself to get DCA into the review, expected a performance worthy of its trust. DCA grew hell-bent on proving its prowess.

"I've spent a lot of time recruiting the best and brightest people I can. I *know* the effort they put into Subaru," Ray Freeman, DCA's American chief operating officer, said in the midst of his preparations. "I've been in a lot of new business pitches. This is no different. It's nights, weekends, frantic phone calls."

And Levine, Huntley, Vick & Beaver; formerly Levine, Huntley, Schmidt & Beaver; formerly Levine, Huntley, Schmidt, Plapler & Beaver? Its objective was simple: The incumbent agency wanted to survive.

Whatever their personal or professional neuroses, though, all the advertising people shared a goal. The courtship of and acceptance by the captains of industry was a ritual that validated their acceptance into the highest echelons of American society. "We're playing every day with the hopes of rich manufacturers," one adman exulted in 1931. In almost sixty years, that thrill had not diminished.

Jim Dale of W. B. Doner, the most reflective of the bunch courting Subaru, put it this way: "Using an idea to overcome obstacles is absolutely addictive. There are few places where sheer power or money are less important than an idea. We get to take a particular business we're not in and change its destiny."

In one of the agency business's favorite games, handicapping, Dale's agency was the front-runner. Over drinks at Positano and at lunches of the Chinese Gourmet Society and in conversations with *Ad Age* reporters, senior account executives and junior copywriters alike assessed the contenders' chances with clinical care. The finalists were particularly engaged in predicting the pattern of the race, for their judgment of their opponents would inevitably shape how they themselves would run the course.

Doner, because it had done auto advertising at the retail level, usually finished first in the commentary sweepstakes. "They're in funny cities, but they have nine fucking dealerships and *know* cars," Jack Taylor worried. But Doner's lead was narrow. Some participants agreed with the street tattle, that DCA had a lock on the account, one to which no other agency held the key. "They've been hired," insisted a former Levine, Huntley executive. "They're doing work that they're showing the Japanese." Then there were the two agencies most ad folk considered mystery dates: Jordan, McGrath and Wieden & Kennedy. Jordan's "nameonics" was much derided but, as Ed Vick of Levine, Huntley put it, the agency was "a good, solid advertising machine. Last of a breed. People underestimate them." As for the Oregon agency, Vick appraised it as a "creative wild card. 'Let's bring them in. They might do something incredible.'" Others believed the Portland hotshots would fade. "Wieden & Kennedy will come in and say, 'We'll make you famous,'" said a Jordan, McGrath executive. Subaru would never fall for that line again.

Subaru's own expectations were more expansive than those of the contestants. "I truly believe any one of them has a shot," Mark Dunn insisted.

That required each to finish the daunting task Subaru had set out. In a letter sent by Gene Van Praag, the consultant, to the six finalists on May 9, the company expressed its belief that it could increase its sales to 150,000 cars in 1992, and 175,000 in 1993. "We want you to convince us that we can meet this goal," the letter read. Privately, Subaru executives doubted that these numbers reflected what the company and its ad agency, new or old, might reasonably accomplish. The figure of 150,000 units—a 36 percent increase over 1990—was established by Tom Gibson, S.O.A.'s president.

When a dubious Mark Dunn asked Gibson how he had arrived at this number, Gibson replied: *Well, we've got to make them stretch.*

MARKETING IS CONSIDERED a science. Few would be foolish enough to make that claim about advertising. "Advertisements may be *evaluated* scientifically; they cannot be *created* scientifically," a distinguished marketing researcher, Leo Bogart, has written. In approaching

Subaru's particular dilemma, both the agencies and the car company needed to make informed, but in the end political, decisions which, decided correctly, might lead Subaru to renewed viability but, decided incorrectly, could hasten its demise. Even more important, the agencies had to ascertain which way Subaru was leaning on these matters and, if necessary, map out the narrow path between the tactics needed to *win* the account and the strategy required to *keep* it.

For the agencies, the first set of choices involved the company, its cars and its markets.

Even the most cursory conversations in and around S.O.A. revealed to the finalists that Subaru's dealers, by and large, despised Levine, Huntley and the last several years of its advertising. Dealers (in the conventional wisdom that prevails in the automobile industry) dislike humor, narrative, irony and urban settings; they like ads with country roads, babies, dogs, leggy women, sheet metal and implied or overt competitor-bashing. Should, then, an agency design a new campaign specifically to mollify the dealers, on the assumption that what the company needed more than anything else was a more satisfied and, therefore, more pliant sales organization? Or should an agency design a long-term strategy, even if it meant leaving out dealer-placating icons?

More important still was how an agency meant to deal with Subaru's reputation for four-wheel-drive engineering. An agency could reasonably suggest that the fastest way for S.O.A. to reach its sales target would be to promote four-wheel drive. Here, the company's renown was strongest and its competition the weakest.

But Subaru's executives believed strongly that the company's future growth would probably come by expanding sales of their front-wheel-drive automobiles. Chris Wackman explained his colleagues' reasoning. "We're third or fourth in front-wheel drive. We have just as good a front-wheel drive as Honda or Toyota. And yet we only do a heck of a job in four-wheel-drive sales. *They* sell a whole lot of front-wheel drives. Why aren't *we* getting our fair share of the front-wheel-drive sales? The theory here is that it's not happening because people think of Subaru only as a four-wheel-drive company, and if you put additional weight and retooled creative behind it"—"it" being a new advertising strategy—"you can change people's impression of the company. 'Subaru? Yeah, they do the great four-wheel drives. And they also do those great front-wheel drives, as well.' "

Subaru of America had its own set of tough decisions to make as it reviewed the agencies and, eventually, their proposals. It, too, had to wrestle with the dealer-pacification problem and its several components. Was it more important to boost sales immediately or create a broader image, even if that resulted in fewer immediate sales? Should S.O.A. choose an agency from New York—that dealer-hated den of advertising iniquity—or a shop from outside Manhattan, which might lack the sophistication and media-buying clout of the Big Apple agencies? Was an agency's previous experience with auto advertising an advantage, or would it mire it in conventional thinking? Should S.O.A. choose a campaign that sold its cars on the basis of their attributes, or should it try an emotional sell?

Subaru's choice, really, was between the old advertising and the new advertising, between relationships and entertainment, or, if it was lucky enough to find it, something in the middle. Subaru of America had to find the proper balance between a strategy (and an agency) that subdued its internal constituencies (current customers, dealers, salesmen, regional sales directors, Fuji Heavy Industries), and an agency (and a strategy) that could grab the eyeballs of the great mass of Americans and keep them glued long enough to the page and the TV to deliver some kind of emotionally and/or rationally relevant message.

But Subaru was not merely looking for a strategy or an agency. As much as anything else, it was looking to fall in love. "Chemistry will be important in this search," said Tom Gibson, on whom the credit or blame for the choice would rest.

To prove their love, the six agencies ultimately had to wrap their political calculations, strategic analyses, market choices and image decisions into one giant, simple-to-render, easy-to-comprehend package with both an "aah!" and an "aha!" built into it. In advertising, this elusive chimera has a name. It is called the Big Idea.

The Big Idea is easier to illustrate than define, and easier to illustrate by what it is not than by what it is. It is not a "position" (although the place a product occupies in the consumer's mind may be a part of it). It is not an "execution" (although the writing or graphic style of an ad campaign certainly contributes to it). It is not a slogan (although a tag line may encapsulate it).

The Big Idea is the bridge between an advertising strategy, temporal and worldly, and an image, powerful and lasting. The theory of the Big Idea assumes that average consumers are at best bored and more likely irrational when it comes to deciding what to buy. The advertisements for one of the better-known toilet tissue brands of modern times could have featured a sober spokesman describing the manufacturing processes and embedded oils that made this tissue exceptionally soft. Instead, they featured a fey grocer who shooed women from a front-of-counter display, importuning them, "Please don't squeeze the Charmin." Now that was a Big Idea.

"The Great Idea in advertising," Leo Bogart has written, "is far more than the sum of the recognition scores, the ratings and all the other superficial indicators of its success; it is in the realm of myth, to which measurements cannot apply."

That's what S.O.A. wanted: a new American myth, an Idea so Big that it would immediately integrate Subaru into the collective national consciousness, where lived already George Washington, Babe the Blue Ox and Snap, Crackle, Pop. If big enough, Subaru's Big Idea would be a golden highway at the end of which the company's new image (whatever it might be) would be as shining and memorable as Oz, an icon of wonderment with four wheels and a dash.

But where would this Big Idea and its destination, the image, come from? Inside the competing agencies, there were two schools of thought.

Some argued that the process of finding an image was rational, perhaps purely scientific. "Don't confuse selling with art," said Jack Taylor of Jordan, McGrath, the "nameonics" agency. "The consumer doesn't think it's art. Technique is not the same as content."

But Taylor was ignoring Bill Bernbach's thirty-year-old dictum: In advertising, form can *become* content. Others involved in the search had not forgotten; they held to somewhat less logical, more mystical, beliefs. "There's a lot of research in there, from which comes an understanding of what people want in a car and how Subaru has linked that in its product line, in its presentation," Wilder Baker said. "If you have a campaign that capitalizes on what you've been and takes that equity"—the marketing term for the sum total of a product's meaning—"and presents that equity in a way that appeals to a broader audience, that comes from human understanding. Is that a science? You use scientific techniques to get that understanding. How you transform that information into a product position and advertising, that's art in my book."

All the ad execs were united, though, in one crucial respect. They believed that a new image, communicated through a Big Idea, would change the car company's world. They believed this despite decades of research that had proved . . . nothing. Some studies have found that advertising builds barriers to entry into a consumer market and therefore restricts competition and furthers monopolies and high prices in that market; others have concluded that increased advertising neither creates nor sustains monopolies, but generally follows sales growth already in progress. Some academics have shown that advertising makes consumers more aware of and sensitive to changes in prices; others have proved that it eases consumers' regard for pricing. Other studies show: that as long as a company's advertising volume is kept on a reasonable par with that of its competitors, a brand's current equity can be maintained, although not necessarily enlarged; that advertising cannot halt the fall of a declining market, although it might (as in the case of the Volkswagen Beetle) speed up an already existing growth trend; that it cannot augment total consumption in a mature product category, but can help shift market shares around in the category.

For all the studies, scholars and practitioners are generally no further along in their conclusive understanding of advertising's effects than was Neil H. Borden of the Harvard Business School, when in 1942 he published his definitive text on the subject, *The Economic Effects of Advertising*.

"Does advertising increase demand for types of products as a whole?" Borden asked. Not really; demand was "determined primarily by underlying social and environmental conditions." "Does advertising increase demand for individual concerns?" he wondered. "It depends upon circumstances." Does advertising increase distribution costs? "Indeterminate." Does it reduce production costs? "Indeterminate." Does it promote concentration of supply? "No clear-cut answer." Does advertising impede price competition? "In no case does it prevent it ultimately."

A half-century after the Harvard professor's inconclusiveness, unable to rely on factual proof of advertising's specific powers, Subaru and the six agencies vying for its account were grounding their belief that a new image would lead the auto company into the Jerusalem of renewed prosperity on one principle: faith.

There was nothing novel in their near-religious certitude. The notion of advertising as "the only faith in a secularized consumer society" has long antecedents, going back at least as far as Bruce Barton (a founder of BBDO) and his contention that Jesus was the world's greatest adman. Many scholars have remarked on the similarities between the hortatory style of ads and preachers, between the fantastical dogma of both marketing and organized religion, between the reverence devout acolytes show toward St. John and the Lubavitcher Rebbe, on the one hand, and to Burnett and Bernbach, on the other.

But among the flock seeking the Subaru account, the doctrinal confidence ran particularly deep. Perhaps the magnitude of S.O.A.'s problems demanded it; perhaps they needed it merely to sustain them through the long nights and heated debates and repeated rejections they would suffer. However consciously they understood their mission, the advertising people felt it almost spiritually.

Wilder Baker spoke for all of them when he casually described Subaru's as-yet undiscovered new image. He called it "the grail."

Chapter 8

Four Out of Five
Dentists Recommend . . .

IN THE GREAT AGE OF DISCOVERY, the exploratory missions of Christopher Columbus, Vasco da Gama, and Henry Hudson generally followed the same form: set a goal, get a royal commission, hire a crew, find a cartographer, pray, set sail, return alive with the treasure.

An advertising account review, with its mix of science, religion, courage and hokum, is little different. Typically, the leader of the expedition—the head of the agency—wheedles his way into the review by flattering and frightening the potential client; he asserts both his magical powers and his scientific prowess. Once in, the agency appoints a navigator—an experienced account executive, or the head of its rainmaking operation, perhaps a freelance executive with knowledge of the would-be client's business—to direct the team preparing the pitch. To this person report individuals with specific assignments. The agency's research department will collect data on the client company, its consumers and its industry; the media department will investigate the venues advertisements have been put and can be placed; a field contingent will leave the office to visit with people in and around the client company and canvass their opinions. All this information is then funneled to the account director who, in consultation with the agency's high priests, will translate it into two written pieces.

The first, a "positioning statement," is a (usually one-sentence) description of where inside consumers' heads the client's company, service or product should be made to fit. The second document provided by the account director is "the brief," a short augmentation of the positioning statement that elaborates on the mind-set, and perhaps the demographics, of the company's, service's or product's target consumers, and provides some hints about the tone the advertisements should take to appeal to those consumers. The brief is then delivered, with due cere-mony, by the account director to the creative teams (there is usually more than one working on a pitch), who will weave from its plain threads the rich tapestry of flackery that envelops a Big Idea! From their work will emerge, almost always, a single slogan to encapsulate the position and virtues of the client; and an "executional style" that will communicate its appropriate emotional character.

It is not a pretty process. New information flows in continually, forcing creatives to junk treasured ideas in midstream. Offhand remarks by the client company's executives are magnified by nervous account di-rectors into pronouncements of vast importance. Junior creative teams seeking more prominence compete fiercely with their seniors to provide the ultimately presentable idea. The battle over the slogan—"Creative people want an anthem, a banner, to create to," DCA's Ray Freeman said, explaining its significance—can be bloodier than Bataan, and just as expensive.

The first task, and the first expense, is getting the facts. In this initial stage, at least, facts come in the form of numbers. In the automobile in-dustry, dozens of marketing research organizations ply their numerical information to anyone with a checkbook. They are called "syndicated research companies" because, while they often do proprietary studies for individual clients, much of their research is made available, or syn-dicated, to a regular client list.

A handful of such firms dominate automotive research. R. L. Polk & Company of Detroit, the oldest, has been selling its data since 1870. The "official scorekeeper" of the automotive industry, it turns state mo-tor vehicle registration records into a complete census of all the cars and trucks on the road in the United States. Each of the nation's 184 million vehicles is in its database. Polk's National Vehicle Population Profile can tell marketers (of everything from sheet metal to tires to sparkplugs) exactly what kinds of autos, of what age, are in whose ga-rages in which zip code districts. Its numbers cost its clients some $240 million a year. Maritz Marketing Research Inc. of St. Louis is 103 years younger and $183 million shorter in revenues than Polk, but it is no less a statistical powerhouse. Maritz talks directly to people—over six hun-dred WATS telephone lines, in forty-one focus group suites and at six-teen shopping malls—and collects their impressions about cars, parts, gasoline and driving. And, of course, there is J. D. Power. Power's Cus-tomer Satisfaction Index, Initial Quality Survey and ten other rankings are cobbled together from the thirty-thousand-odd responses it receives to the eighty thousand questionnaires it mails to car owners each year. That these rankings are influential is undeniable. After the Nissan Maxima finished first among imports in the 1989 quality survey, the car's U.S. sales doubled. Almost every automobile manufacturer and importer in America pays (up to $100,000 or more) to receive Power's surveys; many others disburse more for coaching from Power to achieve higher scores. If they do not, they fear their competitors will.

The six agencies pitching the Subaru account had a wealth of information available to them from such providers. They knew, for example, that the demand for cars was still growing, despite the economy's slowdown. The agencies also learned that consumer confidence and automobile sales generally tracked each other over that same twenty-year period. They had also used the data to figure out that even when the recession ended, Americans probably would not lavish much money on automobility. Consumers' total expenditures on their cars—for gas and oil, repairs and rentals, and on the new autos themselves—had dropped from a peak of 13.1 percent of total expenditures in 1978, to a low of 10.9 percent in 1990. When the figures were broken down further, they revealed that people were increasingly allocating a greater percentage of their total spending to repairs and rentals, and less on new car purchases. From these figures, several agencies concluded that utilitarian considerations, like a car's durability, had become more important than status.

Who were these hidden car buyers? The median age of American adults had risen from 41 years to 41.6 years between 1987 and 1990, and median household income had increased from $26,600 to $29,900. During that same period, though, car buyers had grown older than the total population, from 41 years to 42 years, and their income grew faster, from $35,900 to $43,300. The median auto price during that period had increased from $13,000 to $14,700. On that trend line, in 1992 (the year Subaru wanted to sell 150,000 cars) the middle-of-the-road American adult would be 41.8 years old and earning $32,200. The smack-in-the-center car buyer would be older (43) and wealthier ($47,400 per year) and would spend $15,800 on a new car.

Where did Subaru fit in this scheme? The number of people thinking of purchasing a four-wheel-drive vehicle had soared. In late 1985, four-wheel-drive cars and trucks accounted for 3.1 percent of all "purchase intentions"; by the end of 1990, 4.2 percent of all the vehicles people said they planned to buy would have off-road capability. At that rate, 5 percent of the buyers shopping for cars in 1993 would, at least, be considering the products that were Subaru's specialty. Even better, 8.1 percent of the consumers considering four-wheel-drive cars were planning to buy Asian makes; only 3.1 percent intended to purchase American vehicles, with 5.1 percent preferring European models.

Subaru still ranked low in consumer awareness. Potential buyers were less familiar with the Legacy than with the Honda Accord, Toyota Camry, Nissan Stanza, Volkswagen Jetta and Mazda 626. And Subaru owners were older than the rest, their median age registering at forty-three, against thirty-nine for Toyota, thirty-eight for Honda, thirty-six for Nissan and Mazda and thirty-three for Mitsubishi.

That might have been explained by the rise in Subaru's median price, which was far steeper than those of its Japanese competitors. Subaru's owners also came from different places than purchasers of the other makes. Owners of the subcompact Loyale were older (median age forty) than the owners of small cars taken as a whole (median age thirty-five). They also had a higher household income ($42,000 vs. $35,000), were more educated (55 percent college graduates vs. 43 percent), were more likely to be married (64 percent vs. 54 percent), and were more likely to live in small towns or rural cities (58 percent vs. 40 percent).

The ages and incomes of Subaru Legacy owners were roughly the same as those of other import-compact buyers, but they, too, were more educated, married and rural than the rest. A higher percentage (48 percent) of Legacy owners had once owned another Asian car than the total population of import-compact owners, only 41 percent of whom had previously owned an Asian compact. Likewise, a far smaller percentage of Legacy owners (29 percent) bought the new Subaru compact after owning a domestic car than did other import-compact owners, 40 percent of whom had junked a domestic to try a foreign car.

How each agency analyzed this information would determine the nature of its pitch. Did the data mean that Subaru had greater potential for growth by drawing buyers away from the domestics, in a proportion equal to the rest of the import-compact market segment? Or did it mean that owners of domestic cars had already proved themselves less likely to consider Subarus? Should Subaru target younger and less educated consumers—those who were apparently being passed over by its current marketing efforts—or would it do better by seeking out more of the older, wealthier, better educated and more countrified consumers to whom it already appealed?

Perhaps there were clues in how Subaru shoppers, called "intenders" in ad lingo, saw themselves in relation to their cars. Consumers considering Subaru were less likely than other car buyers to be concerned with the prestige of owning the car, its interior roominess, the joy of driving it, its looks, its dependability or its value. Read one way, this information could have indicated that Subaru intenders were not swayed by the images attached to car ownership. Read another, it could have meant that they just didn't give a damn about cars in general.

The six agencies fighting for the Subaru account could have done their own projectible research, of course, but none did. In one of the more profound changes to occur in the advertising industry during the past three decades, agencies abandoned quantitative research, a form of research which, in the 1950s and 1960s, they dominated. In those years, research was a fundamental service provided to clients by ad agencies. But gradually, client companies began doing increasing amounts of their own research, and agencies reduced their own spending on it. When the recession of the late 1970s and 1980s forced many corporations to cut research expenditures, more of the data collection and analysis fell to third-party purveyors of marketing research. Ad agencies continued to pull back from the field. Grey Advertising, one of the ad industry's most research-intensive agencies, reduced its research staff from more than ninety in 1967 to thirty-five in 1990. The slack inside the agencies was taken up by the independent research organizations, whose prosperity contrasted starkly with that of ad agencies: revenues at the independent research firms increased from 8 to 12 percent annually during the late 1980s and early 1990s, a time when client spending on advertising was growing less than 6 percent a year.

It was not simply economics and the wide availability of syndicated data that moved ad agencies out of quantitative research—fact-gathering whose conclusions could be projected with reasonable certainty across the entire population. There were also the products the agencies advertised. To put it bluntly, they were all alike and there was little to say about them.

In their glory days, American advertising and advertising research tended to be very "brand-specific"; agency researchers asked consumers how, where, when and why they used certain products, what appealed to them about the brands, and what else they wanted to see in stores. The advertising that resulted usually focused on the products themselves, and the attributes that made them appealing to the broadest group of consumers who might want them. Sometimes daring new products—Diet Rite, the first major low-calorie soft drink, was one example—emerged from agency research.

Gradually, though, marketing changed. Retail shelves grew more capacious, encouraging marketers to fabricate quickly new items to fill the space. New research technologies found ever-more-refined niches in the consumer market, too small to warrant massive development expenditures but large enough to justify minor changes in a brand's packaging or composition. By the late 1980s, the nation's largest marketers had stopped trying to develop new products significantly different from those already available; instead, they spent their time and money creating what the marketing consultant William M. Weilbacher calls "new brands and brand variants of unrelieved sameness." In the decade following 1979, for example, the number of canned-soup brands selling at least $1 million at retail grew 42 percent, from twelve to seventeen; the number of million-dollar brewed ground-coffee brands rose 58 percent, from thirty-three to fifty-two; the number of million-dollar toothpaste brands in food stores increased 210 percent, from ten to thirty-one.

Automobiles, while more expensive, were no less immune to the virus of brand proliferation. At General Motors, the number of nameplates tripled between 1960 and 1992, from twenty-one to more than sixty-five. During that same period, in the Oldsmobile division alone, the number of cars offered grew from three—Dynamic 88, Super 88 and Ninety-Eight—to seventeen: Achieva, two versions of the Sport Coupe, Bravada, Custom Cruiser, two versions of the Cutlass Ciera, Cutlass Cruiser, Cutlass Supreme, two versions of the International Series, two versions of the Eighty-Eight, two versions of the Ninety-Eight, Silhouette and the Toronado Torfeo.

Consumers, no fools, inured themselves to the onslaught of new brands. A 1988 study by BBDO showed that 66 percent of Americans believed that most brands in most categories were exactly alike.

Agencies and clients therefore realized that commissioning large-scale research studies to ascertain which features of which products were most useful was a waste of money. Brand proliferation, product similarity, economics and the wide availability of data had conspired to make traditional marketing research irrelevant. There had to be a better way, a different way, a cheaper way, to find something new to say, something *advertisable*, about a product.

Beginning in the late 1970s, agencies figured it out. If there was no longer anything to say about products, they would say something about the people who used them. "Brands have become so similar to one another that the real leverage in the advertising is no longer the content of the product," explained Barbara S. Feigin, the research director of Grey Advertising, "but the placement of the product in the consumer's life."

This, indeed, was the second preparatory stage for the agencies pursuing the Subaru account. To buttress the data they had purchased from the syndicated research services, they began looking for "consumer insights"—for "bonds" (as they called the emotional glue that linked consumers to products) that they could use to strengthen their numbers.

The process by which agencies find these insights and bonds is generally called "account planning." Under account planning, researchers (who call themselves planners) work directly with creative teams for the entire period an ad campaign is under development. Instead of delivering statistical pronouncements about markets and products from on high and then passing judgment on whether the finished advertising meets their standards, as traditional researchers had done, planners constantly shovel new ideas to the copywriters and art directors and work with them to hone not just the text of an ad but its context and supertext as well.

Unlike traditional research techniques, which depend on the collection of hard data, planners' tools are soft. They use "qualitative" instruments, like "focus group" interviews to determine how products and companies fit into people's lives. They use long, individual interviews, called "one-on-ones" or "in-depths," to pull away the layers of detail and artifice that cloud consumers' conscious understanding of why they buy what they buy. Sometimes, they will even call on psychologists or anthropologists to help them understand the symbolic meanings of certain brands and products.

This new form of research has its critics. Some contend that the search for "consumer insights" is little more than a convenient way for agencies to justify their abandonment of quantitative research. Others complain that qualitative research is less rigorous and therefore a potentially inaccurate predictor of people's behavior. Still others argue that many agencies, especially smaller shops whose reputations rest on their graphic and literary originality, use the veneer of account planning to rationalize what are otherwise instinctual creative strategies.

But in the decade since the account planning system was imported to the United States by the Chiat/Day agency—the procedure was introduced in 1968 by Boase Massimi Pollitt, a London agency renowned for its creative output, and by 1987 was in use at more than 90 percent of British agencies—it spread through American advertising like a rumor. In part, its popularity was due to Chiat/Day's success in creative awards shows and account reviews. In part, the system's expansion was clearly attributable to the fact that it allowed small agencies which could not afford real marketing research departments to claim that they now did research.

Most of the ad agencies pitching Subaru used account planning to develop their campaigns. It was the only way they could claim any proprietary knowledge; it was the sole form of competitive advantage, save for the speculative creative work itself, an agency could maintain.

Warwick, Baker & Fiore, for example, retained a research firm with a special interviewing technique "that borders on the hypnotic," Wilder Baker recounted. "Really intensive. We wanted to *understand* the consumers." The procedure, called "Behavior-Link" by the research firm that used it, was concocted to find consumers' motivation in choosing or considering Subaru; the imagery Subaru called to mind; what, beyond the tangible features of the car, consumers were really buying; and the "contextual framework, or 'Subaru-ness,'" that led people to or away from the company's cars. Eighteen people—ten Subaru owners, five Subaru "considerers" and three Subaru "rejectors"—were interviewed in hour-long "in-depths."

"Okay, I'd like to do just a visualization," an interviewer told an owner, a woman named Mamie, who had recently abandoned a Ford Escort to acquire a Subaru, in one of those in-depths. "Just close your eyes and go way back to the first time that you . . . decided that you were going to get a Subaru. . . . Way back, you know, when you talk about how you were dying to have a Subaru for the longest time. . . . Let me know what you have in mind."

"I'm coming to Rising Sun Avenue," replied Mamie, her eyes shut, her mind retreating. "It's a lot of traffic there all the time, it's a lot of traffic and between coming down this road and coming across this bridge, there's an intersection where this lane can turn into it, and my car shook to hell and I had my son in there and he was like 'Mommy, you've got to get rid of this car, you've gotta get rid of this car.' And we had to get out and literally push my car over to the side of the road and just sit there and then just try pressing to get it going again and that's when I said, 'This is it. I've gotta get rid of this, and I want a Subaru. I would die if I would get a Subaru.'"

From this and the sixteen other interviews, Warwick concluded that Subaru owners, like other drivers, were concerned about safety, but articulated it in the context of dependability, not in relation to the car's construction. Buying a Subaru, the agency found, resulted overwhelmingly from conversations with close friends and relatives. And Subaru owners, Warwick determined, took pleasure in talking about their cars and even passing them on to other members of their families. This, said the agency, was a way the owners shared a bit of themselves; Subaru was "a facilitator to the ongoing familial relationship."

None of this could have been gleaned from the statistical data provided by the syndicated research services. "They have a lot of knowledge," Wilder Baker said, "but when we looked through it, we didn't see in it an *understanding*."

Chapter 9

The Real Thing

THIRTY-TWO FLOORS ABOVE 42ND STREET, little evidence was at hand to indicate that DCA Advertising was pumping headlong into the pitch of its life. Giggling secretaries livened the quiet halls. Soft conversations, punctuated by frequent *"hai's"* and less distinguishable Japanese words, took place from one end of the long floor to the other.

Only a frequent visitor to the lobby would have been able to sense DCA's quest for the edge, its search for the Big Idea, its hunt for Subaru's image. On the coffee table where, in late May, had sat well-thumbed copies of *Adweek* there were stacked, by early June: *Car Craft, Hot Rod, Petersen's 4Wheel, Circle Track, Sport Truck*—the library of the grease monkey.

Magazine subscriptions were not the only cost the agency was incurring. More than any of the other finalists, DCA exemplified the ad industry's penchant to throw money at a pitch. Word had even filtered to Tom Gibson, Subaru's president, that DCA "had hired every freelancer in New York" to pitch the account. Ray Freeman, DCA's COO, took umbrage at the characterization. Of the 130 staffers in the office, between twenty and twenty-five had been assigned to the pitch, he claimed: three creative teams working in DCA's New York headquarters, and one creative team scribbling away in California. Of those, only eight were freelancers.

"These happen to be gaijin," Ray said. "All Americans." They were the center of DCA's pitch, not some Asian overlords or a horde of rapacious freelancers. The agency's work, Freeman averred, represented "the hearts and souls of eight brave men." He repeated it again, more softly, a reminder to himself of what was at stake. "The hearts and souls of eight brave men."

That's what it all came down to, of course: people. A pitch was more than pseudoscientific measurement and structured chaos. It was personal fervor and fame and resurrection and salvation, all rolled up into a three-and-a-half-hour presentation and (one prayed) a lifetime's recognition.

DCA had its share of glory seekers, not least among them Ray Freeman himself. With his sky-blue eyes and a white shirt starched stiff as steel, the Lansing, Michigan, native seemed the very model of the upright IBM executive he once had been. But his floral tie was a giveaway, a tipoff that he'd abandoned the straitlaced computer company to enter the looser world of advertising.

Below his serenity, Freeman was burning for a comeback; he resembled the actor Robert Conrad in a memorable advertisement, softly but fiercely daring you to knock a battery off his shoulder. Freeman had been one of the six partners in the respected Lord, Geller, Federico, Einstein agency who, in 1988, rebelled against the acquisition of their shop by a British conglomerate. Years before, Lord, Geller (whose fame rested on its brilliant association of giant IBM with Charlie Chaplin's "Little Tramp" character) had sold itself to the larger J. Walter Thompson agency. The affiliation was satisfactory until 1987, when Thompson became the victim of the ad industry's first hostile takeover, by Britain's WPP Group. The next year, claiming that they had lost their authority to compensate their employees as they saw fit and had suffered other slights, the six men walked out and, with financing from Young & Rubicam, established a new agency, Lord Einstein O'Neill & Partners. The ad industry cheered, seeing the breakaway as Madison Avenue's replay of the American Revolution. Shortly after, in a seeming validation of their effort, Saab, the Swedish automobile manufacturer, gave its lucrative advertising account to the new agency.

The channel between right and wrong soon grew murky, however. The group chief executive of WPP, Martin Sorrell, sued the rebellious group, charging that they had breached their financial duty to their company and conspired with Y&R to take business—notably the IBM account—away from their former agency. Day after day in downtown Manhattan, courtroom testimony depicted a group of admen less concerned about their clients than with their own futures.

IBM, embarrassed by the revelations, took away its account. Before long, Lord, Geller was closed. Saab fired the fledgling Lord Einstein shop, which also was forced to dissolve. Ray Freeman went off to seek renewal—and a car account to replace the one that had sunk them.

Ray's charge at the Dentsu outpost was elemental: to remake it. The Japanese parent company had made it clear that it considered the New

York office a headache and, worse, a drain on corporate resources. Office-equipment manufacturers—like Canon, DCA's only substantial client—were in a slump and reducing their ad expenditures. New clients were needed to take up the slack. Ray was brought in to make rain. "Can we continue to serve Canon and grow? That was the mandate," he said. "Subaru would change the agency forever, which is why I came here."

Like several of the competing agencies, DCA faulted Subaru's old advertising strategy for being too "national." As much as Harvey Lamm had talked about niche marketing and decried "make you famous" advertising, Levine, Huntley had gone off and made arch, slapstick commercials and broadcast them on network TV. DCA planned to tell S.O.A. not to "slug it out with the big boys," Freeman said, but to "fish where the fish are." That meant buttressing an emotional sell with stronger utilitarian arguments; it meant transforming the image of the Legacy compact, making it less a quirky Subaru and more a "mainstream car"; it meant figuring out why people purchased Subarus in the hills of New England and the mountains of Idaho and "carrying that to other regions."

DCA was going to rest a large part of its pitch on an unconventional recommendation for organizing the account. Instead of a substantial central headquarters and a few small branch offices, the agency wanted to create six full regional offices to service Subaru. Each office would combine staff from DCA, a Chicago-based firm that specialized in consumer promotions and a company that specialized in time and space buying. The agency had come up with a logo to describe the concept, an "I-92" encased in an interstate-highway sign. It stood for "integration of resources in 1992."

Freeman knew, though, that DCA would not win the account with organizational suggestions. Strategic brilliance and "breakthrough" creative were the paths to the Subaru account. For that, Freeman turned to an old friend, a man whose name had graced the doors of both the ill-fated Lord, Geller, Federico, Einstein and Lord Einstein O'Neill & Partners agencies, the copywriter Arthur W. Einstein, Jr.

Ad agencies frequently seek out "famous names" when they need to establish or reestablish their credibility in the advertising world. In the Subaru review, Warwick, Baker & Fiore engaged Leonard Pearlstein, whose own well-regarded agency, Keye/Donna/Pearlstein, had closed when the Japanese auto manufacturer Suzuki pulled its account.

Einstein, what with the sad tale of the Lord Einstein breakaway and the Charlie Chaplin–led revival of IBM's personal-computer business, was as eminent a name as an agency could expect to find. So much so that his anonymous work for the minor outpost of a foreign agency seemed a comedown—an interpretation Einstein dismissed.

"I'm very happy being a writer," he said. "I look at this circumstance as an opportunity."

Einstein was in charge of DCA's "war room," a chamber dominated by a whiteboard with a rather ironic World War II–era Kilroy drawn on it in blue marking pen. Less than two weeks before the pitch, the creative teams under his direction had had their showdown, a four-and-a-half-hour meeting, during which each team unveiled its campaign based on the agreed-upon strategy: "value equals price equals engineering." Weeks of round-the-clock work, weeks of Saturday sessions at the Rye house of Kiyoshi (K.C.) Eguchi, DCA's executive vice president and general manager, had come down to this one session.

Ray and his senior colleagues had rejected one slogan—"Engineering for the real world"—as overly utilitarian. They turned down a second, "Take the high road," because it was not self-explanatory. They had finally arrived at their preferred tag line, and the walls of the conference were covered with comped advertisements, in various stages of completion, constructed around it.

Ray Freeman surveyed the cluttered walls. "We have to pare down," he fretted.

THERE WAS A CLASS of less famous, but no less important, names cruising the waters around the Subaru pitch. They were the "car guys."

Agencies seeking accounts in a specific product or service category will, as often as not, hire experts in that category to help prepare the pitch. Occasionally, these virtuosos are executives who have been ousted from a client company; sometimes, they are advertising execs who, through fervor or circumstance, have mastered a single discipline. Airlines, financial services, soft drinks, beer, packaged goods—all have their specialists. But none hold knowledge so arcane or secrets so coveted as the car guy.

The car guys—they are almost always men, known also as "gearheads" or "motorheads"—understand what makes dealers happy and what angers them; they recall the slogans that have worked, and the tag lines that have bombed. They are magnets for automotive gossip, and know whom to call at which buff book for what leads about whose car company. If the creative people are the high priests who invoke God's inspiration in the journey to a car account, the car guys are the navigators who guide them to the temple mount.

But practical knowledge, while the motorhead's strong suit, is not his exclusive value. Automobiles evoke a rapture in car guys that is foreign to the nonbeliever. Like the priestesses of Eleusis, they speak in tongues and writhe in ecstasy, their devotions granting them entrée to a higher realm of knowledge about cars and drivers. To the car guy, heaven is a road, not a destination, and hell is a consumer advocate. The motorhead knows, as Willy Hopkins did, that "automobiles are mechanical sports jackets. They tell people who you are, how you vote, whether you're available to go home with me after the bar closes."

Willy was the consummate car guy, a gunslinger in looks and temperament who lived to pitch automotive accounts. He was four-for-four: Backer & Spielvogel had won Hyundai, Chiat/Day had taken Nissan, Asher/Gould had stolen Suzuki and Lord Einstein O'Neill & Partners had procured Saab with Willy conducting the pitch. Tall and gaunt, with a slow, dreamy drawl and a thick black mustache, he was alternately reviled and feared, but never dismissed, by all the agencies in the Subaru pitch. Save one: Jordan, McGrath, Case & Taylor, for which he was now working.

Late one night as the Subaru review sped to its conclusion, Willy took dinner at Smith & Wollensky, a testosterone-fueled steakhouse and advertising haunt on the East Side of Manhattan. Willy, who was dressed in a conservative blue suit, a blue button-down shirt and a red tie with green polka dots and who appeared, outwardly, a normal businessman, was joined by his friend Jim Williams. The two had met thirteen years before, when Willy worked on the Volkswagen account at Doyle Dane and Jim was in public relations at Volvo. Willy had dragged Jim from his farm in upstate New York to Jordan, McGrath to be a consultant on the Subaru pitch. Jim, too, was tall, and also had a droopy mustache, which, like his hair, was light brown.

As they downed pepper vodka, Willy described a boyhood that should have led him down a straighter path. The son of two scientists, he was planning to become a physician. But during his freshman year at Columbia University, the young Kentuckian bought a Triumph TR-3. From that point on, gasoline flowed alongside the blood in his veins. He roomed with racing champions, worked for racing associations and told people that he was still qualified to certify land-speed records. When he talked about driving, Willy spoke the way some people do about sex. His conversation was peppered with references to "rhythm," "anticipation" and "pace." "There's a physical sensation," he said of driving. "There are noises."

The dinners came (prime rib for Willy, steak au poivre for Jim) and the men turned to the more immediate subject: the Subaru pitch.

"This is the first time we've worked together on a not-done deal," Willy said.

"That's right," Jim said. "A not-done deal."

"Last time was Audi," remembered Willy.

Nonetheless, Willy was feeling cocky. "Most agencies," he said, "don't have the foggiest notion about how to run a car account. They see sixty seconds on the Super Bowl and have visions of billings." Not so, he continued. "Frozen orange juice, you buy it three months ahead of time. It's not selling, you cut the price, get rid of it and face the brand manager. Car business, you're committing a year ahead. Automobile manufacturers don't sell cars to people. They sell to dealers. Dealers sell to people. If dealers don't buy into the marketing program, they won't buy the cars.

"I've briefed, now, two hundred pretty good creative teams—taken them through objectives, what needs to be done. Two things happen invariably when you brief a creative team that has not worked on an auto account. They celebrate with friends and they go to a dealer. And they come back from the dealer with this big breakthrough idea: 'All dealers are assholes, except these.' And they will come up with an idea that will offend the customer—who *is* the dealer."

Hopkins knew that the first task in winning a car account and maintaining it was persuading the dealers that the agency was on their side. "Everybody gets it, except the guys who create the ad. The end receiver, the dealer, takes from it: What does it show me? What does it say about what *they* think I think?"

Willy had been using this knowledge to guide Jordan, McGrath's two creative teams, one led by Jim Jordan, the other by Gene Case. Willy had proved his value in other ways, as well. He knew S.O.A.'s head of public relations. The day after Subaru invited Jordan, McGrath into the pitch, Willy called him and discovered that a Subaru SVX, the company's new sports car (and another product the agencies were going to have to figure out how to market) was stranded out in Portland, where it had been unveiled to a northwestern dealer group. S.O.A. needed to get the car back to Los Angeles. Willy volunteered, hopped onto a cross-country flight with Jim, and got a chance to drive the hell out of an SVX before most of the other agencies even knew they would be pitching the account.

Presumably, an experienced car guy would learn something about his product from a few hours behind the wheel. But the trip was also intended to have another effect.

"Part of what you do in this business is separate yourself off by dint of heroic action," said Jack Taylor, Jordan, McGrath's vice chairman.

"This was heroic action. This is such an intangible process. We're looking for edges everywhere."

W. B. DONER retained no famous names. W. B. Doner hired no car
guys. If the "killer agency" had a role model, it was Clint Eastwood—
tough, stoic, relentless. "We sent in our credentials, they picked us, I
figured they wanted the minds they saw," Jim Dale explained.

A sense of methodical, if nervous, anticipation coursed through
Doner's headquarters. Even before its April credentials presentation to
Chris Wackman, Mark Dunn and Gene Van Praag, the agency had an
idea of where it wanted to take Subaru. Like the other shops, it had
quickly discovered that Subaru buyers were pragmatic people, concerned about functionality more than status. But these buyers were also
proud of their practicality, "harder-nosed" than Honda or Chevy buyers.

"One dealer said the Subaru buyer comes in with *Consumer Reports*
tucked under his arm, a pipe in his mouth, a clipboard and a pen in his
hand," Jim Dale recounted. "He's already decided on a Subaru and now
he's shopping color and price."

"How do I find more of those guys?" was how Dale summarized
Subaru's marketing problem. "God knows, there's more than 140,000 of
them. . . . No matter how you shrink that group, you'll still have a lot of
car buyers. The best way to broaden this market is to find those who are
derivative of those you already have and do it again and again. I think
the best way to sell a million Subarus is to first sell 150,000, then
180,000." His plan for the pitch was to tell S.O.A.: "Let's be realistic.
You need 42,000 more buyers. I'll show you how to find those people.
If we target right, maybe 62,000."

The strategy, however vague its description, was exactly what the
other agencies feared from Doner: a retail campaign. Yet unlike its
competitors, W.B. Doner saw no real distinction between good retail
advertising, with its assumption of a rational consumer, and image advertising, which posits the consumer as a slave to emotion. The agency
believed it could satisfy both requirements with one, well-crafted
campaign.

"I'll tell you what we're going to do," Dale confided. "On Monday,
we're going to take people out for a test drive. People who are
prescreened, under consideration. We're going to put them in a Subaru
Legacy—except all Subaru Legacy identifiers are removed, and replaced with Honda. We'll also do it as a Toyota. And at the end of the
interview, we'll ask them how they like this Honda or Toyota. And how
much they'd pay for it. And when they say 'Eighteen-five,' we'll say, 'I

can save you $3,000 on this car.' How? We'll take off the removable sticker."

The Doner executive smiled at the synergy. "Won't the satisfaction be emotional?" Jim Dale asked. "Yet it's based on rationality!"

CLEAR ACROSS THE COUNTRY, rationality was a tourist at the circus, watching in wonderment as Wieden & Kennedy readied itself for the Subaru pitch.

Wieden & Kennedy had no experience handling automotive accounts. Nor was the agency easily prepared to open an office on the East Coast. Its one previous branch office, in Los Angeles, was closed after its single client fired it. Moreover, some of the staffers who would be crucial to the Subaru account, like the agency's new media director, had just relocated to green, clean Oregon from other agencies in other locales, and were unwilling to uproot themselves for lives back in the Sodom of New York or the Gomorrah of south Jersey.

Headhunters were enlisted to supply names of advertising people who might staff the account should Wieden & Kennedy win it. A freelance creative team with some automotive experience was brought in. It and several creative teams at the agency set to work on the presentation, none with specific assignments but all knowing that, in the end, the agency would have to show work in television, radio, print, outdoor and point of purchase.

Even this procedure surpassed the shop's organizational abilities. A former Wieden & Kennedy copywriter, a young Yale graduate named Peter Wegner, was asked to return for several weeks to team with a longtime agency art director, Larry Frey, to draft concepts for the pitch. But Frey was out of town on a shoot for much of the month, leaving Wegner to toil alone. Another copywriter, Jerry Cronin, a laconic Bostonian, fought his employers' request that he labor on the pitch. Cronin had run into a streak of bad luck with Nike, and in recent months had seen several of his favorite campaigns shot down in the concept stage. He had toiled long and hard on ideas for Swatch, the Swiss watch company (which had briefly retained Wieden & Kennedy), only to sit by as those suggestions, too, went down in flames. His work on several pitches before the Subaru search had also failed to see daylight when the agency was passed over in those reviews. Cronin had no desire to get involved yet again with the heartbreak of speculation. Only with great reluctance and after several pleas by his superiors did he take a partner, the art director David Jenkins, and begin outlining automobile ads.

Once the teams and individuals were conscripted, they toiled quite apart from each other. Unlike Jordan, McGrath, Case & Taylor, where Jim Jordan and Gene Case posted their work for continual competitive review, or DCA, with its war room, at Wieden & Kennedy the creative teams worked on their own. All were fed consumer insights by Chris Riley, the agency's director of account planning, a Brit who had been hired only a few months before. But how the creatives applied those insights remained between each team and Dan Wieden. The disorder led to strategic inconsistencies and duplicated efforts. Early on, one creative team offered Dan a campaign that ridiculed the idea of cars as status objects. Like the other agencies, Wieden & Kennedy had also found Subaru buyers unusually drawn to an automobile on utilitarian grounds. The agency's chairman quashed the satirical concept, though, arguing that it devalued cars more than the research mandated and might anger consumers by mocking their current choice in cars. Yet several days later, when the competing teams assembled for the first and only examination of their different proposals, Dan settled on a strikingly similar recommendation by another team.

In its naïveté, Wieden & Kennedy was unaware of the chaos it was creating for itself. Leaving Cherry Hill one day after a fact-finding visit to S.O.A., Dan Wieden was ebullient. *For a moment*, he said to his mates after he departed, *I really thought of us as a killing machine.*

Others saw it differently.

"To the extent that a pitch can be random," said one creative who worked on it, "it was truly random."

THEN THERE WAS ED VICK, who had assumed the thankless role of chief executive at Subaru's incumbent advertising agency. Ed Vick was quite alone.

It wasn't merely that the other men whose names now enveloped his on the new stationery at Levine, Huntley, Vick & Beaver had died, retired or passed into irrelevance. It was more the debilitating pattern of haphazard events that had conspired to isolate him and his new charges at exactly the time they should have been rallying to save their flagship account.

First there was Frito-Lay. Bob Schmidt had labored long and hard to land the Pepsico snack-food subsidiary as a client. When the Dallas company gave two minor brands to the agency, it seemed a validation of everything Schmidt had been working toward, a recognition that entertaining advertising could sell the most undifferentiated of products. But in late April, less than two weeks after the agency took its solo shot at retaining the Subaru account, Frito-Lay pulled its business from Levine, Huntley and divided it between two larger agencies on its roster.

The second blow came only a week before the final Subaru pitch, when Levine, Huntley's senior vice president and media director, Ed Ronk, and its vice president and associate media director, Andrew Donchin, suddenly quit the agency to join an independent media buying service. Their departures were sudden; only moments after they revealed their intentions to Vick, the men, accompanied by two senior partners of their new company, traipsed over to the *New York Times* to tell Stuart Elliott, the newspaper's advertising columnist, of their new jobs. What was more, they told the newspaper that they planned to ask Subaru to give their new company the account's media-buying assignment, reducing the workload, and the compensation, of whichever agency ended up with Subaru's business. Vick, understandably, lashed out at his departing media director, intimating that Ronk left to avoid being fired. "He saw some handwriting on the wall," Vick said. "I was looking for more creativity in media." To Levine, Huntley's stalwarts, though, the defection was a devastating blow.

Still, Vick fought on. With Grey's backing, he brought in a series of consultants to help with the marketing research. At Vick's behest, two Grey executives forsook their positions, one to take over the agency's leaderless media department and the other to develop a promotional adjunct to the advertising campaign Levine was developing for Subaru. To run the pitch, Vick hired a car guy who had worked on the Ford account at J. Walter Thompson and the Chrysler account at Bozell. He promoted Rochelle Klein, a respected copywriter on Levine's Maidenform lingerie account, to the position of chief creative officer—a bold move, for women were not well represented in senior levels of automobile accounts. There was also a hazy rumor that drifted out to Gene Van Praag, the consultant, that Levine, Huntley had signed a star endorser to appear in the Subaru commercials it planned to present to S.O.A.

The expense was enormous; Levine, Huntley was easily going to spend between $100,000 and $200,000, the same amount as the other agencies, to win the Subaru account. Unlike the other agencies, however, Levine, Huntley, as the damaged incumbent, was presumed to have no chance to prevail. Another CEO might have cut his losses, dropped out and used his time and money to pursue other accounts. Indeed, Harold Levine pleaded with Vick to do just that. An officer at the American Association of Advertising Agencies gave similar counsel, advising Vick to resign the Subaru business in order to try for the Isuzu automobile account, which had also gone into review.

Vick considered their advice, and rejected it. As he saw it, the agency had several advantages the skeptics ignored. His people knew Subaru of America's strengths, weaknesses, warts and beauty marks; presumably, there were hot buttons Levine, Huntley could push that the other agencies could only stumble toward. Furthermore, the agency had already pitched Subaru once this year and knew from the experience what the company did not want. That earlier pitch had also convinced Vick that, for all its talk of image, S.O.A. really did want a strong retail campaign and an immediate sales increase that would force the recalcitrant dealers back into line.

Finally, Levine, Huntley, Vick & Beaver was slated to pitch last, on Friday, June 14, giving it nearly one extra week to perfect its presentation. Warwick, Baker & Fiore had drawn the straw to go first, on Monday morning, June 10. Jordan, McGrath, Case & Taylor and DCA would pitch back to back on Tuesday. Wieden & Kennedy would have Wednesday to itself. Thursday was going to be W.B. Doner's day.

But any leverage Levine, Huntley had was precarious, and Vick knew it. When he was asked why he took the job at the agency, knowing the risks, agony and potential for embarrassment that came with it, Vick grinned an ironic half-grin and cocked a thumb toward a painting that he had brought with him to the agency and had hung in the small, windowed conference room that abutted his office. It depicted two Revolutionary War–era frigates in the violent throes of battle.

The caption underneath it, signed "J.P. Jones, Captain, U.S. Navy, January 16, 1777," read: "I have no interest in any ship that does not sail fast, for I plan to go in harm's way."

Chapter 10

It's the Right Thing to Do

CHRIS WACKMAN was more ebullient than he had any right to be.

"I'll tell you, I'm feeling good about this," Chris said to Mark Dunn, as he absentmindedly shuffled papers around on the top of his desk. "I think we really have an opportunity to change the strategic direction of the company."

Tom O'Hare, the tall, white-haired president of the Subaru Distributors Corp., which had the exclusive right to wholesale Subaru cars to dealers in New York and New Jersey, and which was one of the last two distributors still not owned by S.O.A., strode woodenly into Chris's office as the marketing director spoke. He responded to the predictions dourly. "It couldn't have come at a better time," O'Hare said.

Shortly before noon, the three men and Gene Van Praag drove in three cars to the Cherry Hill Hyatt, a quarter of a mile down Route 70 from Subaru headquarters. In Circles, the hotel's dark restaurant, which was opened for the auto executives' conclave, Chris, Mark, O'Hare and Gene met up with five other members of Subaru of America's advertising agency selection committee.

All were men; all, save Mark, were over forty. The agencies over which they held sway thought of them collectively as "the Subarus." But their personalities, let alone their positions, were quite distinct.

Henry H. (Woody) Purcell was S.O.A. regional vice president for the southern United States, part of a group charged with the unenviable task of selling cars to the company's disenchanted dealers. A backslapper with a drawl, Woody also possessed a fierce intelligence and a sense of corporate politics that would have impressed Machiavelli.

George Muller, S.O.A.'s chief financial officer, was in many ways Woody's opposite. Tall and boyishly handsome, he was also quiet and contemplative, a man with such an obvious seriousness of purpose that his few utterances commanded complete respect. In many ways, he knew more about Subaru than any of the others present. Muller's relationship with the company dated back to the early 1970s, when Malcolm Bricklin had run the company and Muller had been a junior auditor with Arthur Andersen.

Charles (Chuck) Worrell, Subaru's senior vice president of sales, was, for the previous few years at least, the most lamentable of the company's executives; in his office lay the ultimate responsibility for Subaru's declining sales. A Southerner like Woody, Chuck could also flash an engaging bleached grin. But he no longer bantered or told tales; times were too tough for that. Instead, he hammered away ceaselessly about the need for a new corporate image—remonstrations that some took as veiled slaps at Chris Wackman, who oversaw the company's advertising during its years of decline.

Masahiru (Mas) Masumitsu was Fuji's man on the scene, sent by S.O.A.'s parent company to supervise the importer as its vice chairman and chief executive officer. But Mas was a far-from-domineering presence; the gray-haired corporate chief rarely spoke, and when he did, it was usually to defer to "Mr. Gibson." Subaru's American executives believed that Mas's attitude was more laissez-faire than laziness; only after S.O.A. truly failed could Fuji fully impose its will on the company.

Which only put more pressure on Tom Gibson, S.O.A.'s lithe, silver-haired president and, given Mas's deference, the most senior member of Subaru's agency selection committee. Gibson personified grace under pressure. His voice was calm but firm as he called his colleagues together around a cramped assembly of heavy oak tables.

As they lunched on salads and cold cuts from the buffet, Gibson informed the committee of his plan. They would sit through the pitches, meeting after each one for preliminary discussions; spend the weekend of June 15–16 privately mulling over the presentations; assemble again on Monday, June 17, to reach a consensus on not one but *two* agencies; and then negotiate price. The less expensive of the two would become the company's choice.

Gibson asked if the men had met and socialized with the agencies. "This isn't a question of the best presentation," he admonished, "but of a relationship."

Most of the committee's members had met with at least some of the competing executives. They were duly impressed. "They've jumped through hoops, done anything we asked," Mark Dunn excitedly told his colleagues.

"Pardon my French," Chris Wackman added, "but there are no nose pickers in this group."

Shortly before 1:00 p.m., the eight Subarus and Gene got up silently, left the restaurant and walked briskly across the Hyatt's lobby to a side corner of the hotel, where three conference rooms, each named for a different south Jersey county, abutted one another. The men filed into the Burlington Room, a soporific hotel chamber where the carpet seemed as old as the moss on a forest floor. They took seats around several long tables arranged in a horseshoe shape, with its open end facing the back of the room. Within the horseshoe stood three vacant easels.

Almost simultaneously, the Subarus lifted their rumps from the chairs, removed their suit jackets, slung them around the backs of their seats and sat down again. That was the signal for Warwick, Baker & Fiore, seven people strong, to begin its pitch.

"What we hope we have today is truly a dialogue," said Wilder Baker, his voice punching forward through a forced smile. "We're excited because *we've got the answer for you.*"

He turned over the presentation to Leonard Pearlstein, the famous name he had hired to direct the pitch. Pearlstein took off the jacket of his olive suit, revealing the dapper rainbow of summer pastels—blue shirt, white collar, pink bow tie and yellow suspenders—beneath it. He strode to the center of the horseshoe and, following Wilder's lead, proclaimed: "We promise today to look for and find *the missing soul of Subaru.*"

The language was Plato's. So was the certitude: The soul of a product, its image, *exists*, Warwick asserted—exists independently of the poor consumers, wretched producers and flawed products which lived their fallen lives on earth. "On the one hand, we have that which is divine, immortal, indestructible, of a single form, accessible to thought, ever constant and abiding true to itself," Socrates said. "On the other hand, we have that which is human, mortal, destructible, of many forms. . . ." The two were related; a worldly good was but a representation of its supernatural essence and a reminder of divine perfection. Through the miracle of dialectic, the advertising man, the philosopher-king of commercial culture, could, like Socrates himself, lead producer and consumers to an understanding of the Form, the *eidos*, the "soul of Subaru." Together, they would bask in The Good Life—a life in which consumers purchased Subarus because, however imperfect they were, the cars would serve as continual reminders of the "pure, everlasting, immortal" souls that existed outside their metal shells.

Pearlstein continued with a restatement of Subaru's problem.

"You have a low share of voice," he said, as the committee members, expressionless, watched. "You have 5 to 7 percent of the about $1 billion spent by Asian car manufacturers. That low share of voice means you have low share of mind." He shuffled large cards on and off the easels to illustrate the points. "Your sales have declined from a peak of more than 180,000 cars a year to about 100,000 now. You have low road presence. One of the greatest advertisements a car has is road presence. Most of your dealers are dual, which also lowers your presence in the consumers' mind."

Pearlstein performed without a script. Other than his speech, the only sound was the hum of the fans cooling the audiovisual equipment and the Apple Macintosh computer that coordinated and controlled the machines. A short, barrel-chested man, he leaned several times on the slide projector, and used his hands to point, or form "O"s, or, several times, for no reason, to touch his nose.

He returned to the meeting's subject: Subaru's soul. The company, for all its ambivalence, believed its essence lay within the four-wheel-drive transmissions that accounted for half its sales. "You've positioned this feature as an insurance policy—the notion that when you buy a Subaru you get an absence of a negative." This was inappropriate, because it denied the transcendent power of automobility. "Americans," he said, "view cars as a very positive, optimistic experience."

Where, then, was Subaru's inner core? For the answer, Pearlstein turned the pitch over to Susan Small-Weil, Warwick's research director and the only woman in the room. She was dressed in a smart white suit trimmed in black; her hair was pulled back. She seemed very efficient. "We found the soul of Subaru described very succinctly," she said crisply. "There's something Subaru owners know that nonowners don't know. If nonowners knew, there'd be a lot more owners."

What this was Small-Weil did not say, at least not immediately. She wanted to tantalize the Subarus a bit more with videotapes of what the owners knew. The tapes—recordings of Warwick's in-depth interviews with Subaru drivers—were hard to follow. The voices were muddy, the lighting harsh. In one interview, the reflection of the agency staffer monitoring the session was visible in the two-way mirror through which the discussion was taped. Nonetheless, some comments could be discerned: A middle-aged woman wearing pearls and heavy eye liner exclaimed, "A car is a wonderful invention. It gets you places! And whatever." A young woman said of her Subaru: "My kids love it. It's roomy."

Woody Purcell scribbled furiously. A former Ford executive like Chris and Gibson, Woody, like them (and like Henry Ford II) wore half-glasses, which he pushed up the bridge of his sweaty nose as he wrote.

Small-Weil placed on an easel a photograph of a jubilant angler wearing a fishing vest, flannel shirt and jeans and triumphantly holding up a small-mouth bass. This, she said, was the customer S.O.A. and its dealers pictured when asked to describe the Subaru owner. She took the *Field & Stream*–type photo away and replaced it with a photographic collage of different people, mostly young, all active, most in outdoor family settings, many with babies. These, she said, were the true "Subarites."

"On the surface, they buy Subarus for rational, functional reasons. Some have even *experienced* your advertising; they had an accident on a rainy road, and then went out and bought a Subaru." Yet however explicit their expressed reasons for purchasing Subarus, there were "feelings behind their words."

To understand them, Warwick dollied its camera in for a closeup on a number. The other agencies had the figure, too: The percentage of Subaru owners who were married was higher than the percentage of married owners of all Asian compacts and subcompacts taken together. Warwick's additional research, the videotaped in-depths, found that "Subarites" were heavily influenced by or influential over their families; half the Subaru owners randomly called had family members who also owned a Subaru. Only 10 percent had friends who owned one. With an Archimedean "eureka!" crossing her face, Small-Weil declared that *families* were the Big Idea that would lead Subaru to a new image.

"Subarites," she said, were "very family oriented. . . . Subaru gives them peace of mind. There's an emotional comfort they have in the car. The fact the car is dependable means *they* can be a dependable person. When they say 'comfortable' and 'roomy,' they mean they can have a positive family experience." Subaru could quadruple its target market by accenting the fuzzy and familial emotions underlying the purchase. "We believe there are plenty of people 'kindalike' Subaru owners," Small-Weil concluded. A lone fly competed with the buzz of the equipment. She passed the baton to Bob Fiore, the creative director.

Fiore had a pixieish grace. His wide, bald, bearded head rested atop a short body, and he stood with his right hip confidently thrust out and his right hand upon it in the manner of a fairy-tale wizard about to bestow three wishes on a country bumpkin.

His voice rang cocksure and clear. "You have given these people the wherewithal, the freedom, the peace of mind to do what they want to do," Fiore told the Subarus, as he stood before the easels on which were arrayed pictures of families, traffic jams and country roads. "What kinds of cars are those?"

He paused for deliberate dramatic effect and let his eyes sweep across the room. Then Fiore bellowed his slogan for Subaru:

"CARS THAT CAN!"

The line, it transpired, was the inspiration of a Warwick staffer who recalled, in the midst of the agency's preparations, the children's book *The Little Engine That Could*. Fiore pulled from a pile of stiff cards at his side one board on which the words were printed in reverse type, in comforting, rounded letters that clashed with the stiffer, more modern rendering of the company's name.

Swiftly, he shuffled cards on and off the easels in a vertical version of three-card monte. Ad after magazine ad, "every one of them its own little story," all concluding with the punchy "Subaru ... cars that can," Fiore read in a sharp, impassioned baritone. As he finished with each, he passed it to an assistant, who arranged the boards against the room's left wall.

One ad showed a country road, its pavement covered by a dense carpet of slippery autumn leaves. "Why would Phil Ludlow take his family on a picnic in the middle of nowhere?" asked the headline.

Adjacent to it was the answer: "Because he can."

Another advertisement, looking out from inside a dark barn, peered into the back of a Loyale wagon stuffed with heavy bags of earth and other gardening equipment. "Why would Bob Gordon take the family car and treat it like a pickup truck?" the ad queried.

Again it answered: "Because he can."

"I could have done ten thousand of these!" Fiore blurted.

He put up another one, a long view down a snow-saturated street, where the only sign of activity was two lone tire tracks leading to the horizon. "Why does Santa show up every December 24 no matter what?" it asked.

On the opposite page, atop a drawing of a Christmas-costumed Dad next to his Legacy wagon, was the answer: "Because he can."

Fiore beamed. "It just brings all the humanity back into the advertising."

Warwick's television commercials followed the same narrative format: a problem (the world), a solution (Subaru), a consequence (family harmony). The agency recommended that S.O.A. use only fifteen-second spots instead of thirties, which would enable it almost to double its presence on television. Any loss of detail, the agency claimed, would be offset by the punchy memorability of the repeated slogan.

Two creatives, Alden R. Ludlow III and Andy Mendelsohn, unfolded the long storyboard of a commercial they entitled "Pizza," and stood on either side of the black accordion. The lighting and the perspective of the precise watercolor panels were reminiscent of Charles Addams cartoons in *The New Yorker*. There were four scenes: an empty road on a snowy night; an open but vacant pizza parlor; a car pulling up to the restaurant; a man, woman and child walking from the car to the joint.

Andy explained. "The snow keeps coming down, but this family is hungry. So they're going for pizza anyway. Why? *Because they can* in their Subaru Legacy. We will see shots of the car prevailing over the snowstorm, see and hear the family inside the car and also intercut shots of the empty pizzeria save for one employee who searches through the window for any potential customer. He can't believe his eyes when the Subaru pulls up and the people get out."

The voiceover narration was as simple as the copy in the print ads. "Why in the world would Phil Mockler take his family out for pizza on a night like this? Because he can." As the wintry scene faded out and white-on-black words faded in, the announcer concluded, "The all-wheel-drive Subaru Legacy. . . . Subaru. Cars that can."

The Subarus, who until this point had seemed oddly detached, perked up. This was what they had come for. They leaned forward attentively.

Alden and Andy unfolded another storyboard, for a commercial they called "Mesa." The nine painted panels (this time more Roz Chast than Charles Addams) depicted a surreally happy family bumping its way across rutted Arizona roads to stand in wonder before a rock formation. "Why would Ken Schaeffer drive a hundred miles into the desert, braving potholes, 110-degree heat and his wife's nagging just to show his kids a rarely seen mesa?" the creatives read, mimicking the voiceover. "Because he can."

The advertisement was oddly jarring. The mention of "wife's nagging" seemed clichéd; worse, it was a dissonant note in a campaign whose theme was family accord. No matter: Warwick's creatives bulled on. They showed regional, retail advertising, which replaced the "cars that can" line with "dealers that can." The campaign for the new SVX also followed the form. Warwick wanted to launch the luxury car with a six-page magazine insert that depicted the flashy vehicle traversing mud-slicked back roads and snow-covered streets. "Why would you ever take your luxury coupe out on a day like this?" the headline asked. "Because you can."

At this point in the presentation, the Subarus interrupted: they had some questions about the creative that required more immediate resolution. Ever so gently, Chris Wackman started them off.

"These are very—" he paused, "*light* on specific content. Comment?"

Bob Fiore, who had taken his seat while his colleagues presented the television campaign, leapt to his feet to respond. "This whole campaign is made up of what this car is all about. That's a bigger story. *Everybody* talks about horsepower, mileage, and nobody hears it. Our minds are open. But I have that feeling."

Wilder Baker elaborated: "Specific attributes are meaningless unless they're placed in an emotional context."

Tom O'Hare, the most outwardly demanding member of the search committee, bore in.

"When I see commercials, it's on a big screen in a screening room," O'Hare said, straining his Yankee accent in a way that made him sound more street Irish than Boston College M.B.A. "When I see that same commercial in my living room, when I've got the dog that wants to go out and the kids who want to grab me, I have a real hard time getting that commercial. I suspect the real time of that commercial is the first five seconds. What will these commercials do to meet that particular need?"

Fiore nodded vigorously. "I do believe that to be important. We live in a world of zappers."

"Do you," asked O'Hare, "grab me with my eye or my ear?"

"Both," Fiore answered.

Tom Gibson pulled reading glasses from his pocket and slalomed down a page of questions.

"Any discussion of using testimonials"—true, first-person tales—"to tell their stories?" he asked of the fictionalized "cars that can" narratives.

"We thought about it," Bob Fiore answered quickly. "In some way, there is a testimonial quality to these."

Gibson pressed on. "Is this too soft?" he wanted to know. "Or would a more direct testimonial ad make the same point, but not as soft?"

It was a trick question. The visiting Warwick executives did not know whether S.O.A.'s president was testing their resolve, or whether he actually wanted testimonial ads. Fiore, still sitting, took a gamble.

"Testimonials have become a common executional device. It's a judgment call, but I think I'm right. I really do think I'm right."

Gibson sprang his surprise. Chris Evert, the recently retired tennis star, and Andy Mill, her husband and a professional skier, were "friends of the company" and would, Gibson suggested, like to do some ads. "Should we?" he asked.

Fiore snapped at the bait. "We'd love to have Chris Evert tell a real story about why she drives a Subaru."

If the questions about creativity were tough and pointed, the comments about Warwick's media plan were downright captious. The agency presented a simple schedule that involved spending $40 million (roughly half Subaru's ad budget) on national image advertising, most of it on network news programs, sports shows and prime-time series. Woody Purcell, peering over his glasses like a second-grade teacher about to initiate a scolding, wondered, "How do you justify spending so much money on network to reach areas that aren't major?"

Mark Dunn pursued the inquiry. "We have been spending on prime, news and sports before, as much as $100 million annually. Why would your plan be better?"

A note of desperation crept underneath Warwick's earlier ebullience as its executives responded in rapid-fire succession. Their answers were uniform: a media plan did not determine an ad campaign's success; the *advertising* did.

"I don't think it's as much a question of where you're running as what you're running on it," said Warwick's media director, Mike Haggerty.

"You got a battle cry now!" proclaimed Bob Fiore. "Three *very simple* words that have this uplifting impact!"

Three and a half hours after it began, Chris Wackman signaled the session to a close, saying, "I think we've had an afternoon!" Over the Subarus' applause for his agency's effort, Wilder Baker thumped his last point: "You need an agency that can do, as well."

As S.O.A.'s search committee filed from the room, Warwick executives handed each member a box. Inside were white T-shirts imprinted with the slogan "Subaru ... Cars that can."

JORDAN, MCGRATH, Case & Taylor left nothing to chance. Its executives, led by the car guy Willy Hopkins and by Jack Taylor, the agency's vice chairman, had gone to great lengths to visit every member of S.O.A.'s search committee during the previous four weeks. They went so far as to invite the committee to a cocktail party at the Hyatt that Monday evening, the night before their pitch, to break the ice. No other agency had considered so bold a gesture. By the time S.O.A.'s officials took their seats in the Salem Room at 8:30 Tuesday morning, Jordan, McGrath was a comfortable presence in their lives.

The greatest source of the Subarus' comfort was Willy Hopkins, who led the agency's march. He was dressed in a conservative dark suit, but wore a bright tie adorned with license plates and (he claimed) boxer shorts to match. His presentation matched the whimsicality of his garb. At times he was measured and scientific, making copious use of graphs, charts and slides; at other times he veered into the racy but folksy humor of a country mechanic.

Willy stood behind a podium at the front and to the left of the room, and projected a slide on the screen in the center of the agency's rectangular performance area. "What is going on in the marketplace?" it read. The subsequent litany was both familiar and sour. There were 1.4 cars for every licensed driver in America, indicating a lower-than-ever demand for new cars. Prices for cars had soared, but consumers had dealt with it by extending the lives of their loans, to the benefit of banks and other lenders but not of auto manufacturers, which found consumers unwilling to trade their cars in every three years, as in the good old days.

As he recounted the statistics, Willy illustrated them with "Pepper and Salt" cartoons torn from the editorial pages of the *Wall Street Journal*.

Was there any good news for Subaru? he asked rhetorically. There was. Research showed a steady increase in consumers' intent to purchase four-wheel-drive vehicles. A closer look disclosed that the desire to purchase four-wheel-drive vehicles fell during the first quarter of the year but rose during the normal spring and fall selling periods—proof, claimed Willy, that four-wheel drive was not merely a seasonal, snow-related impulse but, now, a natural part of consumers' purchasing patterns. "We don't think the market is running away from you," he comfortingly told the Subarus. "We think the market is coming right at your franchise."

So why weren't consumers marching into Subaru dealerships? To answer that infernal question, Jordan, McGrath held eight focus groups in New Jersey and Los Angeles. Time and again, drivers told the agency that they had bought Toyota Camrys and Honda Accords because they were familiar with them. Subaru's other competitors had managed to compete with the two leaders by carving out distinct images for themselves. Among compact cars, consumers considered the Mazda 626 more "fun" and more "interesting." In the four-wheel-drive category, sport-utility vehicles shouted, "Yes, I'm married, but it doesn't mean I'm not available for consultation," Willy quipped. Subaru, however, had nothing to boast about.

"The brand itself lacks clout, lacks image," Willy said, standing ramrod straight, tapping a pen professorially into his hand. "You've had great ads, but while people liked the ads, they couldn't necessarily associate them with Subaru. You don't have an image problem. The problem is, you don't have an image."

Willy flashed on the screen a "perceptual map," a popular device by which consumers' attitudes toward different competitive products could be visualized. In a perceptual map, two elements of a product's "meaning" are laid out on the opposing axes of a two-dimensional grid; based on consumers' responses in interviews, competing products are assigned places on the grid. Jordan, McGrath wanted to assess how Subaru stacked up against other car makers in terms of price and value, on the one hand, and emotional impact, on the other.

The agency's map looked something like this:

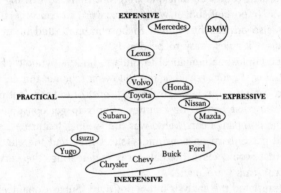

Willy pointed at Subaru's position on the map. "It's perceived as something very pragmatic, logical, *not sexy*," he exploded under his mustache. He dragged his finger to the northeast, to where Honda sat on the map. "If we could get in *here*—be more expressive, as Toyota, don't be as wacky as Nissan—we think you'll be in a wonderful position to take people leaving GM products and flip 'em to Subaru."

How to do that? Jordan, McGrath's focus group interviews showed that consumers' interest in the Legacy grew the more the car and its attributes were explained to them. But, Willy warned, stressing the automobile's mechanical virtues would not suffice to satisfy the dealers, who uniformly believed the advertising should build the owners' pride. Subaru, one disgusted dealer told Jordan, McGrath, had to replace its current image as "a ten-year-old wagon limping down the road with a Greenpeace sticker on it."

Chris Wackman grimaced visibly at the description, but Willy's act was playing well. Tom O'Hare, using the red pen provided by Jordan, McGrath, scribbled at the top of his notepad, *"Very much impressed."*

Jack Taylor, an appealing, glad-handing man with an open smile and an infinite capacity for conversation, took over the presentation, but only briefly and only for a businesslike summation of his agency's positioning for Subaru. Jordan, McGrath had developed and analyzed twelve possible positions for the company and its cars. By position, Taylor meant an emphasis, an overarching element of automobility that S.O.A. might conceivably stress in its advertising. Indeed, Taylor's twelve positions covered virtually everything car manufacturers could accent in their ads: engineering, practicality, durability and reliability, all-wheel drive, workmanship, safety, economy, value, performance, fun to drive, styling and comfort. Of those, Subaru had little reputation for the latter four, Taylor said. Economy, he continued, was "hard to own"—too many other automakers were out there advertising it. Engineering was important, but it was "a buzzword to consumers." Practicality was also critical, but it had to be communicated in an exciting way, because "it's very easy to be dowdy."

Using a complex mathematical formula to build a pyramid of marketable attributes, Taylor arrived at the following scheme: durability, reliability and practicality were Subaru's "cost-of-entry" features, the characteristics that had to be flaunted simply to get consumers interested in the company's cars; value was the "selling feature," the quality that would get Subaru on consumers' short lists; and the clincher, the property that would close the sale, was engineering, the very special way Subaru's cars were made.

Taylor translated the analysis into a position: "Subaru engineering satisfies all the values of drivers who are intelligent and practical."

To turn the statement into advertising, he passed the pitch on to his senior partner, James J. Jordan, Jr.

With deliberate steps, Jordan walked to the center of the room. His face was craggy, his eyebrows bushy, his voice deep and ringing. Like a street-corner evangelist clutching the Bible, he held aloft a copy of a pamphlet the agency had prepared for such occasions. Its cover was blood-red, Jordan's preferred hue. Its title was *Power Copy*, Jordan's gospel.

"The heart and the power of advertising is copy," Jordan preached. "A very few words so skillfully targeted, so clear in their positioning, so vivid in their articulation and so memorable in their identification with a given brand, that they, all by themselves, become not only what people remember about the brand, but also the most important part of the brand's identity and people's principal reason for buying the brand."

He paused, as if to look for where God's lightning might have struck. Seeing the conference room still intact, Jim Jordan looked out on those he was trying to convert and intoned, syllable by syllable: "To our knowledge, we are the only agency that practices this principle."

"Power Copy," Jordan thundered, "is the *exact opposite* of anonymous advertising!" He dismissed with contempt other automakers' attempts to particularize their ads. "You can literally *substitute* the soundtrack from a BMW commercial or an Infiniti commercial!" he said.

The search committee was rapt as Jordan recapitulated the reasoning that had led him to Subaru's Power Copy. First, he dwelt on four-wheel drive. Could Subaru *own* it? Maybe. He modulated his voice with the proficiency of a faith healer. So why not, he asked softly, position Subaru as the leader in four-wheel-drive engineering? Quietly, he answered his own question: because Americans buy cars for reasons other than mechanics. Subaru's Power Copy, Jordan said, lifting his voice up and up and up, had to make four-wheel drive its foundation, but it had to be bigger and broader! "Subaru can effectively preempt all the right reasons for buying a car," he thundered. "*That's* what our Power Copy position says!"

He went to a pile of large cards on a nearby table, and held one up in the crook of his arm. He read, in a towering, precise voice, the slogan he had composed for the Cherry Hill car company.

"SUBARU. FOR ALL THE RIGHT REASONS."

Tom O'Hare, watching intently, shifted his eyes to his pad and scrawled, "I like it." Jim Jordan, if he noticed, did not miss a beat. He was too eager to translate his Power Copy into advertising. He continued his buildup, in an ever more robust voice, proclaiming his discovery of "an Idea so Big, it will plant the Subaru name in the mind of every driver in America!" He went to his stack of big cards and held another one for all to see.

It read: "800-SUBARU-92."

The air hissed out underneath the door as the room deflated. The Subarus, in puzzlement bordering on consternation, realized that they had been led to the top of the mountain to look down, not upon Jerusalem, but upon a toll-free telephone number.

Unaware of any shift in mood, mesmerized by his own brilliance, Jordan continued with unequaled passion. Every Subaru ad, he expounded, should include *this* toll-free number, *this* mnemonically memorable number, for consumers to call to receive *free* information about Legacys, Loyales, Justys and SVXs. The agency, in its confidence, had taken an option with the telephone company on the number. The beauty part was, it was good for at least eight years! A telephone number, Jordan explained breathlessly, only needed nine digits. With *this* number, the tenth digit was extraneous, allowing S.O.A. to update it continually. "Next year, it can be ninety-three! After that, ninety-four!" Jordan shouted. "You can *own* this for the rest of the century!"

He walked over to a tape machine, flipped a switch, and through stereo speakers jangling rock music blared. "Eight OH OH/SU-ba-RU/ NINE-ty TWO," the syncopated radio voices sang. Mark, Chris, Gibson and Kazuhiro Miyake, an executive vice president of S.O.A. who had been absent from the Warwick pitch the day before, leaned forward and rested their heads in their hands, whether out of interest, disappointment or weariness it was hard to tell.

Just as suddenly, though, Jim Jordan slowed down and lowered the pitch of his voice. He walked over to his card pile and began picking up and describing magazine ads. Perceptibly, the presentation again swelled.

The cars in these advertisements were big, bold and beautiful, in action angles that highlighted their best features to an almost prurient degree. When Jordan held up one ad, for the SVX, with the car facing up and to the left at a fifty-degree angle, Woody Purcell, looking like a man ogling a *Playboy* centerfold, whispered to Chuck Worrell, who was sitting next to him, "Nice shot!"

"Subaru reinvents the wheels!" Jordan proclaimed, reading the headline. In a stirring voice, he read his body copy, with its almost poetic explanation of the mechanics of four-wheel drive. With the card crooked in his outstretched right arm and his head turned toward it to read, his left hand held up to his left shoulder for balance, he was a man possessed, as if taken over by spirits and talking in tongues.

With each print ad, the Subarus grew more excited. "The '92 Subaru SVX Sports Coupe reads like a driver's wish list. Right down to the price," read one, which, like the others, had the words "Subaru SVX" in bold, sans-serif letters running vertically up the left side of the page and concluded with Jordan's "for all the right reasons" slogan. The advertisements for the Legacy were just as brassy. One, with a fulsome three-quarter rear view of the Legacy station wagon, featured a photograph of a young woman and the large, boxed caption: "I don't drive off the road on purpose. I sure don't want to do it by accident." Another, for the Legacy sedan and targeted at Woody Purcell's southern region, depicted a rugged gentleman in a cowboy hat. "I haven't seen a snowflake in eight years. Why do I need Subaru's all-wheel drive?"

When he finished his reading of each ad, Jordan handed the card to a little man in a bow tie, who stuck it to the left wall of the room with Velcro. The wall soon filled with a panorama of the most voluptuous automobile photography imaginable. Sensing the spirit (and hearing the whispers) Jordan hit his stride again. He moved on to the retail ads, which were vibrant, strident and competitive. "When you see what's standard on every Loyale, you'll kick yourself in the Isuzu," Jordan read, laughing Red Skelton–like at his own wordplay and drawing an audible chuckle from the Subarus. He showed ads for contrived sales events, each one more unabashedly hype-mongering than the last—"Valentine's Day Massacre," "Spring Clean-Up," "Graduate to a Subaru"—and each one exposing Jordan's relish for salesmanship. Ideas flowed from Jordan like water through a busted dam. He talked about a special sale for the first night of Daylight Savings Time. "God, I'd love to open the dealerships at two a.m.!" he exclaimed. He displayed the storyboards for a regional television spot entitled "All-Weather Test-Drive," which encouraged consumers to come out on rainy days to test-drive a Subaru and concluded with the invitation, "If you don't want to take your car out on a day like this, call us. We'll drive a Subaru to you." Chris Wackman smiled broadly; he *liked* that idea.

Finally, at 10:45 a.m., an hour into his recital, the inexhaustible Jordan finished. Tom O'Hare was enraptured. "Exciting," he scribbled in his notepad. "Makes you feel *good* about Subaru."

As Warwick had done, Jordan, McGrath concluded its pitch with a brief overview of the media plan. The agency wanted to devote $25 million to a national image campaign, $15 million to regional advertising and $20 million to launch the SVX. Like Warwick, Jordan, McGrath favored specific television programs it believed reached the homes of its target buyers, among them the talk show "Late Night with David Letterman" and the drama series "L.A. Law," both on NBC.

The agency's media director returned the presentation to Jim Jordan for its conclusion. With the same passion he had mustered when showing his work, he swiped at the entertainment-oriented advertising that was engulfing his business and beseeched the Subarus not to be swayed by camera tricks and easy laughs. "Among other things, you will hear that Subaru needs to be famous," he said. "You will hear a lot of other pronouncements, all of them solemn and serious and incomplete.

"Remember," Jordan concluded, wagging a finger at the car company's search committee, recalling for them a popular campaign for flashlight batteries. "People talk about the Energizer Bunny advertising. But they think it's for Duracell."

The Subarus applauded lustily and left the room. A Jordan, McGrath representative handed each man a small box containing a silver pen knife with the agency's name engraved on one side and "Subaru of America" on the other.

DCA HAD SPENT THE MORNING setting up its pitch in the Hyatt's Somerset Room. The new chamber was bigger than those used by Warwick, Baker and Jordan, McGrath, but so, in a way, was the agency's goal: to persuade Subaru's American executives that the Japanese shop was not riding a locomotive into the car company's account but deserved the business on merit.

That the atmosphere was different was apparent as soon as the Subarus stepped through the door. The thirteen DCA representatives stood in a "V" formation, like an athletic team waiting for a match to commence, with Ray Freeman, the agency's chief operating officer, at its apex. The DCA executives, who greeted each member of the search committee with a firm handshake, wore large buttons reading "Subaru I-92" pinned to their chests. The same logo glowed from a pair of television sets that stood guard on either side of the room, which DCA had made more intimate by closing off the back with black felt screens.

When the two teams were seated, Ray Freeman explained that "I-92" stood for "Integrated Resources." He introduced executives from the promotions firm and the time- and space-buying operation, and told the Subarus of his agency's plan to bring the three companies' combined faculties to bear on S.O.A.'s problems. (In the agency business, this sort of scheme is called "unbundling," because it involves spinning off to separate companies activities that traditionally were handled by ad agencies alone.)

From the earliest stages, DCA filled its pitch with pomp and glitter which had been missing from the earlier presentations. When Chas Conklin, the agency's resident car guy, took over the performance, the television screens served as coordinated commentators, dramatizing his analysis of Subaru's market position and "share of voice" deficiency with visual and audio asides. The other DCA representatives acted scripted roles in the pageant he was presenting, each one playing a different surrogate consumer. As the members of the cast spoke and finished, they bounced straight up and down in their seats, like choreographed ducks in a shooting gallery. Arthur Einstein, the famous name who directed DCA's creative assault on the account, introduced himself as "the enthusiast." "I depend on editorial, mostly, and most of the time I find advertising talking down to me." K.C. Eguchi, the only Japanese executive visible on the agency's side, presented himself as "the loyal Subaru owner." "I live in the suburbs, thirty miles north of Manhattan," he said, reading haltingly from file cards. "My news sources are print media and some radio. I used to own a Ford Taurus wagon, but it needed towing once. I test-drove a Subaru. My wife liked the styling and handling." Norman Hajjar, DCA's young director of new business development, played the part of the SVX prospect. "I haven't reached my midlife crisis yet, so I'm still interested in practicality. I need a trunk, room, a backseat. But the number one thing that will grab me is loving this car."

To understand what, if anything, linked these stereotypes together, DCA presented its director of planning, Dr. Robert Passikoff.

Dr. Bob, a big man with an appropriately academic mien, began his portion of the pitch with a sweeping justification of account planning, the marketing research system founded on qualitative investigations of consumer attitudes. He claimed that a study by the Advertising Research Foundation had found that "how a consumer bonds to a product"—what emotional ties were formed between the buyer and the bought—"was the most predictive link between a product and its sales." What most agencies, even those that used account planning in strategic development, failed to understand, Passikoff continued, was that consumers could bond to different aspects of a product—its name, for example, or its advertising, perhaps its formulation—in the same way that baby ducks can imprint to a bearded scientist, a fire hydrant or anything else they happen to see upon hatching.

DCA had developed a proprietary research technique, called "Brand Keys," which Passikoff said could identify the ideal emotional bonds for a product in any category, then measure how existing products matched that hypothetical ideal. By asking questions that seemed culled from U.S. Army intelligence tests (sample: "If you were your ideal car, would you be the Master of Ceremonies or a member of the audience?") DCA could determine how to change a product's identity—it could devise an advertising "key" to fit the emotional "lock."

Dr. Bob displayed two images, sequentially, on the television sets in the center of DCA's performance space. The first showed the ideal, the "lock" that explained why drivers purchased compact cars imported from Asia:

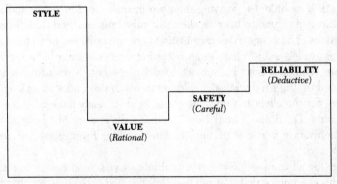

The second image showed Subaru's current "key," which at the time of the pitch looked like this:

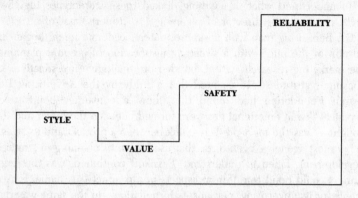

The trick, Passikoff concluded before taking his seat, was to forge a new key for Subaru that would match the compact-car buyer's lock. To determine its shape, DCA conducted sixty in-depth interviews—half with current Subaru owners, half with potential buyers—in Boston, Houston and the Baltimore-Washington area. The conversations led the agency to a five-part advertising strategy for S.O.A., which DCA proudly unveiled on the television screens. "Establish Subaru as an outstanding value," it read. Let consumers know that they "get a lot" for their money, and that part of that "value story" is "advanced technology." Make the car a badge of pride, and, finally, make the auto "the hero of the advertising."

DCA's positioning statement underscored perfectly the agency business's tendency to mask what are essentially well-founded opinions in the language of positivism. Advertising people are continually inventing empirical techniques, gussying them up in quasi-academic terminology, and bringing them to bear on the most subjective and individualistic of decisions. The agencies' determinations are unverifiable, of course; few things are less subject to laboratory testing than consumer behavior. But where opinion would be subject to disagreement, a scientific veneer painted on their judgments enables agencies to suspend a client's opposition, for the client has no similar studies at its ready disposal. Account planning, Dr. Bob's "Brand Keys" studies—these were just hokum, the contemporary versions of the "Unique Selling Proposition" of forty years ago.

Yet for all the pseudoscientific prattling, it was nonetheless true that all three agencies that had pitched thus far had arrived at roughly the same conclusions about Subaru's needs. Either the auto company's problems and the market conditions were obvious to anyone who bothered to spend a few days talking to dealers and consumers, or the incantations and wizardry practiced by the ad agencies had tangible value.

It was left to Arthur Einstein to show how DCA intended to teach Subaru to sing more sweetly than the rest of the car horns in the traffic jam. He wasted no time, immediately disclosing his agency's chosen slogan:

"THE PERFECT CAR
FOR AN IMPERFECT WORLD. SUBARU."

Speaking with an intensity that belied his dry accountant's garb of white shirt, gray slacks and yellow-and-black tie, Einstein proceeded from the unveiling to an impassioned defense of the tag line—a pitch ritual not unlike the congregation's antiphonal answer to the cantor's cry, although here both call and response come from the same person.

"I love it," Einstein said of the slogan. "I love it, first of all, because an art director came up with it, not a copywriter. I love it because I can see it on the sales floor. I think it's value-oriented. It's aggressive. I think it's open-ended. It allows each of you around the table to bring your own agenda to it. And it's both competitive and has style."

"The numbers were astonishing," Chas Conklin interjected from his chair. DCA had tested this tag line and three others. "The readback on this one was style and value"—the missing tine and groove on Subaru's "brand key"—"with just those words!"

Chris Wackman, a bit morosely, asked, "Anyone say Subaru?"

"No," Dr. Bob responded. He waited a beat. "Sorry."

Arthur Einstein carried on with his presentation by piecing together a sample advertisement on a blank board. He hung a photograph of a Legacy on the left; shot squarely from the front, from a height of about ten feet, the car stood motionless, half in shadow, half in bright light, on a cobblestone street. "The car should look like jewelry," Einstein declared. Then he attached the headline to the upper-right corner of the page; it was colored gray because "it looks more editorial"—it better mimicked the conventions of a magazine story's layout. In the lower-right-hand corner of the page, under a solid black rule and in relatively subdued type, he appended the slogan. Voilà! The perfect print advertisement for the "perfect car."

Having cobbled together a prototypical ad in the manner of an artist on a "learn-to-draw" television show, Einstein proceeded to plaster the black felt screens behind him and the side walls of the conference room with dozens of magazine advertisements modeled after it. "Don't worry. It's still a Subaru," screamed the headline of one, which featured an otherworldly full-frontal shot of an SVX. "To understand why your family belongs in a Subaru, take a look at these slides," read another, whose inset box contained drawings of cars without four-wheel drive skidding across slippery roadways. There was the required ad for the forlorn but not forgotten southeastern states: "Where is it written that you don't need four-wheel drive in paradise?" it asked, over a mockup of a Legacy sedan gliding smoothly against a tropical gale. As Einstein and his accomplices ran from wall to wall, hanging the ads by their Velcro backing, they looked like characters from a speeded-up silent movie. Einstein's voice grew strained as he rushed through snatches of body copy: "If you think four-wheel drive is only for snow country, you're missing a big idea." "You have a safety package that only a Mercedes-Benz can match. But don't worry. You can afford a Subaru." By the time they were finished, barely a surface remained uncovered.

Einstein stopped, breathless, between the television sets. The print advertising, he said, was heavy on facts. "But broadcast," he continued, "is the medium where emotion comes first and logic second."

In a fraction of a second, the bright blue glow of the television sets was replaced by something the Subarus had not yet seen in the presentations: a real TV commercial.

A model of the modern, emotion-driven, logic-devoid, rock-video-inspired spot, the advertisement crowded fifty-seven separate scenes into its seventy-eight seconds, all of them backed by a pounding, pulsating, empathetic pop tune. The visuals (which cut starkly from one to the other, except for occasional fades) looked like this:

Long road shot of Subaru Legacy wagon. Closeup of front bumper. Top view of Legacy sedan on the road. Closeup of passenger side mirror. Driver's side of car on road. Young mother and baby. Fade to mother and baby at piano. Blond father playing with young daughter on brass bed. Closeup of Subaru nameplate. Closeup of naked baby with mother. Quick cut of pregnant mother and daughter backlit against doorway. Black grandfather cuddling infant on outdoor swing. Fade to top view of Legacy sedan, traveling down a glowing red road. Three-quarter front view of car on road. Rain-slicked road, seen through the windshield of a fast-moving car. Two children, who wake their father, asleep in a tent, and bring him orange juice, while their mother cooks breakfast on a grill in the back. Metallic blue Legacy sedan, shot from the front and above, mottled by sunlight gleaming through trees. Young teacher with Princess Di haircut teaching two black boys and one white girl to read. Overhead sweep of a college classroom, students raising hands. Quick cut of leaves in trees. Long front view of Legacy sedan traveling down a country road straight toward the camera. Quick closeup front view of the same car. Long view of two farmers in tractors in a wheat field. Medium shot of three farmers in flannel shirts and jeans loading hay bales onto the back of a truck. Two young boys with baseball bats, running. Father in down vest resting hands on the shoulders of his son, circa age ten. Rear view of priest in cassock with arms around two parishioners in a chapel. A bride and groom stepping up to the canopy in a Jewish wedding. Quick cut of a Legacy sedan driving over cobblestones through an arch in a European village. Closeup front view of same car. Closeup view of driver's side of car. Boy in baseball cap and rain slicker repeatedly kissing his mother. Fade to older woman in sunglasses laughing and running on a beach with her husband, who carries a Polaroid camera. Fade to father hugging his newlywed daughter. Fade to youthful lacrosse team, posing before the goal, waving their sticks in victory. Side view of Legacy wagon, traveling fast. Brightly dressed gymnast, shot from below, doing a flip. Quick cut of high jumper clearing the bar. Two very young Little Leaguers, one black, one white, in baseball uniforms, walking in slow motion with their gloves, a ball and a bat. Slow motion of a man in road race, grimacing. Slow-motion closeup of boy taking a swing with a stickball bat. Rear view of two football players, in full uniform, walking slowly from a game. Slow-motion shot of a black Legacy sedan passing other cars on a crowded street. Slow-motion shot of a soldier emerging from a train to greet a waiting woman. Fade to reflection of a woman touching the Vietnam Veterans Memorial. Top view of a Legacy sedan pulling into the screen. Father pushing young daughter in a swing. Two men with mustaches on a rubber raft waving their arms in a cheer. Top view of a traveling Legacy sedan. Man running on beach and throwing a stick for two dogs to retrieve. Two men in cowboy hats looking from the top of a mountain down a deep ravine. Closeup of a car mirror. Man and woman in evening clothes, clutching each other and walking in dawn mist. Long view of a Legacy wagon. Rear view of a Legacy wagon, traveling in golden sunlight down a rain-slicked road in verdant farm country, shot long from the rear. Fade in over scene: "The Perfect Car for an Imperfect World. Subaru." Fade to black.

The commercial was not an original piece of work, but a "ripomatic"—ad lingo for a commercial assembled, or "ripped off," from pieces of existing spots. And although the Subaru executives did not recognize the footage, much of it was theirs: Dentsu had provided to its American affiliate film it had shot for Subaru commercials in Japan and Europe. The tipoff, barely perceptible, was one very fast shot of the driver's side of the Subaru Legacy—the driver and the steering wheel were on the right side of the car.

But the Subarus were not concentrating on whether the cars in this overly long ersatz advertisement were built for American roads. Rather, they were puzzling over what the spot had to do with them. The random scenes—family intimacies, soulful wildernesses, interracial harmony, footfalls on seashores—were familiar from scores of commercials from the latter half of the 1980s, ever since parity products and the account planning system of marketing research had pressed agencies into showcasing the attitudes of consumers instead of the attributes of products. Then there was the musical backdrop. A few lines in the accompanying pop tune—"Here's to the travelers on the open road," for example, and "Here's to the drivers at the wheels"—appeared to refer to the act of driving. Most ("Here's to the babies in the brand-new world" and "Here's to the preachers of the sacred word") seemed aimed at arousing generalized emotions that could easily have been transferred from cars to bubble baths. And while some lines and scenes were no doubt meant to evoke a poignant sense of patriotism, a shot of the Vietnam Veterans Memorial joined to a musical reference to "soldiers of the bitter war" was not the most felicitous image to associate with an Asian car.

As the Subarus left the room, they absentmindedly clutched the big "I-92" buttons DCA had given them as souvenirs.

THE NEXT MORNING, the Burlington Room looked different. The tables were tightly packed together, family-dinner fashion, forcing the occupants to face each other at close quarters. Seat assignments were missing. So were the tchotchkes, like monogrammed agency pens and inscribed notepads. Instead, stationery cadged from the Hyatt's front desk had been hastily placed at each setting. Dominating the room's center was not a computer-controlled multimedia deck but a single, rickety slide projector balanced precariously atop a file cabinet. Up front stood a five-foot-tall, upright, cardboard cutout of a 1930s-style cartoon pitchman, a wide-eyed, bow-tied glad-hander who looked as if he had been pulled from a "You've just won $100" Monopoly game card. It all seemed so . . . odd.

The Wieden & Kennedy staffers milled about uneasily as the Subarus walked in and tried to figure out where around the cramped table assembly to sit. The Oregon advertising people were an eccentric lot, certainly compared to the Scarsdale Galahads and Continental savants who had preceded them. A few wore scruffy beards; several lacked jackets and/or ties; one, a wan young man, had his hair tied in a ponytail that streamed to the middle of his back.

Suddenly, in terror, a thin, nervously energetic man with blond hair and a goatee shouted out: "Do we have enough chairs?" Frantic eyeballs scoured the room and answered in the negative; several agency representatives scurried out and returned hauling metal folding chairs. Without direction, the Subarus gravitated toward the front of the room, near the projection screen, the advertising people crowded the rear seats by the door, and the day's only pitch began.

The Maynard G. Krebs lookalike opened the session. "I'm Dan Wieden," he said, "and you should know my heart is as a writer."

The other agencies had done their damnedest to portray themselves as grease monkeys and stock-car drivers whom misfortune had lured into the seamy world of advertising. Not so Wieden & Kennedy. Everything the agency said and did indicated that advertising came first—not just advertising as a discipline, but advertising as a form of creative expression. After advertising, this agency's next love was itself, which was clear from Wieden's nervous laugh and opening proclamation: "Subaru is an incredibly significant piece of business for this agency. It serves two important goals for Wieden & Kennedy. It brings us outside of Nike and gives us potential to stretch our wings creatively."

The Portland agency was setting off on unsteady ground. Chris Wackman had already eliminated an agency from competition because its credentials presentation had been more about itself than about Subaru. Yet here was Wieden & Kennedy, not ten minutes into its final pitch, and so far, like a refugee from a twelve-step program, it had managed to talk only about its own wants and needs.

Chris's face betrayed no offense, not even when David Luhr, the agency's youthful director of account services, stood up and continued Wieden & Kennedy's spiel of self-interest.

"Diversity has been our key objective for the year and you fit very nicely into that objective," he said. "You'd be a perfect match for us."

Scot Butler, the agency's media director, raised the stakes from self-interest to egocentricity. "I also think," he said, "that the name Wieden & Kennedy has some cachet."

Luhr saw his colleague's egocentricity and upped it to pure obsessiveness. "There's a number of people who would do *anything* to work at our agency," he said. "I've gotten fifteen résumés a day since this review started."

But the Subarus, who had grappled with their share of self-centered ad people over the years, quickly forgave Wieden & Kennedy its transgression, because the agency had the guts, or the foolishness, to overturn pitch traditions and open the formal part of its presentation with a brief discourse on future strategy, not a recap of S.O.A.'s by-now familiar problems, as the others had done. And what Wieden & Kennedy said made the Subarus sit up and pay rapt attention. Talking over the loud whine of the projector's fan and illustrating his assertions with slides, Dave Luhr summarily dismissed virtually everything the other agencies had told S.O.A. about car marketing.

Sixteen new automotive nameplates had been introduced into the United States in the 1980s, and each new maker built four or five different models, he explained. On top of that, the import leaders had instituted a four-year period of replacing and upgrading their cars, vastly speeding up the traditional cycle of automotive obsolescence. All these new cars, he said, were technically equivalent, or at least perceived as such by American auto buyers.

The other agencies had maintained that the proliferation of cars had made it more imperative than ever for Subaru to differentiate its vehicles using tangible product attributes. Not Wieden & Kennedy. "Because of shared technology, because of the models out there, the consumers' perception is that it *doesn't matter* which car to buy, because they're all reliable, all well-engineered," Luhr asserted.

What *did* move consumers to purchase one car over another, he asserted, was "fashion."

For Subaru, the path was clear. The company must end its image reliance on four-wheel drive. "We need to wrap your product attributes around a brand. You cannot define yourself merely by product attributes. . . . When people are in the 'desire ownership' phase of car shopping, *image* dominates their perception of the brand."

Luhr clicked the slide advancer in his hand and projected his agency's "mission statement" for Subaru on the screen. It was a half-sentence reiteration of the radical proposition he had just made: "To position Subaru as the only clear alternative to the mainstream of American car purchasing." Underneath, in slightly smaller letters, the agency explained how it intended to support its mission creatively: By positioning Subaru as "A car built for the individual, not the masses."

The proposal was original, to say the least. Of the four agencies thus far, only Wieden & Kennedy dared posit that engineering was irrelevant, at least insofar as the word centered on tangible properties; only the Oregon agency dared state that image superseded substance in the minds of casual car shoppers.

On a more abstract plane, Wieden & Kennedy was elaborating one of the grander ironies of contemporary marketing. The agency was claiming that in the late twentieth century, a period when more products were more alike than at any other time since the advent of the Industrial Revolution, manufacturers had little choice but to appeal to individualism to sell their mass-produced wares. This postmodern turn-about was not wholly novel; at the time of the Subaru review, The Gap retail clothing chain was selling its jeans and workshirts by throwing them over the torsos of notable furniture stylists and marine explorers, distinctive characters all. But no other ad agency had articulated so clearly the Orwellian thesis undergirding this novel approach, this "personalized" form of mass marketing. In effect, Wieden & Kennedy was proposing to make Subaru the Levi's dungarees of the auto industry.

The Subarus still had their heads turned to the projection screen when Luhr, behind them, passed the clicker to Scot Butler for an expanded discussion of media planning.

Here again, Wieden & Kennedy was unlike the earlier contenders. The other agencies had moved directly from their positioning statements to their creative. The Portland shop, which was (as its competitors saw it) the "creative wild card" in the review, was delaying its creative presentation to provide a detailed schematic for time and space buying, which the other agencies had saved for a hasty endgame.

Of all the Wieden & Kennedy lot, Butler was the most conservative. He wore a baggy dark suit, a white shirt and a narrow tie; he peppered his conversation with frequent references to "you guys" in a low, deep voice. His look and sound gave him a plodding demeanor, but the appearance was belied by his aggressiveness in assailing S.O.A.'s own media-buying routines. Network advertising, he contended, was worthless to Subaru. So were attempts to make inroads where Subaru was currently unknown. "The markets where you have the best opportunities to get higher volume," Butler averred, "are where you should be putting your media dollars."

That short statement was arresting for several reasons. First, it was simply different from what the previous three agencies had recommended. Because S.O.A.'s annual ad spending was only about half that of its rivals, it could not compete for attention effectively on network television. Yet the other agencies had all placed national advertising at the center of any campaign to rebuild Subaru's image. Here, at least, was the glimmer of a different strategy.

More important was what Butler's brief comment indicated about Wieden & Kennedy. Ad agencies preferred network television advertising because of the exposure the medium gave their own work; a New York copywriter couldn't call old college chums in L.A. and Cincinnati and brag, "You see my newest spot?" unless that spot was running on the networks. The Subaru executives, with long experience doing business with a "creative" agency, thus were surprised to find another self-professed creative shop willing to abjure network advertising.

Butler proceeded to give a somewhat lengthy elaboration of what he meant. Subaru's top ten markets, he said, represented less than 1.5 percent of the U.S. population. No matter what S.O.A. did, there simply were not enough people in these areas—places like Bend, Oregon, where Subaru's per capita sales were the highest in the country—to increase substantially the company's sales. Instead, he suggested that the company concentrate on its top fifty markets, which were already responsible for 78 percent of S.O.A.'s sales volume, and try to gain incremental sales in those locales.

Using network television to increase sales in those scattered local markets was like using a blunderbuss to shoot a flea. "Forty percent of your dollars against 18 percent of your volume, the way you're doing it now, is a waste," Butler sniffed. "With your money, to compete using network TV is farfetched."

He then unveiled the pièce de résistance of his presentation, a projected map of the United States with Subaru's "markets of opportunity" shaded in according to their proposed importance. The darkest areas of the country, the markets of greatest opportunity, were the Pacific Northwest and New England. The entire middle of the continent, the flyover, the center of American consumption, the places where S.O.A. absolutely *knew* it needed more recognition to move into the mainstream, was blank.

Butler paused to allow the image to settle. "I hope this isn't upsetting," he deadpanned.

Nervous titters erupted around the room. They were interrupted by Tom O'Hare, who was sitting closest to the screen and had been studying it intently. His tone was less one of consternation than of worry. "We are a national company, if not in sales then in distribution," said the distribution-company president. He pointed to Florida, Texas and California, which were blank—low opportunities—on the map. "To walk away from those! To have a vacuum, a complete denial, in Texas, in Florida. . . . " His voice trailed off. Clearly, Wieden & Kennedy had taken a risk in presenting this strategy, perhaps a fatal one.

As the gravity of the agency's media-spending recommendation was sinking in, the tall, thin man with the ponytail took command of the proceedings. He had a small, round head and rimless glasses and wore a loose-fitting gray suit. His name was Chris Riley. He had joined Wieden & Kennedy as its first director of account planning only six months before. He had grown up in England, where he majored in American Studies in college, having fallen in love with the United States from watching "Kojak" as a boy.

Riley immediately proved a popular figure. He was wry and un-assuming, and dotted his conversation with Britishisms—"telly" for tele-vision, plural instead of singular verbs when used in conjunction with companies and groups—which made him seem alternately funny and intelligent. He described his role as helping the agency and Subaru fig-ure out how to "fill the gap between what consumers believe about cars and how car companies present themselves."

Wieden & Kennedy had conducted several consumer studies which were odder than any others the Subarus had yet confronted. One was a Rorschach-type test in which drivers were asked to compose a caption for a fanciful pen-and-ink cartoon of a person of indeterminate sex standing and musing in front of a car. A man in Chicago wrote, "I'm successful. My company is successful. I like an economy-minded, reli-able car." A woman in Atlanta wrote, "Logical. Practical. And economy-minded." Another caption read: "What's the markup on this car?"

To Riley, if not to the others, the conclusion was clear: the gap between the consumer and the overly glamorized, promise-laden adver-tising of American car companies had widened over the decades. Con-sumers, increasingly, had come to see the luxuries of the recent past—television sets with digital readouts, compact-disc changers—as a right, not an aspiration. Combined with the recessionary economic cli-mate, this attitude meant that consumers now expected quality in every-thing they acquired, yet considered the conspicuous consumption of the 1980s gauche.

"If you go out there with a badge that says, 'I'm into disposable goods,' you look like a wally today," Riley said. He grinned, then went blank when he saw the uncomprehending faces. "An idiot. Sorry." The Subarus laughed, which startled him, which made them laugh more loudly.

S.O.A., because of its historical association with durability and quality, was well positioned to take advantage of the new value-consciousness of the rapidly downscaling American consumer. All the agencies had said that, but Riley gave these consumers a name. He called them "role-relaxed people," men and women who were comfortable in themselves, eager to send a message about their own stability by showcasing the dis-tinctive simplicity and subdued superiority of the products they owned.

His description matched those of the other agencies. Subaru buyers were people for whom rationality provided an emotional kick. But Riley, without knowing that other advertising people were also circling his analysis, argued that rational appeals (like Subaru's "Inexpensive, and built to stay that way" ads) would only reach the people who were *al-*

ready familiar with S.O.A.'s cars. While this burgeoning new consumer class was ripe for Subaru's message, to reach a wider audience that message had to be recast to emphasize feelings over knowledge.

Out of these insights emerged a two-sentence creative brief for the Legacy, which the account planner had provided to the agency's creative teams. Riley projected the brief for the search committee to ponder. It read, "The Subaru Legacy is for people who know their car is only a machine. But what a machine!" For the SVX, a luxury car which had to have a modicum of sex appeal, the brief was slightly different: "The SVX is a fine sports car that grips the road for fabulous performance. How should drivers feel? We want them to feel like Porsche 911 drivers with brains."

With laughter, the group broke for an intermission, and the Subarus readied themselves for the long-delayed creative presentation. Here again, Wieden & Kennedy went about it in a different way. Gone was the bombast of Jim Jordan; banished, the energetic self-assurance of Arthur Einstein; absent, the fiery confidence of Bob Fiore. Instead, a pair of physically mismatched creatives took center stage and mumbled so quietly (out of fear? boredom?) that the Subarus had to strain to hear them.

Jerry Cronin the writer, was a large, chunky fellow with a heavy Boston accent who wore old white painter's pants and a knit tie that clearly was knotted in an afterthought. David Jenkins, his art director–partner, was the only savvily dressed member of the Wieden & Kennedy staff; his black European suit, bright white shirt, floral-patterned black tie and neatly trimmed beard made him the near-twin of Miles Drenttel, the mercurial ad-agency owner in the television drama "Thirtysomething." Awkwardly, without introduction, they held up a sign with their tag line for the car company:

"SUBARU. WHAT TO DRIVE."

Jerry explained it. "The theme is 'the truth.' To get rid of the fluff and myth about cars. The reason you should buy it is the way it's built. What the machine is. The premise is truthfulness and honesty."

Jenkins held up black cards with dark, difficult-to-discern photographs taken inside an auto factory. These or similar scenes, depicting the making of cars, in the manner of an industrial film or newsreel footage, would fill the agency's recommended launch spot. Over the film would run the written text of the ad, which was to be read simultaneously by an unseen announcer.

"A car is a car," Jerry mumbled, reading the voiceover. "And its sole reason for existence is to get you from Point A to Point B. And back again. It won't make you more handsome. Or prettier. Or younger. And if it improves your standing with the neighbors, then you live among snobs with distorted values. A car is steel, electronics, rubber, plastic and glass. A machine. A machine. And in choosing one the questions should be asked: How long will it last? How well will it do the job? Could I get a comparable one for less? And do I like the way this machine feels? And looks? And in the end, with an absence of marketing glamour about the automobile, may the best machine win . . . Subaru. What to drive."

With this spot, Wieden & Kennedy showed that it had, in fact, arrived at the same conclusions about Subaru and its customers that the other agencies had. The cars were well-engineered but unfashionable, which gave owners a perverse pride in driving them. But where the other agencies sought to bolster Subaru's position and attract new drivers by specifying and lauding the company's alleged technical superiority, Wieden & Kennedy judged that the real Subaru consumer did not, and would never, care about the details of engineering. Indeed, this agency believed that slogans like "Cars that can" and "For all the right reasons" and "The perfect car for an imperfect world" were exactly the sort of hype that would repel core Subaru customers. So strongly did Wieden & Kennedy feel this that it developed an advertising campaign not to deify cars but to ridicule car marketing.

The print ads aimed at the same target but shot from a different quiver. With one exception (a long-copy, serious two-page magazine advertisement that was headlined, "The Truth") they were all witty (if slightly obvious) satires of the conventions of car advertising.

Jerry read the headline of one, for the Legacy. "Weld a peace sign to the hood and make believe you're driving a Mercedes that gets really great gas mileage." A chuckle started among the search committee. He read another headline, for an SVX ad. "You can drive it so fast, you'll get so many tickets, you'll lose your license." The chuckle ballooned into laughter. Jerry read an ad for the tiny Subaru Justy. "Going down a very steep hill, it feels a lot like a Ferrari." The laughter exploded into loud guffaws.

Most of the print ads were designed as two-page spreads, and looked somewhat like layouts from *The New Yorker*. On the left, under the name of the model, was the comic headline. On the right were two columns of text, underneath which were the slogan and a drawing of the car. Atop the first column of text in every ad was the same 1930s cartoon character whose effigy stood at the front of the room. Because his mouth always appeared to be open in mid-declaration, he seemed to

beg for the moniker "Mr. Shout." The agency never explained his presence or meaning, nor did it clarify the disjunction between the deadly
serious television commercial and the satirical print ads.

The regional advertising and dealer promotions were also out-and-out
funny. Instead of sales events tied to Valentine's Day, the opening of the
baseball season or the start of Daylight Saving Time, Wieden & Kennedy proposed "Subaru's Lack-of-Pretense Days." Among the gifts it
recommended dealers give away were balloons on which were written
"Large balloon to keep kids quiet while salesman closes deal."

Jerry Cronin concluded his presentation as unspectacularly as he had
conducted it. "That's our thing," he muttered. "We think it would be
different." Scot Butler, the media director, sensing the need for a punctuation mark to end the pitch, shrugged and said from his seat, "That's
our hard sell."

The agency fielded some questions and then offered to show the auto
men its newest Nike commercial with Bo Jackson, which had not yet
been released to the public. The Subarus eagerly waited for the VCR
to be connected to the television set, and stood around as Wieden &
Kennedy ran the spot twice.

Unlike the other agencies, the Portland shop did not provide the auto
executives with trinkets as they departed.

THAT NIGHT, returning to the Hyatt after a Chinese dinner in Philadelphia, Gene Van Praag noticed that a car was parked inside the hotel,
in the lobby just in front of the Somerset Room. It looked to be a
Subaru Legacy. But it was covered by a white shroud, and on top of it
rested a pyramid-shaped placard that read, "What is it?"

"Doner," said Gene, shaking his head and smiling. "A killer agency."

The pageantry began promptly at 8:30 the next morning. Doner had
set up the Somerset Room like a Broadway backers' audition. The
Subarus sat in a line behind tables, with their backs against the right
wall. The agency had arranged its own tables in a row projecting forty-
five degrees out from the far end of the search committee's seats. That
left a playing area shaped like an isosceles triangle, of which Don
Riesett, the Baltimore agency's vice chairman and head of account services, took complete command.

"I guarantee you," the lean man with moussed blond hair declared in
a thick "Bawlmer" accent, "there is a simple idea!"

Riesett picked up a ruler and thrust it to the ceiling. A long, vertical
banner unfurled proclaiming the "Path to a New Idea." Riesett detailed
how Doner had walked it, tearing the coverings from wall cards to un-

derscore the agency's feats. It had interviewed 150 consumers in seven states (*rip*); talked with twenty-one Subaru dealers around the United States (*rriiipp*); met with each of S.O.A.'s regional vice presidents and both independent distributors (*rripp*); debriefed editors of *Road & Track* (*rriipp*), and sent agency staff members to two dealerships for two days each, where one Doner executive actually succeeded in selling a Subaru (*rrrrrriiiiiipppppp*)!

From all these conversations, a pair of conclusions emerged: few Americans cared about Subaru, and those who did fell into two familiar categories, educators and engineers. "Thirty percent of the teachers in this area own Subarus," said one salesman, in a tape recording played for the search committee. "Every person's nightmare," another salesman complained on the tape. "A guy who walks in five minutes before you close with a clipboard and a pipe."

Riesett moved on to another medium. He played a videotape of interviews with selected Subaru owners. In it, a man in a T-shirt protested that "people are sadly caught up in image." A bespectacled woman boasted, "I'm into a car as transportation. I'm not into status symbols." Another woman called Honda owners "dumb" because "they've spent more for less quality."

Doner had identified the same core Subaru consumer that the other agencies had found. Indeed, they sounded like the men and women Wieden & Kennedy had described the day before. Even Doner's assessment of these consumers—"They're tired of the vagaries of slogans like 'Oh, what a feeling!' They want the *truth*!" Riesett said—was markedly similar to the Oregon agency's. And Doner's mission statement, its "simple idea" for Subaru, was similar to, although much broader than, Wieden & Kennedy's. The Baltimore shop proposed that Subaru present itself as "the informed, intelligent choice."

But Doner's style of presentation differed from that of the other agencies. It referred little to hard numbers, demographic surveys or organized qualitative research. Its technique was impressionistic. Its consumer research and market analysis were far more cursory than its predecessors'. W. B. Doner, the "move-the-metal" retail agency, was going to rest its pitch on creative.

Jim Dale stood with his jacket off and his left hand on his hip. His voice was mellow and soothing, like a deejay's on an easy-listening FM radio station. He gestured with his right hand as he spoke. "There's great emotional gratification in making the smart choice. That's what this car is about," he said. So strong was this rational-emotional conjunction that Doner had created a half-dozen separate campaigns to showcase it. The Baltimore agency's simple idea, Dale explained, was not a single slogan, but a way of thinking that it intended to thread through different executions in different media.

He unveiled Doner's first campaign. It comprised a series of magazine executions that utilized a page with a cut-out hole in the center covering another page. The first ad he showed depicted a colonnaded Newport-style mansion whose surrounding grounds (which included several automobiles) reeked of wealth. "There's nothing more satisfying than being obscenely wealthy," read the headline over the opulent setting.

Lifting the page left only a single car, sitting starkly against a plain white background. Underneath was the agency's first theme line:

"GET REAL. GET A SUBARU."

Something about this advertisement and several spinoffs was nagging. It wasn't the "turn-the-page" gimmick; that trick was familiar from novelty greeting cards and *Mad* magazine, but could nevertheless still be used cleverly. There was just something ... familiar about the idea. Of course! The campaign itself was already on the air—not for a car, but for a beer: Heineken beer. The Heineken ads (fashioned, as the Subarus knew, by Warwick, Baker & Fiore) opened on an obnoxious, trendy fellow sitting in a bar and singing the praises of the voguish brew-of-the-moment, until he got squeezed offscreen by an outsized green bottle of the Dutch import, as a dismissive announcer sneered, "When you're through kidding around, drink Heineken."

Doner, slaloming toward its goal, had tripped over a mogul that repeatedly fells advertising agencies: unoriginality. The Baltimore agency was far from alone in its plight. Virtually every creative idea presented to the Subarus was based on recognizable advertising conventions from the past or present. S.O.A. had seen rain-slicked roads and snowscapes; some of the slogans it had heard rang as familiarly as hometown church bells. Even Wieden & Kennedy's seemingly novel campaign proved strikingly similar to the old Volkswagen ads, in its demystification of cars and mockery of traditional auto advertising. But Doner's Heineken-inspired idea was so trite that a palpable feeling of uneasiness swept along the Subarus' row.

Jim Dale, if he discerned the shift in attitudes, ignored it. He introduced another campaign.

"There are more reasons to buy a Subaru than for any other vehicle," he asserted, echoing what Jim Jordan had said two days earlier. "So many facts that they don't fit into thirty seconds. They don't fit into sixty seconds. They don't fit into ninety seconds. *That's* the campaign!"

He explained himself: "Let's run one, very long commercial that runs the whole year. In fifteen installments." Every individual spot would be a cliff-hanger that would compel people to continue watching as the year progressed. The theme, an oblique reference to Subaru's technical talking points, would allude more directly to the continuing serial:

"THE SUBARU STORY. IT NEVER ENDS."

John Parlato got up. The buoyant young creative director began narrating the year-long drama, whose storyboard cells were swathed in black paper and covered the screens that shaded the front and right walls of the room. As he related the tale of a single Subaru driver (the "Spokesguy") and his cross-country jaunt through varied climes and cataclysms, Parlato danced around the room, joyfully tearing the paper from the pictures as he shook his shaggy dark mane and pirouetted on his black cowboy boots.

"We cut to the railroad crossing," he cried out, dramatically imitating the "ding, ding, ding" of the closing gates and the "woo woo" of an approaching train. The "Spokesguy"—Michael J. Fox, the agency hoped—got across the intersection, outgunned an oncoming diesel truck, fit three women from a broken-down car in his spacious backseat and dueled a Honda Accord. In the last installment of the tale, he showed up at a "Subaru Owners' Picnic," where a pregnant woman suddenly stopped the festivities by yelling, "I think it's time!" "Is there anyone whose car can get this woman safely to the hospital?" Spokesguy asked. The "longest commercial ever made" ended with every hand in the picnic shooting straight up.

The ending, like the rest of the year-long ad, was unsurprising and contrived. It was also, like the previous recommendation, unoriginal; serial commercials had been in vogue for several years, at least since the California agency Hal Riney & Partners invented two hicks named Frank Bartles and Ed Jaymes to flack a wine cooler.

The agency led the search committee out into the lobby, where Jim Dale removed the shroud from the car parked on the carpeting. "What is it?" he asked.

The white car had an "H" welded to the front of its hood, but it didn't fool Chris Wackman. "It's a Legacy with Honda nameplates on it," he said, chuckling.

Back inside, the agency revealed its last campaign—retail ads in which the car in the hall was the star. As Dale had disclosed in Baltimore, the agency had recruited consumers for test-drives, videotaped their reactions to the ride, and recorded their shocked expressions when they were told the real make and price of the car they thought was an Accord or a Camry. Those reactions had been spliced into two separate, ersatz commercials, starring John Parlato as a fast-talking car salesman. The highlights of the spots included an older woman slapping her face and screaming, "Give me a break!" when told, "It's a Subaru," and a man laughing in response to the same information: "The Toyota people are gonna get you guys." To augment the campaign, Doner even broached the possibility of purchasing an Accord for every Subaru dealer in the United States, so buyers could be invited to test-drive a Honda at the same time they test-drove a Legacy. The initial expenditure, Dale explained, would be $10 million, but after the Accords were resold the experiment would cost only $1.2 million.

Like the agency's other campaigns, the disguised-car advertising was unoriginal; Tom Gibson even referred to it as the "taste test," in homage to the hidden-camera ads that asked consumers to judge unlabeled products. But unlike Doner's other recommendations, the taste test intrigued Gibson. Subaru's president dominated the question period after the pitch. "Obviously, I think that's a very strong piece," he told Doner. "How real was the reaction?"

"Very real," answered Parlato. "I was the interviewer."

"If you were the agency," Gibson continued, holding the stem of his glasses in his mouth, "who would we get?"

Herb Fried, the agency's chief executive officer, who had been quiet during most of the pitch, responded. "Everyone at this table."

Gibson went on. "How much of the work we've seen today was done by freelancers?"

Dale, his inner excitement growing, replied: "None. We don't use freelancers."

WHEN THEY SWEPT into the Salem Room for the final pitch of their account review, the search committee entered a low-pressure area. The moment weighed heavily on everyone present. As the Subarus took their seats—the tables were set up, inexplicably, in a "V," its apex toward the door, with name tags directing the clients to take the left side of the room—they found ten grim-faced advertising people confronting them. It felt like a session in a divorce attorney's office, a final effort at mediated reconciliation before the papers were signed. It was Levine, Huntley's last chance.

The agency bore little relationship to the one Subaru had known for sixteen years. Just two or three faces were vaguely familiar; of these, only one person, Michael Moore, the research director, had worked closely with S.O.A. Everyone else was a stranger. The Subarus were in-

troduced to an executive with Grey Advertising's direct-marketing affiliate and to a new media director who had also come over from Grey.
The creative director, Rochelle Klein, was also new to them. So was
Tom Benghauser, the big, balding car guy the agency's new chief executive, Ed Vick, had hired. It was kind of like the familiar nightmare,
where the dreamer returns home after a journey only to find a group
of strangers living in his house, bearing his family's name and claiming
to know him. It was very uncomfortable.

But as soon as Vick opened his mouth, it became clear that Levine,
Huntley had done its homework and had formulated a clear and
coherent positioning for Subaru that not only differed from the agency's
past thinking but matched the analyses of several other agencies in the
pitch. "The Subaru target," Vick said, recapping the agency's April 10
presentation, "remains making Subaru an alternative to the mainstream."

As its positioning statement implied, Levine, Huntley's appraisal of
Subaru's opportunities was, in terminology and emphasis, virtually identical to Wieden & Kennedy's, whose presentation had, if nothing else,
amused the Subarus. It stressed the intelligence and individualism of
Subaru buyers. The agency projected a slide asserting, "We must focus
more on"—the word of the week—"value."

But in one crucial respect, Levine, Huntley diverged from Wieden &
Kennedy and the others. This creatively renowned New York agency,
this inheritor of Bill Bernbach's scepter, affirmed that image would not
sell Subarus.

"An image-driven strategy is a classic top-down strategy. It requires
time and money. But we feel we don't have time for a slow build," Ed
Vick said from his seat in the middle of the agency's side. "Here's what
we want to do. We want to mentally and physically intercept the in-
market buyer and give him or her compelling reasons to rethink his car
purchasing plans."

Levine, Huntley was going retail.

In a way, it was sad—sad to see how rapidly an organizational culture
could be transformed. Almost overnight, it seemed, an advertising agency had changed its beliefs, left its faith and found another with no intervening period of anguish or introspection. But the situation also
proved fascinating, for Levine, Huntley, more than any other contender,
was determined to retain this account by deploying science—facts, not
impressions; statistics, not psychotherapy. From a purely competitive
standpoint, it was a brilliant pitch strategy. Incredible as it seemed,
Levine, Huntley was positioning itself to win the image war on the battlefield of positivism.

Tom Benghauser stood at his seat and held a long pointer. The bearded motorhead was visibly nervous. Sweat plastered the swatches of graying hair to his nude scalp as he packed the room with data. He claimed that 38 million American adults fit the profile of the "Intelligent Individualist" at whom the agency wants to aim the cars; and 150,000 of these "eye-eyes" went car-shopping every week. In 1990, Benghauser continued, flashing Maritz and Polk data on the screen, 448,320 of these people left their cars to marry Camrys or Accords. If Subaru had hooked one in fifteen of these "promiscuous brand switchers," the company would have added 30,000 more units to its total sales. Likewise, an additional 23,278 Subaru owners joined the Accord or Camry camps; if S.O.A. had kept one out of every three renegades, it would have toted up 7,759 more cars. If Subaru could accomplish these goals in the coming year, Benghauser affirmed, the company would meet its 1992 sales goal.

Benghauser walked to the screen, which rested at the top of the "V." The projections came from the rear, allowing him to stand directly in front of it without shadowing the numbers. He launched into a discussion of geographic target markets.

The analysis was complex, filled with talk about the Brand Development Index, or BDI, and the Category Development Index, or CDI. These measures were created by media planners to assess the popularity of specific products and product types in different areas of the country. The BDI calibrates a brand's sales in a given locale in relation to the population, and compares it to the sales-to-population ratio in the United States as a whole. It is expressed as a single number, which is found by dividing the percentage of the brand's total national sales that occur in an area by the percentage of the total U.S. population that lives in that area. A Subaru BDI of 100 in Chicago would mean that Subaru's per capita sales in the City of Big Shoulders matched the per capita sales ratio of the entire country; a BDI of 50 would indicate that Chicago per capita sales were half the nation's; a BDI of 200 would show that sales penetration was twice as heavy as in all markets taken together. The CDI, which is arrived at in the same fashion, measures entire product classes. By comparing an area's BDI and CDI, advertisers can judge whether their own brand is more or less popular in a market than all brands in their category combined. The findings can then be used to determine whether to pump more or less advertising and promotional support into a local market, in an effort to bring a company's sales up to the putative market threshold, or to curtail excessive spending in a market that does not require it.

Science, but with a creative twist. For although BDIs and CDIs seem to be objective measures of what *is*, there exists considerable room for interpretation. If the brand, for example, is defined as "all Subarus," the BDI would be quite different than if the brand is defined as "Subaru Legacy." Similarly, if the category is "compact cars," the resulting CDI will bear little resemblance to the CDI for "import compacts," "front-wheel-drive compacts" or "four-wheel-drive compacts."

This was where Levine, Huntley got tangled in the web of its own numbers. All the agency was trying to do was arrive at a discrete set of "opportunity markets," not unlike the one Wieden & Kennedy had presented. But as Benghauser went blithely along, his talk of "beady eyes" and "seedy eyes" began to sound like a lurid melodrama. The transactional details were lost on the Subarus. Woody Purcell and Tom O'Hare paid close attention to the slide screen, but grew visibly more disturbed by the analysis. Finally, Woody blurted out that he couldn't understand it, that the agency seemed to be combining indices for the SVX sports car and front-wheel-drive Legacies.

O'Hare hastily scribbled some notes, then looked up to announce his conclusion. "You want to put half the ad spending in markets that currently account for 30 percent of our sales, where we currently spend 18 percent of our budget, after which you're saying they'll increase to all of 34 percent of sales."

Michael Moore jumped in to try to save the situation. "All we're trying to do," she explained, "is say that instead of giving to all the dealers equally, you allocate more to the dealers selling more cars."

"All *I'm* trying to do," the distributor responded angrily, "is unconfuse myself."

It fell to Rochelle Klein to save the account. In a strong, direct voice that belied her fragile look, she interrupted the silent dirge. "We have a campaign," she said, a small smile playing on her lips, "that's going to feature a personality." Gene Van Praag looked up and brightened—he knew it! "Not a big star, but a personality people in the U.S. have gotten to know." Names bandied about earlier in the week flashed through the Subarus' minds. Chris Evert? Andy Mill? Michael J. Fox? "We decided to look for someone who exemplified the 'Intelligent Individualist.'" The tease was exquisite. "If this was 1985, we would have picked Corbin Bernsen, the guy who plays the handsome divorce lawyer on 'L.A. Law.'" Levine, Huntley had previously used the sexy star in its all-male campaign for Maidenform lingerie. "But in the 1990s, there's another 'L.A. Law' star who personifies the 'Intelligent Individualist.'"

A videotape rolled on the large television that stood toward the front of the room. A montage of scenes from "L.A. Law" flooded forth. The celebrity endorser the agency had chosen for Subaru was Michael Tucker, who played the character of Stuart Markowitz. The ad agency believed that the best way to convey the spirit of Subaru and personalize the aspirations of consumers across the United States was to embody them in a short, balding Jewish tax attorney.

The audacity of the idea was striking; the other agencies had merely suggested advertising *on* "L.A. Law," but Levine, Huntley was suggesting buying a piece *of* it. Rochelle allowed the concept to penetrate the room, then revealed her master stroke. The agency, on its own dime, had hired Tucker and filmed several speculative television commercials. The only original, near-finished spots of the entire review, they consisted of the NBC star walking around a Subaru Legacy and a Subaru SVX, each car gorgeously lit against a charcoal-gray background, verbalizing the inner thoughts of a driver shopping for a new car. Epée-sharp attacks against the pricing and content of Accords and Camrys, the spots were breathtakingly simple . . . and captivating. They ended on a slogan that was both:

"THE CAR THAT WILL CHANGE YOUR MIND."

The Subarus were bewitched. That was clear from their questions. What if Tucker leaves the show? Chris Wackman wondered. Not to worry, Ed Vick answered: Ogilvy & Mather had worried about the same thing when it hired Karl Malden of the cop show "Streets of San Francisco" to promote the American Express Card; now, no one remembered the program and everyone knew the ads. What about the costs, Chris asked? Tucker was asking $700,000 for the year, including all television, radio, print and personal appearances, replied Vick—more than manageable, since the agency was proposing to take no profit if S.O.A. sold 115,000 cars or less in 1992.

Vick nervously eyed the room and took a gulp. "Do you . . . do you *like* the campaign?" he asked.

Tom Gibson could not stop staring at the television screen. Without hesitation, he gave a drawn-out, one-word answer: "Yeeaahh. . . . "

Chapter 11

The Quicker Picker-Upper

THE POSTMORTEMS BEGAN with the vigor and high hopes that had accompanied the start of the review itself. After the Warwick, Baker & Fiore pitch, the Subarus returned to Circles, where they sat in a semicircle around a table. In the near-darkness, the nine men could have passed for a medieval star chamber. For a few minutes they were silent, as they let their pupils enlarge. Then Tom O'Hare (as a distributor, he was the only one who did not have subordinate or superior position to anyone else in the room) disturbed the peace.

He liked the Warwick executives' personalities. He liked the idea of fifteen-second spots. He liked the slogan "Cars that can," but thought it needed more of an edge. He did not like the "Dealers that can" retail campaign.

"On a one-to-ten scale," O'Hare said, "I give them a four or five."

"Oooooh," responded Chris Wackman, only part satirically. "*That* sets the tone."

It did—one which grew increasingly rambunctious. Woody Purcell, for one, despised what he had just seen. He thought Warwick's campaign day-old hash. The snow-filled ads with happy families plowing through drifts for a slice of pizza were just reworked versions of Subaru's old four-wheel-drive ads. They would never play outside the Snow Belt and certainly not in his sales territory in the nation's southern tier. He branded the agency's media plan "ludicrous" and, as his final cut, opined, "I don't think they understand Subaru that well or the challenge that well or the opportunity that well."

Now the beast was unchained. The Subarus complained about the poor quality of Warwick's videotaped interviews. Several criticized the agency for not attempting to contact them during its preparations. George Muller, normally reserved, expressed admittedly ill-defined reservations about Bob Fiore. Tom Gibson concurred. "Whatever question you had, he would 'consider' it," he complained. This was not true; Fiore had held his ground on the desirability of emotional advertising over functional advertising. But he had undercut his resolve by acceding to the Chris Evert endorsement and by developing ads that *talked* about emotion but *showed* traditional, slippery, rocky Subaru scenery. "Who isn't shooting mesas? Coastal highways?" Woody asked derisively.

Warwick had done itself in. In part, its error was one of perception: The agency appeared more malleable than it was; the muddy videotapes seemed to represent muddy thinking. But in part, it met resistance for building a campaign on an uncertain reality: the recondite appeal of family rapport. Not once in their postpitch discussion did the Subarus even mention this positioning, an indication that they considered it irrelevant to the company's true image, whatever it might be.

By the time Chuck Worrell, the company's sales director, chimed in with his lone support for the agency ("I thought their theme was terrific!") it was too late. As far as S.O.A. was concerned, Warwick, Baker & Fiore had failed to find the soul of Subaru.

Tom Gibson turned to the company's Japanese chief executive, who had sat impassively through the entire presentation and postmortem. "Mas?" he asked.

"It was better than Levine," said Mas Masumitsu in a slow monotone. "But it's only the first meeting."

JORDAN, McGRATH, Case & Taylor, on the other hand, inspired something close to bliss, at least in Tom O'Hare. Over a lunch of tasteless fish in an artery-clogging cream sauce, he waxed ecstatically about the agency. A man's man (he felt compelled to explain, without being asked, that he carried a leather purse to prevent wallet-wear on his jacket pockets), O'Hare nevertheless did not shy away from expressing his deep feelings for the agency.

"Their presentation made me feel *good* about Subaru," he said, reading from the notes he had taken. He adored the slogan, "For all the right reasons." He loved the big, gutsy car photographs in the magazine spreads. "I was impressed that they made the car the star. The car looked *super*." He used words like "refreshing" and "exciting" to describe Jordan, McGrath's pitch. "There were moments during those three hours when I felt tingly." He glanced straight ahead and deadpanned, "And I don't get tingly much."

Tom Gibson, however, felt few sparks. At a time when S.O.A. believed it needed to broaden its appeal, Jordan, McGrath placed too much emphasis on four-wheel drive for his taste. And the agency wanted to pour nearly as much money into the (unadmitted) white elephant of the SVX as into the Legacy, Subaru's money car.

Mark Dunn also felt a bit uneasy. "My only problem with 'For all the right reasons,'" he said, "is it could be for any product. It could be a laxative. It could be a cereal." Indeed, although no one mentioned it, it already was a cereal slogan, in a way; Jordan, McGrath, after all, was the agency responsible for "Quaker Oats: It's the right thing to do."

THE SILENCE FOLLOWING DCA's "Perfect car for an imperfect world" presentation was awkward. As the Subarus gathered in the living room of a suite on the Hyatt's eighth floor, the Americans on the search committee pondered what might happen and how they would react. Several men stared out the picture windows at a large flock of Canadian geese gathered docilely around a gazebo on the banks of the Cooper River at the hotel's rear. Would Fuji, finally, impose DCA on them, they wondered? Would it be so terrible if it did? Should S.O.A.'s Americans move against them? If so, how?

Chuck Worrell broke the uneasy quiet. "We're back to the mud, back to the snow," he complained, referring to the print ads that had blanketed the conference room's walls. He grew angrier with each syllable. "It reminded me of the old Levine advertising."

Chuck's words were magnets. From the window, from the dining table, from the bedroom telephone the committee's Americans gathered and joined his stampede. DCA was "conventional," Tom O'Hare chimed in; he didn't think it "got to know Subaru"; the presentation "went to hell in a handbasket" as soon as the agency started showing its creative. "They talked about the car being the star of the advertising, but in the print, the *headline* was the star." There were objections to DCA's copious use of freelancers. The agency was reproached for presenting too much attitudinal research and too little empirical data. The organization of the pitch itself was condemned. "A disjointed, uneven effort," Woody Purcell called it.

Through the censure, Mas Masumitsu and Kazuhiro Miyake, an S.O.A. executive vice president also sent to the U.S. from Japan, sat silent and expressionless on the couch.

The exchanges actually constituted the cathartic scene of a drama that had been playing out, behind closed doors and for the most part silently, a short walk down Route 70 for the better part of a year. Although DCA was the object of the discussion, it was not the target. The agency's presentation had been adequate, certainly energetic and in some instances exceptional. Some of the criticisms, to be sure, were legitimate. Chris Wackman, for one, pointed out that the "perfect car" slogan had been suggested, almost verbatim, by Levine, Huntley and rejected by S.O.A. three years before. But DCA barely deserved the shellacking it was taking in this beige-on-beige hotel room. The carping was actually directed at Fuji Heavy Industries, the unwelcome parent that had taken its unruly child by the ear and dragged it into this account review and then forced it to play with this little agency it didn't want to be friends with.

But if Subaru's American executives expected their aspersions to be met by a scolding from their Japanese partners, they were surprised.

Mas, the chairman, spoke first. "So far, none of the three has impressed me," he said, only the barest aspiration of sadness apparent over his words, "on how we can change the sales trend."

The only sound was the enveloping hum of the air conditioner.

"Yaki-san?" Tom Gibson asked.

Miyake's eyes were half closed. "I expected some more exciting concepts," he responded. "That is all."

THAT NIGHT THE AIR grew heavy with the realization that the review was half over and love had yet to sweep through the hearts of Subaru of America. Over dinner at an Italian restaurant in the thick of gentrifying south Philadelphia, the spirited laughter of the previous night turned to the corporate equivalent of gallows humor.

Chris Wackman, his mouth a half-grin, half-grimace, like an "S" turned sideways, wondered whether he was indeed about to be fired or transferred, "as the Subaru rumor mill has it." Woody Purcell raised what was, to him, the terrifying possibility that the best agency in the review would turn out to be the incumbent. "I'll tell you," he said to the table, "we hire Levine, we better hire a major public relations firm to sell this to the dealers."

Later, after the *tiramisu* and the digestifs, as the men drove back to the Hyatt for a night's sleep before the next pitch, Woody and O'Hare indulged the speculative bent that they, as street-smart participant-observers in automotive politics, shared. Regardless of the quality of DCA's presentation and in spite of the criticism, Fuji would inevitably impose the Dentsu affiliate on S.O.A.

"Maybe not today, maybe not tomorrow," joked Woody, quoting from the end of *Casablanca*.

"But after a year," interjected O'Hare, "if sales don't improve."

. . .

AFTER THE WIEDEN & KENNEDY presentation, the Subarus were finally feeling hopeful—but only briefly.

"I feel like the Volkswagen people must have felt when they were presented by—who? Ogilvy?" said Woody, immediately after the Oregon agency finished pitching its occasionally wacky, sometimes serious "What to drive" campaign.

"Doyle Dane," Chris corrected.

"Doyle Dane," Woody repeated. "I still remember the ad. A broken down car. 'Nobody's perfect.'" He returned to the present. "I like it. I love it. It will really break through. Do we have the guts to run it?"

An electrical impulse seemed to be coursing through the empty restaurant. The Subarus, so sullen just the evening before, were now taking slices of cheese and ham from the buffet and slapping them onto pieces of wheat bread with happy abandon. The chattering at times grew so spirited it was hard to sort out who was saying what.

But after a while, the boisterous palaver gave way to sober reflection. As much as Wieden & Kennedy's intellectual rigor and humorous creativity had captivated them, the search committee worried about the agency's almost willful ignorance of the need to sell cars *now*. Both Tom O'Hare and George Muller doubted publicly whether the agency's campaign had enough immediacy to bring Subaru to its goals of 150,000 cars in 1992. It would take well more than a year to translate the giggles into sales, they calculated—if, that is, the dealers, who expected more traditionalism in their advertising, were willing to accept the odd campaign.

Tom Gibson turned to his Japanese superior for a comment. Mas Masumitsu, normally impassive, came alive. "I agree with Mr. O'Hare," said S.O.A.'s chairman. "In order to live long range, we have to live tomorrow. We need to increase sales of Legacy next year, not three years from now. This is a risky concept."

Was Mas dismissing Wieden & Kennedy, the way the other Subarus had tossed off DCA? No one knew.

"We have to consider," Mas continued, "whether we're willing to take a risk to break through our current sales trend."

"Are you a risk taker?" Chris Wackman asked him softly.

Miyake, jabbing his countryman in the ribs, answered for him. "He's a gambler!" he laughed.

. . .

THE SUBARUS' WORRIES, only briefly allayed by the Wieden & Kennedy pitch, grew darker yet after W. B. Doner's presentation. Expectations were *so* high. Desire was *so* tangible. Which only made the disappointment so deep. Chuck Worrell, the head of sales, pronounced the summary, damning judgment on the killer agency: "I don't think they understood us."

W. B. Doner had been undone by glitz. There was too much of everything—too many slogans ("Get real, get a Subaru," "The Subaru story, it never ends") and too many props. "Too much of the satelliting and filming the dealers and everything but getting to know us," said Woody Purcell with disgust.

It's a funny thing about pitching: when an agency screws up, even the little things, items that would be overlooked in any normal business relationship, are magnified in importance. Mark Dunn was bothered that the Doner executive who was slated to direct the company's account, a young man named Dave Sackey, had not spearheaded the pitch. George Muller was irritated that the agency hadn't once suggested how to appeal to women.

Gene Van Praag, who had been careful throughout Subaru's search to remain neutral, now stepped in to try to support his killer agency. "I know Doner well," the consultant said. "I've seen presentations that were so-so. But whatever ends up on the air *works.*"

There remained the possibility that the taste-test campaign—the "hidden Honda" idea, which Gibson considered the strongest individual execution he had seen—might pull the agency to victory. One search committee member even wondered out loud about the ethics of awarding the account to another agency but offering to buy the idea from Doner.

But the Baltimore agency's presentation had demoralized the Subarus. In each and every pitch (save for Doner's, where the preliminary analysis was so weak) the agencies had led the Subaru into the sanctum sanctorum of advertising, lifting their spirits with rigorous, interesting consumer and marketing research. But when the doors of the Ark were then opened to reveal The Word, the creative, the executions which were to illuminate Subaru for the masses, all that was visible were crudely molded idols, discredited ideas from marketing's past. The Great and Powerful Oz was, so far, just a little sloganeer behind a curtain.

Several heads shook in sad agreement when George Muller finished his lunch and said, "I don't think any of the creative I've seen was outstanding enough to convince me that it will sell cars."

THEY FELT DIFFERENTLY after Levine, Huntley, Vick & Beaver pitched, which created more problems than it solved. As they exited the Hyatt's rear driveway in their line of Legacies and drove east along the Cooper River until reaching S.O.A. headquarters, not a man wasn't wondering whether Levine, Huntley deserved to retain the account because of its simple, conventional but nonetheless dazzling campaign with Michael Tucker, the "L.A. Law" star.

After they arrived and rode the elevators up to the executive floor of the angular, modern structure; proceeded to the conference room across the hall from Tom Gibson's office; took off their suit jackets and hung them on the backs of their leather swivel chairs, O'Hare, the toughest man in the room, addressed the subject directly.

"I found their campaign to be somewhat bold and on the edge," the white-haired distributor said. "They were right out in front of everybody in positioning the car against the two main competitors. They delivered in that campaign a tremendous sense of urgency. No doubt you will sell cars from day one with that campaign."

Chuck Worrell set aside years of antipathy toward Levine, Huntley and agreed. "That was one of the best price-value campaigns we saw," he drawled. "Short-term, that's exactly what we have to do."

For the first time, the Japanese grew loquacious. Miyake was the first to speak. "I am much disappointed today. Much disappointed. We need image, not just pricing. Only competition, not enough." He finished as he always did. "That is all."

"I agree," Mas said. "We need a change. Changing the agency itself has meaning. They changed the people, but that did not give us a new idea." He concluded with a reference to Levine, Huntley's slogan "The Car That Will Change Your Mind." "I don't think Levine is strong enough to change my mind."

Mas, as he had throughout the week, deferred to his subordinate for any final decision. And Tom Gibson, despite his respect for Levine, Huntley's campaign, had few doubts about its potential effect on Subaru of America. Perhaps if another agency had presented the "L.A. Law" endorsement. . . . "It's not revolutionary enough to get rid of the excess baggage," Gibson said, referring with that one vague word to the dealers. "And that will weigh us down like an albatross."

The Subarus exhibited little joy, or anticipation, as they quietly parted. They agreed to reconvene after a three-day weekend to choose their new advertising agency.

. . .

RAY FREEMAN spent four days after DCA's pitch in Cape Cod staring out at the sea.

In Baltimore, Amy Elias, W. B. Doner's public relations director, dreamt that she was in a glassed-in office, from which she could see Jim Dale look up from the telephone and smile at her.

At Levine, Huntley, Ed Vick spent the time negotiating with Michael Tucker's agent over whether the actor would agree to appear at Subaru's annual dealers' meeting.

Mark Dunn drove an SVX north to the Davis Cup tournament in Newport, Rhode Island, and found himself invigorated by the gawking tennis fans who asked about his car.

Chris Wackman stayed at home and wondered whether it was possible to reduce all the sweat and creativity to a set of numbers on a page.

The questions Chris, Mark and their colleagues faced had grown no easier during the week of pitches. S.O.A. still had to decide whether its reputation for four-wheel drive would impel more sales, or hinder its ability to reach new buyers. It still had to judge the political impact of its agency choice on the dealers. The Subarus also faced an additional set of issues they did not have to confront fully before the pitches. Was it better to direct advertising spending into specific local markets, or continue to pump it into national magazines and network television? The local-market strategy seemed an efficient way of boosting sales, but if the market choices were wrong, Subaru would die an agonizing death. And how important was the SVX? Some of the agencies—Jordan, McGrath and Warwick, for example— placed a lot of emphasis on it, arguing that it would alter Subaru's reputation for unfashionability. Other agencies virtually ignored it. How much money should be put behind a campaign of dealer promotions and "buy-it-now" come-ons? Or should all the money (as Wieden & Kennedy had more or less suggested) be poured into brand building? Should Subaru be as feisty as Doner and Levine, Huntley recommended in attacking Honda and Toyota? How significant was compensation? How should the company weigh the value of an idea? Could one campaign be deemed better than another because it cost a million dollars less?

Analysis was easy. Creativity was hard. Decision-making was torture.

Of course, on one thing, broadly, all six advertising agencies agreed: There existed in America a breed of people with an affinity for Subaru cars. They were men and women united not by faith or ethnicity or shared history but by products and by purchases.

The conviction was not a novel one. "The motive at the root of ownership," Thorstein Veblen wrote around the turn of the century, "is emulation." The historian Daniel J. Boorstin has written about advertising's role, beginning in the nineteenth century, in redefining the notion of community around the fact of consumption. Mass production, the department store, the newspaper and public transportation together transformed the procurement of goods from a private transaction between a salesman and a customer into a public activity. In this newly public realm, people's property was believed to communicate something about them to others; in order for the communication to be understood, the language, the meaning of goods, had to be comprehensible. Advertising rapidly developed into the lexicon of acquisition. "The arts and sciences of advertising," as Boorstin rendered them, "were the techniques of discovering consumption communities, of arousing and preserving loyalty to them."

It is, needless to say, in the interests of marketers and the media which depend on them to promote the doctrine that we are united not by what we believe but by what we buy, that our lives are circumscribed not by where we live but by the advertising media to which we attend. "Every advertising medium tries as hard as it can to define a market for itself by making advertisers and audiences alike conscious of something which, for practical purposes, may never before have existed," writes Leo Bogart. "A radio station may establish itself as 'the Voice of Northeast Lower Something,' in order to carve out for itself a lucrative area of doing business, even though the people living in that area may have no sense of common identity other than that created by the medium itself."

This distortion of the meaning of community has leached into the most intimate pores of our existence. We unthinkingly judge candidates for public office not by the content of their policy recommendations but by their standing in public opinion polls, which are devices originally developed to aid marketers. We measure the value of cultural artifacts by survey research technologies invented to help advertisers; in the late 1980s, the *New York Times* began publishing a weekly roundup of the television networks' Nielsen ratings in the back of its culture section, not in its business pages. Following the lead of Ralph Nader, we no longer even identify ourselves as citizens, but as consumers.

Yet this abstraction of the communitarian ideal from denomination and neighborhood into a fellowship of goods reflects more of the ideology of marketing than the reality of modern life. There exists a large body of research which shows that consumers care little about which brands they buy, and, especially in this era of brand proliferation, there is widespread evidence that consumers are swayed more by convenience, price and familiarity than by either conscious or subconscious associations with brand images. Even the small, recurring handful of signal successes trotted out by the advertising industry to prove that images can build consumption communities ignore the porous walls around these shires; after thirty years on the high plains of the American West, the Marlboro cowboy got shot off his horse in 1992 when Marlboro's brand share started plummeting in the competition with low-price cigarettes.

Advertising agencies, of course, must reject this supply-side explanation of consumption, this assertion that, like climbers facing mountains, people buy because a product is *there.* The very foundation of the agency business is a demand-side description of acquisition: people desire emblems of their uniformity; the market responds to their wants; they buy.

So it was that the six agencies battling for the Subaru of America advertising account presented a portrait of a community, whose tens of thousands of members were bonded by common traits. Like all communities invented by advertisers, the dwellings in Subaruville housed people whose calculation of their own interests could be overwhelmed by the irrational appeal of slogans, sex and sounds. Unlike the denizens of many other consumption communities, however, these people were unusually intelligent, strikingly value conscious and markedly uninterested in status and glamour. They did not think about cars. They did not like shopping. They were not concerned about their neighbors.

All of which presented Subaru of America's search committee with the toughest task of all: to choose an advertising campaign that would make people care about the fact that they didn't care. Or, to put it another way, to pick a symbol that symbolized disinterest in symbols.

"WOODY, YOU WANNA START?" Tom Gibson asked.

"I have only two," answered Woody Purcell, "and they are Jordan, McGrath and Wieden & Kennedy."

They were in shirtsleeves, the ten men sitting around the polished table they had abandoned a few days before. There was no charge of excitement in the room. The outside air was still torpid, and no answer to their dilemma had miraculously revealed itself over the weekend. So unsettled were the judgments that Gene Van Praag even argued heatedly for extending the process; he wanted to send a new, nine-point questionnaire to the agencies asking them to justify in more detail their creative and their compensation proposals. He was curtly dismissed by Gibson, who wanted to complete this messy business. So to Woody, who was sitting across the table and to the left of Subaru's president, fell the unenviable task of starting the debate.

"I thought the Wieden & Kennedy approach was the most effective, especially over the long term, but I thought it had some risk in the short term," Woody continued, voicing the concern that had surfaced immediately after the Oregon agency's pitch. "The Jordan, McGrath approach was traditional. But it left hardly anything to criticize as a traditional approach.

"In my heart," he concluded, "I know Wieden & Kennedy is right. But my head tells me to go with Jordan, McGrath."

And so it went, with little disagreement. Chuck Worrell picked Wieden & Kennedy first, Jordan, McGrath second. So did Mark Dunn. Chris Wackman chose Jordan, McGrath first, and Wieden & Kennedy second. Tom O'Hare, who had spent the weekend devising a complex mathematical system of weighted analyses in nine different categories, calculated that Wieden & Kennedy and Jordan, McGrath were separated by only two points. "I boiled all this down and said, 'Shit. I don't want to make a decision.'" When the laughter subsided, he offered one anyway: "Jordan, McGrath, in a *very* close call. I would not be upset with Wieden & Kennedy."

No one would ever have predicted it, for in the Subaru review—indeed, in the advertising industry in toto—no two agencies were more unlike than these. Jordan, McGrath was the priesthood of the word; Wieden & Kennedy was the apostle of the image. The New York agency exemplified the "reason-why" school of advertising; the Oregon shop promised to "make you famous." Jordan, McGrath was buttoned-down, suit and tie, organized and traditional; Wieden & Kennedy was T-shirts and jeans, long hair and insouciance, the-meeting-was-supposed-to-start-an-hour-ago-where-are-they. Jordan, McGrath had asked for a straight 15 percent commission, or a $13 million annual fee; Wieden & Kennedy, although not the lowest bidder (that honor fell to DCA, which offered to take the account for two years at 8.5 percent, or a $4.7 million fee) came in significantly lower, at 13 percent, or $9.12 million.

The session passed to the Japanese. Miyake went first.

"I did eight-point analysis," he said. "Tag line, research, creative, media planning and buying, ability to get to 150,000 sales, organization, compensation, understanding Subaru. My choice, Wieden & Kennedy first. DCA second. That is all."

"Mas?" Tom Gibson asked.

"My recommendation is Wieden & Kennedy," the chief executive said, "only because I thought they'd give us some change. But they are second-highest compensation. Need negotiation. We need some contri-bution for one year, two years." His voice was soft but unhesitating. "I'm not recommending gamble," he said, glancing at Miyake, "but I know they have some risk. I have no number two. Jordan could be, but they are the highest with the fee."

He turned to Gibson. "It is your decision."

And so it was. There had been no single consensus choice, no jump-for-joy elation, just an obvious feeling that the review had sifted down to two agencies whose flaws were more obvious than their advantages. Both agencies were asking for a great deal of money. One was risky be-cause its witty creativity might remind dealers of Levine, Huntley; one was a gamble because it was "another New York agency."

Gibson, staring straight ahead, began musing about money. He had gone over Jordan, McGrath's cost calculations, an eleven-page justifica-tion for the traditional 15 percent commission. If the rationale underly-ing the proposal was real, he fretted, the agency might not be able to staff the account adequately should S.O.A. suddenly reduce its ad spending. Equally troublesome to him was Jim Jordan's infatuation with a toll-free number for consumers to request product and dealer in-formation.

He conceded his judgment was more emotional than rational, but was a secure one nonetheless. The high price and creative orthodoxy of Jor-dan, McGrath, Case & Taylor put it in second place.

"Wieden is a geographic risk, a humor risk, a dealer risk, but they have the best chance of breaking through," Gibson said. "At this point, I'm saying, 'What's the problem with taking a risk?' We've got to do *something* to sell cars."

SOMEWHAT LATER, telephones from Chiat/Day to BBDO to Lintas began ringing with the news. Levine, Huntley, Vick & Beaver was clos-ing. Dozens of staff members had already been fired, but the agency was still bleeding money. Grey Advertising, the parent company, did not want to support it. Levine, Huntley, said its last CEO in a statement re-leased to the trades, had "ceased to be a viable business."

The final embers of the Creative Revolution were extinguished. Mad-ison Avenue was no longer the navel of the world. The Jewish agencies and their Borscht-belt *shtick* were dying. The center of advertising's universe had shifted. The agency business was looking West.

PART IV

THE PRODUCTION

Chapter 12

Somewhere West of Laramie

THEY FLEW. Loop-the-loops, figure eights, bombing dives. There were thousands of them: some long and angular, with pointed noses and turned-up wing tips; others short and stubby, with broad fusilages; still others in configurations that defied geometry's description. What the aircraft had in common was their composition: paper. They were all entries in the First International Paper Airplane Competition.

In the 1990s, such events are called "performance art." In 1967, one crazy adman dared to call it advertising.

But then, Howard Luck Gossage, the San Francisco ad executive who devised the contest, was always ahead of, or at least outside of, his era. At the same time Bill Bernbach and his students back East were fulminating that advertising could be *creative*, that it could be *entertaining*, Gossage would let loose a booming laugh that could be heard throughout the old firehouse that was his office and confide: Advertising didn't even have to be *advertising*. "The real fact of the matter," Gossage said, a stutter lengthening the statement, forcing his listeners to wait, wait, wait for the punch line, "is that *nobody reads ads*."

So it was that from the several advertising agencies that bore his name emerged a peculiar type of advertising, a western advertising, that people did not have to read or watch or listen to. Like the rock music that was pouring from the nearby concert halls and the psychedelic posters tacked to the telephone poles hard by his headquarters, Gossage's advertising could be *experienced*.

There were the sweatshirts with pictures of Ludwig van Beethoven and Wolfgang Mozart—part of an early 1960s campaign for, improbably, Rainier beer. (A Beethoven sweatshirt, Gossage explained, was "a brewer's idea of culture.") For Eagle Shirtmakers, Gossage published a photograph in *The New Yorker* of a two-color striped button-down shirt, designed and made by Eagle but sold in many establishments as the store's own brand. "Is this your shirt?" Gossage asked, inviting readers to write in for their free Eagle label. (More than eleven thousand did.) The First International Paper Airplane Competition was a trade promotion for *Scientific American* magazine that garnered thirty-five pounds of news clippings. When Gossage made conventional advertising, wicked parody was a more likely route than "reason-why" argumentation. He took David Ogilvy's revered automobile ad—"At sixty miles an hour the loudest noise in this new Rolls-Royce comes from the electric clock"—and inverted it. "At sixty miles an hour," read Gossage's ad, mimicking Ogilvy's in look as well as tone, "the loudest noise in this new Land Rover comes from the roar of the engine."

"The buying of time or space is not the taking out of a hunting license on someone else's private preserve but is the renting of a stage on which we may perform," Gossage said of his methods. That philosophy, at first hearing, sounded like a bolder restatement of Bernbach's: that "good taste, good art and good writing can be good selling." Yet it was strikingly, and stridently, different, as distinct from the theories of advertising's eastern savants as the San Francisco firehouse was from the starched, skyscraping offices of Madison Avenue. The Creative Revolutionaries who followed Bernbach, the sons and daughters of Italian and Jewish immigrants, wanted to change advertising, to be sure, but they wanted as well to be accepted by it. Howard Gossage, of English stock, born in Chicago and raised in Queens, Denver, New Orleans and Kansas City, cared nothing for acceptance or assimilation. He was a native American radical, and his goal was subversion. "Our first duty is not to the old sales curve," he said, "it is to the audience." And he wanted that audience to understand that consumerism and capitalism, the forces that supported him, were corrosive.

At every turn, Gossage strived to topple the industry that sustained him. Legend has it that in the late 1950s he rejected an audition for the Volkswagen account. "I've been driving your car for years, and it's a great little product. I don't think you *need* any advertising," Gossage counseled the Germans, who took their account, and the fame and fortune it conferred, to Doyle Dane Bernbach. In 1965, Gossage and a partner invested $6,000 to bring Marshall McLuhan, then an obscure Canadian scholar, to the United States. To magazine publishers and advertising agency executives, the mild-mannered McLuhan delivered his doomsday thesis: Everything they were doing was for naught, their industries were slated for destruction, "the medium," not what was artificially crowded into it, was "the message." Gossage, a monocle in his eye, his wavy, gray hair swept back in the style of a Prussian aristocrat, stood backstage and howled at the destructive fears his charge instilled.

"People wouldn't be any dirtier if soap advertising were stopped," Gossage believed. "And people would still be able to handle their headaches, upset stomachs, or symptoms of neuralgia just as well if all the aspirin derivatives and compounds were to quit advertising."

In July 1969, at the age of fifty-one, Howard Gossage succumbed to leukemia. Whatever influence the "madman impresario," as Tom Wolfe called him, might have had over his industry seemed to die with him. The Creative Revolution was in full flower in New York and nothing else, least of all a singular, subversive San Francisco copywriter, seemed to matter. To the New York rebels, there was no real advertising west of the Hudson, let alone west of Laramie.

"It's not advertising the way I know it," Jerry Della Femina said of the work done beyond New York's borders. "There's no creativity in Cleveland"—his epithet for everywhere else—"very little originality. . . . They live vicariously and get their glamour from New York."

Della Femina and his eastern colleagues were not blind, merely myopic. Something was going on out West that they could not see. By 1990, by which time New York agencies' share of total domestic advertising spending had dropped some 28 percent over a three-decade period, the trend was becoming clear: Advertising was moving off Madison Avenue. Not just a few blocks or even a county or two beyond the street, but to small burgs like Richmond, Virginia, and frozen midwestern outposts like Minneapolis.

Over time, New York ceased to be the cultural capital of the American agency business. Following Gossage's spiritual lead, advertising's westerners continued the Creative Revolution, long after it flickered out in New York, and in a far more virulent, far less tradition-bound manner. If Bernbach and his children nudged agencies away from marketing and into the entertainment industry, the westerners tried to sever the mercenary tether altogether and affirm that advertising had nothing whatsoever to do with marketing.

Their advertising was hype, events, news, fun—a carnival!

Advertising was Disneyland!

Advertising was Hollywood!

Advertising was art!

Advertising was Wieden & Kennedy.

IT STARTED WITH BILL CAIN, an arrogant Californian with a white beard, a barrel chest and a hip-pocket account. He had begun his advertising career in 1952 in San Francisco, where he quickly fell under the thrall of Howard Gossage, who was writing copy at an agency Cain joined as a junior creative. Gossage's message to the young copywriter was succinct: Clients don't matter.

Bill, I write advertising for the presidents of other advertising agencies, Gossage, who had just returned from a sabbatical in Paris and fancied a porkpie hat in those days, told Cain. *If it benefits the agency I work for, so much the better, but that's not the primary purpose. And if it helps the client, that just happens to be good luck for the client.*

For a quarter-century, as he rose through the ranks of small San Francisco agencies, Cain carried Gossage's words with him. Success in advertising depended not on expertise in consumer manipulation, but on media manipulation. It required self-promotion, daring, a flair for hype and, equally important, a venue. A place where people would listen. A quiet depot, not so jaded that it couldn't be shaken up.

L.P. gave him his shot. L.P., Louisiana Pacific, was a timber-products company, spun off by the giant Georgia-Pacific Corp. to avoid federal antitrust action. Cain did advertising out of San Francisco for a small L.P. subsidiary, and in 1979, as he was turning fifty, he heard through his contacts that the parent company was not happy with its current ad agency, giant McCann-Erickson. At a sales conference, Cain gained an audience with Harry Merlow, the mercurial head of L.P., and discovered that Merlow was a connoisseur of wines from northern California, where, as it turned out, Cain was part-owner of a vineyard.

Merlow offered Cain the L.P. account. Cain agreed, on the condition that the wood-products company accept his unusual terms. He handed Merlow a slip of paper. "We refuse to turn out crap," it read. He gave Merlow another piece of paper and asked the executive to pass it back to Cain if he agreed with its clause. "We will take no shit," it read.

Merlow slid the sheet back. And Cain prepared to set up shop—a new agency—in L.P.'s headquarters town, Portland, Oregon.

That a strange, revolutionary creative spark would ignite a fire in San Francisco or Los Angeles or even Seattle was not surprising. Los Angeles was America's tabula rasa, open to all who would cultivate the new. San Francisco was a fabled hotbed of radicalism. Even Seattle, founded by the same open-minded Scandinavians who united farmers, unionists and Democrats in Minnesota, was tolerant of foreign ideas and progressive politics. But Portland was another matter entirely.

Oregon didn't want to know you. Its founders arrived from New England and came from the same repressive Puritan stock that had burned witches and branded adulterers. The first building erected after the settlers formed the Portland city government in 1851 was the jail. New ideas, new people, new methods were not appreciated.

"There was in the character of the people . . . a preference for isolation," a local historian has written. "Oregonians liked the independence which isolation gave, and they still do. Here was a quality that was never to quite disappear, this feeling of isolation and specialness."

The individualism and isolationism of Oregon and its largest city manifested themselves in contradictory ways during Portland's first hundred years. In the nineteenth century, the citizens voted to exclude blacks from the state, and Chinese residents were driven from Portland by angry mobs. At the dawn of the twentieth century, the "Rose City," as it fancied itself, was the West Coast's center of Ku Klux Klan activity.

Yet the green, hilly city and its pastoral environs also provided refuge for radical intellectuals who craved respite from urbanity and its special brand of conformism. An apocryphal story has it that the north-south fork in the Oregon Trail was marked by two signs: the road to California was indicated by an arrow and a drawing of gold quartz; on the sign pointing north, however, was written: "To Oregon." Come the literate did. They started progressive political journals early in the twentieth century. They founded Reed College, whose radical overseers banned sports and fraternities as inimical to scholarship. They made Oregon among the first states to institute laws by initiative and referendum and allow citizen recall of elected officials. Later, Beat poets and experimental artists made the city their home. Portland grew into a counter to the counterculture of San Francisco.

Wherever they sat on the political spectrum, though, Oregonians, and Portlanders in particular, wanted to be left alone. The cultural impact on the city's economy and business community was acute. By the 1890s, four local families controlled twenty-one corporations and partly owned eighteen others, including most of the banks and insurance companies. Few national corporations were able to gain a toehold in Portland, and few Portland companies—with the exception of Jantzen, the swimwear company, and a timber company or two—tried to seek national (let alone international) markets. Whether in wood products, chemicals, food products or metals, Portland businesses thought local and acted local. "The business side was never very big and the thinking never got very big," said Dick Paetzke, an advertising executive who spent his career in the Pacific Northwest.

Whether the look and tone of advertising is influenced by an agency's locale has been debated within the ad industry for decades. But it is undeniable that the organization and interests of a local advertising community are defined by the provincial business culture. In Portland, the ad industry was as narrow in its concerns as the clients it served. By national standards, all the agencies were small. They were little interested in the doings or opinions of their peers in New York, Chicago or California. Few national ad agencies attempted to establish branch offices in Portland. The city's agencies produced little national print advertising and no national television ads.

Well into the sixties, Portland specialized in old-school, relationship-securing, boring advertising. "This New England conservatism, from a business standpoint, was very leery—client-wise, budget-wise—of reaching beyond accepted norms in the development of an advertising product," said Wes Perrin, a longtime Portland agency executive.

Inevitably, however, the restless, antitraditionalist side of Portland's character was bound to assert itself in the agency business. The inspiration was the Creative Revolution, whose woolly advertising made its way to the eyes of young art directors and copywriters via the annual awards publications—the books and magazines in which were collected the honored advertisements of estimable creative organizations. *Look what George Lois is doing in New York!* youthful designers laughed, internally anguishing as they laid out yet another dull trade ad for a paper mill. *Look at Mary Wells!* Silently, they grumbled: *Why can't we do that?*

The catalyst for the change in Portland came from Seattle. Just two hours to the north, Seattle was a continent away in spirit—culturally gregarious, international in outlook, home to numerous large corporations. In the early 1970s, a small ad agency called Cole & Weber (which had been founded in Portland but rapidly found Seattle more remunerative and moved its headquarters there) managed to persuade several of these clients that, if they were to compete nationally, their advertising had to be nationally noteworthy. On behalf of the Boeing Corporation, the agency demonstrated the spaciousness of the new 747 airliner by filming two commercials, one featuring the Harlem Globetrotters basketball team running a drill inside the plane, the other depicting the Seattle Symphony Orchestra playing inside it. The spots were worthy of anything coming from New York, and they attracted new clients.

When two of the only nationally known companies in Portland, Jantzen and White Stag, the skiwear maker, spurned local agencies and sent their accounts out of town, Cole & Weber's leaders thought the time had arrived to export the Creative Revolution from Seattle south, to see if they couldn't work the same magic there. They dispatched to Cole & Weber's languishing Portland office a young creative director named John Brown.

Brown was unlike anyone the Portland ad community had ever seen.

Until his arrival, the Roseys, the local awards given by the Portland Advertising Federation, were a sleepy, backscratching affair. Brown went after them with a vengeance, winning Roseys for the agency's U.S. Bank campaign and its regional work for Porsche-Audi-Volkswagen dealers, knowing that a shelf full of medals would attract good creatives up from California, maybe from back East, who might lure in big clients. His philosophy, which he hammered into his young creatives, was: *You should position yourself in terms of trying to represent the customers' interest, rather than the client. The customer wants to get something out of this message, entertainment or emotion, something he or she can embrace.*

This, truly, was novel. "Until that point in time," recalled Wes Perrin, who was an account man at the agency, "what I really tried to do was find out what the client wanted and tried to deliver it."

But Portland's flirtation with the Creative Revolution was brief. Brown burned out on disputes with his absentee bosses and the difficulties of working in a tiny-minded town, and moved back to Seattle. Cole & Weber sold itself to Ogilvy & Mather. Perrin and two creatives started their own agency, Borders, Perrin & Norrander, to plow the creative fields Cole & Weber had fertilized, but detached, recalcitrant Portland was rocky acreage. With Georgia-Pacific making rumblings about moving its headquarters to Atlanta, and McCann-Erickson, the agency for both Georgia-Pacific and its Louisiana Pacific spinoff, and the only national agency with a branch in Portland, suggesting that it might close up shop and follow, Rose City advertising, after a brief bloom, looked to be wilting again.

Then Bill Cain arrived. His landing was anything but quiet. Even before he had set up an office, word was seeping through the Portland agency business that Cain intended to shake things up. His favorite means of communication was not the telephone or the telegraph but what ad people call the "tele-rep"—magazine, newspaper, radio- and television-station advertising sales representatives who traveled throughout the Pacific Northwest and northern California, servicing accounts, schmoozing new ones, picking up, dispensing and trading on gossip.

Cain played them, and Portland's nervous agency doyens, like cellos. *I'll show these bumpkins how advertising is done!* was the word that filtered through the reps from Cain to Portland. When he finally showed up, Cain sought out the business reporters of the local newspapers and, like his mentor Howard Gossage, handed them hot copy. He called Portland a "provincial town" and reaffirmed his refusal "to turn out crap," like the other agencies did. With his big white beard and shock of white hair, he looked to the staid Portlanders like Santa Claus, but in temperament reminded Mark Silveira, a small-agency art director, of Melville's Captain Ahab: "Swashbuckling. Bigger than life. Loud, hard laughing. Stir up the pot. A crazy man."

Behind the lunacy lay inspiration. Cain wanted to rattle the trees of Portland advertising until a few good creatives fell from the upper branches. "I wanted the very best people I could get for my agency," Cain recalled. "So what I did was go out and pillage." Which was how Bill Cain found Dan Wieden and David Kennedy.

Wieden was an unlikely creative star. His father, Duke, was one of the grand old men of Portland advertising. Tall, prematurely bald, hand always extended, with an ever-present smile that turned appealingly up one side of his face, Duke Wieden was the consummate account man. A onetime celebrity in the local amateur volleyball scene, he had parlayed his winning personality into the chairmanship of Gerber Advertising, the biggest, grayest, dullest agency in Portland. About the only thing provocative anyone ever had to say about Gerber was that its founder, Joe Gerber, once had an affair with the Jantzen girl—the swimsuited diver whose profile graced the company's logo. But that was only a rumor.

Dan was born on the cusp of the baby boom, in 1945. He was as rebellious as his father was establishment. An angular, perpetually energetic kid with a seemingly limitless capacity for wonderment, he cringed at the sight of his father glad-handing and knee-bending his way through business. Dan wanted to be a writer, but not like the writers at his dad's agency. There, the "copy contact" system ruled; ads were virtually dictated by the client. If these subordinated scribes were the best minds of his generation, then they were, as Allen Ginsberg wrote, "burned alive in their innocent flannel suits on Madison Avenue amid blasts of leaden verse & the tanked-up clatter of the iron regiments of fashion." Dan would have none of it.

Advertising is a whorish business, he told his friends. *It's a shell game. An easy way to make a living.* Especially after Duke, the Portland Advertising Federation's 1970 Advertising Man of the Year, decided to leave the agency business to go to work for a utility company, Dan knew he wanted something more—more pure, more honest.

He lived at the beach. He tried his hand at poetry, taking inspiration from Oregon beats like Gary Snyder. He grew a goatee. With his younger brother, Ken, he hatched schemes that drove Duke and their mother, Timmie, to distraction. *We'll bicycle 'cross country!* But, like the screenplays Dan started, nothing ever came of the plans. Married early, with several children arriving quickly, and unable to make a living as a writer any other way, he began writing verbose copy for local wood-products companies and scripting industrial films. At one particularly low point, he wrote headlines and body text for a series of toilet paper ads. He explained it away: *You've got to treat it like science fiction. You've got to suspend disbelief to survive it.*

Eventually, he landed at Georgia-Pacific and in 1978, when the company decided it did not require a writer on staff, at its advertising agency, McCann-Erickson. There, he was teamed with an art director five years his senior, a fellow as subdued as Dan was animated. His name was David Kennedy.

Like Dan, David originally had no plans to go into advertising. The son and grandson of itinerant western oil wildcatters, he intended to be a geologist. Everything he needed to know about ad agencies he learned as a teenager, from the wicked satires of Will Elder, Harvey Kurtzman and their disciples in E.C. Comics and *Mad* magazine.

The Mad *Madison Avenue Primer*
Lesson I

> *See the man.*
> *He does advertising work.*
> *He is called an "ad-man."*
> *See his funny tight suit.*
> *See his funny haircut.*
> *Hear his funny stomach churn.*
> *Churn, churn, churn.*
> *The ad-man has a funny ulcer.*
> *Most ad-men have funny ulcers.*
> *But, then, some ad-men are lucky.*
> *They do not have funny ulcers.*
> *They have funny high blood pressure.*

But geology classes at the University of Colorado paled against the fine-art tutorials. And, what with the difficulties finding a job sculpting, marriage to a flight attendant, a move to Chicago and a quick child (the first of five), advertising beckoned as the only way to exercise his artistry *and* finance a family.

David toiled away for a few years as an underling in large Chicago agencies, waiting for his shot at art directing. As in so many other areas, Chicago in the sixties was the Second City of advertising. The industry there was large and proud, built on the backs of the great American graineries and industrial corporations. Although David learned from some New York expatriates the secret of the Creative Revolution—*It's not just what you say, but how you say it*—the flour and meat accounts he worked on gave him, and others, little chance to perform.

Just how sodden the city was became apparent when David landed at Leo Burnett, Chicago's grandest agency. Founded in 1935 by a potato-faced Michigan native, by the 1960s Burnett was the home of what it pronounced a "Chicago school" of advertising. The agency trafficked in midwestern verities—home, hearth, happiness—and embodied the powers of its clients' products in mythical figures of heroic proportions. The Jolly Green Giant, Kellogg's Tony the Tiger, the Pillsbury Dough-boy, the Marlboro Man, were all Burnett creations. "Leo's critters," the industry called them.

Leo, the man and the agency, disdained the efforts of individual cre-atives. Every advertisement was run through the Plans Board, an inqui-sition that beheaded headlines, disemboweled body copy and slaughtered layouts. All ads were pretested before they were released by the Burke method, which purported to judge advertising effective-ness by measuring consumers' recall of ads. A woman in David's crea-tive group who worked on the Pillsbury account surreptitiously provided newcomers with mimeographed copies of her carefully com-piled "Ten Ways to Beat Burke." Babies and animals—and cartoon crit-ters, of course—were high on the list.

David's introduction to the Burnett way was inauspicious. On his first day at the agency, he was led to a tiny cubicle, its walls just two feet short of the ceiling, in an isolated warren on the twenty-first floor of the Prudential Building. The space was shared by his creative group and by recently fired account executives who were allowed to use the tele-phones to try to find new jobs. David was filling out insurance forms. In the next cubicle, he heard a man in the midst of an emotional break-down.

Man! I can't stand it! I can't draw one more frame of this fucking fag-got in this white suit! the fellow sobbed.

Get hold of yourself, his partner implored in a firm voice. *We'll get through this board. They're not gonna buy this shit anyway. We'll go work on something else. We'll do some award-winning work on Pillsbury. We'll get some other assignment. We'll just get this shit out of the way.* The crying subsided. The staunch-voiced man settled in to work. *Okay, man, now let's see this dude come in on rocket shoes—* The crying man screamed and ran from the office.

In a few moments, David's boss fetched him and introduced him to the copywriter in the next office. *David, we have a problem. We have a very important assignment for the Man from Glad, and we need an art director to take over the project....*

Life in Chicago advertising never really improved after that. An outwardly laconic man, David seethed inwardly over artistic slights and the pettiness of agency politics. Although he found some respite working with a few of the politically charged creative boutiques that opened with the Creative Revolution, hung out with a contingent of radical Irish admen and helped produce the first six months of the black television program "Soul Train," David had no respect, let alone love, for what he did. "It was advertising," he recalled. "I still hated advertising." He hated Chicago, too—its urban corruption and comfortable suburban amorality. When a friend of his daughter's, in their affluent Highland Park neighborhood, received for her sixteenth birthday a Mercedes-Benz, David started looking West for work, and found it at McCann-Erickson in Portland. There, he was teamed on the Georgia-Pacific account with Dan Wieden.

In the vast McCann-Erickson empire, they were nobodies. In New York and its far-flung outposts around the world, McCann had taught the world to sing for Coca-Cola. It had changed the name of Esso to Exxon. It had asked the nation, "Wouldn't you really rather have a Buick?" Wieden and Kennedy were a two-bit creative team working from one of McCann's smallest offices on an account that was thinking of leaving town anyway. They had little impact. "I don't think anybody in the company knew they existed," said Dick Paetzke, a McCann creative director at the time.

Nor was there much to do for Georgia-Pacific. Although they spun out concept after concept, only a handful of their advertisements—all of them print, since Dan had never written television spots—were ever produced. They filled their time (always during working hours, never, because they both had large families, after) with each other. Dan, a font of ideas, a Beat poet whose coffeehouse was now advertising, needed professional discipline, and he got it from David, whose mind and cluttered office were an advertising archive. David kept what was, to outsiders, an incomprehensibly organized collection of every advertisement he had ever appreciated, every typeface he had ever loved, every cartoon and photograph he had ever wished to use. When Dan (or any other creative) spouted an idea he deemed decent, David grunted a happy, *Ooooh, ooooh*, rummaged around his library and emerged with either an antecedent or further inspiration.

And Dan, with his wide-eyed naïveté (*fresh meat*, David considered him), provided his older partner with something professionally priceless. He taught David that advertising could still be fun.

But not fun enough—not for Dan and not at McCann, a colorless Rotary Club of an agency which reminded him of his father's former shop. In 1980, when a blustery newcomer named Bill Cain came calling, having stolen the Louisiana Pacific account from McCann, it was Dan's second nature to jump ship, and to persuade his more settled partner to leap overboard with him.

These were heady, cramped days at the William Cain agency. Cain leased some space in the Crown Zellerbach Building from a timber broker that had gone belly up. Eager to make his mark in his adopted city, Cain plunged the eight staffers he eventually hired into work for L.P. and a search for new clients. There was little by way of equipment. David rigged up an ersatz "Lucy"—a device that throws traceable projections onto blank paper—by staring through a piece of plastic and tracing what he saw on drafting paper taped to a countertop.

The agency's very first campaign for the flagship client made a splash—at least, in the rather small universe of Portlanders who concerned themselves with advertising for wood-products companies. The ads consisted of tight photos of stern men whom the copy represented as building contractors, buyers and wood users, and was further illustrated with a series of confrontational "show me what you've got" quotations. In a category that was accustomed to pictures of smiling, thankful robots, "it was not like anything done," said Mark Silveira.

The campaign served its purpose. It validated Cain's boast that he wouldn't *turn out crap*. It made L.P. happy. And it attracted the notice of other advertisers, including a conspicuously expansive local athletic shoe company, Nike Inc. Peter Moore, a Portland graphic designer who was serving on contract as Nike's design director, had been the creative director of Georgia Pacific when Dan Wieden was writing toilet paper ads there. He liked the look of what Dan and David Kennedy were producing at Cain. More importantly, from his conversations with them, he discovered that "we had some mutual goals and mutual ideas about how things could or should be done."

It was a small account, maybe only $300,000 in billings a year. *It'll grow*, Moore promised. Cain didn't worry. He intended to let Dan and David busy themselves with Nike while he attended to Lousiana Pacific.

THE SPORT OF RUNNING fit perfectly with the character of Portland, Oregon: in this most insular of territories arose the most personal and isolating of activities.

Nike, however, was an anomaly in Portland. In keeping with the city's character, it was standoffish. ("I consider them a Eugene company, not a Portland company," said a local historian, E. Kimbark MacColl.) But in a break with area convention, Nike thought big—very big.

The company was founded in 1964 by Phil Knight, a Stanford M.B.A. and former track star at the University of Oregon in Eugene, and Bill Bowerman, who had been his coach. Like Subaru of America, Nike, then called Blue Ribbon Sports, started with only an exclusive contract to import a product, Tiger track shoes, from Japan. Knight and Bowerman believed that American sneaker companies were ignoring the very specific needs of runners in favor of serving more general consumer markets. They carried that message, with suitcases full of Tigers, to track meets, where they sold the shoes from their cars. Eventually, they tired of the vagaries of the import business; what's more, the foreign shoes they were buying were little better than the American shoes they were denigrating. If runners were to get the arch support, cushioning and grip they needed, Nike (the company officially changed its name in 1978, taking it from the Greek goddess of victory) would have to design its own. In the early 1970s, the company began contracting the manufacture of its own shoes to factories overseas, and developed a reputation for technological innovation that made it a connoisseur's favorite.

Nike was in the right place at the right time. The company's focus on running matched the nation's rising interest in health and jogging. By the late 1970s, almost half of all Americans said they had tried running; a magazine devoted solely to it, *Runner's World*, claimed a circulation of 400,000. Between 1970 and 1977, the number of contestants in the New York City Marathon increased more than thirtyfold, from 156 to 5,000; 3 million more people lined the course to watch them pass. During these years, Nike's sales were doubling annually.

Like the Ford Motor Company under the first Henry Ford, Nike saw no distinction between its manufacturing processes and its marketing. Its shoes were designed, made and sold for one purpose: to make athletes perform better. The company's means of achieving this goal was to improve continually the technology of its shoes, whether through the use of novel materials, new sole design or different support structures. And the way to communicate the product's virtues was to talk directly to the athletes—not to the retailers, and certainly not to financiers—in the athletes' own language, just as the company's founders had done a decade earlier when they hustled shoes at track meets. "We thought the world stopped and started in the lab and everything revolved around the product," Phil Knight, the chairman and chief executive, recalled.

Nike's interest in a corporate image distinct from its product promotions came about purely by accident. In 1977, the bulk of the company's meager advertising budget went into a single, monthly advertisement on the back cover of *Runner's World*. For one of the fall issues, Nike had planned an advertisement showcasing, as usual, some new shoes. When, at the last minute, the availability of the product was thrown into doubt, the company needed a substitute ad. It resurrected one its marketing director had earlier discarded. Under a picture of a lone runner loping down a country road that cut through a forest of soaring pines, the headline read: "There is no finish line." The spare body copy explained the meaning: "Beating the competition is relatively easy. Beating yourself is a never-ending commitment."

The advertisement was written by John Brown, the copywriter who had ignited Portland's little creative insurrection years earlier, then fled to Seattle to form his own agency. Brown had no natural athletic affinity. But he and his art director, Denny Strickland, had spent enough time around the Nike executives to absorb the culture of running. Runners, as represented by Nike's leaders, saw themselves as alone, other, empowered, *better*. "There is no finish line" was written and designed to reify this sense of specialness. When *Runner's World* readers started writing in for copies of the ad to tack on their dormitory and locker-room walls, Nike realized it had touched something deep inside its constituency. From that point forward, the athletic-shoe company put image at the heart of its communication.

At about the same time, the advertising agency, with the guidance of Nike's marketing managers, developed what the company came to call its "personality posters"—advertisements that featured well-known athletes, Nike endorsers, in fanciful poses which, in some unexpected way, captured elements of the endorser's character. One of the first depicted George Gervin, the National Basketball Association scoring champion, whose nickname was "Iceman," perched on a throne sculpted from ice.

Peter Moore, the design consultant, and Rob Strasser, Nike's marketing director, realized that the personality posters lifted Nike's image to another level. All athletes, they believed, not just runners, were imbued with a sense of individuality, of specialness. The "There is no finish line" advertisement had portrayed this sensibility by using an anonymous runner as a consumer surrogate, as Everyrunner. The personality posters, they understood, caught the same mood, but communicated it to a larger audience (gauged by the number of reprint requests they received) by using celebrity athletes as its embodiment.

Moore, especially, saw the personality posters and the aspirational attraction of the athlete-as-other as the two keys necessary to unlock larger markets for Nike. He enjoyed using the tools of graphic design as a psychoanalyst's couch, employing a prop or photographic trick to pull a single, captivating element of an endorser's personality into an ad. He inveighed upon Phil Knight and Rob Strasser to strengthen the advertising to support the company's newly coalescing image. *There are really two halves to the puzzle,* he told them. *You have advertising, but you better have something in back of that advertising that controls the rest of how the image is portrayed, that either adds to it or substantiates it in some way.*

The Nike executives agreed, and in 1980 they gave Moore complete control over the content of the shoe company's communications. Moore, in turn, fired John Brown & Partners—he wanted his creatives in the neighborhood, not on call from Seattle—and hired the William Cain agency and its insouciant creative team of Wieden and Kennedy.

Dan and David's work for Nike initially built on the foundation laid by John Brown and Denny Strickland. That pattern, cultivating and refining intellectual and strategic advances made by others, would remain a hallmark of the team and its agencies for years to come. In their earliest efforts for Nike, the men took the irreverence of the personality posters and applied it to advertising for specific products, linking the image campaign and the product campaigns and communicating product specifications in a witty, light fashion.

Unlike many creatives-turned-agency heads, Bill Cain interfered little with his creative staff's work. He did not second-guess them, did not rewrite copy, did not pretend to be an art director. The attitude inside his agency, in regard to the rest of the Portland agency business, was cheerfully confrontational. A Cain agency promotional advertisement in the Roseys awards show program, an opportunity local shops took to publicize their corporate philosophies, said it all. "I refuse to write a house ad for William Cain Inc.," the headline read. The graphic was a broken pencil.

Nevertheless, Dan and David rapidly grew disillusioned with their new home. Money wasn't the issue; Cain told them he intended to turn over half the agency, 25 percent to Dan alone, within five years. What rankled them was his lack of appreciation for their work. Cain was hogging all the credit.

Credit is the true coin of advertising's realm. Without it, creatives cannot win the awards that gain them the recognition that boosts their value. More significantly, without credit, they cannot call themselves artists or entertainers: they are merely hacks. For Dan, especially, who justified the abandonment of his literary dreams by claiming that advertising was a noble substitute, Cain's self-aggrandizement hurt. Once, when Dan and David were out of the office, the finished version of a

Louisiana Pacific television spot they had produced arrived. Cain tucked it under his arm and ran to L.P., presenting it (unbeknownst to them, until later) as *his* creation. At another point, in one of his frequent newspaper and business journal interviews, Cain described the agency as a "box full of warm puppies." He meant it as a compliment; Dan and David, who considered themselves Dobermans, took it as an insult.

Within a year, they were determined to start their own agency . . . and to take Nike with them. Stealthily, for months, they plotted. Over a nervous lunch with Nike's advertising managers, Dan, fresh from the dentist and numbed by Novocain, mumbled the plan. Nike was so enthusiastic that the company guaranteed the incipient agency its account for a full year. That their scheming to steal business while still in Cain's employ might have opened Dan and David to lawsuits for breach of fiduciary responsibility did not enter their minds. The team enlisted the support of Jane Kirby, the agency's media specialist, and Dennis Fraser, the production manager. The financial arrangements among the four were left vague. Dennis and Jane assumed that once the creative duo left, the Cain agency would collapse, and they did not want to be left on a sinking ship. "They were the creative geniuses, but it wasn't buttoned down until we got away," Jane said years later. "There was a lot of faith."

On March 31, 1982, Dennis and Jane returned to the office after it had closed, packed their property and stored it in their cars. The next day, April Fool's Day, Dan told Cain that the four of them were leaving.

Cain blanched. With a few furious telephone calls, he quickly discovered that Nike was jumping, too. Devastated by the loss, all Cain could do was toss around and around in his head a hoary advertising adage. *My agency*, he repeated to himself, *just went down the elevator.*

Cain contemplated suing his departing staff, but decided that a lawsuit would just drain him financially; he wouldn't get his agency or his lost client back. Louisiana Pacific willingly renegotiated its contract with him, to stem the damage from the loss of Nike's revenue. As if in silent defiance of the rebellion, he maintained his shop until the late 1980s, when he sold it to Gerber, Duke Wieden's old agency, and retired as a prosperous gentleman vintner, dividing his time between Portland and northern California.

Dan and David celebrated their breakaway by commissioning a trophy for themselves and their new partners. Atop a wooden pedestal sat two metal balls, like the ones Captain Queeg massaged incessantly in the Herman Wouk novel. The plaque underneath read: "The Cain Mutiny, April 1, 1982."

Some of the more junior members in Nike's marketing department were aghast. However creative Dan and David may have been, their managerial abilities were . . . questionable. These fellows were long-haired, bearded flower children. *How are these two guys going to start an agency?* several of the client company's young executives wondered.

The answer, thanks to Nike, was: without pain. As a housewarming gift, marketing department personnel pilfered staplers, tape and other office notions from their supply cabinet, and brought them down to the headquarters of the new agency—it was named Wieden & Kennedy, of course—on the first floor of the Grantree Rental Furniture Building. Dan and David had each anted up a bit of cash to get the operation going, but money was coming in from the start from Nike and from Automatic Data Processing, another Cain client that leaped to the new shop.

Time was their only constraint. The partners—Jane Kirby moved to Seattle soon after the startup; her stake was taken by Cindy Taylor, the office manager and the first new person hired—were too busy to go out to buy furniture. For weeks Dennis's card table from home was their reception-area furniture. The telephone, when it was finally installed, rested on an upside-down apple crate; until then, the pay phone outside the delicatessen at the other end of the hall was their only link to clients. Financially conservative, Dan, the ever-moving spiritual force behind the operation, kept them in the tiny space for a year and a half before moving to larger quarters. *Next year, if we do really well,* he confided to Cindy when she signed on, *we can double this agency to ten people!*

Their early work for Nike was virtually all print; the shoe company, which sold $458 million worth of sneakers the year before Wieden & Kennedy took control of its advertising, was leery of television's cost and doubtful of its impact. Nonetheless, the tyro agency soon began adopting the lingo and affectations of larger shops. The ad people stopped talking about meetings, asking instead to make "presentations." At some point, the word "payoff"—meaning the climax or resolution of an advertisement—crept into Dan's vocabulary. The antics reminded some Nike executives of children playing dress-up.

Not that Nike didn't respect Wieden & Kennedy. To the contrary, the company soon came to depend on the agency, Dan especially, for strategic insights and long-term planning. Nike's revenues had increased by a factor of sixteen in the half-decade before Wieden & Kennedy was awarded the account. Now, as valuable members of the company's inner circle, Dan, David and their colleagues believed they would share in its inevitably glowing future—until Nike ran into an army of hopping, skipping and jumping women, all wearing Reebok shoes.

Reebok was Nike's opposite. Where Nike was focused, Reebok was inspirational; where Nike's chief executive, Phil Knight, was educated, directed and disciplined, Reebok's leader, Paul Fireman, a college dropout and onetime fishing-tackle salesman, was mercurial. Fireman managed to quintuple Reebok's running-shoe sales, to $1.5 million, between 1980 and 1981, but fighting against Nike for the feet of runners was a tough business. So in 1981, based purely on observation and hunch, he engineered a change in the company's direction. Fireman was intrigued by aerobics, a heart-pumping exercise fad increasingly popular with young women. He decided to make and sell shoes for that market.

The shoes were the kind that Nike's fanatic runners despised. Reeboks were too narrow for the pounding that runners gave their feet; they were made of soft leather, which was apt to fall apart after a few good beatings on long-distance courses; they were white, which showed the dirt.

But the white footwear was appealing to women who wanted goodlooking shoes not only to exercise in but to walk to work in; the soft leather felt like a slipper; and the narrowness flattered women's feet in ways fat running shoes never could. Reebok's sales curve told the story: from $3.5 million in 1982 to $13 million a year later, virtually without advertising. As the overall American market for branded athletic footwear grew—from $1.8 billion in sales in 1983 to $2.6 billion in 1986—Reebok took the lead, very much at Nike's expense. Reebok's sales nearly quintupled in 1984, to $64 million, and almost quintupled again the next year, to $300 million, then soared again, to $841 million in 1986. Nike's decline was less spectacular, but equivalently steady: from $636 million in 1983, to $625 million in 1985, a year in which the company spent two quarters in the red and saw its profits plummet by 80 percent. In 1986, the company's sales fell to $536 million.

Missing the aerobics boom was only a manifestation of Nike's larger problem. A company built by jocks for jocks, where top executives called their no-holds-barred, locker-room-loud management meetings "Buttfaces," Nike had no understanding of or affinity for women. And women were the primary purchasers of shoes in the United States.

The company also failed to understand one of the more compelling explanations for its own, earlier success. It believed its growth was based on its appeal to athletes. It ignored the fact that sales of athletic shoes in the United States closely tracked cultural trends. The running boom, which was, after all, not a permanent change in the American character but a temporary fad exploited by the media, was the real source of Nike's expansion. Instead of hunting for the next sports-as-culture trend, Nike allowed Reebok to find and market it.

Athletic-shoe sales, in a word, were a function of fashion—a term Nike did not appreciate or understand. "If you said the word 'fashion' in a Nike meeting," said Peter Moore, the company's design director, "you were a really bad guy. You didn't know what you were talking about."

As Nike's sales fell, its top executives agonized over the reasons, and finally came to an understanding. Reebok had defined itself not by technology or by markets, but in terms of a transcendent image; Nike had merely grafted an image onto its existing rigid orientation around its products and runners. The company forced itself to address a question it had never before asked: *What does our brand stand for?* The answer was uncomfortable: *We are a technology company. But technology is fashion. So we are a fashion company.* In order to appeal to the broadest possible market, Nike would have to talk about or present the technology built into its shoes as something fresh. While that novelty presumably made the shoes better devices for athletic performance, it was not the reason the sneakers lured customers: People were attracted to novelty, the company now reasoned, by the novelty *itself*. Thus, advertising, which from its earliest appearance in modern societies was a means of communicating something new, rose in importance to Nike. Indeed, it became central to Nike's redefinition of its mission.

"For years we thought of ourselves as a production-oriented company, meaning we put all our emphasis on designing and manufacturing the product," Phil Knight said, long after the crisis had passed. "But now we understand that the most important thing we do is market the product. We've come around to saying that Nike is a marketing-oriented company, and the product is our most important marketing tool."

But a tool for what? What was Nike *really* marketing if not athletic shoes? The answer was staring the company in the face, embedded in Moore's personality posters. It was selling heroes.

Rob Strasser, the company's marketing director, was the first to advance this odd hypothesis, in a memo explaining the meaning of the posters. "Individual athletes, even more than teams, will be the heroes; symbols more and more of what real people can't do anymore—risk and win," he wrote in 1983. In the middle of its downward spiral, Nike realized that sports heroes, far from being a mere public relations gimmick, might be the very vehicle to drag the company back to health.

These heroes were portrayed in ways that exalted their individualism, however uncomfortable that might be to mainstream America. The false humility with which athletes in older advertisements were imbued, the aw-shucks-I'm-just-like-you attitude they affected, was banished from Nike's posters and ads. John McEnroe, the bad-boy tennis star from Queens, New York, was photographed on New York's 59th Street Bridge, dressed sullenly in black leather à la James Dean. Philadelphia Phillies strikeout king Steve Carlton was shot with a literally blazing baseball in his hand. Moses Malone of basketball's Houston Rockets was depicted in flowing robes reminiscent of his biblical namesake. By individualizing its endorsers, in every element of the company's communications, Nike meant to apotheosize them and implicitly identify itself, their home, as the Olympus of America's 1980s-celebrity-worshipping-hero-adoring consumer culture.

The personality posters were central to Nike's great marketing breakthrough. It was no longer marketing its product—shoes—as heroes. It was selling heroes as its product. The purchase of athletic shoes served the consumer like the communion ritual, as transubstantiation. In buying a pair of Nikes, a man or woman was literally consuming part of a hero, and taking on elements of his (or, later, her) character.

Nike rearranged its business around this transforming idea, signing on as spokesmen, endorsers and contract demigods some of American sports' most individualistic stars, *then* developing product lines around the quirks in their personalities. After the company affiliated with David Robinson and Charles Barkley, two NBA stars whose style of play was aggressive and muscular, it set about developing shoes suited to their tough confrontational tactics. It dubbed the products the "Force" line. When Scottie Pippen, a basketball player who favored quick moves and high-flying passes and dunks, came onboard, Nike developed a more flexible, lighter-weight line of shoes called "Flight."

Selling heroes as products—now *this* was a Big Idea. Obviously, it needed to be communicated to consumers in a big way, by a big-thinking advertising agency with big-time credentials capable of turning out big, hip broadcast advertising—advertising that Nike intended to tie in to the 1984 Summer Olympic Games in Los Angeles, the biggest athletic event in America since . . . since . . . ever!

Unfortunately, Wieden & Kennedy was not that agency. To Nike, in the throes of its life-sustaining redefinition, Wieden & Kennedy was the proverbial underappreciated girl next door. It had done almost no television advertising; its work was stylish but far from "hip," whatever that meant in the frenzied but unfocused minds of Nike executives. "There was the feeling that we were in Beaverton, and they were in Portland," said Cindy Hale, a young exec in the company's advertising department, "and what did any of *us* know about the real world?" The shoe company decided to throw its advertising account into review.

Wieden & Kennedy was invited to participate. But the review included the heavyweights of West Coast advertising. Ogilvy & Mather's San Francisco office, run by the legendary Hal Riney, a gravel-voiced adman who liked to narrate his own spots ("It's perfect.... It's Perrier"), competed. Also asked was the Los Angeles office of Needham, Harper & Steers (which dropped out of the review before its conclusion). The final contestant was Chiat/Day, the irreverent Los Angeles shop that specialized in ballsy advertising for clients like Yamaha motorcycles and Apple, a young company that made desktop computers.

Nike gave all the agencies the same direction, which was less a strategy than a goal attached to a compendium of techniques. It wanted to be considered a hip company. It wanted the campaign to showcase a handful of the athletes in its stable, including John McEnroe and the track-and-field star Carl Lewis. It wanted to concentrate the campaign on the handful of cities it believed were the impetus behind cultural trends in the U.S. And it wanted to center the campaign on Los Angeles, the nation's trend center as well as the home of the forthcoming Olympic Games. All the agencies were provided copies of the music video of the Randy Newman song "I Love L.A.," which Nike wanted included in the campaign in some way. Heroes were the product, hipness was the message and Los Angeles was the medium.

Wieden & Kennedy tried gamely to prove its hipness against the competition. It decorated its pitch room with a palm tree, and the members of its crew all wore Hawaiian shirts and sunglasses. Its ideas were novel. (The agency suggested projecting changing images on the sides of buildings, which Nike finally did a decade later.) But in the end, it couldn't compete with the creative sophistication or organizational firepower of more worldly agencies. Although it wasn't fired outright—it maintained responsibility for several million dollars' worth of ads aimed at the retail trade and the core market of runners—Wieden & Kennedy was eliminated as Nike's agency for image advertising. Nike was going national with Chiat/Day.

Chiat/Day made good on its promise. Beginning in the fall of 1983, Los Angeles itself became a cultural event, sponsored by Nike. The agency fashioned a campaign on the contradictory foundation of large-scale minimalism. It painted giant copies of stripped-down versions of Nike's personality posters on the sides of buildings in L.A. and several other cities; the shoe company's sponsorship was indicated only by a tiny Nike logo in a bottom, brick corner. Billboards were equally bold and wordless, and showed a long jumper in midflight, or a football player in fierce crouch. The launch spot, with Randy Newman "rollin' down Imperial Highway, a big nasty redhead by my side," was indistinguishable from the rock videos then beguiling youngsters on MTV. There was Randy, in his big Buick convertible. Here was McEnroe, arguing with a cop. There was the Hollywood sign. Here was the Nike logo. There was Mary Decker marathoning through the city's sunny streets. *I love L.A.!* they mouthed. The song aside, the commercial was completely copyless. Chiat/Day's innovation was to show that pure visual imagery, sans words, was valid on the page, in the environment, on the screen. The agency proved that subtext and context could substitute for text in advertising. If Nike was responsible for conceiving of the hero as a product, Chiat/Day was the agent that translated the strategy into workable executions and, indeed, a campaign.

But there were difficulties. The first was that Nike's sales in the year after the Olympics improved hardly at all. The second, and by far the more serious, was that Nike hated Chiat/Day.

At first the disturbances were small, like the verbal arrogance of the agency's creatives and their willingness to go to war to protect inaccurate punctuation of copy. Then the real differences became clear. Having worked its entire history with neighbors it considered partners, the company now confronted an agency that looked on itself, not unnaturally, as a separate and distinct entity committed to protecting its own turf, whether that benefited the client or not. Chiat/Day wanted credit for the Nike campaign, and it intended to take credit regardless of whether the shoe company gave it. The painted buildings? *Our idea!* shouted Chiat/Day. (*Hey, wait a minute . . . ,* Nike responded.) "I Love L.A."? *Ours!* screamed the agency. (*No, ours,* cried Nike.) The clincher was an advertisement placed in the *Wall Street Journal* by Guy Day, the agency's co-founder. Day told Nike of his plan to run a full-page ad touting the agency's work for the shoe company. Rob Strasser irately shot him down. *This is our brand, this is our advertising, this is not about you, this is about Nike,* he said. But Day had already booked and paid for the space, so he used it for a message to Strasser: "Rob," it read. "Peace." It was signed, "G."

It was close to the last of many slights. "We grew weary of trying to beat Chiat/Day into submission," recalled Cindy Hale, the Nike advertising executive. "We grew really weary of them using our name to leverage their name. We grew weary of being around people that we really didn't like that much."

At times like these, the little girl next door starts to look mighty attractive, especially if she has grown up.

· · ·

WIEDEN & KENNEDY had been devastated by the loss of the Nike brand-image account. What could be worse than a tiny creative boutique spurned because it wasn't hip enough or novel enough in its thinking? The agency had already moved into its new office space, but couldn't begin to fill it because Nike had pulled so much of its budget. It had even hired a new copywriter, a twenty-five-year-old perpetual student named Jim Riswold, who kept acquiring bachelor's degrees from the University of Washington. Now, with Nike mostly gone, there was barely anything in the agency to keep him busy.

For a year, the Portland agency licked its wounds, surviving but not thriving. Then, around Thanksgiving 1984, Wieden & Kennedy heard that Honda was tossing its motor-scooter account into review. It was worth a fair piece of change—$6 million in billings (although it turned out to be even larger, $12.5 million). But more than the money, the account could provide Dan and David a chance to prove their mettle, their bigness, their hipness to Nike.

Like Nike, Honda had a vague strategy: to turn its scooters into a hip form of transportation. Its Los Angeles ad agency, Dailey & Associates, had tried gamely to meet the challenge, filming MTV-style spots with the fierce black model-singer Grace Jones and the glam rocker Adam Ant. To Wieden & Kennedy, the advertising indicated a client willing to take risks to be hip, so the agency decided to meet Honda's gamble with one of its own.

Jim Riswold, the young Seattle copywriter, headed the presentation. He had not prepared a storyboard. He had not written a script. Nervously shuffling into the room, he propped a record-album cover against a wall and punched a button on a tape recorder. As a group of "colored girls" harmoniously warbled, "DOO-da-DOO-da-DOO-da-DO-DO-DO," a deadened, tuneless male voice poured forth, painting a scabrous portrait of modern urban decay: ". . . but she never lost her head / even when she was giving head. . . ." Wieden & Kennedy was recommending that Honda, a Japanese industrial giant still somewhat skittish about its acceptability to the American mainstream, hire Lou Reed, the dissipated, leather-clad godfather of punk rock, as a celebrity endorser.

What made the suggestion remarkable was not that Reed's musical corpus celebrated psychotics, drug addicts and sexual deviates. Nor was it that "Walk on the Wild Side," the number the agency was recommending to back its spot, was known as an urban gay anthem. It was more that Honda's target market, young men and women in their twenties, were, like Riswold, barely sentient infants when Lou Reed had flamed through the underground music scene in the late 1960s and early 1970s. Wieden & Kennedy, in an apparent paradox, reached back to their unremembered childhood to find its hook.

Riswold's rationale for the spot was simply, "I wanted to meet Lou Reed." Yet somewhere inside this diffident young man's crewcut head was the understanding that using a wasted 1960s outlaw to flack motor scooters in the 1980s, however horrifying a sellout it might be to his generation's older siblings—indeed, *because* it was so horrifying to them—was exactly the kind of entertainment that might engage the post–baby boomers who were just then beginning to drink, drive and vote. It was a political statement stripped of its political meaning by its transformation into a sales tool, a work of intellectual street art divested of any moral relevance. It was pure camp, the perfect advertising device (camp, as Susan Sontag noted, is "a mode of seduction") for the disengaged, amoral generation of youngsters reaching its maturity under the stewardship of President Ronald Reagan. Even better, it was a sort of postcamp, comprehensible only to Riswold's peers, yet taken seriously, or at least at face value, by his elders.

Honda loved it. The company told the agency to produce the spot.

The shoot was a fiasco. Wieden & Kennedy hired an experienced Madison Avenue director to reproduce downtown New York street scenes for the commercial. But the director, who was given little direction by the agency, accidentally underexposed much of the film. More than half the shots seemed too grainy or too dark to use. Some of the scenes had to be reshot. Costs ballooned. In the end, Wieden & Kennedy, whose sole television experience was a couple of Nike spots, dumped the footage of the rocker and the scooter on a Hollywood film editor, and fled.

The editor was Larry Bridges, who ran a postproduction company called Red Car and had achieved notoriety as the editor of the Michael Jackson music-video dance extravanganza "Beat It." At thirty-six, an aging but still-proud member of the sixties counterculture, Bridges was exactly of the generation to be put off by the sacrilegious employment of a rebel rocker to sell mass-manufactured goods. When he sat down with the footage, he recoiled. Lou Reed was a hero. "Walk on the Wild Side" was Bridges's own story. *I can't do this,* he told himself. *I can't make a commercial out of this music. I have to* honor *this music.*

Bridges, however, was also a professional, who had returned to graduate school for an M.B.A. degree to help him transform his hobby, filmmaking, into a business. He had edited other Honda spots, and was not going to turn down a job from a steady client on cultural or political grounds. Instead, he had an inspiration. He could rationalize the sellout by using the dark, grainy footage to construct an homage to the 1960s French New Wave film directors who had stimulated his interest in cinema. Flash pans, jump cuts, abrupt light changes, whip pans—an entire grab bag of film idioms—he threw into the work. His goal was to remove himself (and the spot) from the realm of advertising . . . and make the commercial a *commentary* on advertising.

"I had a sense of reverence that I couldn't shake, and it drove me into the interior of my beliefs and my values," Bridges recalled much later. "Consequently, I had to do the *metacommercial* in order to hide the fact that I was doing a commercial."

The Lou Reed advertisement drew immediate attention in New York and Hollywood. Music-video makers considered themselves underground artists and had recoiled from conventional advertising, fearing it would sully their somewhat dubious reputation for artistry. The Honda spot provided them absolution. Music videos, which usually have lower budgets than national television commercials, thus became a guilt-free entry point to the lucre of the advertising industry and, through it, to feature films. Through these young, experimental video makers, advertising in the latter half of the 1980s became a library of novel production techniques. The hand-held shaky camera, a device designed to communicate home-video verisimilitude, moved from MTV to Maxwell House. Skip-framing (the sequenced removal of frames from film footage to give it a stop-action effect) was another idiom that was translated from one medium to the other. Morphing (computer-generated transformations of people or objects into completely different forms) was yet another. All in the name of art.

Beyond placing emphasis on filmmaking technique, Wieden & Kennedy's Lou Reed ad helped foster the development of a postmodern sensibility in the advertising industry. In the minds of the youngsters who were entering the business, advertising no longer had to be advertising, or entertainment. It could be, in Larry Bridges's phrase, "metacommentary": art that explicated, through irony, camp, iconic reference or self-reference, the commercial itself and the consumer culture of which it was a part. It was a living, evolutionary answer to Walter Benjamin's denial that art could exist in the modern era—"that which withers in the age of mechanical reproduction is the aura of the work of art." Wieden & Kennedy's advertising, which over the years would exploit rising athletes, has-been pop legends, avant-garde outlaws, even fictional cartoon characters, was a picture postcard of the postmodern esthetic, recycling and recombining cultural fragments, often for the purpose of cynical or, at the least, ironic annotation. To the media-drenched generation of consumers that had tuned out both conventional advertising and conventional art, the self-consciously hip come-ons of the Portland shop and its followers coyly called out: "Wish you were here."

Marketers, desperate to reach the disaffected younger generation of consumers, willingly acceded to the recommendations of Wieden & Kennedy and a handful of other agencies operating at the edge of mainstream culture. These shops—Chiat/Day; Goodby, Berlin & Silverstein and Foote, Cone & Belding in San Francisco and New York's Deutsch and Kirshenbaum & Bond—were given free rein to experiment, even to offend, if such experimentation and insult promised to pierce the veil of disinterest that seemed to be settling over the American consumption ethic. Isuzu automobile ads made fun of car dealers—the company's customers—in a campaign featuring an oily salesman telling outrageous fibs while text on the bottom of the screen stated, "He's lying." Reebok borrowed from the language of black urban rappers to tell the nation, "Reeboks let U.B.U." The Reebok ads illustrated the call to freedom with surreal scenes of a fairy princess, strange triplets and other oddballs, all wearing Reeboks.

By popularizing this new insider's advertising, by showing that it could be sold to mainstream clients, Wieden & Kennedy changed the composition of the agency business. Just as Bernbach drew to the ad industry young wisecrackers and other entertainers, the Portland agency and its followers lured a new generation of writers, art directors and commercial producers who believed that advertising could be their art and their criticism. They were "image scavengers," of the same school as the photographer Cindy Sherman and the artist Roy Lichtenstein, roaming the cultural landscape and mining from it bits and pieces of the mass-cult past to use in their pastiches.

It was all false bravado, of course. Wieden & Kennedy's young writers and art directors were no more artists than Bill Bernbach's sloganeers had been entertainers. They were court jesters, toiling at the sufferance of their masters. Although their ads seemed to be open, to promise, in accord with the postmodern ethos, multiple interpretations, depending on the will and wisdom of the interpreter, in the end they still led in one direction: the sale. The act of pulling together references, icons, text from various cultural locations and assembling them into an advertisement with no apparent, directed meaning seemed to symbolize freedom and independence. But it was really an appropriation of the style and form of postmodern pastiche, of camping, for a directed, institutional purpose. It may have looked like "metacommentary," but semioticians term it a "false metacommunication" because, through its production techniques, it pointed the viewer in a wrong direction—

toward the preferred interpretation of freedom and license—in order to mask its covert purpose, selling mass-manufactured goods, which it did by the implicit linkage of the product with the message of independence. Robert Goldman and Steve Papson, sociologists who have studied this school of advertising, refer to it, with good reason, as "the postmodernism that failed."

In other words, the young men and women drawn to Wieden & Kennedy and other such agencies were doing what young, truly creative people who went into advertising had always done. They were selling out. They were creating works that looked like avant-garde art or sounded like hip criticism, but whose "prime goal," as the *Village Voice*'s ad critic, Leslie Savan, has written, "is to take you back to the brand and down the buy-hole."

Larry Bridges understood this from the moment he finished editing the Lou Reed endorsement for Honda scooters. Wieden and Kennedy, he said, have been "the boatmen taking us"—the once-proud members of the political and artistic counterculture—"across the River Styx to selling out." By picking apart the culture—high and low, contemporary and past—to serve the requirements of marketers, "you're going to be subversive," he said, "until there's no more old culture to consume."

For all its impact on the advertising industry, the Lou Reed commercial did little for Honda. Young Americans had little interest in scooters, no matter how hip they were made out to be—not with automobile importers like Hyundai and Yugo selling honest-to-God cars, with roofs, for $4,000 to $5,000. Wieden & Kennedy eventually lost the account and closed the small Los Angeles office it had opened to service it. But the Portland agency won something far greater: the renewed attention of Nike.

Cindy Hale, Nike's advertising manager, who was still working her way past Chiat/Day's arrogance, was at Wieden & Kennedy's Portland headquarters a few days before the Honda spot first aired. One of the agency's account executives offhandedly asked her if she wanted to take a look at the new work. When the reel was finished, she did not hide her thoughts. *God, I'm jealous,* she said. *This is what I wish we could do.*

NIKE FIRED CHIAT/DAY in the spring of 1986 and returned its entire advertising account, without a review, to Wieden & Kennedy. What followed was one of the more remarkable growth spurts—for client, agency and creative experimentation—in advertising history.

Within a year, a pair of young women at Wieden & Kennedy—both in their early twenties, one in the research department, the other in pasteup—had figured out a way to bring the specific attributes of the Honda spot to Nike. The shoe maker had developed a line of sneakers in which a pocket of air in the inner sole was made visible through a clear plastic window on the outer sole. The two junior creatives proposed a starkly simple way to communicate the innovation: position it as a revolution in athletic shoes, and use the Beatles' song "Revolution" to back it.

The commercial was a pristine example of the postmodern ad. There was no dialogue. Only twice, at the opening and the closing, was the sponsor identified, and then in a simple billboard of the logo. The spot incorporated a comprehensive sampling from the toy box of art-film and news idioms. John Lennon's wrenching scream, which opened the spot, was used to augment, playfully, a familiar newsreel shot of Nike endorser John McEnroe arguing with a line judge. The cinema vérité style suffused the commercial: in a grainy scene, shot from below, of a woman doing situps; in frantic whip pans around a gymnasium; in a fuzzed-beyond-recognition close-up of the agonized faces of two opposing basketball players; in blazingly quick shots of seemingly irrelevant objects like treetops and picket fences, which actually stood for a runner's point of view; in the jump-cut that united the shot of a young boy practicing his schoolyard dunk and an NBA star accomplishing the same. Throughout, there were sly cultural allusions to times past. A crowd of swimming-capped and goggled triathletes running, knees up, into a body of water raised the barely conscious memory of 1930s-era newsreel footage of mass antics like the Polar Bear Club's annual New Year's Day ocean plunge. Another scene, enhanced by the "rat-tat-tat-tat" of Ringo Starr's snare drum, used stop-action filming to show runners appearing, one by one, on a track—a cinematic device borrowed from the Beatles' movie *Help*.

There was enough in the spot to support a multiplicity of interpretations. In linking a song about purposeful revolution to Nike, in techniques that communicated both newsy "realism" and artistic license, it overtly celebrated independence even while it covertly argued for conformity. Its stripped-down form was a stark contrast to the multimillion-dollar Hollywood productions, like the Michael Jackson song-and-dance pageant for Pepsi-Cola, that advertisers had recently favored. Yet if it was a political statement (a construction from which Nike did not recoil) it could still be read two ways: as a swipe at the excesses of the Reagan era, or as a commemoration of its "do it yourself" ideology.

Sales of the Nike Air line soared. And the company credited its neighborhood ad agency with the feat. "That commercial helped turn the company completely around," Nike's ad director, Scott A. Bedbury, said.

When Nike signed as an endorser Michael Jordan, a young basketball player with the Chicago Bulls who possessed an uncanny ability to hang in the air for seemingly endless seconds, the agency went to town again. It hired Spike Lee, then an unknown graduate of the New York University film school, to direct several spots featuring himself and Jordan. Wieden & Kennedy consciously aimed the ads at different constituencies. On the surface, the knowing black characters, Spike Lee's Mars Blackmon and Michael, would appeal to a black audience. The advertisements would also engage a larger swath of young Americans, who would be attracted by the use of an avant-garde director and the spots' jabs at commercialism. To this end, Spike's relative obscurity was an advantage. "You don't have to spell things like that out for people, because if they're interested enough, they'll find out for themselves," Jim Riswold, who wrote the ads, explained. "They'd be doing homework on a commercial. You can't ask for anything more. They're thinking about your thing after it's run its course."

As with the Lou Reed and "Revolution" spots, the "Spike and Mike" advertisements, as Wieden & Kennedy dubbed them, were rife with hidden codes, surface misdirections and double meanings. "This is something you can buy," said "Mars" in the first execution. His face was filmed in extreme close-up, as he cradled a pair of shoes to his cheeks and overtly invited the viewer into the commercial. The spot jump-cut to Jordan executing his "patented, vicious, high-flying 360" slam dunk. "This is something you cannot do," informed Mars, impishly denying the ad's implicit, transubstantiating promise. Subsequent commercials in the series employed other elements of the not-ad ad, including reflexive references (like a shot of Spike, yelling out the window at noisy neighbors, "Shut up! I'm doing a Nike commercial here. Shut up!") and pop icons (like Little Richard playing Aladdin's genie).

It may have been the new products. Maybe it was the advertising campaigns, or the godlike endorsers. Perhaps it was nothing more than Dan Wieden's three-word slogan, "Just do it," or the increased ad spending. But between 1987 and 1989, Nike's sales doubled, to $1.7 billion. After a decade-long struggle, Nike finally overtook Reebok again as the nation's number one marketer of athletic shoes—a position the company held as the 1990s opened and advanced.

Other than Nike and its shareholders, no one prospered as greatly from the athletic-shoe company's renaissance than the advertising agency that saw it through its most difficult period. Nike's ad spending ballooned to more than $130 million a year, as it strove to hold back

Reebok in the ongoing "sneaker wars." Wieden & Kennedy took its expanding profits and renovated a one-hundred-year-old former confectionery factory and department store, the Dekum building, in downtown Portland, a few blocks from the Willamette River, in an area just beginning to bud with boutiques and bistros.

Dan and David dusted off the rough sandstone pillars and terra-cotta ornaments on the facade. They started filling the five floors of offices, many of them overlooking, through half moon-shaped windows, the neighborhood's other ornate cast-iron edifices, with dozens of copywriters, art directors, producers, media planners, account executives and juniors. On the third floor they built a basketball court, where they sponsored daily exercise classes, guest speakers from the entertainment and literary worlds, and agency-wide meetings. With the entire youthful staff piled on the bleachers and Dan and David holding court (literally) while new employees were introduced or new advertisements debuted, the environment was reminiscent of nothing less than a high school pep rally. Messrs. Kennedy and Wieden, of course, were the coaches.

Everything reeked of . . . fun. In the back corner of the first floor was a kitchen. Nothing special, but the soda machine was free and offered an ecumenical selection that included Ramblin' Root Beer, Hi-C Lemonade, Diet Coke, Diet 7-Up and Pepsi. In the entrance lobby, where other agencies showcased their Clio awards and One Show trophies, Wieden & Kennedy hung individual portraits, by a local fashion photographer, of every member of the agency's staff. Birthdays were announced—like it or not—over an agency-wide intercom. New employees were expected to blow one full paycheck taking the entire agency out for beer at McCormick & Schmick's, a local fish joint. At least once a week, an itinerant vendor, nicknamed the "Mountain Man," appeared in the lobby to hawk dried fruits and nuts from the Oregon countryside. Everything in the place was designed to remind people that this shop famous for ads that were art was an agency like no other.

It's a slime mold, Dan told new recruits. *All of our cells are interrelated, but we're not in any visible order. We don't do things with what appears to be order. Chaos is creative. We get things done, but it frequently gets crazy.*

Dan and David ruled over their expanding entourage like benevolent dictators. David was the generous one. He adored the process of designing and helping others develop visual concepts. As for Dan, nothing—*nothing*—left the agency until he gave it his final imprimatur; even as the agency grew beyond his ability to track all its movements, he refused to grant subordinate creative directors the authority to sign off on work, as other agencies routinely did. This did not distress his staff, for he was more open to innovation than any other creative director with whom they had worked. Although he was a decade or two older than the men and women he was leading, a modernist in a galaxy of urbane postmodernists, he nevertheless retained his ability to enjoy their work. He summed up his management philosophy with an aphorism: *You're better off walking in stupid every day.*

In his own corner office Dan kept a copy of a book by Aesop Glim, a columnist for the defunct advertising trade magazine *Printer's Ink*. It was entitled *Copy—The Core of Advertising*. It was filled with rules for writing ads ("Don't associate food or drug products with the animal kingdom"), and was inscribed by the author to Duke Wieden. Dan liked to keep the book at hand both as a tribute to his father and as a reminder to himself that there *were* no rules in the business he was building.

Creative people employed elsewhere did all they could for an audience with Dan and David. One English art director went so far as to spend $1,200 for a full-page ad in the local daily newspaper to call the agency's attention to his work. Others put up with endless rounds of interviewing and months of indecision, far more than they would submit to from other agencies, for the license the Portland agency promised. "At just a practical, day-to-day level, it's as much freedom as I can imagine a creative being given," an agency copywriter confirmed.

By the early 1990s, Wieden & Kennedy was recognized throughout the advertising industry as the surpassing influence in the unstable world of advertising creativity, a maker of " 'auteur' commercials . . . a thinking-man's agency," according to *Print* magazine. It had won every prestigious award the ad industry offered, from the Magazine Publishers of America's $100,000 Kelly Prize for the best print advertising campaign to the One Show Gold Pencil for best television campaign of the year. "Wieden & Kennedy, more than any other agency, including my own, more than any there's ever been, has found a way to instinctively create advertising that appeals to the mass mind," affirmed a jealous competitor, Andy Berlin, who led both his own notable San Francisco shop, Goodby, Berlin & Silverstein, and the New York office of DDB Needham, Bernbach's old agency. "Dan Wieden calls it advertising of the id. But it's not of the individual id, not of a single sentient being, but of a single stream of consciousness of the whole fucking planet!"

Yet there was still The Fear. It was a fact of advertising existence, "a thing of muscle and life, of twitching nerves and furtive movements," as Frederic Wakeman, a former copywriter, had written in his Madison Avenue novel *The Hucksters*. As distant as Wieden was from Madison

Avenue, as different as his agency was from the granite-encased New York relationship machines churning out undifferentiated ads, he was still gripped by it. In his private moments—and they were many, for no member of his staff, to anyone's knowledge, not even Kennedy, many believed, had ever set foot inside his house—he dwelled on The Fear.

What if we lose Nike?

The Fear was far from irrational. Wieden & Kennedy had lost Nike once before, when the stakes were much lower. And the late 1980s and early 1990s were seeing a series of solid agency-client relationships worn away by the dour economy. American Express and Ogilvy . . . IBM and Lord, Geller . . . Miller Lite and Backer Spielvogel Bates . . . Prudential and Bates . . . why should Nike be any different? The company was no longer the loose, gym shorts–and–track suits place it had once been. Nike executives wore coats and ties now. *What if Phil Knight retires?* agency staffers whispered worriedly. *What if Nike's stock plunges? What if Reebok catches up?*

Dan put the best face on it. *The agency is an ongoing experiment,* he liked to say. He strove to add a veneer of industrial professionalism to the shop, hiring a director of account planning to make Wieden & Kennedy more attractive to larger clients.

But The Fear did not diminish. Like Wieden & Kennedy's style of advertising, it, too, had a double meaning. It was the last thing that stood between Dan Wieden and the unfettered ability to create metacommunicative art. And it signaled that he was, when all was said and done, still a huckster, like others gripped by The Fear.

Dan Wieden needed to rid himself of it. He needed another big account. Which was why he evinced such desperation when, in June 1991, he told Subaru of America's advertising agency selection committee: "Subaru is an incredibly important piece of business for this agency. It brings us outside of Nike."

The advertising campaign that Dan mobilized his staff to create for Subaru was a distillation of everything Wieden & Kennedy believed about marketing. It was postmodern advertising in its purest form.

Like the Levi's "501 Blues" campaign, which used city-street scenes and Delta blues music to highlight the ragged and rugged individualism of Levi's wearers, Wieden & Kennedy's Subaru campaign promised that a mass-produced product could be sold as a symbol of independence. Its anti-advertising message—if a car "improves your standing with the neighbors," the agency's launch commercial suggested, "then you live among snobs with distorted values"—was to be highlighted by the design of the commercial; like other "not-ad ads," it would use seemingly real documentary footage (of an allegedly real automobile factory) to invite the viewer to abandon the false ideals of modern marketing. The apparent paradox, that scenes of mass manufacturing would be used to send a message about nonconformism, only served to invite the viewer to participate even more deeply in the "metacommentary."

Indeed, the entire Wieden & Kennedy Subaru campaign was filled with ironic symbols of advertising exaggeration—a form of self-reference that literary scholars term "intertextuality." The "Mr. Shout" character, the 1930s-era, Monopoly-style cartoon man who introduced each of the print ads, referred to advertising's all-too-typical hyperbolic gyrations. The fact that Mr. Shout was yelling out such satiric comments as, "In bumper-to-bumper traffic it goes just as fast as a much more expensive car," signaled, in its self-consciousness, that these were ads that could be trusted. So, too, the slowly scrolling type that the agency recommended for the television ads recalled nothing less than the grandiloquent openings of Cecil B. DeMille spectaculars. But again, the contradiction between the visual symbolism and the verbal message was intended to highlight (to consumers savvy enough to understand it) the truthfulness of the message.

Taken together, these print advertisements and television commercials proposed by Wieden & Kennedy were less a promotion for automobile sales than a commentary on automobile advertising itself. Jerry Cronin, the campaign's copywriter, considered car advertising "the Emperor's new clothes—fun, open roads, no traffic, trees . . . *bullshit.*" *Let's talk about cars the way they are,* he told his art-director-partner, David Jenkins. Jenkins, in turn, wanted to use the campaign to pay homage to the Volkswagen campaign, the progenitor of all modern advertising. He filled the campaign with little allusions to Doyle Dane Bernbach's VW ads. Situating the car against a white background in the print advertisements referred directly back to Helmut Krone's innovative design of the VW ads. Both the VW ads (in their Thurberesque tone of the "little man" bedeviled by, but ultimately triumphant over, the modern world) and the Subaru print ads (in their text-heavy, wide-column page design and use of an introductory pen-and-ink cartoon) borrowed heavily from the look and manner of *The New Yorker* magazine. Jenkins even kept a picture book of Volkswagen ads by his side throughout the time he was working on the Subaru campaign.

But for all the citations, the Subaru campaign presented by Wieden & Kennedy differed markedly from the Volkswagen campaign that was its model. The VW Beetle was a humble, simple car noted, and advertised, for providing superior technology at a low, low price. Only as an ancillary matter did Beetles become status symbols for tweedy intellectuals. Wieden & Kennedy, to the contrary, had said in its pitch that it wanted to sell Subarus, like Nikes, as fashion items. Antistatus status appeals were the primary focus of the agency's campaign; engineering talk would come second, if at all. In effect, the agency was accepting Alfred Sloan's theory that the "laws of the Paris dressmakers" motivated automobile buyers, but was employing Henry Ford's utilitarian language to suck the buyers in.

Subaru of America loved it. Of course, the Subarus only caught the surface meaning—here was an advertising campaign that would turn their cars' unimaginative styling into a virtue. No one on the agency search committee stopped to consider that Wieden & Kennedy was trying to make an artistic statement about commercialism and American culture. Nor did S.O.A.'s regional representatives, or the select group of dealers the company invited to meet with the new agency after the pitch was concluded. They only saw a bold campaign, one that might finally help them sell an old car, the Loyale, that had become (in dealer parlance) sale-proof; a new car, the Legacy, that had failed to find its market; and a sports car, the SVX, that would either resurrect the company's reputation or pummel it further.

You guys, one California dealer told Dan Wieden at the end of a contentious, day-long meeting in San Diego a few weeks after the pitch, *will be the last agency Subaru ever has. Because if you turn it around, the loyalty will be so great they'll never look elsewhere.*

And if you don't turn it around, the dealer added, *there won't be anyone here left to beat you up.*

Chapter 13

Just Do It

THE SOUNDS OF BEDLAM filled the air. A dog barked. Cackling laughter bounced from the bare wooden floors and reverberated off the twisting metal staircase and the high, high ceilings. Shouts emerged from nowhere, grew louder, then disappeared into distant whispers. A dog barked again. An intercom constantly blared messages. "There will be a staff meeting in the gym at 11:30. Everybody please attend." Eleven-thirty passed without incident. "There will be a staff meeting in the gym at 11:45. Make sure you're there." No one was. Amidst a hum as constant as a nearby highway's, a dog barked again.

Dan Wieden's office was an island of confusion amid the chaos. Silence and mumbles mixed with bursting half-sentences as Dan; Dave Luhr, the director of the new Subaru account; Bill Davenport, the agency's head of broadcast production; Jerry Cronin, the copywriter and Subaru creative director; and Larry Frey, an art director temporarily assigned to the account, grappled with how to make their video dreams a reality.

"Voiceover?" asked Davenport. "Jerry?"

Jerry, who, like all the others save Dan, was in his mid-thirties and dressed less for success than for softball, stared up at the poster of Ursula Andress that adorned the south wall of Dan's office. "I'm listening to TV," he muttered. He leaned forward and plucked a jelly bean from the mason jar on Dan's oak coffee table.

Davenport, beyond the others, had the least time for indecision. Most commercials take months to complete. This one had only weeks. In his own office, a floor above, a calendar that took up half a wall relentlessly, in green magic marker, reminded him of the schedule: July 9—tomorrow—"Subaru director search"; July 11, "Scout Subaru factory"; July 16, "Award Subaru job"; July 17, "Record Subaru v.o."; July 23–26,

"Shoot Subaru"; July 29–31, "Edit Subaru"; August 1, "Subaru music"; August 2, "Final Subaru approvals." Left blank was the space under August 4—that was the day the agency had to have ready two sixty-second commercials for projection on a giant screen to an auditorium full of car dealers in Denver.

"We're probably going to need someone by next week," Davenport goaded.

But Jerry was determined to avoid the subject. "What about the music?" he interrupted. "Should we use somebody different for the music? Steve Reich, maybe? Who did the music on those new IBM spots?"

No one answered. The meeting, as did all meetings at Wieden & Kennedy, hopped indiscriminately from subject to subject, over bridges made of uncomfortable pauses.

"How's Justy doing?" Jerry asked of Subaru's smallest car. He shook his left knee, bare beneath his gray gym shorts, up and down with nervous energy.

"Dead as a doornail," answered Luhr, who was, after three weeks as account director, a fount of all knowledge Subarunic. "They sell seven thousand. It's ugly. And it's eight thousand dollars of ugly."

Larry Frey, a tousled blond who was wearing torn, faded jeans, parried with another non sequitur. "What happened to Levine?"

Luhr described how the friendship between Harvey Lamm and Bob Schmidt sowed bitterness among the troops in and around Subaru of America, leaving Levine, Huntley, Schmidt & Beaver unprotected when sales started falling. "Dealers felt it was advertising that won awards but didn't sell cars," Luhr said.

A look of utter disgust crossed Jerry's face. He had worked on a car account back in Boston, his hometown. "Dealers!" he spat. "They *never* think you're selling enough cars!"

Now Dan spoke. He was still adjusting to the need to balance his time between his massive existing account—Nike—and his exceedingly large and important new account. He was content to leave the Subaru arrangements to his subordinates, sitting back in his chair, watching with wide eyes and stroking his beard. But every now and then he exploded with worry over a detail. "This voiceover thing is getting me freaked out," he flared. "*So* many people are tied up."

Finally, names flew. Martin Sheen? "No, he does Toyota," someone said. Daniel Travanti, the "Hill Street Blues" star? "No, Honda." They trailed off into stories—a fond recollection of a Burgess Meredith voiceover, an apocryphal tale of Orson Welles winging it for Gallo wines—then they fell silent again. All the names recommended were famous; no one suggested a review of faceless voiceover specialists. Deadline pressures required them to communicate with each other in shorthand, and telecinematic fame was an easily decipherable code. Besides, the new Hollywood culture of advertising silently demanded that they corral a star's voice.

Jack Lemmon?

"He does Honda, too."

They fell silent again.

"Did you ever notice how guys n-n-n-nickname their cars to show emotional attachment?" intruded Jerry. He tended to stutter when extemporizing in group settings. "My gut tells me that w-w-w-women do that, too."

Saved from having to contend with the voiceover question, his colleagues happily joined the discussion.

Dan volunteered that his daughter used to call her maroon Pontiac "the Blood Vessel."

Davenport referred to his Volkswagen as "the Badass Jetta."

Eyes turned back to Jerry, who'd driven them along this tangent. "I call mine," he said dourly, "the Shitbox."

IT ALWAYS CAME BACK to Jerry Cronin. At every turn, his opinion was sought. His words, which often emerged only grudgingly, were attended to with great care. Little happened without his assent. Nothing unexpected about that; he was, after all, the Subaru account's creative director, and in the Wieden & Kennedy school of "auteur" advertising, the creative director's say-so was supposed to be akin to Hitchcock's control over a film.

There was something else to Jerry's character that made his colleagues pay attention. He was tall (over six feet) and walked with the stiff-legged gait of a basketball player. He had the flat nose and plump cheeks of a Southie street tough. Yet there was a fragility about him that belied his imposing physical presence, an Irish cloud of tragedy always hovering over him that made those around him solicitous. His lobby photo said it all: his collar was turned up, his dark hair was confrontationally mussed and perched near the gap in his upper front teeth was a "so's-yer-old-man" toothpick—which, on closer inspection, turned out to be a thermometer.

That sense of doom, edged, it must be said, by a sharp rim of typically Irish sarcasm, had been forged in Marshfield, a small, blue-collar town on the Massachusetts coast southeast of Boston. Burned into Jerry's memory was the sight of his father, a bright, witty World War II veteran, trudging off each morning to a job he hated. *I'm never going to work a job where I don't like going off to work,* Jerry told himself, *where I'm going to dread waking up.*

Reading, unsurprisingly, was Jerry's earliest escape, but for all the possibilities it opened, limits were revealed as well. In the seventh grade he tackled James Joyce's *Dubliners,* and was haunted by the tale of the young boy, hopelessly in love with the older girl next door whose "dress swung as she moved her body and the soft rope of her hair tossed from side to side." When she innocently mentioned to the boy her inability to get to the splendiferous Araby bazaar, he took it upon himself to journey there and bring her back a gift. With impatience he cadged money from his uncle for the trip, with difficulty he traveled by train, arriving at the fair as it was closing. Making his way quickly to one of the few stalls that remained open, he watched as the proprietress, a girl his beloved neighbor's age, flirted with two older lads. The boy, crushed by reality, bought nothing.

More than two decades later, Jerry could still recite by heart the closing sentence of a tale he considered, in some way, personally metaphorical: "Gazing up into the darkness I saw myself as a creature driven and derided by vanity; and my eyes burned with anguish and anger."

He wrote plays and poetry and fled to Connecticut College (which he found full of "overachieving public school kids and underachieving yuppies"), where, short of money, he found himself, in his final year, re-living his father's dreaded life, working in a shipyard in Groton building nuclear submarines.

"I worked the seven-to-five shift. I was pulling cable basically," Jerry recalled. "You get this big piece of cable and you pull it through these stanchions inside the sub. It was so fucking cold! It was right on the Sound. It was winter. You're inside this piece of metal. It's so cold your feet are going numb. You're inside this cigar tube. And inside are these burners and smelters and grinders. The smoke is so thick that every time you blow your nose black comes out. . . .

"Every day, at lunch, ten thousand people would line up before the gate. On the other side of the gate, twenty bars. You go to the bar, the bartender lays out a shot and a beer, a shot and a beer, a shot and a beer. One after the other. The idea was to drink as much as you could in the half-hour lunch break because you hated your job so much."

After college, when he discovered the existence of advertising from an art director, a friend of his girlfriend's—and was told that he could actually make a living with his writing—he ran headlong into the business. Not for him the self-hatred that burdened other artists coerced by circumstances into the world of advertising. The chance to work with words, to play with them, craft them, cut them, move them, and make money doing it, was all he wanted. In a month, without guidance, he wrote 120 speculative ads, and landed a job at one Boston agency, then another, then a third, making the rounds in a town that prided itself on the wittiness of its flackery. Finally, he attracted the notice of Dan Wieden, who invited him to Oregon.

The city's green hills and clear skies were a tonic for Jerry, who loathed his native East Coast. He became known around Wieden & Kennedy for his mordant wit. In his office (where his reference books included *Best American Short Stories, 1990* and the novel *Paris Trout*) he wrote an advertisement for French television to introduce Nike 180s to the Continent. The spot depicted an old man on the subway who looked up to see Death staring at him. The old man ran from Death— wearing his Nikes, of course. Jerry persuaded the agency to hire Jean-Luc Godard to direct it. Advertising, like the short-story collection he was halfway through, like the screenplays he was crafting, was, for Jerry, just another opportunity to tell the truth.

And the truth was this: Jerry Cronin, the new creative director on Subaru of America's advertising account, despised cars. The man whose beliefs and words S.O.A. had chosen over so many others had, shortly after purchasing his first house, in Portland's fashionable Northeast, ripped up his driveway and torn down his garage. In their place, defiantly, he put a garden and a side deck.

"I always hated cars," Jerry said one day in his office. "I didn't own a car until I was twenty-eight. We had no money when I was growing up. We always had these old Ramblers. I always heard the old man complaining about cars. Every time he left the house, he never knew whether the car would get him home. Cars for us were like Bics— disposable. My impression of automobiles was they were a hindrance, a terrible influence on my family. Cars are fun for one year, when you're seventeen. A bordello on wheels: drink in the front seat, screw in the back."

That was the history, the philosophy, the worldview that underlay Jerry's composition of Subaru's advertising. "I want people to know what cars can do. They won't make you feel better or more successful. Stop slinging the shit at people. I want to separate people from their cars, get rid of the emotional bind. People are far too attached to their cars. I want them to see that cars are a hunk of metal. Automotive advertising is the biggest lie of all time. You want to live better, look better—buy a grill, go to the gym!"

It was this antipathy toward automobiles and his abhorrence of moving from verdant, spacious Portland back to the hated, congested East that explained Jerry's hesitation about producing the Subaru spots.

Words needed to be written. Other words, written by others, had to be approved. That and more needed to be completed before the creative and production team traveled halfway across the country three days hence to tour the Subaru factory in Lafayette, Indiana, the as-yet-unexplored site of the commercial they had pitched to S.O.A. a month before.

The most important unsettled issue, and the one for which Jerry's time was most needed, was the SVX television commercial. As originally presented to S.O.A. in June, the sports-car spot was something of an afterthought. Uncharacteristically for Wieden & Kennedy, the ad seemed to replicate a traditional auto advertising convention by featuring the car, beautifully lit but stationary, on an indoor stage, as if it were being presented at the Detroit Auto Show. True, the voiceover, in Wieden & Kennedy fashion, was intentionally ironic ("The Subaru SVX. . . . You can drive it so fast. . . . You'll get so many tickets . . . you'll lose your license") and the spot also featured an animated version of Mr. Shout, the overheated comic character, prancing around the car in an intentional homage to the Tex Avery cartoons of the 1940s. But the commercial seemed somehow lacking.

After shaking hands on their affiliation, Subaru and Wieden & Kennedy agreed that the SVX spot did little to highlight the new car's novelty. S.O.A. had heavily flacked the car to the automotive press, and by July word was filtering back to the company that the buff books, already intrigued by the SVX's fashion-forward Italianate styling, were raving about the car's performance as well. *Automobile* magazine was soon to report that "in seven days of driving, our enthusiasm to get back into the SVX never waned." *Car & Driver* was even more ardent. "If its banzai assault on the heavily defended luxocoupe market is even half successful, it will not only change what the word 'Subaru' means, it will raise the all-around performance ante for subsequent similar cars." The advance praise was confirming S.O.A.'s wildest fantasies that the SVX could, almost singlehandedly, transform the company's image. This was not a car to be wasted, unmoving, on a stage set.

So Cronin authored a new commercial, one which showcased visually what he and Wieden understood was the signal appeal of a sports car—speed—but which also underscored Jerry's own apposite belief that, given the realities of driving, such interests were foolish. The commercial opened on a bare open road stretching into the distance, from the point of view of a driver behind the wheel. As, gradually, the unseen car picked up more and more and more speed, other images were superimposed on the sky above the road—factory scenes, not unlike those in the agency's planned commercial for the Legacy.

Jerry's copy reconciled the visual dichotomy. "In making a sports car, it seems mandatory to mention how fast it could go," the voiceover wearily noted. "All right. . . . With an overhead cam engine capable of producing 220 pounds of torque, the new Subaru SVX has a cruising speed of 131 miles per hour. But how important is that? With extended urban gridlock, gas at $1.42 a gallon, and highways full of patrolmen? Instead, why not mention the things you shouldn't mention about a sports car? An extra layer of paint . . . A deeper weld . . . Sixty-three safety features . . . Engineering that endures . . . The ability to carry four adults . . . Still, if it's speed you want, we promise—you'll be able to use most of the speedometer." Only at the end of the spot did the full car come into view, pulling onto the screen, then zooming off as the announcer gave the tag: "The new Subaru SVX. What to drive."

Jerry, in his haste and distaste, had fabricated some of the statistics he used to fill his spot. Nowhere in the country was gas priced as high as $1.42 a gallon. And no one had counted the number of safety features on the SVX. Still, the spot was much closer to S.O.A.'s desires than the original. When Wieden & Kennedy presented it to the Subarus on July 2, the executives enthusiastically endorsed it.

Now the agency had to figure out how to produce it, which was not as simple as it looked on the storyboard.

"To do this spot 100 percent correctly, it should be made in Japan," Dave Luhr informed his colleagues, still assembled in Dan's office. There was no way to double up the filming of the factory scenes for the two commercials, he said, "because SVXs aren't made in Indiana."

The advertising men had never considered that fact might interfere with their fictions.

"Can we get the skeletons?"—shells and bare drive trains of the sports car—Jerry wondered.

"We'll need a whole car," said Davenport.

"You'll need *more* than a whole car," said Larry.

The solution, to Jerry, appeared obvious: Shoot the SVX commercial's factory scenes in Japan. *Anything* to get out of going to Indiana.

Luhr, who as account director oversaw the budget, momentarily considered the option. "What's the cost, Bill?"

"A one-day shoot in Japan? Three hundred thousand. Maybe two," Davenport answered. That was $200,000 or $300,000 above the budget Subaru had approved. But, Davenport added, "given the time constraints, I think we should shoot in Japan. I think you should go back and ask them for more money."

Under normal circumstances, an account director, certainly an agency chief, would have put a stop to the discussion right there, reasoning (appropriately) that a financially struggling client might find a request from a brand-new agency for a quarter of a million additional dollars, well, disagreeable. But Wieden & Kennedy was confident of Subaru's love. Money, they felt sure, would not be an issue.

"You're looking at $400,000 each," Davenport, the producer, cautioned his colleagues.

This was considerably more than the average cost to produce a single national television advertisement—about $168,000, according to the American Association of Advertising Agencies—and more, even, than the $235,000 average cost of making a car commercial, which was among the most expensive categories. The high cost of producing television spots was a subject of irksome debate among advertisers. In 1970, during the glory days of the Creative Revolution, the most expensive commercials had cost only about $70,000, and marketers were at a loss to figure out why the tariff had tripled as their ability to move their products grew concomitantly difficult. Even as the agency business found itself gripped by the recession of the late 1980s, production costs soared far beyond the inflation rate—by 12 percent in 1988, and by another 8 percent in 1989. Clients, already upset about compensation rates, faulted their agencies, which, by industry tradition, marked up their cost of commercial production by 17.65 percent and, the clients argued, had little incentive to keep costs down. Agencies, in turn, blamed commercial directors (some of whom received fees as high as $25,000 a day for directing an ad) and commercial production companies, many of them owned by directors, which, also by industry tradition, marked up their costs by 35 percent.

But Dan did not flinch from a figure that was already 70 percent higher than the industry's already high average for auto spots.

"We can get that," he said of the $800,000 production tariff. "These guys will give us all the rope we want."

GIVEN TWO TELEVISION commercials which, in their use of footage shot inside an automobile factory, now risked looking too much alike, Wieden & Kennedy needed to find a director who could, in Bill Davenport's words, "plus the boards."

"Plussing the boards" was a term that hid within its incomprehensibility many of the changes that had taken place in advertising and marketing during the 1980s. Even under the reign of Bernbach and his children during television's first two decades, the role of the television-commercial director was circumscribed by agency tradition and the novelty of empowerment. Art directors, only recently elevated from their previously menial status as layout mechanics, were unwilling to relinquish any of their newfound eminence as full partners in the communications process. Several film directors achieved fame during and after the Creative Revolution. But with a few exceptions, they merely realized the concepts of the agency, as drawn by the art director, drafted by the copywriter and mangled by the client.

During the 1980s, though, several developments converged, placing the film director at the center of advertising creation. Products had grown so alike in so many categories that verbal argument declined as an advertising tool; visual imagery, especially in television, grew in importance, making the imaginative director a coveted property. Network television, too, passed its fortieth birthday. No longer a novelty, the medium required inventiveness if it was to penetrate the audience's apathy. Moreover, as sales in many product and service categories began to stagnate, either from the recession or from market maturity, agencies grew increasingly fearful of presenting bold ideas to clients. Instead, they submitted lackluster concepts in storyboard form and relied on the director to save them. They hoped, in the parlance, to find a director who could "plus the boards."

At Wieden & Kennedy, directors were an especially important part of the action. As the nation's preeminent exponent of advertising-as-art, the agency had a special obligation to continue to seek distinctiveness in its work. Directors, in turn, knew that the shop gave great license to filmmakers, and was always willing to experiment with new production techniques, new looks, new colors and new sounds—novelties that could help extend a director's career. There wasn't a rock-video director in America, not a shaky cameraman on either coast, not a hypercolor-quick-cutting-swish-panning-grainy-filming filmmaker anywhere in LaLaLand, London or the Big Apple who wouldn't have killed for a chance to direct for Wieden & Kennedy. The videocassettes that overflowed from two wall shelves and the cheap wooden bookcase in Bill Davenport's otherwise spare office attested to this fact.

The news was not good, Davenport told his colleagues. A handsome, slightly built man with dark hair, smooth skin and long eyelashes, he was operating the controls of a Sony videocassette player with the bare toes beneath his paisley shorts as he spoke. His first choice to direct, Oliver Harrison, was unavailable. "I find it hard to suggest a director who I have confidence in steering this concept through in so little time," Davenport said in his high-pitched voice. He pushed the "Play" button with his big toe, and a General Motors "Putting quality on the road" commercial, filled with giant machines, tiny people, flashing lights and colorful computer screens, started to unwind.

"Matt Mahurin," said Jerry. The California-educated designer and director was not available—Jerry had already been told that. But he kept insisting, and played, for the third or fourth time, a music video featuring the neo-folk singer Tracy Chapman. Jerry was captivated by the look of the video. It used color film with so much of the color washed out that it seemed black-and-white.

"Are you saying you want the spot to look like this?" Davenport asked.

Jerry didn't respond.

"This is the max you can go with the color and still have flexibility with the type," Larry cautioned.

Jerry just watched.

"If you want black-and-white, you should start with black-and-white," Davenport insisted.

Jerry was thinking. What he was looking for was inspiration. He had already decided that the look he wanted derived from the heroic Social Realism prevalent in public and commercial art during the 1930s—the "dawn-of-the-Machine-Age" style popularized in friezes by the Works Progress Administration and photographs in *Life*. That this look was also prevalent in the hortatory art of both Hitler's Germany and Stalin's Soviet Union did not escape the agency men. Larry sent his assistant to a local video store to pick up a copy of Leni Riefenstahl's *Olympiad*, a celebration of Nazi power, to review it for cinematographic stimulation.

Davenport's toes began working double-time. He played a Converse sneakers spot with the basketball star Magic Johnson. "I think it would be better to go creamy, like this, instead of grainy."

Jerry did not respond.

Davenport replaced it with a tape of a BMW commercial distinguished by its cross-dissolves and lighting effects. "It's really choreographed lighting," said Larry, impressed. Still Jerry was silent.

Larry put in a reel of commercials by a director named Dominic Sena, and reviewed a big, gutsy spot for Coca-Cola featuring the teenage pop group New Kids on the Block. "I think Sena is a great talent," he said. "Whaddya think, Jerry?"

The silent one spoke. "Not knocked out by him."

Larry exploded in frustration. "Orson Welles is dead, Jerry! John Huston is dead! John Ford, dead! Stanley Kubrick is unavailable."

By this time, Larry's assistant had returned, sans *Olympiad* but with *Citizen Kane,* another film shot in the heroic style. As Davenport placed a prearranged conference call to a director named Jeffery Plansker (to whom he had sent copies of the Subaru storyboards), Larry put the tape in the VCR and began fast-forwarding through some scenes and watching others with the sound off. Davenport explained to Plansker his agency's plight.

"We were thinking of shooting the factory scenes for 'SVX' in Japan, but it looks like it'll take too much time," he said. "We might have to say, 'Fuck it, we'll shoot SVX in the Indiana factory and fake it.' But we're not comfortable with that yet."

Plansker clearly had given the matter next to no thought. "Having received this yesterday, what I've been thinking about, uh . . . you guys are thinking of black-and-white?"

"We're thinking," answered Jerry. "Not sure."

"What I'm thinking," Plansker improvised, "is using typography as an opportunity to enhance these factory parts. Maybe go so far as to shoot the parts in Super 8. You'll have to help me know how much you want to push this film. Obviously, the imagery can be strong visually, strong film. But the type is an opportunity."

With visible (but not audible) dissatisfaction, Davenport hung up. Almost immediately, he received a prearranged call from Dominic Sena. Sena, too, had not yet had time to review the boards and was forced to wing it.

"There's a lot of robotics, welders, not many people," Davenport explained.

"Really?" said Sena, whose voice seemed poised perpetually on the edge of surprise. "What kind of access can you get?"

"They'll shut it down for us," answered Jerry.

"Really?" Sena repeated. "That's cool."

"We want to debunk the myths of BMW and 'Heartbeat of America' bullshit," Davenport said.

Sena, not unexpectedly, was entranced by the vague concept. "I like the idea of this. I love the idea of black-and-white."

Davenport underscored the need to differentiate between the Subaru commercials. "The two spots should tie together artistically. They shouldn't both look like factory spots, using common footage."

"I'm doing product photography tomorrow, so I'll just be in the studio drinking coffee and looking at lighting and being bored," Sena responded. "It'll be a good time to look at stuff."

Without hope, the three agency men bade good-bye to Sena. They called Tibor Kalman.

Tibor was a long shot. A controversial figure in New York commercial art circles, he was a leader of the postmodern school of graphic design. He and his small firm, M & Co., pillaged from pre–World War II brand trademarks, East Asian pop iconography and even local Yellow Pages directories to "undesign," as he put it, advertisements for hip Manhattan restaurants, David Byrne album covers and Andy Warhol's former magazine, *Interview*. The Hungarian-born Tibor had some directing experience; he had coordinated music videos for the Talking Heads and had worked on a Wieden & Kennedy commercial for Pepe jeans. But Tibor had never directed a thirty-second spot for a major national advertiser. Wieden & Kennedy's notion was to use him only to develop the type treatment for the Subaru spots—until the agency found itself directorless, less than a month before it required finished commercials in hand.

"So you guys are in trouble, right?" Tibor asked over the speakerphone.

"Big trouble," Davenport admitted.

Tibor wasted no time with further introductory chatter. Unlike the other directors, he *had* reviewed the storyboards the agency had sent him, and he had developed opinions and ideas, which he vented, at length.

"The thing I liked best about the spots is the clarity and simplicity of the language," said Tibor. "It's refreshingly free of bullshit. The most important thing is to find a way to make the language the most important part of the commercials."

Tibor was not unaware, of course, that the account's creative director was a copywriter who believed in his politically poetic power. But if he was cozying up to Jerry by praising his words, Tibor also unhesitatingly identified the weaknesses in the campaign.

"But," he continued, "you have to clearly differentiate between the commercials. One is selling a brand, the other a product, a sports car." Yet the ads, as designed, were not distinctive enough. Having the voiceover repeat the on-screen words was also wrong, he said. "It will make people feel stupid. I would advocate not using it. People at the client and the agency will want a voiceover, to reassure them, but you should let the words speak for themselves." Without prompting, he agreed with Jerry's idea of shooting the spots in color, then "desaturating" them, or drawing the color out while cranking up the contrast, to make the film look like 1930s-era postcards—black-and-white, with unexpected splashes of color.

Tibor, indeed, had ideas for everything. Cameraman? "Salgado, the Magnum photographer, who gets a real heroic quality to his work." Soundtrack? "My dream is to get somebody like Philip Glass to compose a piece for this." Moving typeface? "The x-height, the height of the lower case letters, is too small to be legible, at least in the boards you sent me." Tone? "The emotion I want is the wonderment of the Machine Age." SVX spot? "I think it should be entirely different. The typography and some of the music should be identical, but that's it." The SVX-is-only-made-in-Japan problem? "We can shoot everything very tight, so you never get to the point where you don't know you're not in the factory." Man vs. machine? "The emphasis in the images should be that, despite the technology, despite the robotics, *people* make cars."

Hmmm ... Hadn't Jerry said his concept was to *divorce* people from cars? Well, after an hour of listening to nonstop Tibor, perhaps some details *were* obscured.

They returned to Dan Wieden's office to report on their overdue progress. "So what's the difference between the spots?" the agency chief inquired.

Jerry parroted the idea tossed out by Tibor. "The SVX spot would be tighter in parts, the brand spot would concentrate more on the machinery."

Dan was unsatisfied. "That approach works well with what you're saying in the first commercial—'A machine is a machine, and may the best machine win,'" he said. "Can we *please* look at something that talks about the premise of speed for the second commercial? That's the whole *idea* of this spot."

His subordinates, as usual, grew silent. The boss wanted speed; speed, presumably, it would be.

After a pause, Dan plunged into the void. "What did we do about directors?"

Jerry recounted the conferences with the three potential directors. Davenport added what little substance he could, pointing particularly to Tibor's heretical idea not to mix the type with a voiceover. Dan mulled the concept over.

"Has he ever done film before?" he asked.

"Tibor?" responded Davenport. "Yeah. Talking Heads videos, other stuff."

Dan dwelled silently on the cachet of, and potential results from, a commercial affiliation with Tibor. After a moment, he began thinking out loud.

"Is Tibor too far out, too weird, for what we're trying to do here? He understood what we're trying to do? Honesty? Truthfulness?" He paused for a bit more reflection. "He's an exceptional mind." He meditated some more. "I love *Interview*." He mulled again. "I don't think Tibor's a bad idea at all."

No response from the fellows. The boss wanted Tibor; Tibor would direct.

They returned to the last unsolved dilemma, the voiceover.

"How about that famous Irish guy who was in *Miller's Crossing*? The guy who was whistling 'Danny Boy' while they were blowing them all away?" Davenport suggested.

"The skinny guy?" asked Larry.

"No," answered Davenport, "the chubby guy."

"Albert Finney," Jerry said quietly.

"Hey," continued Larry, "how about Miles Davis?" The legendary jazz trumpeter had actually appeared in a Nike spot for the agency. But Larry's imitation of Davis bebopping the slogan "Subaru. What to drive" persuaded his colleagues that the idea was not as cool as Miles himself.

Davenport played a tape of other voices for Dan. They reviewed Fred Ward, who had recently opened as the lusty Henry Miller in the film *Henry and June.*

"Wow!" said Dan, breaking into an ingenuous, toothy smile. "There's a really nice energy to him."

They played a tape of John Goodman, the fat co-star of the television sitcom "Roseanne."

"I'm really intrigued by him," Dan said.

They paced through Jeff Bridges, who, appropriately enough, had played a failed, idealistic automaker in the movie *Tucker.*

"Bridges. I *like* Bridges," Dan said. "Finney, he's too theatrical. Jeff Bridges, he's hard to top."

"He sounds believable when he talks," Larry agreed.

Entranced, almost like a child, by the wonder of doing advertising, Dan dwelled on the prospect of buying Jeff Bridges's voice.

"I like Bridges," he repeated. "He's not real regional. Is he a fortune?"

Davenport responded. "We don't know yet."

But Dan had already moved on. "Hey!" he shouted. "Have we thought about Brando?"

Chapter 14

Come Alive

ONE MIGHT CLAIM that the era of modern image-making began before television, before radio, before the rotogravure press; began, in fact, in the year 1811 on a field not far from what is now Interstate 65, about midway between Indianapolis and Gary, Indiana. It was there that William Henry Harrison, an undistinguished career soldier from Virginia by way of Philadelphia who had married into some land in Ohio, fought the battle of his career . . . and lost.

He was lucky to get away with his life, for at dawn on November 7, Harrison and some eight hundred men under him were surprised at their encampment on Tippecanoe Creek by a force of Shawnee warriors under the command of the Prophet, the brother of the Indian leader Tecumseh. Sixty-one of Harrison's soldiers were killed and 127 wounded.

Yet somehow, as time passed, Harrison managed to make people think he had *won* the Battle of Tippecanoe. Persistence was his ally: He wanted nothing more than to gain political office, and over the years, he ran for several positions; although he generally lost, people tended to remember his overblown biographical claims because, ever cautious, he rarely was cornered into taking memorable political positions. Which was how, in 1840, financially insolvent and reduced to serving as the clerk of the court of common pleas in Hamilton County, Ohio, he managed to persuade the Whig party to nominate him and the American people to elect him President of the United States. The campaign slogan that propelled him to victory, as every schoolchild to this day knows, was "Tippecanoe and Tyler, too."

So it was only appropriate that Subaru of America and Wieden & Kennedy should choose Tippecanoe County, Indiana—site of the creek, and the battlefield, and Purdue University, and the Triple XXX Restaurant's Duane Parvis All American Burger ("¼ lb. of 100% ground sirloin served on a toasted bun with melted cheese, lettuce, tomato, pickle, Spanish onion and peanut butter"), and, not incidentally, the Subaru-Isuzu Automotive manufacturing plant (known as SIA)—to begin the job of repairing Subaru's image.

About two miles from the plant, in Room 109 of the Homewood Suites motel, as dawn broke sullenly over the sweaty summer landscape, the organization of that repair job was well under way. Taped to one wall were ten manila envelopes containing all the information needed to make the next week in the personal and professional lives of several dozen refugees from New York and Los Angeles smooth: "Indiana Maps," "Call sheets," "Tibor's Itinerary," "Maps to Airport," "Maps to SIA," "Messages," "Vendors List," "Menus," "SVX Boards" and "Shot Lists." Stuck to another wall were five penciled sheets detailing all the flights in and out of the Lafayette airport from and to New York and L.A. A handwritten weather forecast tacked nearby disclosed little respite from the weather—"Heat index 100+!"—which only made the Amberglow log in the fireplace seem more incongruous. Next to it, a television set silently played an old Hollywood newsreel story about the motion picture *The Diary of Anne Frank.* A Mita copier churned out documents nonstop. And a procession of people not-from-these-parts, each accompanied by numerous flies definitely-from-these-parts, wound their way through the door. The flies remained glued to the twisty yellow death strands hanging from the ceiling. The people asked questions and left.

"Do you have the boards?" a muscular young man asked no one in particular. He and his partner were the detailers, charged with such tasks as clipping rubber nubbins off tires, jacking up back ends, buffing hoods and the other makeup and wardrobe chores that ready a car for a commercial.

"Can we find out when the shift breaks occur?" a bearded, horse-faced fellow wanted to know. He was the second assistant director, whose job was coordinating and maintaining the schedule so the first assistant director was free to assist the director.

They and forty others were brought together in less than ten days' time by a film-industry hiring chain that can operate fast and furiously when the need, like the two-week-turnaround Subaru relaunch campaign, arises.

The linkages began when Tibor Kalman, the director retained by Wieden & Kennedy, called Maribeth Phillips, a New York producer in her late twenties with whom he had worked, and told her to put together a crew. Maribeth called Becky Coleman, a production manager from New Jersey. Becky called George Billard, a production coordinator with whom she worked frequently, and Kristine Jelstrup, a production assistant in L.A. who had grown up in Indiana. Together, they located eight more production assistants and sundry other personnel, and began the effort of readying a film site inside the factory.

Tibor also called Fred Elmes, a wan man with a perpetual squint and a way with a camera. Fred had served as director of photography on several of David Lynch's surreal descents into the dark side of Middle America, and was literally instrumental in giving those films their languid, dark look—a look Tibor considered appropriate for Subaru's "Factory" spot. In hiring-chain tradition, Fred then engaged the gaffer to supervise all the lighting and electrical setups and a key grip to guide all the construction necessary to move the camera and focus the lights. Each of them hired a best boy, or chief assistant. And on it went, until the entire crew—a large one, by advertising standards—was found. "The premise of the business," said George Billard, a casual, ebullient young man who favored khaki shorts and pink polo shirts, "is that everything is rented—equipment and people."

Although the members of the crew knew the individuals who had hired them, there were few longtime friends and many strangers in the group. Once assembled, however, they betrayed the easy familiarity of old acquantainces. All knew their roles and responsibilities; all knew whom to command and to whom to defer. Thanks to the rigidly compartmentalized organizational structure of the movie business, they were an army of mercenaries so expert at their singular tasks that they needed none of the seasoning a real army receives from barracks life and training exercises. They were ready to hit the ground filming, under the command of their general, Tibor Kalman.

Tibor had arrived the night before in typically noisy fashion. He had flown into Chicago shortly before midnight, where he was met by the car service which was to drive him the hundred miles to Lafayette. The driver, however, arrived in Chicago without a map, and with Tibor babbling, fuming and directing in the backseat, wound up delivering the director to the Homewood Suites not at 1 a.m., as scheduled, but at 3:30 a.m. Further, the driver demanded a cash payment, which Tibor, assuming, correctly, that payment had already been arranged, refused to provide. A loud argument ensued, which ended only when the local police made an entrance in the motel's lobby. To forestall an overnight stay in jail, Tibor woke Maribeth (whose job as producer made her his alter ego) who woke Becky, who woke Kristine, who somehow, circa 4 a.m., settled the dispute.

Tibor was tired. But that did not stop him from talking. Rarely did anything stop Tibor from talking. And everything Tibor was telling Wieden & Kennedy about his plans for the shoot seemed, well, *wrong.*

He told the agency men that he planned to use nine separate shots in the "Factory" spot, for which he would shoot eleven. "That's not much of a fail-safe," Jerry Cronin said.

He told them that he wanted more encompassing views of the factory in the commercial. "I thought it was interesting real tight," Jerry said.

He told them he was thinking about concluding the spot with a shot of the six-star Subaru emblem being implanted on a car. It reminded Jerry of another, despised auto spot that concluded with the embedding of a nameplate. "It's just like the Ford commercials where the lady takes the thing and does the Ford logo," he complained.

Worse yet was what Tibor saw when he first walked through the factory with the agency executives. A cavernous, corrugated metal box covering 2.3 million square feet, the equivalent of thirty-five football fields piled against each other, the plant was a jangling, hissing, clanking asylum of modernist madness, 167,000 cubic yards of concrete and 20,000 tons of structured steel set amid the cornfields of the American midwest. It was unnaturally clean, its gray, stone floors completely empty of the scraps and skid marks that tell of a human presence. Within its walls giant robot arms moved with the canny rhythms of jazz dancers, darting their pincers and drills out and in and around to a cacophonous beat. Enormous beige-and-blue vaults accepted 10,000 pounds of steel coils at a time and, applying 500 tons of pressure, flattened, washed, cut and pinched them into 3,600 car parts each hour. Giant sparks flew from inside grated metal enclosures and sizzled into nothingness.

Amid this dazzling display of electromechanical wonder, all Tibor could talk about were the people. "We went into the factory and were kind of blown away by the *machinery*," Jerry chafed.

Jerry and his colleagues worried among themselves that Tibor was going to put a smiling person in every shot and turn the Subaru brand-image spot—which Wieden & Kennedy saw more clearly than ever as a celebration of the automobile's inanimate verities—into an idolization of the faces, "each sealed in its hunger / for a different life, a lost life," of the men and women who made the cars. Even before filming began, the Wieden & Kennedy execs had given a name to Tibor's presumed predilection for people over machines, a name taken from the solicitous title character in the long-running General Motors parts-and-repairs advertising campaign. Tibor, they believed, wanted to "goodwrench" the Subaru spots.

Whatever the toll, they—the advertising men, Subaru of America's agents on the scene—would have to prevent that.

WHEN JERRY, art director Larry Frey and John Adams (a broadcast producer who had joined the agency less than a week before to help with its burgeoning commercial production efforts) wound their way through the factory's maze to observe the start of filming Monday morning, their worst fears were realized. For his very first shot, Tibor had chosen to focus not on the machinery but on an affable young SIA worker named Randy Ferguson.

Randy's cinematic task, mimicking his job, was to bolt together two parts of the right side of the car, heedless of the sparks flying at his face, then leave the drill hanging from the ceiling, turn and walk up and off left, like Glenn Ford after a gunfight. The camera was going to add its own drama to the action: the film speed was set at forty frames per second, much higher than the normal speed for filming and playback, which is twenty-four frames per second. Filmed at forty and played back at twenty-four—a technique, favored by postmodern agencies, called "overcranking"—Randy's bolt-and-stroll would become slow and ever so poetic.

Tibor was intent on capturing every nuance of the man and his action. He peered intently at one of the two small video monitors that sat atop a metal cart not three feet from the action, staring at a screen that had been divided with electrical tape into two sections. On the right one-third, the agency's scrolling text was to cover most of the scene; on the left two-thirds, the action was to be visible. The camera, with Fred Elmes, his key grip and several assistants attending it, floated smoothly around the action on a dolly that looked like a metal golf cart without sides.

"Go!" yelled Tibor, starting in on a close-up of Randy's hands as the worker pivoted to grab the hanging drill. "Hit it!" he continued, ordering the camera to pull back to capture the start of the drilling. "Go!" he said, commanding a close-up of the drill hitting and sparking. "Beautiful," he said, as the camera drew back again to watch Randy walk off into the distance. "Beautiful. Great."

Then Tibor filmed the scene again. And again. And again. Not until 11:15 did he finish.

The crew began dismantling the camera rig, the viewing station, the scaffolding, lights, filters and scrims, to move them to another area. Despite the 108-degree temperature inside the factory, the men and women, per plant regulations, wore long-sleeve shirts, long pants and white plastic hard hats. To keep cool, most had tied around their necks blue or pink Handi-Wipe strips soaked in a bucket of Sea Breeze, a cooling astringent. In these sweat-stained ascots, they looked strangely elegant, blue-collar gentlefolk off for a rollicking day at the machine shop.

There was little merriment in the mood of Wieden & Kennedy's road crew, though. One scene down, they asked to take a meeting with Tibor.

They walked past a collection of buffed car shells which, in their embryonic pallor, looked like fetuses in the womb. They walked past a line of giant, sparking robots. "This is fucking amazing," marveled John Adams, a lanky young man with a soft voice who resembled a long-haired version of *Mad* magazine's Alfred E. Neuman. "I keep expecting to see Ridley Scott or *Blade Runner* or *Terminator 2*." Tibor disagreed but slightly. "It's like Fritz Lang's *Metropolis*," he said.

They arrived at one of the few cool places inside the plant, Body Meeting Room 1, an air-conditioned conference room, windowed on all sides, visible to but apart from the factory floor. A tray of sliced vegetables and fruits and a picnic cooler filled with Perrier and spring water were wheeled in.

Jerry wasted little time getting to the point. He pulled out notes he had been taking. "W-w-we think there might be too many people in the shots," he said.

On Jerry's normally impassive face, a slight frown, a glance down betrayed real worry. But Tibor glided right through Jerry's concerns. In looks, he seemed of Wieden & Kennedy's easygoing ilk. Unlike other New York graphic designers, who favored blocky black Italian suits, Japanese ties, hair mousse and ponytails, Tibor preferred jeans and flannel shirts and a short, irrelevant haircut. His pudgy face and thick, round glasses lent him a babyish innocence. Yet he was a relentless talker; in a sharp, deep, hard-to-interrupt voice, he let loose sly asides that flew over people's heads or landed to grate on them. Although he and the Wieden & Kennedy men were, ostensibly, both part of advertising's casual avant-garde, in truth they could not have been more different. The agency execs were soft-spoken Middle American radicals. Tibor was a quick-talking New York Jewish anarchist.

"It's going to be less people-looking than you think I want to make it and less metal-looking than you want to make it," he replied, not exactly reassuringly, to Jerry.

Jerry then questioned, gently, the robot Tibor had chosen to shoot in another scene, and suggested several alternatives.

"I prefer to use the robot I got," Tibor said. "But I want to keep you happy. I want to get paid."

"Oh, you'll get paid," Jerry said, not catching the irony.

"I'm just being an asshole," Tibor responded, compounding the tension. He began skimming one hand over the surface of the conference table in faster and faster circles as he chain-smoked Marlboros. "Am I done with you guys?" he asked, his voice growing quicker, louder, more frantic. "Am I done with you guys?"

The answer was yes . . . and no. Wieden & Kennedy let Tibor return to filming. But barely four hours into the shoot, the agency had other problems with its director.

At the root of their dispute was the issue of preparation. Tibor had not, as commercial-production protocol demanded, delivered to Wieden & Kennedy shooting boards—detailed storyboards, based on but not necessarily completely faithful to the agency's original story-boards, describing each shot the director planned to make. Tibor blamed the lapse on the agency, claiming that Dan Wieden had not re-turned his calls. To the agency creatives, this was no excuse, especially when Tibor appeared to be countermanding their designs.

"His vision is more cluttered than our vision. And the composition, the things he wants to put in the shot, are superfluous," John Adams ex-plained. "And there's no plan, no storyboard. That adds to the element of uncertainty."

Beyond the questions about readiness, clutter and goodwrenching, Tibor and the agency also disagreed about the SVX spot. Tibor wanted more of a plot line to the commercial. He persuaded the agency to use a split screen—a device they had already employed in spots for Anne Klein fashions and Pepe jeans. The top half of the screen would not feature disconnected scenes shot inside the factory, as Jerry had written it, but a car under construction, progressing from a bolt to a finished auto.

Their argument was over the bottom half of the screen. The director and the agency agreed that it should show a road, from the driver's point of view, as the car gradually picked up speed to match its degree of completion on the top half. But Wieden & Kennedy wanted to con-clude the piece with what Jerry called "an out-of-body experience" and what Tibor labeled "the impossible idea"—the transformation of the open road into the SVX itself. In effect, the agency envisioned the sports car pulling into the open road visible through its windshield.

How to accomplish this? Well, *that* was the director's job. But when Tibor suggested variations on the theme—the road going dark, followed by a flash of light and the sudden appearance of the SVX, as if, he said, it was "leaving the birth canal"—the agency turned him down. It wanted—it demanded—out of body.

Tibor believed the agency was taking advantage of him. He hadn't "bid that board"—had not factored into his cost calculations the special equipment necessary to obtain this effect. "We didn't get a board that says, 'The car materializes,' " he fumed, outside the agency's hearing. "Their board says, 'The car passes the camera truck.' As a director, I think that sucks. But we can't do a shot we don't have the technology for. It would take Industrial Light and Magic"—George Lucas's Hollywood special effects company—"to pull it off."

The agency executives had little sympathy for their director. Another director had filmed Bo Jackson walking out of a television set for them. Tibor was getting paid a director's fee of $10,000 a day, an extraordinarily high sum for a novice. Certainly he could figure out a way to make the SVX come into view. "I don't know what's difficult about that," Jerry said ingenuously.

Even more than the goodwrenching debate, this contest of wills over the last shot of the SVX spot symbolized their division. Wieden & Kennedy saw it as a simple creative dispute, one on which, as the agency, it had an unquestionable right to prevail. Tibor saw it as a power play, an effort by philistines to triumph over an artist. "The bit with Jerry, I just find the attitude kind of hard to take," he said later that day. "He doesn't want to listen to another idea and he hides behind the point-of-view thing. I think it's basically an ego thing. 'I'm not letting you win this one, Tibor.' "

On this point, Tibor was wrong. Wieden & Kennedy was simply suffering from a malady known in the advertising business as "demo love."

Demo love describes an agency's or client's infatuation with a ripomatic, a song or some other creative device shown in a presentation, and the desperate, often impossible, effort to replicate it in the finished commercial. Frequently, an agency will present a demonstration ad backed by an existing piece of popular music, only to discover later that the rights to the song cannot be had at any price. If the client is suffering from demo love, the agency has no choice but to find a way to steal the music.

Sometimes, the theft is literal. In 1989, a federal district court awarded the singer Bette Midler $400,000, judging that Young & Rubicam had deliberately copied her singular vocal style in a commercial for the Mercury Sable. The ad agency had presented to the Ford Motor Company a demo commercial backed by Midler's rendition of "Do You Want to Dance?" Only after the client gave the green light did Y&R discover that the singer would not sell it the song. The agency then hired one of Midler's backup singers and asked her to mimic the singer's style.

The Portland agency freely admitted that it was suffering from demo love. "We've had a bad case of it," Jerry conceded. He and his colleagues had become captivated by a videotape that Larry Frey had shot during the agency's first walk through the SIA plant two weeks earlier. As edited, Larry's demo was a seamless, flowing, moving documentary about the mechanics of automobility. It featured grainy closeups of bolts, slowly moving robot arms, a measured pan across the inside of a bare car door, lights glowing through ceiling mesh, a car frame on a dolly, flying sparks, all backed by a haunting, repetitive mandolin piece by the New Wave composer Steve Reich. It was a pure, unadorned visualization of Jerry's antistatus, a-car-is-just-a-car philosophy.

"The idea is simple as a rock," the copywriter maintained. "Emotionally, it's not complex. We knew what we wanted. Inventory. Pieces of goods to be sold. We just wanted Tibor to plus our boards." Instead, Jerry complained, "Tibor wants something more *artistic.*"

Sometimes, though, the line between art and mechanics, or, in this case, between commercial production and automobile production, can grow quite blurry. Both, after all, demand an initial concept. Both require mastery of complex machinery. One may exemplify the information-era economy into which we are ostensibly moving and the other may symbolize the industrial age from which we are passing, but both tasks call for an awful lot of people to repeat a large number of mindless movements in order to disgorge a fairly simple product at the end.

Tibor and his crew reconvened at the head of an assembly line identified by signs reading "REAR DOOR LH" and "FRONT DOOR LH." To visualize the shot, Fred Elmes climbed inside the hull of car as it moved from inside an enclosed clean room, where rough spots and welding bumps were sanded down, and slowly rolled down the line. Crouching, Fred peered through a lens he had brought with him, watching the action. First, two women bolted on the rear doors. The car moved on. A pudgy fellow named Bernie, with holes where his front teeth once were, pivoted his body back on his hips, grabbed a clamping contraption that hung from a mess of wires and pulleys and, swinging it back, pushed the right front door into place. He pressed two black buttons, there was a *whoosh* of air, and the door was secured in its position. Taking a drill attached to the unit, he gave two quick *craaannnks*, and bolted the door on. Finally, he laid the front-right fender in place, reloaded the drill, flipped a piece of metal from the fender back to the door post, bolted it in place, reached back and attached another door to the frame-holder-bolter gizmo, and secured the front and rear doors to the frame with heavy magnets. The whole process took about four minutes.

Fred got out of the car, and with his assistants set up the shot. A camera loader stood in front of the camera, which was at right angles to the clean room. She held up a card with a gray-scale on it as Fred adjusted the camera's lens aperture. Meanwhile, the key grip set about constructing a high hat, a support structure made up of two metal circles bolted to two metal plates with pillars. The camera was to be mounted on the high hat inside the car.

During the eight minutes it took the grip to finish the high hat, a camera assistant removed the camera from its dolly and brought it to the head of the line. There, she, the grip and some production assistants quickly mounted it on the rear seat of a sedan as it slowly made its way down the line, and surrounded the precious camera with blankets. Fred moved to the car and crouched again in it, his butt sticking out the rear-left door. With the camera assistant adjacent to him on the front seat, Fred pointed the camera through the front windshield and slowly panned it to the rear-right window and back to the front. An assistant grip stood behind them holding the camera's red power cable, which snaked through the trunk. Fred swung the camera back and forth and back and forth. After about a minute of this, Tibor yelled, "Cut!"

The principals gathered around the TV monitor and waited as the videotape, an instantly readable substitute for the film inside the camera, rewound. Then they watched as the shot slowly moved from a view straight down the lines outside the windshield to a view of a woman riveting the door.

"I like her," Fred said.

"What do *you* think?" Tibor solicitously asked Jerry Cronin.

"I like it, but I'm not sure about her," Jerry replied.

Tibor turned around to face the waiting crew and rotated his arm in a circle.

"Again?" asked the second assistant director.

"Again," said Tibor.

WIEDEN & KENNEDY DECIDED the time had come for a showdown. At 9:40 p.m., the agency convened a meeting of pertinent personnel in an inner room in Suite 109 at the Homewood, a small chamber cluttered with a film editing console, three-quarter-inch and half-inch videocassette players and the backseat of a Plymouth minivan.

If not rested, the attendees at least looked cleaner than before. Short and spunky Maribeth had put on white jeans, a clean T-shirt and a blue blazer. Larry had traded his sweaty T-shirt for a clean blue one and white cotton twills. John Adams wore a white, high-necked T-shirt, khaki shorts and moccasins, while Jerry, his wet hair slicked back from a desperately desired shower, wore rubber-soled windsurfing shoes beneath his gym shorts. Tibor had simply traded his black jeans for blue ones. Of them all, only Fred Elmes had not changed. But only Fred had shown no ill effects from the factory's heat.

The showers, however, did little to wash away the somber moods. Bantering unsmilingly, the participants filed over to a tray of sliced cheese, carrots, grapes and honeydew melon that Kristine, the P.A., had brought in. Finally, Tibor broke the uneasy détente. He had arrived at a new resolution to the SVX spot, a way to reveal the car and to pay off the plot line.

"In a stretch of road where we have a dotted line," he said, drawing the scene in pen on a napkin, "what happens is, we're driving along, and we want to see fairly far in the distance. The Subaru is coming toward us in the other lane, the *opposite* direction. What we do, as it comes by, we do a whip pan, okay? So we just follow the car, and it gets right next to us, coming in the opposite direction." He drew a picture of the camera, mounted on top of a truck, slowly swiveling to meet the oncoming SVX, then holding for a second on a full profile of the sports car as it pulls adjacent to the truck. "Then, once it gets past the camera car, the Subaru just stops."

"It just stops?" Jerry repeated, puzzled.

"It just stops," Tibor emphasized. "Dead across the road. The reason I want that is it then gives me the opportunity to structure this in a certain way. Subaru is square in the frame, across the road. We get closer with the camera, we lose the edge. We get it to the right size, sitting essentially on the horizon. And the type comes up in the sky.

"It's a contextual product shot," he explained, "that comes out of the plot of the piece."

All eyes turned to Jerry, who had been drinking this in. "Ummm," he started. "I-i-i-t seems kind of fucked up, to be honest with you."

For a second, everyone, even his colleagues, were stunned into silence. Maribeth broke it with a quip. "Tell us what you *really* think," she said.

But it was no joke to Jerry. He had already emphasized to Tibor his idea for the spot—that the bottom of the screen depict the road from the perspective of the car, the speed increasing to match the construction of the car on the screen's top. Tibor apparently had not listened. "I really think all movement should be taken from the perspective of the SVX," Jerry reiterated. "To give you the out-of-body feel. Because you're on the road. Nothing's happening in the very initial stages of being built. And as it's more and more built, movement picks up. On and on."

The tension was dissipated by the arrival of dinner—prime rib and barbecued chicken in Styrofoam containers. The room filled with the high-pitched squeaks of plastic knives and forks against the polystyrene. Above the painful noise, Tibor, haltingly at first, pleaded his case.

"Let's forget about your idea for a minute, Jerry. Let's talk about why mine is fucked up."

"Because I think that the bottom thing should be the Subaru SVX, as it's being built, coming to life," said Jerry. "Then when it's fully completed, it fully comes to life, and it's like an out-of-body experience."

"Are you open on this at all?" Tibor asked.

Jerry pondered. "I mean, a little. Sure."

Tibor launched into a passionate defense of his "vision." "See, what I think makes the commercial more challenging and more interesting is two things. One is to end up combining the upper and lower frames. I think clearly the perception will be, because of the nature of the copy, that we're in this car. I think the surprise of it is that we see *another* car coming toward us. It unifies the top and bottom of it. Which to me is important. I think it's the kind of commercial that is very much worth paying off with a shot of the car. The car has never been seen before. It's not like a car that's been around for two or three years and is being updated. The car is pretty striking in profile, with the window and stuff like that."

His logic was unassailable. It was also unnecessary, as Larry pointed out. "So why don't we just cover that in the top shot? Do a profile of the car, and then do whatever we want on the bottom?"

"Because I'd like to bring them together," answered Tibor. "I'd like to let that last top shot fade, and suddenly, there's like a moment, a brief white sky, and then wham! it comes on, in a stunning way. I think it's like a big shock that pays off the spot. I just want it to have a solid, grounded, exciting ending. As this car whips past us, and we whip with it, it crosses the road from the camera, and the whole thing just feels integrated and paid off to me."

There was a long, uncomfortable pause. "Is this the usual course of events?" Tibor asked. "You have this conversation with the director at this stage?"

"What do you mean?" John Adams responded.

"These disagreements."

"Sure," John replied, ingenuously. "All the time. We just normally have these discussions a couple of days sooner, that's all."

Tibor had done himself a grave disservice with the question. Already, Jerry was suspicious of, and not a little intimidated by, his fast talk. Now Tibor had revealed his insecurity. Nevertheless, instead of demanding that Tibor toe the line, Jerry tried to reason with the director.

"I just feel as it's being built, it's coming to life, picks up more speed, and then"—Jerry gave a *whoosh*ing motion with his hands—"it's gone. I like the very simple, linear 'the car comes to life as it's being put together' theme. Speed, power, life."

The copywriter was handing the director a baton of conciliation, but Tibor refused to run with it. Under his breath, but loud enough for all in the small room to hear, he said, with withering condescension, "It's so fucking like *Star Wars*." To force the agency to see it his way, he tried one last tactic: the Socratic method.

"What do you think a person watching this commercial will think is on the bottom of the screen, as you take the driver's point of view and go down that road?" he asked.

"I think normally they'd associate it with the car on the top," replied Jerry, "just because of all the talk about cars and speed."

"So why," Tibor continued, with a "gotcha" in his voice, "is changing the direction of the car on the bottom anything but an interesting surprise? Why is it, like, wrong?"

At this, Jerry lost his temper. He was in no mood to play befuddled Gorgias to Tibor's Socrates. He was a nice guy, an easygoing guy. He had gone out of his way to describe his concept to the director, to explain how the commercial's plotting supported its theme. Jerry was presenting an artistic vision. So was Tibor. But Tibor had forgotten an essential fact: Unlike feature filmmaking (at least under the auteur theory), advertising is not a director's medium. It is the agency's. And no agency needed to defend itself to a director—certainly not a first-time director.

"I'm not saying it's *wrong*," Jerry responded, contempt rising in his voice. "I don't think anything is *wrong*. I don't think it's *wrong* if the car blew up on a mound of gasoline. I don't think that would be *wrong*. I don't think it would be *wrong* if it hit a tree. I just think the other way's better. The ascension, my payoff, just feels better to *me*—better than having something come on from the other direction."

Tibor, plaintively, tried to continue the argument. "I have a feeling this is bogus," he said. But he had lost—the battle *and* the war. He had driven Cronin to the breaking point, a place the reserved Bostonian rarely went, and from which it would be difficult to bring him back.

"We'll talk tomorrow," Jerry concluded.

TUESDAY DAWNED hot and ugly. The night before, Jerry had tried to calm himself by plunging into a copy of Mark Twain's *The Innocents Abroad*, and, like the author, he "soon passed tranquilly out of all consciousness of the dreary experiences of the day and damaging premonitions of the future." Larry had tossed fitfully all night, in pain from an ankle sprain suffered during a pickup basketball game several nights earlier with some Lafayette teens. And John just stared into the night, wondering whether his new career at his new agency was crumbling just as it was beginning.

They gathered uneasily at the factory's Metal Closure cage that morning to observe the commitment of a simple shot to film. Two metal arms were to swing around from the left and lock into place underneath an incipient Subaru Legacy, which sat face forward, front and center, in the screen. Slowly, the arms would lift the vehicle skyward, as another car moved into view farther down the line.

As uncomplicated as the shot was—the camera would remain stationary throughout—the setting required complex lighting maneuvers. Three assistant electricians, their motions as fluid and synchronized as an acrobatic team's, slid and screwed a lamp to a lightpole, secured its base with sandbags, and *allez-oop*ed the extending rod twenty-two, twenty-five, thirty feet toward the roof. The men all wore blue work shirts; on the front pockets were stuck clothespins, which were used to attach gels to the lights. The gels were colored orange and flame. One of the electricians, a ponytailed man known as J.B., explained that these colors would balance the fluorescent lights inside the factory, which to the eye appeared white but which the film picked up as green.

The grips, meanwhile, set up their own array of materials to absorb, reflect or diffuse the light. They talked in a code that other crew members termed "grip talk." The pure black screens, which soaked in all the light that came their way, were called "flags"; "nets" were cloth screens of various densities; the more reflective acrylic screens were called "silks"; any big rag was referred to as a "butterfly."

It took close to an hour for the grips and electricians to hang their network of gels, flags, nets, silks and butterflies to Tibor's and Fred's satisfaction. Finally, Peter Replier, the assistant director, signaled the start. "Rolling!" The arms swung around, grabbed the Legacy, and lifted it to the ceiling, as the camera slowly zoomed in on the next car down the line. "Cut!" yelled Peter. The shot took all of ten seconds. "That's nice," said John Adams. "Let's move."

But Tibor was dissatisfied. He wanted to do the shot again. "Let's moooove," John repeated, mostly to himself. Then he saw why Tibor was repeating the shot: The director wanted to focus the camera not on the succeeding car's roof, but on the worker attending to it.

John walked over to Larry, who was sitting in a wheelchair, his ailing leg extended. "Larry, hang out by the camera today."

"We're putting Tibor on a short leash?" Larry asked.

"A very short leash," the producer replied.

Tibor saw what was occurring but was powerless to stop it. He commandeered one of the beat-up bicycles which were the preferred, low-tech form of transportation around the high-tech plant. While the crew was dismantling the rigging at the Metal Closure cage and transporting it to the Car Trim line, he rode furiously and aimlessly around the plant. "I'm angry. I'm angry," he seethed.

He refused to blame himself for his difficulties. Yet, having spent the previous night ridiculing the agency's plans for the SVX spot, here he was, the very next morning, contravening their "metal, not people" dictum. The agency would not stand for it.

"People will see it and they'll say, 'Oh, I know what this commercial is about. It's about the people who make Subarus,' " Larry complained.

Jerry unhappily agreed. "You've seen so many people working on cars, it brings back all that *baggage*. It's been done."

Tibor saw only one way through his dilemma: John Adams. John, the agency producer, had gone to the College of William & Mary with Maribeth, Tibor's producer. John would be sympathetic. So Tibor asked John to meet with him and Maribeth in the cafeteria, away from the factory's din and prying eyes.

"My idea of creative work is one person loving it. If there's no one in the world who loves it, it's shit," Tibor pleaded, leaning in on John from across a dining table. "If there's one thing that's going to happen, sure as shit, we'll turn out a piece of work Subaru thinks is shit and blame me. Or I'll hate it and blame you."

Throughout the speech, John, exuding gentle concern, nodded his head and repeated, "I understand."

Tibor delivered his ultimatum. "Let me direct. Or let me stay here for guidance and turn the leadership over to someone else."

"I understand," John said.

He understood enough to seek out Jerry and Larry to tell them that Tibor was now threatening to quit.

Jerry smiled a crooked grin. "He has no idea what we're trying to do. He keeps adding people, cluttering up the shots." He held his head in his hands.

"God," Jerry said, "this is awful."

As the drama unfolded in the back rooms, the crew did what most crews do on commercial shoots: they horsed around.

Their primary form of merriment, a tradition on production sites, was Teamster jokes, a category of entertainment which, like ethnic humor, traded on the presumed laziness and stupidity of its subjects.

"What did the Teamster say when his kid came home from school?" asked Blaise, the ablest wiseacre among the P.A.s. The answer: " 'Go out and watch the other kids play.' "

Mike, the second assistant director, switched to another class of jokes of which his ilk were the butts. "What's the difference between a proctologist and an assistant director?" he queried. "The proctologist only deals with one asshole at a time."

Maribeth chimed in with a piece of gallows humor appropriate to the day. "Hey," she wondered. "Who do I have to fuck to get off this job?"

THE CREW HAD ESTABLISHED its base camp outside Gate N5, a gaping maw that confronted a sea of some two hundred trucks, and which usually served as an entry point for the raw materials of which automobiles were made.

These days, though, the seeds of future Subarus had been swept away, replaced by the raw materials of image-making. A white Cadillac Sedan De Ville—Tibor's car—sat just outside the gate. Seven minivans—black, blue and maroon Chevy Luminas and Plymouth Voyagers, looking like a family of obedient South American capybaras—were lined up in a row leading toward the gate, waiting to take exhausted crew members back to their motels. Two large yellow trucks, rented from Hertz and Ryder, contained the lights, filters, screens, struts and scaffolding necessary to prepare reality for film. From a third truck, abutting the factory's wall, spilled the event's fuel: junk food.

Bill Davenport sat alone on the grass next to the food truck, deliberately chewing on a bowl of Kellogg's Raisin Squares. He was tired. He was angry. Wieden & Kennedy's head of broadcast production had arrived from Portland late the night before, summoned by his colleagues to help solve their crisis. He had reviewed the dailies—the raw film shot each day—and deemed it mediocre and insufficient. He was steeling himself with cereal to prepare for a confrontation with Tibor.

Davenport got up and walked the entire width of the factory. He passed the crew members who, like him, were distinguishable from the factory workers only by their shirts, which invariably advertised a film, a production company, a postproduction house, a supplier or a union. He entered the cafeteria, where Tibor already sat with Maribeth. "What exactly is your disagreement on vision?" Davenport asked, pronouncing the final word with a slight hint of distaste.

Tibor, still hoping, somehow, to find a way to overrule Cronin's directives, appealed to Davenport.

"I think mine has a larger emphasis on people," Tibor said. "I don't think people give a rat's ass about machines. On the other hand, it's not a GM film, a 'we're working together to build America' film. In SVX, we have a disagreement about how the car is being built. I think screws are bullshit. There's a huge difference between a screw floating in air and a forklift lifting a coil of steel. One is a fuck-you, pretentious attitude shot. To pan over a bolt, or over a thing of parts, is Design 101. It's not scratching the surface of what these things can be."

"As much as you say you didn't like that," Davenport responded evenly, "the creatives say they like it."

Tibor turned contentious. "I think you guys are full of shit on this. But I'm not angry. I know what you're protecting."

Now it was Davenport's turn to get mad. "We're not protecting anything," he said. "Our confidence was shaken early. It was lost when we didn't get the storyboards. We have no creative confidence in what's happening. We're in deep, deep shit. In my ten years in this business, I've never seen anything so ill-prepared and chaotic. We *must* pick up the pace. Light it, shoot it and move on. All this talk about vision—your vision, our vision—right now it's the *agency's* vision that must be followed."

Tibor absorbed the producer's ire, then issued a warning which was, by this stage, rather toothless. "The way I interpret what you're telling me: You will tell me what will be shot. I'll do my best to accomplish it. So *you* lead. But I can't guarantee that the commercial will be what I thought it could be, for Subaru."

Now Davenport understood why his colleagues were so drained after only a few days in Indiana. "I agree," he said wearily. "We take full responsibility."

Even a titular shift in responsibility could not gain for Wieden & Kennedy all the components it believed it needed to construct two commercials for Subaru. As the fourth day of production began, the shot boards—two blackboards listing the scenes filmed—registered a paucity of material.

For "Factory," the Legacy image spot, there were fourteen shots, but the ad agency considered many of them unusable. Tibor had filmed a close-up of a man, a robotic arm, two men feeding a metal stamping press, the attachment of a car door, the car lift, a conference room, a Legacy driving inside the plant, the underside of a car passing down the line, an auto entering the paint room, a headlight pan, a sparking grinder against a hood, a pan along a gutter, a pan to a gas tank and the inside of a car door. For SVX, only seven shots (aside from "Factory" footage which was to be reused) had been filmed: a welding torch, a dynamometer, the engine, a buffer, a man working on the wheel well of a stripped sports car, the windshield and the "beauty shot"—the finished SVX. For an agency that liked to fashion its advertisements in the editing suite, this was not nearly enough material to stitch even a threadbare patchwork quilt.

The activity taking place before Fred Elmes's Arriflex 35BL4 camera did little to reassure the agency. Fred, still dressed elegantly in his khakis and his ACA Joe shirt, was squinting and focusing on a bolt that was being tossed—over and over and over again—against a board.

Tibor might have called shots of screws "bullshit." But he also still insisted that "this"—the filming of a television commercial—"is not commerce. It's, I hate to say it, art." Together, he and Fred were going to give that goddamn bolt the most artistic rendering a fastener had ever received.

This was Annie McDermott's big moment. Heavy, ebullient, ready for work, Annie had been severely underutilized during the shoot. She was a professional props person, and there just wasn't that much call for her expertise at fakery inside an honest-to-goodness auto factory.

"Remember the manhole cover that blew up in the new Kentucky Fried Chicken spot?" Annie boasted. "That was me. I figured out how to do it. And we did it in only *two* takes. The only way we get our jobs is from the tricks we know. I'm known in New York as the 'scum queen.' I developed the grime on the bathroom walls that Procter and Gamble uses in all its commercials. They fly me to Cincinnati all the time. The agencies and production companies hire me because I make it work. The only thing I won't give away are my formulas. Procter stole my bottles once—I had ten of them lined up on the set—to have them analyzed. But I learned to spit in my bottles because the enzymes in saliva break down some of the chemicals. I make them in different colors. Bathroom scum is white, kitchen brown, garage black. I spray 'em on, they say, 'We like that one,' I say, 'Okay, I'll make six bottles.' "

Among her specialties, it turned out, was tossing bouncing objects. Annie took a piece of white foam board and glued a rubber mat to its underside to act as a shock absorber. She then taped the rectangle to a cafeteria table the P.A.s had lugged out for the job, and marked off a five-inch square in the center of the board with adhesive tape. With the camera poised only a foot from the action, Annie practiced her technique, flicking the 1⅛-inch golden bolt onto the white board so it would rest, and roll. Rest, and roll . . . She tried a drop from the top. She tried a pinch-toss from the side. Each time, she attempted to achieve the perfect rest, and roll.

Nine times—with breaks—Annie and the film crew repeated the action. This was too much for the advertising executives. With their last day in the plant ebbing away, they saw only one way to extricate themselves from the looming disaster: a second unit.

Second units are separate, smaller film crews, dispatched with their own camera to obtain additional footage to buttress the work being shot by the first unit. Initially, Tibor and his crew had resisted the agency's suggestion that they deploy a second unit. Maribeth warned that, without special lighting and attention to color correction, the second unit's film would look entirely different from the first unit's. But the agency brushed aside the objections. "A big crew tends to make the camera rigid, like it's frozen in cement," Larry Frey said of the existing footage. "The principle of the second unit, it's just one man, one camera. The shots are so personal. It's like you're a fly on the wall. It's hard to do that with fifty people. Jerry's word for what we want is 'stolen'—we want stolen moments. This commercial is about being truthful. The more set up it is, the more we defeat our own goals."

Larry had a personal stake in the argument. The second unit was to be his big break. Ever since the Creative Revolution, when art directors began the leap from the sketchpad to the camera, nary an agency art director has not contemplated a career as a film artist. Larry had proven his ability with his videotape demo. Now, his colleagues, in desperation, were going to give him a chance with a real camera and some real film.

Assisting Larry was Tom Zimmerman, a young cameraman from Indianapolis and a living example of the extended reach of the industry hiring chain. Zimmerman was one of numerous film professionals who resist moving to Hollywood or New York, preferring instead to eke out a living from their comfortable, less expensive homes in the flyover. He owned his own equipment—a $75,000 camera and a $50,000 zoom lens—and used it on whatever came up: a John Cougar Mellencamp movie, retail ads by Milwaukee agencies and, most recently, a commercial entitled "Party with the Animals" for the Indiana State Fair, for which he shot flying pigs in harnesses. Kristine, the Indiana-bred P.A., had known him since junior high school. So frantic was Wieden & Kennedy about the need for more film that it hired Zimmerman merely on the production assistant's say-so, without even asking to review his work. "To go from filming pigs to a national auto spot!" the cameraman marveled. "Only in Indiana."

There was something heroic about the second unit. Larry was still limping badly from his sprained ankle, but that did not prevent him from moving at breakneck speed through the factory, leading a sweaty Zimmerman on a Keystone Kops–paced chase through the plant. Up ladders, across beams, underneath chassis, down lines they clambered. Lissome Kristine, ponytail flying, bicycled back and forth between the unit's shifting outposts and its base camp back by the first unit, delivering exposed film and picking up fresh film for the camera. Everyone performed triple duty. Zimmerman not only did the shooting, he marked the slate identifying each shot and, no grips or gaffers here, dragged a dolly with his camera, tripod and lens cases behind him. Kristine held the slate for focusing and took Polaroid pictures of and obtained releases from the factory personnel caught by the second unit's lens.

By 4:30 p.m., at about the time the first unit was just wrapping up the bouncing bolt shot, the second unit had completed six shots. With each one—a metal press, dye cables, steel coil—Larry's confidence grew and his mood lightened. The extra footage was tantamount to peace of mind. Indeed, as he scurried to the Car Final plant, with Zimmerman and the camera dolly trailing right behind him, Larry looked uncannily like Linus, dragging his security blanket with him from room to room. By 6:00 p.m., Frey's second unit had completed eighteen shots. Tibor and the first unit were finishing their fourth.

They were back at Gate N5, filming a long line of Legacies heading from the darkened factory out into the bright sunshine. Fred Elmes was crouched inside the camera dolly as several grips slowly pulled it along a track which ran parallel to the row of cars. He panned smoothly across the queue until a burst of light washed out the scene. Tibor wanted a "birth canal" shot, and this was it. For once, it worked to the agency's satisfaction.

"That was a great shot," John Adams said to Fred, with real gratitude, after reviewing it on videotape.

"I think you'll like it," Fred replied, equally sincerely.

Peter Replier, the assistant director, called the day to a halt, with instructions to the crew to assemble at the Homewood Suites at 6:30 the following morning to begin the long drive to southern Indiana to film the SVX road footage. There was a mild smattering of applause.

John Adams turned his eyes skyward. To no one in particular except, perhaps, his God, he whispered, "It's wrapped."

Chapter 15

Perception/Reality

WHENEVER JERRY CRONIN became agitated or otherwise needed to transport himself to another plane of existence, he wrote a letter to President Bush. The letters, which identified Jerry as "a registered voter from Oregon," gently mocked the Ivy League president's faux populism by suggesting various ways he might improve his political or personal fortunes. When Jerry saw the Bushes in the audience at the televised Country Music Awards, he wrote to advise the president on getting better seats the next time around. When he read that the administration employed two people to search for the perfect White House Christmas tree, Jerry, citing his residence in woodsy Oregon as an advantage, applied for the job.

After departing the horrendous Indiana shoot, driving with his colleagues to Louisville, Kentucky, and flying from there to Los Angeles, Jerry fell, exhausted, into his hotel room where, at 10:30 p.m., he decided to exorcise the previous week's demons by drafting a letter to the president. He set up on the bed the portable Macintosh computer he was lugging along with him and was hardly through the "Dear George" when he heard banging on the wall. Fearing he had awakened the people in the next room, he started tapping the keys ever so lightly, sketching a fable about a new inheritance he wanted to donate to the Republican party. The banging persisted. He put the computer away, turned off the lights and tried to get some rest. Only then did he hear the groans. Jerry drifted off to sleep, the first good one in a week, to the sound of people screwing next door.

He arrived at Red Car Studios some twenty-four hours later, rested and looking like the kind of fish you're supposed to choose when shopping for seafood. A bright shine had replaced the dead look in his eyes. He was clean and colorful, a pressed pink polo shirt and gray sweat shorts having substituted for the dirty jeans and perspiration-soaked tops of the previous week. He was ready to make magic.

Red Car was the place where Wieden & Kennedy and its increasingly popular brand of postmod advertising had been created seven years before, where the film editor Larry Bridges had taken a mess of underexposed footage of the rocker Lou Reed and turned it into an homage to French New Wave cinema. The Portland agency had rewarded Bridges and his company by making Red Car its official L.A. home-away-from-home. Other agencies, from both coasts and between, followed suit, turning Red Car—which was located, along with numerous other cinema industry suppliers, on an old movie studio lot a few blocks from the intersection of Melrose and Highland avenues in the heart of Hollywood—one of the ad industry's more favored postproduction houses.

Postproduction, or simply "post," is the place where it all comes together, where the disparate bits of light and sound are sewn into a fabric of meaning. Thousands of feet of exposed film are developed and cut into individual scenes and takes. The best takes are selected and the ad agency, assisted by a film editor, compiles them into a rough cut. Special effects—animation, computer distortion, superimposed text ("supers")—are added, as are a voiceover, a musical track and any other desired sound. Finally, the finished advertisement's color is corrected, its sound modulated and the ad is transferred onto a videotape master from which endless numbers of copies can be made and then shipped to TV networks and stations.

In the old days—that is, before the 1980s—postproduction was an uncomplicated procedure, in design if not always in execution. An agency and its director looked for editors and aides who could help them realize a deliberately crafted and approved storyboard. But the advent of wondrous new computer-controlled tools for the manipulation of film images had added layers of complexity and possibility to the postproduction process—layers in which young agencies like Wieden & Kennedy, so enamored of the artistic and political opportunities of advertising, liked to swath themselves. To Wieden & Kennedy (an agency, after all, that had once presented a proposed ad to a client not in the form of a storyboard but as an album cover), post was everything.

Red Car (its name was taken from the Pacific Electric Railway's trolleys, the "Big Red Cars" that had plied Los Angeles in the early twentieth century before the tracks were torn up to make way for the automobile) was a hive of activity by the time Jerry and his cronies arrived to complete their work on the Subaru spots. In room after room, video screens blazed and speakers blared with the sights and sounds of modern culture—soda cans sweated and cereal boxes poured; jazz, New Wave and classical strains mingled in a huckster's choir. Casually attired copywriters, art directors, producers, directors and editors popped out from their cool, dark suites to grab handfuls of the M & Ms and Reese's Peanut Butter Cups that filled the hollow porcelain dinosaurs which sat on pantry shelves in the airy lobby.

Jerry had prepared himself for the start of postproduction by spending several hours at a nearby Tower Records store. There, he pulled from the stacks $330 worth of compact discs, which he dragged to Red Car in a shopping bag, expecting to find in it a suitable soundtrack for the "Factory" spot.

Erik Satie, Béla Bartók, Bach sonatas, the Kronos Quartet, Rachmaninoff, Schoenberg, Mozart and Schumann consorted with Steve Reich, Miles Davis, "Great Blues Guitarists" and the scores to *Blue Velvet, Blade Runner* and *Silence of the Lambs.* "I like Aaron Copland, but I don't think he's right," mused Jerry, who had spent the earlier part of the morning listening to "Appalachian Spring" on a portable boom box he had also purchased.

John Adams and Larry Frey were listening intently to several cuts from the Pink Floyd album "Dark Side of the Moon." "When I was in college," Larry said, as the tune "Brain Damage" lasered toward its conclusion, "every party, if you stayed late enough, ended with that side of the album."

With no conclusions reached nor, yet, wanted, they ended their musical deliberations and filed into Rob Watzke's editing room.

Rob was to be the creatives' spiritual guide for much of the coming week. An accomplished editor who resembled the actor Kevin Costner, he had managed to maintain the sweet temper and boundless patience he learned during the first twenty-two years of his life in Iowa City, despite spending the succeeding nine years in the two-faced environs of L.A. He needed an even temperament to cut film for Wieden & Kennedy, for, as he knew from previous episodes with the shop, editing a spot for the Portland ad people required interpreting their silences, divining meaning from their rambles and experimenting endlessly with novelty.

Rob's first task with the agency was to review the film—some eighteen to twenty thousand feet of it—that had been shot in Indiana by the Tibor Kalman–Fred Elmes first unit and the Larry Frey–Tom Zimmerman second unit. At twenty-four frames per second, it takes twelve minutes for a thousand feet of film to work its way through a movie projector, which meant that Rob and the agency had to choose from over four hours of footage the two minutes that would wow an audience of dealers and, after them, a country full of consumers.

He threaded a reel onto his Moviola—a triple-screened console with more spindles and rolls than a textile mill—and, after taking a long swig from a bottle of Arrowhead mineral water, played the film. The first shot showed activity inside the Subaru plant reflected in a large globe hanging from the factory's ceiling. Jerry quaffed Diet Pepsi from a glass; the only voice heard was Henry Fonda's narration of Copland's "Abraham Lincoln," which came from the boom box. The second scene unwound: the beauty shot of the Subaru Legacies emerging from the factory into the blinding light of day. Finally, after a ninety-second eternity, Rob delivered the first outside judgment on the agency's hell week.

"It's nice," he said. "It's nice film."

That signaled the start of running commentary. As Rob's right fingers danced across the console's buttons—playing, rewinding, freezing—he, John and Larry stared straight ahead at the unit's center screen and judged the work.

"That's real cool," Rob said, viewing a second-unit scene of two men rotating a car shell 360 degrees on a dolly.

"But I'd crop it so you can't see their heads," Larry responded.

"Why?"

"Because bodies rotating bodies—that seemed interesting to me."

Rob wrote with a thin marker directly on the film, indicating that this take was to be included in the batch used for assembling the final spots. Later, all the marked takes would be transferred onto three-quarter-inch videotape, creating a "dirty dupe" that the agency and the editor would use to build the spots.

Another second-unit shot came up: two rows of arc welders, leaning in on a production line like a military honor guard with blue, green and yellow flames shooting from its rifles. "It's wild!" exclaimed Rob. "I like these shots, Larry. They're busy, but they're cool-looking. It sure looks like industry."

To an untrained observer, the excitement seemed premature, if not out of place. The construction of the scenes seemed interesting enough, but the film itself appeared jumpy, with lighting that ebbed and flowed in intensity and blemishes that often marred the action. The admen, however, were not worried. Most of the defects, they believed, were not in the film but in the playback machinery. What's more, many of the real flaws could be fixed in the on-line editing process, where the color would be corrected, the "chatter" steadied and the film transferred to broadcast-ready videotape.

Then they moved on to review the bulk of the first-unit footage. Their cheering stopped. Many of the shots seemed overdesigned— "fake-y," as Rob put it. And, as Jerry had feared, many shots were over-populated. "Too goodwrenchy," Jerry said, breaking his Pepsi-sipping silence.

When Rob threaded on the film from southern Indiana—comprising the last-day footage of the SVX on the road and the SVX driver's P.O.V. scenes—their enthusiasm ratcheted down even farther. Much of the material appeared useless.

After all their arguing and some $18,000 in scouting and site-preparation costs, the agency and Tibor had agreed that a road in Orleans (the self-proclaimed "dogwood capital of Indiana") was the perfect showcase for the SVX. They agreed to spend $3,000 a day (plus drivers' and camera rental costs) to bring up from Georgia the one-of-a-kind, specially outfitted, reinforced-everywhere gray Ford F-250 Custom camera truck from which much of the movie *Robocop* had been shot. They also agreed on how they would obtain the desired effect of the SVX racing out from the driver's own vision of the road speeding by in front of him. They started the camera truck just ahead of the SVX, with the camera laced to the end of the truck's seventeen-foot swinging boom. The camera was thus held steady, a few feet off the ground, in front of the SVX, then slowly raised to allow the race car to zoom out toward the horizon.

The film fell short of their expectations. There were a few decent shots, including a side view of the SVX holding steady in the center of the field of view, with only its fast-spinning wheels and the racing greenery to indicate its movement. Overall, though, the film was bumpy. And in the final emergence-from-nowhere shot, the beautiful, unusual, Ferrari-like SVX was so small that it made only the barest impression.

The SVX footage ended. "Okay, Rob," said Larry. "The truth."

"The truth?" the editor responded. "It's in the design. I don't think the stuff is killer. But the words are strong. It'll be in the design."

The agency men left Red Car confident. So it was going to be in the design, was it? Well, that was what they had always planned, wasn't it? Especially in their use of on-screen type, they were going to *shock* the advertising industry.

John, Jerry and Larry drove in a rented Subaru Legacy to a rundown part of Hollywood, at the foot of the hills. They parked in front of an unmarked red door, behind which lay, in an unexpectedly bright and airy space, Pittman-Hensley Composite Image Systems, the two-person operation that would obscure their advertisements' cinematic deficiencies with type.

Like Red Car, Pittman-Hensley had a towering reputation in the rarefied world of advertising hipsters. It had taken a once menial task—putting words on film—and turned it into high art, using various new pieces of software and other tools to transform on-screen typography into a sophisticated form of animation. Wieden & Kennedy had used the firm to create the erotically engaging type in ads for Anne Klein fashions. BBDO New York (the only large creative agency) hired Pittman-Hensley to do the jumpy, rhythm-and-blues-and-rap typography for the "You got the right one, baby, uh-huh" Pepsi-Cola campaign starring the singer Ray Charles. In the early 1990s, with the recession forcing a new simplicity upon American culture and (naturally) the agency business, on-screen type—simple, cheap and oh-so-basic—was becoming quite the thing. Pittman-Hensley thus had more than enough work to keep itself busy, but not so much that it wouldn't drop most of it to help its friends from Oregon.

The admen dug into a plate of deli sandwiches the type house had ordered for them and played a tape that contained four different versions of Larry's "Factory" demo. In one, the scenes cross-dissolved into each other; in another, they faded out and faded in. Three versions were black and white; one had color dialed into it. Some versions had the factory scenes bleeding out to the edge of the frame; others put thick borders around the scenes. In each demo, the music was different, and ranged from New Age tinkling to driving rock.

Donna Pittman, a petite Asian-American woman who wore a springy, pastel frock, viewed the demo coldly.

"The music seems to be driving it. Do you have a track you like yet?" she asked.

"No," John answered.

"What about a scratch track of the voice?"

Larry and John looked at each other. "No," John responded.

"When will a cut of the film be available?"

"Tuesday afternoon."

"When do you go into on-line?"

"Friday."

Donna glanced at her partner, Mark Hensley, a quiet man with stringy blond hair, who was wearing white jeans and a white T-shirt. The look said everything: Normally, they received months to work on a type treatment. Here, they were being asked for one in three days.

Larry, ever the problem solver, launched into his outline of the issues Pittman-Hensley faced. Reverse out the type—white against a black background? Should they use a background panel at all, or print it directly over the factory scenery? If a panel, soft-edged or hard-edged? Should the words crawl up the screen, or bloom in and fade off?

Donna, gently but seriously, waved him off. "We need to have the scratch track and the real picture before we can do anything. We need to know where the voice is falling. That kind of thing." In other words, little was possible until Wieden & Kennedy made some decisions about the final look and sound of the spot—both spots, since there was to be moving type on the SVX ad, too.

They talked, idly, about other options. Donna's one solid thought was that the type treatment needed to be simple, to offset the busy nature of the factory scenes. Jerry offered up a variation on a story layout he had seen used in *Rolling Stone*: a simple box, smack in the center of the screen, in which one or two words at a time, not the entire text, would be pulled from the voiceover. A playful graphic idea like that would, he thought, defuse some of the "preachiness" of his copy. "It sounds a little like a sermon at times," he conceded to Donna and Mark, a bit sheepishly.

"I think we better get to work," Donna said.

"Scribble down the options, start crossing out the stuff that's unworkable and give us a recommendation," Larry pleaded.

"All right," Donna said with an exasperated laugh, as she led them to the stairs leading down to the door. "Now get out of here."

The enormity of their task did not strike them until they were halfway back to Red Car.

"Pepe jeans," said Jerry, citing another Wieden & Kennedy client with on-screen text, "they've been working on the type for two and a half months."

"Anne Klein, they spent *months*," Larry added. "This is hopeless."

John, the most level-headed of the trio, tried to inject a note of calm into the proceedings. "We'll have time after the dealers' meeting to change things."

The black cloud of Irish despair which had moved with Jerry Cronin across the state of Indiana but dissipated after he had landed in California once again settled over his head, darkening a small, moving plot of Hollywood Boulevard.

"But if it's not right for the dealers' meeting, we're fucked," Jerry whispered hoarsely. "These guys have all the power. That sets the tone for the future." He fell silent. "Fuck. This is no time."

"This is barely enough time," Larry said, "to put a super on the end."

By the time they arrived back at Red Car, the agency men were in a state of high agitation. They needed the type to save the pictures, but they needed the pictures and a voiceover to fashion the type, and they needed a soundtrack to determine which voice and which pictures to use.

They began snapping cassettes and C.D.s into their boom box, frantically sorting through the possibilities. A voiceover casting service had sent over several dozen tapes of actors famous and unknown. Some of the voices were drawn from movie tracks, others were actually reading Jerry's copy—an act for which the performers received about $150 each, according to actors union rules requiring the payment of audition fees.

Snap. The voice of Ed Asner, Lou Grant from "The Mary Tyler Moore Show," began slurping, "A car is a car. . . ."

"Too serious," said Jerry. "Turn it off."

Snap. Peter Gallagher, a co-star in the film *Sex, Lies and Videotape*, started reading. Jerry rejected him, too.

"It should be thrown away," he said of his own words. "Tossed off."

Snap. A demo tape by a Portland rock band opened on a driving blues piece. Jerry frowned. "I don't know," he sighed.

Larry grabbed his shoulders and shook him. "Whaddya mean, you don't know? Jerry, *you don't have time not to know!*"

The creative director was saved from injury by the announcement that Rob had prepared a demonstration of how the SVX spot would look. The admen repaired to Red Car's basement, to an off-line editing room where they could review and tinker with the cut, which was done on easily manipulable three-quarter-inch videotape. The spot had been cut exactly to their storyboards. The screen would show a running shot of the open road, as seen from the SVX; superimposed onto the top of the screen, into the blue sky above the road, would be views of car parts and the factory, symbols of the caring construction of a sports car. The off-line editing console would allow them to test various types of superimposition—hazy bleeds, full bleeds, perhaps a distinct line between the road shot and the factory shots—as well as different overlapping shots from the plant.

A young editor named Billy ran the tape, and for the first time, the advertising men noticed that the open road shot, which had seemed correctly bumpy when viewed on Rob's Moviola, chattered continually, even on the presumably stable medium of videotape. Their contemplation of this problem ended abruptly when Billy began superimposing the factory shots. The first one showed a whirring, hand-held polisher hovering above the clouds and burnishing the hood of an SVX.

The agency crew laughed uproariously.

"It looks like the buffer of God!" cried Larry.

"Sky buffer," Jerry called it.

As Larry began singing the words, "Buffer in the sky," to the tune of The Doors song "Riders in the Storm," Billy stopped the tape and went over to a stationary camera that sat at right angles to his console and placed under its lens a page of SVX copy. He angled it so the camera fed the words in a vertical row down the right side of the screen. He returned to his seat, tapped a few keys and began playing the spot as it might look in its finished form: running footage, inset factory pictures up top, copy on right.

The singing and the laughter stopped. Jerry was the first to speak.

"God!" he said. "It's awful."

Their SVX spot looked so reverential that it was ridiculous. "Looks like the 'Lord's Prayer Before I Drive and Buff,' " said Larry, through laughter. " 'I have entered the Valley of Auto Repair and I will fear no evil.' "

They turned somber again only when John Adams pointed out that they not only had to find a voiceover artist and two soundtracks, they now had to figure out how to compensate for the shaky SVX road footage and the sheer absurdity of the concept itself.

Perhaps they could move the type crawl to the center of the screen?

That offset the bumpiness . . . but it covered up the factory scenes, which had been set up with a heavier left side to make room for the type on the right.

So why not flop the factory shots so they were heavier on the right?

Because it still wouldn't be balanced.

So maybe they shouldn't use scrolling type at all, but have the words bloom in and out, as Jerry had suggested earlier?

It might look better, but it was not what they had proposed to Subaru.

Their decision was to make no decision. Instead, they asked Billy to prepare four different roughs that they could ship to Dan Wieden and David Kennedy in Portland. Three would use type variations to obscure the problems with "Buffer in the Sky." But the only way *really* to save the spot, and it would be so obvious that Dan and David would naturally agree, was to split the screen with a heavy line in the middle, dividing the factory scenes from the road footage instead of superimposing them on top of the empty sky. They would show that in the fourth demo.

John and Larry left Red Car apprehensive. Jerry, as was his wont, was more despairing. The day had begun full of hope, his masterly concept for the struggling little car company finally taking form, but it was ending with his vision crumbling, bit by bit.

"I see my career," Jerry said, as he headed back to his hotel for a long shower, "falling into the abyss."

· · ·

ROB WATZKE worked through the night, concentrating his efforts on cutting "Factory" and ignoring, until the agency could make up its own mind, "SVX."

Rob was considered one of the better editors at Red Car. He had spent several years at Chiat/Day but had grown frustrated with life as an agency captive, continually confined by one shop's style and subjectivity. Film editors consider themselves storytellers who need a certain distance—from directors and, in advertising, from clients and agencies as well—to free themselves from the financial and political pressures constraining the other characters in order to piece together a compelling tale. "Editing must be detached," said Larry Bridges, who had hired Rob for Red Car and took pride in his protégé's professional maturation. "An editor looks at film and says, 'Here is something that will allow me to tell this story.' A good editor knows all the moves and idioms and all the phonemes and morphemes and sentences and syntax and rhetoric of film." And Rob was good. "He is a value-added editor," Bridges said. "He makes the ad a little film, a little work—more in editing terms than in advertising, marketing or directing terms."

That was fine as far as Wieden & Kennedy was concerned. In its television work, at least, the agency considered itself a collection of filmmakers, not advertising types, so an editor who thought about film, about light, about shapes and stories and form was a perfect companion.

Rob was among the diminishing collection of advertising editors who still preferred to cut on film, not on tape, which was quicker and more forgiving. He liked the feel of the film, and believed it connected him more directly to the images. So for hours, long after the agency executives had departed Red Car, he sat hunched over his console, splicing, cutting and resplicing bits and pieces of Indiana, thinking all the while of the philosophy expressed in the copy and the storyboards.

"First, I tried to cut it with real long takes," he said after he was finished. "I found that the film didn't sustain it long. It really wasn't that interesting. So I kept making it a little shorter, adding other scenes. It's still very languid." Initially, Rob did not even think about the copy. "I just wanted to work on it visually. Then I put a dummy voice track on top of it, to see where it would fall. At first I thought, 'Well, the pictures are really going to work with the voice.' But really, the pictures work as a counterpoint."

That was the revelation that urged him to his final cut. When he *heard* the reading of Jerry's words, he understood Jerry's disdain for the consumerism that was supporting him. "The pictures have a different thing going than the voice does. It wasn't until I put them together that I could see that," Rob said. "The visuals are working very specifically and the voice is working philosophically. The visuals are working at making a car. What the guy's talking about *seems* to be about that, but also, 'Let's not make this into something more than it is.' When he says, 'It's not going to make you more handsome,' or this or that, there isn't anything in the visuals that corresponds to that. It's that anti-advertising stuff that they seem to do a lot of."

Rob was proud, if tired, the next morning, when he presented his rough cut of "Factory" (backed by Larry's own voice track and the music from the demo, the polyphonic Steve Reich mandolin piece) to the Wieden & Kennedy crew. Rob had compensated for the poor quality of the film by shortening the scenes and increasing their number, fitting twenty individual scenes into a spot that had been designed for six or seven. Although Larry Frey was surprised by the editor's changes in his art direction, he liked them, and suggested that any languidness lost by the addition of the new scenes could be recaptured by cross-dissolving, instead of abruptly cutting, between scenes.

John Adams agreed. "It's a really nice edit," the producer told Rob. He turned to the copywriter and creative director. "Jerry, what do you think?"

Jerry, who was still clutching his copy of Mark Twain, shook his head. "Too many cuts. *Too* many people. Too goodwrenchy."

Without argument, Rob rewound the spot to the beginning. He and the agency began the process of excising scenes. A woman wiping a windshield—*out.* The reflecting orb—*cut.* Fred Elmes's painstakingly acquired shot of a worker attaching a door to a Legacy, filmed from inside the car—*gone.* Rob snipped the offending scenes from his cut and handed the strips of film to an assistant, who hung them on a rack on the back wall.

Pretty soon, the editing suite looked like a pasta factory, and the commercial was substantially depopulated. Seven scenes, with at least as many people, were cut and thirteen, almost equally split between Tibor's and Larry's work, were left. Rob agreed to prepare two versions of the commercial for satellite beaming to Portland for approval. One would contain the agency-preferred central text box. The other would feature the text crawling up the right side of the screen. The creatives had little doubt that their superiors would approve the "blooming words" version, but they had no choice but to show them the alternatives. "Dan and David are 'gotta-see-it' kind of guys," Larry said with a shrug. They broke for lunch, called Portland to say they were sending the "Factory" rough cuts, and agreed to reconvene at 1:45 p.m. for a scheduled call from Dan Wieden, who was to give his pro forma approval on it and "SVX."

Dan called exactly at 1:45.

"Hey," he said over the speakerphone. "I really *liked* that one where you had that whirring buffer up in the sky."

Down in Hollywood, the Wieden & Kennedy road crew broke into loud laughter. "Did Davenport set you up?" someone asked.

"Huh?" Dan responded.

No one had set him up. No one had told him anything about the SVX ad. He really *did* like buffer-in-the-sky.

"It seems elegant and important," Dan continued. "It doesn't look like it was done in somebody's garage. The rest," including the absolutely-he'll-buy-it-no-question-about-it split-screen version, "looks like it was done at independent station Channel Twelve."

Jerry, Larry and John grew silent. Not hearing any objections, Dan rambled on. "The SVX running footage is unusable. The bumpiness of the shot speaks to the car's ride. I won't go to the sales meeting with it."

The men in L.A. still said nothing. "I just got a quick look at 'Factory,' " Dan went on. "I like the original idea—the crawl on the right. The box in the center seems like we're trying too hard."

Hearing nothing, Dan concluded with a quick, "I gotta go," and hung up.

All was quiet. Wieden—their boss, their mentor, their friend, advertising's inscrutable genius from the Pacific Northwest—had just shot down every single recommendation they had forwarded.

No one moved or spoke until a dial tone flowed from the speakerphone. Rob reached over and shut it off. Only then did Jerry Cronin let out a long sigh that seemed to rise from the pit of his soul. "We're fucked. We're absolutely fucked." He sat in Rob's swivel chair and cradled his head in his left hand, then draped the hand over his eyes. Over and over, he repeated: "Fuck." Either Dan was crazy, and he would bring the spots as designed to Subaru and be fired by the disbelieving auto executives, or Subaru would accept and air the awful commercials and end the creatives' careers in a hail of ad industry ridicule.

Rob Watzke immediately began reviewing all the factory footage that might possibly suffice as insets in the "SVX" spot. Larry, meanwhile, assumed his command position. Suggestions poured from him. Give the inset "SVX" shots a harder matte and they'll appear cut out, minimizing the ridiculous "from God" look. As for the shaky road shot, maybe they could just reduce its length, by cutting into it other shots of the SVX roaring straight into the camera. Or maybe they could artificially speed up the running footage, eliminating the chatter that way.

Jerry, still perched on Rob's swivel chair, could only say, "I just think we're on a fuckin' road leading to disaster."

"Let's do a body count," Larry continued, ignoring his depressed colleague. "We have no voiceover. We have no music. We don't have a cut—yet. We'll have one soon for 'Factory.' We haven't started a cut for 'SVX'—yet. And it's due in three days—"

"For a brand new client that expects brilliance," Jerry interrupted. He lowered his head back into his hands. "We're fuckin' dead meat."

Larry ran to the Red Car lobby and returned with two copies of *TV Guide*. He intended to force Jerry to find a suitable voice.

"Peter Falk," Larry said, scanning the television listings.

"No," Jerry replied. He still had his heart set on Jeff Bridges, whose name had first surfaced several weeks before in Portland.

"John Forsythe," Larry continued.

"Too old," said Jerry.

"William Hurt."

"Yeah. He's a good speaker. He'd be an absolute fortune. I bet he wouldn't do it."

"Peter Horton—'Thirtysomething.' "

"Too wimpy. Too sensitive."

"John Cusack."

"He'd be all right. I like John Cusack."

Larry wrote his name on a yellow legal pad. "James Spader," he continued.

"He sounds too young."

Flipping pages, Larry became a Gatling gun of names. "David Letterman. Bob Hoskins. Albert Finney. Richard Crenna."

Now Jerry began looking through his copy of *TV Guide*. "Nick Nolte?" he asked.

"Very gruff," answered Larry.

"Ed Harris?"

"Ed Harris has a nice voice." Down went his name.

"Ernest Borgnine?"

Larry realized they would not get very far with Jerry suggesting names, so he took over the process once again. "Robert Loggia," he said.

"No," Jerry answered.

"Ron Howard. James Coburn. Tony Curtis. Harry Shearer."

"Ed Marinaro?" Jerry said.

"From 'Hill Street Blues'? What about Charlie Haid?"

"Hey," said Jerry, lighting up briefly. "What about the guy who played Belker? I'd write him down."

The phone rang and John Adams answered it. "Uh huh. . . . Uh huh . . . Uh huh," he said. He hung up and turned to Jerry. "Jeff Bridges has no time."

Jerry threw his big head back into his hands.

"Fuck," he said. "Fuck, fuck, fuck, fuck."

ROB ARRIVED at 7:30 the next morning and demanded to be left alone in his darkened studio while he tried still another cut for "SVX." Meanwhile, in a different studio, his assistant played, rewound and re-played a rough cut of "Factory," while the agency men, joined over the night by Bill Davenport, who had again flown out from Portland to ease them through the crisis, tried different soundtracks against it.

John Adams programmed the boom box to play "Time" from Pink Floyd's "Dark Side of the Moon" album.

"Too ominous," said Jerry, looking at the video screen through the dark, hollow ditches that contained his eyes.

John tried another cut from the album, a boozy, melodic saxophone piece entitled "Us and Them."

"Mellow," Davenport said.

Consumed by demo love, Jerry still preferred the repetitive, Steve Reich mandolin number.

Despite the unchanging visuals—bolts, welders, the side of a door—the different accompaniments completely altered the tone and the intent of the Subaru commercial. Backed by some tunes, the factory footage seemed simple and heroic, a tale of modernism triumphant. To other melodies, the same scenes appeared dark and forbidding, prewar German Expressionism transported to northern Indiana. There was a time in advertising when a simple jingle ("Hot dogs / Armour hot dogs / What kinds of kids like Armour hot dogs?") or perhaps a heart-tugging wordless riff from the likes of Mantovani was the standard fare for television commercials. In the new world of postmodern advertising, though, where every image contained multiple meanings and where every audience member was a knowledgeable interpreter in good standing, the choice of a soundtrack was even more important than the selection of the film clips, for not only the music but the identity of the artist communicated crucial hermeneutic information to the consumer: Camp? Hip? Hip-modern? Hip-arcane? Hip-recherché?

John cued up "Rainfall," a cello-guitar duet to a steady two-quarter beat pulled from a New Age sampler entitled "Narada Artists."

"Too wimpy," Jerry said.

Rachmaninoff's Opus 34, No. 14 by the Philadelphia Orchestra came next.

"No," said Jerry, after only five seconds. He pressed the "stop" button.

John replaced it with a piece entitled "Wind, Rain and Fire" from the film *The Last Emperor.* The three-quarter-time tune sounded as if a Bangkok bar band was trying to play a country/western song.

"I kinda like that, to tell you the truth," Davenport said. "Conceptually, it says something kinda interesting."

"It sounds like Japanese guys who moved to Indiana," John agreed, urging Jerry toward a decision.

Jerry shrugged.

They were in the middle of several blues guitar and boogie-woogie pieces by the Portland rock band when Dan Wieden called. He had thought about the SVX spot overnight, and he had found yet *another* problem with it. "The P.O.V. stuff," he told his charges, "somehow, that has to indicate speed."

Dan was obsessed with the issue of speed. That was the end-all and the be-all of "SVX"—Subaru's newest car had to look fast. Why this was so was something of a puzzle. The SVX's ability to move quickly was the least interesting of its attributes, and not one that either distinguished it from other cars in its class or had figured prominently in any of the research Subaru of America had done during or since the car's development. Certainly the vehicle's sleek, unusual design set it far apart from every similar car on the road. Its engineering was also singular: The SVX was going to be the only four-wheel-drive luxury coupe on the market. But S.O.A. seemed torn by indecision over how to define the SVX. Should the company market it as a sports car, a product category whose aficionados naturally looked to speed, pickup and horsepower when shopping for an auto? Or should S.O.A. sell it as a luxury car, where styling, handling and comfort influenced buyers' decisions more? Wieden & Kennedy handed Subaru its answer in the form of Jerry Cronin's speed spot—a commercial with no rational basis. No matter, though. S.O.A. had given speed the green light, so the agency was going to produce it, with all deliberate speed.

Davenport listened to Dan's concerns. In the twenty-four hours since his arrival from Portland, he had become a convert to his L.A.-bound colleagues' views. He tried to communicate them to their boss. "We hate the SVX stuff," he said. "We basically feel miserable about it."

"Do we have good-looking product stuff?" Dan asked.

"No," Davenport answered. "I don't think so."

"What I've got looks fucked," Dan continued.

"We can clean it up a little bit," Davenport warned, "but it won't ever be top-notch product photography."

There was a long pause (not unlike the long pauses that punctuated their face-to-face meetings in Oregon), so Davenport attempted to lighten the mood by updating Dan on the status of the more nearly completed "Factory" ad. Dan, who had been reviewing that commercial as well, verbally waved him off.

"It's too sleepy. I've presented the concept for two weeks in meetings to Subaru dealers. It's a sharp concept. You can see it even in our slides. There's a fuck-you attitude to it. I think this music"—the Steve Reich mandolin number—"is just not right. When it's done, it's like, 'Fine. So what?' The attitude of this spot was always, 'It's time to tell the god-damn truth about cars.' Right now, it's like a lullaby. The music, the whole tone of voice, is 'la de da da.' It needs bite and sting." His tone of voice was not tough; nor was it soft. He did not worry whether he caused discomfort among his employees. "I think it should feel the way Jerry felt when he wrote it," he continued. "He didn't feel like 'Ode to a Car.' I think this thing should have an attitude."

Attitude. It was *the* word in the new advertising. Every commercial had to have it. For a spot to succeed, it had to be—this was the adjectival form of the word—*edgy*.

Problem was, nobody knew what it meant.

Oh, Dan Wieden had his synonyms. He wanted "barbs"; he wanted "irreverence." And David Kennedy (who, in deference to the blossoming crisis, had also arrived from California) knew attitude when he saw it, letting loose a "cool" or a "neat" as an identifier. Larry Bridges, Red Car's founder, believed "attitude advertising" to be a distinct category of marketing communication, and defined it as "advertising that knows better." But what that meant in practice was anybody's guess, or opinion.

They crowded into Davenport's rented blue Chevy Lumina and drove the half-mile to Editel, the on-line editing house at which the finishing touches would be put on the Subaru spots. The facility was as clean and polished as Red Car was raw and funky. The on-line editing suite to which they repaired looked like the control room of the Starship *Enterprise*. Up front and to the left was an enormous console with more than two hundred buttons and six small black-and-white television monitors. At the front and center was a large computer screen for visual and audio-level testing; above it sat a color TV monitor. The setup also included two Macintosh computers; a device for superimposing text on videotape, called a Chyron; an Ampex ATR-700 reel-to-reel tape recorder; a Graham-Patten systems Model 712 audio equalizer; and a video effects generator. To the right, in a cool room, were the actual videotapes on which the finished spot was to be built, kept separate to protect them from the heat of the machines.

Jerry slumped into a brown leather armchair at the back of the editing room. "Maybe," he said, continuing a discussion about "Factory" that had begun immediately after Dan's call, "we just watered the fuck out of it."

"This is more Infiniti than Subaru," Kennedy, the gray beard, said. When Nissan introduced its luxury-car division to the United States in 1989, the commercials featured nothing but long, unbroken takes of rocks, trees and seashores, backed by a zen-like poetic monologue and no music.

"We were doing more homage," Davenport agreed. "We've got to shift gears."

Larry Frey leaned on Jerry who, as creative director, was charged with the authority to make decisions. "You gotta get a voice, man. Voice is ninety-nine percent of attitude."

Painfully, Jerry drank in the criticisms. With as much energy as he could muster, he softly asked Davenport, "Can we get Albert Finney?"

Davenport muscled on by him. "Let's think of smart-aleck voices who are here in L.A. What about Ray Sharkey?"

Jerry grimaced.

"Ken Wahl?" asked John Adams.

"He is *the* wise guy," Davenport responded. Jerry did not react. "Sean Penn? Ray Liotta?"

"Sean Penn would be okay," Jerry grudgingly replied.

"Think of all the guys Madonna's gone out with," Davenport said, without irony.

"Hey!" exploded David. "What about Harry Dean Stanton?"

Dennis Hopper. Nicolas Cage. Danny Glover.

"What about Robert Prosky?" Davenport asked. "You know, when the guy died on 'Hill Street Blues,' he took over."

Danny Aiello. Eric Bogosian.

"He's really strong. He's really edgy," Larry said.

Hundreds of dollars an hour—the cost of the Editel facility and the on-line editor—were ticking away as they debated a subject they could have discussed in a coffee shop. When the agency people realized this, they turned their attention to more immediate remedial efforts to gain attitude.

They fiddled with the color of the spot. Within certain constraints, color, color tone and color intensity can all be modified, a procedure known (because of the controls) as "dialing." First, the editor dialed out almost all the color, leaving the factory scenes a stark blue and white. But the pictures were too muddy. The editor removed a little more color and rendered the footage in a sharply contrasted black and white. Then, he reversed the on-screen type, so the letters were also in white. At Jerry's suggestion, he moved the text scroll from the right side directly into the center of the screen, tripled the size of the letters, and changed their color to orange. It looked good—very good. The viewer's eye was drawn to the center of the television screen, where it absorbed both words and images simultaneously.

Inspiration struck David Kennedy. He asked the editor to blow up the centered text even more, but to run a smaller duplicate of the text down the right side of the screen. The look of the spot changed yet again. "Neat," David said. "It's like three-D."

They laid the text crawl on a videotape and returned to Red Car, where their type advisers, Donna Pittman and Mark Hensley, were waiting for them (and for some final word on the design of the commercial). David placed the tape in a deck in the Red Car lobby, and for once, all the activity in the place halted. Even the Red Car housekeeper stopped to watch.

Donna's reaction was terse. "It's a lot of words."

But the normally restrained David was energized. He began one of the longer extended monologues anyone had ever heard from him, the gist of which was a recommendation: run *all* the words in the smaller, right column of type, and only *selected* words in the larger, center scroll.

The typographers thought about it a moment. For the first time, Mark Hensley spoke. "Hypnotic," he said.

HUNCHED OVER and bleary-eyed, Rob Watzke emerged slowly from his dark studio, just in time to receive his several-times-weekly back rub. Mack, a tall, freelance masseur with a droopy mustache, was waiting for him. Mack's massages were one of the perquisites of employment at Red Car, but as Rob had learned over the years, they were less a display of Hollywood excess than an unfortunate necessity. Like many film editors, who spend their lives bent over Moviolas, Rob suffered from chronic back pain. He went regularly to a chiropractor and to a sports-medicine specialist. Mack's rubs provided him with a blessed ten minutes of relief.

He had finished a new cut of "SVX," Rob told the Wieden & Kennedy executives and their assorted minions, as Mack ran his thumbs up

Rob's spine. They all (save Mack, who moved on to help another editor) piled into Rob's room.

The rough cut that Rob showed them was more than a new edit, it was a totally different commercial. He had eliminated both "buffer in the sky" and the split screen, and spliced together a spot that moved from a driver's P.O.V. shot of the open road to factory scenes, back to the open road, to a profile of the moving car, to a front view of the moving car. It was supported by a driving rock-and-roll tune that gave the advertisement needed energy. "This is the way the footage wanted to be cut," Rob explained. "It wasn't meant to be split screen. Too many images."

For the first time that week, the admen glimpsed salvation. "I think," said Larry, who was counting up the number of car shots in the cut, "Subaru would love it. Whaddya think, Kennedy?"

David answered, "It's nice."

But the disembodied voice of Dan Wieden disagreed. Shortly after the group in Los Angeles saw Rob's cut for the first time, Dan, thanks to the miracle of satellite transmission, got a chance to watch it in Portland. He was not pleased. The P.O.V. shots still chattered. The product shots were brief and undistinguished. And the style of the commercial . . . Dan had seen it a hundred times. "This spot, when you see the car, it should be terrifically awesome. You should say, 'Fuck!'" he told his partner and their employees by phone. Larry, ever the idea man, started rat-a-tat-tatting suggestions for refining Rob's cuts. None were to Dan's liking. "I think you're gonna have to reshoot. You'll have to reshoot the product," Dan said.

There. It was finally out in the open. It had been hiding in the backs of their minds all week, a haunting specter, but they'd kept it boxed up. The time, the money, the red flags that would go up at auto dealerships (and rival ad agencies) around the country if the word got out. Now they knew they had no choice: a reshoot was the only way to save the SVX spot. It would be horrendously expensive—$300,000 perhaps, including shooting costs, the director's fee and the postproduction tariff—and would put the total bill for the two Subaru spots near $1 million.

"I'm so shell-shocked and feel so awful, I don't know what to think," Jerry said thickly.

But Davenport did, and he said it: *Pytka.*

Get Joe Pytka to reshoot it.

Get Joe Pytka to film new P.O.V. footage, a beauty shot, close-ups of car parts and fake factory footage.

"He can't do all that in a *day!*" Rob blurted.

"He can do it," Davenport replied calmly. "He shot Bo Diddley in a day."

JOE PYTKA was the wild man of American advertising. He had worked his way up from the depths of boilerplate smiling-mom spots for Procter & Gamble to the top of the directorial pantheon, where he was renowned not only for the delirious Bo Jackson Nike ads and multimillion-dollar extravaganzas for Pepsi, but for smaller, starker work, like the Partnership for a Drug-Free America's famous "Frying Egg" commercial. "This is your brain," a no-nonsense standup said in that spot, as he held an egg up to the camera. He cracked it into a hot frying pan, where the white and yolk sizzled. "This is your brain on drugs. Any questions?"

Pytka (who called himself "anti-smoking, anti-drugs, anti-abortion, anti-Bush, anti-Thatcher, anti-killing the animals") had executed these and hundreds of other thirty-second filmettes with an exquisite eye for color, light and detail, the product of years of art training in his native Pittsburgh. He had also shattered the egos and damaged the psyches of dozens of production assistants over the years, for the sensitive soul that his friends and longtime colleagues insisted resided within him was encased in the outer shell of a Shining Path guerrilla—demanding, heartless, without remorse. He loved nothing better than to taunt the newest, rawest workers on his sets. If he found a weak spot—a stutter, a look of fear, the barest hesitation before responding—he pounced. The aide's intelligence would be impugned, his taste excoriated, his cinematic future dismissed. One story, most likely apocryphal, related the tale of an assistant director on a shoot somewhere in the middle of a desert. Pytka was berating him mercilessly, attacking his skills, his dress, his managerial ability. After several hours of this torment, the A.D., it was said, simply removed his headset and walked off toward the sandy horizon, and was never seen again. People—mostly the agency executives on whom he depended for work, and the remarkably loyal and well-paid staff of his production company—said he had mellowed after his marriage to a gorgeous French model, the birth of their angelic blonde daughter and the critical dismissal of his first foray into feature filmmaking, a Runyonesque farce. But many of the grunts still thought Pytka was a bully, "the kind of guy who, you feel, would go out at night and beat up a crippled person," as Larry Bridges put it. But Pytka got the shots.

He arrived at 6:30 p.m. Everyone knew it was him. No one else in publicly genteel L.A. would slam a door so resolutely, or pound his way up the stairs so heavily.

He was larger than life. He was dressed entirely in black—black Nikes peeking from under black jeans, atop which was a black T-shirt that covered his muscular chest and read "Homme Inoubliable." Above these words, more than six feet up from the shaky ground, was his head—a massive, broad, weathered block of flesh over which his jutting brow forced a deep shadow. His nose looked several times broken and there was a scar on the right side of his right eyebrow. On top of it all was the hair—gray, long and untied—which breezed out like a fan below his shoulders. He was Cecil B. DeMille crossed with Paul Bunyan.

He looked at Jerry and said in a booming, mocking voice, "How are you?"

Jerry gave him the "SVX" storyboard. "Miserable," he replied.

"Calm down," Pytka responded, with contempt. "Nothing's that bad."

The director quickly eyeballed the board, on which Larry had drawn yet another variation on the buffer-in-the-sky concept. "It's difficult," Pytka said.

"We've got seventy-two hours!" Davenport said, with feigned brightness.

"Are you kidding?" Pytka exploded. "That's impossible!" But even as he was denying them, the tone of his voice made clear that he was testing the agency men, goading them into pleading publicly for his help. Instead, they explained Rob's new concept to him, then drew him over to a nearby video deck and played Rob's newest cut. Pytka appreciated the editor's effort, but not the film it comprised.

"This is terrible. This is awful," he said. The dealers' conference was only days away. Nothing artful could be accomplished in so short a time. "It's a great fuckin' idea. But this Denver meeting, it's a . . . it's a fuckin' disaster." He sank into a soft couch. "Who shot this?" he demanded.

"Tibor Kalman," Davenport answered.

Pytka narrowed his eyes. "Who's he?" he shot back.

"Fred Elmes was the D.P.," continued Davenport, hoping to show Pytka that the agency had managed to snag a brand name from the world of big-cinema. The director wasn't biting.

"No wonder," he said. "Did you see his movie?"

He didn't wait for a response. Instead, he launched into recommendations for "SVX." "If the car is beautiful, one of the things you don't get from this spot is how beautiful it is. So why don't you do *aspects* of the car, of the finished car, instead of pieces of it being built?" As the Wieden & Kennedy execs pondered this idea, Pytka went on, dazzling them with his theories of automobile advertising. "I think there's something really elegant about aspects of the car shown against a blown-out background. You have to design the shots so the horizon line, where the car is, is blown out, or white. It has to be shot in such a way that you can blend these things. Which is no problem if you have the right postproduction time. There has to be a natural bridge between the object and the horizon. You have to have a flat horizon where you can matte out what you don't want, so it goes off into infinity.

"It's slightly different from your concept," he continued, referring to buffer-in-the-sky. "I'm concerned about what you sold your client. But if it's done beautifully, I don't think they'll care. It will take someone with wit, taste, intelligence and patience." He grinned a wicked grin. "Certainly no one in this room."

He looked at Jerry, who was still sitting, as he had been for much of the day, with his elbows on his knees and his head in his hands. "I don't understand. Why did you have parts of the car in the sky? What was the point?" Pytka asked him.

Jerry glanced up. "We were trying to reduce the car to its elements," he mumbled.

"You look tired," Pytka needled. "Are you tired?"

Jerry repeated his favorite word of the evening. "I feel miserable."

Pytka moved to mollify him and his colleagues. He agreed to reshoot the spot. But he could not do it until Saturday—three days away, and only two days before the finished advertisements were scheduled to debut before several hundred skeptical Subaru dealers in Denver, Colorado. His location scouts would spend the intervening time finding an appropriate place for the shoot. The timing was tight, he told them, but the agency had little choice.

"The thing you got is such a piece of shit that whatever you get will be better," Pytka said.

THEY STILL NEEDED an attitude, and they had forty-eight hours to find it.

After dithering for most of the week, Jerry finally agreed to audition several voiceover artists. Thursday morning, he and John Adams hightailed it halfway up the Hollywood Hills to start.

Like every other place in which they had spent the warm, sunny week in Los Angeles, L.A. Studios was a windowless, airless box, as removed from its environment as a bomb shelter. And like a shelter, it was stocked with the provisions necessary to support the lives of its denizens: a Pyrex jar filled with hard candies and Tootsie Rolls in the lobby, an espresso-cappuccino maker adjacent to the soundproof recording studios, and 4 p.m. frozen margaritas for all inhabitants, courtesy of the management.

Jerry and John sat expressionless as Chris Lemmon, the first actor sent by the voice casting service, walked in. Tall and strapping, dressed in faded jeans and a pink polo shirt, he bore only slight resemblance, physically and in his desultory career, to his famous father, Jack (who had recorded Honda voiceovers in the same studio).

Without looking at him, Jerry gave him the "Factory" script. "Oh, it looks like prose," Lemmon said, making small talk. "I like that." He got no response. He walked into the recording room, behind a glass wall, and began to read. "A car is a car. And its sole reason for existence is to get you from Point A to Point B and back again. . . ."

His reading was mannered, not at all the conversational tone Jerry wanted. "Try it again," the copywriter intoned through a microphone piped into the recording room, "and try not to take it so seriously. Just tell people that all that stuff about cars is crap."

"You're the boss," said Lemmon, who proceeded to try to follow the vague directions.

He was still too mannered. "Make it more sarcastic," commanded Jerry.

"I don't want to get cutting or nasty," objected Lemmon, who nevertheless tried his best. Finally, after six takes, he left.

"He sounds a bit weak to me," John worried.

Almost immediately, Charles Kimbrough sauntered in. He was a co-star of one of the most popular series on television, CBS's "Murphy Brown," on which he played a stiff, repressed television news anchorman. But although the voice was unmistakably that of his character, in his green T-shirt, tan slacks and fluid movements, Kimbrough appeared younger, looser, thinner, hipper, far more the actor than his fictional counterpart.

Jerry, exhaustion in his voice, provided him the barest direction. "You're sick of the bullshit about cars."

With only that as guidance, Kimbrough stabbed at the text, vigorously and well. "Do it again," Jerry ordered, slightly enlivened, "maybe not so tough."

Kimbrough complied. "It won't make you handsome. Or prettier. Or younger," he read, punching the air with his right hand as he stared down at the page clipped to an easel in front of him. "And if it improves your standing with the neighbors, then you live among snobs with distorted values."

"He's *flying*," John Adams whispered to his partner. Through the glass, the actor took no notice.

"And in the end," Kimbrough concluded, shaking the long fingers of his right hand from side to side in a moralistic commentary, "with an absence of marketing glamour about the automobile, may the best machine win."

He looked up. They thanked him. He left.

Waiting for the next actor to show up, it occurred to John that maybe Jerry, imbued as he was with a hatred for cars and filled with anxiety and depression about the commercials they were trying to complete, might provide the perfect voiceover for the Subaru spots. The suggestion was not without precedent. One former Wieden & Kennedy creative was well into a new career as an advertising voice, and even Jerry, with his thick "Bahston" accent, had provided the vocals for the agency's sexy Anne Klein fashion spots. So at John's urging, Jerry took the mike.

"A car is steel, electronics, rubber, plastic and glass," Jerry read, standing limply before the easel. "A machine." His voice was flat, filled with the tired disgust his colleagues had heard in his normal conversation throughout the week. It was almost perfect. But he read too quickly (he came in at forty-one seconds for the sixty-second version of the spot) and he riffled the script and moved his head around the mike, causing sound-level changes. John asked him to do it again.

"In choosing one, the questions should be: How long will it last? How well will it do the job? Could I get a comparable one for less?" Jerry read, leaving the papers untouched and stabilizing his head.

John liked it. "He almost sounds defeated," he said approvingly.

IF THE AGENCY was to obtain the elusive attitude, it had to find the right soundtrack—one connoting speed for "SVX" and one indicating who-knew-what for "Factory." Back at Editel, the Wieden & Kennedy crew continued its haphazard search for the slippery strains. Stretched prone on couches in the on-line facility's lobby, Jerry and John contemplated a work by the group Art of Noise.

"It has potential," John told the ceiling.

Like parasites, he and his partners had taken over the Editel anteroom. On the coffee table in front of them, which was littered with popcorn boxes, half-filled mineral-water bottles, CDs, a boom box and wrappers from a nearby fried-chicken franchise, two telephones rang continually. In answering, the four agency men progressed from "Editel" to "Wieden & Kennedy" to their individual names to "hello" to, giddily, "Skybuffer Productions."

Ring. Portland. They've located Steve Landesberg, once-upon-a-time the co-star of the sitcom "Barney Miller." He'll do a voiceover demo for $500. *Get him.*

Ring. Auto Cosmetic Incorporated, the company that preps cars for filming. They've located the paraphernalia for the "SVX" reshoot. *We'll see you there.*

A messenger arrived. "Wieden & Kennedy?" Davenport signed. It was a new audiotape from the voice casting service. He snapped it into the boom box. The voice of Telly Savalas emerged. "A car is a car . . ."

"I just can't believe he came in," Davenport said, shaking his head.

Brian Keith. "And its sole reason for existence is to get you from Point A to Point B and back again."

"If it weren't for him," Jerry said wryly, recalling the 1960s sitcom "Family Affair," in which Keith had starred, "Buffy would still be alive."

William Daniels. Chad Everett. Charles Rocket.

"He was in a really good episode of 'Parker Stevenson Can't Lose,' " Davenport observed.

Jerry Orbach. "It won't make you handsome. Or prettier. Or younger."

"Hey, he's okay," Jerry Cronin said of the Broadway musical star.

Davenport laughed. "Hey," he shouted to nobody in particular, "somebody just got an okay from Jerry!"

A young woman walked up to them from the back of the studio. Several editors had completed an on-line version of Rob Watzke's "SVX" cut, she told them. They were ready for The Client.

The Client. Her name was Karen Allen. She was a short, round woman with reddish-brown hair, a friendly manner and a thick Philadelphia accent. She was a Subaru lifer. Having joined the company as a part-time secretary during high school, she had inched her way slowly up the ranks until she had achieved the position of director of broadcast production.

In many ways, Karen was the ideal client. Although her job required her to be present at most of S.O.A.'s commercial shoots, she was determinedly unobtrusive. *Let the advertising agency do what it does best* was her attitude. In Indiana, at the factory, she sat quietly through most of the storm, seeing and understanding much of it but interfering only when it came time to film the "SVX" beauty shot. *I want a shot that shows the sheet metal,* she had insisted at the time. *This is the intro spot for the SVX, so we owe it to the car and the consumer*—and, although she didn't say it, the dealers—*to show it. In the past, that didn't matter. We were perceived as small and boxy, and we were. With this, we want to show that metal.* No one dared argue.

During the postproduction week, though, Wieden & Kennedy, per-

haps sensing the trouble that eventually did befall it, determinedly kept
The Client (as they always referred to Karen) far from the proceedings.
A young agency account executive named Elena accompanied her everywhere. They sat together by the side of the pool at their Santa
Monica hotel. They shopped Beverly Hills. They did everything but interrupt the ad boys while they rushed toward the finish line. As far as
The Client knew, on this evening a bit more than three days removed
from the Subaru spots' Denver premiere, all was right with the advertising world.

The Client arrived, and with the four agency men she proceeded to
the editing suite. With little introduction, the three editors unveiled the
sans-music-sans-voice-but-otherwise-nearly-finished "Factory" spot. The
color looked burnished. The transitions were smooth. The camera ten-
derly caressed the bolts and the raw metal. The commercial was, in a
word, gorgeous.

Larry Frey, something of a perfectionist, jumped in with notes. Reverse the shot of the arc welders, because a flash of light from their
torches would obscure the type crawl on the right. The quick cuts, or
"wipes," separating the first three scenes were fine, but between the
medium shot of the factory line and the close-up of the grinder should
be a slow dissolve.

The Client was less critical. She said a single word: "Great."

The agency decided to try potential voices on her, and played tapes
of its current favorites, Charles Rocket and Brian Keith.

The Client was completely agreeable. "I don't mind any one of
them," she said.

The agency determined that the time was right to ease The Client
into the "SVX" situation. At Bill Davenport's nod, the Editel editor
played for her the on-line version of Rob Watzke's cut of the
commercial—the one that shifted among shots of the open road, shots
inside the factory and shots of the car. Then he ran two other variations
of the spot—the original buffer-in-the-sky rendering, in which car parts
and factory scenes mysteriously floated in the air above the road, and
the split-screen version, with the footage from the plant clearly delin-
eated from the running shots.

To the agency's vast relief, The Client gave her approval to Rob's cut.
The others, she believed, were too busy, too complicated and didn't uti-
lize the television screen fully. She had one problem, however, with the
new "SVX" cut, a problem she was sure would be solved as the editing
progressed. There was no beauty shot, no long, lingering view of the
gorgeous new Subaru luxury car, wheels spinning, traversing the verdant Indiana terrain. "Where's the car?" The Client asked. The agency

executives stared at her blankly. "What's the angle of the car?" she insisted.

Ah, yes, well, footage here chatters a bit, somewhat bumpy, you know, tried to correct it on-line but hard to do, anyway need better shots of car parts so maybe thinking reshoot but no problem there got Joe Pytka best director in the business he's made time for us on Saturday we'll get all the footage we need. . . .

The Client stared dumbly at Larry Frey and Bill Davenport through this dialogue before interrupting in a voice that grew with the intensity of a fire siren.

"Of all the film we have of the SVX, we can't use diddly-squat, it's useless, that's what you're telling me? *All that stuff in the factory?* IT'S THURSDAY, A QUARTER TO EIGHT, AND WE'RE CHANGING A WHOLE SPOT—A WHOLE SPOT! *YOU'RE TELLING ME WE'RE GOING TO SHOOT THIS TOMORROW NIGHT AND SATURDAY MORNING?*"

Jerry Cronin sat slumped in an armchair, cradling a can of apple juice. Davenport and Larry babbled. The Client cut them off with a lower, angrier voice.

"My priority right now is to get a commercial to the dealers' meeting. If we have to go back and make changes before it airs, okay. But the priority is getting the visual of the car on the road. If Dan Wieden wants to redo the whole spot later, that's fine with me, because I'm not paying the bill. . . . It scares me to death to reshoot a whole commercial in two days. *It scares me to death! This is the SVX intro spot! It's an image spot. You're talking to a GROUP OF DEALERS!*"

Don't worry we can do it we guarantee it if anyone can do it Pytka can do it we'll get the spots both spots on the last plane from El-A-Ex to Denver at nine pee-em on Sunday no doubt about it if not we will charter a plane at our own expense and have the spots there by Monday morning without—

"Guys," The Client interrupted, with disgust dripping over the rim of her lips, "I don't have a problem with it. If you want to do it, do it. Guys, it makes me a little nervous. *It makes me a lot nervous.*"

JOE PYTKA was like a steamroller.

"I saw Tony Scott at a party. Shocking! . . . The studio abandoned my movie. I have no rancor. They were too stupid to understand it. So stupid. Shocking! . . ."

The time was 3:45 a.m. Some eight and a half hours earlier, he had wrapped a spot for DuPont never-stain carpeting that featured a rambunctious baby and her young mother. ("Did you see how long her legs were? Shocking!") About six hours earlier, he had finished a meeting with Michael Jackson about a new Pepsi commercial. He was now pumping himself with coffee while members of his crew drove him past the outer edges of Los Angeles to California's high desert near El Mirage. The Client and her handler, Elena, snoozed open-mouthed in the back of the minivan. No matter. Pytka did not need respondents.

"Lemme tell you. Every car shot has been done. There's no shot that hasn't been done. Except the exploding car. And I'm going to save that for last. An agency I did work for once decided it wanted to shoot a car spot in Italy. In Amalfi. Most beautiful spot in the world to film a car commercial. Cliffs plunging into the sea. Blue water. Vines coming up the cliffs. Roads cut into the cliffs, with tunnels and covered bridges. We get to Amalfi, the agency comes over and says, 'Do you think we can make this look like southern California?' Shocking!"

At 5 a.m., with the sun beginning to peek above the eastern mountains, Pytka's van arrived in the middle of nowhere. It moved past several cars and trucks parked adjacent to a patch of saguaro cactuses. Pytka snorted derisively. "There are no saguaros outside Arizona," he told his driver. "Somebody else is shooting here." They rode on and finally arrived at a desolate corner identified by an unneeded street sign as the intersection of Avenue G and 200 Street.

To the southeast, the San Bernardino Mountains rose from the mist. To the west, a road stretched for unbroken miles into the foothills near El Mirage and the Dry Lake. A silver SVX pulled up. So did a Chevy 3500 camera truck. A large tanker truck filled with water for wetting down the road rumbled to a halt. Another minivan filled with crew arrived.

Pytka left his van and stalked wordlessly off the road into the thistly underbrush, his long stork legs crushing the dry plants and ant hills in his way. He looked east, his arms folded across his chest, and contemplated the sky. To a casual passerby, he would have seemed engaged in an ancient religious rite. But he was actually hunting the unpredictable north light, the best light for art ("Ask Vermeer") and for car commercials. "It's soft," Pytka explained. "It gives that liquid look to the car. The only time a car looks good is when it's lit yellow or red." North light gave it that look.

He returned to the camera car, sat on its back platform, peered through a lens and held his hand about fourteen inches off the ground. "Camera right here," he barked. Two grips hurriedly complied. "Come on. Come on!" he said after barely fifteen seconds had passed. They finished, but the camera car did not start. "What the fuck is wrong with

the camera car?" he yelled. The slight, young production coordinator
tried to tell him, quietly, that the camera car was experiencing engine
trouble, but Pytka bit his sentence in half. "I don't want to use him anymore," he shouted to his producer, sending the young man scurrying
away.

The grips moved the camera to the center of the road as the assistant
director commanded the driver of the SVX to head about a mile into
the mountains. Pytka, who was his own cameraman, gazed through the
lens. "Quiet," Pytka said to the few chatterers around him, all shivering
in the early desert cold. "Shut up!" he screamed when they didn't . . .
and they did.

"Go!" ordered the A.D.

Off in the distance, the SVX's headlights blinked on. The car moved,
and after a split-second delay, its roar could be heard in the distance.
It bore down straight on Pytka, who crouched motionless behind the
camera in the middle of the road. The car hit seventy, eighty, ninety
miles an hour. Twenty feet from Pytka, it veered to the left and passed
him. Only then did the director stand. He walked over to the camera
truck, where video monitors provided an immediate taped playback of
the scene recorded by the camera. "Nice shot, huh?" Pytka said smugly.
"I wonder who thought of it."

After several additional takes, the grips quickly moved the camera to
the camera car's front platform, to allow Pytka to film running footage
from the driver's point of view. Every thirty seconds for the next four
minutes, as they secured the camera in place, Pytka interrupted with an
impatient "Let's go" or "Why are we waiting?" With each overbearing
decree, the distinctions between his steady crew and the day laborers
became apparent. His own crew ignored him, but perceptibly increased
its speed. The newcomers glanced up with fear in their bleary eyes.

"Do you want a safety bar across you, Joe?" the camera-car driver
asked.

"No," the director responded with disdain. "Let's go." His hair flying
behind him, they went. Several more takes, and they were done for the
morning. It was 7 a.m. "The light is too shitty for the P.O.V. anyway,"
Pytka told Bill Davenport. "And the road is too patched up. We gotta
find a better road around here."

BACK IN HOLLYWOOD, John Adams and Jerry Cronin were coming
to the end of their tether. One actor's nasal, snide voiceover reading was
good but not great. Another actor was too mannered, but he had a nice
way of reading the tag line, "Subaru. What to drive." Using the

Macintosh-controlled sound-editing equipment, several composites were created—the first actor's take 18 with his take 19 tag line, his take 18 with his take 20 tag line, his take 18 with the second reader's tag line. But no one was terribly happy with any of them.

Then Brian Keith walked in. Keith was an iconic figure to children of the 1960s like Jerry and John. The treacly sitcom "Family Affair," like much prime-time network programming of that period, was burned into their memories for no reason other than the force of repetition. Afterward, he had disappeared into gueststardom, an undistinguished series or two and summer stock (he was currently rehearsing a dinner-theater production of Neil Simon's *The Sunshine Boys*). But when he appeared at L.A. Studios before the Wieden & Kennedy representatives, he was anything but the faded has-been. A strapping, glad-handing man, he was dressed to ride: brown suede cowboy hat, boots, jeans and a western shirt with the tail hanging out. At a glance, John knew that Keith understood how to record voiceovers—his clothes were soft and did not rustle.

The first thing the actor said upon entering the recording studio was disarmingly earthy. *This place looks like a sushi bar.* It was uphill from there. While the engineer was setting up the equipment, Keith regaled the young admen with memories of his twenty-two-day trip back home from Guadalcanal in 1944. *I was puking most of the way.* As he and the other vets stepped from the boat in San Francisco, some unknown benefactor handed each sailor $100. *"Be back in the morning" was all we were told.*

Keith did forty takes without complaint. To Jerry, his voice was perfection. Gruff. No nonsense. Just a hint of cut-the-bullshit to it. By lunchtime, Jerry knew: He had found the voice of Subaru.

Back at Red Car, the men burrowed through a new armful of CDs. Under relentless, if unspoken, pressure from his colleagues, Jerry finally conceded that the Steve Reich New Age mandolin piece, with its high, sweet notes and repeated phrases, was too winsome for "Factory"'s gritty realism. In defiance, though, the copywriter refused to settle on an alternative, until, eager to resolve the issue and move on to more technically complex matters, the Red Car assistants who were supervising the on-line edit, cut in one of the blues tracks on the demo tape by the Portland rock band. It wasn't the driving blues-rock tune the agency had considered and set aside earlier. This one was simpler—acoustic guitar, electric bass, a Mississippi Delta blues, written and recorded in Oregon, laid down in California, about an Indiana factory. It seemed so *right*.

But the "SVX" score still bedeviled them. The agency worked its way through Bang Tango, Big Guitars from Texas, ZZ Top, and Bach's Sonatas. The best the creatives could come up with was a piece by the Irish rock band U-2. But David Kennedy hated it. The tune opened on a long, sustained organ chord that David considered too funereal, especially for a commercial intended to celebrate a speedy new luxury car. So they called Jud Haskins, a local composer and musician with whom Wieden & Kennedy had worked before, to see if he could do better.

"How about this?" responded the incorporeal voice. The agency execs crowded around the speakerphone. Within seconds, what sounded like a six-piece heavy-metal band stuck in some kid's garage launched into a thunderous, pounding imitation of Black Sabbath.

"I wonder if we should build in the beginning," Jerry mused, mostly to himself. But rather than supervise Jud and his players over the telephone, Jerry and John opted to pay him a visit.

They looped up and over the Hollywood Hills and parked their Legacy at a pink stucco apartment complex in Studio City. Instead of heading to the garage, though, they went through a light green wire-mesh gate, past a tiny, empty swimming pool and up an elevator to a small, immaculate duplex apartment. This was the home of Jud Haskins—the man *and* the band.

Jud had converted a second-floor bedroom into a studio and packed it with Macintosh-controlled digital sampling equipment, a red Fender Stratocaster guitar, an enormous reel-to-reel tape recorder, three keyboards, a metal sawhorse stacked with sound emulation devices, a three-quarter-inch VCR, tape decks, a graphic equalizer and a machine capable of mimicking the acoustics of various concert halls, including Carnegie. Above the commode in his bathroom was a blown-up rendering of an audiotape that explained it all. "Jud and the Cassettes/The One-Man Band of the Future," it read. "Enter a universe of sound. Experience an entire orchestra. From a single artist." Jud Haskins was a solo commercial soundtrack company.

Sitting behind his keyboards, Jud listened to the copywriter and the producer explain their musical needs. He wore horn-rimmed glasses and had a conservative haircut; his head was the size and shape of a granite block turned on its end. He looked more like an accountant than an artist. But his easy, booming laugh (he actually articulated the words "Ha, ha!") and his frequent ejaculations of "Cool!" betrayed little hint of actuarial sobriety.

John handed him a tape of the U-2 track. "I'd like to get something from you that takes it out of that churchlike realm," the producer told Jud, after they had listened to it. "I don't know what to suggest, other than some Hendrix-like fuzzy guitar over it."

Jud picked up his Fender, tuned it, fiddled with a distortion box and began playing acid-rock riffs lifted from "Purple Haze." "Less fuzzy," John requested. Jud tried a more staccato vamp that alternated between a steady bass undertone and pingy high notes, to which he gave a concert-hall echo. He played it over the U-2 tape, using his improvisation to heighten the band's ecclesiastical organ until its own rock guitar drove the song forward. Then, with his bare toes, Jud pushed the "play" button on his VCR and watched the "SVX" rough cut progress as he and U-2 played their soundtrack behind it. "Cool!" he exploded.

Jud laid his doctored version of the U-2 track on tape and handed it to John and Jerry. "You are roadworthy, baby!" he said by way of farewell.

As they descended, the elevator stopped on the third floor of Jud's apartment complex and a young woman, her head piled high with red tresses and her large breasts spilling out from her flowered sundress, stepped on. When she exited at the first floor, the producer and the copywriter gave each other a knowing look.

"Fake," declared John.

"Really?" replied Jerry.

"I know, I've seen enough."

"How?"

"Last job I did was the Swedish bikini team for Stroh's," John Adams answered. "Wardrobe woman told me four out of five were fake."

SIX P.M. Golden hour was approaching. The high desert sky was a canvas of red, yellow, blue with flecks of green. "Let's move it. Why are we waiting?" screamed Joe Pytka. To the east, an endless road, a broken yellow line up its middle stretching to infinity. To the west, the sun at ten o'clock, the road bulging and curving, a snake digesting a rat. On both sides, fulsome Joshua trees, one clump looking like Stonehenge, "like that scene in *The Right Stuff*," mused the A.D. "Come on, let's go!" yelled Pytka. The SVX took off, heading into the sun, followed two feet behind by the camera car, Pytka and his camera strapped to the front platform. The truck swerved to the driver's side of the luxury car, the camera panning along the entire length of the car and back again, then zooming in for a surgical close-up and repeating the pan. Zoom up the tailpipe, zoom on the driver's window, zoom on the front left tire. The camera car swerved from the left to the back to the right of the SVX and repeated the shots on the other side. Holding on in the back were Bill Davenport and Larry Frey, eyes glued to the three TV sets that recorded what Pytka's camera saw. They rooted like sports fans. "All right!" "Nice move!" "Pretty!" The sun sank to nine o'clock. The shadows deepened. The desert brush turned into a rippling gold tidal pool. "What the fuck are you doing? Can we do this for Christ's sake?" screamed Pytka. A full tracking shot of the racing car with the camera truck glued to its side. The camera truck racing off on its own, Pytka crouched six inches off the ground filming the road that passed sixty miles an hour beneath him. Another pan of the driver's side. A close-up of the driver's-side window electronically rising and sinking and mysteriously gold-and-black against the grainy texture of the silver body and the glowing, Martian landscape colored red by the sun, and Elena watching silently and responding sexually, licking her top lip with her tongue and saying "oooh" in unison with Davenport and Larry, smiling beatifically watching the monitor capture it live. The only sound as azure fell and the last faint rays of the sun were squeezed like a dishrag into Pytka's camera was the hum of the car's generator as it powered the camera that recorded the desert road sweeping before it and off into the endlessness of space.

Pytka collapsed into the back of a minivan. "Thank you, everybody," yelled the A.D. They had shot four thousand feet—forty-eight minutes' worth—of film.

"Dear George," the creative director on Wieden & Kennedy's Subaru of America account wrote shortly afterward to the President of the United States. "Recently, I wrote to tell you that I had inherited a large sum of money and wanted to donate a big chunk of it to the Republican Party and your next campaign. Unfortunately, I . . . reinvested my entire fortune into a new line of car fresheners. (They're in the shape of the fifty states and each one is scented with a smell associated with the particular state.)" The letter was signed: "Jerry Cronin, a registered voter from Oregon."

Chapter 16

You Get a Lot to Like

"COFFEE?" ASKED SUBARU DEALER Jack Pring, holding up the pot. Then he chuckled. "Oh, you're Mormons. You don't drink coffee, do you?"

Nate Wade, the owner of Nate Wade Subaru, 1207 South Main Street, Salt Lake City, Utah, and his wife, Bonnie, smiled politely. That was about all they and the 250-odd other Subaru dealers, spouses, sons, in-laws, and sales managers intended to muster, until they got to look at the new campaign.

In the lobby outside the main auditorium of the expansive and dully dark Hyatt Downtown in Denver, two SVXs, one white and the other maroon, sat astride an easel bearing a placard that read, "Our New Look: Subaru." Chris Wackman, Subaru of America's marketing director, and Mark Dunn, its advertising manager (both dressed in the S.O.A. dealers meeting uniform of blue slacks and white polo shirts with a red "SVX" embroidered over the left breast), engaged in friendly chatter with the casually attired dealers. Beneath the executives' bonhomie, though, their nerves tingled. The annual dealers meeting was an important event for any car company, a chance to appeal directly to its real customers. For S.O.A., with a new agency and a new image ads in tow, this one was life or death.

"This was unusual for me," Mark conceded, his words, as usual, bouncing around his throat before tumbling out. "I used to get to see dailies or rough cuts from shoots. But this one had to finish so quickly, I didn't get to see anything." Nonetheless, he was expectant. On the plane carrying him west from Philadelphia, he sat next to a trade magazine writer who, hearing Mark's profession and travel purpose, confidently declared that he was one of those consumers unaffected by auto advertising. *To me*, the fellow said, *a car is just a car. I only need one to get me from Point A to Point B.* " 'Just wait until you see our new commercials,' I told him," Mark recounted. " 'Just wait.' "

The dining dealers were less confident. "Advertising...," Bonnie Wade pondered, "all you can really hope is that it'll get people in the front door."

Nate Wade, a soft, parental presence, as was his wife, dug through his scrambled eggs and listened. He and Bonnie were among Subaru's original franchisees, going on twenty-three years now. Maybe, just maybe, Subaru used to create effective advertising, but by Nate's calculation, that time was long past. "Subaru's biggest year was when they were number two in customer satisfaction, behind Mercedes-Benz, in 1985," he said sternly. "Then they came out with a product, it was terrible, they didn't stand up to it, and sales went down." The lesson, Salt Lake Nate proclaimed, was self-evident: Advertising didn't sell cars, people did. "The bad mouth is a lot more important than the good mouth."

Jack Pring, the Wades' genial religious tormentor, agreed. His father started the family's Spokane, Washington, dealership in 1922. "I figure every car we put out, every bit of service, has a bit of me in it," said Pring, a large man with an overpowering handshake and a face creased with smile lines. "You live in a community. Word of mouth sells cars." But not, he added, without support from the manufacturer. "You're looking at a team. If the team isn't successful, you won't sell cars. You gotta have the product. You gotta have the location. You gotta have the people—people who know how to sell a car."

"It's the *factory's* responsibility to create interest in the car and *our* business to sell 'em," said Nate.

"The *factory*," Pring elaborated, "has the responsibility to create the image—"

"To get people in the front door of the dealership," Bonnie chimed in.

The Wades' dour son-in-law and heir, Kirk Schneider, stopped chewing long enough to conclude the discussion with a summary dismissal. "Subaru, way back, they won all those Clio awards. Cute ads, but business kept going down. In retrospect, it would have been better to have no advertising, and let the car sell itself."

Tough crowd.

In the back of the auditorium, Wieden & Kennedy's Subaru account management and media team, for the most part peacefully unaware of the torment its colleagues suffered during the previous two weeks, stood in a silently tense clump. Hal Carlson, the head of media planning, and David Luhr, the director of both the agency's new account and its newly opened Philadelphia office, wore SVX polo shirts. Scot

Butler, the media director, augmented his with a green, blue and black SVX jacket. They did not talk to each other. And they did not go out of their way to glad-hand with the dealers. They were too skittish for that.

Somebody cued the stage manager. The lights dimmed and a tape started playing. A mock-rock choral group, assembled (no doubt) from the same chorus of pop singers who jingled their way through commercials when commercials still had jingles, sang, "Subaru SVX! Subaru SVX!" Tom Gibson, Subaru's president, took the stage and introduced Isamu Kawai, the president of Fuji Heavy Industries, who introduced Takeshi Higurashi, the chief executive of Subaru of America, who introduced Chuck Worrell, Subaru's sales director, who introduced Chris Wackman, the man who started it all a long, long four months earlier.

This was Chris's big moment. During his nine-year career at S.O.A., he had always been somebody's servant—Harvey Lamm's or Alan Ross's or Bob Schmidt's. Now here he stood, in front of the dealers, the customers, ready to unveil the fruits of *his* search, *his* sweat, *his* intellect.

He introduced his speech by calling for a blackout and running a video clip—a segment from a failing television series entitled "My Life and Times." In the clip, two men were trapped in a Jaguar upended in the San Francisco earthquake, injured, endangered and waiting to be rescued. "I wanted a Jaguar," the morose, dying driver told his companion. "But if I'd gotten a Subaru like you, I'd still be back at the office."

The lights brightened slightly, a spot illuminated him, and Chris continued in an exquisitely articulate voice. "The message," he proclaimed, "is clear. The decade of conspicuous consumption is over. And all of its symbols—the junk bonds and Wall Street, insider trading and the 'greed is good' mentality, even the extravagances of 'The Donald'—all are now passé.

"Ostentatious living is out and practicality is in. And all of us, as consumers, are rediscovering basic values. . . ."

His voice picked up momentum as he transformed himself into a creature unfamiliar to all but his closest colleagues, who had seen him do this before: an evangelist. "What's really important," Chris continued, "is for us to recognize these trends and position ourselves to communicate product benefits to a more receptive market.

"And for us, it's a golden opportunity. Why? *Because we're one of the few companies that truly have the right products at the right time.*"

There was a smattering of applause.

"As you know," he went on, regulating his voice to a lower pitch again, "we recently brought on board a new advertising agency—the result of an extensive process that began back in early April. After looking at nearly thirty of the country's best advertising agencies, we narrowed the field down to a group of six finalists who made presentations to our management committee. . . . All six had, as their assignment, the task of not only identifying the problem"—he meant, of course, selling Subarus—"but recommending a solution as well.

"The agency we chose, Wieden & Kennedy, really separated themselves from the others when it came to 'closing the loop.' "

At the back of the room, Luhr, Butler and Carlson nervously glanced from Chris to the seated dealers. Chris plunged ahead, offering the dealers a raft of information about the new SVX, the marketing support S.O.A. intended to offer to back its introduction, the media plan the company was proposing. Then he returned to the subject at hand.

"Wieden & Kennedy from Portland, Oregon, has just the ideas and Subaru spirit to provide the exciting, refreshing, but most of all straightforward communications we need for the nineties.

"You know, in this industry, advertising feeds on recycled ideas and clichés and a fire-sale approach that consumers have grown tired of. We think *this* agency is approaching *our* challenge with a clear perspective—one not unlike the approach they used with Nike."

He had bought into it. Chris was using Nike the way Wieden & Kennedy used it: as the unkickable crutch, the unassailable explanation, the rationale and the support for everything and anything that needed a justification.

"The famous athletic shoe company," Chris continued, "is now recognized as one of the most innovative and creative of all advertisers. But, most importantly, its advertising has improved their bottom line. Since Wieden & Kennedy began working with Nike, its sales have climbed from $800 million to over $3 billion in just three years.

"That's advertising that works. And that's the kind of advertising we need."

Dan Wieden ambled, slightly hunched over, to the podium. His nervousness was tempered by sheer exhaustion. He had spent the day before in Los Angeles, frantically urging his weary charges toward the completion of Subaru's two commercials, then barely making the 9 p.m. flight from LAX to Denver. Then, on the runway, the plane developed mechanical trouble. For hours, the agency chairman sat, with his tapes, on the tarmac, telling himself over and over, *Please God, just let this plane take off.* . . . Finally, at 11 p.m., it did.

As he walked to the podium, Dan felt his sphincter muscles tighten. *I can make it, I can make it,* he told himself. Eternity concluded, and he was on stage.

"For an advertising agency," Dan read, hesitantly, "there is no better place to be than in this room, on this stage."

He looked up. There was no reaction from the audience.

"For an advertising agency," he repeated, "there are few more pivotal people to be talking to than the men and women assembled here."

He had been told to stroke the dealers, although coddling was not in his nature, and he had done so. Now he could find his voice, and did. He began to think of the dealers the way he did his employees: malleable, metaphor-poor but inspiration-prone.

"Because in spite of a sick economy," Dan proceeded, "in spite of impoverished consumers, credit frustration, dealer insecurity and everything else the automotive industry has been through, this—this room, this fine August morning—this is where the promise is. *This is where something surprising, something profound has a chance to unfold.*"

He stood rigidly, his hands glued to the sides of the podium in a death grip. His goatee bobbing up and down, he propelled himself into a five-minute summary of everything his agency had told Subaru of America in its pitch the previous June.

"The time has come to tell the truth," Dan maintained. "The time has come to stop making ads and start making a *connection*—a real, honest connection with our customers. We've got to stop shoveling the same language, the same series of images that every other automaker and advertising agency in the world is dumping into the magazines and onto the airwaves."

At this, the dealers became attentive, and apprehensive. *Was he going to pull an Infiniti?*

"The car still represents the most powerful statement you make about yourself and your relationship with society," the ad executive went on, picking up speed. "What is no longer the same is the statement many of us would love to be making."

Will there be metal in the spots?

"It's no longer about display—big fins, chrome and machismo."

Was he going to make Legacy a woman's car?

"It's no longer true that I want my car to speak for me."

Was he planning on showing people or not?

"Frankly, today, I want my car to work *for* me. I'm more interested in practicality, durability and honest value."

Durability? Was he copying the Levine, Huntley campaign?

"And I'm proud as hell if that makes me seem a bit quirky."

That New York agency did quirky and we suffered!

"Because it shows that I'm an individual."

Well. . . .

"A very, very smart individual and cool enough to be in tune with *these* times."

. . . Yeah. . . .

"The proposition?" Dan asked with a rhetorical flourish. "The Subaru Legacy is for people who appreciate that a car is only a machine, but what a great machine!"

The lights dimmed again, and the large screen in the middle of the stage came to life. An acoustic guitar riffled into a circular, twangy blues and settled into a thumping, repetitive walking beat while, simultaneously, the camera panned lovingly across the burnished bare metal along the inside of a car door. It wiped to a pile of copper-colored bolts. White words, written in Bernhard Modern, the same typeface used in "The Twilight Zone" logo, started scrolling up the right side of the screen, and that famous gruff voice—Uncle Bill!—repeated them for emphasis.

"A car is just a car. And its sole reason for existence—"

The word **existence,** blown up four times larger than the type on the right, rolled up and over the center of the screen. The scene wiped to a tracking shot of faceless workers toiling on an assembly line.

"—is to get you from Point A to Point B"—a large **A** with an ↓ pointing down to a large **B** floated up the middle of the screen, under which appeared a grinder, sparks flying in slow motion, filing down a car fender—"and back again. It won't make you handsome. Or prettier"— a giant **prettier** rolled up the center—"or younger. And if it improves your standing with the neighbors"—the camera slowly zoomed in on the empty headlight cage of an unfinished car—"then you live among snobs with distorted values."

A loud, spontaneous laugh engulfed the auditorium, obscuring the sound of the next words: "A car is steel, electronics, rubber, plastic and glass. A machine." But no matter. The dealers could still read the words, and see the scene dissolve into a view of the arc-welding line, and appreciate that this agency they had never heard of, from Oregon for God's sake, had maybe come to understand Subaru as well as *they,* the men on the lots, understood it.

The action dissolved to a worker on the assembly line, shot from ground up, hanging up his drill. Brian Keith continued: "And in choosing one, the questions should be: How long will it"—A car's underbelly, shot from below, passed over the camera's eye—"last? How well will it do the job?" **The Job** scrolled up. "Can I get a comparable one for less?" The camera closed in on an assembly line, shot from the front. "And do I like the way this machine feels? And looks?" **Feels and Looks?** crawled up and over the screen's edge. There was a cut behind it, to a man pushing a car hull on a dolly. "And in the end, with an absence of marketing glamour about 'the automobile'—" Keith read the last two words with a kind of withering scorn that gave new emphasis to Jerry Cronin's own disgust, as the phrase **marketing glamour** passed over the center of the field of view. The scene beneath it shifted to a fast tracking shot, through a dark obstruction, of a bare, unfinished Legacy shell.

Finally, the beauty shot—the finished Legacies, a red sedan and a blue wagon—leaving the factory's birth canal.

"May the best machine," the voiceover said, "win."

The blues ended on a dominant chord and the screen faded to black as the words **Subaru. What to drive,** repeated assertively by Brian Keith, appeared.

The auditorium exploded into applause and cheers. Dan Wieden left the stage and made his way to the back of the room, where Chris Wackman pumped his hand. Mark Dunn came over, and the three of them, smiling in relief, conferred.

A dealer walked up to the three men and grabbed Dan's hand. "That," the car guy told the advertising man, "was as good as an orgasm."

PART V

THE CAMPAIGN

Chapter 17

It Keeps Going . . .
and Going . . .

HIS TRIUMPH BEHIND HIM, Chris Wackman settled back with his colleagues into the daily mundanities of marketing automobiles to American consumers.

The critics were raving about Subaru's new campaign. "Smartly written, directed and compelling," wrote Barbara Lippert, *Adweek*'s reviewer. "The creators dipped into the zeitgeist and have come up with the perfect ratio of truth, graphics and earnestness for the moment."

Bob Garfield, the frequently caustic critic for *Advertising Age*, was equally enraptured. "Graphically, literally and psychologically," he wrote, "this is perfect advertising for the Greed Generation in recession."

The plaudits were not inconsequential. While people do not buy tickets to watch commercials, advertising critics wield real influence over the fate of agencies and advertisers. In the absence of any quantifiable measure of a new campaign's merits, the critics can establish how the significant constituencies—headquarters executives, retailers, the advertising industry—judge a campaign. A negative review can be deadly. *Advertising Age*'s Garfield was widely blamed for dislodging the $200 million Burger King account from N. W. Ayer, after his scathing front-page review of the agency's first campaign for the fast-food company inflamed the franchisees. The review ran before the ads even appeared on television.

S.O.A. was having its own prerelease problems with the press. The *Wall Street Journal*'s advertising columnist, noticing how the SVX advertisements that had been sent to her by Subaru seemed to glorify speed, decided to call several consumer groups to gauge their reactions to the new luxury car's ads. They were mightily displeased. Charles A. Hurley, vice president of the Insurance Institute for Highway Safety, called the campaign "offensive and totally inappropriate." Representatives of the Center for Auto Safety and Advocates for Highway and Auto Safety asked Subaru, through the *Journal*, to modify or withdraw the ads.

The columnist failed to report that none of those quoted had seen the SVX ads, but were reacting to headlines ("Experience the feeling of having your head flattened out by g forces") that she had read to them over the telephone. They were unaware of the body copy ("the average responsible driver . . . isn't swayed by rpms and speed") that showed the advertisements to be satires of typical sports-car ads.

S.O.A. and Wieden & Kennedy protested what they considered a misinterpretation of the campaign. "These ads are sarcastic references to the kind of advertising that is generally done for this kind of car," Chris explained. He quoted to a reporter one ad's admonition that "it's stupid, dangerous and a waste of precious fossil fuels to be breaking speed limits." "I can't see that there's anything subtle about this campaign," Chris said.

He was being a tad disingenuous. During postproduction, after all, Dan Wieden had insisted that his staff do everything they could to emphasize the SVX's swiftness. The damage was done; the three major broadcast television networks, which had earlier accepted the SVX commercial without question, reacted to the controversy by threatening not to air the spot unless changes were made to its copy. So Brian Keith was rushed to a studio to record a new conclusion to the ad. Instead of finishing with Subaru's "guarantee that you'll be able to use *all* of the speedometer," as Jerry Cronin had originally written, the spot now ended with a toothless promise that "you'll be able to go as fast as the law allows."

Of course, some inside S.O.A. and its agency, Chris among them, secretly exulted over the public imbroglio. *What a perfect way to show that we're no longer dowdy old Subaru!*

Still, if Subaru of America was now suffused with an unfamiliar hopefulness, any public expressions of it were muted by the company's beige surroundings. In the Cherry Hill headquarters' marketing department, the padded walls, the carpeted floors, the textured dividers that separated junior executives from secretaries blocked all sounds from traveling very far. Not that any exultant yelps or anguished cries ever parted the Subarus' lips. Far from it. The Americans and the Japanese (who now wandered in greater volume among the floors) nodded politely to one another on the elevators, but they rarely conversed. The men and women who had once toiled long hours for the greater glory of streetwise Harvey Lamm now, under his successors, came quietly at 8:30 a.m. and left quietly at 4:30 p.m., no lingering.

Between those hours, though, there was much to be done. Once upon a time in the auto business, when summer slipped into fall, a marketing department's work wound down, the preparations for the October 1 new-model introductions well near completion by Labor Day. Now, the toil was year-round, what with late-winter incentive pushes, spring model introductions and the endless rounds of dealer programs and consumer rebates.

Subaru executives were now confident that, after five years of steady decline, this labor was about to bear profit.

"It's not just the product, it's not just the marketing of it, but the factors that you have no control over, the major one of which is the competition—and I think they've done some very good things for us," said Mark Dunn, ever the optimistic advertising manager. "Toyota and Honda have really gone upscale. They've gone into the intermediate class, really vacated the compact class, where we are. In the sedan market, we can now make comments that 'we're $3,400 less than those guys.' I mean, $1,000—well, when you look at it from a four- or five-year financing standpoint, on a monthly basis, it's no big deal. But when you start saying $3,400, that's a lot of money. And financed over four or five years, you're really talking $4,500. Say, now you're talking a *lot* of money. In other words, those things have to fall into place, and they are."

Also falling were the company and its new ad agency—for each other.

Wieden & Kennedy was helping to redesign the binders that held the pricing and merchandising information that Subaru provided its dealers. With the agency's guidance, Subaru was also refashioning its Monroney Labels, the government-mandated stickers glued to every car's side window. The labels were required to be a certain size and to list gas mileage and pricing information. But the typeface used, the graphics, the order of the features and how the company added and subtracted the prices of those features to enhance the vehicle's appeal were the manufacturer's prerogative. This was but a bit of the minutiae that S.O.A. had put off in the whirlwind agency search, but which required the company's zealous attention if its message to consumers, through its distributors and dealers, via its agency, was to have an effect. "You wouldn't think a Monroney would do that much, but when you see the difference between the old and the new, it's *significant*," said Fred Adcock, a senior Subaru sales executive.

In many ways, the relationship between Subaru and Wieden & Kennedy was like the relationship between two teens in the first crush of puppy love. The agency's willingness to take on dishwater-dull assignments like the Monroneys and the binders—the advertising equivalents of carrying a girl's books home from school—was but partial evidence. There were, as well, more formal, senior-prom-like efforts at building rapport.

S.O.A. executives held weekend barbecues for their new Philadelphia neighbors. Mark Dunn even sponsored a combination road rally and scavenger hunt, in which Wieden & Kennedy staffers were paired with Subaru personnel, given a Legacy, a map, and a list of questions ("Rank the five major import companies in order of sales") and told to locate a list of area landmarks while putting no more than thirty miles on the odometer.

The task of managing this budding alliance fell to the advertising agency's Subaru account director, David Luhr, who was also responsible for starting, staffing and running Wieden & Kennedy's Philadelphia office, the agency's first branch on the East Coast and an operation its founders clearly expected would grow beyond its single account. "It's the Kissinger of the agency business," Luhr said, describing his obligations to his new client and to his colleagues. "You have to make both parties feel good."

In fact, though, Luhr's burdens were not so evenly balanced. During advertising's great growth periods, after World Wars I and II, account directors were trained to become one with their clients, at the sacrifice of all personal satisfaction and of others in the agency, if need be. Preserving the relationship—and its profits—was paramount. Not infrequently, an account director grew so close to the client and so distant from the agency that he stuffed the account in his hip pocket and waltzed it to another shop.

Wieden & Kennedy, and Dave Luhr, came from a different school. "One good thing about this agency: It's focused internally," Luhr admitted. "Not to say we don't focus on our clients. But we focus on our organization first."

Luhr interpreted his main challenge as exporting to and sustaining on the East Coast Wieden & Kennedy's corporate culture of insouciance, originality and artistry. Clients footed the bill and provided certain constraints, but they could not be allowed to get in the way, lest the agency's entire raison d'être crumble. It was a worldview shared by most of the postmodern ad agencies, like Chiat/Day, Fallon McElligott and Goodby, Berlin & Silverstein, which also believed their role was to create intellectually challenging, short-form cultural expressions.

Those agencies were like religious cults, Luhr believed, as any good agency had to be. He saw himself not only as a disciple of the masters, Dan and Dave, but as their warrior, conquering new territory, making new converts, carrying their message to distant ports. "All Wieden &

Kennedy is, is an environment. That's the most important thing we own. An environment for doing great work," Luhr said.

A thirty-seven-year-old who stood a powerful five-foot-ten and wore his dark hair in razor-cut spikes, Luhr seemed to have his head on a swivel. He could not talk without shifting his gaze from side to side, to beyond and back, in search of the next problem or, perhaps, the next solution. Yet he maintained an ability to concentrate his mind completely on his interlocutor's words, even as his clear, blue eyes focused on the next converser.

Such schizophrenic skills were necessary to achieve success in the agency business of the eighties and nineties, where creatives had to be coddled and clients held at bay, and Luhr had learned from the best. The California-bred, Arizona-educated son of a chemical engineer and a housewife, he came to advertising when he realized he lacked the temperament and talent for journalism, his college major. He spent four years at the Los Angeles office of Dancer-Fitzgerald-Sample, long enough to know he loved the ad game but hated traditional agencies. Fortunately, it was 1980, and Chiat/Day was beckoning.

Chiat/Day was the West Coast's rebel agency and a transitional shop in advertising history. It was the last bastion of pure, Bernbachian entertainment and the first of the postmodern artists colonies. Founded in the early 1960s and led by an ex-Easterner, Jay Chiat, the agency was still small when the Creative Revolution died in New York and thus didn't need to turn its back on the creative impulse the way so many of the larger New York agencies did. Through the seventies, Chiat/Day attracted attention with its introductory work for Honda cars ("The Hatchback of Notre Dame"), Suntory whiskey ("From the bonnie, bonnie banks of the Yamazaki") and Pioneer stereo systems ("Have an eargasm"). By 1980, its work had earned Chiat/Day election as *Advertising Age*'s Agency of the Year. Dave Luhr was joining a hot shop.

Watching the agency win, and build, Apple Computer and Yamaha motorcycles and other prestigious accounts taught Luhr the essential lessons of account management in the era of postmodern advertising. To do good work was the purpose of advertising, he learned. And good creative people don't operate by the same rules by which, say, good bankers do. And clients don't always recognize the value of good creative work or good, quirky creative people, so an account exec had to be prepared to fight the client, anger the client, even risk dismissal or fire the client if the going got too debilitating.

Serendipitously, it was that kind of fighting that landed Luhr his job at Wieden & Kennedy. He was a manager on Chiat/Day's Nike account when the company canned the agency.

During the years that Chiat/Day and Wieden & Kennedy shared the Nike account, Luhr had come to know several people at the Portland agency quite well. When Wieden & Kennedy won back the brand-image portion of the account, it fell to Luhr to perform the uncomfortable job of flying to Portland to brief the new agency on its tasks. He made his presentation directly to Dan and David, who were so impressed with his efficiency, candor and humor that they offered Luhr a job.

Wieden & Kennedy was small and barely known; Chiat/Day was America's most famous ad agency. It was like being asked to leave the Vatican for a parish priesthood. But Luhr was as taken with the men from Portland as they were with him. "Jay Chiat's a brilliant guy; he'd be a real shitty neighbor, and there were a lot of people like him at Chiat/Day," Luhr explained. "Dan Wieden is not only a brilliant guy, he'd be a great neighbor. I'd gotten to the point where I wanted some nice neighbors." He took the job.

Luhr rapidly became Dan's and David's most trusted manager and organizer. His goal was to clone the home office and grow its Philadelphia branch into a genetically identical offshoot. "I want to have a place," Luhr said, "where the Portland people will come and be jealous that they aren't part of it."

The first task was finding office space that would spur their envy, no easy matter considering that everyone in Portland's Dekum Building worked but a few yards from an in-house basketball court and a few blocks from a riverside park. Luhr assigned Christine Barrett, a funny, brash young woman, to this duty. She knew the drill. The new office had to be in downtown Philadelphia, not far from the Vine Street Expressway to the Ben Franklin Bridge (for easy access to the client); it had to be reasonably close to the 30th Street Station (for quick Amtrak exits to New York); and it had to be on a large, open floor (to enable people to yell down the hall to each other). Finally, and most importantly, it had to be environmentally appropriate to the creative mindset. In other words, said Christine, "It had to be cool."

"Those who can, do. Those who can't, work in cubicles," she said, without apology. "We're in the image business, and this is our image."

After several weeks of searching, she led Dan and David (both dressed, inappropriately, in wool suits) through the same sweltering August heat that had nearly killed the Continental Congress 215 years earlier, to a selection of downtown Philadelphia's finest and funkiest edifices. They settled, tentatively, on a thirteen-thousand-square-foot cavern on an upper floor of Wanamaker's Department Store. No place could have been more appropriate. It was the store's founder, John

Wanamaker, who was reputed to have said almost a century before: "I know I waste half the money I spend on advertising. The problem is, I don't know which half."

Meanwhile, as other agency executives haggled over the lease and renovation questions, Luhr settled his Portland pioneers into temporary quarters seventeen flights up a nondescript glass tower on the corner of 16th and Market streets in the heart of Center City. To lend the viewless, colorless space a semblance of character, the men and women of Wieden & Kennedy/Philadelphia set at the apex of the "V" that marked the border between the creative department and the account services department the life-size cardboard cutout of Mr. Shout that, several months earlier, had adorned the pitch room at the Cherry Hill Hyatt. With his finger raised, his lips curled and his eyebrows arched, the cartoon man looked to be in the throes of a good idea.

Luhr's next and most crucial duty was to find the thirty-five to forty people who would *be* Wieden & Kennedy/Philadelphia.

At another agency, this might have been a reflexive action; thousands of advertising people, most of them midlevel, midcareer account managers, more than a few with automotive experience, had been laid off by New York agencies during the media recession that began in 1988. Moreover, almost immediately upon release of the news that Wieden & Kennedy had won the Subaru account, the agency was deluged with applications.

Luhr ignored most of the entreaties. He was looking for a special class of personnel: misfits. "People that normal companies will not hire, they'd be scared to hire" was how he described his quarry. "I want advertising enthusiasts, not car enthusiasts. A good advertising enthusiast can switch from cars to soda pop very quickly, because he's in love with the process. It's people who see more, see different colors, and people who have a passion to prove that they can make it. Because maybe they wouldn't survive at IBM, but goddamn it, they're going to make it in the agency world."

Luhr called several old friends from Chiat/Day and put the word out to a network of executive recruiters. Advertising people, by nature, are gypsies, accustomed to moving from job to job and city to city, in search of greater challenges, higher salaries or more congenial colleagues. Luhr quickly located a host of candidates.

Account executives, or A.E.s, were his first priority. Luhr wanted relationship managers, stamped from his own solipsistic mold, who could comfort the client and carry its concerns back to the agency without becoming the client's captives. "Here," said Luhr, "the work comes first, agency-client relationships come second." He needed enough account execs to cover, or "bracket," as ad people say, all of Subaru's senior marketing and sales executives, as he bracketed Chris Wackman and as Dan, in his role as agency head, in theory bracketed S.O.A.'s president, Tom Gibson.

The national account team was easy to find. A headhunter located the national account director, Walter Mills, an unflappable, mid-thirties M.B.A. off the Boston agency circuit. Walter's job was to bracket both Mark Dunn and Chris Wackman, and to serve as the outside overseer of Subaru's brand image—to nurture it, nudge it this way and that, but keep it consistent, however the immediate merchandising requirements might shift.

To Luhr, Walter was perfect for the job; he evinced disdain for "credit-card management," the agency term for account execs who spend their time wining and dining the client but remain distant from the creative product, and maintained that "a good account executive has to be somebody who recognizes what is right for the client, but knows that many times what is right for the client isn't always what the client thinks is right."

Finding the regional account management team was more difficult. These were the account execs charged with visiting Subaru's seven (later consolidated to six) regional vice presidents and the dealers under their purview. They had to explain advertising strategy to them, field their complaints and help devise ads that would run in conjunction with the national image ads, but were tailored specifically for their respective parts of the country.

Regional advertising sits in a cheerless netherworld between national brand advertising, which the manufacturer pays for and controls, and the dealers' own advertising, which the dealers finance and manage. Where a national campaign is supposed to create an overarching image for a company and its cars, and dealer advertising promotes specific stores and prices, regional ads aim at creating a sense of urgency—a reason (a special sale, short-term factory-to-dealer incentives) to buy now. The factory provides a large portion of the money for regional campaigns, but the rest comes from a tariff paid by the dealers—in Subaru's case, 1.5 percent of the sticker price of each car sold. This meant that Subaru's regional advertising had many masters. Luhr wanted to make sure that the regional account executives he brought in served none but the agency.

To direct the regional staff, he hired a brash veteran of the Ford account at J. Walter Thompson, Jeff Greenberg, who had spent a fair portion of his professional life providing succor to dealer associations in places like western Illinois and eastern Iowa. Under him, Luhr hired three A.E.s to serve in the regions themselves, stationing one each in Atlanta, Portland and Philadelphia.

The next requirement was to hire the media department. Subaru, in Wieden & Kennedy's new construct, may have been "what to drive," but if no one heard or saw or read that message, would it make any difference? The media people were to see that it did.

In the era of three television networks and *Life*, *Look* and the *Saturday Evening Post*, media was the sleepiest backwater in the agency business. During the 1980s, however, with the growth of cable television, the creation of a score of TV networks and the fragmentation of the magazine industry, media departments had become their agencies' strategic nerve centers. The wiliest tacticians and the toughest negotiators inhabited them, living their lives behind a curtain of computer printouts, before which periodical publishers and network sales reps supplicated themselves.

S.O.A. demanded more strategic effulgence than most accounts. The car company had $10 million to get the word out during the last four months of 1991 and another $70 million to spend in 1992—less than half the media budgets of its major competitors, and only 1.2 percent of the total amount automotive companies planned to spend on advertising in 1992. To Scot Butler, the challenge was delicious.

Butler was a representative advertising gypsy. A forty-one-year-old college dropout from New Jersey, he wandered into the media side of advertising to satisfy his love of pro sports (sales reps are always plying media buyers with tickets) and his fascination with statistics. A man with the deep tones and loping features of a basset hound, Butler had learned the numbers during ten years at Backer Spielvogel Bates in New York, then jumped to Fallon McElligott in Minneapolis and, after less than a year there, to Wieden & Kennedy in Portland. He moved to Philadelphia to fulfill a professional dream: to prove to Nike, which had pulled its network-television buying from Wieden & Kennedy before his arrival, that the agency was capable of handling a multimillion-dollar network account.

To assist him, as director of media planning, Butler brought east from Portland Hal Carlson. Together, they found eight men and women with what Hal called "a real logical way of looking at the world" to help supervise the department; and they hired several spot buyers to cut deals with local television stations and newspapers.

During the preparation for Wieden & Kennedy's Subaru pitch, Butler and Hal had immersed themselves in state-by-state, county-by-county data weighing Subaru's brand popularity against the popularity of all imported compact cars. From this information, they divided the 210 U.S.

media markets in which Subarus were sold into five tiers. Tier 1 markets were those where Subaru cars had the highest per capita concentration—and, by the agency's reasoning, the greatest potential for additional sales. There were thirteen of these Tier 1 markets in the U.S., and although they held only 20 percent of the nation's population, they accounted for nearly 40 percent of Subaru's sales. Tier 5 markets were those where Subaru was the least known and least viable; the 142 markets in this ranking had almost 40 percent of the population, but only 18 percent of Subaru's sales.

In the pitch, the agency had told S.O.A. that it wanted to allocate about 70 percent of Subaru's media budget according to this tiering strategy, with the rest going to pay for network TV ads. Through careful planning and negotiating and buying, the agency believed it could give the Tier 5 markets only marginally less advertising than they had received before, while pumping enough additional advertising into the top tiers to make it seem as if Subaru were spending the equivalent of $150 or $200 million a year—on a par with Toyota and Honda. The core of the plan would be the network buy; the regional money would augment it with purchases of time on local stations. The commercials would run on the same programs (networks and affiliates divide the advertising time on network programs), so the effect on the viewers' perceptions of Subaru would be profound.

Now Butler, Hal and their new crew of media planners and buyers had to make their strategy real—and quickly. They investigated seasonal purchasing patterns, demographics, television viewing habits and reading preferences in the different tiers.

Given the target audience of Subaru consumers—educated, "role-relaxed" men and women ages twenty-five to fifty-four who consciously abjured status seeking to pursue more socially and intellectually constructive pursuits—certain media assumptions were easy to make. Time-Warner, for example, had an attractive group of magazines (*Sports Illustrated*, *People*, *Fortune*) that it was willing to package together at a discounted price. But the agency considered the publisher's flagship newsmagazine less appealing than its arch-rival.

"I think *Newsweek* is more the innovator now than *Time* is," Butler said. "They hired Frank Deford"—a former *Sports Illustrated* writer whom Scot particularly liked, "which was a big step; they're going to have a big series of excerpts from Norman Schwarzkopf's book next year, which is a big deal. They're going to hold back their presidential election issue for a week until they can do a whole issue on the election, which we're going to get a feature position in. *Time* . . . they're not doing that stuff." So, while Wieden & Kennedy put about 35 percent of

Subaru's magazine budget into Time-Warner books, for subjective reasons of editorial quality it stayed out of *Time*.

In television, NBC's "L.A. Law," a sexy ensemble drama, was deemed a better choice for Subaru than, for example, "Golden Girls," a geriatric sitcom. But other considerations also influenced buying decisions.

"NBC, when we're in the marketplace, might offer us a great deal on 'L.A. Law' if we do some 'Quantum Leap' as part of it," Hal Carlson explained. "It might be a second-tier program for us, but we want to be doing 'L.A. Law' and this will enable us to get it. On the other hand, if NBC says you can't have 'L.A. Law' unless you buy 'Matlock,' we won't do it. We won't cannibalize the plan because NBC is holding 'L.A. Law' ransom."

Instead of assembling a rigid media plan, then, the agency opted to articulate a set of broad principles—*here are the people we're trying to reach, here are the shows we like*—and allow the networks to come up with their own recommendations. Butler also hired a well-connected freelance time-buyer in Los Angeles to spearhead Wieden & Kennedy's efforts, and granted the buyer flexibility to achieve the best network deals he could, even if it meant slotting in some secondary program choices. The objective was to hit the right people and for Subaru to be a dominant presence in the shows those consumers were watching.

Subaru was blocked from buying time on many of the most desirable programs, particularly major sporting events, like NBA basketball games and NFL football. Months earlier, the car company had decided not to get involved in television's "upfront market," where the networks sell big chunks of time on the fall schedule to the largest advertisers and their agencies. Network sports, particularly coveted by automotive advertisers because they reach men, were snapped up by the other car makers.

Still, the networks proved eager to negotiate with Butler and his crew. The broadcasters' once-unfamiliar competition from national cable networks had turned television into a buyer's market. The broadcast nets' willingness to deal also had another foundation: Nike. Even though Wieden & Kennedy was not responsible for the shoe company's network time-buying, there was always a chance. *Make nice now, we might benefit later,* the sales reps thought. Working with the agency's L.A. buyer, the networks even made available some coveted commercial slots, including the season premieres of the Candice Bergen sitcom "Murphy Brown" on CBS and NBC's comedy "Cheers," which they had held out of the upfront market. NBC also offered to sell Subaru one quarter during each Notre Dame football game it broadcast. Hal knew the networks were bribing the agency for some future Nike business. "I mean, these guys aren't dummies, you know?"

Wieden & Kennedy determined that the best places to reach Subaru's target consumers were on early morning news, late-night programs, prime time and sports, in that order. Evening news, S.O.A.'s most significant buy under its previous agency, was virtually eliminated in the new plan, because Butler and Hal judged its audience too old.

For late night, the agency bought ABC's "Nightline" and NBC's "The Tonight Show," "Late Night with David Letterman" and "Saturday Night Live"—by far the most popular shows for the midmarket intelligentsia. In the early morning slot, it purchased time on ABC's "World News This Morning," because it complemented "Nightline." The agency bought marquee sponsorship of the Ryder Cup golf tournament on NBC to launch the SVX and picked up a significant presence on the 1992 Winter Olympics on CBS. Blocked from other network sports programming (save Notre Dame football), the agency turned to cable, purchasing slots on college football and basketball on ESPN, and on the TNT and TBS pro basketball shows. In prime time, Wieden & Kennedy turned to some of the newer programs that seemed demographically correct, like the ABC sitcom "Home Improvement" and the wacky CBS ensemble show "Northern Exposure." Rounding out the schedule were various cable buys: "Letterman" reruns on the Arts & Entertainment Network, "Crossfire" and "Moneyline" on CNN and nature specials on The Discovery Channel.

AS SUMMER GROUND swiftly into fall, the new campaign was prepared to enter America's homes. The agency was well staffed. The only stumbling block was *doing* the new campaign.

The two television commercials and the half-dozen magazine advertisements that Wieden & Kennedy had produced in July and August were only the first missiles in what was supposed to be a long, articulated assault on the automotive market. The Legacy needed its own brand-image television spot; S.O.A. considered "Factory" more about corporate image than about its flagship car. A complete regional campaign—TV and newspaper ads explaining why consumers in the Northeast, Northwest, Southeast, Mid-Atlantic, Midwest and Southwest should buy Subarus *now*—also had to be created. That took copywriters and art directors.

Unfortunately, there was nothing Dan Wieden enjoyed less than hiring copywriters and art directors. Creative was the soul of his agency. Everything Wieden & Kennedy was grew out of a creative philosophy that required immersion in the convolutions of American culture; everything the agency could *be* depended on the collegial spirit of the men and women who filled its offices. Although hundreds of creatives at other agencies across the land would have overturned their lives for a chance to work, however briefly, at Wieden & Kennedy, Dan was not an easy mark. *You can't just . . . just . . . hire people overnight! You have to talk to them, again and again and again, test them, tease them, scrutinize their work and their philosophies.* Since it was difficult enough to schedule time with Dan (his insistence on approving everything that went on in the agency made him difficult to pin down) Wieden & Kennedy generally took months to hire even relatively junior copywriters and art directors.

On the Subaru account, the delays took their toll. Dan dawdled over a top-name art director who had worked on the Schweppes soft drinks campaign at Ammirati & Puris; the designer eventually took a job doing Isuzu ads for Goodby, Berlin & Silverstein. He dawdled over a talented youngster from Hill, Holliday, Connors, Cosmopulos, Jerry Cronin's old Boston shop and the agency for Infiniti cars, until the kid gave up. Finally, with the deadline for the regional campaign looming, Dan brought in a Portland freelancer.

Serendipitously, though, a partner for Jerry came on the scene rather quickly. Vince Engel looked like, and was, a surfer. Not yet forty, he had dark ruddy skin, a slender, graceful body, and a large head with outsized features: translucent blue eyes, shiny, white teeth and a shock of dark hair that crested and rolled like a wave over his forehead. He was beach culture incarnate; he had spent his boyhood in Santa Barbara, studied art at U.C.L.A., and done freelance lettering on record-album covers before succumbing to the call of the Australian surf.

In eight years down under, Vince became one of advertising's best-known expatriates in the southern Pacific. He landed jobs art directing at Ted Bates and Ogilvy & Mather in Australia, and later crossed the Tasman Sea to work for the N. W. Ayer office in New Zealand. He was a frequent award-winner and displayed a pronounced willingness to underdesign his ads, to fly resolutely in the face of prevailing trends. He shared a gold award from the New York Festivals, an international competition, for an Ayer house ad that ran only once on a satellite TV service. It consisted of plain, black sans-serif type that sat against a white background. "Karl Marx once described advertising as maggots feeding on the rotting corpse of capitalism," read the first screen. The next screen responded, "Let's do lunch."

Vince's voice rarely rose or fell from a deep monotone, but the apparent imperturbability masked a passion for all things advertising. He knew the players, eagerly sought and shared agency-world gossip across several continents and littered his conversation with talk of awards—which ones were most prestigious, which ones were worthless. His ardor contrasted sharply with Wieden & Kennedy's feigned indifference to such temporal matters. In New Zealand, Vince was known for his immodesty; when two of his former Ayer juniors were named associate creative directors at another Auckland agency, his letter of congratulations noted that they "had a great teacher."

But Vince was of Wieden & Kennedy's ilk in more substantive ways. Like its other creatives, he was an artist who had made peace with the duplicity of his craft. "It sounds corny, but products I really believed in have always been my best work," he droned. "Stuff I did on American Express, I really believe in the American Express card, the service they offer. People will look at you differently when you put down an American Express card as opposed to a Visa card, no matter what anybody says."

What's more, he adored Jerry's Subaru campaign, and saw in it the righteousness that was so absent from other automobile advertising. "Tell the truth, with a lot of 'fuck you' in it, that's what the campaign is, it's really about," he said shortly after seeing it for the first time. "You look at the stuff, it's really 'fuck you.' I worked on Toyota in Australia, and God, what garbage! And they go on about cars! Come on, guys—it's a hunk of steel, and overpriced." He paid Jerry the highest compliment: "Without doing a disservice to the campaign in its own right, I think there is that element of honesty you found in the old Volkswagen campaign."

Jerry saw in Vince the perfect partner, and quickly the two set about to develop the Legacy brand-image spot—a commercial that Jerry intended to satirize consumers' status concerns. Vince's contribution was to suggest modeling it on a device Woody Allen used in his movies *Take the Money and Run* and *Annie Hall*, and have laughably unappealing men and women reveal, seriously and straight to the camera, their deepest, inner thoughts, in this case, about what a luxury car meant to them.

Vince and Jerry thought alike about advertising, which is the linchpin of an enduring creative partnership. They would work very, very well together. "As long as the whole thing is, 'Ah, that's neat,'" Vince said, summarizing the philosophy they shared, "that's all that matters."

Chapter 18

All Aspirin Is Alike

SUBARU MAY NOW HAVE BEEN "what to drive" to its headquarters' executives and its advertising agency, but the message still had to be communicated to its seven hundred dealers, a good chunk of whom hadn't made it to the annual dealers meeting. That was the job of the regional campaign.

In theory, but only in theory, there need be no differentiation among types of advertising. Research would provide insights into consumer needs and desires, agencies would devise ads to meet them, and those ads would run everywhere, with exceptions made only for important local variations in price or demographics.

Theory has never met an automobile dealer. Dealers—there were 14,850 of them in the United States in 1991, and they owned 24,000 franchised new-car dealerships—sold and serviced cars for a living, bringing in more than $300 billion in revenues a year for themselves and the manufacturers, virtually all of it through one-on-one, face-to-face transactions between a salesperson and a customer. Tell them how to market cars? Hah! Dealers wanted their own campaigns.

And for most of the first half of this century, dealers got their own campaigns by doing them themselves. They advertised price and location, the factory advertised image and features, and together, uneasily, they sold cars to a motor-hungry public.

Then, in the late 1940s, according to ad-industry lore, J. Walter Thompson, the Ford Motor Company's lead agency, grew inspired by the notion that there was a missing link in automotive advertising: ads urging consumers to buy their cars immediately; ads that added to the manufacturer's "what" and "why" and the dealers' own "where," the crucial, urgent "when." Thompson persuaded Ford's dealers to band together in regional sales associations and pool their money to finance this extra layer of advertising. When World War II ended, the nation's factories began making consumer goods again, and the returning veterans and their booming families started purchasing homes and cars, these dealer associations and their novel form of advertising received much of the credit. Pretty soon, regional auto campaigns, paid for and supervised by the dealers themselves or co-sponsored by the manufacturer with plenty of dealer input, were a standard in the industry. And ad agencies had another source of 15 percent commissions.

So it was simply a given that Subaru of America was going to have a regional advertising campaign. Wieden & Kennedy put responsibility for its creation in the hands of Peter Wegner.

Wegner was a freelancer, a fact that might have dismayed a new client were it not for his special status. The twenty-eight-year-old Yale fine-arts graduate had been a full-time Wieden & Kennedy copywriter who had left the agency the previous May to recapture his independence. A keen cultural observer and a somewhat cantankerous intellectual, he liked advertising but was unable to give it the cultish devotion that Wieden & Kennedy desired. He wanted to spend more time with his family, and more time creating his Gary Larsenesque editorial cartoons. In the months since his resignation, though, save for a long vacation in Italy, he had been working virtually full-time for the Portland agency. The only things he lacked that his former colleagues still possessed were health insurance coverage and a sense of indentured servitude.

Wegner had never worked on an automotive campaign before. His ideas were intuitive, and informed in no small part by the experience he had recently had shopping for and purchasing a Volvo. He found it demeaning. *I don't want to have anything out there with my name on it that's going to indicate to people that they're going to be hit on,* Wegner told Chris Wackman. With the S.O.A. executive's approval, he intended to paint a portrait of a company that would not pressure its customers.

The slight, sandy-haired young writer did not have much help. Vince Engel had only just joined the agency and was spending almost all of his time either in Philadelphia or arranging his family's move there. Jerry Cronin was also transferring his pregnant wife and his life back East. The agency hired a freelance creative team from Seattle to help Wegner with his brainstorming. They worked together for a week, producing ads that ranged from broad, light humor to more obscure narratives, but before they could settle (or receive approval) on one style, the team left for vacation.

Finally, with the deadline looming, Dan Wieden mandated the approach. The regional campaign, he dictated, should follow closely the national campaign, at least in the print ads. Synergy virtually demanded it: If the national ads and the regional ads looked and sounded alike, they would reinforce each other in the consumer's mind. Otherwise, Subaru ran the risk of running advertisements that looked as if they came from two different campaigns.

Wegner studied the national magazine advertisements that Jerry had developed months before with his old art director. These were the ads with the funny, Bernhard Modern headlines on the left that subtly ridiculed the status-consciousness of Mercedes-Benz drivers and their ilk, and the long, *New Yorker*–style copy on the right extolling Subaru's virtues with the same dry wit. Wegner and Susan Hoffman, a Nike art director whom he grabbed for design help, made some obvious changes, like condensing the two-page magazine spreads into small spaces for newspapers. He also focused the body copy much more specifically on the price and attributes of Subaru's cars, throwing in technical details which he believed would "regionalize" the advertisements. But he tried to stay true to the sensibility and tone of Jerry's national campaign.

Others in the agency joined in the effort. David Kennedy devoted himself for more than a week to the point-of-purchase displays—collateral materials that were usually fobbed off on junior creatives and which rarely, if ever, engaged an agency principal. Toward the end of the week before the mid-September meeting at which the campaign was to be unveiled to Subaru's regional vice presidents and their senior staff, whose jobs were to interact, directly and daily, with the dealers, Dave Luhr flew in from Philadelphia to inspect the progress. He found the campaign nearly buttoned up. Wegner and his helpers had created fifteen executions each in newspaper, television and radio, augmented by dealership exhibits, brochures and other materials. Luhr was euphoric. He publicly pronounced it the best presentation Wieden & Kennedy had ever prepared.

More important, the client felt the same way. Wackman and Dunn traveled to Portland the day before the meeting and were given a quick, preliminary run-through. Mark loved the TV ads. As illustrated in the storyboards, they showed heavy metal—just the car against a plain, white background. But they retained the humor of the print ads by featuring an animated version of Mr. Shout cartoonishly miming various activities, from driving fast to playing the violin. Chris had a few reservations about the print ads as they were described to him. *Is it*, he wondered, *retail enough? Does it clearly state that you can get a Legacy for $2,000 less than a Camry?* But he kept his questions to himself. Copy could always be fixed. *Let's see what the RVPs*—the regional vice-presidents—*say.*

THE SUBARUS FILED into the agency's gym and took seats on the basketball court. Tom Gibson, Chris Wackman, Mark Dunn, senior vice president for sales Chuck Worrell, the sales executive Fred Adcock and several Japanese executives had come from Cherry Hill. Woody Purcell from Atlanta, Portland's Tim (Parzy) Parzybach and the other regional vice presidents accompanied them, as did representatives from the independent distributors in New York and New England, and several other regional sales and marketing executives. With the Wieden & Kennedy personnel (some from Philadelphia, some from Portland), they occupied about thirty-five folding chairs.

The RVPs could not begin to imagine how completely, how perfectly plotted this presentation was. The boards and the print-ad comps had been expertly dummied up by a professional illustrator. Poster-size versions of the newspaper advertisements, neatly wrapped in brown paper to preserve the surprise, hung, in a row, by nearly invisible thread from the gym's ceiling. Underneath each, also wrapped, was a one-sentence explanation of its strategic rationale. It was so unlike any other meeting Wieden & Kennedy had ever held.

Peter Wegner opened the meeting. Newspapers were a vital medium for the regions (they could quickly change the details and placement of the ads as needed), so Wegner had decided to lead the presentation with these ads, then describe how each one became a television spot, a radio ad and a point-of-purchase display. He began to unwrap the posters. He read the headlines and the body copy of each one for the benefit of those in the audience too far back to see.

"Solve urban gridlock," Wegner recited, going over one headline. "Throw your Legacy into all-wheel-drive and go over the BMW in front of you."

Silence.

"Buy a Porsche . . . or buy a Loyale," he read.

No reaction.

One after another after another, he unwrapped the posters and read the ads, but not a sound could be heard. The headlines that had elicited so much laughter from Wieden & Kennedy staffers, the copy that had drawn so much satisfaction from Luhr, pulled nothing but blank stares from the Subaru executives.

Finally, after twenty minutes, Worrell spoke up. *These aren't retail,* he said in his high southern drawl. *They don't have the price big enough.*

Woody Purcell, widely considered the first among equals of the RVPs, at least in terms of political savvy, was more emphatic. *This is* not *gonna sell cars,* he complained.

The plug had been pulled and the criticism flowed. There was *no sense of urgency* to the ads, one RVP protested. That was right, carped another, the ads didn't have a *call to action.* Wegner tried to answer the objections, but each time he was cut off by another. One RVP got up and pointed to the poster headlined, "If you find yourself choosing between car payments and food, maybe you should think about another car." It was, the sales executive said, *insensitive to the homeless.*

Tired of acting the target, Wegner responded with sarcasm. *You know,* he heckled the increasingly unruly mob, *we were told you guys were going to be unresponsive, so this comes as a big surprise.* The RVPs and their staffs refused to take the bait. *Where are the starbursts?* several asked, referring to the graphic highlights they expected in the layouts. *Where are the grids comparing us to the competition?*

Tom Gibson held back, watching, saying nothing. Too often in auto companies, marketing and sales meetings, especially those where the bosses are present, are quiet, acquiescent affairs. Here Gibson had a rare chance to find out what his men in the field were really thinking about the new agency, and he was of no mind to interrupt them. After all, the RVPs were responsible for communicating the company's line to the dealers. If the RVPs were unhappy, the dealers would pick that up. The whole marketing program could be subverted. Better to find out now.

Wackman, too, was content to allow his agency to become a punching bag. He was surprised by the RVPs' vociferousness, but figured the lesson was a good one for the agency to learn. He had warned Luhr and Dan that dealers and regional execs were different from headquarters people, had different needs, demands, standards. The agency had ignored the warning. Now it was discovering the hard way.

"You can talk until you're blue in the face, and the message just won't get through," Chris sighed later. "You know, you hear it from the client, the agency thinks, 'Well, yeah, but the client is just nervous because they don't think it's the right thing, but *we* know it's the right thing.' " Wieden & Kennedy required taming. "Sometimes, you need to get hit right between the eyes with a two-by-four before you recognize that you're serving two different clients."

The criticisms flew for the better part of an hour. *Funny? That's not funny! . . . You never talk about the deal! . . . We gotta sell cars today!* Peter Wegner, still taking most of the heat, felt like a comedian playing before a crowd of drunken, uncontrollable Rotarians. Luhr, who had believed the presentation represented the light at the end of the four-month-long tunnel that had begun with the agency's credentials presentation, started thinking that the illumination was a train bearing down on him.

Finally, Dan Wieden could take it no more.

What the fuck do you guys want? he cried. *You say you want price and features—you want value. Well, that's this campaign—that's what it's all about!* He leaped to his feet and began justifying the work. He read sections of the copy that spoke glowingly of the cars' attributes. He showed the RVPs how many times the word "value" was used. He tried to tell them about the TV commercials—Wegner hadn't even been given a chance to present them before the outburst started—and how wonderfully the spots showcased the gorgeous, gleaming metal.

But Dan did not help his cause. He seemed defensive, agency blood to auto-sales sharks. Besides, the regional vice presidents felt betrayed by the shop. They had been told that finally they had an ad agency that understood consumers, knew Subaru, grasped its problems. They didn't expect to see "hey-come-on-down-deals-deals-deals" ads, Wieden & Kennedy was too classy for that, but they did anticipate some compelling advertisements. What they got hit them on their blind side: another take on the national-image campaign.

The meeting was called to a halt. After some desultory discussion, the agency staff and the Subarus drifted to a cocktail party, and then to dinner at the Alexis, one of Portland's classier hotels. Surprisingly, the same men who had acted like rabid dogs at the presentation grew chummy with the agency. *Nothing personal,* one exec told Peter Wegner. *That's just the way the regional business goes.*

WIEDEN & KENNEDY had been trapped by its own inexperience. Dan Wieden assumed that the best way to transform Subaru's image was to infuse all the company's communications with the same tone, even the same design. But all advertising, to paraphrase an old aspirin commercial, is not alike.

Auto-industry tradition held that national advertising and regional advertising were different; S.O.A.'s regional sales executives needed a distinctive campaign to bring back to their dealers for no other reason than the dealers expected it. In advertising, territoriality is its own demand. Mark Dunn assessed the failure of the agency's regional campaign this way: "It was more a problem of form over function."

The regions were also reacting to their loss of power. Under its previous advertising agency, Subaru paid for much of its regional advertising by assessing the dealers 1.5 percent of the retail price of every car

they sold. Each region's "accrual money" went into a pot that Subaru's
RVPs, in close consultation with their dealers, largely controlled. S.O.A.
had used the financial crisis of the late eighties to dismantle this system
and place authority over the regional advertising with Cherry Hill. The
company still made and collected the assessments, and it guaranteed
that the total dollars taken from a region would flow back into that region, although they would not necessarily be allocated to individual media markets within each region so democratically. Other car companies,
like Nissan, had done the same thing several years before. The dealers
and the RVPs were publicly in favor of the move; after all, it *would*
make the company's advertising more consistent. Privately, though, they
chafed at the loss of power.

Wieden & Kennedy was also a pawn in a game it was only beginning
to understand—a survival game that included dealers, distributors,
manufacturers and consumers and revolved around their competing
needs, motivations and subterfuges. Subaru of America had decided to
eliminate the use of seasonal sales, incentives and gimmicks to sell its
cars. The regional advertising campaign was the company's first attempt
to ram this unpalatable strategy down its dealers' throats.

The idea was a simple one. S.O.A. was going to equip the base model
of the Legacy, the lowest-priced version offered, with all the options
that people normally wanted in a car, including air-conditioning, an
AM/FM cassette radio, power windows and power locks. The company
would set a price for the package and it would not deviate from that
price. No haggling, no hassling. *What we say is what you get.*

Subaru was taking on a hallowed auto-industry tradition. It intended
to eliminate incentives (technically, the term for factory money that
goes to dealers, on a per-car basis, to be pocketed or used by them to
give discounts to consumers) and rebates (the term that describes
money given by the manufacturer directly to consumers). Instead,
S.O.A. was going to take that money and "bake" it into the car, at the
plant. At $12,999 retail, the Legacy would cost $2,000 to $3,000 less
than a similarly equipped Toyota Camry or Honda Accord.

This strategy was, in a word, radical. Manufacturers' advertised retail
prices were usually for stripped-down models of their cars—manual
transmission, no A.C., small engine, no radio. Only those who read the
fine print knew this; others discovered the uncomfortable fact at the
dealership, often only after they found themselves agreeing to pay thousands of unexpected dollars for options. Subaru hoped such disaffected
consumers would applaud its pay-one-price strategy.

"What it means to the consumer in terms of perception is: 'A car,
priced right, with the stuff you want on it.' That's Subaru—stuff priced

right. 'Subaru. What to drive,'" explained Jeff Greenberg, Wieden & Kennedy's regional account director. "Subaru is 'what to drive' because it comes at the right price with all the stuff on it, as opposed to being the car of the iconoclast, which is what it's always been—a funky, goofy car that you gotta be left of Gene McCarthy and living in a tree to own."

But changing Subaru's image was only an ancillary motivation for the new pricing strategy. The company's primary rationale was to eliminate incentives and rebates, which were eating away at the auto industry, particularly small players like S.O.A.

Automobile manufacturers simply could not continue to give back to consumers $1,500 to $2,000 per car; their profit margins were not high enough. In order to finance incentives, the major manufacturers had gotten into the habit of raising their prices and rebating the increases back to buyers. Subaru could not do that. When it had raised its prices in the late eighties to offset the appreciation of the yen, it lost customers. Raising its prices even higher to play the rebate game would drive away its remaining, loyal customer base. To compete with other manufacturers, S.O.A. had little choice but to pay for its incentives out of its cash reserves. If it continued to do that, the company would die.

The pricing strategy seemed the only alternative. Although it cost the company good money to build into the Legacies a "special value package" of options at the factory, it was much less than the cost of the incentives. "Whether it is a dealer incentive or a customer-cash rebate or a 'special value package,' they're all price adjustments," Tom Gibson explained. "But if I give you a '$1,500 special value package,' it doesn't cost me $1,500, because there's a markup on all that equipment. If I give you a $1,500 dealer cash incentive or customer rebate, it costs me $1,500. That's *real* money. So the 'special value' approach is a way to start to ratchet down your incentive moneys."

S.O.A. had introduced a similar pricing strategy a year earlier, on its Loyale. The six-and-a-half-year-old car was dead, "sale-proof." Then the company announced that it was adding consumers' favorite options to the base model sedan, and charging $9,700—a very low price—for the car. In the 1990 model year, sales doubled. That emboldened Subaru to try the program on the 1992 Legacy—as soon as the company could move the remaining 1991 Legacies off dealer lots. When, in the spring, Wieden & Kennedy pitched S.O.A. the idea of making Subarus intellectually fashionable, the company thought the idea the perfect umbrella under which to shelter its new corporate pricing strategy.

That strategy needed protection. For as soon as they heard about it, even before Wieden & Kennedy had assumed charge of the account,

S.O.A.'s regional sales executives began complaining that it wouldn't work. The problem was consumer debt.

People who bought cars at the tail end of the economic boom, between 1987 and 1989, paid top dollar for them. Japanese cars were scarce and expensive because of the voluntary restraint agreement, and domestic manufacturers took advantage of the barriers by raising their prices. Consumers, feeling flush, willingly paid sticker prices for their new cars; from 1980 to 1990, the average retail selling price of a new car more than doubled, to $15,900 from $7,530. To finance them, drivers took out longer loans: the average maturity of a new-car loan was 54.6 months in 1990, up from 37.4 months in 1970.

But automobiles depreciated in value more quickly than consumers paid down their loans. The result: with increasing frequency, cars were worth less than the money owed on them. If a driver wanted a new car, she was in a double bind: She needed to come up with a down payment *and* additional cash to pay off her loan. The auto industry referred to consumers with negative equity in their cars as "upside-down" on their loans.

Government statistics indicated that a substantial number of drivers, up to half, were upside-down. In 1971, the average driver put 14 percent down on her $3,370 car, and financed it at 11.6 percent for about three years, at the end of which her car was worth $1,716—enough, on a trade-in, for a down payment on a new car. In 1988, the average driver put 6 percent down on a $14,100 car, and financed it for just under five years at 12.2 percent. If that driver wanted a new car after three years, she still owed $5,635 on the old vehicle, far more than it was worth.

Incentives and rebates, then, were not only an enticement to consumers; they were a necessity, the only way to get drivers out of their loans. A dealer who was being given cash by the factory for every new car he sold could take all or part of that money and offer it to the consumer to help her pay down her auto loan. Or a consumer could take the factory rebate and use it for a down payment. Even if the vehicle's price was higher than a competitive model's price, the higher cost was worth it to many consumers—*if* it was accompanied by larger incentive moneys. That was the only way they could pay off their old loans and buy into new ones. Dealers called these customers "getmeboughts." *I'll buy this car,* they announced when they walked into a dealership, *if you can get me bought.* "Trading money" was often the only way to get them bought.

The dealers were not necessarily being greedy in their demands for factory cash to help consumers purchase cars. They had to get those vehicles off their lots. Under the floor-planning system, every day a car sat in a dealership it cost them money—the interest they paid on the loans they took to buy the cars at wholesale. A car with a wholesale cost of $13,000 financed at two points above the late 1991 prime of 6.5 percent cost the dealer $1,105 a year, or slightly more than $3 a day. As a rule of thumb, dealers liked to keep a two months' supply of cars on the lot, and ordered from the manufacturer accordingly. If a dealership accustomed to selling thirty cars a month saw sales suddenly drop to ten cars a month, its floor planning expenditures could rapidly rise from $180 per day to $300 or more per day.

Needless to say, dealers deemed trading money necessary for their survival. A Subaru corporate strategy of eliminating incentives and rebates, which threatened to hamper a dealer's ability to make deals with customers, made it likely that the dealers would curtail their orders from S.O.A. The RVPs, in turn, would not meet their individual sales goals, which meant that their compensation would decline or they would be fired.

Hence the RVPs' angry reaction to Wieden & Kennedy's regional campaign. No way was it going to convince a customer who was upside-down to buy an incentive-free Subaru instead of a rebate-laden Pontiac. No way would it persuade a dealer—the real customer—to buy more cars.

Yet Tom Gibson was adamant that S.O.A. was going to stick with the strategy. *We're going to take hits on this, from dealers, from the regions, from the press, for being stubborn,* he told his headquarters executives. *But we've got to stay the course, because it's the right thing to do— especially in these tough economic times.*

Up until its regional presentation, Wieden & Kennedy was hardly aware of the divisions in the company. Peter Wegner did not even know what "factory-to-dealer incentives" were, and he had just purchased a car! After the shouting, the agency understood.

IN ADVERTISING TERMINOLOGY, an agency that has endured a bad meeting is said to have been "thrown under a bus." Wieden & Kennedy's tread marks were still smarting when, a day after the regional presentation, the agency's senior executives met to assess their failure.

Regional automotive advertising was as awful a process as they had heard. It was rife with politics; it had nothing to do with quality; communicating to consumers was not its goal.

Yet there was no question that Wieden & Kennedy would fight to keep the regional business. The $20 million in billings was but a part of its reasoning. Even at that early stage in the relationship, long-term security was at stake. "If you let somebody else do the dealer business, and they start doing a good job, suddenly you got guys sitting and saying, 'Hey, pretty good ad came out of Nashville last month for the dealers' association. Let's run that,'" Jeff Greenberg said.

How could an agency prevent this kind of disaffection? Wieden & Kennedy's execs agreed that they had learned an essential lesson about automotive clients: always take pains to presell the work. Find out where the power centers are, schmooze them, get them on your side.

Wieden & Kennedy and its partisans in Subaru's marketing department also believed they could turn the fiasco to their advantage. The agency could show the RVPs that it could stomach criticism, trash an entire campaign and return immediately with a new one.

Luhr, Wieden and Kennedy called Peter Wegner in for a private meeting in Dan's office. Dan closed the door—an uncharacteristic action that prompted Wegner to announce, *You guys can't fire me. I quit last May!* They reassured him that not only did they not blame him for the debacle, they believed that only he could help them save themselves. *We need you to go to Philadelphia.*

Could he take his wife and infant son? he asked.

Absolutely, they said.

He agreed to go. *But what,* he wondered, *will we substitute for the campaign?*

Luhr had spent much of the previous evening talking to the car company's regional representatives, teasing from them the reasons for their displeasure. The agency was not lost, Luhr told his colleagues. The regions still approved of the agency's corporate image campaign, especially its determination to "tell the truth" about cars. They wanted to maintain that theme in the regional advertising, because they believed it might be persuasive enough to surmount the problems caused by Subaru's elimination of factory incentives.

The solution was staring right at the agency, Luhr maintained. In fact, Wieden & Kennedy had presented it to S.O.A. back in June, only to abandon it, unthinkingly, months later. Subaru's dealers were going to participate in one of the best sales events ever devised for the auto industry, a sales event that would expose the duplicity behind the heavily advertised Toyotathons and Dodge Days and Chevy Summers and their empty promises of something for nothing.

For its regional campaign, Subaru of America was going to sponsor "Lack-of-Pretense Days."

Wegner started from scratch. Wisely, he decided to eliminate from the new regional creative any vestiges of the rejected campaign. Why give the RVPs an opportunity to accuse the agency of protecting its preserve?

He scrapped the cavorting Mr. Shout and replaced him with an actor who would play a dealer-salesman. The surrogate's character was vitally important. Dealers were sensitive about their image; they knew the public mistrusted them, and feared anything that might remind consumers of pressure tactics, bait-and-switch and I'll-ask-my-manager-he's-in-the-back-room gambits.

Wegner ran in the other direction. The "Lack of Pretense" campaign, at least the television ads, would be humorous, but gentler and less threatening than the famous Isuzu campaign with the lying salesman. He wanted his dealer to be deadpan, honest and knowing, not oily.

As before, Wegner wrote fifteen commercials. By early October, Subaru, constrained by its tight budget, asked him to reduce the number to five, each one showcasing a different car: the Legacy sedan, the Legacy wagon, the Legacy four-wheel-drive wagon, the Loyale sedan and the Loyale wagon. An introductory spot explaining the meaning of "Lack-of-Pretense Days" was cut from the plan, because both the company and the agency believed the background was obvious from the context and the dialogue.

The spots were simplicity exemplified. As scripted and designed, they opened on a plain black screen, with the words "Subaru Lack-of-Pretense Days" written in white. The scene shifted to an unadorned room, in which an automobile rested, in three-quarter view from the front. The salesman walked around the car (in some spots he would carry a hand-held microphone, trailing the cord behind him) and explained Subaru's "special value package" of options, available at one, low, no-gimmicks price.

"Your local Subaru dealer is pleased to announce," the salesman said in one spot, "that we won't be offering any factory-to-dealer incentives. You know, that's where the factory basically gives us money and we in return"—he paused—"uh, *keep* it.

"We're going to instead try to sell you a great car like the '92 Loyale. It's got, uh, air-conditioning, great stereo, power locks and windows. And it comes in a variety of nice colors. And it costs just $9,299, which for some reason"—he fumbled again—"sounds a lot cheaper than $9,300. It's only a dollar difference." As the final text-on-screen "super" with the "Subaru. What to drive" slogan appeared, the salesman, in voiceover, concluded with, "Test drive a Subaru today, won't you?"

To play the salesman, the agency found a New York standup comedian and improvisational actor named Jim Meskimen. With his thinning hair and high, boyish voice, he was deliciously nonthreatening, so much so that the agency thought it could play a bit more forcefully with some of the conventions of automobile dealer advertising. In one spot, Jim (he introduced himself by name in the ads) told viewers that the Legacy wagon "comes with A/C, power windows, great AM/FM tape deck . . . and a very handsome dashboard. And it undercuts the competition, whoever they are"—a super revealed that it was the Honda Accord LX model—"by . . . by . . . plenty.

"Oh," Jim continued, "it doesn't come with fuzzy dice or those annoying stuffed animals with suction cups on the bottom of their feet. But that stuff"—he held up an example—"*is* available in our special Nerd Value Package. You might want to look into that."

The commercials were unusual, so Luhr and his regional staff were methodical about preselling them. Their first stop, naturally, was S.O.A.'s marketing department. Chris Wackman and Mark Dunn embraced the campaign. Once burned, though, the agency was now cautious.

My concern is to get this sold in, and there will be regions that don't like it, Luhr warned Chris. *What's going to happen when they start saying "nay"?*

Don't worry, Chris reassured him. *You've got us.*

But in the weeks since the disastrous Portland presentation, Luhr had done his spade work, and learned more about Subaru's corporate politics. "The way to lock this thing in is to get Woody," he told his staff after returning to the Philadelphia office. "There's a chain. If Woody nods off on it, the others will, too."

The way to obtain Woody Purcell's approval was to get Chuck Worrell's. And the way to assure Chuck's assent was to secure Tom Gibson's endorsement. All this the agency did. By the time Wegner, Jeff Greenberg and Bruce Buchanan (Greenberg's assistant for the crucial New England and New York regions) took the campaign out to the field to the RVPs and the independent distributors, all of S.O.A.'s personnel knew that Cherry Hill was enthusiastic about "Lack-of-Pretense Days."

"Individually, the regions are not going to sit there and kill this campaign" the way they did in Portland, Bruce Buchanan said as he prepared to leave for a trip to Boston. All the RVPs and the independents could do was give the agency guidance. "We want to know, do we have the proper elements in there? Are we attacking the right things?"

The regional sales executives greeted the campaign with moderation. The newspaper ads, as written, noted that a Legacy was some $3,000 less than a Camry or an Accord. The RVPs and the dealers to whom they spoke questioned whether the new advertisements shouldn't quote the actual retail price of the car, not just the savings. Wieden & Kennedy willingly tinkered with the wording.

But the agency refused to doctor the television commercials. Some RVPs complained about their mild, whimsical tone. *Bob Uecker jumps out at you!* one regional exec worried, citing the baseball announcer whose clownish antics were used by other agencies to sell beer and autos. Wieden & Kennedy dismissed the concern. *Do you remember what product he was advertising?* the RVP was asked. *Because he sounds just the same as Toyota and Buick and everything else.*

"We're not changing the tone," Bruce confidently maintained. They did not need to. By mid-October, "Lack-of-Pretense Days" was sold in.

Producing the campaign presented only minor problems. Although Subaru was pouring what little end-of-year money it had into its two national image spots, it wanted its regional campaign quickly, if for no other reason than to keep spirits high among regions and dealers that Cherry Hill was on their case. On such a tight schedule, several directors the agency desired, including Joe Pytka, could not accommodate Wieden & Kennedy.

Happily, Gary Johns was available. Johns was a partner in Johns & Gorman Films, one of commercial directing's up-and-coming operations. He, however, was no greenhorn. A one-time political science graduate student, he went into advertising in the early seventies in his hometown of Pittsburgh because, he freely admitted, in those days advertising creative people did drugs, and he liked doing drugs. His career choice within the agency business was equally haphazard: he became an art director, instead of a copywriter, because he had once considered studying architecture.

His history with Wieden & Kennedy was intricate and revealing. He and Gorman were the creative team at Chiat/Day that had helped steal the Nike account away from the Portland agency back in 1983. The team went on to fashion most of Nike's 1984 Olympics campaign. But they were older than many of the kids coming into Chiat/Day (Johns was then in his late thirties, Gorman in his early forties), and they decided that becoming film directors would give them more security and satisfaction.

As directors, Johns and Gorman made their marks by doing the first "Joe Isuzu" ads. But they still did not feel, and indeed were not, at Pytka's level. Perhaps Wieden & Kennedy's new Subaru campaign would be their ticket.

Johns, a thin man with graying hair and a clipped mustache, was less a visual technician and more an advertising ecologist than other directors. Coming from an agency background where he created and maintained ad campaigns, sometimes for several years, he concentrated his efforts on figuring out how the work he was directing fit into a larger campaign. His goal was to make his spots congruent with the agency's purpose.

From his review of Subaru's national image spots and his discussions with Wegner and Vince Engel, Johns understood that the underlying theme of the Subaru campaign was truthfulness. He set out to translate that motif into every facet of the "Lack of Pretense" spots.

In practice, this meant contravening virtually everything Gary Johns had ever learned about directing a commercial. First, he messed up the lighting. Most auto commercials, especially those for European and Japanese models, use a technique called "liquid lighting" to illuminate cars. A director suspends a light box, some forty feet long and twelve feet wide, from the ceiling above the car. Inside the box, light is diffused through soft fabric. By shifting the position of the box, the director can make the light flow around the vehicle, to caress its curves, hug its hood, drip from its doors.

Johns refused to use liquid lighting. "It's almost deceiving somebody," he said.

He told his production designers: "Let's not get too uptight about making the car look as good as it can possibly look. Let's make it look just very matter-of-fact." They, in turn, lit the car the old-fashioned way, by putting a large light above the vehicle and letting the rays fall where they did. "Very unpretentious," the director called the technique. "A much more honest approach to lighting."

He wanted the set to be equally modest. Automobile ads frequently display cars in front of rippling gray curtains, or against austere black backgrounds, the better to showcase a vehicle's distinctive features. Johns wanted the "Lack of Pretense" commercials to look as if they were filmed in an out-of-the-way warehouse, with the auto set against a plain cement wall.

Unfortunately, no real warehouse that he knew of in the Los Angeles area fit his conception. They were all too glamorous, in a film noir kind of way. One location he had used, a warehouse in South Bay, was a favorite of auto-ad directors because of the way the light streamed in through its high windows. "It just looks beautiful," Johns said. "It looks too planned." To get the "cruddy look" that he preferred, the director had no choice but to build his warehouse on a stage.

Johns wondered whether his unconventional ideas for the regional spots were appropriate. But on reviewing the campaign's national launch spot, he retained little doubt that he was doing what Wieden & Kennedy wanted. "I noticed that was sort of their technique also when they shot that first factory spot," he said after he finished filming. "There was not a lot of attention to making the cars look as good as they could possibly look. So I tried to stay in that vein."

Wegner and Vince had heard the horror stories about the Indiana shoot. But because neither man had been on the scene in Indiana to witness the battles between the agency and Tibor Kalman, they had no idea that the "Factory" spot, especially its poorly lit, concluding beauty shot, was largely accidental—the agency's effort to make do with available footage. They willingly acceded to Johns's directorial notions, and retained "Factory"'s inadequacies into a second generation of advertising. A foul-up had become a genetic flaw.

The faux cement wall, the overhead lighting and Jim's mild demeanor lent a muted tone to the "Lack of Pretense" commercials. Although they were shot in color, in the mind's eye they appeared as gray-scale tableaus. It was strenuous work for the director. "It was a bit difficult for me actually to light it and not go with my instincts based on all these other car spots I had done, where we worked for hours trying to make sure that the light caresses the car in just the right way," Johns said. But he was proud of the outcome.

"The method I was using to shoot these spots," he said confidently, "was *totally* different than any other way I shot any other ones."

WHEN MILES F. DALY, the president of the Crain Daly Volkswagen and Subaru auto dealership, arrived at the Marriott Hotel near Atlanta's Hartsfield Airport for a viewing of Subaru's new regional advertising campaign, he had every reason to be hopeful. At last, *one* of his two manufacturers was listening to its dealers.

He had been sitting on this pair of turkeys for so long he was beginning to gobble. Volkswagen was the worst. He had surfed the Beetle wave from the 1950s to the early 1970s and grown rich. Sold a hundred VWs a month as recently as 1975. Now he was down to ten a month, and Volkswagen still wouldn't listen. Arrogant Germans *never* listened.

Once upon a time, Volkswagen sold more than 500,000 vehicles a year in the United States. Now, it would be lucky to break 100,000. Sales continued to plummet. Sold only 6,935 cars in October 1991, down from 10,251 a year before. VW was paying for its haughtiness. Unfortunately, Miles Daly was paying for it, too.

For the longest time, S.O.A. wasn't much better. Daly had taken on Subaru in 1975, when Volkswagen wasn't willing to sell him enough product. It was a nice little Japanese franchise, even if it never did catch on in the South. When times got bad, though, Harvey Lamm was as bad as the Germans. *All you do is talk about four-wheel drive, which doesn't mean nothin' to folks down here. Can't you give us our own regional ads?* Daly, part of a chorus of southern dealers, asked. But Harvey wouldn't do it. *That ad agency of yours doesn't know how to do anything but act cute. Please dump them and get another,* Daly requested. Harvey wouldn't even dignify the criticisms of his agency with a response.

S.O.A. had suffered as badly as VW, and Daly along with it. In the mid-eighties, the dealer was selling thirty to thirty-five Subarus a month. Now, for 1991, he was going to average out at eleven per—with only five, six or seven cars moving each of the past few months.

But Subaru, at last, had gotten the message. It brought out a new vehicle, the Legacy. *A beautiful car, a good car,* Daly thought, and he wasn't shy about praising Cherry Hill. And it had switched ad agencies, *thank God.* Finally, they could all get back to the business of selling automobiles.

Daly settled back in the conference room at the Marriott/Airport in College Park, Georgia, and watched the reel of new Subaru regional spots unspool. He was a little unsettled by Jim's reference to a "Nerd Value Package." *That humor could offend some people,* the dealer thought. *He's saying that the general public, if they don't buy this car, they're stupid—in so many words.*

Then, as he watched the rest of the spots, he began to boil. *They're hardly showing the car at all* . . .

"You know," he told the agency, "we've got a good-looking car at a hell of a price. People need to know that."

It's cute, he thought. *Has a little humor to it.* . . . In Daly's world, that wasn't a compliment. "I still believe you need to show the car and sell the benefits, the quality, the price of the car."

And the lighting, the glare on the side of the vehicle—it makes it look like it's a two-tone car! . . .

He could not contain himself. "You know," Miles Daly, the dealer, complained to Woody Purcell, the regional vice president, "the quality is filthy!"

Chapter 19

If It's Out There,
It's In Here

FAITH, WHILE HARD WON, is easily lost. It can be shaken by many things: misguided words, obstinacy, an inability to grow along with one's partner, suddenly seeing the partner through eyes unblinded by desire. Relationships, of course, are maintained by faith. No matter how fervently contemporary ad agencies insist that they are entertainers or artists, advertising is still founded on relationships. So in advertising, as in marriage, a loss of faith can be debilitating. It is the only quality, really, that binds a client to an agency.

Wieden & Kennedy had barely been granted a chance to realize its strategy for Subaru. The tiering system, by which media expenditures were to be allocated to the most expandable markets, was not yet in place. Because the company had little to spend, American consumers had seen little of the new campaign. Yet by late 1991, some of the Subarus were already losing faith.

The agency believed that Woody, ever the politician, was planting poisonous bugs in others' ears. He was exacting vengeance, some thought, for Luhr's refusal to hire "his guy," the former agency's Atlanta-based account executive, to serve as Wieden & Kennedy's regional representative for the Southeast.

Chuck Worrell, too, was becoming an obstacle. He vacillated, the agency claimed. Yes, he supported the pricing strategy (he had no choice), but in the face of his RVPs' complaints, he failed to provide ardent enough support for the "Lack of Pretense" campaign, which was the strategy's voice. "Chuck has a tendency to believe exactly what the last person he talked to told him. And Woody is constantly whispering in his ear," complained an exasperated Jeff Greenberg.

But by far the biggest and most surprising difficulty was Tom O'Hare. O'Hare had been a supporter of the agency choice, having arrived at his decision after a multifactor mathematical analysis. But he fell out of love as quickly as he fell into it.

O'Hare was thoroughly Boston Irish. But he had long ago replaced the emotional component of his heritage with a rigorous, methodical approach to life. A Marine who had spent ten days in a troop carrier off Guantanamo Bay during the Cuban missile crisis, O'Hare still stood and thought rigidly. With a B.S. in accounting and an M.B.A., both from Boston College, he fervently believed that with enough information, all problems could be understood and solved.

That had always been his way with the automobile business. He started in it with the Ford Motor Company, as an auditor of dealerships partly owned by Ford. His assignments took him to different dealerships for two weeks at a stretch, full-time. Always, he rushed through his audits in order to spend time with the new car manager, the used car manager, the general manager, the finance manager, the lease manager, the service manager, the parts manager, always asking questions. He eventually worked his way into Ford's corporate hierarchy, rising to become one of the company's four regional sales managers, responsible for the entire northeastern United States. "There's only one person in the Ford Company who ever worked his way up to a position of responsibility from an auditing job," he said proudly, "and that's me."

O'Hare considered himself different—and better—than the typical Ford executive, including the Ford executives who later defected to Subaru of America. The conventional career path at Ford "would be all from a wholesale point of view. A typical executive never knew what made the dealership work. He never helped develop ads. I helped develop ads. I saw them work or not work. I knew the mistakes that were made."

When he accepted an offer from the owner of the Subaru Distributors Corp. to run the independent New York area distributorship, O'Hare soon came to believe himself one of the few men around Subaru who understood car marketing from both a wholesale and a retail standpoint. "I'm a student of this business. I really am. I read anything and everything I can get on the car business and the economy, because they're so interrelated. I must know what's going on. I must know. I must formulate my plans a year in advance."

Which was O'Hare's complaint with Wieden & Kennedy. He simply did not see a plan to its actions. He did not understand what its campaign *was*. "Either they don't have a campaign, or it hasn't been communicated to me so that I can understand it," he said. "If they can't communicate the campaign to me, there's no way they're going to communicate it to the dealers."

To O'Hare, there was little that made the agency's print advertisements and television commercials a *campaign*. The launch commercial talked vaguely about the old themes of durability and reliability. The introductory SVX advertisement idly addressed the same themes and added speed to the quotient. He had recently gotten a glimpse of the new Legacy brand spot, the one for which Vince Engel and Jerry Cronin had used Woody Allen for inspiration, and saw that it did not address any of these themes. All it did was feature a series of unattractive men and women revealing how luxury cars eased their neuroses: "Mine says I'm witty beyond belief." "Mine says I'm the product of superior genes." *What does that have to do with the Legacy?* O'Hare wondered. *The Legacy is not a luxury car.*

The regional spots were as ineffective as the national ads. Despite their gentle tone, he considered them negative. Several of the executions compared the Legacy directly to the Accord and Camry. While some dealers wanted those head-to-head comparisons, O'Hare recoiled from them. Instead of "here's why Legacy is better than Camry," he preferred "here are forty-three reasons to buy a Legacy." He called the "Lack of Pretense" campaign "underwhelming."

"The marketplace today requires, in my opinion, not only the establishment of a value story, but it also must establish a price relationship with that value. 'What can I buy? What is it going to cost me to buy that value?' " O'Hare believed. "They've got nothing."

Nor was the agency willing to listen—a cardinal offense by his rules. When he suggested holding a national, or at least a regional, sales event—keeping all dealerships open for twenty-four hours, and running ads trumpeting on-the-spot financing for qualified buyers—the agency spurned him. *That is against our campaign,* Bruce Buchanan told O'Hare's sales manager. *We don't want to do the sales thing. Our approach is to tell the truth.*

O'Hare was livid. "You can have a sales event and tell the truth, too!"

In no small way, the distributor was reacting to Subaru's continued fall from grace among consumers. The company sold only 4,487 cars in October, down from 7,135 a year earlier; November was looking no better, with only 5,129 cars sold, compared to 7,907 in 1990. S.O.A. kept telling O'Hare and others like him that the fall was due to a lack of advertising, not the content of the advertising or the pricing strategy.

That was the real issue, thought the Subarus: Tom O'Hare was actually rebelling against the pricing strategy and his loss of control over regional advertising. "I think we're playing power politics here," was Chris Wackman's analysis of the distributor's complaints. "O'Hare bought into the agency but not necessarily into the loss of control over the money.

He is also less than enthusiastic about some of the regional creative. He feels we're bashing the competition. I think we're being tough, but not bashing. Bashing to me is when you say, 'Gee, why do you want this piece of junk over here when you can get this great car for $2,000 less?' We're not saying the competition is junk. We're saying they're *both* good cars. But ours is a better buy. It's an area where Tom, an extremely aggressive person, becomes somewhat of a mystery to me."

A mystery, perhaps, but a very public one who, if he was really attacking S.O.A., was nonetheless making its advertising agency his scapegoat. By December, O'Hare was reminding anyone who cared to ask that Wieden & Kennedy had been his *second* choice in the agency search.

"I think they are out of control," he said of the shop. "I think they have been given too much latitude. I liken it to the fact that we've got some sheep there in the barn. A good farmer puts up a corral and says, 'Okay, sheep, you can wander all around here,' but at some point in time they're going to bump into the fence and can't go anymore. S.O.A. said to Wieden & Kennedy, 'You're sheep in this barn,' then opened the door, and there was no corral, no fences."

GRIDS. The answer was grids. Take a newspaper page. Draw a bunch of vertical lines, a bunch of horizontal lines, you've got a grid. Up top, you list the competition's vehicles and your vehicle. Down the side, you put all the features a loaded car ought to have. In the boxes, you check off which features they don't have that you have at no extra charge. The perfect auto ad!

"A hunk of fuck," Jerry Cronin called it.

"Stupid," Vince Engel said.

Nonetheless, grids were going to be Wieden & Kennedy's way out of the morass. Woody wanted a grid ad, and if that would keep him from carping about the "Lack of Pretense" spots, well then, Wieden & Kennedy was going to do a grid ad, Dave Luhr decreed. How about a grid ad for each car, then, Chuck Worrell wanted to know? *No problem*, said the account director . . . whose creatives were beginning to refer to him as "Yep-We-Can-Do-That Luhr."

"They want an ad that talks about every price and all the features of all the competition. Gross," said Jerry, as he sat at his Macintosh, trying to devise an inventive way to compare air-conditioning, power locks, power steering and AM/FM cassette radios inside a fifteen-block box. "It may be what they want, but it's certainly nothing I ever wanted to do." He snorted. *"Grid ads."*

Five feet away, Vince sat on a stool, hunched over his easel, meticulously structuring the grid. He said little as Jerry vented spleen.

"It's like buffing a turd," the copywriter continued. "You just cannot make it good. There's nothing you can do with it. You got a car. You got a grid. You got a big price. There's nothing. You can write a semi-clever line. But it's still a hunk of fuck."

"It's a festering disease," Vince said, without looking up.

Although most of Wieden & Kennedy's makeshift Philadelphia headquarters still had the spare look of a holding pen, the room behind the receptionist's desk that Vince and Jerry shared was beginning to take on the character of its occupants.

On the right wall, immediately upon entering, was a photograph of David Ogilvy, inscribed to Vince. Beneath it were three R-rated postcards. Above Jerry's desk was a nerf basketball hoop that emitted a cheer each time a basket was sunk, and a Xerox of a 1930s nightclub ad advertising "Fun Galore—The Town's Gay Spot." Behind his desk, Jerry hung a three-foot-by-four-foot velveteen wall covering, the kind usually found in wood-paneled suburban basements, of a lake in the Pacific Northwest.

Otherwise, Jerry's domain was filled with the detritus of his current profession. On the credenza next to his desk were copies of *Autoweek, Car & Driver, Motor Trend, Sporting News, Road & Track* and several ski magazines, alongside of which were blank "Wieden & Kennedy Philadelphia Creative Time Sheets." Appended to one sheet was a Post-It Note asking Vince to "please fill out for weeks ending 10/6, 10/13, 10/20, 10/27." There were copies of *USA Today*, a loose-leaf-bound "Subaru Product Information and Specifications 1992 Model Year" fact book and a job application from a young graduate of the Portfolio Center of Atlanta, addressed to Jerry ("I've admired the cutting-edge quality of your work for some time").

Against the window above the credenza, stacked like a house of cards, were twenty-six videotape reels. Some were from commercial directors (Ron Travisano, Brian Coyne), some were Subaru product shots ("Subaru Select Edit 2nd Choices," "Subaru Select Edit 1st Choices"), some were from other agencies and suppliers ("Chiat/Day/Mojo," "Margarita Mix") and some included material for Wieden & Kennedy's public service campaign for the American Indian College Fund ("Pytka-Indian PSA," "Western Images Demo Reel"). Next to the reels were books that reflected Jerry's mixture of interests: *Elizabeth Bishop Complete Poems 1927–1979*, a loose-leaf notebook entitled "Wieden & Kennedy: Subaru Marketing Proposal, June 12, 1991," a volume of Crow Indian stories entitled *Uuwatisee, The 31st Annual Francis W. Hatch*

Awards for Creative Excellence in New England Advertising Annual, a copy of the "Subaru of America Quarterly Competitive Review, Prepared by Wieden & Kennedy, Nov. 1, 1991," a book on Native American culture entitled *Sacred Ways of Knowledge, Sources of Life* and "Subaru of America: Overview of Advertising Production Procedures."

Vince's territory more properly reflected the eclectic sensibilities usually associated with advertising creatives, especially art directors. On the radiator by the window adjacent to his desk he kept a plastic inflated snake, copies of *Backstage Shoot*; *Lurzer's Int'l Archive: Ads, TV and Posters Worldwide*, a British advertising publication called *Creative Review*, the British magazine *The Face, Vanity Fair, Sports Illustrated*; eighteen-by-twenty-inch sketch pads, the sixty-sixth and sixty-eighth editions of the *Art Directors Annual, One Show Annuals* no. 7 and no. 12, *Australian Writers and Art Directors Annuals* from 1989 and 1990, *Directory of Illustration*; *CA Advertising Annuals* for 1988, 1989 and 1991, an unopened can of Rolling Rock beer, a snifter full of magic markers, a Hawaiian hula dancing doll, and *The Oxford Paperback Dictionary*. There were reels from Subaru, NFL Films, CBS News, several directors, a copywriter, Wieden & Kennedy's Nike ads and Vince's own Australian spots; a dozen collections of typefaces, a history of cowboy images in the movies, color spec books and a chronicle of life in an automobile factory, *Rivethead*. Bracketing it all, like bookends, were a stuffed armadillo, a wooden pencil from a British advertising association, a plastic coffee mug from the Au Bon Pain restaurant and a ceramic bull.

Vince had taken over a pillar opposite his desk and taped to it business cards from producers, photographers, type houses, comp makers, car detailers, graphic designers, computer-image systems reps, cinematic designers and illustrators. He also commandeered the entire bookshelf along the wall adjacent to the door, which he filled with the books *This Is New York*, *'50s American Magazine Ads*, *Printing Types: A Second Specimen Book*, *The Graphic Language of Neville Brody*, *New Zealand! New Zealand!*, *Corvette Catalogs*, *Cars Detroit Never Built*, *U.S. 1: America's Original Main Street*, *Only in America*, *Flashing on the 60s*, *Weird Wonderful America: The Nation's Most Offbeat and Off-the-Beaten-Path Tourist Attractions*, *Route 66: The Mother Road*, *Close Cover Before Striking: The Golden Age of Matchbook Art*, *Diners*, *The Collected Verse of A. B. Paterson*, *Zen and the Art of Motorcycle Maintenance* and *Gray's Anatomy*. Next to the tomes, framed but unhung, were a Ronald Reagan magazine ad for Chesterfield cigarettes, an advertisement from an early-twentieth-century British magazine headlined "Learn To Write Advertisements" and individual photographs of the

Three Stooges. At the end of the collection, also framed, was a simple statement: "What others may think of as danger, we refer to as a challenge."

Outside the office, on the wall, was a plaque left over from the previous tenant, a local AT&T operation. It read—and the team's lair would forevermore be known as—"Quality Room."

Jerry's sullen contemplation of grids had lasted so long that his white computer screen went black and the screen-saver, the program that prevented stationary images from burning into the phosphor, kicked in. Words, endlessly repeating, scrolled from right to left across the machine's face. " 'I thought he was going to run. Then I didn't think he was going to run. Then I did. Now I don't care.' Democratic analyst Bob Beckel on Mario Cuomo."

Jerry hit a key and tried to return to the grids. "It's not as gross as the shit beside it in the auto section," he sighed. "Well-art-directed gross."

"A hunk of fuck," said Vince.

IN A WAY, the hated grids were Wieden & Kennedy's penance for its own inexperience. Among other matters left unattended, the agency never bothered to take its June pitch to Subaru's selection committee and turn it into a formal statement of purpose and extended plan of action. This was a standard feature on car accounts—a book that provided brand statements for each of the manufacturer's models, explained how specific vehicles fit into the maker's product galaxy and included mission statements detailing the short- and long-term objectives for each car. By failing to assemble such a document, Wieden & Kennedy lacked ammunition to use against the regions, to show how individual advertisements fit, or did not fit, into its overall marketing strategy for Subaru.

Also lacking was an account planner. Chris Riley, whom S.O.A. accorded an almost mystical reverence, was based in Portland and only came East for major presentations to the client. Without a Philadelphia-based account planner, the agency had no one on call to provide the seemingly scientific research that consumer-products companies require to calm their fear of creativity.

But what hurt Wieden & Kennedy more than anything else was its collective lack of passion for automobiles. Car companies and their dealers can sense such ardor; when it is present, they can forgive advertising people their flakiness and other transgressions. Its absence, however, sows mistrust.

Wieden & Kennedy treated the subject of automobiles offhandedly.

Leslie Koyama, an experienced young automotive A.E., noticed this as soon as she arrived in Philadelphia from the West Coast. Jerry drafted some copy for a magazine ad and included the claim, left over from his original SVX work, that the car had sixty-three safety features. When he presented it in an agency meeting, someone asked him where he got the statistic from. "I made it up," Jerry answered. Everyone started laughing. Leslie, who had worked with automotive marketing executives for several years, thought to herself: *He just decides to make things up! Car people don't like that.*

This aloofness was taking a toll even in Cherry Hill, where the agency's strongest support lay. Kei Ono, the Americanized product planner from Japan, was livid when he saw how the early SVX print advertisements highlighted the luxury car's independent suspension. "That cheapens the car!" he complained. "Independent suspension is the norm even for subcompacts. More involved people could have pointed that out. That's where progress needs to be made."

The agency was also suffering from Subaru's earlier, misguided conviction that a new advertising campaign would somehow surmount exchange rates, voluntary restraint agreements, economies of scale, an attenuated product-development cycle and rising U.S. unemployment rates. When the new advertising campaign failed to accomplish its unrealistically lofty goals within its first ninety days before the public, S.O.A., desperate to get the dealers off its back, readily buffeted the agency with additional work and contradictory instructions, anything to buy more time.

The "Lack of Pretense" commercials were victimized by this indecision. Originally, most of S.O.A.'s senior executives wanted the regional campaign to proffer head-on comparisons between the Legacy and its two main rivals, the Camry and the Accord. The spots were scripted and filmed accordingly. Only after they were in the can did several executives, their ears bent by Tom O'Hare and several others in the field, have second thoughts.

"As I see this car now on the road, more and more, I think to myself, 'That's not a fair comparison, between a Legacy and a Camry,'" said Fred Adcock, the field sales manager and one of the converts. "And for us to say that we're $3,000 less—I'm just not comfortable with what that message is. Someone can interpret that as, 'Shit, for only three thousand more bucks, I can go get a Camry!'"

Subaru was also allowing its regional vice presidents to undermine the media tiering system, the strategic foundation of the agency's campaign. Under its old system of media spending, Cherry Hill provided subsidies to some individual dealers, through a cooperative advertising budget; the more cars a dealer ordered, the more co-op money he received. Under Wieden & Kennedy's tiering system, the co-op money was dumped into a single pot for each region, and the regional budget was allocated market-by-market according to a given market's "opportunity index." The RVPs no longer had money with which to reward a "good dealer"—a dealer who ordered and sold a lot of cars—who happened to be stuck among a bunch of duds in a Tier 4 market.

Several RVPs were refusing to acquiesce to the new system. Instead, they shifted the spending around within their advertising budgets, taking money out of Tier 1 markets, say, and putting it into a Tier 4 market in order to continue the old reward scheme. In the Penn/Jersey region, for example, so much media money was removed from Philadelphia, which was ranked as a high-opportunity Tier 1 market, that the city's advertising budget fell below that of a Tier 2 market. This meant that Philadelphia consumers were not seeing Subaru television ads with the frequency Wieden & Kennedy believed was necessary in order for them to remember the "what to drive" message.

All the rigamarole in the regions led Luhr to comment, half sadly, half angrily: "The regional business is not a question of advertising. It's a question of power."

From the agency's standpoint, their biggest problem was the sales department, under Chuck Worrell. Worrell publicly supported the program and the agency, but he consistently backed the regions and their requests, which Wieden & Kennedy argued weakened the campaign. The marketing department was not blameless, however. While it upheld the agency, the ad executives believed it was not willing to join its battle.

"The hardest thing in this account right now is the split," Luhr said. "I like Chris Wackman a ton. He's a great guy to us, he's a great guy to be friends with. But he is the great healer; he's not necessarily the great opinion leader or, more than that, even a great leader. It makes it hard."

More than hard. Chaotic. "We try, you know, but it's like whirling out of control," said Leslie Koyama, the account exec. "From Thanksgiving on you're supposed to be able to kick it all the way and cruise, because you should have your plan done for the next year. You should have everything done. We're so far behind in the normal schedule of things."

Jim Heidt was feeling the powerlessness and chaos more than most at the agency. Heidt, thirty-one, was Wieden & Kennedy's regional account executive based in Atlanta; in that capacity he dealt with Subaru's two weakest regions, the Southeast and the Midwest, on a daily basis.

His job, as he described it wearily in winter's depths, was "struggling to get the balance between what we say as an agency, 'this is the way it should be done, guys, this is what we feel is a good, regional ad,' " and the never-ending demands by his RVPs for starbursts, the graphic fillips that, along with the grids, were the agency's bête noire.

"The reason that they hired Wieden & Kennedy is to bring something different to the table, and not do the basic '$1,200 cash back' and starbursts, but to come out with some totally, totally different advertising," said Heidt. But every day, it seemed, he was fighting a debilitating battle to remind his charges of that.

One major Chicago-area dealer did not want to run the "Lack of Pretense" advertisements, or hang the posters in his store. *Does this mean we were pretentious before and now we're not?* he demanded of Heidt. In the newspaper ads, the account exec was constantly being pressured to make the name "Subaru" larger and to expand the size of the featured cars. Frequently, dealers presented him with dummied ads, and demanded that he execute and publish them. Heidt had taken to repeating a line he had picked up from a colleague when he worked on the Lincoln-Mercury regional business at Young & Rubicam: *Don't write the ad for me, don't do a layout, because we're not waiters and waitresses asking, "Do you want cream with that coffee?"*

His colleagues in Philadelphia, though, were often little better. He would approach them with requests for minor changes in advertising copy or design, only to receive scorn in return. *Can't you sell this stuff? What's your problem?*

His skirmish with the Mid-America region was typical. For years, the region ran a full-page advertisement once a week in the *Chicago Tribune*. The agency's media department wanted to wean the region from its newspaper fix in order to put more money into television. When the dealers screamed bloody murder, the sides compromised: a full-page ad every other week.

As to the content of the ad—that required Heidt to exhibit the patience and negotiating skill of a third-party mediator in the Middle East. Vince Engel, who loved the naïve, vernacular design style exemplified by Mr. Shout, put together a page that lovingly and wittily resembled a 1940s-era advertisement. "Attention," it said in large, speedy, white, sans-serif letters encased in a black circle on the top. Underneath was copy, with illustrations, worthy of a Jersey Shore salt-water-taffy concession:

Right now you can buy a reliable Subaru Legacy and save $2,605. This Legacy comes equipped with A/C, AM/FM stereo cassette,

four-wheel disc brakes, tilt steering, & power windows & locks.
With the money you save you can also equip it with a blender, a
microwave, a washer and dryer, and a 32" color TV, and the friends
only money can buy.

The text was sprinkled with amusing nuggets: the admonitions "Do it
today" and "It's great!" drawn in cartoon type, matchbook-cover illustrations of a man counting his money and a happy couple clutching, and
a drawing of a Legacy. On the bottom, beneath ample white space, was
the slogan "Subaru. What to drive."

S.O.A.'s RVP in Chicago and his marketing manager both liked the
ad, but felt they ought to show it to some of their larger dealers. The
dealers did not appreciate the whimsy.

"Jim, are you crazy!" a dealer in Park Forest, Illinois, complained, by
fax, to Heidt. "Look at my very rough copy and play off of it."

The dealer had scrawled an ad that was largely indistinguishable from
other ads in newspaper automotive sections. On the top right he
wanted a photo of a Legacy. Stretched diagonally down from the top
left he wanted a copy of the Legacy's window sticker. "Subaru Value"
was the headline across the top. "Compare! This car against the Honda
Accord LX." The body copy was basic: "We build dependable, quality
cars in our Lafayette, Ind. plant and we back them with a 3-yr.
36,000-mile bumper-to-bumper warranty plus 5-yr. 60,000-mile power
train warranty with no deductible plus 100,000-mile rust protection."
Across the bottom, the ad said, "Plus! $500.00 REBATE. Save!
$2605.00." The advertisement concluded not with the slogan but with
"Contact your local Subaru dealer today!"

The RVP wanted to mollify his dealers. When Heidt reported the
contretemps to the creatives in Philadelphia, they thought a "Lack-of-
Pretense Days" grid ad—comparing Legacy to Accord, Camry, Mazda
626, Nissan Stanza and Mitsubishi Galant—would do the trick. Vince
even topped it with a drawing of Mr. Shout punching another cartoon
character in the mouth.

But the Chicago marketing manager figured the new ad would not
satisfy his dealers. He made some changes. "Subaru: To Compare Just
Isn't Fair," he wrote across the top of the grid. "The best for LESS!"
he added, in a suspiciously starry enclosure, on the bottom. Heidt faxed
it back to Philadelphia, which excised both additions, resurrected the
words "Subaru Lack-of-Pretense Days," and drew up a new headline.
"Subaru: More for Less," it read in large letters.

Chicago was still worried. *How about a drawing of the little guy with*
a megaphone, shouting out the price in a starburst? the marketing man-

ager asked. He provided his own rendition, which also included a drawing of a Legacy set across from a picture of Mr. Shout screaming the
Legacy's price, inside a starburst, through a cone. Heidt sent this latest
request to Philadelphia, which adamantly refused to do starbursts. Instead, it sent back to Atlanta a new version, which eliminated Mr. Shout
and the starburst, but kept the drawing of the car, which was now centered along the bottom. Chicago was now ready to go along—*if* Wieden
& Kennedy would add a box on the bottom center of the page, beneath
the car illustration, that emphasized the offer of a $16,389 Legacy for
$13,784.

After two weeks and seven variations on a theme, Wieden & Kennedy
was willing, exhausted but willing.

"It's going to be interesting to see how far we go. How far are we going to give in?" Jim Heidt wondered. "Are we going to stick to our guns
and say, 'Look, we know good advertising, we know what we do is
good?' "

DAVE LUHR WANTED TO KNOW the answer himself. On a Friday in
December, he convened a meeting of the creatives and his account staff
in the agency's "Blue Room"—the conference chamber, named for its
azure walls, sparsely furnished but for the beat-up table and chairs and
the video equipment—and put the question to them bluntly. "Okay,
what's the lowest we will go? How big of a whore will we be?" Were
they ready to put a halt to the starbursts and the grids by telling
Subaru, "If you want this, farm it out to another agency"?

The consensus was: No. Not yet.

They were being tough. They were also being realistic. This was no
time to put pressure on a client, particularly an automotive client.
Earlier in the week, the leading forecaster in the agency business, Robert Coen of McCann-Erickson, announced that ad spending in the
United States had declined in 1991, for the first time in thirty years.
Automobile companies, hammered mercilessly by the recession, were
among the worst culprits; up 13 percent in 1990, auto advertising fell
by 9 percent during the first half of 1991, with the second-half figures,
still to come, assuredly worse.

You could hardly blame the car makers for cutting their budgets.
Americans simply were not buying automobiles. General Motors recorded a $1.1 billion loss for the third quarter of 1991 and Ford a $574
million loss; already, the domestics were saying that their annual losses
would be greater than the $4 billion they'd lost in 1980, the industry's
worst year ever. Nor were the once-invincible Japanese immune. Toyota

and Honda, the two biggest Asian brands in America, were on their way to finishing the year down 4.5 percent and 6 percent, respectively, in sales.

Car makers were bumping into each other as they wandered on and off Madison Avenue, seeking new agencies to help save them from the economy. Isuzu had fired Della Femina, McNamee in late August. In mid-November, Mercedes-Benz of North America announced that it was throwing its account into review, after twelve years at McCaffrey & McCall and a 20 percent sales drop in 1991. The advertising rumor mill was feverishly pumping out tales of other imperiled auto accounts. The whispers would become reality over the next year, with Nissan's Infiniti division firing Hill, Holliday, Connors, Cosmopulos; Porsche leaving Fallon McElligott; Ammirati & Puris quitting the $67 million BMW account instead of submitting to a review; and Geer, Dubois shutting down after its dismissal by Jaguar.

Luhr decided not to threaten Subaru but to continue fighting the good fight—for the campaign and against compromise. Time, for now, was on his side. "I think we have a year's halo," Luhr said, "and then the shit will hit the fan."

With the advertising news around them growing as cold as Center City's sidewalks, Jerry and Vince took to trading insecurity stories, the agency-business equivalent of the ghost tales that campers tell to exorcise their nighttime fears.

Over lunch one day at Magnolia, a Cajun restaurant not far from their office, Vince told of an Australian agency that called a staff meeting to announce a management reorganization. Ordering his employees and managers into a conference room, the agency president unrolled an organization chart and told his people, *This is how you all fit in the new structure.* The head of production raised his hand. *Excuse me. I don't see my name here.* The president brightened. *Oh, that's right. Paul, Sally, can you come with me?* Several people followed him into the hall, where they were handed severance checks and commanded to leave the premises immediately.

Jerry and Vince finished their spicy shrimp and blackened tuna and returned to Quality Room. In every nook, another Subaru task awaited their attention.

There was the U.S. Ski Team voiceover. Wieden & Kennedy had produced a television spot to help the team, Subaru's long time sponsoree, raise cash. The narration, as recorded by Brian Keith, concluded with the line: "At sixty miles an hour, it's hard to ask for money." But ESPN, the cable network for which the commercial was intended, refused to allow it to air with the word "money" in the copy: Network rules forbade overt fund-raising. Jerry rewrote the line. Unfortunately, Brian Keith's contract called for him to provide eight voiceovers and no more. *Is it worth it,* Jerry had wondered, *to pay the guy an extra $10,000 for a spot that's only budgeted at $25,000?*

There was also a print ad stressing the SVX's four-wheel-drive transmission. Jerry opened up a file on his Mac on which he had already begun to draft headlines. His thin patience was evident from his earlier entries: "The All-Wheel-Drive Subaru SVX. The Only Thing That Sticks To Asphalt Better Is Road Kill"; "Buy a Subaru. Because Brightly Colored Lycra Already Makes You Look Wimpy Enough."

He attempted some serious efforts. "Live Life on the Edge," he typed. He paused and rocked back and forth in his chair, then batted the keys. "Any Other Car Would Send You Over the Edge." Hunched over and motionless, he stared at the screen. He typed again: "For Those Who Prefer Not to Live Life on the Edge."

Vince, balancing a sketchbook on his lap, drew tiny treatments of the ad, writing Jerry's alternate headlines at a forty-five-degree incline, from lower left to upper right, with a Pilot razor-point pen. When, he wondered, was Dan Wieden going to review the portfolios of the copywriters they had forwarded to him? That would remove at least some of Jerry's burden.

Jerry was being a stoic about the work. His wife, Kim, was in the final days of her pregnancy, and he intended to take some time off, whether or not Wieden & Kennedy hired a copywriter to assist him. Frankly, the only creative exercise that interested him these days was devising a name for the baby. If a girl, he and Kim were agreed on Maya, after the poet Maya Angelou. If a boy . . . they were still arguing. The debate interfered with headline-writing.

Reminded by Vince that an additional body would help him breathe, Jerry halted his efforts and picked up from the credenza a portfolio that had been sent to him by a copywriter at Warwick, Baker & Fiore. One ad, for Barneys men's store, was headlined, "A Man in a Tuxedo Is a Man at His Best."

"Jeez," said Jerry, reflecting less on the ad than on the effect it had on him, "that's awful."

He flipped through the work more rapidly, and was about to toss it back on the credenza when another advertisement caught his eye. It was a storyboard for one of the commercials in Warwick's failed pitch for the Subaru account. The graphics depicted a blinding snowstorm and a small car pulling up to an isolated eatery. "Why would Phil Mockler go out for pizza on a night like this?" ran the copy. "Because he can."

Jerry was unmoved. "What kind of reason is that to go out for pizza?" he wondered.

THROUGH THE PRESSURE, there was still opportunity for glamour and glory. Chris Wackman had directed the agency to return its attention to the SVX. The luxury car was supposed to redefine Subaru's image, but neither the flurry of favorable coverage in the buff books nor Wieden & Kennedy's launch commercial had generated many sales. S.O.A. had hoped to sell twelve thousand units in the year after the vehicle's introduction. It was barely achieving half that number.

"The plain, hard facts are that it takes time for people to recognize this car, and to recognize that it's a Subaru, and the economy sure as hell isn't helping," Chris said. "And also the time of year is not really right to introduce this kind of car. People don't think about purchasing these kinds of cars till the buzz of spring gets in their bonnet and they start thinking about the open road again."

To prepare for that buzz, Chris asked the agency to develop a new national SVX campaign to replace the original spot from the late summer.

Vince, particularly, threw himself into the task. In automotive advertising, nothing feels better than crafting a sports-car campaign. With their sleek lines and associations with wanderlust and eroticism, sports cars provide the widest creative latitude. Vince had missed his chance to launch the SVX, but now he could help guide the relaunch.

Chris's comments about springtime and the open road touched a chord in Vince, who had been deliciously afflicted by vagabond dreams his entire adult life. Eyeing his shelf of Americana books, he picked up *Route 66: The Mother Road* and began paging through it. The photos of tawdry motels and roadside attractions and bare, open highway called to his mind the brush snare and jazz strains that defined the early 1960s for him. *You get your kicks / On Route 66. . . .* The perfect concept!

Jerry, attracted by a retro charm that was pure Wieden & Kennedy, put aside his cynicism about cars and embraced the idea. So did Dan Wieden and David Kennedy—David especially. Ever since he worked on the Harley-Davidson account in Chicago in the sixties, he had wanted to do ads with a Route 66 theme.

But on December 8, in the early stages of the new campaign's development, Jerry's son was born. Even before Jerry and Kim could settle on a name, the baby developed a fever and had to be rushed back to the hospital. The doctors said it might be meningitis. Jerry possessed neither time nor inclination to dwell on sports cars. On his recommendation, Wieden & Kennedy hired Bill Heater to serve as the SVX campaign's freelance copywriter.

Heater was a modern legend in the agency business. Jerry's mentor at Hill, Holliday, he was responsible for some of the decade's most singular and memorable advertising. He popularized the shaky camera-video vérité form in commercials for Wang office systems—a campaign that seemed to train a hidden camera directly on a management information systems conference and dared to leave the incomprehensible technical language untranslated. He took the style even further in his campaign for John Hancock life insurance, an effort so audacious (one ad focused on a father cradling and cooing to his newborn daughter, without music, without schmaltz, without finance talk) that it was booed by the audience when the judges awarded it the top prize at the International Advertising Film Festival at Cannes. Undaunted, Heater continued to defy convention, a trait that reached its zenith with the famous "rocks and trees" launch campaign for Nissan's Infiniti luxury car division, in which the car was never shown.

Heater left the agency business shortly thereafter to try his hand at screenwriting. But he was still available to friends in need like Jerry. Heater liked the Route 66 idea for the SVX campaign, and showed his value almost immediately when he suggested adding a literary twist to it: Jack Kerouac. Underneath visuals glorifying the open road, he wanted words drawn from the novel *On the Road*.

The concept related only marginally to the original positioning statement for the SVX—"The SVX is a fine sports car that grips the road for fabulous performance. How should drivers feel? We want them to feel like Porsche 911 drivers with brains"—but the agency and Subaru had long since veered from that path. Emotion was the way to sell a sports car, not intellect. Speed, tramping, lost youth seemed worthy successors to the initial position. The necessary parties endorsed Heater's concept, and the new team started shaping its ads—with Heater flying down from his home in Milton, Massachusetts, for a day or two a week, otherwise communicating with Vince via phone and fax.

If Vince now had a project that removed him spiritually from the chaos, his colleagues felt, more and more, as if they were sitting in the middle of the maelstrom. Baby Cronin's illness shook the office. Even Mark Dunn's attempt to lighten their mood with a congratulatory reminder—at a December 17 account meeting in Cherry Hill, he happily announced that *today is Wieden & Kennedy's six-month anniversary with Subaru!*—sent them reeling. No one from the agency applauded, no one said a word. *I can't believe it's been so much time,* a weary Scot Butler said to himself, on hearing Mark's words.

Butler freely admitted to suffering from depression over the turns the account had taken, and he was not alone. Even the invitation to the agency's Christmas party, a lighthearted solicitation drafted by Jerry before his baby's illness, was suffused with a melancholia drawn, without subtlety, from the shop's situation. It took the form of a long-sleeve gray cotton T-shirt, with the summons written in red on the front, underneath an entomologically correct drawing of a giant black insect.

"The 'African Dung Beetle' (*Putrido Giganticus*)," it read. "One of the largest members of the beetle family, this defenseless and offensive-smelling insect lives in the Sahara sands where it subsists solely on a diet of dung. So if the nineteen million Hindus are correct in their beliefs, any one of us could someday return as a dung beetle ourselves. Which is reason enough to fully enjoy yourself now at the first ever Wieden & Kennedy/Philadelphia Christmas Party."

The partyers, gathered at Dave Luhr's rented house in Radnor, Pennsylvania the night after the six-month anniversary, tried to be festive. Vince's young son debated whether to go upstairs or down, and Luhr's cherubic daughter demanded a kiss from her dad before going to bed. David Kennedy had flown in from Portland for the affair, and with his long, white hair, white beard and face burned red by the cold, he looked like Santa Claus incarnate.

But joy came hard. Luhr's rented house was sparsely furnished, a reminder to them all that they had chosen a career circumscribed by temporariness. And between bites of bacon-wrapped scallops and stuffed mushroom caps, tension popped like champagne corks. *The car business sucks,* an account man said. *And it's going to get worse,* another rejoined.

Luhr was trying to enjoy himself. But even he, an expert at putting the varied components of his life in separate boxes on his desk and in his head, could not distance himself from the office. He had spent the day in conversation with Chris Wackman, discussing Subaru's dangerous sales slide. Unlike his colleagues, though, Luhr was not depressed. He was angry.

"The regions have far too much power in this company," he said, his tongue loosened by wine. "They control too much money, they have too much say." The problem was compounded by the fact that the regions were essentially answerable to the dealers, whom Luhr considered, as a class, "dinosaurs."

"They're drive-in movies. They've got all this expensive real estate, which they fill with cars they've taken out loans on. It makes no sense whatsoever. It adds all these people, all this bureaucracy, all this expense, to a simple process. Ten years, they'll all be gone. People will walk into a shopping mall, say, 'I want that one, in brown, with leather upholstery,' and it will be delivered to them."

Ten years was a long time. Until then, Wieden & Kennedy had to survive Subaru of America.

"Dealers," said Luhr. "If you only knew."

THE DEALERS, fortunately, had nothing to do with the new SVX campaign. They could not complain, they could not delay it, they couldn't kill it. Nor was it likely they would have tried, because the campaign was perfect.

Vince and Heater superbly captured the romance of the open road in three print advertisements and three television commercials. In one spot, entitled "Streamliner," they depicted a man dozing in the passenger compartment of a train traveling across the open fields of the Midwest. Next to him, his wife was reading a magazine. Their two children slept, sitting, across the aisle. The man woke, and in his sleepy gaze he caught a glimpse of the SVX creeping up alongside the train. He watched wistfully as the SVX pulled ahead. The scene shifted to the exterior and to a close-up of the SVX as it passed the train, then drove into the distance and out of sight.

On the screen, a small super appeared—"*On the Road*. Jack Kerouac"—and the narration, from the book, began, the voice reading the words that scrolled up the screen, in the style of the earlier national spots.

"In no time at all we were back on the main highway and that night I saw the entire state of Nebraska unroll before my eyes. We drove straight through, an arrow road, sleeping towns, no traffic, and the Union Pacific streamliner falling behind us in the moonlight." The commercial concluded with: "The Subaru SVX all-wheel-drive sports car. Subaru SVX. What to drive."

The agency sent the storyboards to Joe Pytka, who jumped at the offer to direct the spots. Wackman was dazzled by the campaign. Rather than delay a presentation into the New Year (Wieden & Kennedy was giving itself a vacation during the week between the two holidays), Chris arranged for the agency to unveil the work to Tom Gibson on December 23.

At 2 p.m. that Monday, a procession from the agency filed into the boardroom adjacent to the Subaru president's office, the same chamber in which they had been awarded the account six months and one week before. Walter Mills, the national account director, led the charge. Jerry was sick and sniffling, but he was present; his son, named Gage by his mother with his father's acquiescence, had recovered completely, to everyone's relief. Chris and Mark Dunn completed the group.

Walter explained the strategy. Then he turned the floor over to Vince, who had been more intimately involved with the campaign's creation than Jerry. The art director had also overcome fatigue and a bad cold to come. He placed the boards and the print comps on easels and described the scenarios. Jerry then read the copy.

Gibson listened impassively. When it was over, he shook his head.

Why in the world are we doing this? he asked. *Where's all this stuff coming from? I've got to sell Legacies! I've got to sell six thousand a month.*

He shot a puzzled look at Chris and Mark. Were they crazy? Why had they spent so much time and energy on something so unnecessary?

I can't waste money on a television campaign for SVX, Gibson said. *I just can't afford it.*

Chapter 20

We Are Driven

AUTOMOBILE SALES in the United States in 1991 were the lowest in eight years. Sales of light vehicles dropped 11.2 percent for the
year. Even the twelve Japanese automakers that exported cars to the
United States, the powerhouses of the previous decade, saw their sales
drop a collective 4.6 percent. Because General Motors, Ford and
Chrysler did so much worse, the Asians actually picked up a bit of market share; even Subaru of America added a fraction of a share point.
But market share gains were only of interest to manufacturers. To
Subaru dealers, who sold only 1,888 Legacies in December (about half
the number sold a year earlier, when the Persian Gulf War was looming
and Americans were presumably staying home), the situation looked
bleak.

Automotive News blamed "wars, rumors of wars, economic recession
and a total lack of consumer confidence." As they rested their weary
brains during the holiday week, however, the staff of Wieden &
Kennedy/Philadelphia knew that, in the extended Subaru family, they,
too, were among the villains.

This sat poorly with Vince Engel. Coming in from the outside, he saw
how hard the agency had been working and how little control it had
over Subaru's destiny. He was bothered beyond belief that Subaru, even
by implication, would blame Wieden & Kennedy for the state of the
economy, the inadequacy of its dealers and the company's inability or
unwillingness to tame its own regional executives. Even more, he was
vexed by the agency's compliance; instead of fighting back, instead of
telling off S.O.A., his colleagues, with the absentee support of Dan
Wieden, kept proffering their chins for additional punching. Wieden &
Kennedy talked tough, he realized, but it was not hardened enough.

The agency needed a rabbi. Dan was too distant to understand how

grim the situation in Philadelphia was. Luhr was too much Dan's amanuensis to overrule the boss. Vince took it upon himself to lead the tribes
to Jerusalem.

His efforts on the now-dead Kerouac campaign had left Vince with an
easel full of other, unfinished work, so he came into the deserted office
several times during the holiday week to complete it. One day he was
joined by Luhr. Normally unflappable, the account director needed
someone with whom to commiserate. *Things are coming at us from all
corners, without coordination,* Luhr complained.

Vince had been dwelling on the problem. *Why don't we present them
with a year's schedule?* he said.

Luhr agreed to offer Vince's notion to the rest of the crew. On January 2, the first day back from the holidays, he called a staff meeting.
Jerry, rested and relieved from his professional and personal ordeal,
spoke first. *We're getting caught up in the particulars. All-wheel-drive
ads, ski team ads, SVX ads,* he said. *It's time for us to give them direction. Time to get back to what we originally presented: a good car, for
a good price. "What to drive."*

They went back and forth about how to do that. Just giving them a
year's schedule of advertising was not enough; S.O.A. could always vio-
late it, once the regions started complaining. Luhr believed the agency
had dispensation from Gibson to go even further. The company president's complaint at the disastrous pre-Christmas meeting that he
needed to sell Legacies seemed, to Luhr, a tacit acknowledgment that
everyone, agency *and* company, had veered from the course they had
agreed upon in June.

Luhr even steered his staff into territory generally left uncharted by
Wieden & Kennedy: self-criticism. In their haste and confusion, the agency had allowed itself to create inferior advertising for Subaru. The Legacy
brand spot, the Woody Allenesque rococo of ugly people admitting to
their innermost fantasies about luxury cars, was *too ad-y,* Luhr said.

His creatives conceded the point. The original "Factory" spot, at Jerry's insistence, was virtually devoid of people, in order to concentrate
the consumer's attention on machinery, engineering and the realities of
driving. The Legacy spot not only consisted entirely of people (with
only one brief shot of the car at the end) but it ridiculed consumers in
a haughty, unappealing way. Brian Keith, the voice of tough reason in
the original ads, had become the voice of reverse snobbery. "I look at
it and realize we were trying to be too cute," Vince said.

Somewhere in Subaru's cars lay an image. The "Factory" commercial
captured it, but somehow, the subsequent advertising failed to reify it.

Walter Mills put words to their feelings about what they had done and now needed to do. "Somebody once said to me, and I never forgot it, that when you're talking about an image, think about it as a person. If you know Walter Mills, and he's five-foot-nine, and now two months later someone tells you that Walter Mills is going to be starting center for the Los Angeles Lakers, you'll say, 'No way! I know Walter Mills and there's no way he can do that!' That's what I think this is like. It's like you have to build—particularly for a product that's been around, you have to build from who you are. It's like a person; you grow and change, but you're always that same individual. And that's kind of what this is about."

By the end of the conclave, the notion of a year's schedule was dismissed as inadequate. What Subaru of America needed was a new campaign, advertising that forced the client to recommit to the original positioning for the company and its cars. Vince summarized the agency's goal. *We need,* he said, *to bring them back to basics.*

THE AGENCY'S "BACK-TO-BASICS PLAN" had several components, all of which aimed to undergird S.O.A.'s corporate goals. First, the agency wanted to provide backing for Tom Gibson's pricing strategy—the no-haggling, pay-one-price scheme to stanch the flow of cash reserves. Second, the agency wanted to preserve the regional advertising campaign (which was the voice of the pricing strategy), even if elements of the ads had to be changed. Third, Wieden & Kennedy wanted to persuade Subaru to allocate more money for media in 1992 than the company intended. Finally, the shop needed to create a slam-bang new advertising campaign that still fit the original positioning. Wieden & Kennedy wanted to keep the umbrella's steel skeleton but stretch a new, waterproof skin over it to protect the vital but fragile components of Subaru's system to sell cars.

Preparations began immediately. All were kept secret from the client, for the client's own good. Subaru was so rent by internal politics that any leaks would inflame the divisions. Wieden & Kennedy did not want this. It intended to provide a rallying point. If that meant playing politics, something at which the shop, unlike older and more established agencies, was unskilled, then Wieden & Kennedy would learn to play politics. Tactically, it knew it had to get the sales department in Cherry Hill to buy into the new idea. Then Chuck Worrell and his people would sell it to the regions and the dealers. Even Chris Wackman was going to be kept in the dark; like the rest of S.O.A.'s executives, he was going to be told that the agency was working on a new promotional campaign.

The maneuvering was delicate and tense, for Subaru was divided within itself. S.O.A. already had in place an existing program to pay consumers directly a $500 rebate on Legacies (all except the highest-priced model). That program was supposed to end, to make way for the new pricing strategy. Now, however, under pressure, the company was considering not only extending it, but taking the money and flipping it into dealer cash—giving it to the dealers so they could use all or part of it to help customers pay down negative equity on their trade-ins. Dealers and distributors were clamoring for the change.

Some inside S.O.A. considered this a minor tweaking of the pricing strategy. Others insisted that it was a return to the top of the slippery slope that would inevitably lead the company to raise its prices in order to provide larger incentives. In the process, Subaru would then lose whatever price advantage it had left over its rivals, which would eventually force the company to provide even greater incentives to remain competitive.

"The automotive side of me that's spent most of my time out in the field says, 'Let's raise the prices and get some money out there for the dealers to make their deals,'" said Chris Milhous, the young S.O.A. marketing executive. "But the corporate side of me says, 'Let's stay the course, bite the bullet, give this thing time and give Wieden & Kennedy a chance to get the advertising message out there.' It's a tough call."

Even Wackman was unsure who, in the contest between S.O.A. and its dealers, was right.

"Now," Chris said in early January, "it's a test of nerves. Who's going to blink first? And I don't know, if we blink first, if that's bad. Should we stick to a long-term plan, if that means we don't survive in the short term?"

WIEDEN & KENNEDY had no doubts. A new purposefulness saturated the agency, which came down on the side of those who wanted to stay the course. Staffers readily acceded to a new rule, instituted by Jeff Greenberg, that required anybody caught slurring the client to pay one dollar into a pot, which would finance agency parties. Meetings were now routinely interrupted by shouts from back-benchers—*That's a slur!* and *That's a rip!*—and the sight of the offenders, laughing, pulling bills from their pockets.

On Monday, January 6 at 11 a.m., Greenberg assembled the Subaru account group in the Blue Room to discuss the plot.

The regional account director handed out photocopies of S.O.A.'s December sales report. The tables showed that, despite the fall from a year earlier, Subaru sold some five hundred more units in December than in November. "The fabulous Worrell himself attributed it to the advertising finally getting into the market," Greenberg said, recounting a meeting earlier that morning with S.O.A.'s sales chief and Tom Gibson. "That's as close as Worrell will get to wrapping his arms around anything."

From around the table and in the back, the room erupted with *ho*s and *yeah*s. "So for those of you out there wondering when Subaru's going out of business," Greenberg continued, as the cheering subsided, "it's not on anyone's game plan right now."

There was bad news, too. At the earlier meeting, Greenberg discovered that Tom O'Hare planned to put together a guerrilla promotional campaign for the New York area—a Presidents Day Sale, in mid-February, replete with advertising and hoopla and whatever incentive or rebate program the distributorship could muster. To prevent O'Hare's scheme from winning acceptance throughout the country, S.O.A. was thinking about preempting it by announcing a national promotional campaign tied to the opening of baseball spring training.

The specter of ads heralding "Grand Slam Savings" incited as many groans as there had been cheers. Greenberg tried to mollify the troops.

"They're very positive," he reassured them. "They're holding with the pricing strategy."

"So they believe in the tone of the ads?" Vince asked.

"The tone. The strategy. The only thing that's holding up the pricing strategy is three words: 'Lack of Pretense.' . . . I think Woody, McGinty in Penn/Jersey and Worrell really don't understand the word 'pretense.' They really don't understand what it means. O'Hare, too, complained that people would not understand it. It's a small but vocal minority, led by Chuck, that is against the retail campaign."

To Vince, Chuck Worrell was the nemesis—the living embodiment of everything wrong with Subaru of America. In his deep monotone, the art director launched an attack on the sales director that concluded with a blast of his own invention. "You know," Vince said, "hair dye has a high lead content." Someone shouted, "Slur!" but Vince protested, "Seriously. I knew a guy in Australia who used Grecian Formula, and he went wacko." But, caught in a churlish fabrication, he pulled out a dollar and slapped it on the conference table.

An account executive pursued Greenberg's analysis to a potentially unsettling conclusion. "In terms of a new campaign to replace 'Lack of Pretense,' assuming no change in strategy, what happens?" she asked.

"The first thing we have to do is figure out what this spring promotional event is," Greenberg replied. "But we also have to figure out an evolution of the 'Lack of Pretense' campaign, probably without those words."

All eyes turned sideways to Vince and Jerry, to gauge their reaction. But their faces remained impassive. They were prepared to sacrifice their copy, *if* they could save the strategy.

TOM O'HARE, in his disillusionment with the ad agency, had unwittingly handed it the tool it needed to put its scheme into action.

His desire to stage a Presidents Day promotion was not irrational. Although the rest of the country tended to ignore them, on the eastern seaboard, north of the Mason-Dixon line, George Washington's and Abraham Lincoln's birthdays had long been a fruitful selling period for automobile dealers. Subaru had little choice but to contend with O'Hare's plan, which it did through the vague idea of an early spring baseball promotion.

Although Wieden & Kennedy recoiled from the gimmickry of the baseball idea, it readily accepted the assignment to devise an alternative promotion. By doing so, the agency believed it could buy itself the time it needed to develop, in secret, a new and fully integrated advertising campaign for Subaru. The agency reasoned that S.O.A. would hold off on ordering any precipitous changes in either the "Lack of Pretense" campaign or the pricing strategy in the interim.

To sweeten the deal, Wieden & Kennedy also suggested a minor repair to strengthen the regional advertising: a new television commercial, starring the surrogate dealer Jim Meskimen, to explain the meaning of "Lack-of-Pretense Days." Wackman enthusiastically supported the production of this "bridge spot," and sold it to Tom Gibson, who got O'Hare to delay the implementation of his Presidents Day Sale. Thus the agency received two solid weeks to work without threat. Publicly, the shop was working on a new, national promotional campaign. Privately, it was plotting the "Back to Basics" campaign.

The tactics appeared to pay off when the agency unveiled its own promotional concept in mid-January. Instead of a sales event with a baseball theme, Wieden & Kennedy suggested a promotion structured around the slogan "What to drive." Among its gimmicks could be a trip to the Indianapolis 500 for the top five Subaru salesmen, T-shirts and racing flags with the slogan emblazoned on them, and other gimcracks and geegaws to excite dealers and their personnel—anything and everything they could think of short of new incentives and rebates. Luhr even invited S.O.A.'s own sales-promotion staff to work with the agency to develop the campaign, nullifying the shop's earlier insistence that creativity was its province alone. Along with the bridge spot, the new promotional campaign would hold the dealers, the regions and the distributors at bay, Wieden & Kennedy maintained.

The ploy worked. Subaru's sales department was captivated. "This is critical! This is absolutely critical," Fred Adcock exulted after the presentation. "This in my mind is the missing piece of the puzzle that makes the picture complete. That makes the campaign work. That ties the whole thing in, as far as 'Subaru. What to Drive.'" Go forth, he and the other executives said, take another week, give us a promotional campaign!

Gleeful in its duplicity, the agency magnanimously accepted the challenge.

"It's one of the things I've learned on the retail side," Jeff Greenberg explained. "If you can't win the game, get the rules changed."

JERRY AND VINCE silently pored over a package of material that Chris Riley had sent them from Portland. As they read copies of a cover story from *Time* entitled "The New Frugality," the only sound in Quality Room was an occasional *boing* from Vince's computer—each one signaling that a piece of electronic mail had just been delivered.

"Jerry, it's almost like you could paraphrase it," Vince said when he finished the article. He read from a yellow legal pad on which he had scribbled notes from the piece. "'Upscale is downscale; downscale is in.' 'Flaunting money is considered gauche.' It's like my father. He always told me, 'You guys—where does the money go? I raised eight kids, and I never made more than $60,000 a year.' We used to think, 'Oh God, there he goes again.' But in a way, he was right."

Jerry riffled through Subaru's large "Product Planning Information Book" and read aloud from a list of awards the Legacy had won. " 'Easy Maintenance Car of the Year—*Home Mechanix* magazine.'"

"Hey, we could do that!" Vince blurted. "You just see a yuppie standing there, in a suit, with a briefcase. Then a Legacy runs over him."

Television was confounding the partners. The "Back to Basics" message seemed clear, but translating it into a compelling thirty-second visual message flummoxed them. Every time they came up with something appealing, Dan Wieden, by fax from Portland, shot it down.

"It's fucking obvious what we have to do," Jerry said. "It's putting it together in an interesting way." He turned his attention to a print advertisement he was attempting to compose. In a sketchbook with hard black covers, he had scrawled the outline of a magazine spread. Atop the left-hand page, he had written the headline, "How to Buy a Car During Prosperous Times." In large letters underneath, in quotation marks, he wrote: "I don't care how much it costs, just give it to me in {fill in the color}." On the right page was the headline, "How to Buy a Car in a Recession." Beneath it was long but as-yet-unwritten copy.

Vince tried to keep Jerry from slipping into despair. "We're making it overly difficult. The basic message is simple."

"You're right. Somehow, you want to get at, 'Bad times are the right time for Subaru.'" Jerry sipped on a Fresca and wrote again in his pad. He looked up at Vince. "Could you do a print ad that just asks, 'Who'd you buy your last car for?'"

The art director wanted to stay focused on television. "Here's my concern. The 'Factory' ad and 'SVX,' too, there's no trickery, no gimmicks in the execution. Maybe the scrolling type, an art director, would say, 'Wow!' But there's no trickery to the message. It's like when we presented that group of ads to Dan, and he said, 'They're fine. They're great ads. But none of them have that plain honesty, with the "fuck you" to it.'"

"It's much easier in print," Jerry sighed. "TV should be print come to life."

"That's what the 'Factory' spot is."

It was dawning on Jerry how flawless Subaru's old slogan was. "You start with, 'It's inexpensive.' Then it lasts and lasts. It's the most durable car out there. It doesn't get stuck. You get great value for your money."

Vince, the enforcer, grew agitated. "Jerry, you say stuff like that and I say *write it down*! When we do the ads, they come out sounding *like ads*. The facts are far stronger than anything we've written."

Jerry doodled in his sketchbook. "It's fuckin' tough."

IT WAS EVEN TOUGHER given the daily shifts and twists in public attitudes and events. The recession, America's worst since the early 1980s, was the agency's hook. But how Subaru could or should exploit it was open to debate.

As 1992 dawned, economic growth was at a standstill and unemployment was high and persistent. Thanks to General Motors—in particular its announcement, just before Christmas, that it was going to close twenty-one factories in North America and lay off 74,000 workers—the auto industry had come to represent the recession. At the recommendation of several advisers, President George Bush determined to show the public that he was tackling the problem by inviting the chairmen of the Big Three American automobile manufacturers to accompany him on a long-scheduled state visit to Japan. The officials and their entourages arrived on Tuesday, January 7, with plans to impress on the Japanese government and the country's auto executives the severity of the U.S. industry's plight.

The Americans' goal was to persuade Japan to erase its $41 billion automotive trade surplus with the U.S. by 1997, in part by redressing the imbalance in market share—29 percent of the American market for Japanese cars and parts, a mere 0.2 percent of the Japanese market for American auto products.

But a funny thing happened during Bush's trip, along with several not-so-funny things. Far from being conciliatory, the Japanese were unyielding. The Asian automakers bluntly told the Americans that they had agreed to a decade's worth of voluntary export restraints, only to watch as the American manufacturers squandered the opportunity by raising prices and abjuring market-share gains. Furthermore, the Japanese turned a cold eye to the high salaries commanded by American auto executives, which far exceeded those of their Japanese counterparts and which, the Japanese implied, affected the morale and productivity of American factory workers. Finally, the major Japanese automakers had already announced plans to increase their purchases of American parts and machinery; they saw no need for further concessions.

The inability of the American manufacturers to sell cars to Japanese consumers, the Asians declared, was less the result of protectionist trade policies than Detroit's own arrogance. The Americans, for example, insisted on exporting left-hand-drive vehicles to Japan, when Japanese consumers overwhelmingly preferred right-hand-drive vehicles. Indeed, none of the Big Three maintained a design center in Japan to research and fabricate cars to Japanese tastes. "If the Big Three are to expand in the Japanese market, they first and foremost have to offer a car that is the right size and the right feel for Japanese consumers," Yutaka Kume, the president of the Nissan Motor Company, said. "They have to improve their marketing."

Back home, the American press not only reported the Japanese criticism, it added its own independent verification of it. "American Auto Makers Need Major Overhaul to Match the Japanese," the *Wall Street Journal* declared in a front-page headline.

To the American public, the entire Bush mission appeared uncomfortable, indecorous, almost like begging. The unseemliness of the trip was crystallized by the sight of President Bush, apparently suffering from the flu, throwing up at a state dinner hosted by Prime Minister

Kiichi Miyazawa, who cradled the sick president's head in his lap. Television cameras captured the whole unsightly mess which, to the American public, looked like a tableau of their nation's decline.

Detroit tried to use the trip to inflame public sentiment. "I for one am fed up hearing from the Japanese—and I might say some Americans, too—that all our problems in this industry, all our problems, are our own damn fault," a defiant Lee Iacocca, the chairman of Chrysler, told an audience of five thousand businesspeople at the Detroit Economic Club after his return. But American consumers did not buy the act. In fact, in their own despair, vexed by Detroit's insolence and Tokyo's stubbornness, Americans seemed to declare a pox on both houses. If American cars were not selling, it was America's own fault . . . and Japan's, too.

How Subaru should react to the debacle was not at all clear. S.O.A. executives were none too happy about an editorial cartoon by Dan Wasserman of the *Boston Globe*. In it, two doctors, trying to diagnose the cause of President Bush's illness, peered intently at an X ray of the chief executive's stomach and a mysterious object lodged inside it.

"Is it sushi?" asked one physician.

"It's a Subaru!" declared the other.

JEFF GREENBERG, dressed in executive-style braces, straightened his tie. Then he straightened it again. "Nerves aren't running high," the account exec said. "Frustrations are running high."

Outside, a flurry of late-January snow dusted the Center City pavement. Around him, a commotion was reaching its last-minute crescendo. Commercial scripts slid from the photocopier into waiting staplers and hands. Portfolios were unzipped and inspected for the appropriate storyboards and comps. The "Back-to-Basics Plan" was no longer the issue. Selling it was.

"Let me get it straight," said Walter Mills, rushing into Quality Room to converse with Jerry. "You and I are going to stand up together, right?"

"Who's Melrose and who's Milhous?" Luhr asked, unable to distinguish between two Subaru executives. "Is one Jim and one Jeff?"

In from Portland, dressed in a dark suit, Dan Wieden paced the narrow hallway, until he joined the blur of underlings who zipped out the door, down the elevators, into the parking garage and, in several Legacies, across the Delaware to Cherry Hill. They were greeted in S.O.A.'s lobby by Chris Wackman, who escorted them into a large conference room that overlooked the snow-sprinkled parking lot.

Nervously and without introductory chatter, Luhr opened the meeting. "We're really excited—"

Dan interrupted. The agency chief could not contain himself. As Luhr pulled a strained smile over his teeth, Dan raced into his own, unscripted screed about cars, markets, consumption and creativity. He alerted the Subarus—Chris, Mark Dunn and three sales-promotion executives—that, while they were expecting to get a promotional campaign, they were actually going to witness something greater. "This agency a lot of times tries to think hard and come up with a larger, global solution," Dan said. "I think we've done it with what we're presenting today."

Walter got up and stood to the left of a large easel. Jerry, who was wearing jeans, a green corduroy shirt and a garish floral-print tie, shifted uneasily from foot to foot on the right.

The national account director calmly explained how the "disastrous pre-Christmas meeting" set the agency thinking about how it had allowed its advertising campaign for Subaru to drift off course. Using large presentation cards as visual aids, he described Wieden & Kennedy's continuing quest to understand how the vicissitudes of the economy were reshaping the American character. Citing data from the Yankelovich Monitor, a respected marketing- and opinion-research report, he identified the 1990s as the emerging era of "neotraditional values," which the recession, with its many pressures, was hastening. He explained that the agency initially sought to develop a promotional campaign, an event that would galvanize the regions and the dealers. But all the research, and their intuition, favored a loftier and more heretical concept:

Why not do a new national campaign that would make Subaru the most talked-about car company in America? Why crowd into the Winter Olympics or the opening of baseball spring training with dozens of other consumer-products marketers? Why not find an event that Subaru, and Subaru alone, could own? Why not turn the *recession* into that event? Why not make America's economic turmoil into the Super Bowl of automobile marketing, with Subaru of America as its sponsor?

Walter sat down. Jerry lifted a shrouded presentation card onto the easel. "In short," the copywriter said, picking up seamlessly from the account executive, "the Legacy is the perfect car. Or, as we would like to say—"

Vince stood up and ripped the covering from the card, revealing the new slogan Wieden & Kennedy wanted to introduce. Jerry read it for his audience:

"THE OFFICIAL CAR OF THE RECESSION?"

The line, printed in white type on black foam-board, was Dave Luhr's invention. Returning to Philadelphia from the pre-Christmas debacle, he had begun venting to his colleagues about S.O.A.'s blindness to reality. *There's no way with all these little ads they want us to do, these ski team ads, these four-wheel-drive ads that we can move Legacies in the numbers they want,* he protested. *We ought to do something crazy, like call it "the official car of the recession."* His friends laughed. But they continued to use the line as a reference point in their conversations. Finally, when alternative ideas proved unsatisfactory, Vince decreed that the line would *be* the campaign. *There's no one out there on the street who can disagree with it,* he argued. Dan Wieden, by fax, assented, and the campaign thereafter fell into place.

As his colleagues passed around copies of the text and Vince placed a mockup of a full-page print advertisement in the easel, Jerry flatly read the text he had been laboring over for three weeks.

We're about to reintroduce our Subaru Legacy as the Official Car of the Recession. And we're afraid, no, we're almost certain, some people are going to attack us for that. The reason (as if we need to tell you): because we're Japanese. It doesn't matter the company was started by two Jewish salesmen from Philly. Or that 63 percent of our employees are Americans. Or that nearly 70 percent of all Legacies sold in the U.S. are built in Axl Rose's hometown— Lafayette, Indiana. It just doesn't matter. And it doesn't matter the products are well made and the company was American-owned and -run for 19 of its 21 years and that the Japanese have never made a penny of profit from it. (Since the 1990 buy-out, Subaru has lost almost 200 million dollars in the U.S.) No. The only thing that matters are Japanese owners and the fact that it's an election year and Japan will be bashed for many of America's problems. We're not going to debate the issue or pass blame or scream "Uncle." All we want to say, like many companies, the recession has hurt us badly. And to survive we need to think and work harder than ever before. And part of that is by repositioning the Legacy as the Official Car of the Recession. We can't think of a better positioning. Or a more relevant one. (In these times you can't get by with, "The Subaru Legacy. Excitement and a whole lot more." Or "The Subaru Legacy. Engineered for the really smart driver like you.") Or a more honest positioning. It's simply the truth. Everything we hear says consumers now demand well-built products that are inexpensive to buy, inexpensive to maintain, that'll last for years. Which sums up the Subaru Legacy. The Legacy is so well built reviewers often claimed it was "overengineered." Its starting price is just $12,999. It was 1990's "Easy Maintenance Car of the Year." And as for longevity, it's a Subaru and 93 percent of all Subaru vehicles registered in the last ten years are still on the road and running today. Now, we know this explanation probably won't reverse thousands of opinions or win us hordes of new admirers. After all, it's hard enough just to sell cars with an ad.

The advertisement concluded with the new slogan, "The Subaru Legacy. The Official Car of the Recession?" Underneath it, Wieden & Kennedy's original "What to drive" slogan, identified now with the brand more than any individual model—still stood.

The Subarus silently sucked in the new advertising. It was vintage Wieden & Kennedy. With its talk of "positioning" and "repositioning," of "truth" and selling, the advertisement was more about advertising than about Subaru. In every other respect, though, it was . . . different. Even the look of it was changed. Vince had replaced the florid, Bernhard Modern typeface, to which he had always objected, with solid, blocky, sans-serif letters that he believed better reinforced the underlying theme of simplicity and honesty. The two-column *New Yorker* magazine-style layout was gone, supplanted by a solid page of text, broken up only by a few small line drawings (the Liberty Bell, an Indiana map, some architectural renderings of cars) and an unadorned photograph of the Legacy on the bottom. All in all, the "Back to Basics" print advertisements looked like political posters hastily assembled by radicals, which, in a sense, they were.

The national TV commercials were equally direct in design and language. The neurotic men and women who populated the Woody Allen–"Luxury Car" spot were absent. The camera focused instead on exterior and interior elements of the Legacy—its grille, a window, a hubcap, the speedometer. "For years, they've been saying we've overengineered our cars," Brian Keith was to say. "Made them too durable, too functional, without a surplus of extras. Now, the recession's come and everyone's proclaiming, 'We have a strong tradition of making cars that last, we make them durable, we make them practical.' . . . The Subaru Legacy. From the car company that believed in a trend . . . when there wasn't one."

The Subaru executives reviewed the pages of material handed them by the admen. They said nothing. Abhorring a vacuum, Dan leaped to fill it.

"What gets me so goddamn excited about this campaign is it takes us from talking about the ethics of advertising and selling and takes us back to the car as hero again! It really gets me jazzed up!"

Still, the auto marketers made no remarks. Were they overwhelmed by the advertising's gutsiness?

"Keep in mind," Scot Butler, the media director, told them, "every magazine they see these in, they'll just have read a story about the recession."

Finally, a response.

"Why is the question mark after 'Official Car of the Recession' so big?" Chris Wackman asked. "Why don't we *assert* it?"

"We *had* a period," Jerry answered. "But it looked like it would offend people."

"We thought by asking it as a question," Vince added, "it would make people think."

Chris did, for a moment. "I guess you could ask it as a question and answer it with 'Subaru. What to drive.' Period," he mused.

That was it, the only objection. As they tossed around the potential political problems—how to sell it to the regions, how to get the dealers behind it, how to manage the transition from the current campaign to the new one—the Subarus grew increasingly excited by Wieden & Kennedy's "Back-to-Basics Plan."

Ron Shangle, the company's sales promotion director, approvingly called it "the hardest sell you can get with the strategy we're employing."

Chris Milhous, the sales promotions manager, said, "It *does* push all the hot buttons."

Later, back in Philadelphia, the advertising men were overjoyed. Finally, they had managed to hold a meeting with Subaru where they weren't run over by a bus. Far from it. Wieden & Kennedy was driving the bus.

"A bad meeting, they tell you, 'No, sorry, we appreciate the work but we just can't do it.' A good meeting is a meeting where they tell you, 'We like it, but can you change the tag line?'" Walter Mills explained. "This was a great meeting."

CHRIS WACKMAN was intrigued by the Back-to-Basics Plan. He was also nervous. *We can say whatever we want in the backup to the advertising, but how many are just going to pick up on that headline,* he wondered, *and change one word, from "Official Car of the Recession" to "Official Cause of the Recession?"* The campaign, Chris figured, was a risk.

But not so risky that Tom Gibson shouldn't see it, and see it unencumbered by his marketing director's opinions. "When we take something to Tom, I try to leave my feelings out of it, recognizing that I'm only one person," Chris explained. "This is whether it is creative or almost anything. Then, if he is in concert with me, I end up supporting it. If he's not in concert with me, then what I end up doing is presenting a devil's advocate point of view. I won't generally kill something unless it is something I couldn't live with."

Chris did ask the agency to come up with a new advertisement before presenting the campaign to Gibson. The ad about "two Jewish salesmen from Philadelphia" and "repositioning" and Japan-bashing was a little too harsh; it did not serve Wieden & Kennedy's purpose well. A new introductory ad which formally and fully explained the concept of the campaign and provided more detail about the Legacy would, Chris suggested, sit better with S.O.A.'s president.

Since Gibson was traveling, Wieden & Kennedy also took time to devise regional television spots, the better to head off any territorial objections from the RVPs. The commercials starred the salesman-surrogate Jim Meskimen. But gone were the words "Lack of Pretense" and Jim's ambivalence about the art of selling. Even he attested to the new sobriety.

"The human brain's capable of understanding the structure of the atom," Jim was to say in one of the new spots, holding up a large glass container with an apparently real brain in it. "But there's one thing it can't comprehend: Car advertising. Enough! So we're taking into account that you have one of these"—he nodded toward the brain—"and we're simply going to say, 'During these tough times, you can buy a Subaru Legacy wagon that should last for years . . . at a price thousands less than the competition.'"

The agency presented its Back-to-Basics Plan to Gibson one week later. Chuck Worrell and Fred Adcock from the sales department were present. The room was tense; the advertising executives could not shake the memory of how they had been blindsided by S.O.A. before the holidays.

Dan Wieden, who flew East for this second presentation, spoke first. *You came to this agency because you knew it was going to be different,* he told Subaru's president. *We're not going to do advertising that's going to pass in the night. Keep that in mind when you look at what we're going to present. Keep in mind that it's crisis time.*

The agency ran the presentation and Gibson loved it. So did the senior sales executives. *Crisis,* Gibson said, by way of dispensation, *that's a good word. Because I can't think of anything stronger.*

But Subaru's chief operating officer did not yet want to give the agency the final go-ahead. The possibility of a backlash against the company was evident. While he thought that a controversy would benefit S.O.A.—externally, by calling attention to the company; internally, by reinstilling the underdog energy that had galvanized it under Harvey Lamm—Gibson believed his Japanese colleagues ought to review the campaign.

We don't normally go through the Japanese, Gibson told the agency, *but this time we should, because of the repercussions.*

Wieden & Kennedy prepared to make its third "Back to Basics" presentation a week later.

PUBLIC OPINION, aided by clumsy politicians, ardent capitalists and hungry correspondents, can turn quickly. During the period Wieden & Kennedy was preparing and presenting its "Back-to-Basics Plan," it swerved and dipped like an errant roller coaster.

First, the Speaker of Japan's Diet, Yoshio Sakurauchi, declared in a speech that American workers were "lazy" and that one-third of them were illiterate. Somewhat later, trying to settle the brewing controversy, Prime Minister Miyazawa averred that the United States "may lack a work ethic." As a capper, the owners of the Seattle Mariners, a financially ailing Major League Baseball team, attempted to sell the franchise to the family that founded Nintendo, the Japanese video-games giant. For average Americans, or, at least, for the correspondents who fed them and the capitalists who sought them, it was all a bit too much.

Since the automobile industry now symbolized the competition between Japan and the United States, some companies extended to their workers incentives to purchase American cars—setting aside, for the time being, the fact that many "American" cars, like GM's Geo Storm, were made overseas, while so many foreign cars, like Honda's Accord, were manufactured mostly in America. Provenance was less important than patriotism. Monsanto Chemical offered $1,000 to each of its twelve thousand employees toward the purchase of a Big Three vehicle. So did the Tosco Corporation, an oil-refining firm, even though its chairman owned two Mercedes-Benzes. "I got mad," the executive said, explaining his proposal.

American automobile dealers rushed to exploit the tensions. The metropolitan New York Pontiac dealers association charged onto the air with a commercial that angrily highlighted, against a rising sun, the Diet Speaker's comment about American literacy. Chrysler-Plymouth dealers in Anchorage, Alaska, ran print advertisements with photographs of Pearl Harbor. Pat Domenicone, an Atlanta dealer, urged people into his Cadillac store with full-page newspaper advertisements that declared, "We don't have to take it anymore! Companies are closing! JOBS ARE LOST! Families are homeless! Buy American! Let's keep American companies in business & American workers working!" Domenicone did not mention in his ads that he also owned a Subaru franchise.

Takeshi Higurashi, Subaru of America's chairman and chief executive, reviewed the "Back-to-Basics" campaign in early February. He was scared to death, but he was fascinated as well.

"I think campaign is like earthquake in Tokyo last week," he told Dave Luhr. "It shakes a lot of people up."

Listening to the apprehensions of his Japanese colleagues, Gibson decreed that there would be a fourth "Back to Basics" presentation. Because so much of the new campaign rested on the public's reaction to its political message, S.O.A. decided to bring in two public relations specialists to review it. If the p.r. experts gave their assent, the Subaru Legacy would become the Official Car of the Recession.

At 1 p.m. on February 6, Wieden & Kennedy gathered in Subaru's boardroom and presented the campaign to a public relations authority S.O.A. had called up from Washington, a former network newscaster who had served in the Middle East.

This can create a lot of controversy, he told Tom Gibson and the other auto executives in attendance. *But it might create human interest.*

To the agency's relief, the p.r. man backed the strategy fully. It was *based on truth,* it could be *backed up with facts.* He told them the campaign *wouldn't be so much like a Japanese company, but a small company fighting for its survival.* He had suggestions to enhance the advertising's effectiveness: make Tom Gibson the spokesman, contrast S.O.A. to Honda, which didn't have the guts to stand up against Japanbashing.

Give me a risk assessment, Chris Wackman commanded.

With everything properly in place including an accompanying p.r. campaign—*there can be great positives,* the expert answered.

What if you take away the tag line? Chris asked.

Then you got nothing.

The advertising men—Walter, Luhr, Jerry, Vince and Jeff Greenberg—spent the next several hours excitedly chattering about the production schedule. At 4 p.m., they reconvened for their last presentation, to Edelman Worldwide.

Edelman was the largest independent public relations firm in the United States. It was one of the business's oldest and best. Its founder had invented the Toni Twins for the hair-care company, helping to make "Which twin has the Toni?" part of the vernacular. The firm was the p.r. industry's leading producer of video news releases, publicity tools disguised as television news stories.

Edelman sent several representatives to Cherry Hill. Wieden & Kennedy showed them the full-page print advertisement headlined, "The Subaru Legacy. The Official Car of the Recession?" The agency described the television commercial that depicted how Subaru "overengineered" its cars. The admen played out the spot that featured Jim holding the brain.

The head of the Edelman delegation had one word for the campaign: *dangerous.*

Give me a risk assessment, Chris Wackman said.

The p.r. executive responded, *Fifty-fifty.*

I think it's sixty-forty negative, chimed in his assistant. *Maybe seventy-thirty.*

He looked to the advertising people and recommended an alternative strategy. *Have you ever thought of using a Japanese spokesman on TV?*

The agency representatives, despair welling up within them, looked blank.

You know, the p.r. man prodded, *like Tony Bennett would be the spokesman for an Italian company.*

Luhr could not mask his disgust.

How about Yoko Ono? he retorted.

After the public relations specialists left, Gibson told the agency what it already knew. Without unanimity from the experts, he could not in good conscience recommend the advertising to his Japanese superiors and colleagues. With regrets, he killed the "Official Car of the Recession" campaign.

JERRY DROVE to a bar on South Street in Philly, tipped a few beers, shot pool, and did not call his office. Around midnight, he telephoned Vince. Every other word in his monologue was *fuck.*

He stayed away from Quality Room for a few days, prompting Luhr to drive out to his neighborhood to drag him to lunch and play psychiatrist. What they did was commiserate with each other. Jerry talked hopelessly about moving back East, an area he despised, living in a city he hated, in *somebody else's house,* putting up with *shit he abhorred.* Luhr had little stomach to placate his copywriter.

"Can you imagine a company, its president wants to go with something, its sales director wants to go with something, and it still has to go and ask not one but *two* outside p.r. companies for their opinion? And takes two weeks to get to *that*?" he asked, less in exasperation than astonishment.

Wieden & Kennedy now had nothing. By embarking on a new national advertising effort, the ad agency and its client had agreed implicitly that the original national campaign was no longer viable. The agency, on its own, had sacrificed the "Lack of Pretense" regional campaign on the altar of its "Back-to-Basics" plan, which died at birth. And S.O.A., bowing to pressure from its dealers, scuttled its pricing strategy. It agreed to give dealers $1,000 in trading money to get upside-down consumers out of their bad auto loans, and to raise the Legacy's base price to account for part of the incentive.

The no-gimmicks marketing approach was dead. So was the agency's mood. And energy. And ambition.

The advertising agency watched helplessly as other companies rushed forward with programs Subaru had abandoned. Volkswagen introduced a "Payment Protection Plus" plan guaranteeing car payments to any buyer idled by the recession. A Palm Beach, Florida, Pontiac dealer, introduced a pay-one-price, no-haggling sales policy and tripled his sales to more than a hundred cars a month. Toyota went on the air with commercials extolling its American workers.

"I feel worse for them," Jerry said of his client, "than for me."

To clear the air, Wieden & Kennedy and Subaru of America congregated in neutral territory, at a hotel not far from Cherry Hill, for a daylong meeting to discuss long-term product planning, marketing strategy, and the convolutions in their eight-month relationship. Several Japanese executives were there—only the third time, after the original pitch and the penultimate "Back to Basics" presentation, that the agency had been present at a binational client meeting.

The first hour of the conclave was torturously slow. No one wanted to get to the point, to address Subaru's fearful conservatism or Wieden & Kennedy's stubborn ignorance or what had gone so wrong with Subaru's marketing during the last half-year. Everyone was too polite.

Finally, Dan Wieden addressed Higurashi and Miyake directly. *Who do you build your cars for?* he asked. The longtime Fuji executives responded with clinical details about the age range, educational attainment, and economic status of their consumers.

No, Dan demanded. *When you build your cars,* who *do you have in mind?*

The Japanese auto men were not accustomed to thinking that way.

They fumbled around a bit, then were joined in the halting answers by their American counterparts. Some among the agency crew believed it was the first time the two sides of Subaru had ever discussed the issue together candidly.

Tongues loosened. Gibson mentioned that the company always took pride in the way the cars were made. Higurashi recounted the fervor with which Fuji's engineers designed their engines. One of his colleagues joyfully described the company's "concept cars," the futuristic vehicles that most companies simply displayed at auto shows and never produced in quantity. With the SVX, Fuji had brought a concept car to market more quickly than any other auto manufacturer in memory. But the corporate executives admitted that in nearly twenty-five years, they had never set on paper a corporate platform, a position, a philosophy that explained their passion, and that told people inside and outside their now-joined organizations what they and their company were about.

The advertising agency lifted itself from its depression to take on the assignment. "We've got to understand," Vince Engel told his partners and client, "the true image of Subaru."

PART VI

THE IMAGE

Chapter 21

I Think in My Legacy

IN AN OFFICE BUILDING not far from the Tsukiji fish market in Tokyo, Kosuke Mori was also dwelling on the image of Subaru. For him, as for David Luhr, his counterpart in the United States, it was a problem. Mori was the Subaru account director at Dentsu, Japan's largest advertising agency. And his Subaru campaign, the advertising he had sweated over, argued about and assented to, was not working.

The campaign had been designed to highlight the new Subaru, to show drivers in Roppongi and other fashionable Tokyo neighborhoods that Fuji Heavy Industries no longer made cars only for farmers and shopkeepers. The Legacy was a junior executive's car. Even a senior manager could drive one!

Fuji had its own ideas of what the campaign should include, of course, and its executives did not shrink from providing Kosuke Mori their recommendations. From their first meetings in Fuji's windowless, tobacco-stained conference rooms atop its Shinjuku tower, Akira Yamaguchi, the general manager of Subaru's domestic advertising and marketing department, was insistent.

We must focus on the Legacy four-door sedan. Mori agreed with that; only the sedan would draw consumers away from the Toyota Camry. *We must set new road-rally records, to show consumers how durable the Legacy is.* Mori tried gently to explain to Yamaguchi-san that that was unnecessary, that consumers did not question the durability of a Subaru. *We must tell them of our technological superiority.* Mori could be blunt; he had taken to heart the last of Dentsu's Ten Working Guidelines, as promulgated by the advertising agency's fourth president, Hideo Yoshida: "When confrontation is necessary, don't shy away from it." So the account director tried to disabuse his client of the need to address technology. Subaru's slogan, for the longest time, had been

"Advantage: Technology," Mori reminded Yamaguchi-san. Technology wasn't Subaru's problem. Subaru's cars lacked status; that was the problem. Subaru's cars were ugly; that was a *big* problem.

In the end, they compromised. If Mori had gleaned anything from his years at Dentsu, it was that a good account director must learn the art of compromise. "Welcome difficult assignments," President Yoshida's fourth guideline counseled. "Progress lies in accomplishing difficult work."

Yamaguchi-san and Fuji got their way—a campaign to market the new Legacy sedan by its durability and technology. The company emphasized the Legacy four-wheel-drive Turbo Sedan's new 100,000-kilometer world speed record of 447 hours, 44 minutes and 9.887 seconds, and the Legacy's first-place finishes in the Group N divisions of the Acropolis Rally and the Safari Rally. The advertising showcased the 2.0-liter, 16-valve DOHC Turbo engine, with two camshafts for each right and left cylinder—much more powerful than any engine ever placed inside a Subaru.

But Mori and his fourteen-person Subaru account team at Dentsu managed to inject a dose of style into the Legacy's launch campaign. They persuaded Fuji to promote the concept of *hashiri*—the vehicle's invisible attributes, like the feeling of the ride, its comfort, its stability. Not only that, but the television commercials and print advertisements implied that *hashiri* was a luxury which only beautiful people with a surfeit of leisure time could afford. In a striking departure from earlier Subaru advertising, the TV spots featured a man and woman in evening dress posed by their Legacy as Spanish music, a new rage in Japan, played in the background.

Now, as he chain-smoked Hope Lights at his desk in the Sumitomo Irifune Building, in the upper corner of Dentsu's twenty-four-building campus, Mori had to confront the truth: The campaign was not working. Legacy sales were disappointing. Dentsu's three-year marketing plan to turn Fuji around from its long slump by focusing on the car the first year, the places it could go the second year and its drivers the third year was, two-thirds of the way in, bearing little fruit. "The sedan, regrettably, hasn't improved its image over Toyota and Nissan," Yamaguchi, the client, said.

The problem was compounded by the deep trouble in which Fuji Heavy Industries was mired. Fuji liked to think of itself as a diversified conglomerate. Its annual reports never failed to feature the Boeing and Fokker jets for which it made parts, the unmanned space shuttle it was helping develop for the government, the luxury buses it exported to the Middle East and the industrial engines it produced for factories throughout Europe and the U.S. But, truth be told, these other activities accounted for only 20 percent of its business. The rest came from Subaru cars. And Subaru was in a shambles.

Fuji blamed much of its trouble on Subaru's severe sales slump in America, its largest market. But the Subaru division was encountering problems at home, as well. Fuji was late in taking advantage of the Bubble, the economic upsurge initiated in late 1986 by the Japanese government's decisions to keep interest rates low and spending high. By early 1987, euphoric economists were predicting that the Bubble would surpass the Izanagi Boom of 1965 to 1970, when Japan achieved the second-highest gross national product in the free world and Japanese consumers first began to enjoy the "Three Cs" of modern life: cars, color television sets and air-conditioners.

The Bubble money easily found its way into the pockets of consumers, who used the cash to fill their lives with vacations, imported foods, household extravagances and cars. Always new cars; especially luxury cars. Benz (as the Japanese call Mercedes-Benz) was particularly popular. When Benz cars became a status symbol for the *yakuza*, the criminal element, the affluent turned to the new luxury models made by Toyota, Nissan and their competitors.

The Bubble was upsetting years of business and social stability. In Japan, the lifetime sales system, through which an automobile salesman tended to the needs of his customers for years on end, had given the major automakers generally firm market shares over long periods. But the new growth in disposable income (and a change in the tax code which reduced the cost of owning luxury cars) was agitating this delicate balance. Once-loyal customers were defecting to other companies' cars. With only its old workhorses—the Leone subcompact, the Rex minicar and the Sambar microbuses—to sell, Fuji's Subaru division was threatening to sink from view.

The Legacy was supposed to revive the fortunes of the Subaru line. But the Legacy's introduction in 1989 had failed to capture the imagination of the Bubble-crazed public. And now, two years later, Fuji's timing was off again; the Bubble was bursting. Auto sales would finish 1991 down 6.5 percent.

Japan's major automakers were contending with the bursting Bubble by shifting production out of small cars and into more profitable regular-sized cars, while reducing their total production volume. Fuji, still expecting, always so smugly secure, that it would be among the winners, was among the few to increase aggregate production.

Saving Fuji from itself was not the only pressure weighing upon Kosuke Mori. He was also responsible to Dentsu. And even mighty

Dentsu was facing difficulties. "Search for large and complex challenges," President Yoshida admonished in his third guideline. He would have appreciated this one.

The advertising industry soared to even greater heights than the rest of business during the Bubble. The government, under pressure from America and Europe to reduce Japan's surging trade surplus, became advertising's benefactor. Its decision to hoist the value of the yen against the dollar and European currencies drew imported luxury goods to Japan like a magnet. Consumer-goods manufacturers also aided the government in its mission, shifting their attention from exports to the domestic market. All these new wares required advertising. By 1988, in the Bubble's early stages, advertising was accounting for 1.2 percent of the gross national product, up from 1 percent in the earlier part of the decade.

No agency prospered more than Dentsu. It was only fitting. Dentsu was not only the largest agency in Japan, it was the largest agency in the world. Its billings were more than twice those of its nearest competitor, Hakuhodo. But even the billings did not begin to describe its dominance.

Dentsu placed 20 percent of all the newspaper advertisements in Japan and almost 17 percent of all the magazine ads. It produced one-quarter of the eight thousand television commercials broadcast in Japan each year. Because of its supremacy in advertising spending, Dentsu's power over media content was unparalleled; it was said the agency could persuade news organizations not to cover stories harmful to its clients. It even controlled Japan's television ratings system, and allegedly forced from the air programs of which it disapproved by claiming low ratings for them.

What Dentsu could not accomplish indirectly it did directly. The agency was involved in the production of half the prime-time television series, for which it was jokingly called "the editing bureau of Tsukiji." More than 3,800 employees scurried around its Tokyo campus. Hundreds of subcontractors in graphic arts and film production were beholden to the agency. It claimed to have four thousand clients, with three thousand of them cared for by account executives and creatives in Tokyo. The Bubble validated Dentsu's omnipotence. In 1990, billings stood at a record $9.7 billion. Profits rose 29 percent, to $140 million.

But even mighty Dentsu was not immune to the effects of the Burst. In 1989, gross advertising expenditures in Japan rose almost 15 percent. In 1991, expenditures were rising at an anemic 2.9 percent rate. In automotive products, Kosuke Mori's area, the category which more than any other stood for the glories and excesses of the Bubble, spending was basically flat.

Kosuke Mori was keenly aware that he, although one account executive among hundreds, was obligated to help Dentsu through this period of uncertainty. "Lead and set an example for your fellow workers," President Yoshida's sixth guideline admonished.

Mori had to save Fuji Heavy Industries from itself and for Dentsu. Already, Fuji had given the account for its newest car, the replacement for the subcompact Leone, to the Asatsu agency. Hakuhodo handled the Vivio minicar. He could not let the Legacy account fall to a competitor.

It wasn't like the old days, when all he had to do was chat up a client, take him drinking or golfing, to give ballast to an unstable account. Now, account executives were expected to be marketing experts, too. And Kosuke Mori's marketing judgment was: Subaru needed a new image.

Mori knew that a corporate image possessed a surpassing power. Japanese consumers consistently said that the second worst handicap a company faced, after providing poor products or services, was not being known. Shoppers almost always knew the name, the size, the reputation, even the history of the manufacturers that made the products they bought. Some researchers traced this phenomenon to Japan's history as a land-poor agricultural nation, in which dependance on the community and knowledge of its members determined the size of the crop and the community's very survival. Others believed the significance of corporate branding had a more spiritual foundation, grounded in the concept of *wa*, or harmony.

Even before the Legacy launch, Mori had tried to tell Fuji that it needed to renovate its image. But the company resisted. Fuji executives possessed a snobbery that was, to say the least, misplaced. *We manufacture good cars. Our cars are technologically superior. Why aren't they selling?* they would ask. *Excuse me,* Mori would reply, *don't you think that a good car is one that sells?*

Mori knew that, to many people in Japan, the word "Subaru" did not call up technological greatness, but was, instead, virtually synonymous with "minicar." To others, it had no meaning at all. ("If you say 'Toyota' or 'Nissan' or 'Honda,' people immediately have an image," said Amano Yukuchi, the nation's leading advertising critic. "But Fuji Heavy Industries? Subaru? Not too many people have a distinct image of that.") Mori suggested, delicately, that the company establish two sets of dealerships—one for its minicars, the other for its more upscale models—so as not to taint the Legacy with a low-class image. *The cus-*

tomers who buy Legacies are different from the customers who buy the minicars, he told Fuji. *Everything is different—the way the dealer talks to them, the subjects that he brings up. They have nothing in common.* But Fuji did not listen. And the Legacy did not sell.

So, two years into the Legacy launch, Mori went back to Fuji and repeated his argument. To save the Legacy, he told his client, Subaru needed a new image. To his great relief, Fuji now agreed.

The goal image, Yamaguchi-san granted, *is to become a company that makes small cars, not a small-car maker.*

But when they began to discuss ways to change the image, the Fuji executives fell into their old patterns. *Let's talk about four-wheel drive,* they said. *Let's talk about our technology.*

Kosuke Mori could take no more. *Please excuse my vulgar analogy,* he told his client, *but selling a car in the 1990s by talking only about technology is like trying to win a woman by saying you have a large penis—and nothing else. You've got to sell her on your clothes, your mind, your job, your prospects,* not just the size of your cock!

That shut them up. But the lesson was not lost on Mori. As much as Fuji Heavy Industries acceded to the need for a new image for Subaru, no new image could be created without deference to the company's culture. And to understand culture, one had to know history. . . .

WHEN CHIKUHEI NAKAJIMA was born on January 11, 1884, his father was overjoyed. A son! The future of the family business—a wheat farm, indigo plants, silk worms, all in Gunma Prefecture, about 150 kilometers north of Tokyo—was assured. But young Chikuhei disappointed Kumeyoshi Nakajima. From an early age, he told his father, his four younger siblings, anyone who would listen, that he wanted to be a soldier.

His fervor was unsurprising. War with China broke out in Chikuhei's eleventh year. Nationalism rose to a pitch. Soldiers from neighboring families returned to Gunma and told of glorious tragedies and triumphs in Manchuria, the Pescadores, in the Straits of Formosa. Once, Chikuhei left home and traveled to Tokyo on his own, without telling a soul, to take the military academy's entrance examination.

Eventually, his father relented. He allowed his eldest child to forgo the family enterprise. In the spring of 1902, with his family's blessing, young Nakajima returned to Tokyo for sixteen months of hard study. At the end of the period, he passed the officers' qualification test and entered the Naval Academy at Yokosuka Bay.

During Nakajima's four years at the academy, his nation was in turmoil. The Russo-Japanese War was raging. Although Japan's navy was able to vanquish the Russian fleet off the Tsushima Islands, the navy suffered grievous damage, losing ninety-one ships in the war. While growing chary of the vulnerability of large ocean vessels, the young sailor learned that two bicycle mechanics in the United States had flown an engine-powered craft through the air, and landed it safely. Nakajima quickly grew convinced that only superiority in this new form of transportation would secure Japan's safety and, indeed, its supremacy.

Aerial defense was Japan's destiny, Nakajima maintained early in his career, because the Japanese people were light and agile—they were built to fly. Even more significantly, airpower would relieve the pressure on the ragged, war-torn Japanese economy.

Japan is involved in a competition to build ships and more ships, which looks like it will last forever, Nakajima concluded. *One battleship costs millions of yen, which the Japanese people must pay in taxes. Japan has been made poor by competing in the warship race with nations of great wealth. We will be destroyed economically if we continue. If we can build aircraft capable of dropping bombs and launching torpedoes, we will have enough military power to dispense with ships and lighten the population's tax burden. Airplanes are a much more economical way to make our nation strong and stable.*

Nakajima was not shy about sharing his opinions. Nor were his superiors put off by them. Not long after his graduation from the Naval Academy, they named him the Japanese navy's student representative on a joint army-navy commission to study the military uses of balloons. In 1913, Nakajima served on the Naval Aviation Research Committee, and the next year he was appointed chief of the new Yokosuka Naval Aircraft Arsenal, where he supervised the construction of the navy's first charter plane. Nakajima also traveled to France and to the United States. In America, he earned his pilot's license.

Witnessing firsthand the progress the U.S. was making in air transport frightened the young officer. He came to believe more strongly than ever that Japan's national defense could only be assured if its offensive capabilities were second to none. Like General Billy Mitchell in the United States, Nakajima understood this required his nation, Japan, to supersede all others in its aeronautical proficiency. That required a dedication to research, development, manufacturing and, above all, to engineering.

But the Japanese military was too slow, too hidebound, to understand this tenet of survival. *Japan is far behind the Western nations,* Nakajima fretted. *The main reason for this is governmental management. The government decides on aircraft production plans one year and doesn't get around to executing these plans until a year later.* Although a military career was an honorable one, second only to finance in the cultural hierarchy, it was no way to secure his nation's future. *With citizen management we can make plans and improvements many times a year or more. That's the way it is done in the West.* Patriotism demanded that Chikuhei, barely into his thirties, become an industrialist.

On December 12, 1916, Nakajima resigned from the navy. Shortly after, with six younger acolytes, several of them engineers, a few his subordinates at the Yokosuka Arsenal, he founded the Nakajima Aircraft Research Laboratory. He located the company in Ohta, a small city in his beloved Gunma Prefecture. *It is my duty and my vocation to pursue the development of aircraft,* Nakajima told colleagues at the time. *Protecting and defending our motherland must be our most sincere aim.*

Nakajima had it in mind to create around him and his family a *zaibatsu*. These were the giant industrial groups, each controlled primarily by a single family, that united vast financial strength with diversified manufacturing and trading companies, and wielded enormous influence over the government. Several of the *zaibatsu* dated back centuries, although it was only after the Emperor Meiji was forced to open Japan to the West in 1868 and introduce a form of Western capitalism to the country that the *zaibatsu* achieved economic mastery over the nation. For almost a century after the Meiji restoration, little of consequence occurred in the government or private economy without *zaibatsu* involvement.

At the time Nakajima's vision was coalescing, several of the oldest and most powerful groups exercised great authority; the Mitsui, Sumitomo and Mitsubishi *zaibatsu* were well on their way to controlling more than 50 percent of the nation's significant industrial production. But the introduction to Japan of new industrial technologies around the turn of the century, and the stories the Japanese read of Westerners like Henry Ford and Andrew Carnegie, provided ambitious young entrepreneurs opportunities and impetus to dream about vast wealth and power. A youthful engineer named Aikawa Yoshisuke turned his fantasy of a "new *zaibatsu*" into the great Nissan combine. Chikuhei Nakajima had the same objective.

From its founding, Nakajima Aircraft sprouted airplane and engine factories throughout Japan, in a pattern clearly intended, by the company and its patrons in the military and the government, to grant the nation air superiority in any Pacific war. Nakajima Aircraft was instrumental in introducing assembly-line manufacturing and scientific management to the aircraft industry, rationalizing the production process in order to put Japan on a war footing.

Nakajima's dream imbued his company. Japan's supremacy required aeronautical excellence, and to dominate the air, the nation and the company needed new, strong engines and novel aircraft designs. Engineers, particularly those who specialized in engines and materials research, were Nakajima Aircraft's most revered employees. Although the company's headquarters remained in Gunma, its Mitaka facility on Tokyo's outskirts, where its engine research and design center was located, housed its soul.

With backing from the Industrial Bank of Japan, a development bank closely tied to the government, Nakajima Aircraft built one plant a year between 1939 and 1941. It added a spate of additional factories by 1945, at which time the corporation comprised six main factories, twelve construction arsenals and a half-dozen plants under subcontract. Hundreds of other firms cooperated with this new *zaibatsu*. By the time Japan launched its attack on Pearl Harbor in December 1941, Nakajima Aircraft and the older Mitsubishi *zaibatsu* dominated airplane construction. Between them, the two groups accounted for almost 46 percent of the aircraft bodies and 68 percent of the airplane engines made in Japan during the war. Among the planes Nakajima Aircraft wholly or partly produced were the feared *Zerosen*—the deadly Zero fighter.

The war, though, dashed Nakajima's dream. In January 1944, with fighting in the Pacific reaching a crescendo, the Japanese military designated the company a first-class military-supply corporation and took full control of its management. Stripped of his authority, Chikuhei still worked for the glory of his motherland, designing aircraft intended for direct attacks against the American mainland. But before such planes could be built, Allied B-29 bombers struck Ohta, destroying some of Nakajima Aircraft's facilities and damaging others, including the main building which, seen from above, took the form of an eagle with its wings outstretched.

On August 17, 1945, three days after Japan's surrender, the nation's minister of military supplies sent telegrams to the heads of each military supply arsenal informing them of the war's end. The same day, Nakajima reassumed command of his company, which he renamed Fuji, after the beloved national symbol, Mt. Fuji. The company's headquarters were moved from the damaged Gunma complex to the main office of the Industrial Bank of Japan in Tokyo's Maranouchi district. Prevented by the occupational government, the General Headquarters of the Allied Forces, or "GHQ," from designing or building aircraft, the firm dedicated itself to rebuilding a civilian economy for Japan.

But this reformation did not satisfy the occupiers. As the GHQ acclimated to the task of purging Japan of its warlords and rebuilding the economy along Western lines, it soon set its eyes on the former Nakajima Aircraft *zaibatsu*. On July 2, 1946, the GHQ issued a memorandum "proposing" the company's reorganization. Its managers were forced to resign and the company was split into a dozen smaller firms. As part of its policy to dismantle the *zaibatsus'* entrenched authority, the GHQ spread ownership of the companies that once made up Nakajima among dozens of parties. The Industrial Bank, whose executives' jobs, for the most part, the GHQ spared, was a source of financing for many of them.

Using their undamaged industrial capacity and the skills of their engineers and workers, these little Nakajimas tried to adjust to a post-war world in which needs were high but incomes low. One firm specialized in building motor scooters, to give men and women transport over Tokyo's rutted roads. Others manufactured engines to power the new factories that were replacing those destroyed in the war. Still others made buses. To maintain their dignity in the face of their national and corporate humiliation, the staff in these companies continually strove to apply the techniques and standards of aircraft engineering to their new tasks, no matter how humble they seemed.

Eventually, the occupation government loosened its restrictions on Japanese industry. To facilitate innovation and production, companies were allowed to join together. Two former Nakajima factories united to form Prince Motors. And in 1953, five other companies that had been part of the Nakajima *zaibatsu* merged. This new corporation took the name Fuji Heavy Industries. Its symbol was five small stars, linked by beams of light to a larger, gleaming star. This was the *Subaru*, the group of six visible stars known in the West as the Pleiades. In Japanese, *Subaru* means "unite." Written in Chinese characters, it can also be interpreted as "the star that rules."

Fuji Heavy Industries was one of numerous former *zaibatsu* that managed, despite the GHQ's wishes, to recongregate after the war in a different, looser form, called *keiretsu*. Collections of affiliated companies, these new groups were centered not around a single, all-powerful family-controlled holding company, but (generally) around a bank or a trading company. The firms in a *keiretsu* held small percentages of shares in each other. No one firm dominated, but collectively the group's components held the controlling interest in any single company.

The three strongest *keiretsu* were, not surprisingly, remarkably similar in composition to Japan's most powerful prewar *zaibatsu*, and were built around the Mitsubishi, Mitsui and Sumitomo holdings. Diversified, older, not beholden to the government or its banks, these *keiretsu* were well positioned to take advantage of any opportunities that might arise as the Japanese economy was restructured.

Keiretsu constructed from the remnants of the "new *zaibatsu*" were not so lucky. Concentrated around single industries, dependent on government-affiliated banks for financing, they were less able to avail themselves of the entrepreneurial freedoms the new economy presented.

History determined that Fuji Heavy Industries would never compete successfully with its larger, older rivals. "Nakajima ... wasn't resilient enough to cope with the new situations developed after the war," said Naohiro Amaya, a former official of the Ministry of International Trade and Industry (MITI), who negotiated the auto industry's voluntary-restraint agreement in the early 1980s. "Nakajima depended too much on the military. The conversion to the civil industrial economy was pretty difficult for them."

At the center of the Fuji Heavy Industries *keiretsu* was the Industrial Bank of Japan, the bank that had helped finance much of Nakajima's expansion before and during World War II. The Industrial Bank was a private institution, but one intimately linked to the government and its economic wishes. Earlier in the century, the bank was responsible for helping war-related industries, like trucking and aircraft, get the long-term financing they needed to expand but which they could not obtain from the capital markets. The bank became a principal source of financing for many of the newer corporations which were unaffiliated with the old *zaibatsu*.

Although deeply involved in Japan's war effort, the Industrial Bank was not dismantled by the GHQ, which considered finance a less venal occupation than armaments manufacturing. Left relatively intact, the bank became an essential institution in the revival of the Japanese economy. It maintained some of its early privileges—it could issue bonds that other banks could not—but it also kept its special responsibility to aid industries and companies deemed by the government to be of the national interest.

Its wartime affiliations and its postwar obligations led the Industrial Bank into formal alliances with several corporations. When the Nissan combine was broken up by the GHQ, the bank rushed in and bought shares in the reorganized company, becoming one of Nissan's largest shareholders. The bank provided the loans Nissan needed in 1949 to continue operating in the midst of a debilitating strike by the auto company's workers.

In like ways, it supported and bought into Fuji Heavy Industries. By

1956, the Industrial Bank of Japan was Fuji's largest shareholder, with 10 percent of the stock. The Nakajima family held less than 5 percent of the shares. As years passed, the Nakajimas disappeared from the list of major Fuji shareholders. The bank remained among the largest. Over the next three decades, several of Fuji's most senior executives would come not from the ranks of industry, but from the Industrial Bank.

The bank also helped arrange for Nissan's takeover of Prince Motors, another remnant of the Nakajima *zaibatsu* and, like Fuji, a company fanatically devoted to engineering excellence. The Prince merger helped smooth the Industrial Bank's way to bring Fuji into Nissan's fold, which finally occurred when Nissan made a major investment in the smaller manufacturer in 1968. But the Prince merger was an acrimonious affair, a drawn-out battle that ended with the dismantling of Prince's labor union and, uncharacteristically for Japan, the dismissal of numerous workers. The lingering bitterness left Nissan and the Industrial Bank unwilling to force the other, fiercely independent piece of Nakajima into a merger with Nissan.

So Fuji Heavy Industries remained independent, although it came to consider itself the major component in the Industrial Bank's *keiretsu* and a member of Nissan's *keiretsu* as well. Naohiro Amaya described the confederation as "a very loose, little European Community." Its peculiarities were everywhere evident. Years later, when DCA, the tiny Dentsu affiliate in New York, was pitching the Subaru of America account, one of DCA's senior Japanese executives went out and purchased a Nissan Infiniti luxury car. "It was political," he said. "Subaru is in Nissan's group. So I bought an Infiniti Q-45."

No relationship is more important in Japanese business than of a company to its *keiretsu*. The strong groups supported their automobile manufacturers. The entry of the former cork-products firm Toyo Kogyo, called Mazda in the United States, into the motorcycle and then the automotive business would not have been possible without the backing of Sumitomo, whose steel company provided metal at bargain prices and whose bank shored up Mazda when its inefficient rotary engine failed to find an audience during the 1973–74 oil shock.

Fuji's connection to the Industrial Bank of Japan would shape the company's destiny in a way that would prevent it from realizing the grand dreams of its founder. For the bank was a conservative organization, accustomed over the decades to following government policy, not its own initiative. The executives it sent to run Fuji rarely started the company down new paths or brokered dramatic changes. They refused to forge alliances that could help the company find new markets. Although Fuji and Isuzu managed to build a factory together in the

United States, Isuzu's membership in the Dai-Ichi Kangyo Bank's *keiretsu* prevented a more formal affiliation, one that might have gotten Subaru of America the sport-utility vehicles and pickup trucks it later would need so desperately.

Takeshi Higurashi, who joined Fuji after graduating from Hitotsubashi University in 1954 and later rose to the chairmanship of its American importer, explained the Industrial Bank's influence over Fuji succinctly. "A banker does not like drastic change, unless the situation requires it," he said. Because of the Industrial Bank's influence, Fuji was destined to remain a small company, a minor manufacturer, surpassed by both the descendants of the major prewar *zaibatsu* and by newer, entrepreneurial companies like Honda.

Nonetheless, Fuji was left with one bit of residue from the glorious history of Nakajima Aircraft: a burning conviction that engineering was the apogee of the mechanical arts, and that aircraft engineering was its highest manifestation.

Unfortunately, neither Fuji nor its engineers were allowed to work on aircraft. They had to turn their talents elsewhere—to smaller products, like motor scooters. Fuji began building motor scooters immediately after the war. In 1946, even before the company was split apart by the GHQ, an engineer in the Oizumi plant, in Gunma, realized that the monocoque, chassis-less, construction of an airplane's fuselage could apply well to the manufacture of passenger buses. That summer, buses started rolling out of Oizumi.

Some in the Japanese government were content with this development. Other forces, however, wanted more than buses. In 1955, MITI announced through the *Asahi Shinbun* newspaper a competition for manufacturers to develop a Japanese Volkswagen. MITI wanted to spur the development of a domestic and, eventually, export-oriented auto industry. The ministry believed that a "people's car" was a necessary first step.

MITI decreed that the vehicle should hold four passengers, have an engine displacement of no more than 500 cubic centimeters, be able to reach a cruising speed of 60 kilometers an hour and a top speed of 100 kilometers an hour, and get gas mileage of 30 kilometers a gallon. Among several additional requirements, MITI wanted a car that could be built for ¥150,000, or $417. It also wanted a company capable of manufacturing 24,000 cars a year.

The contest excited little interest. The smaller manufacturers already made three-wheel minicars—covered motorcycles, really—and they saw no reason to cut into their own businesses. Several of the major automobile manufacturers were adjusting to the postwar economy by establishing joint development arrangements with larger, better-financed foreign producers; these companies did not want to jeopardize the ventures or steal time from them. It was also unclear what, if anything, a company would gain by winning the minicar competition. There were hints of government financial aid, but with the government and the banks divided within themselves over the future of the auto industry, the offers seemed insubstantial.

Fuji, eager to reassert its primacy, accepted the challenge. It was a chance to show the nation that the spirit and ingenuity of Nakajima still lived. The company mobilized employees at the Isesaki plant, in Gunma, to start research on frame design and materials. They developed a lightweight body by employing the monocoque design, aluminum alloys and plastics they knew from aircraft construction.

The engine, which was to be based on the company's existing motorscooter engine, was to be designed and built at Mitaka. Technicians there called the challenge "The Great Adventure."

Organization of the task fell to an engineer named Momose, who had started at the company in the aircraft division. Under him, a project team began experimenting with engine design. At the time, engines under 500 cubic centimeters were thought too small to propel a four-passenger car. Momose's men found a way to move the engine and transmission from the front to the rear of the vehicle, thereby reducing the car's length and weight and making it light enough for a 360-cubic-centimeter engine to power. The rear engine also increased the vehicle's interior space by eliminating the drive shaft, which in other cars ran from a front engine to the rear axle. Momose's team also positioned the engine in a strikingly unconventional way; they placed it in the vehicle sideways, in a configuration the company would later call "horizontally opposed." This lessened the space needed to contain the engine block and added room to the passenger compartment. The engine designers also experimented over and over with methods to prevent carbon clogging in the exhaust vents, eventually settling on a system of air cooling to improve heat distribution and alleviate the problem.

For his efforts, which continued for months, seven days a week, hour upon hour, his colleagues in Mitaka bestowed on Momose a nickname. They called him "Endless." To them, "Endless" Momose was the personification of the old Nakajima ardor.

Fuji dubbed its prototype car "The Ladybug." In the winter of 1956, MITI designated it the winner of its people's-car competition. Emboldened, Fuji quickly set about putting the vehicle into production. On March 3, 1958, it was unveiled to the public with a new name, the Subaru 360, at the Shirogiya Department Store in Tokyo's Nihonbashi district. In May, the car went on sale. The little vehicle quickly became a national hit. Several celebrities (including the head of Matsushita, the electronics firm, and Yama Yoshiba, the sumo wrestler) purchased one. The Subaru 360 sold about a thousand units its first year of production, and nearly six thousand units in its second year.

To Fuji, the victory in the minicar contest, a competition forsworn by the larger, richer manufacturers, validated the company's heritage. No challenge was too severe for Fuji's engineers. Engineers could conquer all!

Fuji's engineers disdained the methods rival companies used to make cars. Others finished crankshaft pins on lathes; Fuji's engineers finished them by hand, using fine powder and leather belts, to prevent the pins from sticking at high speeds—as they had done on airplane engines during the war.

That the engineering spirit ruled Fuji Heavy Industries was made clear to everyone who accepted employment at the company. When Yasuo Furuno, a young marketing planner, joined Fuji in the 1950s, a senior manager, meaning to be helpful, informed him: *You have come to the engineer's kingdom, so you will never be the president or a director.*

For years to come, Fuji Heavy Industries would respond best to technical challenges, but hardly at all to market needs. Did the electric company require a four-wheel-drive passenger car? Fuji would build it. Did Tokyo want a beautiful sedan? That was Toyota's province; Fuji was not interested. Such haughty dismissal of market demands and styling requirements was unusual in the Japanese auto industry, which tended to favor design over function. As early as the late 1950s, Toyota was sending survey teams to the United States to investigate the desires and gaps in the American auto market. Fuji's sales force and its marketing executives were rarely if ever consulted about what consumers wanted in their cars, either at home in Japan or abroad. The engineers knew best.

"Many engineers believe that engineering, not styling, is the best element of the car," Furuno, the marketing executive, came to understand. "They believe the best-engineered car should be the best-selling car. They believe that design should facilitate the engineering, not the other way around. If there is one best way for the suspension to be, the design should promote that, not be irrelevant to that. How the tire steers, how the tire stops, the door design, the door dimensions—what is necessary should be decided from the engineering point of view."

It was a recipe for irrelevance.

In 1967, Honda, until then a successful motorcycle manufacturer with backing from the Mitsubishi *keiretsu*, began selling a minicar which it dubbed the N360. The vehicle had a four-stroke engine, more powerful than the two-stroke engine in the Subaru 360. Honda positioned its faster vehicle as a car for young people, consumers who were ready to step up from its motorcycles. Fuji decided not to battle Honda for the youth market, but to position its automobiles as family cars—a "changeless change," in the company's terminology, that would assure it a lasting place in the market.

Fuji's decision (which had the miserly Industrial Bank's blessing) meant that the company would not invest in faster engines or modern body styling. A family-car manufacturer had no need to do so. Like Volkswagen in the 1960s and Ford in the 1920s, Fuji believed that functional engineering was all it had to provide consumers. Ford, of course, was overtaken by the more stylish cars of General Motors, and Volkswagen was superseded in the United States by the small luxuries offered by Toyota and Nissan. In the same way, Fuji's Subaru line lost its primacy in the Japanese domestic market. The company became a niche manufacturer, saved from obscurity only by its willingness to build odd cars, like its four-wheel-drive wagons, in which other manufacturers were not interested. Indeed, the wagon was the symbol of Fuji's self-image: inexpensive and drab, but invisibly superior.

Inside Fuji, employees would always think of the company as the avatar of automotive technology. Among the Japanese public, though, Subaru's cars, and its drivers, possessed a quite different image: dreary, durable autos for farmers, shopkeepers and middle-aged white-collar dullards.

"The average diehard Subaru enthusiast," said Aritsune Todaiji, Japan's leading auto critic, "is between the ages of forty and fifty, he is a college graduate, he is employed in a relatively intellectual profession—engineers, schoolteachers, all types of journalists. His children have grown up, he is a nature lover, and that leads him to believe that in some cases it's not good to drive cars in general."

It was the same image and the same market Subaru had in the United States, right down to the teachers and engineers the Baltimore ad agency W. B. Doner had identified in its market research. Which was no surprise: This was the image Fuji's own technicians had been building into the vehicles since 1958.

AS HE REVIEWED Fuji's history, a solution became clear to Kosuke Mori. First, the new Subaru campaign should focus not on the Legacy sedan, but on the Legacy wagon. Station wagons were not glamorous, but they were what Subaru was about, after all. Then, get an American celebrity to serve as the company's spokesman, because clients liked it when Western celebrities endorsed their products, considering it a validation of their place in the social hierarchy. (Dentsu hired Bruce Willis, the star of the *Die Hard* action movies, and provided him with the slogan "I think in my Legacy.") Finally, Dentsu's advertising for Subaru, although stylishly filmed in American settings, still concentrated, at least obliquely, on the company's engineering—its turbo-powered engine, in the horizontally opposed configuration, that powered the four-wheel-drive transmission. Sales went up, too, nearly doubling to ten thousand vehicles a month before too long, because Fuji and its Subaru sales force were so excited by the new ads.

For Mori knew an essential rule of advertising, one not listed in President Yoshida's guidelines: history equals culture equals destiny. A corporate image, he understood, is formed by the collective beliefs of all the men and women who make, sell, buy and contribute to a product.

Or, put another way, perception is reality—although not the consumer's perception, but the client's.

Or, rendered even more simply: The client is always right.

Chapter 22

Have It Your Way

THE NEW YEAR DAWNED anything but happy. Subaru's total sales for January fell well below those for the same month in 1991: 5,621 cars vs. 7,064. February, despite its Presidents Day hoopla, did not herald a pickup: Subaru's dealers sold 7,284 autos, down from 8,054 in the war-jittery month of February 1991.

S.O.A.'s market share was also sliding, to 1.1 percent of the American car market, down from 1.3 percent in 1991. The company's inventory was so high—50,500 cars on January 1—that on a per-dealer basis it had more unsold vehicles than any other manufacturer, a 224-day supply, against an industry average of 78 days. Fuji Heavy Industries, though, gave no indication that it planned to curtail production. By the middle of February, the SIA plant in Indiana had already churned out more than 6,300 Legacies, almost the same number as a year earlier.

More ominous yet was how Japan was reacting to the continuing pressure from the U.S. government and automakers to redress its trade surplus with the U.S. In mid-February, the Ministry of International Trade and Industry disclosed that it planned to reduce Japan's "voluntary" export quota to the United States, from 2.3 million vehicles a year to 1.6 million or 1.7 million. On the surface, this news appeared salutary; perhaps now Fuji would be forced to curb production and stop contributing to S.O.A.'s excess inventory. But in fact, any reduction in Fuji's export allocation could damage S.O.A. irreparably. If MITI cut Fuji's exports to a level commensurate with its recent American sales, the company might never be able to export enough cars to return it to profitability in the United States. It would be doomed to life—and death—at the industry's margins.

The company's smallest competitor provided an inauspicious foundation for its fears. Daihatsu, Japan's tiniest auto exporter, announced al-

most simultaneously with MITI's disclosure that after four years of
trying, it was ceasing auto sales in the United States. Industry watchers
said the company had little choice; without volume, a bantam's chances
of battling the Toyotas and Nissans and turning a profit were slim.
Openly, auto executives, analysts and dealers began to question whether
Subaru was next.

In the midst of all the melancholy, a curious thing happened. Both
Advertising Age and *Adweek*, the two leading marketing trade publications, named Wieden & Kennedy their Agency of the Year. *Ad Age*
(which was known on Madison Avenue as the "clients' magazine," and
thus packed the most clout) commended Wieden & Kennedy's "artistry
in generating and maintaining creative momentum during an economic
recession." The magazine called the agency's work "brilliant" and
claimed for it a "special creative 'voice.' "

The journal did not exempt the Subaru campaign, however controversial it might have been on the inside, from its praise. "Its first campaign
for this highly visible client brought a refreshing new voice and a knowing, candid premise to automotive advertising," *Ad Age* maintained.
"With the Subaru work, Wieden laid to rest any lingering notion it was
a one-trick pony."

The magazines were merely certifying what the ad industry was already demonstrating. Creative copycats were beginning to storm over
the Subaru campaign, appropriating its "honest" tone and many of its
fillips and flourishes. On-screen scrolling type, a device that Wieden &
Kennedy insisted on maintaining through the national image ads, became a particularly pronounced creative rage, with giant corporations
like Coca-Cola and AT&T among the many to float, spiral and unravel
written words on the couch-bounds' cathode-ray tubes.

The accolades had a curious effect on Wieden & Kennedy. Publicly,
they filled the agency's personnel with renewed bravado, a we-can-do-
anything spirit that bordered on arrogance. Privately, several of the
shop's leaders, especially in the Philadelphia office, wondered why, if
their work was so fresh and so vibrant, it was having so little effect—on
consumers and on Subaru's people.

The reactions of Subaru and its far-flung constituencies varied. Some
headquarters executives thought Wieden & Kennedy's accolades might
help validate the campaign and buy them some time to develop new
marketing and advertising strategies. But in the field, more than a few
dealers seethed. All the praise for the agency's creativity and originality
supported their contention that the agency was interested only in winning awards, not in selling cars.

Whatever criticism there was fell, not surprisingly, on Chris

Wackman. For dealers, RVPs and the sales department in Cherry Hill, he was the likeliest scapegoat. If the agency's advertisements did not contain a call to action, the blame was his. If they did not signal urgency, he was accountable. If they showed no understanding of Subaru, Chris was the reason.

Chris, of course, had no one to lash out at but the agency. And although it was in his character to find forgiveness, not fault, even he began to chafe under the barrage of bad industrial news and his agency's unwillingness to bend even a little to the ill tidings thrust its—and his—way.

"It's something that we as a company have to face up to," he said, venting his frustrations over an amber beer at Zip City Brewery, a New York pub, one day in late March. "I think Wieden & Kennedy has to be maybe a little bit more aware of the political surroundings and just the whole climate we're dealing with." Chris was willing to share the blame for the complaints lodged against the agency and its poor relations with the field; S.O.A. had to "loosen up a little bit more," he conceded, and recognize that there was a difference between "dancing with the girl across the street and moving in with her." But the agency's lack of automotive experience and the relationship-building that necessarily came with it were proving, Chris believed, a severe hindrance.

"They've got to recognize that cars are not sneakers and that there is a whole new dynamic going on here."

Chris was willing to exempt most of the agency from his dissatisfaction. He had, in fact, a specific object in mind: the creative department and what he now saw as its disdain for selling—for selling cars, in particular.

"I think Jerry and Vince are still coming at this as purist creative directors," he said. " 'I'm creating something for a brand and that brand could be automobiles or that brand could be dog food.' . . . I think it's real important that they get out to dealerships and talk with not only dealers, but kind of follow through and see how a transaction happens, and spend some time in the service department talking to some mechanics who can tell them, 'Oh, this is the easiest car to work on,' or, 'Look how this is placed.' " Jerry Cronin, especially, disdained such efforts. He would rather trash an entire speculative campaign than tinker with it to sell it through to the dealers and the regions. Chris dwelled on the creative director's attitude. "It takes somebody who can get up in front of a room with some storyboards and kind of 'gee' and 'jaw' and sell that stuff in, and if the dealers ain't buyin', got to be quick enough to pull back and say, 'Hmmm, you ain't buyin' this shit, are you? Okay, well, what do you want to do?'" Jerry, clearly, could not do that.

Chris returned to his more natural, conciliatory state. "It's not just us," he said of S.O.A.'s unhappiness. "The agency's feeling is the same—that we're not hitting grand slams here. We may be hitting doubles, we may be doing a couple of triples, but we are not emptying the bases. And we need to do that."

The need grew even more severe a short while later. On March 31, the *Wall Street Journal*'s advertising columnist ran her second story in eight months attacking the Subaru campaign. Headlined "Subaru's New Ad Campaign Isn't Working," the column, like the newspaper's earlier salvo against the company's SVX ads, omitted data that would have softened the conclusion. The columnist noted that Subaru's market share had slipped in the fourth quarter of 1991, after Wieden & Kennedy's campaign was introduced, but failed to record that S.O.A. had eliminated most of its national advertising in the last few months of 1991 and had finished the year up a tenth of a share point anyway. Subaru's volume was off 3.2 percent for the year, but that was far better than the average drop of 4.6 percent for all Japanese cars. Most galling of all, in March, sales of the Subaru Legacy (the vehicle that was, after all, the primary subject of the new campaign) finally appeared to be turning a corner—up 42 percent from a year before, the best month for the Legacy in a year and a half. The *Journal*'s ad columnist included none of these numbers.

Nor did the data make any difference to Subaru's embattled sales department and the dealers with whom they wrestled. Journalists are the gatekeepers of the nation's opinions, however flawed those opinions may be. On the day the *Wall Street Journal*'s column appeared, a Wieden & Kennedy account executive showed up for a meeting at S.O.A.'s Penn/Jersey regional sales office in Pennsauken. The RVP in charge of the region greeted the account exec by throwing down the newspaper and shouting, *You see? We told you the campaign wasn't working.*

A reassessment of Subaru's image and its ad campaign was now no longer an academic exercise. If open corporate rebellion were to be averted, it was a requirement.

"OKAY, WHAT I WANT you to do now is introduce yourself to the person next to you and make a friend for five minutes, and then I'll ask you to introduce your new friend to the group."

The eight women complied, punctuating their chatter with laughs. There was nothing in the room to distract them. It was purposefully bland, its mottled walls, gray carpeting, blond oval table and blue fabric chairs designed to facilitate conversation by giving no resting place for wandering eyes. Lisa, their leader and the ninth woman in the chamber, was attired in like fashion, in an ochre turtleneck and black slacks; aside from the flaming red hair that fell in curls below her shoulders, she was utterly indistinct.

The point of a focus group, after all, was to get people to focus. And Wieden & Kennedy had trekked north from Portland, to an unadorned low-rise office building adjacent to an undistinguished intersection in a nondescript suburb of Seattle, to get people to focus on cars.

The eight women constituted the first of twelve focus groups the advertising agency planned to convene, four each in Seattle, Chicago and Atlanta. The overt purpose was to determine whether the agency's advertising was having its intended effect on various types of consumers and to glean insights that would help it shape the next phase of the campaign.

From their meeting after Tom Gibson killed the proposed "Official car of the recession" campaign, the advertising people knew that the next generation of ads would have to focus on engineering. But what aspects of engineering? Which attributes, if any? And in what tone of voice? Watching and listening to real consumers would presumably provide some answers.

Covertly, though, the ad executives also hoped to use the focus groups to gain more control over the content and direction of their advertising. The prospect of an engineering-oriented campaign filled many at Wieden & Kennedy with dread. *Engineering? Technical details? Jargon? That's more of the bullshit about cars that consumers don't trust anymore.* Perhaps the focus groups would give them the evidence they needed to modify the plan.

Chris Riley, Wieden & Kennedy's planning director, knew the agency stood to benefit from convening the groups, and had politicked assiduously for months to get S.O.A. to finance the research. He knew that his agency's campaign for Subaru was too new to have had any substantial impact on public perceptions. Thus, any judgments about Subaru to emerge from the focus groups would probably reflect the company's long-standing image in the public mind—and match the conclusions from the research the agency had conducted in pitching the account. In short, Wieden & Kennedy expected the focus groups to endorse its handling of the campaign and allow it to fashion the new ads according to its own, not Subaru's, whims.

Riley was among the seven men and women crowded into a small chamber that was separated from the meeting room by a one-way mirror. He was joined by another account planner whom he had recently hired to work full-time in Wieden & Kennedy's Philadelphia office, the account executive who handled Subaru's western regions for the agency, an executive from S.O.A.'s northwestern regional office; another "facilitator" (as focus group moderators are called) from the company Riley had hired to conduct the groups; a young man who was videotaping the proceedings and Mary Ellen Smith, a marketing research executive with S.O.A. in Cherry Hill.

In front of the mirror, their introductory conversations over, the eight women in the focus group prepared to introduce each other to their momentary colleagues. They knew they were there to discuss cars; their names had been culled from lists of people between the ages of twenty-five and thirty-nine who were in the market for a new one, and they were offered about $50 each to discuss the process. They did not know they were chosen specifically because the Subaru Legacy was *not* on the list of models they were considering.

Helen, an animated woman, introduced Elizabeth, who seemed quiet and serious. "She's a little concerned," Helen said, "that she's the only one here without kids. She's an environmentalist, so she likes clean cars." Elizabeth, in turn, described Helen as having "two kids and three cars, two of them Japanese, and they're on their last legs." Patty, a trim woman who wore a running suit, introduced Karen, a heavy-set woman. "Karen works at a financial institution. She has two grown children and drives a Honda." Of Patty, Karen said only: "She runs a swim school." Jenny, a bland woman, and Susan, an articulate but subdued type, said even less about each other, and Cheri and Christy merely mentioned the number of each other's children.

There seemed to be no bellyacher in the group, no one loquacious individual who dominates a session with complaints and sends the conversation veering off into uncharted and barren territory. Research professionals were familiar with the type—Mary Ellen Smith of Subaru called them "Jessicas," after a colleague of hers—and the observers were relieved that none was present. Nor were there any actresses. In New York City, where it was difficult to find real people to give up two or three hours of an evening, research companies were known to keep lists of theatrical professionals who could play the role of Mr. or Ms. Consumer for unsuspecting clients behind the mirror.

There were also no focus group veterans. A subsequent Seattle group would include members who had recently participated in discussions about talk radio, flower arranging and mushrooms. But these women were unaccustomed to sharing their thoughts with strangers. So Lisa, the facilitator, decided to draw them out immediately on the subject of the moment. "What is the role of the car in your life?" she asked. "Thinking back ten years, in the broadest sense, was it different?"

The women grew animated. "With kids," Christy volunteered, to nods from several others, "the car always serves the same purpose."

Helen, the most talkative of the group, took the facilitator's role. "What about pre-kids?" She answered her own query: "Pre-kids, it was more flash."

"I got a kid and a car at the same time, so I don't think I was ever into image," Cheri said.

"When you have kids," said Susan, "you don't have a two-door."

Lisa pushed them to abandon the practicality of the present, to imagine a future when the children were grown and their fantasies could reign.

It was a difficult assignment, if Christy's response was any indication. "I drove with some friends in a little Honda," she recounted. "Every time you stopped to buy something you strangled yourself in the shoulder harness getting in and out."

Lisa tried again. "Do me a favor," she requested. "Close your eyes and just imagine what it's like to have a new car. What does it feel like when you're in the car? What gives you the most pleasure?"

This tactic began to bear results. "I can see a nice high-tech dash. Leather. I want something real tactile," Karen replied.

"What does a high-tech dash *mean* to you?" Lisa prodded.

"A reward," Karen answered.

The facilitator looked around the table. "Do others feel that way?"

"Yes," said Helen. "You feel *pride*."

Lisa continued the line of inquiry. "I want to put you through a game. I want you to think of the feelings and emotions of each stage of this process—before, during and after shopping for a car. I want you to talk with each other and put it down on yellow lined pads, huddling together in teams."

The women shifted their chairs and paired off. Amid subdued conversation, occasional murmurs of "yes" and "it's exciting" and "it's overwhelming" could be heard. After five minutes, Lisa called their efforts to a halt and asked what they had found.

"We all agreed that it's simultaneous excitement and dread," Jenny responded.

"What's worst about it?" Lisa wondered.

The eight women shouted in unison. "Dealers!"

Animus toward dealers was, indeed, the residue of car shopping, the experience's toxic waste. There was not an automotive advertising executive in the land who hadn't heard the protests voiced in focus group after focus group, and sat back, helpless to do anything about a dilemma that bedeviled every manufacturer from Ford to Hyundai. These women were no different from any other subjects. They complained about "gamesmanship" and "screwing," they talked of their "vulnerability" when buying and their "remorse" after they had bought.

All of this was interesting, in a prurient sort of way, but it was also meaningless. The Wieden & Kennedy and Subaru representatives had heard it all before, and what they heard applied equally to all automakers. What they wanted to know, needed to know, was how Subaru and its advertising stacked up against other brands. Lisa, sufficiently persuaded by now of the group's comfort level, eased it into this territory.

"Tell me all the car brands you can think of," she said. "Just shout them out. I'll write them down."

Tentatively at first, then with more gusto, names—some of manufacturers, others with models attached—came tumbling from the women's lips. Ford Explorer, Dodge Caravan, Plymouth Voyager, Chevy Suburban—if there was a pattern to their list, it showed they were child-centered, and favored the minivans and 4x4s that had replaced the station wagons of their mothers' generation. But as the roster grew, so did the diversity of the names. Chrysler. Honda. Buick. Mercury. Nissan. Volvo. Volkswagen. Mazda. Toyota. Quietly, someone said Subaru.

Lisa wrote the names (with Isuzu, Hyundai and Geo thrown in, as a last gesture, by Helen) on individual cards with a black marking pen. She then asked Jenny, a former schoolteacher, to lead the group in a categorization game. Organize the manufacturers into groups, as many as you want, in any way that makes sense, Lisa instructed them, but be prepared to explain the criteria. "You have two minutes," she said.

For all their earlier tentativeness, the women proved quite adept at the exercise. When they stumbled, it was over topics that troubled even seasoned car guys—"Should Geo be grouped with foreign or domestic?"—and when finished, their "brand sorts" (as research pros termed the ritual) proved remarkably coherent.

The women had divided the manufacturers into four groups: "Basic Expensive Cars," "Basic American Cars," "Basic Quality Japanese" and "Cheap Stuff." In the first group, they placed Infiniti and Volvo. "Expensive," "classy," "safe" and "yuppie" were the words they used to describe them. The "Basic American Cars" included Chevy, Olds, Buick, Jeep and Mercury; their descriptors included "stability," "midsized on up," "family," "grandma and grandpa," and "boring." Hyundai and Geo were identified as "Cheap Cars"; among their attributes were "good mileage," "inexpensive" and "kinda cute."

The "Basic Japanese Cars" were, after some debate, divided into two subcategories. The first, comprising Mazda, Mitsubishi and (inappropriately) Volkswagen, were "not quite as reliable," "I don't know much about those" and "less known." The second category, which held Nissan, Honda, Toyota and Subaru, were "workhorses," "fairly small," "nice," "affordable" and "they start things first and the Americans follow."

All in all, not a bad place for Subaru to be, and again, not terribly enlightening to the advertiser or the agency. The "brand sorts" tended to match the broad categories found in other surveys, including syndicated research. What was important was how consumers saw themselves in relation to the classifications. To elicit that information, Lisa engaged the women in another game. She again divided them into groups of two, gave each pair a card with a single brand name on it, and instructed the participants to develop a stereotype of the brand's owner and act out that stereotype, in a verbal version of charades, for the others to guess.

Jenny took a card. "Single woman," she offered. "Educated. Modern. Conservative in dress. Has a medium-small dog. Healthy. Has quite a social life and uses the car a lot."

Helen, the chatty one, responded. "Sounds like me. Sounds like Honda." And it was.

Cheri went next. "Great family car. Outdoor activities. People who insist on buying American. Bigger people. People who go camping. Bacon and eggs for breakfast. Middle-aged. Financially secure." The answer came back severally: Ford vans.

Helen took a turn. She looked at her card and launched into a stereotype. "They're outdoorsy. They're interested in fuel economy. They're athletic—they like to ski and bicycle. They could be a teacher or an engineer."

This time, Cheri leapt in with the answer. "That's easy. Subaru. That's the person they target in the ads."

"What would we like about that person?" Lisa asked.

"They're free. They can do what they want," answered Jenny, a bit wistfully.

"What don't we like about them?"

"They're free," wisecracked Cheri.

Behind the glass, Chris Riley perked up. Here in the Pacific Northwest, Subaru's image was just what it always had been. But Subaru drivers were seen to boast a degree of self-possession that other consumers found enviable. It was just what the agency had been telling its client since last summer.

Cheri's mention of advertising allowed Lisa to shift the discussion in that direction. She asked the women if they recalled any auto advertisements. Immediately, television commercial plots and themes (print ads are rarely recalled spontaneously) tumbled forth: "This is not your father's Oldsmobile"; a Nissan spot in which a man named Bob fantasized a world made especially for him; a Volvo advertisement extolling the car's safety in crash tests.

"Can you remember any ads for the cars we've discussed here?" Lisa asked.

Helen did. "I remember the Subaru ad"—the crew behind the mirror perked up—"with the old ugly one in the garage and the new one." The crew behind the mirror perked down; the "farmboy" commercial for the Subaru XT had not appeared on television for nearly five years.

The time had come for the centerpiece of the session: the advertising itself. Two by two, Lisa played contemporary auto commercials on a large-screen TV, and followed by asking the women to share their impressions.

She played the Volvo crash-test commercial, then a Honda spot that showed a sleek Accord moving with clocklike precision on a turntable as music simulating the ticking of a watch played in the background. The spot was obviously created to showcase the Honda's workmanship, but it also elicited a few groans. "The music—it's so *annoying*!" one woman said. The Volvo ad also had detractors. "The front smashes and the back smashes, but you never see anyone walk out," another participant complained.

Lisa ran two more spots. One, for Volkswagen, publicized its financing scheme that guaranteed to underwrite buyers' VW payments if they got laid off from their jobs. The other was Subaru's several-months'-old national image spot for the Legacy, the satirical take on luxury car buyers' inner fantasies. The VW ad met skepticism—"I wonder about the hidden costs," Christy mused—and outright hostility. "The word 'layoff' really turned me off," Helen said.

What about the other one, Lisa asked them? "What does it say about Subaru?"

Christy ventured a response. "They're saying, 'Go beyond the feelings.' Besides the feelings, you have a dependable car."

Lisa pushed them for more. "Which ad talked most directly to you?"

"Subaru. I can see me in there. And other people I know," answered Elizabeth, who was more sober and reflective than the others.

But it was Susan who told the invisible men and women behind the mirror what they wanted to hear. After watching several other commercials created by Wieden & Kennedy, she counted herself a convert.

"When we did the first groupings"—the brand sorts—"I would never have looked at a Subaru. But the Subaru ads, they make me think I'll look at a Subaru the next time I'm looking for a car."

AS ONE GROUP LED TO ANOTHER, then another, as the observers wound their way east and south across America, the reaction was largely the same. Subaru Legacy owners (who made up three of the twelve groups) loved the advertising and found it reinforcing. "It's the BBC approach to advertising," said one man, praising the intelligence and the wit. Although some found the humor a bit overwhelming—"It just made me think it was a good ad," was one northwesterner's response—others believed it served its intended purpose. "It's a good imaging thing for people who think Subarus are cheap cars," said a fellow who placed himself in that category.

But what the focus group participants *didn't* say was equally important. After completing the sessions and reviewing the tapes, the company that conducted the research gave its final report to S.O.A. and Wieden & Kennedy. Although S.O.A. was becoming successful in building a "context" for wider recognition of the Subaru name, the researchers concluded, it was still not providing drivers with anything concrete with which to identify the company and its products. In particular, the researchers found in the reactions to the commercials little evidence that consumers had learned anything about Subaru's cars. They found that while the ads appealed to people's rational sides, the work did little to touch their emotions or egos, which played important roles in directing consumers away from some cars and toward others. And while most people appreciated the humor in the television and print ads, for the most part they did not understand it.

"The net effect," the researchers determined, "was that Subaru makes entertaining commercials."

Chris Riley, the skinny Brit whom S.O.A. trusted more than it ever had any other ad agency researcher, took from the focus groups a more positive conclusion. The message from Helen, Elizabeth, Jenny, Susan, Christy, Cheri, Karen, Patty and the hundred-odd other discussants was: Stay the course! Don't get dragged into the mire of conventional auto advertising. The current advertising was successfully broadening Subaru's quirky allure. If the campaign appealed to the head at the expense of the heart, all it needed, Riley believed, was a stronger emphasis on the consumer, not the machine. After all, in the original brief Riley presented to S.O.A. back in June—"The Subaru Legacy is for people who know their car is only a machine. But what a machine!"—people came first.

"Reemphasize the brief," Riley said after one focus group. "Reinstitute the focus on the consumer."

Subaru of America, however, was looking beyond, or perhaps over, the focus groups, to the drumbeat of demands it was hearing from its regions and dealers and from its Japanese owners. Those entreaties were consistent and loud: Show the car. Talk about engineering. Tell people who we *are*.

Chris Wackman rendered the final judgment. "We've come to the conclusion that in order to help bring our image back to where it really was in the early eighties, when we had a car that people absolutely revered, that we've got to show them more of what's under the hood. And show them that there is a lot more behind the car than what they just see looking at it."

WIEDEN & KENNEDY accepted the task of reconciling its own consumer-focused brief and Subaru's functional-engineering requirements without relish. With one campaign—the regional "Jim" spots—reviled and several others drowned before birth, the agency was nothing if not skeptical about the client's ability, let alone willingness, to greet new recommendations with anything other than argument or complaint. The shop signed on with Subaru believing it could provide the same creative direction it had supplied Nike. It now realized that, in automotive accounts, mediocrity tugged at advertising like the North Pole at a compass needle.

"We have to pull the utilitarian image into good, functional engineering. What's tough for us is, it's a real hard area for us to break through the clutter," Dave Luhr fretted. "It has a tendency to be boring advertising. And people perceive Japanese cars to be the same. We have to get through that."

To prepare for the challenge, the advertising agency did something it should have done nine months earlier. It hired a resident car guy for the Philadelphia office, an automotive expert versed more in torque and gear ratios than in the politics of advertising. "I now understand where the power in this company is," Luhr admitted. "It's with the engineers. So now we have somebody who can talk to the engineers."

Out in Portland, Chris Riley prepared a revised brief for the Philadelphians, a one-page guide to the ad campaign's next phase that tried to satisfy the conflicting requirements of the agency, the client, and the client's various factions.

"What is the issue that the advertising must address?" the brief asked. That was simple: "The Subaru image—while positive—does not reflect the full strength of the products themselves."

"Who are we talking to?" the brief went on. Riley provided the same invented jargon he used nearly a year earlier: "Role-relaxed people who are pragmatic and responsible in their decision-making."

"What do we want them to do as a result of the advertising?" the brief concluded. The answer: "To realize that Subaru (Legacy) is the better machine, using all-wheel drive (and its multipurpose applications) as the lead example of functional engineering."

The creative department took the brief. After one false start (a campaign entitled "Engineers" that was filled with mechanical gibberish provided by Wieden & Kennedy's new car guy, and which even dared feature Japanese auto engineers) the agency was ready with its new campaign. It scheduled a presentation to Subaru on April 23, one year and one week after S.O.A. commenced the search that led it to Wieden & Kennedy.

For all the miscues, missed signals and mistakes in its relationship with Subaru, the one element over which Wieden & Kennedy had no control was presentation dates. This was unfortunate, for Subaru's senior executives had a habit of springing bad news on their subordinates, especially the cantankerous regional vice presidents, just prior to Wieden & Kennedy presentations.

As the agency went blithely on its way preparing a new national campaign for the car company, Tom Gibson, S.O.A.'s president, was nearing an unhappy decision. Ever since MITI had made it known that it intended to cut the Japanese auto companies' export quotas to the United States, Fuji Heavy Industries had waited to see whether it would be granted relief. In early April, the answer was communicated—as ever, indirectly—to Fuji's management, and by them to S.O.A. Fuji's future quota, it appeared, was going to be based on the number of cars it exported to the United States in 1992.

The problem was, beginning in 1993, Fuji was planning to send a new subcompact to the States to replace the Leone/Loyale. The new, as-yet-unnamed vehicle was supposed to be a car that would sell in volume and bring new profits to S.O.A., its dealers and its manufacturer. To protect the 1993 quota, Fuji decided that S.O.A. had to take more cars—between thirty and forty thousand more cars—from the manufacturer. Immediately. And unload them on its dealers, in a down market for automobiles, in the middle of a recession.

Gibson argued with his superiors. The new sales goals were unrealistic, he told them, and unrealizable. Worse, they virtually guaranteed that S.O.A. would be left with an inventory of unsold 1992 cars just as the 1993 model year was beginning and the new subcompact was coming in. The directive heralded a repeat of 1989, when the inventory of Loyales prevented Subaru from launching the Legacy with fanfare.

Fuji, as ever, was unyielding and Gibson acquiesced. "You play poker every day for real big stakes in this business," he sighed. "Only you play the hand three years before you see the results." The good soldier, he delivered the message—"For me to get the quota I need, I need to pump out a lot of iron"—to his RVPs, the men in charge of selling cars to dealers, the day before Wieden & Kennedy's presentation.

Agitated, fearing for their jobs, the RVPs joined other senior Subaru executives and several Wieden & Kennedy staffers for dinner that night. Chuck Worrell, the senior vice president for sales, addressed the dissension in the company with a toast. *Everyone's been talking behind everyone else's back in this company,* he said to the assemblage, his drink raised. *Tomorrow, we're gonna have a meeting. Let's lay it all on the line. You got a problem, say it. Don't say it after tomorrow's meeting to anyone else.*

The men and women from the ad agency were surprised, and glad, to hear it. As far as they were concerned, headquarters had done next to nothing over the months to tame the unruly regional representatives, preferring instead to let Wieden & Kennedy suffer the blame for Cherry Hill's decisions. Worrell was the worst culprit, publicly supporting the agency but (so it believed) deriding it privately every time an RVP voiced a complaint. It was time for S.O.A. to corral its ornery and destructive sales force. Finally, Worrell appeared to be doing it.

The RVPs, however, weren't about to submit. Trying to be helpful, Woody Purcell, the southeastern regional vice president, warned Dave Luhr that the troops were restless. *You should open tomorrow's meeting by offering us a peace pipe,* Woody advised him.

Luhr, not realizing the scope of the RVPs' anxiety, and not believing that his agency had done anything that required conciliation, was not amused.

THE ADVERTISING AGENCY spent the next morning preparing for what it believed to be the most important presentation of its brief, tumultuous relationship.

"It kind of evolves out of where we've been, but with more car and more emotion—the things we got back from the research," Walter

Mills, the A.E. in charge of the national account, told Jim Heidt, who had flown up from the agency's cubbyhole of an Atlanta office.

Heidt, who spent his days as a protest antenna for dealers and sales executives in the Southeast and Midwest, wanted reassurance. "But you *will* see the car, right?" he asked anxiously.

Like a coach before the big game, Luhr reviewed the strategy with his team. He pulled papers and slide decks from his metal briefcase, which was balanced on his lap as he sat in S.O.A.'s lobby, and offered inspiration to Jerry Cronin. "Jerr . . . one thing. Be yourself. But also be confident," Luhr told his copywriter. "If they start going after you, be confident."

The Wieden & Kennedy crew elevatored up to the top floor of S.O.A. headquarters. Chris Wackman, Worrell and the RVPs were still locked in Tom Gibson's conference room, so the agency staffers waited nearby, surrounding but not touching a table full of picked-over cold cuts, half-eaten croissant sandwiches, cole slaw, potato salad and brownies left over from the lunch headquarters had tossed for its visiting regional reps.

Vince eyed the victuals bitterly. "All the time I've been here, they've never even offered me a cup of coffee," he said.

Jeff Greenberg, the account executive in charge of the regions, paced nervously. The others checked their anxieties with aimless banter. A pregnant national account executive recalled first dates. A regional A.E. talked of his abandoned dream of becoming a drive-time disc jockey. Vince remembered an art director he knew in Australia named Art Black, who named his son Matt.

Jerry could only recount rejection. "Remember when we did that presentation to Swatch, and they absolutely couldn't understand anything I said because of my accent?"

"Did you produce it?" asked Greenberg.

"We didn't produce *anything*," Jerry responded.

Luhr corrected the copywriter. "We produced a lot of storyboards."

The conference room's heavy door swung open and Chris Wackman beckoned his agency. Chris's head glistened with a thin veneer of sweat; he and some dozen contentious colleagues—headquarters executives, RVPs, independent distributors and Japanese execs—had been locked up since the early morning. Luhr took a seat at the head of the room, next to Chris, who was running the meeting in Tom Gibson's absence. Chris nodded to Luhr, and the presentation began.

"As I seem to do at every RVP meeting," Luhr began, reading from remarks he had prepared, "last night at dinner I sat next to Woody. As usual, we were talking about our jobs, our goals and, more importantly, our frustrations. We talked about the client-agency relationship. We talked about the RVP-W.& K. account rep relationship. What was working. And, more importantly, what wasn't. Woody suggested we start the meeting off today bearing either a peace pipe or an olive branch."

Luhr looked up from his page at the Subarus. "Both are hard to find in Philadelphia. So instead, you will get my opening remarks."

He started reading again. His voice shook with uncharacteristic nervousness, but he did not back down. "First of all, if you remember one thing today, remember that this agency cares. We, too, have an enormous stake in the future of Subaru.

"The comment that bothered me most last night was that we are inflexible, arrogant and stubborn. I will take some responsibility for this. And for that, I apologize and pledge to you that we will change our attitude where needed. But I also want to explain why we are stubborn on some issues.

"Make no mistake about it, Subaru is in trouble. If this statement startles anyone, you've been living in dreamland. I don't say this to scare anyone, but rather to motivate us. The future of Subaru rests solely in the hands of this group today. If we solve our problems, we can and will prosper. If we can't, the fat lady will soon be singing. For all of us.

"The biggest problem we collectively face is that we seem to have no plan for the future. We are all at fault for this. We have all let personal agendas get in the way of the development and implementation of an overall plan. We desperately need a plan of attack. And once developed, we need to rally behind it. In the past, as soon as any plan was implemented, it seemed to be immediately torn apart—by people at S.O.A., by people in the field and by people at W. & K. This has to stop. We need a wake-up call. For this company to have a future, we must all work together behind that future. Behind that plan. The goal of today's meeting should be to develop that plan. And once we have that plan, we must go out and sell in the plan."

Luhr looked up from his papers one more time. "Those people who don't support the program should find something else to do."

An agency account executive leaned in on the person next to him. "Ballsy thing to do," he whispered. But, whether foolhardily courageous or breathtakingly arrogant, Luhr's speech was anything but a rapprochement. The Subarus greeted it in silence, with stony faces. Which provided Walter Mills with his cue to take over.

Walter was unflappable, stolid and, in tone, soft and conciliatory. He immediately established himself as good cop to Luhr's bad cop by affirming that Wieden & Kennedy could and did respond to its client's criticisms. The tenor and content of his remarks made clear the agency's political strategy for the meeting and for the campaign it hoped to sell: *Be tough enough to let them see we know what we're doing, but pliable enough to let them see we listen and learn.*

Walter recounted how the agency had scrapped the Japanese engineers campaign in light of the RVPs' objections. He then played excerpts from the focus groups, carefully culled from some thirty hours of videotape to show both positive and disapproving reactions to the agency's advertising. "The negatives," Walter said, "were not unlike some of the negatives you told us. We've got to tell people *why* Subaru is 'what to drive.'"

Hence, the campaign that Wieden & Kennedy was about to unveil was constructed, as per the RVPs' own advice and the agency's best judgment, to do two things: "convince car buyers why Subaru is a better machine, and evolve out of 'Factory' and do it in a tone we already have, but show more of the car."

Jerry and Vince were already standing on either side of an easel. Both had made slight concessions to fashion by donning sport jackets with their jeans. Jerry began by continuing Walter's theme of accommodation. Like Luhr, he wanted nothing left to chance, so instead of improvising his comments, he read from his notebook. He affirmed that "we do not think this is a time to be cute or fancy. To do so would be stupid." Vince, following him, answered another oft-expressed complaint by asserting that the advertising agency knew how to make ads that car people liked.

"We're *not* afraid to show the car off, either from the image side or the engineering side," Vince said.

Chris Wackman, his fingers splayed across his mouth, scanned the table, back and forth, looking for a reaction. There was none.

Jerry and Vince had worked hard to harmonize the new campaign's two opposing requirements, to emphasize consumer desires and Subaru's engineering, while retaining what Vince called the "family feeling," a style consistent with the earlier advertising. They accomplished their goals by constructing the television commercials around an internal monologue, a car buyer's conversation with himself about what he wanted in an auto. Vince preserved the on-screen type, although he now intended to move it in from the sides, not from the bottom. He eliminated most of the florid Bernhard font, which he hated, replacing most of it with a bastardized version of Franklin Gothic, a clean and simple sans-serif face that he considered more appropriate to the advertising's message. He also incorporated graphic symbols, like road signs and arrows and boxes, into the text scroll, because he believed they heightened audience interest, especially on repeat viewing. Jerry's copy came close to the no-nonsense tone of the "Factory" spot, which had captivated the company and ad critics alike. With Jerry reading his words, it was almost as if Brian Keith's nephew were asking his gruff uncle for advice.

"So how do you like this new car?" Jerry recited, as Vince displayed placards with the Subaru emblem and a front view of the Legacy. "I love it. I adore it. It's great." Close-ups of the wheel well, the Legacy in profile, the engine and the underside of its chassis followed. "It's new! Nobody's spilled anything on the seats yet! The engine's new and running nice.

"But tell me," the copy continued, "what it's going to be like when I've paid off the loan, eight years later when my son's driving it. Tell me, 'cause anyone can make a nice *new* car, but not a nice new car that's gonna be a nice *used* car. Tell me"—the refrain was becoming hypnotically poetic—"like a Subaru Legacy, it has a horizontally opposed engine that can rack up the miles. An automatic transmission I can drive in first and not burn it out. That it's got tough bumpers like the Legacy and offers antilock brakes, so I don't crash my new car so easily. So it can become an old car. Tell me, I don't want a new car every few years. I want to save money. I want to have money. Tell me. Give me the facts. A fact like Subaru has, that 93 percent of all their cars registered in the last ten years are still on the road today. Give me the names, a name like Bill Sandstrom, who's driven his Subaru 300,000 miles. Stop talking new. Stop talking shiny. Start talking sense.

"Tell me. I got the money. I want to know"—Vince held up a placard with the ten-month-old slogan—"what to drive."

The creatives finished but remained standing.

"Who will speak first?" Chris asked. He looked directly at Ernie Boch, who was sitting far down at the other end of the crowded table. "Ernie, I know you're itching to make a comment."

Chris had not selected Ernie by accident. Ernie was a legend inside S.O.A. One of the last two independent Subaru distributors, the excitable New Englander was a millionaire many times over from his investments in auto distribution, dealerships and broadcasting. But it wasn't his wealth that had made him a subject of constant conversation inside Subaru for the better part of two decades. It was his avariciousness. Ernie would do anything for money, including torture his dealers.

The silver-haired, flashily dressed distributor had been the object of a class-action suit by nine of his dealers, who alleged that he had forced them, under threat of withholding cars, to buy freight handling, advertising and other services from him at unfairly high prices. That suit was later settled. He had weathered his own reputation and S.O.A.'s decline by insisting that his dealers sell nothing but Subarus, forcing them to buy cars from him or wither away. His demands on S.O.A.'s top executives were incessant. He was a perpetrator of "terrible things," in Tom Gibson's words. Ernie was roundly despised.

Chris figured that Ernie would denounce the new campaign, and that the others, in their hatred of him, would leap to its defense. On the first count, he was correct.

"A truthful comment?" Ernie replied. "I've got to say, I'm not impressed with what I've seen. Really not impressed."

As he continued, it became clear that Ernie's dissatisfaction had less to do with the campaign he had just been presented with than with S.O.A.'s strategy of boosting the Legacy above all other models.

"I've been a distributor for twenty years," Ernie continued, his voice rising. "I've seen Subaru start from nothing, go up, come down. I'll tell you, we're fighting for our life. I'm gonna lose a distributorship! We need a hell of a lot more than what you've got here. When you talk about the car, you're saying what everyone else is saying!"

Ernie's solution to Subaru's problems was a broken-field run against Cherry Hill. "The SVX, I tell you, what we've got here in the SVX is an all-season sports car!" His voice by now was an unrelieved shout. "NO ONE ELSE CAN SAY THAT! BUT YOU SAY *TEN* THINGS! THIS IS A UNIQUE CAR! YOU CAN GET 100 MILES AN HOUR AND NOT HEAR A THING!"

Through the tirade, Dave Luhr's head sank lower and lower to the table, until his chin was nearly touching it. He turned his eyes up at Ernie and watched.

"You can't imagine the competition on the floor of these dealerships now; it's like war!" the distributor continued, pronouncing the word, in his thick Boston accent, as "wah." "It *is* war!"

But if Chris thought Ernie's opposition would spur support, he was wrong. The sales executives just traveled along in the distributor's wake.

"I found the visual fighting the text," said one RVP.

"We need a sense of urgency. We gotta start selling the cars tomorrow!" said another.

" 'A car for the next eight years' may not be the right line," said another.

"We want them to think of coming in every three or four years," another agreed.

Luhr calmly reminded the assembly that among Subaru's abiding values, as the men in the room had long been telling him, was durability.

That was the reason to mention what the car would feel like "eight years later, when my son is driving it." Chris Wackman supported his account director. "Even when we come out of the recession, it won't be the way it used to be," he warned the RVPs. "We won't go back to the three-, four-year cycle. Durability is and will be *in*."

But these men were in no mood to think of the future. With the new quotas, they were not going to have one, not with this company, unless they started moving the metal immediately. If they were going to be victimized by the new sales goals, then so was the marketing department. And so was Wieden & Kennedy.

Tom O'Hare tried to inject a note of reason into the proceedings. O'Hare, like many of the others, detested Ernie Boch, and loved few things more than to set himself up, in opposition to the other independent distributor, as the voice of wisdom. For all his complaints about the agency's handling of the account, he did not believe Wieden & Kennedy was to blame for the stagnation in sales or the lack of an effective advertising message. Indeed, he appreciated the agency's attempt to resurrect durability as an advertising motif. Nonetheless, O'Hare, like the others, thought the new campaign missed the target. Moreover, he now disagreed with the advertising's *original* premise, the premise the agency had been pressured to return to.

"I think a car is more than just transportation," O'Hare opined. "That belief was brought home to me when three people I tried to sell a Legacy to said, 'It's not for me,' and bought a Mazda. They viewed their car as something more than just rubber and metal that gets them from Point A to Point B. We need a transformation in thinking. We have to build on our reputation for durability. But we need to have on top of that sizzle and style. Our car is beyond that and our advertising has to take us beyond that."

O'Hare began picking at the copy. The reference to money in the commercials' last line—"Tell me. I have the money, I want to know what to drive"—was unappealing. So was the mention of "used cars." Then O'Hare began redirecting the visuals. "You need people. People having fun with the car. Give it life!"

By now, the Wieden & Kennedy staffers were numbed by the assault. Again, the agency was being held hostage to the diverse opinions of a group of salesmen who could not decide whether wholesaling cars was art, science or alchemy. One account executive wore a Mona Lisa smile; the others just stared blankly. Luhr tried to respond.

"I know we can make the cars look better, Tom. But if we get in a style war, we lose."

"I agree," O'Hare replied. "But sizzle and style will help us sell it. *People take pride in their cars.* It is *more* than going from Point A to Point B."

Chuck Worrell, who had been silent while his subordinates and independent distributors assailed the work, finally put forward his own thought. "Are we still totally opposed to a spokesperson for the cars?" he asked. "Nike does it."

Luhr, his patience wearing thin, responded. "There's more"—he searched for the appropriate word—"credibility there. Michael Jordan wears Nikes." Wearily, he turned to Jerry and Vince. "What do the creatives think?"

Jerry was thinking about how much he hated these people, this account, this area of the country. "We can look into it," he answered dryly.

RVPs leapt into that opening. One after another, they shouted names of famous Subaru drivers who, in their fantasies, they could hire as endorsers. "Peter Jennings!" was followed by "Andy Mill!" "Chris Evert!" someone bellowed.

Woody Purcell ventured another thought. Perhaps they should not even do a new image campaign on television. TV viewership declined during the summer, anyway. Maybe the company should take the money it was budgeting for the new advertising and throw it all into radio and newspaper—media which were, unsurprisingly, used primarily for local, retail, price advertising.

At this, Luhr lost his cool. Despite his tough introductory remarks, he had offered an olive branch of sorts to the RVPs. The entire presentation had been structured to show that Wieden & Kennedy knew how to listen and respond to criticism. But all S.O.A. did was change the criticism.

"I'm not concerned about *where* we're gonna say it," the account director told Woody sharply. "We need something to say *about* it. But some of you say 'styling,' some say 'value.' We need one consistent thing to say *and this company can't agree!*"

As if to underscore his point, the two independent distributors started a side-argument with each other.

"We can sell this car on a combination of two features: engine and all-wheel drive!" insisted Ernie Boch angrily.

"I disagree completely," O'Hare retorted. "Ernie, you must believe that a car's purpose is only to get you from Point A to Point B, because that's what the engine and all-wheel drive promote. But people buy cars for other reasons!"

Chris Wackman attempted to keep the meeting under control. "Well, there are some conflicting beliefs here—" But his effort went for

naught. The quarrel careened off in another direction, with Woody, Ernie, O'Hare and several others arguing about eliminating the media
tiering system and reallocating the ad spending. The agency executives
merely watched. Jerry Cronin sat with his head bowed. Vince leaned
impassively on the slide projector. Two account executives cradled
their heads in their hands. Walter Mills crowded himself against a
windowsill, as if looking for an escape from the bus bearing down
on him.

The conflict escalated and twisted. Finally, inevitably perhaps, it settled on the only two people who had remained silent throughout the
session: Kazuhiro Miyake, the executive vice president and a member of
the committee that had chosen Wieden & Kennedy a year earlier, and
Yasumi Mizuno, a senior member of the sales and marketing staff. They
were Japanese. To Subaru's Americans, they might as well have been
personally responsible for boosting the quotas and bringing on the afternoon of rage.

"Our Japanese friends must answer to this," O'Hare said, making no
attempt to soften his accusatory tone. "We need to strike a balance between production and demand. We have fought the battle of unrealistic
sales goals because of overproduction since 1987. And we have not had
a new model launch in years. Next year will be the *seventh* year without
something to sell but too much of it to sell."

He faced the Japanese executives directly. "I think the job that's been
done by the people in this building is nothing short of a miracle. To sell
forty thousand eight-year-old Loyales will take money. To blame the advertising and marketing is wrong. The blame lies with the people who
made the decision in 1987 not to change the Loyale."

Mizuno, who spoke better English than his compatriot and who, as a
member of the marketing and sales staff, well understood the Americans' plight, ignored the request for financial relief but tried to answer
the rest of the charge with what he considered the responsible, corporate point of view. "I agree," he told O'Hare. "But to survive for the future, we need to change our strategy. To do that, image is very
important. Just saying 'basic transportation' is not good enough. We
need image. We need something more."

"Like a miracle," interjected Chris Wackman.

"Finish what you're saying," interrupted Luhr, suddenly awakening
from his stupor. "What is the 'something more'?"

But Chris, suddenly inspirited and mad, was not ready to relent. He,
too, was willing now to blame the Japanese publicly for the company's
descent. "Yes, *what is it?*" he yelled at Mizuno. "Ernie thinks it's the
engine. You don't think that's it. So what is it? *I'd love to know!*"

Mizuno, chastened, said nothing. Chris, emboldened, moved to draw the meeting to a close. If Chuck Worrell refused to discipline his RVPs, then he would do it himself.

"Keep in mind," Chris told the sales reps, "the agency is carrying the corporate flag. *We're* the ones who made that decision. *They* should not be a punching bag. The media tiering structure was *our* decision. It was *our* decision to do the image creative the way it was done. If it hasn't been communicated well, it's shame on *us*. They are *our* flag carriers.

"I'd like to say something about the image advertising," Chris continued, with a strength unfamiliar to most in the room. "With the exception of one person down the room, who believes we should focus on the engine, the image advertising seems to be on the right track. There will be changes, but not wholesale changes. And the decision on it will be made by me, Chuck and Tom Gibson. We got seven different opinions on image today. I hope and expect that whatever the decision is, when we pull the trigger, you will all support it."

He looked around the room and smiled wanly. "I'm exhausted," he said, signaling the session's close. He pointed to Luhr. "Okay. It's back to you guys."

The advertising executives and the automotive men got up from their chairs, stretched and slowly ambled from the room. One RVP, though, had a final recommendation. He walked briskly over to Jim Heidt, Wieden & Kennedy's Atlanta-based account executive, to deliver it.

"Really," the rep told the A.E., "all you need is Chrissie Evert or some girl with big tits standing next to the car to sell it."

THE THROUGH-THE-LOOKING-GLASS DEBATE freed Wieden & Kennedy. So did Wackman's endorsement—the strongest support given the agency by any Subaru executive since the beginning of the relationship. The ad executives returned to their office determined to produce the new advertising as they saw fit. Cherry Hill was behind them. The regions simply did not matter.

The agency threw a few bones to the RVPs. It eliminated the reference to "eight years," and changed the line about a "nice used car" to a "nice old car." For Ernie, Jerry added a few words about the engine. For Woody, he threw a line into one spot about all-wheel drive and "Miami rain." But he and his colleagues refused to budge on the other complaints, like Tom O'Hare's objection to the mention of money. *That's how people think when they're buying cars,* the agency maintained. *The line stays.*

More important, Wieden & Kennedy made sure that the television commercials would turn out literally picture-perfect. It hired a seasoned auto advertising director whose previous work included Lexus and Acura spots, to direct. Instead of abjuring liquid lighting, as it had in the "Lack of Pretense" ads, this time during filming the agency brought in a huge light box, some sixty feet long and thirty feet wide, and made sure that its beams flowed over the subject cars, bathing them in a loving glow. The camera, too, embraced the autos and their components, showing off the vehicles (which were shot against a gray canvas backing) to their best advantage.

One big change did have to be made, however. The additions to the already-long copy were too much for Brian Keith. When the actor tried to squeeze in all the words, he came off as loud and aggressive, *in your face*, in the words of Dan Wieden, who insisted that the former sitcom star be replaced. So Dan's subordinates chased after another voice for Subaru, sorting through 143 of them before landing on one of their own, Mark Fenske.

A former Wieden & Kennedy creative who had left the agency to establish himself as a freelance copywriter, radio-commercial producer and voiceover artist, Fenske and his Los Angeles minishop, The Bomb Factory, remained close to the Portland agency. His slightly loopy, nasal voice was, Dan and David and Jerry and Vince agreed, perfect for new ads. "Fenske is the 'everyday man' of the nineties," Vince affirmed. "Hal Riney"—the agency chief whose voice graced Gallo, Perrier and Alamo rental car ads, "is the voice of the eighties. Fenske is the voice of the nineties. He sounds like a real guy."

Surprisingly, the agency's resilience in fashioning the campaign and its sturdiness in sticking to its plan converted a few former critics. Tom O'Hare was impressed with the new creative. "I think the advertising is moving in the right direction," he said shortly after the contentious meeting, as the agency was beginning production of the new work. "Then again, the final judge will be when it's out, and then how people react to it."

For the first time in a year, Wieden & Kennedy began to feel confident in its relationship with S.O.A. Dave Luhr hung outside his office a framed note from the client. "Jusho Omedeto Gozaimasu!" it read, in transliterated Japanese. "What to say! What to be! What to drive! Subaru and W. & K., looking forward to many years of friendship and success. Congratulations on being selected Agency of the Year." It was signed by dozens of men and women at S.O.A.

On June 18, just as the new advertising was beginning to appear on television screens and in magazines, Wieden & Kennedy and Subaru celebrated their first anniversary together. Dozens of staffers from both companies gathered at a Philly entertainment park called The Beach Club, which (per its name) resembled a Malibu seashore spot, with sand, barbecues, canvas chairs and bungee jumping, albeit on the banks of the Delaware River.

Moods were buoyant. Jerry Cronin, bouncing his plump, seven-month-old son, Gage, on his lap, was uncharacteristically jovial, retelling stories about Wieden & Kennedy's ill-fated relationship with Swatch, the Swiss watch company, but this time to show how good Subaru was by comparison.

"I'll never forget the two-hour debate we had about what was funny," he recalled. "It turned out that to the Swiss, the funniest thing on earth was a man running down the street in a bear suit. So no matter how bad it is, I *know* it can be worse."

Chuck Worrell arrived and made a beeline for Jerry. "Hey, Mr. Creative!" he said, extending his hand. "Great spots! Ernie says he likes them, so it's fine with me."

Dave Luhr, who had just reviewed Subaru's sales for the early part of the month, was ebullient. "First ten-day period since we got the account that we're above projections," he exulted. All was right with their world.

Then the real figures starting pouring in.

Subaru finished June virtually even with the year before. Although it managed to sell some eleven thousand vehicles, more than half of them were Loyales, which moved off lots not because of image or advertising, but because S.O.A. had initiated a discount plan that dropped the price of the old workhorse by as much as $2,000. Many of the buyers were already Loyale owners who, attracted by a direct-mail promotional campaign, traded in their old subcompacts for new ones, instead of trading up to the compact Legacy. Indeed, Legacy sales were down for the month, to 5,647 units, from 6,416 cars in June 1991. July was somewhat the same: Total sales were up sharply (to 12,491 vehicles from 10,686) but Legacy sales were down. The specter of unsold Legacies hindering the introduction of the forthcoming subcompact was hardening into reality.

It was easy to locate the culprit: the advertising, of course. It tried too hard to be . . . *creative*. It was . . . *irritating*. "The copy should work, but instead the words as voiced by The Bomb Factory's Mark Fenske are whining and obnoxious," declared *Adweek*.

Some dealers were mildly supportive. "It's jazzier than the old campaign," ventured Sal Barbagallo, the sales manager at Milla's Subaru in Arlington, Massachusetts. Others were downright caustic. "The whole campaign was flat to begin with. There was nothing to build on. That's why we're not seeing any traffic in the showroom," said Andrew Bennett, the Subaru sales manager at Wilkie Buick, Chevrolet and Subaru in Philadelphia. "It's not the economy, it's the advertising."

No one blamed the economy, which was still stuck in a recession that would soon topple a president. No one bothered to point out that the competition was suffering a worse fate than Subaru. (Volvo, which also dumped its longtime ad agency for a new hot shop in 1991, was, by the end of summer 1992, trailing its year-earlier sales by some two thousand units, twice Subaru's decline.)

No one mentioned these things, because no one was home. In July, Tom Gibson resigned as president of Subaru of America to run a Philadelphia company that managed athletic stadiums and concert arenas.

Publicly, Gibson attributed the shift to the grand opportunity. Privately, he told colleagues that he was tired of arguing all the time with foreign overlords who refused to acknowledge the market conditions in the United States. "It wasn't fun anymore," he said. "There's just so long you can beat your head against the wall. They kept saying 'yes, yes, yes' and then not doing anything about it." He doubted that companies like Fuji could survive in their present form. "The small guy that thinks he's going to go head-to-head with the big guy," Gibson declared, "is going to lose."

Fuji did not name a replacement for the popular president and COO. Instead, it decided that Takeshi Higurashi, the chief executive who had largely deferred to Gibson, would take a stronger role in operations. His first move was to promote two senior executives to share some executive responsibilities.

They were George Muller, the chief financial officer, and Chuck Worrell, the head of sales, who from here on in would be Chris Wackman's boss and S.O.A.'s ultimate advertising overseer.

When he got the call, Dave Luhr took the news in stride. *Honey,* he said to his wife, *this has been a roller coaster ride for the last twelve months and it's just one more hill to go up and down.* As he dwelled on the ramifications of the changes at his client, he tried to remain sanguine.

Troublesome as Worrell had been to the agency, in a position of authority he might prove more decisive than Chris, especially now that sales and marketing were united under him. "Not that from an advertising standpoint he has better taste than Chris, because clearly he doesn't," Luhr said, "but I think from a leadership standpoint this maybe is more beneficial." There was another bright spot: Dan Wieden had dawdled for so long over approving the agency's move to a permanent office space and hiring additional members of the creative department, that the Philadelphia office stood a chance of turning a profit. "Most agencies would lose money their first year," Luhr said. "We're going to make some money."

Luhr even figured that if the unthinkable happened, if Subaru fired the agency, Wieden & Kennedy would still emerge with its reputation intact. "I'd rather worry about the ads. If they fire us, they fire us; if they don't, they don't. I mean, Chiat's been fired from a ton of things and they move on. It's like, 'Let's go, next.' I think we'd feel pretty damn good, actually. I continue to say that the biggest challenge we have in Philadelphia is to duplicate the environment we have in Portland. Because then you have a fertile ground and something can grow. If Subaru fired us, it would be like, well, we had fertile ground but it didn't rain all winter and the crops didn't rise, okay?"

The media and marketing trades, however, did not want to let the agency off the hook that easily. Sharks began circling Wieden & Kennedy and its car account, some looking to dislodge it, others just seeking sport. The *New York Times* printed in its Sunday Business section an opinion piece by a Connecticut marketing consultant entitled "A Subaru Ad That Should Be Buried." *Business Week* magazine identified Wieden & Kennedy as one of "Three Shops With Plenty to Sweat About." *Philadelphia* magazine published a vicious attack on the agency that declared, "Arrogance is a full partner at Wieden & Kennedy."

DCA Advertising, now renamed Dentsu Corporation of America, sent several representatives to Cherry Hill to check whether Subaru might be interested in a promotional campaign it was cooking up.

Chris Wackman, Wieden & Kennedy's client, managed to hold the Japanese agency at bay. But he was not optimistic about his, his company's or his agency's future. Not only had Worrell been promoted above him, but Chris had been stripped of some authority. He considered the demotion a payback, a response to his willingness to challenge the Japanese publicly. It was a sorry signal to S.O.A. He doubted that Chuck or anyone else in the company would ever question Fuji's authority again.

"Tom was the high-ranking voice of reason who was willing to stand up for what's right and for what makes sense and for the realization that there are certain things we can do and certain things we can't do," Chris said, his cadence dredged in unhappiness. "And I have this major concern that with his departure, for whatever reason, we're not going to stand up. We're just going to say, 'Yes, sir.'" His predictions for the company were dire: S.O.A. was going to end the year with unsold Legacies flooding the company's lots; several thousand SVXs, the image cars that were supposed to transform Subaru's reputation, were also going to close the year in company hands; Fuji would never understand the American market until it was forced to abandon it.

Chris was completely demoralized. "It just seems to me that it's taking a very decidedly spiraling twist down. . . . We have lost our direction."

But Worrell, George Muller and Higurashi, the CEO, did give Subaru one important bit of direction by summer's end. They declared the effort to reintroduce the Legacy a loss. An auto company could not "unveil" a three-year-old car—not in a down market, not with angry dealers, not with the competition outspending them three-to-one. S.O.A. would never reach its goal of 132,000 cars for 1992.

Subaru of America's last, best hope, its management decided, was going to be the new subcompact. Fuji had christened it the Impreza. It was a pretty car, as rounded and jaunty as the newly redesigned Honda Civic and Toyota Corolla. It was a powerful car, with the Legacy's engine and transmission. It was, Fuji and Subaru believed, the ultimate expression of their historical verities: a small car, exquisitely engineered, but with stylistic virtues that could, at last, move them into the mainstream.

It was Wieden & Kennedy's job to launch it.

ON THE FIRST DAY OF AUTUMN, 1992, Wieden & Kennedy's personnel again convened in Subaru's conference room. They did not resemble the original freewheeling band from Portland.

The women were attired in understated dresses. The men wore dark suits with white shirts. All wore ties, except for a boyish young copywriter named Izzy.

Izzy represented the biggest change of all. He had assumed the copywriting duties of Jerry Cronin. Jerry had decided to return to the Pacific Northwest. He had hung his head in his hands too many times, moaned "it's awful" so repeatedly it had become an anthem, fled home to his wife and baby in a depressed torpor too often, to stay. He wanted out—and his colleagues, who loved him, knew that if they pressed him to stay in Philadelphia, they would lose him. He went back to Portland, never to touch a Subaru advertisement again.

The mood was subdued, not from fear but excitement. Fuji Heavy Industries and S.O.A. were on the verge of agreeing to spend $100 million to launch the Impreza, more than they had ever spent to advertise a new car. They were debating (and would soon assent to) an agency proposal to inaugurate the advertising with a series of fifteen-second spots during the Super Bowl, giving the new model a boost unlike any the companies' previous cars had received. Fuji and S.O.A. had also lowered their sales goals; they were now saying they wanted only to sell 111,000 cars in the United States during the next year, 42 percent of them Imprezas. The hurdles were still high, but for the first time since Wieden & Kennedy had assumed the account, it believed Subaru's targets were realistic and realizable.

At 11 a.m., George Muller and Chuck Worrell entered the conference room. They circled the table, shook hands with the dozen adagency representatives, then took seats near the door. Down the table on their side stretched a row of Subaru marketing and sales executives. The advertising men and women sat opposite them, their backs to the windows and the racetrack across the street.

Dave Luhr, as ever, opened the meeting. But he did not confront the Subarus. Far from it. He reassured them.

"Dealer concerns—they're in here," Luhr said. "So are your concerns."

Indeed they were. Wieden & Kennedy had finally constructed an advertising campaign for Subaru, not for consumers. With the help of a promotional marketing specialist, it had built a campaign to appeal to "stakeholders." They included, according to a document prepared by the promotions company, S.O.A. employees, Subaru dealers, dealership personnel and suppliers. The campaign's objective was to "create awareness, build excitement, build commitment" and "motivate action" among the faithful.

The advertising agency had learned an essential lesson about advertising: It must look inward before it looks outward.

Linda Casey, the Philadelphia office's new resident account planner, took center stage to discuss the agency's consumer research. Wearing black, owlish eyeglasses, she presented a picture of scholarly propriety. With charts and pictures to support her, she outlined the conclusion drawn from her agency's latest round of surveys and focus groups: The consumers whom the company could lure to the new subcompact liked the same kind of advertising the dealers did.

"Impreza considerers get a little more jazzed about cars than our current owners," Linda said. "They identify a bit more with the car than our current franchise. They expect more of car quality. They like to be marketed to." In other words, Subaru could still talk about the quality of its technical craftsmanship, but with the sizzle that Wieden & Kennedy had avoided in advertising the Legacy.

But sizzle was not a pure part of Subaru's heritage. The advertising agency understood that now. It had to be added for the dealers. Subaru stood for other verities. Jim Piedmont, Wieden & Kennedy's car guy, got up to explain them.

"The Impreza is a product planning achievement, but a marketing dilemma," he warned S.O.A.'s executives. "Despite exceeding competitors in many, if not most, feature variables, the Impreza is still a Civic-class formula car that lacks a buyer-swaying hook. . . . Its upscale refinement qualities are mostly intangibles, such as great ride quality, that consumers have a hard time understanding and believing. . . . Our challenge is to cut through the advertising clutter and position the car so we can get on the shopping lists of Civic-class intenders."

To anyone who understood the history of Subaru, the solution to the "marketing dilemma" was clear. "The campaign you are about to see," Piedmont said, "accomplishes this by touting the Impreza's strength: its many incrementally superior product attributes."

Walter Mills, ever stoical, picked up from the car guy. The handoff— all the handoffs—were seamless, as clean as an Olympic relay team's. The presentation was perfectly structured, down to the code words, with important underlying meanings, that were sprinkled through the text like raisins in bran flakes.

"And so this campaign really does explain the key features of the car," Walter said, "in a very simpleminded way, not unlike the way Lexus is doing it." (*Features*: That meant Wieden & Kennedy had learned to talk about engineering. *Simpleminded*: That showed the agency was not striving to be creative. *Lexus*: That proved the agency had learned to sell by overselling.) "It hits on something we learned in the research: Impreza considerers need to be sold." (*Research*: That meant the work wasn't the invention of artsy types. *Sold*: That spoke again to the agency's new willingness to huckster.) "It also has a new tactical element, a videotape that we'll send consumers and ask them to respond to, via a toll-free number." (*Tactical*: That showed Wieden & Kennedy was ready to deploy gimmicks. *Toll-free number:* The kind of gimmicks used by the big, boring agencies in New York.)

"With that," Walter concluded, "let me turn it over to Dan."

Dan Wieden had flown in from Oregon for the presentation, underscoring its importance. He was a rare enough presence on the East Coast, there when needed but otherwise difficult to pin down. His delays in making decisions on hiring and creative concepts had often frustrated his otherwise-adoring Philadelphia staff. But it was his lack of attentiveness to the client, especially relative to what S.O.A. had been used to under its previous agency, that most disturbed Subaru. Chris Wackman had worried for months about Dan's unwillingness to keep close with anyone at the company. Early on, the agency president had traveled to Japan with Tom Gibson, but Dan failed to make good on the expectation that he would develop a real relationship with S.O.A.'s chief. Dan's distance only augmented the perception among Subaru's constituencies that Wieden & Kennedy did not comprehend the dynamics of an automobile account.

But now, here he was. He had, in fact, been around a lot the past few weeks, flying in from the West Coast for stretches of several days to work with his Philadelphia branch on the Impreza campaign. Dan's mere presence was enough to renew the dispirited agency's vigor. His advice, delivered not by phone or fax but in person, was inspiring.

Dan remained seated. He looked down at the conference table and shook his head slowly from side to side. His mumbling grew into a low roar. "This ... is ... really ... a ... GREAT CAMPAIGN!" he said, finally glancing up. The room erupted in laughter. The Subarus and the agency staff both appreciated that Dan was sounding like an adman. And Dan knew that they knew. The laughter animated him.

"In this campaign," he continued, "what I really like is, it really *does* focus on the product."

Vince Engel stepped to the front. When Jerry had announced that he was leaving, Vince was named creative director for the Subaru account. Operationally, the appointment made little difference; Vince and Jerry thought as one about creative, that it had to be captivating, startling and, most of all, original. Vince was an acolyte of the postmodern advertising ethos—that, as he put it, "sacred cows make great steaks."

But Vince liked to do something that Jerry Cronin did not: sell. He loved to show off his work, describe the visuals, read the copy, explain its reasoning and push it through. With the Impreza advertising, the first campaign created fully under his tutelage, he had his chance to sing.

Waving his hands in little circles, Vince declared that Subaru was ready to go head-to-head with the competition.

"The Civic-like buyers out there, we're going to give them a lot of little reasons that add up to one big reason for why they should buy Impreza," he said. He held up, so all twenty-eight people in the room could see, a gorgeous rendering of a motor. It was the initial shot of the first Impreza television commercial. "It opens like the current Legacy spots, with the camera drifting over the horizontally opposed engine. But it hangs there, without cutting. It's almost sculptural."

Izzy, the new copywriter, read the copy in a squeaky voice.

"Introducing the new Subaru Impreza's horizontally opposed engine.

This engine's configuration helps give a car a lower center of gravity for better stability and cornering. That's why the Porsche 911 has it, and the Honda Civic doesn't."

Vince unveiled a placard for the next shot of the commercial, a full reveal of the new car. Izzy continued.

"It's one of the 12,621 reasons the new Subaru Impreza is not just another dumb car."

Vince held up the last card, which read: "The new Subaru Impreza. What to drive."

The copy was flawless. It answered the objections Subaru's RVPs, distributors, dealers and salesmen had voiced since the early fall, that Wieden & Kennedy's advertising never told consumers *why* Subaru was "what to drive." It also corrected the flaw in the agency's recent, jargon-heavy "Tell Me" campaign by explaining *how* Subaru's engineering benefited the driver.

Vince and Izzy ran through a score of fifteen-second television commercials, each one showcasing a different part. The Impreza's ABS brakes, chip-resistant paint, interior room, hill-holding clutch and computer-controlled gas pedal were extolled and compared to a competition that was found lacking in every way. These teaser spots were supposed to lead up to one grand spot, a sixty-second commercial depicting how the parts become the whole.

"Wherever there's a competitive advantage, we use it," said Izzy.

"We purposely attacked the competitors in this class," affirmed Vince, "showing everywhere where Subaru is superior. It may only be incremental. But the total picture is to show that Subaru is better."

The rest of the advertising matched, even exceeded, the television commercials in its attention to automotive detail and tradition. The print campaign was to start with a four-page double gatefold in glorious color. The other magazine ads were to be distinguished by the most beautiful product photography the agency could buy. The point-of-purchase posters for the dealerships rendered the parts in muted pastels. All the print advertisements closed with an 800 number for consumers to call for more information about the Impreza. In the salesrooms, the agency suggested that Subaru put real parts on display—a museum exhibit of technical superiority.

"We want everything to work together," Vince concluded. "Which would be quite a change."

The nervous laughter only underscored the inescapable truth: Wieden & Kennedy had finally crafted the campaign Subaru's culture demanded. Setting aside the attractiveness of the product photography (which stood in contrast to the gritty utilitarianism of the company's cars), the new advertising was the consummate distillation of Subaru's—and Fuji's—history.

S.O.A.'s executives had only one objection.

"Let me ask you," Chuck Worrell said after the creatives were through. " 'Not another dumb car.' Can we change that to 'not just another subcompact car'?"

Vince demurred gently. "Well, the reason we have that is to talk the way consumers talk. Use everyday language."

Chuck was not persuaded. "Maybe I'm overly sensitive. But we always hear from dealers that consumers don't like to have their current car choices attacked. They want to feel good about their last choice. So you don't attack it, but you give them new reasons why yours is better."

Vince's reply was strong and enthusiastic. "Sure," he said.

The agency left it to its co-founder and spiritual leader to put a final stamp on the presentation.

"The dealers should love this," Dan Wieden concluded. "It's a hard sell. We've never taken shoes apart like this. Why, it's the hardest sell this agency has ever done!"

Wieden & Kennedy had been tamed.

PART VII

THE CONSUMER

Chapter 23

We Do It All For You

SUPER BOWL SUNDAY, 1993. Evening. Twelve adults, most in their thirties, and three children, between the ages of one and five, congregated in the den of an English Tudor house situated on a bluff in an upper-middle-class neighborhood in Maplewood, New Jersey.

The hostess, a tall, striking, transplanted Californian named Diane, served her guests Sausage Stars, a meaty canapé made with Hidden Valley Ranch Salad Dressing. Diane, a twenty-nine-year-old public relations executive, had torn the recipe from a glossy advertising insert in the *New York Times*.

"I don't enjoy football," said Val, a thirty-five-year-old human resources executive at Johnson & Johnson. Val drove a Nissan 200 SX, preferred Pepsi to Coke, drank Coors Light beer, wore Reeboks and held Visa and American Express cards in her purse. "I watch the Super Bowl for the commercials."

A Budweiser beer advertisement came on. It was the first installment of the 1993 Bud Bowl, an animated contest between a team made up of Bud Light bottles and another composed of regular Budweiser bottles.

"I hate the Bud Bowl," said Bill, Val's thirty-eight-year-old boyfriend, who also worked in human resources and drove a Toyota Camry, drank Coke and Corona, carried an AmEx card and wore Avia sneakers.

Craig, the thirty-three-year-old host, a communications director, shouted over the growing din. "Listen, if you guys want more drinks, get them yourselves."

The NBC network's pregame show began, and just as quickly cycled into the first commercial break. John Cleese, the British comedy star, flacked Magnavox ("Smart. Very smart.") electronics. Subway ("Sandwich Artists") hero sandwich shops followed. Chrysler ("Advantage

Chrysler") came next, announcing its presence with white-on-black type that scrolled magisterially up the screen. Super Bowl XXVII returned. The announcers introduced the Buffalo Bills, in blue, and the Dallas Cowboys, in white. That accomplished, Prudential ("1-800-THE ROCK") lauded its financial-planning service. Aspen ("Aspen. For men.") cologne visualized its aromatic power over women. Coopers & Lybrand ("Not just knowledge. Know-how.") explained how its accounting services made chief executives' lives easier. The pregame festivities resumed, country/western star Garth Brooks sang the national anthem while Marlee Matlin, the deaf star of NBC's "Reasonable Doubts," signed it. When they were finished, Pepsi-Cola ("You've never seen a taste like this") introduced Crystal Pepsi to America with scenes of a naked baby, a space walk and a rhinoceros. The baseball pitcher Nolan Ryan promoted Advil ("Advanced medicine for pain") ibuprofen tablets. U.S. Air ("Everything we do we do for you") extolled its friendly employees. The basketball greats Michael Jordan and Larry Bird began a free-throwing contest, which would last through most of the game, for McDonald's. The coin toss was done by O. J. Simpson, the former NFL running back who went on to star in Hertz advertisements. Buffalo elected to receive, and later punted to Dallas. Another Crystal Pepsi commercial came on. Servistar ("Good neighbor. Good advice.") hardware stores followed. When the game returned, Buffalo scored, so it was time for the Bud Bowl installment that introduced the coaches of the two bottle-teams, Corbin Bernsen of "L.A. Law" and the former Jets quarterback Joe Namath, whose many commercial endorsements included the Nobody Beats the Wiz consumer electronics chain. Goodyear ("The best tires in the world") promoted antiskid tread, and Dallas punted to Buffalo, which took possession, after a touchback, on its twenty-yard line.

Through it all, the suburban friends were yelling at and over each other and the television set in order to be heard. Then Pepsi came on to promote its regular soda ("Gotta have it") and Carla, a forty-five-year-old marketing director who did not drink cola, drove an Oldsmobile Cutlass Supreme, owned a pair of Keds, enjoyed Miller Lite and carried a Visa card, called for quiet. She *liked* Pepsi commercials.

The spot, which depicted a young boy's morose speculations about his adulthood, generated a great deal of laughter and comment—enough to overwhelm the thirty-second Master Lock ("Master Lock Tough") commercial that followed it. And the very short, fifteen-second Subaru Impreza ("What to drive") spot that came next.

With all the chattering, no one noticed that it was about the car's horizontally opposed engine.

The game resumed and quickly led to Dallas's first score on a thirty-yard pass to Jay Novacek and a penalty-lengthened extra-point kick. The network broadcast another Pepsi commercial and a second Servistar spot, before returning to the Super Bowl and Buffalo quarterback Jim Kelly's fumble into the hands of lineman Jimmy Jones, who ran the football back for another Dallas touchdown. Buffalo fumbled again on the kickoff, but managed to recover and run down the clock to the end of the first quarter. The break began with an advertisement for the Mark VIII ("Drive everything else first") from Lincoln, a rousing spot for Miller Lite ("C'mon, let me show you where it's at") beer, and a humorous executive-in-crisis ad for Federal Express ("Our most important package is yours") overnight delivery. The second quarter opened with a Buffalo drive that was nipped by a Dallas interception of a short Jim Kelly pass in the end zone. Gillette ("The best a man can get") took the opportunity to debut a spot, replete with naked babies, weddings and girls jumping on their boyfriends' backs, for its new line of aftershave and deodorant products. Lee jeans ("The brand that fits") ran a funny, wordless narrative which revealed the problems that can ensue when a woman tries to squeeze into tight dungarees.

During the Gillette and Lee ads, one guest ran to the upstairs bathroom, another repaired to the downstairs toilet, four went into the kitchen with the host and hostess, and the rest argued about Buffalo's dismal performance. They did not return or calm down until well after the second fifteen-second spot for the Subaru Impreza whizzed by.

No one really focused on its gorgeous portrait of antilock brakes.

And so it went. Dallas ran roughshod over Buffalo. Tony, a thirty-four-year-old phys. ed. teacher with a penchant for Coke, New Balance sneakers, Corona beer, Visa cards and the Buick Century, sang the praises of the Larry Bird–Michael Jordan basketball tossing contest for McDonald's. Diane—the Keds-wearing, Sam Adams–and-Pepsi-drinking, American Express–carrying, Hyundai Excel–driving hostess—finally noticed the Bud Bowl on its third spot. Greg, thirty-five, an engineer who liked Pepsi, Volvo, Beck's, Nike and American Express, shushed the crowd when a Lay's potato chip commercial, with the legendary football coaches Mike Ditka and Tom Landry, appeared.

Nobody said anything about the Subaru advertisements. Most of them went by too quickly for the talkative suburbanites to notice.

Three of the couples, uninterested in the Michael Jackson song-and-dance half-time extravaganza, took their leave before the second half opened. Most of the others drifted out shortly after, as it rapidly became clear that Buffalo was not going to find a way to get back into the game.

Buffalo lost the Super Bowl, 52–17.

Subaru of America lost the Super Bowl, too. A *USA Today* survey of viewers' reactions to the telecast's 43 commercials found that the favorites, by a wide margin, were McDonald's, Lee jeans, Pepsi and Reebok.

Subaru's ads were dead last.

Epilogue

CHRIS WACKMAN resigned from Subaru of America in late October 1992, after the Impreza campaign was approved but before the advertising could appear. The company said it did not plan to replace him. He was soon hired to direct the marketing efforts of a firm that specialized in selling automobiles to American military personnel stationed overseas.

David Luhr also left Subaru's immediate orbit before the end of the year. He followed Jerry Cronin back to Wieden & Kennedy's Portland headquarters, and turned the management of the agency's Philadelphia office and its Subaru account over to another account executive.

Subaru did manage to sell almost 65,000 Legacies in 1992, about the same number it sold the year before. And it held its market share at 1.3 percent. Considering the sorry state of the automotive market, it wasn't a bad performance. But few people paid attention to model sales or market share, for Subaru of America had publicly announced that it planned to sell 150,000 cars in the United States in 1992. Even when it modified its goal to 132,000, it could not come close. Only 104,803 Subarus were sold in America in 1992, 249 fewer than in 1991.

Nor did the Impreza prove to be the volume car Subaru needed. Through May 1993, only 8,648 of the new subcompacts had been sold, at which rate S.O.A. would sell less than half the number it had declared as its goal. With Legacy sales in a severe slump, Subaru reached mid-1993 nearly 13 percent below where it was a year earlier.

So in July, Fuji Heavy Industries forced the retirement of Chuck Worrell, S.O.A.'s head of sales and marketing, and appointed George Muller president of its American import arm. As his first move, Muller renounced Subaru's strategy of moving into the mainstream. "We are not a mass marketer," said the tall, handsome finance man, "and it's time we refocus on the core strengths of our products and dealer body."

As his second move, Muller fired Wieden & Kennedy.

After a lengthy and private search for a new advertising agency and after an informal, months-long association that SOA executives referred to as a "trial marriage," Subaru hired a Texas advertising shop, Temerlin McClain, to be its offical agency of record.

Temerlin, a subsidiary of the giant Bozell advertising network, boasted qualities that Wieden & Kennedy lacked. It had extensive experience with retail accounts; its executives were versed in handling automotive clients; it didn't shrink from market testing its advertising executions. But the biggest difference was in how Subaru of America treated Temerlin: this time, the client knew what it wanted, and told the agency to deliver it.

In February 1994, SOA introduced its new tag line, a slogan that summed up everything the company had avoided during much of its life: "The Beauty of All-Wheel Drive." The television campaign, which began that August, trafficked in all the conventionalities from which the auto maker and its advertising agencies for years had shied. The commercials featured computer animation to show how Subaru transmissions operated. They repeated, several times per spot, the company's name, and concluded with a beauty shot of the shiny and stellar Subaru nameplate. They talked of four-wheel drive as "the ultimate safety feature"—a claim that, for presumed liability reasons, the company had shunned. They were backed by a jingle. They even included dogs and kids.

Equally notable were the absences: of comedy, postmodern self-reference, on-screen type, or any of the elements that the judges of advertising awards shows prefer.

By the end of 1993, thanks in large part to the recovering economy, SOA's fortunes were already improving. Retail sales were up slightly, the first time since 1986 that Subaru had posted a year-on-year increase. The company also recorded four consecutive months of 10,000-plus sales. But even the most optimistic executives were unprepared for the turn of fortune that greeted them after the return-to-the-niche strategy took hold in 1994.

The Legacy station wagon became the best-selling compact wagon in the U.S., beating out Ford's Taurus, according to R. L. Polk. In October, SOA sold 10,691 cars, more than 8,000 of them Legacies, the company's best sales month in two years and its best Legacy month in four. The sales, combined with headquarters cutbacks, enabled SOA to post its best monthly financial performance in almost eight years. Retail sales fell precipitously during the last three months of 1994; executives attributed the plunge to a price increase, born of cockiness after Legacies started selling out earlier in the year, that coincided with price reductions by their competitors. Although the sales falloff showed that Subaru was still a price-sensitive automobile, SOA execs took solace that their dealers were solidly behind their strategy. Sales to dealers in December stood at 18,828 units, a record.

Subaru of America finished 1994, its twenty-fifth full year of operations, with sales up 5.6 percent. But the spirit at the company's headquarters in Cherry Hill was boosted far more than the figure indicated. Employees in the newly "all-casual" workplace could be heard laughing in the elevators again. Secretaries brought their bosses and visitors cookies they'd baked. The vitality, not to mention the sales, emerged directly from what the company alternately called its "rededication" and its "return to our roots."

Subaru of America had learned the lesson of advertising. Advertising did not work by entertaining or assaulting the intellect of its audience, as the company's previous ad agencies had believed. Nor did it work through subliminal manipulation, as so many Americans, ever on the lookout for conspiracies, misguidedly thought. Instead, advertising, as the great ad man Bruce Barton had acknowledged decades before, was "something big, something splendid . . . something which goes deep down into an institution and gets hold of the soul of it."

To succeed, advertising cannot seek to invent a new soul. Instead, it must reinforce and redirect the existing image. It must serve as a form of mythology, providing the corporation's various and often competing constituencies—of which consumers are only one of many—heroes, villains, principles, rules of conduct and stories with which they can rally the faithful to remain true to the cause. Only then, with luck and effort, can they win new converts.

Subaru had found its soul. Its image, as George Muller, the new president and chief operating officer said in the early spring of 1995, was "in the product."

"It starts with the image we have," said Muller, who was lunching on a sandwich at the conference table at which so many of SOA's most important decisions had been made. "And it has a little bit of the flavor of the culture of our business, too. And some of our culture goes all the way back to the engineers who designed the product, and why they designed it the way they did."

"A lot of the last two years," he added, "have been spent telling that story to employees, dealers, and consumers."

AUTHOR'S NOTE

I undertook this book with the full cooperation of Subaru of America. I wrote to Thomas Gibson, the president of Subaru, shortly after the company announced that it was putting its advertising account into review, in April 1991, and asked to cover the process from the inside for the *New York Times Magazine*. He and his marketing director, Christopher Wackman, agreed to my request, and then allowed me to continue my research into the campaign's development. They never flinched, they never backed down, they never hindered my access to anybody or anything. At no point did a Subaru staff member, senior or junior, ask to go "off the record," or request that I not reveal the source of a document or an anecdote.

The same is true with Wieden & Kennedy, the advertising agency, which opened its door to me for meetings, private discussions among principals, productions and postproductions. Thanks to these two companies, the scenes described and the dialogue recounted in this book are, by and large, based on my contemporaneous reporting. In other words, I was there; I reported what I saw and heard; and I have set it down in this book as truth.

In a few instances I have reconstructed scenes at which I was not present. This is particularly true, obviously, in the historical sections of the book, notably Part II, on the development of Subaru, and Chapter

12, on the growth of Wieden & Kennedy, but it was also necessary in portions of the contemporary narrative. In these cases, any dialogue is based on the direct recollection of the participant or participants. Where I interpolated dialogue—for example, from a written text into somebody's mouth, or from one person's recollections of another's words—or where I have taken a subject's description of an event and rendered it as a quoted thought or belief, I have set this text off in italics. In all these instances, as well as in all others where the derivation of information might not be apparent in the text, I have provided the sourcing in the notes that follow.

NOTES

1: WHERE'S THE BEEF?

PAGE 6: "Men said that they are in the advertising business": Daniel Pope, *The Making of Modern Advertising* (New York: Basic Books Inc., 1983), p. 175.

Pope's book is among a handful of comprehensive histories of advertising that seek to place the industry's development in both an economic and a sociocultural context, and thus avoid the pitfalls of participants' memoirs, which are usually devoid of economic understanding, and economists' treatises, which recoil from cultural analysis. Other recommended books include:

Stuart Ewen, *Captains of Consciousness: Advertising and the Social Roots of the Consumer Culture* (New York: McGraw-Hill Book Co., 1976). Dense and provocative, Ewen's work is the earliest among contemporary advertising histories to explore the industry's influence on our notions of truth, individualism and community. His thesis, that modern advertising developed as a means of social control in a new industrial economy that required the dissolution, re-creation and subjugation of the interdependent farm family, is loosely argued but supported by fascinating turn-of-the-century accounts.

Stephen Fox, *The Mirror Makers: A History of American Advertising and Its Creators* (New York: William Morrow & Co., 1984). A popular history, Fox's book is invaluable for his archival research into the thoughts and activities of the industry's leaders during the past century.

Roland Marchand, *Advertising the American Dream: Making Way for Modernity, 1920–1940* (Berkeley: University of California Press, 1985). Marchand's book is considered seminal by cultural historians, who say it provided, for the first time, a rigorous methodology for using advertising's creative product to explore the broad culture of an era. The book is also distinguished by its exploration of the beliefs of average agency employees, as distinct from agency founders, during the period of its research.

Michael Schudson, *Advertising, the Uneasy Persuasion: Its Dubious Impact on American Society* (New York: Basic Books Inc., 1984). Despite its questioning title, this book is one of the best at assessing the economic claims of the ad industry against its performance. His conclusion, that advertising is a form of "capitalist realist art" that serves a purpose similar to that of socialist realist art in the former Communist regimes of East Europe, follows on Ewen's, but Schudson casts a wider net for evidence.

PAGE 6: " 'Fear and loathing' ": "Shifts in marketing Strategy Jolting Advertising Industry" by Randall Rothenberg, *New York Times*, October 3, 1989, p. A1.

"Nearly a century earlier": Martin Mayer, *Madison Avenue U.S.A.* (New York: Harper & Brothers Publishers, 1958), p. 6. This book is the best journalistic account of the ad industry ever written, a rich feast of observations made all the more bountiful by its appearance near the height of America's postwar boom, when advertising was at the peak of its industrial influence. See also: Pope, p. 175; Marchand, p. 7.

"Athlete's foot": Fox, p. 98.

"The avenue's high rents": "Madison Avenue Quits Madison Avenue" by Randall Rothenberg, *New York Times*, February 2, 1989, p. D1.

PAGE 8: "J. Walter Thompson agency's New England Room": "Martin Sorrell's Tough-Guy Act Is Playing Well on Madison Avenue" by Walecia Konrad, *Business Week*, November 21, 1988, p. 82. "WPP's Martin Sorrell Struggles to Revive J. Walter Thompson" by Joanne Lipman, *Wall Street Journal*, December 22, 1987, p. 1.

Needless to say, these and other observations of the ad industry during the late 1980s and early 1990s also derive from my own reporting on advertising for the *New York Times* during that period. For the three decades preceding, there is probably no better source than the reporting of Philip H. Dougherty, my predecessor as advertising columnist for the *Times*.

PAGE 12: " 'Imagery is the conversion of an idea' ": George Lois, *What's the Big Idea?: How to Win with Outrageous Ideas That Sell* (New York: Doubleday Currency, 1991), p. 55.

" 'The right name is an advertisement in itself' ": Claude C. Hopkins, *My Life in Advertising/Scientific Advertising* (Chicago: Crain Books, 1966), p. 276.

" 'Photographs sell more than drawings' ": David Ogilvy, *Confessions of an Advertising Man* (New York: Atheneum, 1984), pp. 100–101, 118. Ogilvy's work is, arguably, the most famous among a raft of memoirs and how-to manuals by advertising executives, a literary form that dates back at least sixty years. Other advertising leaders whose books have managed to attract a general readership are George Lois and Jerry Della Femina.

" 'An image . . . is not simply a trademark' ": Daniel J. Boorstin, *The Image: A Guide to Pseudo-Events in America* (New York: Harper & Row, 1961), p. 186. More than thirty years ago, before cable television, VCRs, political media consultants, digital image manipulation and a host of other modern appurtenances, Boorstin wrote this seminal study of the influence of imagery on American culture. Journalists, especially, would do well to read it, if only to discover how old so many of their "discoveries" are.

Milton quotation: John Milton, *Paradise Lost*, Book I, lines 254–55.

The material on the rise and fall of Subaru comes from several sources. General history:

" 'We Want to Be Like Audi and BMW': Fuji Heavy Industries Company Profile" by Andrew Tanzer, *Forbes*, June 16, 1986, p. 114.

"It's Tough, but It Isn't Doomsday: Subaru Company Profile" by Richard Phalon, *Forbes*, May 4, 1987.

"The Corporation: Subaru Gets Out of the Fast Lane" by James B. Treece, *Business Week*, July 20, 1987, p. 112.

"At the Crossroads: Subaru Strives to Get Back Into Gear" by Richard Rescigno, *Barron's*, March 28, 1988.

"Counterattack: Subaru Company Profile" by Subrata N. Chakravarty and Gale Eisenstodt, *Forbes*, November 13, 1989, p. 56.

On Harvey Lamm's exit:

"Who's News: Fuji Executives to Succeed Lamm at Helm of Subaru" by Krystal Miller, *Wall Street Journal*, September 5, 1990, p. B12.

On Fuji's bid:

"Fuji Heavy Industries Bids $147 Million for the 50.4% of Subaru It Doesn't Own" by Bradley A. Stertz, *Wall Street Journal*, January 17, 1990, p. A4.

On the stock split:

"Dividend News: Subaru of America Declares 8-for-1 Split," *Wall Street Journal*, May 26, 1986.

On 1987–88 results:

"Dividend News: Subaru of America Omits Its Dividend After Weak Results," *Wall Street Journal*, February 18, 1988.

PAGE 13: "Stopped greeting each other": Interview with Chris Milhous, Subaru of America sales promotion manager, January 14, 1992.

PAGE 14: " 'This is a bet-your-company car' ": *Forbes*, November 13, 1989.

" 'The real problem that Subaru has' ": *Barron's*, March 28, 1988.

PAGE 17: " 'The dialectician selects' ": From Plato's "Phaedrus," Edith Hamilton and Huntington Cairns, eds., *Plato: The Collected Dialogues* (Princeton, N.J.: Princeton University Press, 1973), p. 522.

2: I'M NOT A DOCTOR, BUT I PLAY ONE ON TV

PAGE 21: On advertising spending in the 1970s and 1980s and the ad industry crisis of the late 1980s: *New York Times*, October 3, 1989.
See also:

John Philip Jones, *How Much Is Enough? Getting the Most From Your Advertising Dollar* (New York: Lexington Books, 1992), pp. 21–43.

"A Blizzard of Pink Slips Chills Adland" by Mark Landler, *Business Week*, December 10, 1990, p. 210.

"What Happened to Advertising?" by Mark Landler, *Business Week*, September 23, 1991, p. 66.

PAGE 22: Agency research expenditures: "The Economics of the Advertising Agency Business" by Harry Paster, executive vice president, American Association of Advertising Agencies. Speech at the University of Pennsylvania, November 21, 1989.

4: CHEAP AND UGLY

PAGE 41: The Harvey Lamm–Malcolm Bricklin conversation is reconstructed from several sources, including: Interview with Malcolm Bricklin, May 19, 1993; interview with Harvey Lamm, October 21, 1991; "Face-to-Face: Auto Entrepreneur Harvey Lamm" by Steven Pearlstein and Bruce G. Posner, *Inc.*, June 1988, p. 45; "Would You Buy a New Car from This Man?" by Barry Rosenberg, *Philadelphia Magazine*, April 1975, p. 96.

PAGE 43: " 'Transmission view of communication' ": James W. Carey, *Communication as Culture: Essays on Media and Society* (New York: Routledge, Chapman and Hall, 1992), pp. 13–36. The work of Carey and other cultural studies scholars was instrumental in shaping my reading of the history of Subaru and the lessons I drew from it. I've taken their research, which attempts to show how products emerge from a broad national or transnational culture, and applied it to my own conclusion: That "little cultures," of an industry or a company, are both the targets and sources of media products.

Other books I found useful include:

Warren I. Susman, *Culture as History: The Transformation of American Society in the Twentieth Century* (New York: Pantheon Books, 1984).

James Naremore and Patrick Brantlinger, eds., *Modernity and Mass Culture* (Bloomington: Indiana University Press, 1991).

Horace Newcomb, ed., *Television: The Critical View*, 4th Edition (New York: Oxford University Press, 1987).

James W. Carey, ed., *Media, Myths and Narratives: Television and the Press* (Newbury Park, Calif.: Sage Publications, 1988).

" 'Occupied one-third the road space' ": Pedr Davis and Tony Davis,

Subaru: The Innovator Down Under (Blakehurst, Australia: The Marque Publishing Co. Pty Ltd., 1991), pp. 17–19.

PAGE 44: Volkswagen engine details: Walter Henry Nelson, *Small Wonder: The Amazing Story of the Volkswagen* (Boston: Little Brown & Co., 1970), pp. 305–11.

See also: Subaru of America Public Offering Prospectus, March 22, 1968, p. 4. Unless otherwise noted, all details of Subaru's incorporation and initial stock offering come from this prospectus and from the Subaru of America "Notice of Annual Meeting of Shareholders, to be held on May 21, 1969," issued May 12, 1969.

See also: James J. Flink, *The Automobile Age* (Cambridge, Mass.: MIT Press, 1988), pp. 214, 323–26. Flink's book was the most dispassionate, broad and comprehensive of the three chronicles of the automobile industry on which I relied in attempting to put Subaru's development in the context of automotive history.

The others are:

David Halberstam, *The Reckoning* (New York: Avon Books, 1987). A brilliant comparative analysis of Nissan and Ford Motor Co., Halberstam's book, more than any other, captures the social forces that guided automotive development, and particularly the fall of the American auto industry, after World War II.

Robert Sobel, *Car Wars: The Untold Story of the Great Automakers and the Giant Battle for Global Supremacy* (New York: E.P. Dutton, 1984). Sobel's book is wider in scope, freer in its use of statistics and more sparing in exploring personalities than Halberstam's, while covering much of the same ground.

PAGE 45: "The market . . . was good for maybe 25,000 cars": Interview with Harvey Lamm.

"Harvey put up $25,000": "A Slippery Road Ahead for Subaru" by David Diamond, *New York Times*, November 10, 1985, Section 3, p. 12.

"Hastily negotiated contract": SOA Offering Prospectus, p. 4.

PAGE 46: "Wouldn't touch the issue": Interview with Ronald Glantz, automotive analyst, April 22, 1992.

"300,000 shares of stock": See *Inc.*, June 1988, p. 50, where Lamm says, "We raised about $900,000." Also see May 21, 1969, Management Proxy Statement, Annual Meeting of Shareholders, which discloses that 1,807,000 shares were outstanding, 607,000 more than those initially owned by the four inside directors. Of those, 100,000 were acquired by H. L. Federman & Co., an investment bank, and 1,500 by Marvin Kaufman, an accountant and business associate of the men.

PAGE 47: "Bricklin's mother": Rosenberg, *Philadelphia Magazine*, April 1975, p. 102. For "Bala Cynwyd," see "Annual Meeting," May 12, 1969.

"Ed whined": Interview with George Muller, Subaru of America's chief financial officer, October 12, 1992.

PAGE 47: "The first shipment of Subaru 360s": Interviews with Harvey Lamm and Malcolm Bricklin.

"They had been tricked": Interview with Marvin Riesenbach, former Subaru of America comptroller, May 4, 1992.

PAGE 48: On the renegotiated contract: "Subaru of America, Notice of Annual Meeting of Shareholders, to be held on April 12, 1971," March 29, 1971, p. 24.

"Selling about a thousand of the 360 minicars": Pearlstein and Posner, *Inc.*, June 1988, p. 46.

"Hired his brother-in-law": Rosenberg, *Philadelphia Magazine*, April 1975, p. 102.

Description of Bricklin's office: Interview with Michael Sanyour, former Subaru of America president, November 25, 1991; interviews with Paula Green and John Glucksman, former principals of Subaru ad agency Green Dolmatch, March 5, 1992.

PAGE 49: The *Consumer Reports* criticism of the Subaru 360: "The Subaru 360: Not Acceptable," *Consumer Reports*, April 1969, p. 220.

"There were some six thousand Subaru 360s": *Consumer Reports*, April 1969, p. 223.

"Two thousand at S.O.A.": Rosenberg, *Philadelphia Magazine*, April 1975, p. 158.

"Negative cash flow": Rosenberg, *Philadelphia Magazine*, April 1975, p. 158.

PAGE 50: "The pyramid was collapsing": "Notice of Annual Meeting of Shareholders," March 29, 1971, pp. 8ff.

"Sales slowed to a trickle": "Notice of Annual Meeting of Shareholders," March 29, 1971, pp. 18, 31.

"Dealers were able to buy rusting 360s": Interview with Marty Pizza, owner, Pizza Saab and Subaru, April 28, 1992.

PAGE 51: "Len Epstein, the agency owner": Rosenberg, *Philadelphia Magazine*, April 1975, p. 103.

"Ma Bricklin," "A woman in Oklahoma": Interview with George Muller.

"The problems helped delay": "Notice of Annual Meeting of Shareholders," March 29, 1971, p. 2. Also: Interview with Michael Sanyour.

"Malcolm would then pull a gun": Interviews with George Muller and Malcolm Bricklin.

PAGE 52: "You won't have an export market": Pearlstein and Posner, *Inc.*, June 1988, p. 51.

On FasTrack, the Koffmans and the efforts to force Bricklin from the company: Rosenberg, *Philadelphia Magazine*, April 1975, pp. 161–62. Also: Interviews with Michael Sanyour and Malcolm Bricklin.

See also: "Bricklin Again Rises From Past Debacles" by Doron P. Levin, *Wall Street Journal*, May 16, 1986, p. 1.

PAGE 53: "They gave Malcolm all 'assets and equipment' ": "Notice of Annual Meeting of Shareholders," March 29, 1971, p. 12.

Malcolm did not go far. Some half-dozen FasTrack franchises eventually opened around the country, a few lasting into the late 1980s. At the same time he began developing FasTrack Leisure Land, he struck a deal with the government of New Brunswick to bring an automobile factory to the poverty-stricken Canadian province. With $14 million plus land and buildings from the Canadians, plus millions more from Canadian and American banks, he announced—at a party at New York's Four Seasons restaurant, where, decked out in jeans and a western shirt, he took a branding iron and tried to imprint his initials on the plastic prototype—the introduction of the Bricklin, a sporty-looking but completely safe automobile. He produced fewer than three thousand of the gull-wing cars, which leaked water, before declaring bankruptcy in 1975, with liabilities of $32 million. Among his creditors was Leon Stern, who had won a $2.3 million judgment against Bricklin over the abandoned FasTrack Leisure Land project. For years after, in New Brunswick, wild financial deals were referred to as "another Bricklin."

Bricklin resurfaced again in 1985 with a deal from Yugoslavia's Zavodi Crvena Zastava to import the manufacturer's subcompact car, which he dubbed the Yugo. Hailed as "the next Volkswagen" for its base price below $4,000, the little car sold as many as 49,000 units in 1987 before reports of shoddy workmanship sent sales plunging and the breakup of the Yugoslav federation shut down the export operation entirely. Long before the end, though, Mal Bricklin sold his interest in the company. He walked away with $14 million. In 1993, he and several partners were involved in starting a company in California that intended to remake existing gas-powered automobiles into electric vehicles. They also planned to open electric-charging stations up and down the state. See: *Wall Street Journal*, May 16, 1986, p. 1; "Yugo Minicar's Importer in Chapter 11; Infusion by Manufacturer Is Expected" by Paul Ingrassia, *Wall Street Journal*, January 31, 1989; "Can Malcolm Bricklin Really Sell Cars for $3,990?" by Amy Dunkin and William Hampton, *Business Week*, February 11, 1985, p. 32.

PAGE 54: " 'Motorist's paradise' ": Flink, p. 140.

PAGE 55: "A third of Subaru drivers rated dealer service as 'poor' ": "If Only the Dealers Were as Good as the Economy and Handling" by Michael Lamm, *Popular Mechanics*, July 1974, p. 120.

PAGE 55: " 'Oriental mysticism' ": Interview with Marvin Riesenbach. Also: Interview with Thomas Gibson, Subaru of America president, October 29, 1992.

"The mutual independence was illusory": Interviews with Marvin Riesenbach, Harvey Lamm and Tom Gibson.

5: INEXPENSIVE, AND BUILT
TO STAY THAT WAY

PAGE 57: "Jews learned the art of innovation": Paul Johnson, *A History of the Jews* (New York: Harper & Row, Publishers, 1988), pp. 284–86.

PAGE 58: "Madison Avenue was as much a product of the Industrial Revolution": For a history of early advertising and its relationship to the development of industrialism and mass marketing, see the aforementioned books by Ewen, Fox, Marchand, Mayer, Pope and Schudson.

Other excellent books on modern marketing's "prehistory" are:

Daniel J. Boorstin, *The Americans: The Democratic Experience* (New York: Random House, 1973). In this book, Boorstin introduced the concept of "consumption communities," a theory of self-identification, borrowed in part from Thorstein Veblen, that has been adopted implicitly by the ad industry itself. The former Librarian of Congress's bibliographical essay at the end of this book is invaluable for anyone wishing to study early marketing.

James D. Norris, *Advertising and the Transformation of American Society, 1865–1920* (New York: Greenwood Press, 1990). A very good treatise on the history of advertising content.

Susan Strasser, *Satisfaction Guaranteed: The Making of the American Mass Market* (New York: Pantheon Books, 1989). An enjoyable, scholarly exploration, useful particularly for its chronicle of the transformation of retailing and distribution.

Another excellent history, surprising in its scope given its picture-book format but all the more valuable for it, is: Charles Goodrum and Helen Dalrymple, *Advertising in America: The First 200 Years* (New York: Harry N. Abrams Inc., 1990).

"The telegraph was used to transmit": Mitchell Stephens, *A History of News* (New York: Viking, 1988), pp. 226–27. Too often, the history of advertising has been analyzed separately from that of the media in which it has run and, more recently, spurned. Stephens's book was one of several I consulted to rectify the problem, at least in my own thinking.

Other books to which I referred include:

Erik Barnouw, *The Sponsor: Notes on a Modern Potentate* (New York: Oxford University Press, 1978).

Erik Barnouw, *Tube of Plenty: The Evolution of American Television*, 2nd Revised Edition (New York: Oxford University Press, 1990). This Columbia

University historian's work remains the definitive chronicle of the rise of electronic media in the United States.

Daniel J. Czitrom, *Media and the American Mind: From Morse to McLuhan* (Chapel Hill: University of North Carolina Press, 1982). Useful for those who want to trace media theory along with media history.

Richard Kluger, *The Paper: The Life and Death of the New York Herald Tribune* (New York: Alfred A. Knopf, 1986). A lively narrative of the early days of American newspaper publishing.

Marshall McLuhan, *Understanding Media: The Extensions of Man* (New York: McGraw-Hill Book Co., 1964). The overhyped classic, referred to more than it is read—its brilliance is marred by a glib reading of history—yet indispensable because it has seeped into our culture and affected the development of the technologies about which McLuhan was writing.

PAGE 59: "The number of newspapers in America": Ralph M. Hower, *The History of an Advertising Agency* (Cambridge, Mass.: Harvard University Press, 1949), p. 10. Hower's book remains the definitive study of a single company in the marketing-communications industry, thanks to the access granted him by the N.W. Ayer agency some fifty years ago. Unless otherwise noted, the details of Ayer's early history come from this book.

Ayer, along with a handful of other agencies (including J. Walter Thompson; Lord & Thomas/Foote, Cone & Belding; and Benton & Bowles); felt so secure in its historical position that it maintained voluminous archives over the decades, capturing everything from rejected campaigns to consumer complaints to clients' bills. The financial pressures of the late 1980s induced some of these agencies to throw away their archives. Fortunately, some far-seeing academic institutions rushed in to save what they could. Part of the Ayer archives are now held by the Center for Modern Advertising History at the Smithsonian Institute's Museum of American History. The Thompson and Benton & Bowles archives are preserved at Duke University.

PAGE 60: "James Rorty, a former copywriter": James Rorty, *Our Master's Voice* (New York: The John Day Company, 1934), p. 36. Rorty's book is an early, critical, insider's exposé of the industry, another standard product on advertising's bookshelf through to the present day.

"The creative side of the agency business": Albert D. Lasker, *The Lasker Story: As He Told It* (Chicago: Advertising Publications, Inc., 1963), pp. 16–18.

PAGE 61: " 'The time has come' ": Claude C. Hopkins, *My Life in Advertising/Scientific Advertising* (Chicago: Crain Books, 1966), p. 213. Advertising's efforts to advertise itself—to clients and to the nation—have been little studied, yet books like Hopkins's, which are essentially self-promotional exercises, are a trove of insight into the culture of the business and its duplicities.

One of the grand self-promotional products was: Bruce Barton, *The Man Nobody Knows* (Indianapolis: Bobbs-Merrill Company, 1925). In it, Barton, a founder of the BBDO agency, puts forward the thesis that Jesus was the world's first and greatest adman. Warren Susman's short biography of Barton in *Culture as History* provides wonderful background on the man and his mission.

" 'The consumer tends to remember just one thing from an advertisement' ": Rosser Reeves, *Reality in Advertising* (1960; reprint, New York: Alfred A. Knopf, 1961; seventeenth printing, 1990), p. 34. Despite its name, Reeves's thin book, whose long publishing history attests to its influence, has nothing to do with reality. Rather, it is an argument for repetition in advertising. For more on Reeves and the Unique Selling Proposition, see Mayer's *Madison Avenue U.S.A.*, and Denis Higgins, *The Art of Writing Advertising: Conversations with William Bernbach, Leo Burnett, George Gribbin, David Ogilvy, Rosser Reeves* (Chicago: Advertising Publications Inc., 1965).

PAGE 62: "Heavy users": Schudson, pp. 26–27.

" 'Rather than any *trivial product difference*' ": Mayer, p. 58.

" 'Fear is as much a part of the air' ": Patricia E. Tierney, *Ladies of the Avenue* (New York: Bartholomew House Ltd., 1971), p. 33. Another exposé by a former creative person.

PAGE 63: " 'Yes, sir! No, sir! Ulcer!' ": Samm Sinclair Baker, *The Permissible Lie: The Inside Truth About Advertising* (Cleveland: World Publishing Company, 1968), p. 8.

"Ninety-two with identifiably Jewish names": Marchand, p. 35.

"Four Roses whiskey": Fox, pp. 273–74.

" 'Advertising is fundamentally persuasion' ": Bob Levenson, *Bill Bernbach's Book: A History of the Advertising That Changed the History of Advertising* (New York: Villard Books, 1987), pp. xvi–xvii.

" '*What* you say in advertising is more important than *how* you say it' ": Ogilvy, p. 93.

" 'Execution can *become* content' ": Mayer, p. 64.

" 'Creativity can make one ad' ": Nelson, p. 224.

PAGE 64: " 'An almost limitless sense of possibility' ": Thomas Hine, *Populuxe* (New York: Alfred A. Knopf, 1989), p. 12.

"Forty-four pounds": Goodrum and Dalrymple, p. 242.

"One typical 1956 Dodge ad": Auto advertising has been collected and assessed in numerous books. The best by far is: Jane and Michael Stern, *Auto Ads* (New York: Random House Inc., 1988).

Other books on the history of auto marketing include:

Stephen Bayley, *Harley Earl* (New York: Taplinger Publishing Co., 1990). A biography of GM's longtime head of automotive design and styling, and the genius behind streamlining, tail fins and other auto-design features with which we still define our fantasies.

Q. David Bowers, *Early American Car Advertisements* (New York: Bonanza Books, 1966). A picture book.

John Keats, *The Insolent Chariots* (Philadelphia: J. B. Lippincott Co., 1958). A splenetic criticism of automotive marketing, written at the height of Detroit's power.

Alfred P. Sloan, Jr., *My Years With General Motors* (New York: Doubleday, 1963). The autobiography of the founder of the modern industrial corporation. In it, Sloan explains how he came to understand that the "laws of the Paris dressmakers" had overtaken utilitarianism in auto sales.

On the Volkswagen campaign in particular, in addition to Walter Henry Nelson's *Small Wonder*, see: *Is the Bug Dead?: The Great Beetle Ad Campaign* (New York: Stewart, Tabori & Chang, 1975).

" 'When you take a photograph' ": Mayer, p. 115.

On the design of the Volkswagen ads: *Graphic Design in America: A Visual Language History* (New York: Harry N. Abrams, Inc., 1989), p. 54. Also: Interview with Bob Levenson, former Volkswagen creative director at Doyle Dane Bernbach, April 26, 1992.

See also: Fox, pp. 256–57.

PAGE 65: " 'Honest car' ": Nelson, pp. 219–25.

PAGE 66:" 'Once the campaign was launched' ": Larry Dobrow, *When Advertising Tried Harder* (New York: Friendly Press, 1984), p. 27.

" 'Without advertising, without big deals' ": Nelson, p. 225.

" 'The campaign caught the crest of a sales wave' ": Schudson, p. 36.

" 'In the beginning, there was Volkswagen' ": Jerry Della Femina, *From Those Wonderful Folks Who Gave You Pearl Harbor: Front-Line Dispatches from the Advertising War* (New York: Pocket Books, 1971), p. 28. Della Femina's book remains the single most representative chronicle of advertising's Creative Revolution of the 1960s, and deservedly so. It is a funny, unaffected and accurate portrayal of how the social convulsions of that era engulfed and changed a fundamentally conservative industry.

I have done numerous interviews over the years about the history of advertising's Creative Revolution and the transformation of the industry in the period 1950 to 1980. For this book, sources who proved particularly helpful included: Harry Paster, executive vice president of the American Association of Advertising Agencies, January 20, 1992; Steve Frankfurt, principal, Frankfurt, Gips & Balkind, January 23, 1992; Carl Spielvogel, co-founder, Backer Spielvogel Bates, February 5, 1992; George Lois, co-founder of Papert, Koenig, Lois, November 1, 1991; and Bob Levenson.

PAGES 69–70: On front-wheel-drive transmission: Sobel, pp. 213–14; Davis and Davis, pp. 23–25; Flink, p. 239.

PAGE 70: On the Green Dolmatch advertising campaign: Interview with Alan Ross, former Subaru of America advertising director, May 4, 1992.

Also: Interviews with Malcolm Bricklin, Michael Sanyour, Paula Green and John Glucksman.

"In the 1972 calendar year, Subaru dealers sold 24,056 cars at retail": S.O.A. sales figures come from the company's annual reports and notices of annual meetings, unless otherwise noted.

PAGES 70–71: " 'An atmosphere of physical violence' ": Della Femina, p. 77. Other information on Lois and his campaign comes from Lois's own *What's the Big Idea?*, and the interview with Lois.

PAGE 71: "Climbed out on a third-story ledge": Philip B. Meggs, *A History of Graphic Design* (New York: Van Nostrand Reinhold, 1983), p. 422.

" 'Advertising is poison gas' ": Lois, p. 4.

PAGE 72: "He was Korean": Interview with Alan Ross.

"Ross was a man": Interview with Joe Barstys, director of S.O.A. owner loyalty program, November 6, 1991. Also: Interviews with Alan Ross; Harvey Lamm; Robert Schmidt, former chairman and chief executive, Levine, Huntley, Schmidt & Beaver, October 13, 1991; and Lee Garfinkel, former Subaru creative director at Levine, Huntley, November 12, 1991.

PAGE 73: "Subaru's advertising and promotion spending in 1975": Unless otherwise noted, these figures come from S.O.A.'s own annual reports.

PAGE 74: "That mechanism was four-wheel drive": Davis and Davis, pp. 29–30. See also: *Fuji Heavy Industries: A 30-Year History* (Tokyo: Fuji Heavy Industries, 1984). For more on the history of four-wheel-drive transmissions, see Flink.

PAGE 75: " 'Little bastards' ": Interview with Michael Sanyour.

"A Los Angeles public relations executive": Interview with Ron Rogers, founder, Rogers & Associates public relations agency, August 17, 1992. For more on the ski team sponsorship: Interviews with Alan Ross and Marvin Riesenbach. Also: Interview with David and Audrey Wager, former S.O.A. marketing executives, February 10, 1992.

PAGE 77: "In Bob Schmidt he had hitched up with a man": The history of the Bob Schmidt–Harvey Lamm relationship and the development of the Subaru–Levine, Huntley alliance is based on extensive interviews with numerous participants, including previously cited interviews with Bob Schmidt, Harvey Lamm, Lee Garfinkel, Marvin Riesenbach, Marty Pizza, Alan Ross, Chris Wackman, David and Audrey Wager, Tom Gibson and Mark Dunn.

In addition, the following interviews were helpful:

Don Peppers, former Levine, Huntley executive vice president for new business development, October 23, 1991; Ed Ronk, former Levine, Huntley media director, October 15, 1991; Harold Levine, co-founder of Levine, Huntley, December 3, 1991; Jay Taub, former Levine, Huntley creative director, October 22, 1991; Larry Plapler, Levine, Huntley co-founder, April 14, 1992; Michael Moore, former Levine, Huntley research director, December 13, 1991; Philippe Krakowsky, former Levine, Huntley communications director, October 16, 1991; Sal DeVito, former Levine, Huntley art director, October 28, 1991; Terry Bonaccolta, former Levine, Huntley Subaru account director, December 10, 1991; Tony DeGregorio, former Subaru creative director at Levine, Huntley, October 29, 1991; Mary Treisbach, former S.O.A. ad manager, November 6, 1991.

PAGE 79: " 'The main outlet for a sense of pride' ": Marchand, p. 41.

"Fifth best-selling import": Subaru 1978 Annual Report, p. 6.

"Fuji made some minor adjustments in the design": Subaru 1977 Annual Report, p. 2.

"Introduced the 'GL' series": Subaru 1978 Annual Report, p. 3.

Road & Track and *Car & Driver* quotations: Subaru 1979 Annual Report, p. 11.

"60 percent of those were retailed in small towns and rural backwaters": Subaru 1978 Annual Report, p. 5.

On 1980 rural sales: Subaru 1980 Annual Report, p. 7.

PAGE 80: "Between 1978 and 1981, gasoline prices at the pump increased 109 percent": These and other statistics on the gasoline price rise, small-car and import-car penetration are from Flink, pp. 390–91. See also David Halberstam's *The Reckoning* and Robert Sobel's *Car Wars* for additional detail on this period.

6: WE BUILT OUR REPUTATION BY BUILDING BETTER CARS

PAGE 85: "*Forbes* magazine ranked Subaru": Subaru 1981 Annual Report, p. 3.

"Unloading 72,000 of his own shares": "Subaru of America, Notice of Annual Meeting of Shareholders," February 26, 1981, and "Notice of Annual Meeting of Shareholders," February 25, 1982.

"Harvey's holdings were worth $8.4 million": *New York Times*, November 10, 1985.

"Institutions owned some 60 percent": Interview with Marvin Riesenbach.

PAGE 86: On the Voluntary Restraint Agreement between Japan and the U.S.: Halberstam, pp. 625–28; Sobel, pp. 296–99.

"The company reassured shareholders": Subaru 1981 Annual Report, p. 21.

PAGE 87: "Worked out to $250 for every car sold": *New York Times*, November 10, 1985.

PAGES 88ff: On Lamm's abandonment of plans to build a sport-utility vehicle and a minivan in favor of the XT: Interviews with David and Audrey Wager, Terry Bonaccolta, Marvin Riesenbach and Harvey Lamm.

Also: Interviews with Kei Ono, Subaru of America senior product planner, November 8, 1991, and Ron Will, S.O.A. senior product planner, November 8, 1991.

For information on the growth of the sport-utility market, see: "For Drivers, the Fun Is Back" by John Holusha, *New York Times*, June 17, 1986, p. D1.

PAGE 89: " 'A formidable market share' ": *New York Times*, November 10, 1985.

" 'An uninspired effort' ": "Subaru Alcyone: Rounding Out the Wedge" by Yasutoshi Ishiwatari, *Car & Driver*, October 1987, p. 31.

PAGE 91: "They would do anything for us": Pearlstein and Posner, *Inc.*, June 1988.

On Shoji Kikuchi: Interviews with Tom Gibson, Harvey Lamm, Marvin Riesenbach and Michael Sanyour. See also: Pearlstein and Posner, *Inc.*, June 1988; and "We Want to Be More Like Audi and BMW," *Forbes*, June 16, 1986.

PAGE 92: "To finance Harold Levine's retirement": Interview with Harold Levine. It is notoriously hard for an agency to cash out a founder. As a general rule of thumb, ad agencies are valued at one year's gross income, the aggregate of the 12 to 15 percent commissions (or equivalent fees) it receives from clients. In 1985, Levine, Huntley was billing $70 million; its gross income, and its worth, would have been at least $8.4 million. By this measure, Harold's share in the former rag-trade agency was worth more than $5 million.

See: "Wells, Rich, Greene Deal Shows Strength of French" by Randall Rothenberg, *New York Times*, April 16, 1990, p. D1.

"The average price of a Subaru rose": *New York Times*, November 10, 1985.

PAGE 93: "Subaru offered the GL-10": Subaru 1982 Annual Report, p. 2.

"Harvey named the car for the Bo Derek movie": Interview with David Wager.

"Its old sedan in a 'turbo-traction model' ": Subaru 1984 Annual Report, p. 6.

"Add a line on the window sticker": Interview with Marvin Riesenbach.

"Close to one-third of the cars S.O.A. imported": "Marketing: Subaru Hopes to Get Sales Back into Gear with Switch to Unorthodox Transmission" by Paul Ingrassia, *Wall Street Journal*, November 18, 1988.

"Finance ministers and central bankers": "U.S. and 4 Allies Plan Move to Cut Value of the Dollar" by Peter T. Kilborn, *New York Times*, September 23, 1985, p. A1.

On the decline of the dollar and the rise of the yen: "Yearlong Decline of Dollar Fails to Cut U.S. Trade Deficit" by Clyde H. Farnsworth, *New York Times*, September 19, 1986, p. A1; "A Year After Plaza Accord, Currency Issues Remain Divisive" by Susan Chira, *New York Times*, September 22, 1986, p. D1.

PAGE 94: On the 1986 auto finance wars: "G.M. Seen Offering 2.9% Rate," *New York Times*, August 28, 1986, p. D1; "Chrysler and Ford Cut Rates, Too," *New York Times*, August 30, 1986, p. 34; "A.M.C. Adds Free Financing," *New York Times*, September 4, 1986, p. D1.

PAGE 95: " 'C' and 'D' counties": Jane Imber and Betsy-Ann Toffler, *Dictionary of Advertising and Direct Mail Terms* (New York: Barron's, 1987), p. 1.

"Twelve thousand 1986 models were still left on dealer lots": Interview with Mark Dunn.

"Stripped the frills from their compact cars": "For Subaru, Luxury Is a Necessity" by Doron P. Levin, *New York Times*, January 26, 1989, p. D1.

"Its wholesales to dealers dropped 8 percent": Subaru 1987 Annual Report, pp. 20–23.

"Inventories worth $133 million": Subaru 1989 Annual Report, p. 17.

"Proffered S.O.A. money": Subaru 1989 Annual Report, p. 21.

PAGES 96–97: On the building of Fuji's Lafayette, Indiana, plant and the production of the Subaru SVX: Interviews with Tom Gibson, Chris Wackman, Marvin Riesenbach, Harvey Lamm and George Muller.

Also: Interview with Eiichi Hongo, Fuji Heavy Industries managing director, May 29, 1992.

PAGE 97: " 'Trying to take on Camry, Accord and 626' ": *New York Times*, January 26, 1989.

PAGE 98: "We'll market the Legacy as the most powerful Subaru": Interview with Tony DeGregorio.

PAGE 99: "S.O.A. was adamant about not promoting four-wheel drive": Interview with Tony DeGregorio.

"Produced, at a cost of several hundred thousand": Interview with Sal DeVito.

PAGE 100: "Fuji Heavy Industries bid $6 a share": *Wall Street Journal*, January 17, 1990.

PAGE 101: "Harvey resigned from Subaru": *Wall Street Journal*, September 5, 1990.

"When Subaru put its advertising account into review": "Advertising: Subaru Puts $60 Million Account in Review" by Kim Foltz, *New York Times*, April 12, 1991, p. D7.

7: WHEN YOU'RE HAVING
MORE THAN ONE

PAGE 106: Statistics on size of advertising industry in 1991: "Tokyo Supplants N.Y. as Ad Capital" by R. Craig Endicott, *Advertising Age*, April 13, 1992, p. S1.

PAGE 109: " 'We're playing every day' ": Marchand, p. 47.

PAGE 110: " 'Advertisements may be *evaluated* scientifically' ": Leo Bogart, *Strategy in Advertising: Matching Media and Messages to Markets and Motivations*, Second Edition (Lincolnwood, Ill.: NTC Business Books, 1990), p. 10. Despite its clinical title, Bogart's book is a joy—an anecdote-rich compendium of everything one needs to know about how advertising is constructed. Most surprising, Bogart, a distinguished researcher, casts a skeptical eye on research and reserves his accolades for the creative side of the business.

PAGE 114: "Conclusive understanding of advertising's effects": Neil H. Borden, *The Economic Effects of Advertising* (Chicago: Richard D. Irwin, Inc., 1942), pp. 837–82. David Ogilvy was once asked what one job, other than his own, he would like to have. He replied that he wanted Neil Borden's job at the Harvard Business School. It's doubtful that Ogilvy had read Borden's book, for in spite of financial support from the ad industry, Borden's work reeks with suspicion about advertising's effects.

For more on the economic effects of advertising, see Bogart, pp. 17–35.

" 'The only faith in a secularized consumer society' ": Schudson, p. 225.

8: FOUR OUT OF FIVE
DENTISTS RECOMMEND ...

PAGE 117: On R. L. Polk & Company: "R.L. Polk & Co; Company Profile," *Chilton's Automotive Marketing*, December 1991; "Paper Tiger" by Caroline Price, *Michigan Business*, March 1988, p. 28.

On Maritz Marketing Research: "Top 50 Research Firms Profiled; the 1991 Honomichl Business Report on the Marketing Research Industry" by Jack Honomichl, *Marketing News*, May 27, 1991.

On J. D. Power & Associates: "Expanding Beyond Automobile Surveys, J. D. Power Defends Its Methods" by Neal Templin, *Wall Street Journal*, September 5, 1991, p. B1; "More Power to J.D. Power" by Alex Taylor III, *Fortune*, May 18, 1992, p. 103; "The Business Built on Power: Numbers Made an Automotive King Out of James David Power" by Cheryl Eberwein, *Corporate Detroit Magazine*, May 1, 1992, p. 14.

PAGE 121: " 'New brands and brand variants of unrelieved sameness' ": William M. Weilbacher, *Brand Marketing: Building Winning Brand Strategies That Deliver Value and Customer Satisfaction* (Lincolnwood, Ill.: NTC

Business Books, 1993), p. 3. This book is far and away the best, most read-able and most comprehensive analysis of the brand proliferation problem yet published. Unless otherwise noted, the statistics on brand extensions come from Weilbacher's book.

"The process by which agencies find these insights and bonds is generally called 'account planning' ": "Building a Market for Ohio Wines" by Randall Rothenberg, *New York Times*, November 21, 1988, p. D9; "Good Fortune for Account Planners" by Randall Rothenberg, *New York Times*, November 18, 1988, p. D17.

9: THE REAL THING

PAGES 125–26: "The Japanese parent company had made it clear": Interview with Kunihiro Sakurai, deputy director, Dentsu Inc. Overseas Management Division, June 4, 1992.

PAGE 133: "Traipsed over to the *New York Times*": "Advertising: Two New Defections at Levine, Huntley" by Stuart Elliott, *New York Times*, June 5, 1991.

10: IT'S THE RIGHT THING TO DO

PAGE 137: " 'We have that which is divine' ": R. Hackforth, trans. Plato's *Phaedo* (Cambridge: The University Press, 1955), pp. 83–84.

11: THE QUICKER PICKER-UPPER

PAGES 180–81: " 'The motive at the root of ownership' ": Thorstein Veblen, *The Theory of the Leisure Class* (1899; reprint, New York: Viking Penguin Inc., 1989), p. 25.

PAGE 181: " 'The arts and sciences of advertising' ": Boorstin, *The Americans*, p. 146.

" 'Every advertising medium tries as hard as it can' ": Bogart, p. 127.

"Consumers care little about which brands they buy": See Weilbacher, *Brand Marketing*, and Schudson, *Advertising*, for lengthy discussions of this subject.

12: SOMEWHERE WEST OF LARAMIE

PAGE 188: "Thirty-five pounds of news clippings": Jerry Mander, George Dippel and Howard Gossage, *The Great International Paper Airplane Book* (New York: Simon & Schuster, 1967), p. 8.

Howard Gossage bio: Kim Rotzoll, Jarlath Graham and Burrows Mussey, eds., *Is There Any Hope for Advertising?* (Urbana and Chicago: University of Illinois Press, 1986), pp. xi–xxvii.

See also: *Newsweek*, July 21, 1969, p. 74; Tom Wolfe, *The Pump House*

Gang (New York: Farrar, Straus & Giroux, 1968), pp. 130–66; "The Adman Who Plays with Paper Airplanes," *Business Week*, February 11, 1967, pp. 74–80.

PAGE 189: " 'It's not advertising the way I know it' ": Della Femina, pp. 126–29.

"New York agencies' share of total domestic advertising spending": These statistics were provided by the American Association of Advertising Agencies statistics.

PAGE 191: " 'There was in the character of the people' ": Terence O'Donnell and Thomas Vaughan, *Portland: An Informal History & Guide* (Portland: The Oregon Historical Society, 1984), p. 19.

"The citizens voted to exclude blacks from the state" and "the West Coast's center of Ku Klux Klan activity": O'Donnell and Vaughan, pp. 30, 55–56, 71.

"Four local families controlled twenty-one corporations": E. Kimbark MacColl, *Merchants, Money and Power: The Portland Establishment, 1843–1913* (Portland: Georgian Press, 1988), p. xvi.

On the development of the Portland advertising industry and Bill Cain's arrival in Portland: Interviews with Wes Perrin, co-founder, Borders, Perrin & Norrander, February 12, 1991; Bill Borders, co-founder, Borders, Perrin, Norrander, February 13, 1992; Dick Paetzke, creative director, McCann-Erickson Seattle, February 7, 1992; Mark Silveira, executive creative director, Ogilvy & Mather, February 5, 1992; William Cain, founder William Cain agency, February 18, 1992; Phil Stevens, president, Gerber Advertising, February 13, 1992; Jane Kirby Shanklin, former media director, William Cain agency, February 5, 1992.

PAGE 194: The Duke Wieden information came from several sources, notably interviews with Wes Perrin, Bill Borders and Phil Stevens.

Also: Interview with David Kennedy, Wieden & Kennedy co-founder, February 20, 1992.

See also: "They Know Bo" by Warren Berger, *New York Times Magazine*, November 11, 1990, pp. 36ff.

" 'Burned alive in their innocent flannel suits' ": The line is from the Allen Ginsberg poem "Howl."

"A whorish business": "Good Guys" by Margaret Richardson, *Print*, Spring 1990, pp. 76ff.

"A shell game": Interview with David Kennedy. Other sources on Dan Wieden include: Interviews with Mark Silveira, Wes Perrin, David Kennedy and Bill Cain. Also: Interview with Peter Moore, former Nike creative director, February 15, 1992.

See also: *New York Times Magazine*, November 11, 1990.

PAGE 195: "E.C. Comics and Mad Magazine": Maria Reidelbach, *Completely*

Mad: A History of the Comic Book and Magazine (Boston: Little, Brown and Company, 1991), pp. 42–55.

PAGE 198: "Nike, however, was an anomaly in Portland": For histories of Nike Inc. and running, see: J. B. Strasser and Laurie Becklund, *Swoosh: The Story of Nike and the Men Who Played There* (New York: Harcourt Brace Jovanovich, 1991); Jim Naughton, *Taking to the Air: The Rise of Michael Jordan* (New York: Warner Books, 1992).

PAGE 199: " 'We thought the world stopped and started in the lab' ": "An interview with Nike's Phil Knight" by Geraldine E. Willigan, *Harvard Business Review*, July 1992.

PAGE 200: "Brown had no natural athletic affinity": Interview with Wes Perrin.

" 'There is no finish line' ": Interview with Peter Moore. See also: Strasser and Becklund, pp. 269–70.

"Moore, especially, saw the personality posters": Strasser and Becklund, pp. 372–73.

PAGES 201–2: "The finished version of a Louisiana Pacific television spot": Interview with Jane Kirby Shanklin.

Other sources on Wieden and Kennedy's dissatisfaction with and eventual defection from Cain include: Interviews with Bill Cain, Peter Moore, David Kennedy and Mark Silveira.

Also: Interviews with Cindy Hale, former marketing executive, Nike Inc., February 14, 1992, and Dennis Fraser, Wieden & Kennedy print production director and co-founder, February 12, 1992.

PAGE 202: "Numbed by Novocain": Interview with Jane Kirby Shanklin.

"The company guaranteed the incipient agency": Interview with Peter Moore.

PAGE 203: "The more junior members in Nike's marketing department were aghast": Interview with Cindy Hale.

"$458 million worth of sneakers": Strasser and Becklund, p. 439.

"The tyro agency soon began adopting": Interview with Cindy Hale.

PAGE 204: "All wearing Reebok shoes": For the "sneaker wars" between Nike and Reebok, see Strasser and Becklund, pp. 503–504; "The Sneaker Game" by Fleming Meeks, *Forbes*, October 22, 1990, p. 114; *Harvard Business Review*, July 1992; "Nike Catches Up with the Trendy Front-Runner" by Barbara Buell, *Business Week*, October 24, 1988, p. 88.

"It ignored the fact that sales of athletic shoes": Interviews with Peter Moore and Cindy Hale. Also: Interview with Steve Sandstrom, former Nike creative department executive, February 13, 1992.

PAGE 205: "What does our brand stand for?" Forbes, October 22, 1990.

"Technology is fashion": Interview with Peter Moore.

" 'For years, we thought of ourselves as a production-oriented company' ": *Harvard Business Review*, July 1992.

" 'Individual athletes, even more than teams' ": Strasser and Becklund, p. 516.

PAGE 206: "Nike rearranged its business": *Harvard Business Review*, July 1992.

PAGE 207: "The shoe company decided to throw its advertising account into review." For information on the review, I have relied on interviews with Peter Moore and Cindy Hale.

Also: Interview with Gary Langstaff, former Wieden & Kennedy Los Angeles office head, February 6, 1992.

"Projecting changing images on the sides of buildings": Interview with Cindy Hale.

PAGE 208: "So he used it for a message": Interviews with Cindy Hale and Peter Moore.

Other information on the Chiat/Day–Nike relationship came from an interview with Jay Chiat, founder, Chiat/Day, March 6, 1992; and from Strasser and Becklund, p. 521.

PAGE 209: "The agency had already moved": Interview with Gary Langstaff.

"Honda had a vague strategy": Most of the information on the Honda scooters review and production came from my interview with Gary Langstaff and an interview with Larry Bridges, founder, Red Car Productions, November 15, 1991.

PAGE 210: "It was pure camp": Susan Sontag, *Against Interpretation and Other Essays* (New York: Octagon Books, 1982), pp. 275–89.

PAGE 211: "The development of a postmodern sensibility in the advertising industry": The material on postmodernism in advertising and marketing came from several sources. These include:

"The Postmodernism That Failed," draft paper by Robert Goldman, Department of Sociology and Anthropology, Lewis & Clark College, and Stephen Papson, Department of Sociology, St. Lawrence University.

"Levi's and the Knowing Wink: Realism, Reflexivity and Individual Authenticity in TV Ads," draft paper by Robert Goldman and Stephen Papson.

"Hypersignification: Television Ads in the 1980s," draft paper by Robert Goldman and Stephen Papson. Goldman and Papson's work is the most advanced in looking specifically at advertisements through the lens of postmodern theory. I am indebted to them for allowing me to read their work.

Another scholar who has studied the phenomenon, albeit more broadly, is Morris Holbrook at Columbia University. Among contemporary journalists, no one has done more writing on the subject than Leslie Savan, the advertising critic for the *Village Voice*.

A very useful book on postmodernism and appropriationism is:

Steven Heller and Julie Lasky, *Bonehead Design: Use and Abuse of Historical Form* (New York: Van Nostrand Reinhold, 1993).

People who helped me put Wieden & Kennedy's work and development in this context included: Rob Watzke, a film editor at Red Car studios, whom I interviewed on July 29, 1991; Andy Berlin, a principal in the San Francisco agency Goodby, Berlin & Silverstein, interviewed on February 5, 1992; Jim Riswold, Wieden & Kennedy copywriter, interviewed on July 7, 1991; and Larry Bridges.

PAGE 212: "They were 'image scavengers'": "Appropriating Like Krazy: From Pop Art to Meta-Pop" by Jim Collins, in Naremore and Brantlinger's *Modernity and Mass Culture*, pp. 201–23.

PAGE 213: "'Take you back to the brand and down the buy-hole'": "Adblisters" by Leslie Savan, *Village Voice*, June 30, 1992, p. 48.

PAGES 214–15: "'That commercial helped turn the company'": *New York Times Magazine*, November 11, 1990.

PAGE 215: "Nike's ad spending ballooned": For Nike's renaissance, see:
"Advertising: Presenting of Effie Awards" by Philip H. Dougherty, *New York Times*, June 5, 1986, p. D18.
"Advertising: Second Shoe Drops for Image Ads" by Randall Rothenberg, *New York Times*, February 10, 1989, p. D17.
"High Tops: High Style, High Tech, High Cost" by Glenn Rifkin, *New York Times*, January 5, 1992, Section 3, p. 10.
"Reebok Fights to Be No. 1 Again" by Kim Foltz, *New York Times*, March 12, 1992, p. D1.
See also: *New York Times Magazine*, November 11, 1990.

PAGE 217: "Aesop Glim": Aesop Glim, *Copy: The Core of Advertising* (New York: Dover Publications Inc., 1963), p. 13.
"'Auteur' commercials . . . a thinking-man's agency'": *Print*, Spring 1990.
"'A thing of muscle and life'": Frederic Wakeman, *The Hucksters* (New York: Rinehart & Company, 1946), p. 291.
Thanks in part to the subsequent film starring Clark Gable, Wakeman's novel remains the public's iconic reference for the ad industry. Nearly fifty years after its publication, it's still a pretty good rendition of what the ad game is really like.

PAGE 219: "Their Thurberesque tone of the 'little man'": "Volkswagen as 'Little Man'" by Bruce G. Vanden Bergh, *Journal of American Culture*, Winter 1992, p. 95.

13: JUST DO IT

PAGE 228: "The average cost to produce a single national television advertisement": The American Association of Advertising Agencies, A.A.A.A. Television Production Cost Survey System: Report of 1989 Findings, May 1990. "The most expensive commercials had cost only about $70,000": Lincoln Diamant, ed., *The Making of a Television Commercial: The Story of Eastman Kodak's "Yesterdays"* (New York: Hastings House, Publishers, 1970). This little gem of a book explains, and illustrates with copious photographs, the entire commercial production process. Even with technological advances in production, it is still a remarkably up-to-date portrayal.

"Marked up the cost of commercial production by 17.65 percent": Herbert S. Gardner, Jr., *The Advertising Agency Business: The Complete Manual for Management and Operation* (Lincolnwood, Ill.: NTC Business Books, 1988), pp. 50–52.

14: COME ALIVE

PAGE 238: " 'Each sealed in its hunger' ": From the poem "Every Blessed Day" by Philip Levine, *What Work Is: Poems* (New York: Alfred A. Knopf, 1992), p. 8. Levine, a Pulitzer prize–winning poet, once worked in an auto factory.

PAGE 242: "A federal district court awarded the singer Bette Midler": "Style Is One Thing, Defining It Is Another" by Michael Rubiner, *New York Times*, July 5, 1992, Section 2, p. 23.

PAGES 247–48: " 'Soon passed tranquilly' ": Mark Twain, *The Innocents Abroad* (Signet Classic Edition, New York: Penguin Books U.S.A., 1980), p. 26.

15: PERCEPTION/REALITY

PAGE 256: "Its name was taken from the Pacific Electric Railway's trolleys": Interview with Larry Bridges.

See also: Flink, p. 142.

PAGE 273: " 'You'll have to reshoot the product' ": Wieden & Kennedy subsequently withheld a portion of Tibor Kalman's compensation for the commercial shoot, prompting Tibor to take the agency into arbitration. The arbitrator ordered the agency to pay the director everything he was under contract to receive.

PAGE 274: "Pytka was berating him mercilessly": Interview with Bill Davenport, Wieden & Kennedy production manager, February 15, 1992.

17: IT KEEPS GOING ... AND GOING ...

PAGE 297: " 'Smartly written, directed and compelling' ": "Subaru Drives Home Point That Cars Are Machines" by Barbara Lippert, *Adweek*, August 26, 1991, p. 16.

" 'This is perfect advertising' ": "Subaru Revs Up" by Bob Garfield, *Advertising Age*, August 19, 1991, p. 46.

PAGE 298: " 'Offensive and totally inappropriate' ": "Critics Attempt to Put Brakes on Subaru Ads" by Joanne Lipman, *Wall Street Journal*, August 20, 1991.

Also: "ABC Puts Brakes on Speedy Subaru" by Kathy Brown, *Adweek*, August 26, 1991, p. 5.

PAGE 305: "Only 1.2 percent of the total amount automotive companies planned to spend": "Subaru of America CY 92 Regional Media Recommendations," p. 2.

PAGES 305–06: "They divided the 210 U.S. media markets": "Subaru of America CY 92 Regional Media Recommendations," pp. 11–16.

Also: Interview with Scot Butler, Wieden & Kennedy media director, November 19, 1991.

PAGE 310: "They 'had a great teacher' ": "Look Who's Talking," *Ad/Media* (Auckland, New Zealand), vol. 7, no. 12, February 1992, p. 33.

18: ALL ASPIRIN IS ALIKE

PAGE 311: "Dealers—there were 14,850 of them": " '1991 NADA Data: Economic Impact of America's New-Car and Truck Dealers." A special report prepared by the National Automobile Dealers Association's Industry Analysis Division, Washington, D.C., August 1991, p. 25.

"The Ford Motor Company's lead agency, grew inspired": Interview with Jeff Greenberg, Subaru regional account director at Wieden & Kennedy, January 6, 1992.

PAGE 314: "The Subarus filed into the agency's gym": The account of this presentation is based on several interviews. The subjects were: David Luhr, Wieden & Kennedy's Subaru account director, January 8, 1992; Peter Wegner, Wieden & Kennedy freelance copywriter, November 11, 1992; Scot Butler, Chris Wackman, Tom Gibson and Mark Dunn.

I was also helped in my understanding of the tension between S.O.A. and its dealers—indeed, between auto companies in general and their dealers—by the following interviews: Bruce Buchanan, Wieden & Kennedy account executive for S.O.A., January 6, 1992; Tom O'Hare, Subaru Distributors Corp. president, December 4, 1991; Charles Worrell, S.O.A. executive vice president for sales and marketing, July 30, 1992; Woody Purcell, S.O.A. regional vice president, January 29, 1992.

PAGE 317: "All the options that people normally wanted in a car": The details of Subaru's pricing strategy come from several sources, including Tom Gibson, Chris Wackman, David Luhr, Jeff Greenberg and Bruce Buchanan. Also: Interview with Fred Adcock, Subaru field sales manager, January 14, 1992.

PAGE 319: "The average retail selling price of a new car": NADA Report, pp. 29, 45.

"In 1971, the average driver put 14 percent down on her $3,370 car": "The Affordability Dilemma" by Tom Webb and Jake Kelderman, *Automotive Executive*, January 1992, pp. 18–19.

19: IF IT'S OUT THERE, IT'S IN HERE

PAGE 339: "Ad spending in the United States had declined in 1991, for the first time in thirty years": "Advertising: A Forecast for '91 Is Revised to Show a Decline" by Stuart Elliott, *New York Times*, December 10, 1991, p. D1.

"Auto advertising fell by 9 percent": "Automotive Advertising Revenues Increase 13% in 1990," press release issued by the Television Bureau of Advertising, New York, April 8, 1991.

Also: "Automotive Advertising Revenues Down 9% in First Half of '91," press release issued by the Television Bureau of Advertising, New York, September 23, 1991.

"In 1980, the industry's worst year ever": "Big Losses for Top 2 in Detroit" by Doron P. Levin, *New York Times*, October 23, 1991, p. D1.

"Nor were the once-invincible Japanese immune": "Auto Sales Fell 11.2 Percent Last Year" by Adam Bryant, *New York Times*, January 7, 1992, p. D1.

20: WE ARE DRIVEN

PAGE 347: "Automobile sales in the United States in 1991": " '91 Sales Are Lowest in Eight Years" by Joseph Bohn, *Automotive News*, January 13, 1992, p. 1; "Even Asian Sales Fall in Rough '91" by Kristine Stiven Breese, *Automotive News*, January 13, 1992, p. 27; "Domestic Car Sales, December & YTD," *Automotive News*, January 13, 1992, p. 28.

PAGES 354–55: "President George Bush determined to show": The material on President Bush's trip to Japan comes from the following sources:

"In Japan's View, U.S. Car Companies Should Be Blaming Only Themselves" by David E. Sanger, *New York Times*, January 6, 1992, p. A12.

"American Auto Makers Need Major Overhaul to Match the Japanese" by Joseph B. White, Gregory A. Patterson and Paul Ingrassia, *Wall Street Journal*, January 10, 1992, p. A1.

"Blunt Talk by Iacocca, Just Back From Japan" by Barnaby J. Feder, *New York Times*, January 11, 1992, p. D1.

"Japan Torpedoes Big 3 Hopes" by Richard Johnson and Mary Ann Maskery, *Automotive News*, January 13, 1992, p. 1.

PAGE 362: "American workers were 'lazy' ": "Japan Premier Joins Critics of Americans' Work Habits" by David E. Sanger, *New York Times*, February 4, 1992, p. A1.

"The owners of the Seattle Mariners": "Japanese Bid for Seattle Team Gets Baseball's Cold Shoulder" by Timothy Egan, *New York Times*, January 24, 1992, p. A1.

"Monsanto Chemical offered $1,000": "The New Buy-American Auto Sweepstakes" by Matthew L. Wald, *New York Times*, January 24, 1992, p. D1.

"New York Pontiac dealers": "Anti-Japan Auto Ads May Backfire" by Stuart Elliott, *New York Times*, January 30, 1992, p. C18.

PAGE 363: "Pat Domenicone, an Atlanta dealer": Advertisement in *Atlanta Journal/Atlanta Constitution*, January 24, 1992, p. S7.

PAGE 365: "Volkswagen introduced a 'Payment Protection Plus' plan": "VW Payment Plan Sparks Calls" by Arlena Sawyers, *Automotive News*, February 3, 1992, p. 6.

"A Palm Beach, Florida, Pontiac dealer": "New Game Plan" by Phil Frame, *Automotive News*, February 3, 1992, p. 3.

21: I THINK IN MY LEGACY

PAGE 369: "Kosuke Mori was also dwelling on the image of Subaru": The material on the launch and relaunch of the Subaru Legacy in Japan derives from several interviews: Akira Yamaguchi, the general manager of marketing and advertising in Fuji Heavy Industries' Subaru domestic sales and marketing division, May 27, 1992; Kosuke Mori, Dentsu management supervisor and Subaru account director, June 2, 1992; Tetsuo Wada, Dentsu associate marketing director, June 2, 1992; Take Takeichi, the Subaru account's creative director at Dentsu, June 2, 1992; and Takao Saito, the general manager of the Subaru Overseas Planning Dept. at Fuji, May 29, 1992.

"Draw consumers away from the Toyota Camry": Interview with Akira Yamaguchi.

"Consumers did not question the durability of a Subaru": Interview with Kosuke Mori.

"Dentsu's ten Working Guidelines": Dentsu Inc. Dentsu Data Book, undated public relations material, p. 3.

PAGE 370: " 'Advantage: Technology' ": Interview with Kosuke Mori.

"100,000-kilometer world speed record": Fuji marketing brochures and documents.

"Hashiri": Interviews with Kosuke Mori and Takao Saito.

"Man and woman in evening dress": Interview with Takao Saito.

PAGE 370: "Dentsu's three-year marketing plan": Interview with Tetsuo Wada.

PAGE 371: "These other activities accounted for only 20 percent of its business": "Company Takeover, Tokyo Style" by David Sanger, *New York Times*, June 27, 1990, p. D1.

"The economic upsurge initiated in late 1986": For a history of the Bubble, see Kazuo Izawa, ed., *Japan 1992 Marketing and Advertising Yearbook* (Tokyo: Dentsu Inc., 1991), pp. 93ff. These books, which are published by Dentsu annually, in English, provide some of the best information available on marketing and advertising in Japan.

"Izanagi Boom of 1965 to 1970": Izawa, *1992 Yearbook*, pp. 94–95.

"The lifetime sales system": Interview with George Fields, chairman, ASI Market Research (Japan) Inc., June 1, 1992.

The information on sales, marketing and advertising in Japan also comes from the following interviews: Takeshi Matsamura, Dentsu marketing division deputy director, June 5, 1992; Tsutomu Okahashi and Yoshito Maruoka, Dentsu marketing project planning office, June 5, 1992; Derek A. Hall, executive vice president, Dentsu, Young & Rubicam, May 27, 1992; Kiyoshi (KC) Eguchi, executive vice president, Dentsu Corp. of America, April 17, 1992; Kunihiro Sakurai, deputy director of Dentsu's overseas management division, June 4, 1992; Shunji Nakanishi, the director of Dentsu's corporate communications division, June 2, 1992; Toshio Naito, Dentsu managing director, June 4, 1992; Amano Yukuchi, editor, Senden Kaige, June 9, 1992; Donald J. Dillon, chief executive officer of McCann-Erickson Hakuhodo, May 27, 1992.

See also: "About Japan Series 7: Japan's Mass Media" (Tokyo: Foreign Press Center, March 1990); Karel van Wolferen, *The Enigma of Japanese Power* (New York: Vintage Books, 1990).

"Reduced the cost of owning luxury cars": "Automakers Are Stepping on the Brakes" by Takeshi Sato and Shu Watanabe, *Japan Times*, June 2, 1992, p. 4.

PAGE 372: "Advertising was accounting for 1.2 percent of the gross national product": "In the Land of the Soft Sell" by Alice Rawsthorne, *Financial Times*, February 9, 1990, p. 20.

"Its billings were more than twice those of its nearest competitor": *Financial Times*, February 9, 1990.

"Dentsu placed 20 percent of all the newspaper advertisements": *Financial Times*, February 9, 1990.

"One-quarter of the eight thousand television commercials": "Dentsu Rising" by Betsy Sharkey, *Adweek*, February 3, 1992, pp. 27–31.

"Forced from the air": Van Wolferen, pp. 176–78.

"Half the prime-time television series": *Financial Times*, February 9, 1990.

" 'Editing bureau of Tsukiji' ": Van Wolferen, p. 176.

"More than 3,800 employees": *Adweek*, February 3, 1992.

"Hundreds of subcontractors": Van Wolferen, p. 176.

"Claimed to have four thousand clients": *Adweek*, February 3, 1992.

"Billings stood at a record $9.7 billion": *Adweek*, February 3, 1992.

"Gross advertising expenditures in Japan": "1991 Advertising Expenditures in Japan," Dentsu Information Series, published by Dentsu Inc., Tokyo, p. 4.

PAGE 373: "The second worst handicap a company faced": "Seven Crucial Viewpoints to Understand the Japanese Consumer" by Masaru Ariga, *Japan 1991: Marketing and Advertising Yearbook* (Tokyo: Dentsu Inc., 1990), p. 88.

"Shoppers almost always knew the name": "Developing Creative Advertising Strategy for the Japanese Marketplace" by C. Anthony di Benedetto, Mariko Tamate and Rajan Chandran, *Journal of Advertising Research*, January/February 1992, p. 43.

"Japan's history as a land-poor agricultural nation": Interview with Yoshito Maruoka.

"The concept of *wa*, or harmony": "Branding in Japan" by Hiroshi Tanaka, *Admap*, November 1991, p. 15.

PAGE 374: "When Chikuhei Nakajima was born on January 11, 1884": The Nakajima biography and corporate history, including the material on the Industrial Bank of Japan, unless otherwise noted, comes from: Tairyu Takahashi, *Nakajima Aircraft Research* (Tokyo: Nihon Keizai Hyoronsya, 1988). I am indebted to Lisa Prevenslik for the translation.

This material also comes from several interviews. In addition to the aforementioned Fuji executives, the subjects include: Ryuichiro Kuze, president of Subaru Tecnica International, May 26, 1992; Yasuo Furuno, the director and general manager of Subaru Tecnica's business planning and operation department, May 26, 1992; Takeshi Higurashi, chairman, Subaru of America, May 12, 1992; Yasumi Mizuno, Subaru of America sales and marketing senior staff, May 12, 1992; Michiaki Fujino, director and general manager, Fuji's Gunma manufacturing division, May 25, 1992; Hitoshi Maeda, general manager, Fuji's Oizumi engine and transmission plant, May 25, 1992. Other people who proved helpful on Fuji's history included: Naohiro Amaya, chairman and chief executive, Dentsu Institute for Human Studies, June 1, 1992; and Aritsune Todaiji, car critic, June 9, 1992.

PAGE 376: "To create around him and his family a *zaibatsu*": For more on Japan's *zaibatsu*, see Halberstam's *The Reckoning*, Van Wolferen's *The Enigma of Japanese Power* and Michael A. Cusumano, *The Japanese Automobile Industry: Technology and Management at Nissan and Toyota* (Cambridge, Mass.: Harvard University Press, 1989).

"Turned his fantasy of a 'new *zaibatsu*' ": Cusumano, p. 27.

PAGE 377: "Mitaka ... housed its soul": Interview with Takao Saito.

PAGE 378: "Split into a dozen smaller firms": Fuji corporate histories and documents differ on whether the company was split into twelve or fifteen separate companies.

"Whose executives' jobs ... the GHQ spared": Halberstam, p. 132.

"The group of six visible stars known in the West as the Pleiades": The information on the Subaru name comes from company documents. Fuji histories differ on whether five companies or six companies came together from Nakajima to form Fuji. Most say five.

"A different, looser form, called *keiretsu*": For information on *keiretsu*, see, generally, Halberstam, van Wolferen and Sobel, particularly pp. 182–83 of the latter.

PAGE 379: "An essential institution in the revival of the Japanese economy": Halberstam, pp. 131–33.

"It could issue bonds that other banks could not": Interview with Takao Saito.

"When the Nissan combine was broken up": Cusumano, p. 55.

PAGE 380: "The dismantling of Prince's labor union": The information on Nissan, Prince and Fuji comes from: Cusumano, pp. 76, 148, 177, 257; Halberstam, pp. 411–14; interviews with Takeshi Higurashi, Tom Gibson and Naohiro Amaya.

"Without the backing of Sumitomo": Sobel, pp. 182, 274; Flink, pp. 334–35.

"Fuji and Isuzu managed to build a factory": Interview with Takeshi Higurashi.

PAGE 381: "Takeshi Higurashi, who joined Fuji": "Takeshi & Me" by Tom McGrath, *Delaware Valley Magazine*, May 1992, pp. 30ff.

"Destined to remain a small company": Interviews with Eiichi Hongo and Aritsune Todaiji.

"Announced through the *Asahi Shinbun* newspaper": Cusumano, pp. 19–21; official Fuji documents.

PAGE 382: "The task fell to an engineer named Momose": The Momose story was told to me by Yasuo Furuno and Ryuichiro Kuze.

PAGE 383: "Tended to favor design over function": Interview with Aritsune Todaiji.

"Toyota was sending survey teams": Sobel, pp. 156–57.

"The engineers knew best": Interviews with Thomas Gibson and Eiichi Hongo.

PAGE 384: "The vehicle had a four-stroke engine": Interview with Ryuichiro Kuze.

"The company became a niche manufacturer": Interview with Takao Saito. See also: Sobel, pp. 167–77.

PAGE 385: "Dentsu hired Bruce Willis": Interviews with Akira Yamaguchi, Kosuke Mori and Take Takeichi.

"Doubling to ten thousand vehicles a month": Interview with Yasumi Mizuno.

See also: "Automaker Earnings Show Sharp Decline," *Japan Times*, May 30, 1992, p. 9; "Fuji Heavy Industries Reports Loss of $237 Million for Fiscal Year," *Asian Wall Street Journal*, June 4, 1992, p. 3.

22: HAVE IT YOUR WAY

PAGE 386: "The new year dawned anything but happy": The January–February 1992 auto sales and inventory statistics come from: *Automotive News*, February 10, 1992, p. 126; *Automotive News*, March 9, 1992, p. 38; *Automotive News*, January 20, 1992, p. 34; *Automotive News*, February 10, 1992, p. 130.

"Planned to reduce Japan's 'voluntary' export quota": "MITI May Cut Export Ceiling" by Richard Johnson, *Automotive News*, February 17, 1992, p. 1.

PAGES 386–87: "Daihatsu, Japan's tiniest auto exporter": "Daihatsu Throws in the Towel in U.S." by Kristine Stiven Breese, *Automotive News*, February 17, 1992, p. 1; "Daihatsu Sinks Under Catch-22" by Richard Johnson, *Automotive News*, February 24, 1992, p. 4.

PAGE 387: " 'Artistry in generating and maintaining creative momentum' ": "Wieden & Kennedy: Keeping Ad Game Fresh" by Cleveland Horton, *Advertising Age*, April 13, 1992, p. S3.

"A particularly pronounced creative rage": "TV Spots You Read Have Become a Popular Production Technique" by Stuart Elliott, *New York Times*, February 19, 1993, p. D18.

PAGE 388: " 'Something that we as a company have to face up to' ": All this material comes from a March 20, 1993, interview with Chris Wackman, except the final quotation beginning, "That takes somebody who can get up in front of a room," which comes from the January 20, 1993, interview.

PAGE 389: "Like the newspaper's earlier salvo": "Advertising: Subaru's New Ad Campaign Isn't Working" by Joanne Lipman, *Wall Street Journal*, March 31, 1992, p. B4.

"Subaru's volume was off 3.2 percent": "Make Meetings: Subaru" by Jim Henry, *Automotive News*, February 17, 1992, p. 33.

"Up 42 percent from a year before": *Automotive News*, April 13, 1992, p. 45. Also: Interview with Tom Gibson, April 15, 1992.

"You see? We told you the campaign wasn't working": Interview with Bruce Buchanan.

PAGE 398: "Fuji decided that S.O.A. had to take more cars": Interview with Jeff Greenberg, April 23, 1992.

PAGE 399: "Tomorrow, we're gonna have a meeting": Interview with Lucinda Jones, Subaru account executive at Wieden & Kennedy, April 23, 1992.

PAGE 403: "The object of a class-action suit": *Automotive News*, December 3, 1979, p. 6.

PAGE 410: "Legacy sales were down for the month": The Subaru sales figures for June 1992 and June 1991 come from: *Automotive News*, July 13, 1992, pp. 34–35. Also: Interview with Chris Milhous, June 18, 1992.

The Subaru sales figures for July 1992 and July 1991 come from: *Automotive News*, August 10, 1992, pp. 36–37.

" 'It's jazzier than the old campaign' ": I am indebted to Mark Landler, media editor of *Business Week*, for this material.

" 'The whole campaign was flat to begin with' ": "Just Do It Again" by Scott Raab, *Philadelphia Magazine*, September 1992, pp. 70ff.

PAGE 411: "Volvo, which also dumped its longtime ad agency": *Automotive News*, September 7, 1992, p. 44.

PAGE 412: "The *New York Times* printed": "A Subaru Ad That Should Be Buried" by David Essertier, *New York Times*, July 12, 1992, Section 3, p. 13.

"Three Shops with Plenty to Sweat About": "Three Shops with Plenty to Sweat About" by Mark Landler, *Business Week*, July 20, 1992, pp. 74–75.

" 'Arrogance is a full partner' ": *Philadelphia Magazine*, p. 72.

PAGE 414: "It had built a campaign to appeal to 'stakeholders' ": "Subaru Impreza Launch Platform Preview, Executive Summary," Carlson Marketing Group, August 20, 1992.

EPILOGUE

PAGE 425: "Subaru did manage to sell almost 65,000 Legacies in 1992": The figures on Subaru's total sales and Legacy sales for 1991 and 1992 come from: *Automotive News 1992 Market Data Book*, May 27, 1992, pp. 17–21; *Automotive News 1993 Market Data Book*, May 26, 1993, pp. 19–22.

"Only 8,648 of the new subcompacts had been sold": "Worrell Will Leave Struggling Subaru This Month" by Jim Henry, *Automotive News*, July 5, 1993, p. 1.

PAGES 425–26: " 'We are not a mass marketer' ": "Subaru Sheds Its Hopes for the Mass Market" by Jim Henry, *Automotive News*, July 12, 1993, p. 1.

ACKNOWLEDGMENTS

From the moment I became interested in advertising, which long predates the time I took on the assignment to cover the industry, I coveted the chance to write about an advertising account review from the inside. Here, I thought, all the clichés of business-as-warfare were realized. And here, too, loose talk about creativity—a word tossed about with equal meaninglessness by artists, entrepreneurs and, yes, journalists—would take formal shape, on an easel made of dollar bills. Gradually, I came to understand that an account review, together with its aftermath, the reification and evolution of a corporate image, could also serve as a grand backdrop for a portrait of a nation's culture of acquisitiveness. This is the story I set out to tell.

None of it would have been possible, of course, were it not for the courage of Subaru of America's senior executives. From the very start, they were well aware that their quest to revive their company's fortunes would be arduous, and as likely to end in heartbreak as in triumph. But they believed that having an observer witness and question the proceedings would keep them sharp, and provide a service to the many others in American business who will, inevitably, follow along this same path. (Indeed, the hard lessons the company learned appeared, in early 1994, to be earning a payback. Through April, S.O.A.'s return to a niche strategy, together with the rebound in the U.S. economy, had raised Subaru sales by 32 percent from the same period a year earlier.)

More than a score of present and former Subaru executives helped me. Without slighting any, I'd like to single out Thomas Gibson, the former president, and Christopher Wackman, the former marketing director, for their unflinching support and openness. Marvin Riesenbach, the company's longtime chief financial officer, also lent me documents from S.O.A.'s early years that proved invaluable. And Richard S. Marshall, the company's corporate public relations manager, was unflagging in his willingness to track down people and information.

The executives of S.O.A.'s parent company, Fuji Heavy Industries, belied the assumptions that Japanese corporations are impenetrable. Like its U.S. subsidiary, Fuji opened itself to me and my occasionally uncomfortable questions. Among the many executives who smoothed my path, special thanks go to Takeshi Higurashi, chairman and chief executive of Subaru of America; Eiichi Hongo, Fuji's managing director; and Ken Honda, manager of the public relations department, whose comparisons of American and Japanese corporate culture regaled me during long rides back and forth between Gunma and Tokyo.

My research in Japan would not have been possible without the advice and intercession of dozens of others, too numerous to name. However, my appreciation to the staff of the International House of Japan, which graciously allowed me a residency of several weeks, is boundless. So is it as well to David Halberstam, who connected me to I-House, and to Yasutoshi Ikuta, who helped me find my way around Tokyo. And were it not for Hiroshi Ishikawa, a staff officer at the Foreign Press Center in Tokyo, several crucial interviews would never have taken place. (I'm still somewhat miffed, though, that Ishikawa-san knew more New York City magazine gossip than I did.)

The other crucial linkage for understanding the history of Subaru's image was Dentsu Inc. The world's largest advertising agency acted like a neighborhood grocer, welcoming me and offering me virtually a free run of its senior executives. For this, the path was smoothed by Kiyoshi "K.C." Eguchi, the general manager and chief creative officer of the agency's New York office, and approval came from Toshio Naito, the managing director in Tokyo. But I reserve my strongest *domo arigato gozaimus* for Tetsuji Shimizu, the manager of Dentsu's Overseas Communications Department, who was a tireless and engaging shepherd.

Obviously, though, it was the generosity of advertising agencies, throughout my career writing about the media, that helped me bring this project to fruition. My goal was not to shine a harsh spotlight on them, but to explore the culture of an industry that has contributed so much to our nation's perceptions of itself. I could not have done this without the help provided by hundreds of advertising and marketing account executives, researchers, copywriters, art directors and media planners, during and after my stay at the *New York Times*.

For this book, of course, Wieden & Kennedy gave me access to precincts previously unseen by aliens. I thank Dan Wieden and David Kennedy, who even during the darkest times never seemed to worry about how they or their charges would fare in the retelling. I value most, however, the open-door policy of David Luhr, chief of the agency's Philadelphia office, and the quality time spent in the Quality Room with Jerry Cronin and Vince Engel, who—along with dozens of colleagues in Philadelphia and Portland—opened their hearts and histories to me.

Beyond Wieden & Kennedy, it would be impossible for me to cite the many advertising people who contributed, directly or indirectly, to this book. But I'd like to thank the executives of the other agencies that pitched the Subaru account, as well as the former executives of Levine, Huntley, Schmidt & Beaver, particularly Harold Levine, Bob Schmidt and Allan Beaver, who permitted me to visit with them during times of great financial and personal strain. In addition, Mary Warlick of The One Club, George Lois, William Weilbacher, Harry Paster, Carl Spielvogel, Roy Bostock, Alan Gottesman and my friends and fellow dim-sumaniacs at the Chinese Gourmet Society provided or connected me to crucial insights about the agency business.

My methods in researching and telling the tale of Subaru's image were shaped by numerous scholars and scholarly institutions, who helped put history behind my suspicions and provided me the courage to walk down some rocky intellectual paths. Although their contributions may not be entirely evident in the rough-and-tumble of the narrative, their inspiration is there.

Robert Goldman of Lewis & Clark College gave me several unpublished papers prepared by himself and Steve Papson, which were invaluable in helping me understand postmodern literary theory in relation to contemporary advertising. The Center for Modern Advertising History at the Smithsonian Institution's National Museum of American History is a culture vulture's nesting area. Stacy Flaherty, Scott Ellsworth and John Fleckner helped me find my way around the boxes, tapes and transcripts. At Duke University, Ellen Gartrell and Mack O'Barr helped me wind through the J. Walter Thompson archives; indeed, Mack was among the first to tell me there was such a thing *as* advertising history. Jan Kurtz of the American Advertising Museum gave me a home-away-from-home (with library!) in Portland. And my friend and neighbor Stuart Ewen, together with his body of research, forced me to check my assumptions against the history of mass production. My two researchers, Karen Grossman in New York and Lisa Prevenslik in Tokyo, were indefatigable in finding, explaining and translating their materials, and much more. And my typist, Wendy Scheir, put their thoughts—and so many others'—on paper.

I must add special thanks to Morris Holbrook at Columbia University's Graduate School of Business, who allowed me to audit his seminar on semiotics and marketing. My conviction that advertising can, finally, only be understood as an element of corporate mythology was based largely on his research and the work conducted by his associates on the "Consumer Odyssey."

My colleagues at the *New York Times* provide the largest set of "without-whoms" this book has. Indeed, the project really began with a troubling question asked me by Joseph Lelyveld, then the deputy managing editor, who wanted to know why men and women in advertising were so passionate about what they did. Unable to answer, even after two years and some five hundred advertising columns, I eventually wandered across three continents, a dozen states and some 150 interviews to find the reasons. Joe and the other senior editors of the newspaper—particularly Max Frankel, John Lee and Allan Siegal—showed continuing interest in my media reporting, without which my own passions might never have been ignited.

I benefited from the wisdom of other bosses in my stay at the *Times*, notably Ed Klein and James Greenfield. And I was aided by Warren Hoge, Bruce Weber and James Atlas at the *Times Magazine*, who published the story that grew into this book, and by my associates in the Financial News department. But it was my dozen colleagues in the Media News department, especially Martin Arnold and Jan Benzel, whose association I most treasured and most miss.

As with any project of such length, friends were a crucial link to reality . . . and in some cases, to bed and board. Jesse Milan and Bill Roberts, Jon Maas, Steve Fried and Diane Ayres, and Mike and Carla Lev provided shelter. Richard Bernstein, Judy Prouty, Mark Landler, Joan Kron and Jerry Marder, Doug McGill, Matt Winkler and the Bloombergers, among many others, gave succor. Ida Giragossian at Knopf cheerfully knocked down obstacles for me. Gail Hochman was my guide and adviser through the thicket of publishing puzzles. And Jonathan Segal was not only my editor but my voice of reason, my goad, my scold, my cheerleader and my pal.

This book was completed during a fellowship year at the Freedom Forum Media Studies Center at Columbia University. Certainly, no journalist was ever so lucky as to be associated with such smart, supportive people! The Center exposed me to the practical and the profane, to the mustiness of media history, the intricacies of cultural studies and the novelty of new technology. Among the staff and other fellows, there are too many to name. But my thanks to Everette E. Dennis, the executive director, and to Duncan McDonald, the deputy director, extend over many levels of personnel.

Finally, of course, there is my family. In this case, their influence on the book is long and seminal. From my parents, Marvin and Janet

Rothenberg, marketing professionals both, and from their friends, especially Muriel and the late Jack Vilinsky, I first heard the names Bernbach and Wells associated with the words "creative" and "genius." To them, my siblings and their spouses and children, my appreciation and love are deep.

But, in the end, this book has one true benefactor, Susan Roy. Our relationship was forged by advertising. On our very first date, when I went to pick her up at her Hoboken apartment, I spied on her coffee table a copy of *Advertising Age*, and thereafter I became a faithful reader—of account-review coverage, especially. Later, after we were married, as I was about to start my beat as an advertising reporter, she asked me a question: "Can you find out what a copywriter does all day?"

'Ll', I did. Thanks for asking.

INDEX

ABC, 308

Absolut vodka, 9–10, 26

account executives, 60, 227, 300–5, 334

account planning, 121–3, 151, 156, 334

account reviews, 20–1, 106–23; choice of agencies, 23–37, 43, 105–84

account-switching, 20–1

Acura, 97, 409

ad agencies, 23–4, 179–80; account planning, 121–3, 151, 156, 334; account reviews, 20–1, 106–23; account-switching, 20–1; auto advertising budget cuts, 339–40; "car guys," 127–30, 397, 398; choice of, 23–37, 43, 105–84; -client relationship, 20–1, 27, 66, 74, 116, 190, 218, 299–301, 328, 334, 385, 397; commission system, 59–61, 68; credentials visits, 25–37; early history of, 58–67; Jewish, 57–8, 63–7, 184; market research, 117–23, 305–6; media department, 116, 305–8; mergers, 6; of 1980s, 21, 211–13, 218, 228–9, 301, 303; of 1990s, 21–3, 106, 218, 260, 301, 339; postmodern, 211–20, 231–2, 268,

300; regional campaigns, 76–80, 126, 160–1, 304–5, 308–46, 349–66, 387–9; retail campaigns, 106–7, 130, 134, 164, 168–9; TV commercial production and postproduction, 227–8, 235–87; westward movement of, 189; *see also specific agencies and cities*

Adams, John, 239–49, 254, 257, 261–5, 268, 277–8, 283–6

Adcock, Fred, 299, 314, 335, 353, 361

ad spending, 21–3, 59–61, 73–4, 87, 215, 228, 305, 339; early 1990s decline in, 339–40; *see also specific agencies and products*

Advertising Age, 24, 106, 109, 297, 301, 387

advertising industry, *see* ad agencies; ad spending; magazine advertising; newspaper advertising; radio advertising; television advertising; *and specific agencies, cities, and products*

Advertising Research Foundation, 151

Adweek, 9, 124, 297, 387, 410

airline industry, 8, 22

Ajroldi, Paolo, 8

Allen, Karen, 25, 279–81